Signature
SERIES

MICROSOFT®
WORD
2000

NITA RUTKOSKY

Pierce College at Puyallup
Puyallup, Washington

MICROSOFT OFFICE
Microsoft®
OFFICE®
USER SPECIALIST

APPROVED COURSEWARE

EMCParadigm

Senior Editor	Sonja M. Brown
Developmental Editor	Michael Sander
Art Director	Joan D'Onofrio
Cover and Icons Designer	Chris Vern Johnson
Text Designer	Jennifer Wreisner
Desktop Production	Desktop Solutions, Leslie Anderson, Julie Hansen, and Michelle Lewis
Copyeditor/Proofreader	Sharon R. O'Donnell
Indexer	Donald Glassman

Publishing Team—George Provol, Publisher; Janice Johnson, Director of Product Development; Lori Landwer, Marketing Manager; Shelley Clubb, Electronic Design and Production Manager.

Registered Trademarks—Microsoft, Windows, and the MOUS icon are registered trademarks of Microsoft Corporation in the United States and other countries. IBM is a registered trademark of IBM Corporation.

Permissions—Material for selected documents has been excerpted from *Introduction to Computers and Technology*, by Robert D. Shepherd, published by Paradigm Publishing Inc., 1998; "Exploring the Internet," by Joseph Habraken, *EMC/Paradigm Profile*, Fall 1995; *Telecommunications: Systems and Applications*, by William Mitchell, Robert Hendricks, and Leonard Sterry, published by Paradigm Publishing Inc., 1993; *Advanced WordPerfect: DesktopPublishing 6.1 for Windows*, by Nita Hewitt Rutkosky, Judy Dwyer Burnside, and Joanne Marschke Arford, published by Paradigm Publishing Inc., 1996; and *Desktop Publishing: Technology and Design*, by Holly Yasui, published by Paradigm Publishing Inc., 1989.

Acknowledgments—The author and publisher wish to thank the following reviewers for their technical assistance: Susan M. Capecchi, EMC/Paradigm Publishing, St. Paul, MN; Darlene Forsman, Pierce College at Puyallup, Puyallup, WA; Renton Technical College, Renton, WA; Mary A. Walthall, Ph.D., St. Petersburg Junior College, Clearwater Campus, Clearwater, FL.

Library of Congress Cataloging-in-Publication Data

Rutkosky, Nita Hewitt.
Microsoft Word 2000 / Nita Rutkosky.
p. cm. -- (Signature series)
ISBN 0-7638-0249-2 (text). – ISBN 0-7638-0250-6 (text, CD-ROM)
1. Microsoft Word. 2. Word processing. I. Title. II. Title:
Word 2000 III. Series.
Z52.5.M52 R93   2000   99-31328
652.5'5369—dc21   CIP

Text + CD: ISBN 0-7638-0250-6
Order Number: 04335

© 2000 by Paradigm Publishing Inc.
Published by **EMC**Paradigm
875 Montreal Way
St. Paul, MN 55102
(800) 535-6865
E-mail: educate@emcp.com
Web Site: www.emcp.com

Printed in the United States of America
10 9 8 7 6

Contents

Unit 2 Formatting and Enhancing Documents 181

Introduction

When students prepare for a successful business career, they need to acquire the skills and qualifications essential to becoming a productive member of the business community. Microcomputer systems are prevalent in business offices, and students will encounter employment opportunities that require a working knowledge of computers and computer software. Microcomputers, with the appropriate software, are used by businesses in a variety of capacities. One of the most popular uses of a microcomputer system is word processing—the creation of documents.

Word processing certainly belongs in the business world, but it is also a popular application for home computer use. People will want to learn word processing to write personal correspondence, keep personal records, provide support for a home-based business or cottage industry, write term papers and reports, and much more.

This textbook provides students with the opportunity to learn word processing for employment purposes or home use and to utilize a microcomputer as a word processor. The Word 2000 program together with an IBM or IBM-compatible microcomputer system must be available for students to practice the features of the program. Word 2000 needs to be installed on a hard-drive or network system. To properly install the program, please refer to the Word or Microsoft Office documentation.

This textbook instructs students in the theories and practical applications of one of the most popular word processing programs—Microsoft Word. The text is designed to be used in beginning and advanced word processing classes and provides approximately 80 to 120 hours of instruction.

Structure

The book is divided into five units. Chapters within units each contain:

- Performance Objectives that identify the specific learning goals of the chapter.
- Introductory material that provides an overview of new concepts and features.
- Step-by-step exercises at the computer, integrated within the chapter, that allow students to practice using the feature(s) presented in the chapter.
- Chapter Summary.
- Commands Review.
- Thinking Offline, a short-answer knowledge self-check.
- Working Hands-On, skill assessments that require students to complete exercises without step-by-step instructions.

Performance Assessments at the end of each unit contain:

- Demonstrating Your Skills, simulation exercises that require students to make decisions about document preparation and formatting; these practical exercises provide ample opportunity to apply new features as well as to practice previously learned material.
- Creating Original Documents, writing activities that provide students with the opportunity to compose and format business documents, requiring the demonstration of problem-solving, critical, and creative abilities as well as hands-on computer skills.

Completing Computer Exercises

Some computer exercises in the chapters require the student to access and use an existing file saved on the CD that accompanies this textbook. The files are contained in individual folders for each chapter. Before beginning the chapter, the student should copy the folder from the CD to a preformatted disk. After completing the exercises in a chapter, the student should delete the chapter folder to ensure adequate storage space for the next chapter's files, subject to the instructor's instructions. Detailed instructions on how to copy and delete folders are provided on pages xxv-xxvi of "Getting Started" and, for added convenience, are repeated inside the back cover of the book.

Approved Courseware for the Microsoft Office User Specialist (MOUS) Program

The logo on the cover of this text means that Microsoft has approved this text as courseware that teaches all the skills students need to master to pass the Core certification exam in Word 2000. These skills and the corresponding page numbers of related instruction in the text are listed on the page that precedes the first chapter of each unit.

The MOUS program is used to test and validate a student's skills and thereby supply objective proof to an employer or prospective employer that the student knows how to use a program efficiently and productively. For more information on the MOUS program and where to take the certification exam, visit Microsoft's Web site at *www.Microsoft.com* or the specific MOUS site at *www.mous.net*.

Industry Standards from the SCANS Commission

This textbook covers important SCANS (Secretary's Commission on Achieving Necessary Skills) goals. The SCANS report was the result of a commission from the Department of Labor. The goal of the commission was to establish the interdisciplinary standards that should be required for *all* students. SCANS skill standards emphasize the integration of competencies from the areas of information, technology, basic skills, and thinking skills. The SCANS committee agreed that all curricula can be strengthened by emphasizing classroom work that is more authentic and relevant to learners, i.e., connecting context to content. Teaching in context helps students move away from subject-specific orientation to integrative learning that includes decision making, problem solving, and critical thinking. The concepts and applications material in each unit of this book has been designed to coordinate with and reflect this important interdisciplinary emphasis. In addition, learning assessment tools implement the SCANS standards. For example, the skill assessments at the end of each chapter reinforce acquired technical skills while providing practice in decision making and problem solving. The performance assessments at the end of each unit offer simulation exercises that require students to demonstrate their understanding of the major skills and technical features taught in the unit's chapters within the framework of critical and creative thinking. The addition of writing activities at the end of each unit makes it clear that students are not just producers, but editors and writers as well.

Emphasis on Visual Learning

Microsoft Office programs such as Word operate within the Windows operating system, a graphical user interface (GUI) that provides a visually oriented environment by using icons to represent program features. This textbook also emphasizes a graphical environment with icons that represent specific learning components.

In keeping with Windows' graphical environment, figures that illustrate steps performed at the computer are labeled with "bubble" callouts corresponding to the steps. The student can easily follow the steps by seeing the exact spot in the computer screen where a certain action is required. Icons offer additional visual learning cues. For example, a computer icon appears next to Demonstrating Your Skills, visually representing that the exercises are done at the computer. A hands-at-keyboard icon identifies the Creating Original Documents activities.

By the time students have completed the textbook, they will have mastered the basic and intermediate features (Core Level MOUS skills) of Word 2000. In addition, they will have mastered a number of advanced features (Expert Level MOUS skills) of the program as well. They also will have practiced some basic skills in using Windows and acquired a solid foundation in the problem-solving and communication abilities so important in the contemporary workplace.

Learning Components that Accompany This Text

The following products for instructors and students correspond to this text and enhance its teaching possibilities. These products may be ordered by contacting an EMC/Paradigm Publishing Customer Care representative by phone at (800) 535-6865 or via e-mail at *educate@emcp.com* and supplying the order number as follows:

Publisher's Web site at *www.emcp.com*. Watch for updates and tips for students and instructors at the text's Resource Center link.

Microsoft® Word 2000, Signature Series, Instructor's Guide with CD-ROM, order number 41335. The Instructor's Guide contains suggested course syllabi, grade sheets, and assignment sheets for Core and Expert levels; comprehensive Word tests and answers to use as final exams; Supplemental Performance Assessments; and a list of PowerPoint slides available on the CD. For each chapter, the Instructor's Guide also provides a summary of chapter content, Teaching Hints, Thinking Offline answers, and model answers for all exercises in the text. The Instructor's CD-ROM contains everything found in the printed Instructor's Guide plus model answer files for all exercises and PowerPoint slides for classroom use.

Microsoft Word 2000, Signature Series, Test Bank, order number 59335. The Paradigm Test Generator is a full-featured test-creation program that offers instructors a wide variety of options for generating and editing tests. Instructors can create custom tests that include questions from the existing test banks or insert new questions. The test bank provided on this disk offers more than 1,300 questions that range in difficulty and discrimination levels. All of the standard question types plus graphic and procedure-oriented items are included.

OnCourse Word 2000 Web site. OnCourse is a program that allows instructors to create a personalized Web site for the course easily and quickly. Available on a CD-ROM, the onCourse program offers self-study quizzes for students, lecture notes, study aids, Internet links, and a discussion forum tool. To facilitate the instructor's Web site development, course information is already included. Instructors can easily add information or change any of the information already on the template in order to directly match the exact needs of a particular course.

Melina Tanner
235- 3525

Melina Tanner
235- 3525

Getting Started

As you work your way through this textbook, you will learn functions and commands for Microsoft Word 2000. Microsoft Word 2000 is a word processing program that is one application within the Microsoft Office 2000 suite. To operate the Microsoft Word 2000 program, you will need access to a computer.

Identifying Computer Hardware

The computer equipment you will use to operate the suite of programs is referred to as *hardware*. You will need access to an IBM PC or an IBM-compatible computer. This computer system should consist of the CPU, monitor, keyboard, printer, disk drive, and mouse. If you are not sure what equipment you will be operating, check with your instructor. The computer system displayed in figure G.1 consists of six components. Each component is discussed separately in the material that follows.

figure

G.1 *IBM Personal Computer System*

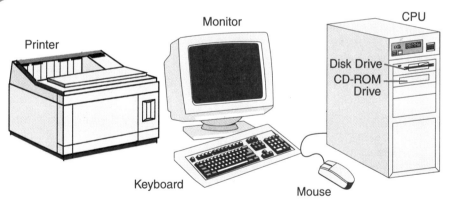

CPU

CPU stands for Central Processing Unit and is the intelligence of the computer. All the processing occurs in the CPU. Silicon chips, which contain miniaturized circuitry, are placed on boards that are plugged into slots within the CPU. Whenever an instruction is given to the computer, that instruction is processed through circuitry in the CPU.

Monitor

The monitor is a piece of equipment that looks like a television screen. It displays the information of a program and the text being input at the keyboard. The quality of display for monitors varies depending on the type of monitor and the type of resolution. Monitors can also vary in size—generally from 14-inch size up to 21-inch size or larger.

Keyboard

The keyboard is used to input information into the computer. Keyboards for microcomputers vary in the number and location of the keys. Microcomputers have the alphabetic and numeric keys in the same location as the keys on a typewriter. The symbol keys, however, may be placed in a variety of locations, depending on the manufacturer. In addition to letters, numbers, and symbols, most microcomputer keyboards contain function keys, arrow keys, and a numeric keypad. Figure G.2 shows an enhanced keyboard.

Microcomputer Enhanced Keyboard

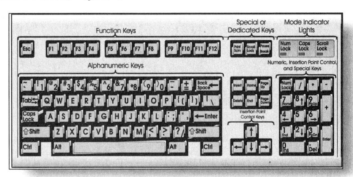

The 12 keys at the top of the enhanced keyboard, labeled with the letter F followed by a number, are called *function keys*. These keys can be used to perform functions within each of the suite programs. To the right of the regular keys is a group of *special* or *dedicated keys*. These keys are labeled with specific functions that will be performed when you press the key. Below the special keys are arrow keys. These keys are used to move the insertion point in the document screen.

In the upper right corner of the keyboard are three mode indicator lights. When certain modes have been selected, a light appears on the keyboard. For example, if you press the Caps Lock key, which disables the lowercase alphabet, a light appears next to Caps Lock. Similarly, pressing the Num Lock key will disable the special functions on the numeric keypad, which is located at the right side of the keyboard.

Disk Drive

Depending on the computer system you are using, Microsoft Word 2000 is installed on a hard drive or as part of a network system. Whether you are using the suite on a hard drive or network system, you will need to have a disk drive available for inserting a 3.5-inch disk, on which you will save and open documents.

The memory capacity for disks varies depending on the density of the disk. Disk memory is measured in kilobytes (thousands) and megabytes (millions). The memory capacity for a 3.5-inch double density (DD) disk is 720,000 bytes (720 kilobytes, which is written as 720Kb). The memory capacity for a 3.5-inch high density disk (HD) is 1,440,000 bytes (1.44 megabytes, which is written as 1.44Mb).

Printer

When you create a document in Word 2000, it is considered *soft copy*. If you want a *hard copy* of a document, you need to print it. To print documents you will need to access a printer. Printers are either *impact* or *nonimpact*. Impact printers have a mechanism that strikes the paper to create text. Nonimpact printers use a variety of methods—heat, ink jet, laser—to print characters. These printers are much quieter and faster than impact printers.

Mouse

Many functions in Word 2000 are designed to operate more efficiently with a *mouse*. A mouse is an input device that sits on a flat surface next to the computer. A mouse can be operated with the left or the right hand. Moving the mouse on the flat surface causes a corresponding mouse pointer to move in the screen. Figure G.1 shows an illustration of a mouse. For specific instructions on how to use a mouse, please refer to the "Using the Mouse" text later in this section.

Properly Maintaining Disks

You will be copying chapter folders onto a 3.5-inch disk and then saving and opening files from this disk. To ensure that you will be able to retrieve information from the disk, you need to follow certain rules of disk maintenance. To properly maintain a 3.5-inch disk, follow these rules:

- Do not expose the disk to extreme heat or cold.
- Keep the disk away from magnets and magnetic fields. They can erase the information saved on the disk.
- Do not wipe or clean the magnetic surface of the disk.
- Keep the disk away from food, liquids, and smoke.
- Never remove the disk from the disk drive when the drive light is on.
- Carry the disk in a plastic case to prevent damage to the metal shutter.

The 3.5-inch disk on which you will open and save files must be formatted. Most likely, any disk you purchase will already be formatted. Formatting is a process that establishes tracks and sectors on which information is stored and prepares the disk to accept data from the disk operating system (and erases anything previously saved on the disk). If you are using a disk that is not formatted, check with your instructor on the steps needed to format. (You can also look up the steps to format using the Windows Help feature.)

Using the Mouse

Microsoft Word can be operated using a keyboard or it can be operated with the keyboard and a mouse. The mouse may have two or three buttons on top, which are tapped to execute specific functions and commands. To use the mouse, rest it on a flat surface or a mouse pad. Put your hand over it with your palm resting on top of the mouse and your wrist resting on the table surface. As you move the mouse on the flat surface, a corresponding pointer moves in the screen.

When using the mouse, there are four terms you should understand—point, click, double-click, and drag. When operating the mouse, you may need to *point* to a specific command, button, or icon. Point means to position the mouse pointer on the desired item. With the mouse pointer positioned on the desired item, you may need to *click* a button on the mouse. Click means quickly tapping a button on the mouse once. To complete two steps at one time, such as choosing and then executing a function, *double-click* a mouse button. Double-click means to tap the left mouse button twice in quick succession. The term *drag* means to press and hold the left mouse button, move the mouse pointer to a specific location, and then release the button.

Using the Mouse Pointer

The mouse pointer will change appearance depending on the function being performed or where the pointer is positioned. The mouse pointer may appear as one of the following images:

The mouse pointer appears as an I-beam (called the *I-beam pointer*) in the document screen and can be used to move the insertion point or select text.

The mouse pointer appears as an arrow pointing up and to the left (called the *arrow pointer*) when it is moved to the Title bar, Menu bar, or one of the toolbars at the top of the screen or when a dialog box is displayed. For example, to open a new document with the mouse, you would move the I-beam pointer to the File option on the Menu bar. When the I-beam pointer is moved to the Menu bar, it turns into an arrow pointer. To make a selection, position the tip of the arrow pointer on the File option, and then click the left mouse button. At the drop-down menu that displays, make selections by positioning the arrow pointer on the desired option, and then clicking the left mouse button.

The mouse pointer becomes a double-headed arrow (either pointing left and right, pointing up and down, or pointing diagonally) when performing certain functions such as changing the size of a picture.

In certain situations, such as moving a picture or clip art image, the mouse pointer becomes a four-headed arrow. The four-headed arrow means that you can move the object left, right, up, or down.

When a request is being processed or when a program is being loaded, the mouse pointer may appear with an hourglass beside it. The hourglass image means "please wait." When the process is completed, the hourglass image is removed.

The mouse pointer displays as a hand with a pointing index finger in certain functions such as Help and indicates that there is more information available about the item.

Choosing Commands

Once Word is open, several methods can be used to choose commands. A command is an instruction that tells Word to do something. You can choose a command with one of the following methods:

- Click a toolbar button with the mouse.
- Choose a command from a menu.
- Use shortcut keys.
- Use a shortcut menu.

Choosing Commands on Toolbars

Word provides several toolbars containing buttons for common tasks. Generally, two toolbars are visible on the screen (unless your system has been customized). One toolbar is called the Standard toolbar; the other is referred to as the Formatting toolbar. To choose a command from a toolbar, position the tip of the arrow pointer on a button, and then click the left mouse button. For example, to print the document currently displayed in the document screen, position the tip of the arrow pointer on the Print button on the Standard toolbar, and then click the left mouse button.

Choosing Commands on the Menu Bar

The Menu bar, located toward the top of the Word screen, contains a variety of options you can use to perform functions and commands on data. Functions are grouped logically into options, which display on the Menu bar. For example, features to work with files (documents) are grouped in the File option. Either the mouse or the keyboard can be used to make choices from the Menu bar or make a choice at a dialog box.

To use the mouse to make a choice from the Menu bar, move the I-beam pointer to the Menu bar. This causes the I-beam pointer to display as an arrow pointer. Position the tip of the arrow pointer on the desired option, and then click the left mouse button.

To use the keyboard, press the Alt key to make the Menu bar active. Options on the Menu bar display with an underline below one of the letters. To choose an option from the Menu bar, key the underlined letter of the desired option, or move the insertion point with the left or right arrow keys to the option desired, and then press Enter. This causes a drop-down menu to display. For example, to display the File drop-down menu shown in figure G.3 using the mouse, position the arrow pointer on File on the Menu bar, and then click the left mouse button. To display the File drop-down menu with the keyboard, press the Alt key, and then key the letter F for File.

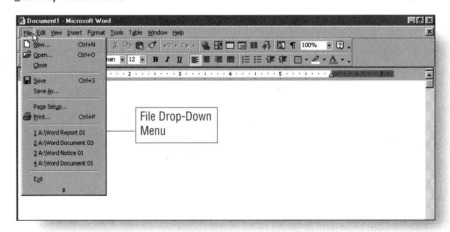

File Drop-Down Menu

Choosing Commands from Drop-Down Menus

To choose a command from a drop-down menu with the mouse, position the arrow pointer on the desired option, and then click the left mouse button. At the drop-down menu that displays, drag the arrow pointer down the menu to the desired option, and then click the left mouse button.

To make a selection from the drop-down menu with the keyboard, key the underlined letter of the desired option. Once the drop-down menu displays, you do not need to hold down the Alt key with the underlined letter. If you want to close a drop-down menu without making a choice, click in the document screen outside the drop-down menu; or, press the Esc key twice.

If an option can be accessed by clicking a button on a toolbar, the button is displayed preceding the option in the drop-down menu. For example, buttons display before the New, Open Save, and Print options in the File drop-down menu (see figure G.3).

Some menu options may be gray shaded (dimmed). When an option is dimmed, that option is currently not available. For example, if you choose the Table option on the Menu bar, the Table drop-down menu displays with dimmed options including Merge Cells and Table AutoFormat.

Some menu options are preceded by a check mark. The check mark indicates that the option is currently active. To make an option inactive (turn it off) using the mouse, position the arrow pointer on the option, and then click the left mouse button. To make an option inactive (turn it off) with the keyboard, key the underlined letter of the option.

If an option from a drop-down menu displays followed by an ellipsis (...), a dialog box will display when that option is chosen. A dialog box provides a variety of options to let you specify how a command is to be carried out. For example, if you choose File and then Print, the Print dialog box displays as shown in figure G.4. Or if you choose Format and then Font from the Menu bar, the Font dialog box displays as shown in figure G.5.

figure G.4

Print Dialog Box

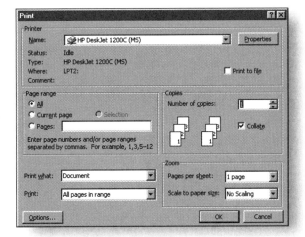

figure G.5

Font Dialog Box

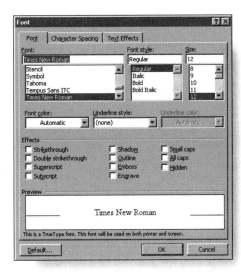

Some dialog boxes provide a set of options. These options are contained on separate tabs. For example, the Font dialog box shown in figure G.5 contains a tab at the top of the dialog box with the word Font on it. Two other tabs display to the right of the Font tab. The tab that displays in the front is the active tab. To make a tab active using the mouse, position the arrow pointer on the desired tab, and then click the left mouse button. If you are using the keyboard, press Ctrl + Tab or press Alt + the underlined letter on the desired tab. For example, to change the tab to Character Spacing in the Font dialog box, click Character Spacing, or press Ctrl + Tab, or press Alt + R.

To choose options from a dialog box with the mouse, position the arrow pointer on the desired option, and then click the left mouse button. If you are using the keyboard, press the Tab key to move the insertion point forward from option to option. Press Shift + Tab to move the insertion point backward from option to option. You can also hold down the Alt key and then press the underlined letter of the desired option. When an option is selected, it displays either in reverse video (white letters on a blue background) or surrounded by a dashed box called a *marquee*.

A dialog box contains one or more of the following elements: text boxes, list boxes, check boxes, option buttons, spin boxes, and command buttons.

Text Boxes

Some options in a dialog box require text to be entered. For example, the boxes to the right of the Find what and Replace with options at the Find and Replace dialog box shown in figure G.6 are text boxes. In a text box, you key text or edit existing text. Edit text in a text box in the same manner as normal text. Use the left and right arrow keys on the keyboard to move the insertion point without deleting text and use the Delete key or Backspace key to delete text.

figure
G.6

Find and Replace Dialog Box

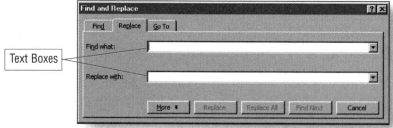

List Boxes

Some dialog boxes such as the Theme dialog box shown in figure G.7 may contain a list box. The list box at the left side of the dialog box contains a list of themes. To make a selection from a list box with the mouse, move the arrow pointer to the desired option, and then click the left mouse button.

figure

G.7

Theme Dialog Box

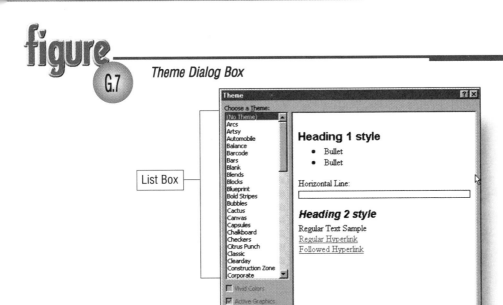

List Box

Some list boxes, such as the one in the Theme dialog box, may contain a scroll bar. This scroll bar will display at the right side of the list box (a vertical scroll bar) or at the bottom of the list box (a horizontal scroll bar). Either a vertical scroll bar or a horizontal scroll bar can be used to move through the list if the list is longer than the box. To move down through a list on a vertical scroll bar, position the arrow pointer on the down scroll triangle and hold down the left mouse button. To scroll up through the list with a vertical scroll bar, position the arrow pointer on the up scroll triangle and hold down the left mouse button. You can also move the arrow pointer above the scroll box and click the left mouse button to scroll up the list, or move the arrow pointer below the scroll box and click the left mouse button to move down the list. To move through a list with a horizontal scroll bar, click the left scroll triangle to scroll to the left of the list or click the right scroll triangle to scroll to the right of the list.

To make a selection from a list using the keyboard, move the insertion point into the box by holding down the Alt key and pressing the underlined letter of the desired option. Press the up and/or down arrow keys on the keyboard to move through the list.

In some dialog boxes where there is not enough room for a list box, lists of options are inserted in a drop-down list box. Options that contain a drop-down list box display with a down-pointing triangle. For example, the Underline style option at the Font dialog box shown in figure G.5 contains a drop-down list. To display the list, click the down-pointing triangle to the right of the Underline style text box. If you are using the keyboard, press Alt + U.

Check Boxes

Some dialog boxes contain options preceded by a box. A check mark may or may not appear in the box. The Font dialog box shown in figure G.5 displays a variety of check boxes within the Effects section. If a check mark appears in the box, the option is active (turned on). If there is no check mark in the check box, the option is inactive (turned off). Any number of check boxes can be active. For example, in the Font dialog box, you can insert a check mark in any or all of the boxes in the Effects section and these options will be active.

To make a check box active or inactive with the mouse, position the tip of the arrow pointer in the check box, and then click the left mouse button. If you are using the keyboard, press Alt + the underlined letter of the desired option.

Option Buttons

In the Print dialog box shown in figure G.4, the options in the Page range section are preceded by option buttons. Only one option button can be selected at any time. When an option button is selected, a dark circle displays in the button.

To select an option button with the mouse, position the tip of the arrow pointer inside the option button, and then click the left mouse button. To make a selection with the keyboard, hold down the Alt key, and then press the underlined letter of the desired option.

Spin Boxes

Some options in a dialog box contain measurements or numbers that can be increased or decreased. These options are generally located in a spin box. For example, the Paragraph dialog box shown in figure G.8 contains a variety of spin boxes located after the Left, Right, Before, and After options. To increase a number in a spin box, position the tip of the arrow pointer on the up-pointing triangle to the right of the desired option, and then click the left mouse button. To decrease the number, click the down-pointing triangle. If you are using the keyboard, press Alt + the underlined letter of the desired option, and then press the up arrow key to increase the number or the down arrow key to decrease the number.

Paragraph Dialog Box

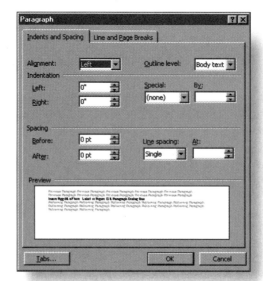

Command Buttons

In the Find and Replace dialog box shown in figure G.6, the buttons at the bottom of the dialog box are called *command buttons*. A command button is used to execute or cancel a command. Some command buttons display with an ellipsis (...). A command button that displays with an ellipsis will open another dialog box. To choose a command button with the mouse, position the arrow pointer on the desired button, and then click the left mouse button. To choose a command button with the keyboard, press the Tab key until the desired command button contains the marquee, and then press the Enter key.

Choosing Commands with Shortcut Keys

At the left side of a drop-down menu is a list of options. At the right side, shortcut keys for specific options may display. For example, the shortcut keys to save a document are Ctrl + S and are displayed to the right of the <u>S</u>ave option at the <u>F</u>ile drop-down menu shown in figure G.3. To use shortcut keys to choose a command, hold down the Ctrl key, key the letter for the command, and then release the Ctrl key.

Choosing Commands with Shortcut Menus

Word includes shortcut menus that contain commands related to the item with which you are working. A shortcut menu appears right where you are working in the document. To display a shortcut menu, click the *right* mouse button or press Shift + F10. For example, if the insertion point is positioned in a paragraph of text in a document, clicking the *right* mouse button or pressing Shift + F10 will cause the shortcut menu shown in figure G.9 to display in the document screen.

G.9   *Shortcut Menu*

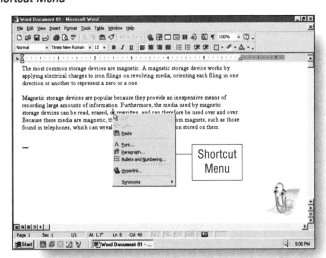

To select an option from a shortcut menu with the mouse, click the desired option. If you are using the keyboard, press the up or down arrow key until the desired option is selected, and then press the Enter key. To close a shortcut menu without choosing an option, click anywhere outside the shortcut menu or press the Esc key.

Using the Microsoft Office Assistant

Microsoft Word 2000 includes an *Office Assistant* that is a link to the on-screen Help feature that anticipates the type of help you need and suggests Help topics related to the work you are doing. The Assistant will also point out ways to perform tasks more easily and provide visual examples and step-by-step instructions for specific tasks. When you open Word, the Assistant displays, by default, in the lower right corner of the screen as shown in figure G.10. The default Assistant is named "Clippit," and is an image of a paper clip. (This image can be changed.)

Office Assistant

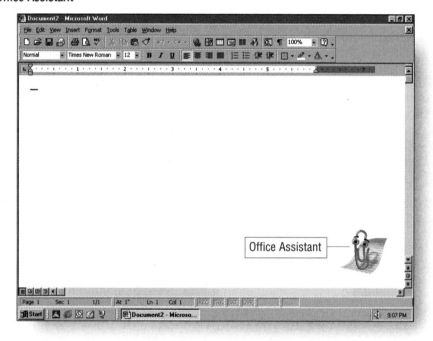

The Assistant will perform a variety of functions. For example, if you try to close a document without saving it, the Assistant will make a sound to get your attention and display a question box like the one shown in figure G.11. At this question, click the desired response.

figure

G.11

Office Assistant Question Box

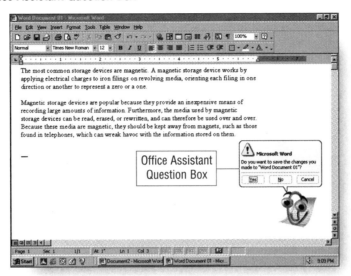

If you are completing a task that Word will automatically format, the Assistant will specify what Word is doing. For example, if you key a numbered paragraph, Word will automatically format this numbered paragraph. As you are keying the numbered paragraph, the Assistant will tell you that Word is automatically formatting the text and ask if you want to learn more about the feature.

If you are working on a task and want help, just click the Assistant. The Assistant will guess what kind of help you want and display a list of Help topics like the list shown in figure G.12. If the desired topic does not display, key a question in the text box that displays below the list of topics, and then click the Search button.

figure

G.12

Office Assistant Help Topics List Box

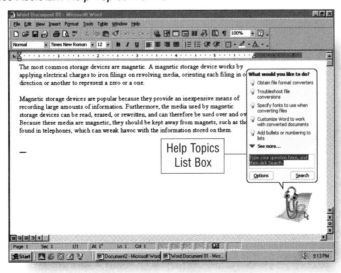

Occasionally, a light bulb will display above the Assistant. Click this light bulb and the Assistant will display a tip about the type of work you are doing.

Hiding/Turning Off the Office Assistant

To hide the Office Assistant, click Help and then Hide the Office Assistant. Redisplay the Office Assistant by clicking Help and then Show the Office Assistant. The Office Assistant can also be turned off for the entire Word session. To do this, click the Office Assistant and then click the Options button that displays in the yellow box. At the Office Assistant dialog box that displays, click the Use the Office Assistant option to remove the check mark, and then click OK.

Changing the Assistant

A variety of other Office Assistants is available. To display and choose another Assistant, position the arrow pointer on the Assistant, and then click the *right* mouse button. At the shortcut menu that displays, click Choose Assistant. This displays the Office Assistant dialog box shown in figure G.13. At this dialog box, the current Assistant displays. To display other Assistants, click the Next button. You can choose from The Dot, F1, The Genius, Office Logo, Mother Nature, Links, and Rocky.

Office Assistant Dialog Box

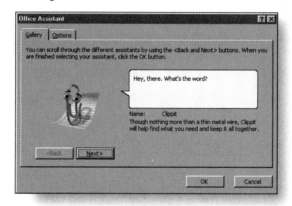

You can customize the Office Assistant by clicking the Options tab at the Office Assistant dialog box. This displays a dialog box with a variety of Help options. Insert a check mark before the features you want active and remove the check mark for those features you want inactive.

Installing Additional Features

During a standard installation of Microsoft Word, all features and applications may not be installed. To install additional features or applications, you would complete the following basic steps (you may want to refer to the Microsoft Word documentation for specific information):

1. At the Windows desktop, double-click the *My Computer* icon.
2. At the My Computer window, double-click the *Control Panel* icon.
3. At the Control Panel window, double-click the *Add/Remove Programs* icon.

4. At the Add/Remove Programs Properties dialog box, click Install.
5. At the next screen, insert the Microsoft Office setup CD-ROM in the appropriate drive. Follow the steps provided by the Install Wizard to install additional features or applications.

Completing Computer Exercises

Some computer exercises in this textbook require that you open an existing file. Exercise files are saved on the CD that accompanies this textbook. The files you need for each chapter are saved in individual folders. Before beginning a chapter, copy the necessary folder from the CD to a formatted disk. After completing exercises in a chapter, delete the chapter folder before copying the next chapter folder. (Check with your instructor before deleting a folder.)

Copying a Folder

The CD-ROM that accompanies this textbook contains numerous files you use to complete some exercises and assessments in chapters. As you begin working in a chapter, copy the chapter folder from the CD to your disk by completing the following steps:

1. Open Word 2000.
2. Insert the CD that accompanies this textbook in the CD-ROM drive.
3. Insert a formatted 3.5-inch disk in the disk drive.
4. Click the Open button on the Standard toolbar.
5. At the Open dialog box, click the down-pointing triangle at the right side of the Look in list box.
6. At the drop-down list that displays, click the drive where the CD is located.
7. In the list box, position the mouse pointer on the chapter folder you want to copy, and then click the *right* mouse button.
8. At the shortcut menu that displays, click Copy.
9. Click the down-pointing triangle at the right side of the Look in list box and then click the drive where your disk is located.
10. With the drive active where your disk is located, position the mouse pointer in any white area in the list box, click the *right* mouse button, and then click Paste at the shortcut menu.
11. After the folder is copied to your disk, click the Cancel button to close the Open dialog box.

The CD that accompanies this textbook contains a folder for each chapter. There are three chapter folders on the CD that do not contain documents. These folders are Chapter 12, Chapter 15, and Chapter 23. Before completing exercises in these chapters, either copy the empty folder to your disk or create your own chapter folder on your disk.

Deleting a Folder

Before copying a chapter folder onto your disk, delete any previous chapter folders. Do this by completing the following steps:

1. Open Word 2000.
2. Insert your disk in the disk drive.
3. Click the Open button on the Standard toolbar.
4. At the Open dialog box, click the down-pointing triangle at the right side of the Look in list box.
5. At the drop-down list that displays, click the drive where your disk is located.
6. Click the chapter folder in the list box.
7. Click the Delete button on the Open dialog box toolbar.
8. At the message asking if you want to remove the folder and all its contents, click Yes.
9. Click the Cancel button to close the Open dialog box.

Step 6

Step 7

Unit *one*

MICROSOFT® WORD 2000

MOUS SKILLS—UNIT ONE

Coding No.	SKILL	Pages
W2000.1	Working with text	
W2000.1.1	Use the Undo, Redo, and Repeat command	25-27, 93-94
W2000.1.2	Apply font formats (Bold, Italic, Underline)	37-38
W2000.1.6	Insert page breaks	115-117
W2000.1.10	Copy formats using the Format Painter	80-81
W2000.1.11	Select and change font and font size	39-43
W2000.1.13	Apply character effects (superscript, subscript, strikethrough, small caps, outline)	44-48
W2000.1.15	Insert symbols	51-54
W2000.2	Working with paragraphs	
W2000.2.1	Align text in paragraphs (Center, Left, Right, Justified)	70-74
W2000.2.2	Add bullets and numbering	81-89
W2000.2.3	Set character, line, and paragraph spacing options	48-51, 74-75, 91-93, 114-115
W2000.2.5	Use Indentation options (Left, Right, First Line, Hanging Indent)	75-80
W2000.2.7	Create an outline style numbered list	88-90
W2000.3	Working with documents	
W2000.3.1	Print a document	7, 11, 152-157
W2000.3.2	Use print preview	122-125
W2000.3.4	Navigate through a document	14-19
W2000.3.6	Set page orientation	117-119
W2000.3.7	Set margins	105-111
W2000.3.11	Align text vertically	120-121
W2000.3.14	Prepare and print envelopes and labels	157-165
W2000.3.16	Create sections with formatting that differs from other sections	112-113
W2000.3.17	Use click and type	128-129
W2000.4	Managing files	
W2000.4.1	Use save	6-7, 10-11
W2000.4.2	Locate and open an existing document	12, 17, 144
W2000.4.3	Use Save As (different name, location, or format)	20-21
W2000.4.4	Create a folder	136
W2000.4.9	Use the Office Assistant	55-61
W2000.4.10	Send a Word document via e-mail	165-166
W2000E.1	Working with paragraphs	
W2000E.1.2	Use text flow options (Widows/Orphans options and keeping lines together)	113-115
W2000E.7	Collaborating with workgroups	
W2000E.7.2	Protect documents	145-146

Chapter 01

Creating, Printing, and Editing Documents

This textbook provides you with instructions on a word processing program using a microcomputer system. The program you will learn to operate is the *software*. Software is the program of instructions that tells the computer what to do. The computer equipment you will use is the *hardware*. You will be learning to operate a software program named Word 2000 on a microcomputer system. Before continuing in this chapter, be sure to read the *Getting Started* section at the beginning of this textbook.

Opening Microsoft Word

Use Microsoft Word 2000 to create, edit, save, and print documents. The steps to open Word may vary depending on your system setup. Generally, to open Word, you would complete the following steps:

1. Turn on the monitor and the CPU. (Depending on your system, you may also need to turn on the printer.)
2. After a few moments, the Windows 98 (or Windows 95) screen displays (your screen may vary). At the Windows 98 (or Windows 95) screen, position the mouse pointer on the Start button on the Taskbar (located at the bottom left side of the screen), and then click the left mouse button. This causes a pop-up menu to display.

3. Point to <u>P</u>rograms. (To do this, drag up until <u>P</u>rograms is selected—do not click the mouse button.) This causes another menu to display to the right of the first pop-up menu.
4. Move the mouse pointer to *Microsoft Word* and then click the left mouse button.

Creating a Word Document

When Microsoft Word is open, a clear document screen displays as shown in figure 1.1. The features of the document screen are described in figure 1.2.

figure
1.1

Clear Document Screen

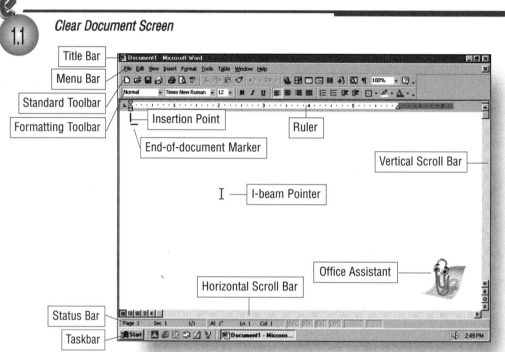

figure
1.2

Microsoft Word Screen

Feature	Description
Title Bar	The document name displays at the left side of the Title bar followed by the program name (such as *Microsoft Word*).
Menu Bar	The Menu bar contains a list of options to manage and customize documents. Word functions and features are grouped into menu options. For example, functions to save, close, or open a new document are contained in the <u>F</u>ile option on the Menu bar.
Standard Toolbar	The Standard toolbar contains buttons that are shortcuts for the most popular commands. For example, buttons are available for opening and saving a document. Position the mouse pointer on a button on the Standard toolbar and, after one second, a *ScreenTip* displays with the name of the button.

Formatting Toolbar	The Formatting toolbar contains buttons that can quickly apply formatting to text in a document such as bold, italics, and underlining. Position the mouse pointer on a button on the Formatting toolbar and, after one second, a ScreenTip will display with the name of the button.
Ruler	Set margins, indents, and tabs with the Ruler.
Insertion Point	The insertion point indicates the location where the next character entered at the keyboard will appear.
End-of-document Marker	The end-of-document marker indicates the end of the document.
Scroll Bars	Use the scroll bars to view various parts of the document.
Status Bar	The Status bar displays information about the text in the document and whether certain working modes are active. The Status bar also displays the current location of the insertion point by page number, section number, line measurement, line count, and column position. At the right side of the Status bar, working modes are displayed. When the working mode is dimmed, it is inactive. When the working mode is active, it displays in black.
Taskbar	The bottom line on the screen is the Taskbar. Information on the Taskbar was presented in the *Getting Started* section.
Office Assistant	The Office Assistant is a link to the on-screen Help feature that anticipates the type of help you need and suggests Help topics related to the work you are doing. The Assistant will also point out ways to perform tasks more easily and provide visual examples and step-by-step instructions for specific tasks.

At a clear document screen, key (type) the information to create a document. A document is any information you choose; for instance, a letter, memo, report, term paper, table, etc. Some things to consider when keying text are:

- **Word Wrap:** As you key (type) text to create a document, you do not need to press the Enter key at the end of each line because Word wraps text to the next line. A word is wrapped to the next line if it begins before the right margin and continues past the right margin. The only times you need to press Enter are to end a paragraph, create a blank line, or end a short line.

- **AutoCorrect:** Word contains a feature that automatically corrects certain words as they are being keyed (typed). For example, if you key the word *adn* instead of *and*, Word automatically corrects it when you press the spacebar after the word. There are many other automatic corrections. You will learn more about this feature in a later chapter.

- **Spell It:** A feature in Word called Spell It automatically inserts a wavy red line below words that are not contained in the Spelling dictionary or automatically corrected by AutoCorrect. This may include misspelled words, proper names, some terminology, and some foreign words. If you key a word not recognized by the Spelling dictionary, Word inserts a wavy red line below the word. If the word is correct, you can leave it as written. If, however, the word is incorrect, you have two choices—you can backspace over the word using the Backspace key and then key it correctly, or you can position the I-beam pointer on the word, click the *right* mouse button, and then click the correct spelling in the pop-up menu.

- **Automatic Grammar Checker:** Word includes an automatic grammar checker. If the grammar checker detects a sentence containing a grammatical error, a wavy green line is inserted below the sentence. At this point, leave the wavy green line. You will learn more about the grammar checker in chapter 6.
- **Spacing Punctuation:** Typically, Word uses Times New Roman as the default typeface. Times New Roman is a proportional typeface. (You will learn more about typefaces in chapter 2.) When keying text in a proportional typeface, space once (rather than twice) after end-of-sentence punctuation such as a period, question mark, or exclamation point, and after a colon. Proportional typeface is set closer together, and extra white space at the end of a sentence or after a colon is not needed.

Saving a Document

When you have created a document, the information will need to be saved on your disk. When a document is keyed (typed) for the first time and is displayed in the document screen, it is temporary. If you turn off the computer or if the power goes off, you will lose the information and have to rekey it. Only when you save a document is it saved permanently.

Save

A variety of methods can be used to save a document. You can save by clicking the Save button on the Standard toolbar; by clicking File and then Save; or with the shortcut command, Ctrl + S. For many features in this textbook, instructions for using the mouse will be emphasized. (For information on using the keyboard, refer to the "Choosing Commands" section in *Getting Started*.) To save a document with the Save button on the Standard toolbar, you would complete the following steps:

1. Position the mouse pointer on the Save button (the third button from the left) on the Standard toolbar and then click the left mouse button.
2. At the Save As dialog box shown in figure 1.3, key the name of the document.
3. Click the Save button located in the lower right corner of the dialog box.

Save As Dialog Box

1.3

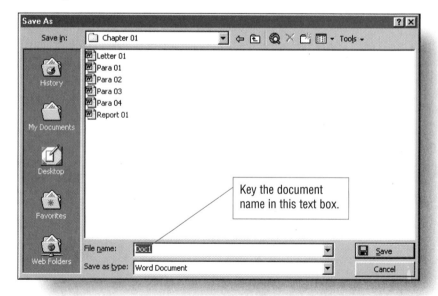

You can also display the Save As dialog box by clicking File on the Menu bar and then clicking Save As at the drop-down menu.

Naming a Document

Document names created in Word and other suite applications can be up to 255 characters in length, including drive letter and any folder names, and may include spaces. File names cannot include any of the following characters:

forward slash (/)	question mark (?)
backslash (\)	quotation mark (")
greater than sign (>)	colon (:)
less than sign (<)	semicolon (;)
asterisk (*)	pipe symbol (|)

Canceling a Command

If a drop-down menu is displayed in the document screen, it can be removed with the mouse or the keyboard. If you are using the mouse, position the I-beam pointer in the document screen (outside the drop-down menu), and then click the left mouse button. If you are using the keyboard, press the Alt key. You can also press the Esc key twice. The first time you press Esc, the drop-down menu is removed but the menu option on the Menu bar is still selected. The second time you press Esc, the option on the Menu bar is no longer selected.

Several methods can be used to remove a dialog box from the document screen. To remove a dialog box with the mouse, position the mouse pointer on the Cancel command button, and then click the left mouse button. You can also click the Close button located in the upper right corner of the dialog box containing the "X." A dialog box can be removed from the document screen with the keyboard by pressing the Esc key.

Close

Closing a Document

When a document is saved with the Save or Save As options, the document is saved on the disk and remains in the document screen. To remove the document from the screen, click the Close button located at the far right side of the Menu bar (contains the X) or click File and then Close. (If you close a document with the Close button, be sure to use the Close button on the Menu bar, not the Close button on the Title bar. The Close button on the Title bar will close the Word program.) When you close a document, the document is removed and a blank screen is displayed. At this screen, you can open a previously saved document, create a new document, or exit the Word program.

Printing a Document

Many of the computer exercises you will be creating will need to be printed. A printing of a document is referred to as "hard copy." (Soft copy is a document displayed in the document screen and hard copy is a document printed on paper.) A document can be sent immediately to the printer by clicking the Print button on the Standard toolbar or through the Print dialog box. Display the Print dialog box by clicking File and then Print.

Print

Exiting Word and Windows

When you are finished working with Word and have saved all necessary information, exit Word by clicking File and then Exit. You can also exit the Word program by clicking the Close button located at the right side of the Title bar. (The Close button contains an X.) After exiting Word, you may also need to exit the Windows program. To exit Windows, you would complete the following steps:

1. Click the Start button located at the left side of the Taskbar.
2. At the pop-up menu, click Shut Down.
3. At the Shut Down Windows dialog box, make sure *Shut down* is selected, and then click Yes.

Completing Computer Exercises

At the end of sections within chapters and at the end of chapters, you will be completing hands-on exercises at the computer. These exercises will provide you with the opportunity to practice the presented functions and commands. The skill assessment exercises at the end of each chapter include general directions. If you do not remember how to perform a particular function, refer to the text in the chapter.

Copying Data Documents

In several exercises in each chapter, you will be opening documents provided with this textbook. Before beginning each chapter, copy the chapter folder from the CD that accompanies this textbook to a floppy disk (or other folder). Detailed steps on how to copy a folder from the CD to your floppy disk are presented in the *Getting Started* section. Abbreviated steps are printed on the back cover of this textbook.

Changing the Default Folder

At the end of this and the remaining chapters in the textbook, you will be saving documents. More than likely, you will want to save documents onto a disk. You will also be opening documents that have been saved on your disk.

To save documents on and to open documents from your disk, you will need to specify the drive where your disk is located as the default folder. Once you specify the drive where your data disk is located, Word uses this as the default folder until you exit the Word program. The next time you open Word, you will again need to specify the drive where your data disk is located. You only need to change the default folder once each time you enter the Word program.

You can change the default folder at the Open dialog box or the Save As dialog box. To change the folder to the Chapter 01 folder on the disk in drive A: at the Open dialog box, you would complete the following steps (see figure 1.4):

1. Click the Open button on the Standard toolbar (the second button from the left); or click File and then Open.
2. At the Open dialog box, click the down-pointing triangle at the right side of the Look in text box.
3. From the drop-down list that displays, click *3½ Floppy (A:)*.
4. Double-click *Chapter 01* that displays in the list box.
5. Click the Cancel button in the lower right corner of the dialog box.

figure
1.4

Changing the Default Folder

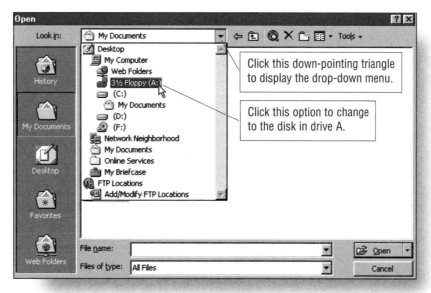

Click this down-pointing triangle to display the drop-down menu.

Click this option to change to the disk in drive A.

If you want to change the default folder permanently, make the change at the Options dialog box with the File Locations tab selected. To permanently change the default folder to drive A, you would complete these steps:

1. Click Tools and then Options.
2. At the Options dialog box, click the File Locations tab.
3. At the Options dialog box with the File Locations tab selected, make sure *Documents* is selected in the File types list box and then click the Modify button.
4. At the Modify Location dialog box, click the down-pointing triangle at the right side of the Look in list box, and then click *3½ Floppy (A:)*.
5. Click the OK button.

Changing the Default Type Size

Typically, Word uses 10-point Times New Roman as the default font. (You will learn more about fonts in chapter 2.) Exercises in this and other chapters will generally display text in 12-point size. If the system you are operating uses a point size other than 12, you can change the default type size to 12 by completing the following steps (see figure 1.5):

1. Click Format and then Font.
2. At the Font dialog box, click *12* in the Size list box.
3. Click the Default command button located in the lower left corner of the dialog box.
4. At the Office Assistant message box asking if you want to change the default font, click Yes.

figure

1.5

Changing the Default Font

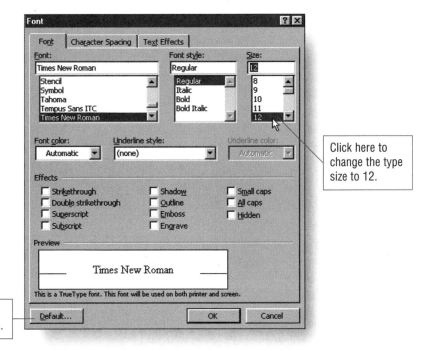

Click here to change the type size to 12.

After clicking the 12 in the Size list box, click the Default button.

Once the default type size has been changed in this manner, the new type size will be in effect each time you open the Word program. You only need to change the default once.

Creating and Printing a Document

1. Follow the instructions in this chapter to open Windows and then Word.
2. At the clear document screen, change the default folder to the drive where your disk is located by completing the following steps: (Depending on your system configuration, this may not be necessary. Check with your instructor before changing the default folder.)
   a. Click the Open button on the Standard toolbar.
   b. At the Open dialog box, click the down-pointing triangle to the right of the Look in option.
   c. From the drop-down list that displays, click 3½ Floppy (A:) (this may vary depending on your system).

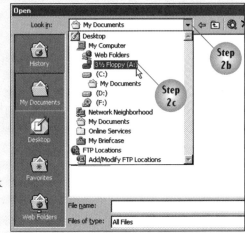

d. Double-click the *Chapter 01* folder that displays in the list box.
e. Click the Cancel button to close the Open dialog box.

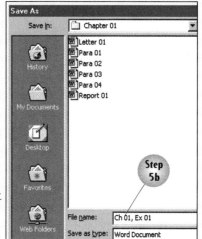

Step 2d

3. At the document screen, make sure that 12-point Times New Roman is the default font. (If not, change the default type size to 12 following the directions listed in the "Changing the Default Type Size" section of this chapter; or, check with your instructor.)
4. Key (type) the text in figure 1.6. If you make a mistake while keying and Spell It inserts a wavy red line, backspace over the incorrect word using the Backspace key, and then rekey the correct word. Ignore any wavy green lines inserted by Word. (Do not worry about doing a lot of correcting—you will learn more about editing a document later in this chapter.) Remember to space only once after end-of-sentence punctuation when keying the text.
5. When you are done keying the text, save the document and name it Ch 01, Ex 01 (for Chapter 1, Exercise 1) by completing the following steps:
    a. Click the Save button on the Standard toolbar.
    b. At the Save As dialog box, key **Ch 01, Ex 01**. (Key a zero when naming documents, not the letter O. In this textbook, the zero, 0, displays thinner than the letter O. As you key **Ch 01, Ex 01**, the selected text in the File name text box is automatically deleted and replaced with the text you key.)

Step 5b

    c. Click the Save button located in the lower right corner of the dialog box or press the Enter key.
6. Print the document by clicking the Print button on the Standard toolbar.
7. Close Ch 01, Ex 01 by clicking File and then Close or by clicking the Close button located at the far right side of the Menu bar. (This displays a blank screen, rather than a clear screen.)

figure

1.6   *Exercise 1*

Computer systems consist of hardware, or machinery, and software, or instructions that run on the machines and process information. A piece of software that performs a particular kind of function is called an application. Business applications can be roughly categorized into three types: vertical applications, individual applications, and workgroup applications.

A vertical application is integrated software that performs functions central to many different parts of a business. Vertical applications are usually custom built for particular industries. Examples of industries that use vertical applications are banking, insurance, and retail merchandising.

Opening a Document

Open

When a document has been saved and closed, it can be opened at the Open dialog box shown in figure 1.7. To display this dialog box, click the Open button on the Standard toolbar or click File and then Open. At the Open dialog box, double-click the document name.

Open Dialog Box

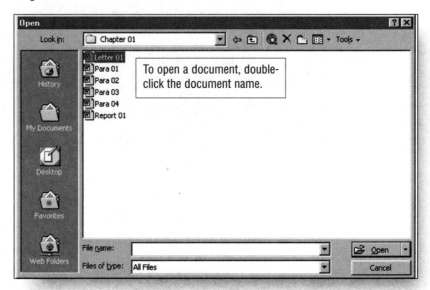

To open a document, double-click the document name.

Creating a New Document

New Blank
Document

When you close a document, a blank screen is displayed. If you want to create a new document, display a clear document screen. To do this, you would click the New Blank Document button on the Standard toolbar (the first button).

Creating and Printing a New Document

1. At a blank screen, create a new document by clicking the New Blank Document button on the Standard toolbar (the first button from the left).
2. At the clear document screen, key the information shown in figure 1.8. (Correct any errors highlighted by Spell It as they occur and remember to space once after end-of-sentence punctuation. Ignore any wavy green lines inserted by Word.)
3. Save the document and name it Ch 01, Ex 02 by completing the following steps:
   a. Click the Save button on the Standard toolbar.
   b. At the Save As dialog box, key **Ch 01, Ex 02**.
   c. Click the Save button (or press Enter).

4. Print the document by completing the following steps:
   a. Click File and then Print.
   b. At the Print dialog box, click OK (located in the lower right corner of the dialog box).
5. Close the document by clicking File and then Close or clicking the Close button located at the right side of the Menu bar.

Make sure correct printer name displays here.

Step 4b

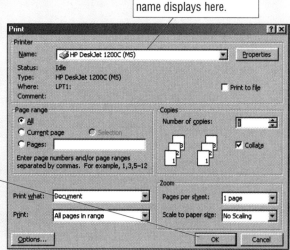

Exercise 2

An individual application is designed to be used by a single person, generally on a workstation, PC, laptop, palmtop, or PDA. Types of individual applications used in business include spreadsheets, word processors, databases, graphics programs, electronic mail, personal productivity programs, and software suites.

Large corporations often adopt a standard set of commercial software programs for their employees. Sometimes, businesses also have customized applications written to perform highly specific tasks. For example, an environmental engineering firm might have a program written specifically to help the company's hydrologist analyze the potential for groundwater contamination at construction or manufacturing sites.

Displaying and Moving Toolbars

The Standard and Formatting toolbars display below the Menu bar at the top of the screen. These toolbars may display side by side with only a portion of the buttons visible. To display the hidden buttons, click the More Buttons button (displays with two right-pointing arrows). Clicking the More Buttons button displays a palette of buttons.

The Formatting toolbar in the figures in this textbook displays immediately below the Standard toolbar. At this display, all buttons on the toolbars are visible. To move the Formatting toolbar below the Standard toolbar, complete the following steps:

1. Click <u>T</u>ools and then <u>C</u>ustomize.
2. At the Customize dialog box, click the <u>O</u>ptions tab. (Skip this step if the <u>O</u>ptions tab is already selected.)
3. Click the *Standard and Formatting toolbars <u>s</u>hare one row* option. (This removes the check mark.)
4. Click the Close button to close the dialog box.

The display of the Standard and Formatting toolbars (as well as other toolbars) can be turned on or off. To do this, position the mouse pointer anywhere on a toolbar, and then click the *right* mouse button. At the drop-down menu that displays, click the toolbar name you want turned on or off. You can also turn on or off the display of a toolbar by clicking <u>V</u>iew on the Menu bar, pointing to <u>T</u>oolbars, and then clicking the toolbar name.

Expanding Drop-Down Menus

Microsoft Word personalizes menus and toolbars as you work. When you click an option on the Menu bar, only the most popular options display (considered first-rank options). This is referred to as an *adaptive menu*. To expand the drop-down menu and display the full set of options (first-rank options as well as second-rank options), click the down-pointing arrows that display at the bottom of the drop-down menu. A drop-down menu will also expand if you click an option on the Menu bar and then pause on the menu for a few seconds. Second-rank options on the expanded drop-down menu display with a lighter gray background. If you choose a second-rank option, it is promoted and becomes a first-rank option the next time the drop-down menu is displayed.

If you want all menu options displayed when you click an option on the Menu bar, turn off the adaptive menu feature. To do this, you would complete the following steps:

1. Click <u>T</u>ools, expand the drop-down menu by clicking the down-pointing arrows that display at the bottom of the menu, and then click <u>C</u>ustomize.
2. At the Customize dialog box, click the <u>O</u>ptions tab.
3. At the Customize dialog box with the <u>O</u>ptions tab selected, click in the *Me<u>n</u>us show recently used commands first* check box to remove the check mark.
4. Click the Close button to close the dialog box.

Editing a Document

Many documents that are created need to have changes made to them. These changes may include adding text, called *inserting*, or removing text, called *deleting*. To insert or delete text, you need to be able to move the insertion point to specific locations in a document without erasing the text through which it passes. To move the insertion point without interfering with text, you can use the mouse, the keyboard, or the mouse combined with the keyboard.

Moving the Insertion Point with the Mouse

The mouse can be used to move the insertion point quickly to specific locations in the document. To do this, position the I-beam pointer at the location where you want the insertion point, and then click the left mouse button.

Scrolling with the Mouse

In addition to moving the insertion point to a specific location, the mouse can be used to move the display of text in the document screen. Scrolling in a document changes the text displayed but does not move the insertion point. If you want to move the insertion point to a new location in a document, scroll to the location, position the I-beam pointer in the desired location, and then click the left mouse button.

You can use the mouse with the *horizontal scroll bar* and/or the *vertical scroll bar* to scroll through text in a document. The horizontal scroll bar displays toward the bottom of the Word screen and the vertical scroll bar displays at the right side. Figure 1.9 displays the Word screen with the scroll bars and scroll boxes identified.

figure
1.9   Scroll Bars

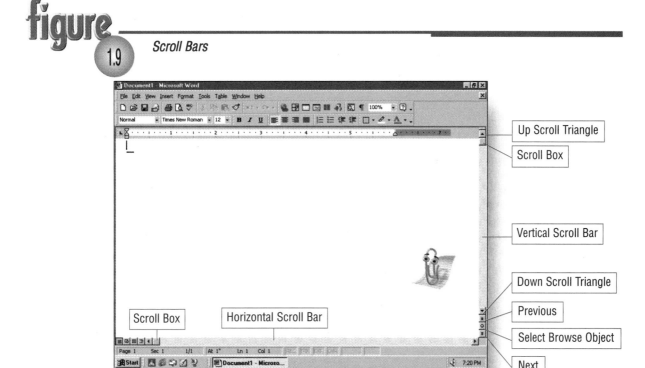

Up Scroll Triangle
Scroll Box
Vertical Scroll Bar
Down Scroll Triangle
Previous
Select Browse Object
Next
Scroll Box
Horizontal Scroll Bar

Click a scroll triangle to scroll the text in the document the direction indicated on the triangle. The vertical and horizontal scroll bars each contain a scroll box. A scroll box indicates the location of the text in the document screen in relation to the remainder of the document. To scroll up one screen at a time, position the mouse pointer above the scroll box (but below the up scroll triangle) on the vertical scroll bar, and then click the left mouse button. Position the mouse pointer below the scroll box and click the left button to scroll down a screen. If you hold down the left button, the action becomes continuous. You can also position the mouse pointer on the scroll box, hold down the left mouse button, and then drag the scroll box along the scroll bar to reposition text in the document screen.

As you drag the scroll box along the vertical scroll bar in a longer document, page numbers display at the right side of the document screen in a yellow box. (You will notice this when completing exercise 3.)

Moving the Insertion Point to a Specific Page

Along with scrolling options, Word also contains navigation buttons for moving the insertion point to a specific location. Navigation buttons are shown in figure 1.9 and include the Previous button, the Select Browse Object button, and the Next button. The full names of and the tasks completed by the Previous and Next buttons vary depending on the last navigation completed. Click the Select Browse Object button and a palette of browsing choices displays. You will learn more about the Select Browse Object button in the next section.

Previous

Select Browse
Object

Next

Word includes a Go To option you can use to move the insertion point to a specific page within a document. To move the insertion point to a specific page, you would complete the following steps:

1. Click Edit, expand the drop-down menu by clicking the down-pointing arrows that display at the bottom of the menu, and then click Go To; or, double-click the page number at the left side of the Status bar.
2. At the Find and Replace dialog box with the Go To tab selected, key the page number. (If you are using the 10-key pad at the right side of the keyboard, make sure the Num Lock key is on.)
3. Click the Go To button or press Enter.
4. Click the Close button to close the Find and Replace dialog box.

Browsing in a Document

The Select Browse Object button located at the bottom of the vertical scroll bar contains options for browsing through a document. Click this button and a palette of browsing choices displays as shown in figure 1.10. Use the options on the palette to move the insertion point to various features in a Word document. Position the mouse pointer on an option in the palette and the option name displays below the options. For example, position the mouse pointer on the last option in the top row and *Browse by Page* displays below the options. When you click the Browse by Page option, the insertion point moves to the next page in the document. Use the other options in the palette to move to the next specified object in the document.

Select Browse Object Palette

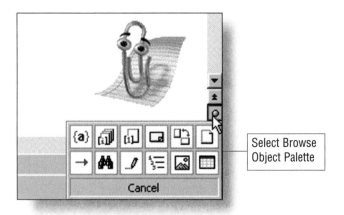

Select Browse
Object Palette

exercise 3

Scrolling, Browsing, and Moving the Insertion Point in a Document

1. At a clear document screen, open Report 01.
2. Practice moving the insertion point and scrolling and browsing through the document using the mouse by completing the following steps:
   a. Position the I-beam pointer at the beginning of the first paragraph and then click the left mouse button. (This moves the insertion point to the location of the I-beam pointer.)
   b. Position the mouse pointer on the down scroll triangle on the vertical scroll bar and then click the left mouse button several times. (This scrolls down lines of text in the document.) With the mouse pointer on the down scroll triangle, hold down the left mouse button and keep it down until the end of the document displays.
   c. Position the mouse pointer on the up scroll triangle and hold down the left mouse button until the beginning of the document displays.
   d. Position the mouse pointer below the scroll box and then click the left mouse button. Continue clicking the mouse button (with the mouse pointer positioned below the scroll box) until the end of the document displays.
   e. Position the mouse pointer on the scroll box in the vertical scroll bar. Hold down the left mouse button, drag the scroll box to the top of the vertical scroll bar, and then release the mouse button. (Notice that the document page numbers display in a yellow box at the right side of the document screen.)
   f. Click on the title at the beginning of the document. (This moves the insertion point to the location of the mouse pointer.)
   g. Click the Next Page button located at the bottom of the vertical scroll bar. (This moves the insertion point to page 2.)
   h. Click the Next Page button again. (This moves the insertion point to page 3.)
   i. Click twice on the Previous Page button located immediately above the Select Browse Object button on the vertical scroll bar. (This moves the insertion point to the beginning of page 1.)
   j. Move the insertion point to page 4 by completing the following steps:
      1) Click Edit, expand the drop-down menu by clicking the down-pointing arrows that display at the bottom of the menu, and then click Go To; or, double-click the page number at the left side of the Status bar.
      2) At the Find and Replace dialog box with the Go To tab selected, make sure the insertion point is positioned in the Enter page number text box, and then key 4.

      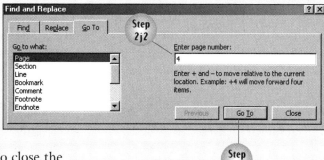

      3) Click the Go To button or press Enter.
      4) Click the Close button to close the Find and Replace dialog box.

k. Move the insertion point to page 1 by completing the following steps:

1) Click the Select Browse Object button (bottom of the vertical scroll bar).
2) At the palette of browsing choices, click the first choice in the second row (Go To).
3) At the Find and Replace dialog box with the <u>G</u>o To tab selected, press the Delete key to delete the *4* in the <u>E</u>nter page number text box, and then key **1**.
4) Click the Go <u>T</u>o button or press Enter.
5) Click the Close button to close the Find and Replace dialog box.
l. Move to the beginning of page 2 by completing the following steps:
1) Click the Select Browse Object button.
2) At the palette of browsing choices, click the last choice in the first row *(Browse by Page)*. (This moves the insertion point to page 2.)
3) Click the Select Browse Object button again and then click the last choice in the top row (Browse by Page). (This moves the insertion point to page 3.)
3. Close Report 01.

Moving the Insertion Point with the Keyboard

To move the insertion point with the keyboard, use the arrow keys located to the right of the regular keyboard. (You can also use the arrow keys on the numeric keypad. If you use these keys, make sure Num Lock is off.) Use the arrow keys together with other keys to move the insertion point to various locations in the document as shown in figure 1.11.

Insertion Point Movement Commands

To move insertion point	Press
One character left	left arrow
One character right	right arrow
One line up	up arrow
One line down	down arrow
One word to the left	Ctrl + left arrow
One word to the right	Ctrl + right arrow
To end of a line	End
To beginning of a line	Home
To beginning of current paragraph	Ctrl + up arrow
To beginning of previous paragraph	Ctrl + up arrow twice
To beginning of next paragraph	Ctrl + down arrow

Up one screen	Page Up
Down one screen	Page Down
To top of previous page	Ctrl + Page Up
To top of next page	Ctrl + Page Down
To beginning of document	Ctrl + Home
To end of document	Ctrl + End

When moving the insertion point, Word considers a word to be any series of characters between spaces. A paragraph is any text that is followed by a stroke of the Enter key. A page is text that is separated by a soft or hard page break.

If you open a previously saved document, you can move the insertion point to where the insertion point was last located when the document was closed by pressing Shift + F5.

Moving the Insertion Point Using the Keyboard

1. Open Report 01.
2. Practice moving the insertion point using the keyboard by completing the following steps:
   a. Press the right arrow key to move the insertion point to the next character to the right. Continue pressing the right arrow key until the insertion point is positioned at the end of the first paragraph.
   b. Press Ctrl + right arrow key to move the insertion point to the next word to the right. Continue pressing Ctrl + right arrow until the insertion point is positioned on the last word of the second paragraph.
   c. Press Ctrl + left arrow key until the insertion point is positioned at the beginning of the document.
   d. Press the End key to move the insertion point to the end of the title.
   e. Press the Home key to move the insertion point to the beginning of the title.
   f. Press Ctrl + Page Down to position the insertion point at the beginning of page 2.
   g. Press Ctrl + Page Up to position the insertion point at the beginning of page 1 (the beginning of the document).
   h. Press Ctrl + End to move the insertion point to the end of the document.
   i. Press Ctrl + Home to move the insertion point to the beginning of the document.
3. Close Report 01.

Inserting Text

Once you have created a document, you may want to insert information you forgot or have since decided to include. At the default document screen, Word moves existing characters to the right as you key additional text.

If you want to key over something, switch to the Overtype mode. You can do this by pressing the Insert key or by double-clicking the OVR mode button on the Status bar. When Overtype is on, the OVR mode button displays in black. To turn off Overtype, press the Insert key or double-click the OVR mode button.

Deleting Text

When you edit a document, you may want to delete (remove) text. Commands for deleting text are presented in figure 1.12.

Deletion Commands

To delete	Press
Character right of insertion point	Delete key
Character left of insertion point	Backspace key
Text from insertion point to beginning of word	Ctrl + Backspace
Text from insertion point to end of word	Ctrl + Delete

Splitting and Joining Paragraphs

Paragraphs of text can be split or joined by inserting or deleting lines. To split a large paragraph into two smaller paragraphs, position the insertion point on the first character that will begin the new paragraph, and then press the Enter key twice. To join two paragraphs into one, position the insertion point on the first character of the second paragraph, and then press the Backspace key until the paragraphs join. More than likely, you will need to then press the spacebar to separate the sentences.

Saving a Document with Save As

Earlier in this chapter, you learned to save a document with the Save button on the Standard toolbar or the Save option from the File drop-down menu. The File drop-down menu also contains a Save As option. The Save As option is used to save a previously created document with a new name.

For example, suppose you create and save a document named Yearly Report, and then open it later. If you save the document again with the Save button on the Standard toolbar or the Save option from the File drop-down menu, Word will save the document with the same name. You will not be prompted to key a name for the document. This is because Word assumes that when you use the Save option on a previously saved document, you want to save it with the same name. If you open the document named Yearly Report, make some changes to it, and then want to save it with a new name, you must use the Save As option. When you use the Save As option, Word displays the Save As dialog box where you can key a new name for the document.

exercise 5

Editing and Saving a Document

1. Open Para 02.
2. Save the document with the name Ch 01, Ex 05 using Save As by completing the following steps:
   a. Click File and then Save As.
   b. At the Save As dialog box, key **Ch 01, Ex 05**.
   c. Click the Save button or press Enter.
3. Make the changes indicated by the proofreaders' marks in figure 1.13. (Proofreaders' marks are listed and described in Appendix A at the end of this textbook.)
4. Save the document again with the same name (Ch 01, Ex 05) by clicking the Save button on the Standard toolbar or by clicking File and then Save.
5. Print and then close Ch 01, Ex 05.

figure

1.13   Exercise 5

Flyers are generally used to advertise a product or service that is available for a limited amount of time. ~~Frequently, you may find~~ flyers _may be found_ stuffed in a grocery bag; attached to a mailbox, door handle or windshield; placed in a bin near an entrance; or placed on a countertop for prospective customers to carry away. Examples of businesses that use flyers for advertising services include lawn maintenance companies, babysitters, window washers, cleaning services, realtors, dentists, doctors, lawyers, and more. ~~As you can see, this form of advertising is used by just about anyone.~~

~~In a flyer,~~ a headline _in a flyer_ should be a dominant visual element, set significantly larger than the words that follow. Standard headlines are usually 36 to 48 points in size. However, depending on your document, the headline may _even_ exceed 72 points. ~~To use a type size larger than 72, display the Font dialog box, and then key the desired point size in the Size text box.~~

_no ¶_ Besides increasing the point size for headlines, you may want to change the shading and/or color of the ~~font~~ _text._ Depending on your needs, you may choose a large, thick typeface or change the color of the headline. A flyer with a large, color headline ~~is an eye-catching way~~ to announce an event or present important information. _effectively_

Selecting Text

The mouse and/or keyboard can be used to select a specific amount of text. Once selected, you can delete the text or perform other Word functions involving the selected text. When text is selected, it displays as white text on a black background as shown in figure 1.14.

Selected Text

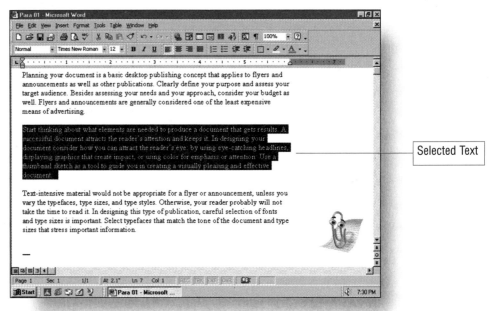

Selecting with the Mouse

You can use the mouse to select a word, line, sentence, paragraph, or the entire document. Figure 1.15 indicates the steps to follow to select various amounts of text. To select specific amounts of text such as a line, the instructions in the figure tell you to click in the selection bar. The selection bar is the space at the left side of the document screen between the left edge of the screen and the text. When the mouse pointer is positioned in the selection bar, the pointer turns into an arrow pointing up and to the right (instead of to the left).

figure

1.15

Selecting with the Mouse

To select	Complete these steps using the mouse
A word	Double-click the word.
A line of text	Click in the selection bar to the left of the line.
Multiple lines of text	Drag in the selection bar to the left of the lines.
A sentence	Hold down the Ctrl key, then click anywhere in the sentence.
A paragraph	Double-click in the selection bar next to the paragraph or triple-click anywhere in the paragraph.
Multiple paragraphs	Drag in the selection bar.
An entire document	Triple-click in the selection bar.

To select an amount of text other than a word, sentence, or paragraph, position the I-beam pointer on the first character of the text to be selected, hold down the left mouse button, drag the I-beam pointer to the last character of the text to be selected, and then release the mouse button. You can also select all text between the current insertion point and the I-beam pointer. To do this, position the insertion point where you want the selection to begin, hold down the Shift key, click the I-beam pointer at the end of the selection, and then release the Shift key.

To cancel a selection using the mouse, click anywhere in the document screen outside the selected text.

Selecting with the Keyboard

To select a specific amount of text using the keyboard, use the Extend Selection key, F8, along with the arrow keys. When you press F8, the extend selection mode is turned on and the EXT mode button on the Status bar displays in black letters. (You can also turn on the extend selection mode by double-clicking the EXT mode button on the Status bar.) As you move the insertion point through text, the text is selected. If you want to cancel the selection, press the Esc key, and then press any arrow key (or double-click the EXT mode button on the Status bar and then press any arrow key). You can also select text with the commands shown in figure 1.16.

figure
1.16
Selecting with the Keyboard

To select	Press
One character to right	Shift + right arrow
One character to left	Shift + left arrow
To end of word	Ctrl + Shift + right arrow
To beginning of word	Ctrl + Shift + left arrow
To end of line	Shift + End
To beginning of line	Shift + Home
One line up	Shift + up arrow
One line down	Shift + down arrow
To beginning of paragraph	Ctrl + Shift + up arrow
To end of paragraph	Ctrl + Shift + down arrow
One screen up	Shift + Page Up
One screen down	Shift + Page Down
To end of document	Ctrl + Shift + End
To beginning of document	Ctrl + Shift + Home
Entire document	Ctrl + A or click Edit, Select All

exercise
6

Selecting and Deleting Text

1. Open Letter 04.
2. Save the document with Save As and name it Ch 01, Ex 06.
3. Delete the name, *Dr. Jennifer Salo*, and the department, *Office Technology Department*, using the mouse by completing the following steps:
   a. Position the I-beam pointer on the *D* in *Dr.* (in the address).
   b. Hold down the left mouse button and then drag the mouse down until *Dr. Jennifer Salo* and *Office Technology Department* are selected.
   c. Release the left mouse button.
   d. Press the Delete key.
4. Position the insertion point at the left margin on the line above *Greenwater Community College* and then key the name, **Mrs. Gina Thompson**.
5. Delete *Dr. Salo* in the salutation (after the word *Dear*), then key the name **Mrs. Thompson**. (You choose the method for deleting.)
6. Delete the reference line, *Re: Desktop Publishing Course*, using the Extend Selection key, F8, by completing the following steps:
   a. Position the insertion point on the *R* in *Re:*.

    b. Press F8 to turn on select.

    c. Press the down arrow key twice. (This selects the reference line and the blank line below it.)

    d. Press the Delete key.

7. Delete the first sentence in the first paragraph using the mouse by completing the following steps:

    a. Position the I-beam pointer anywhere in the sentence, *The Southern Computer Technology conference we attended last week was very educational.*

    b. Hold down the Ctrl key and then click the left mouse button.

    c. Press the Delete key.

8. Delete the first sentence in the second paragraph (the sentence that reads, *The interest in the class has been phenomenal.*) using the keyboard by completing the following steps:

    a. Position the insertion point on the first letter of the sentence (the *T* in *The*).

    b. Hold down the Shift key and then press the right arrow key until the sentence is selected. Be sure to include the period at the end of the sentence and the space after the period.

    c. Press the Delete key.

9. Delete the third paragraph in the letter using the mouse by completing the following steps:

    a. Position the I-beam pointer anywhere in the third paragraph (the paragraph that begins, *The instructor for the course...*).

    b. Triple-click the left mouse button.

    c. Press the Delete key.

    d. Press the Delete key again to delete the extra blank line before the last paragraph.

10. Save the document again with the same name (Ch 01, Ex 06).

11. Print and then close Ch 01, Ex 06.

Using the Undo and Redo Buttons

If you make a mistake and delete text that you did not intend to, or if you change your mind after deleting text and want to retrieve it, you can use the Undo or Redo buttons on the Standard toolbar. For example, if you key text and then click the Undo button, the text will be removed. Word removes text to the beginning of the document or up to the point where text had been previously deleted. You can undo text or commands. For example, if you add formatting such as bolding to text and then click the Undo button, the bolding is removed.

Undo

If you use the Undo button and then decide you do not want to reverse the original action, click the Redo button. For example, if you select and underline text, and then decide to remove underlining, click the Undo button. If you then decide you want the underlining back on, click the Redo button. Many Word actions can be undone or redone. Some actions, however, such as printing and saving cannot be undone or redone.

Redo

In addition to the Undo and Redo buttons on the Standard toolbar, you can use options from the Edit drop-down menu to undo and redo actions. The first option at the Edit drop-down menu will vary depending on the last action completed. For example, if you click the Numbering button on the Formatting toolbar, and then click Edit on the Menu bar, the first option displays as Undo Number Default. If you decide you do not want the numbering option on, click the Undo Number Default option at the Edit drop-down menu. You can also just click the Undo button on the Standard toolbar.

Word maintains actions in temporary memory. If you want to undo an action performed earlier, click the down-pointing triangle to the right of the Undo button. This causes a drop-down menu to display as shown in figure 1.17.

Undo Drop-Down List

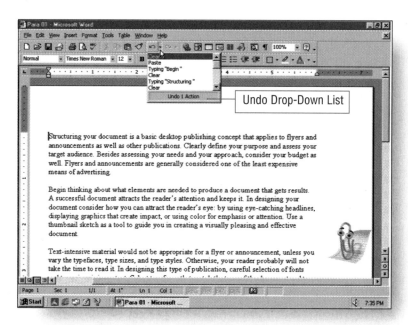

To make a selection from this drop-down menu, click the desired action. Any actions preceding a chosen action are also undone. You can do the same with the actions in the Redo drop-down list. To display the Redo drop-down list, click the down-pointing triangle to the right of the Redo button. To redo an action, click the desired action. Any actions preceding the chosen action are also redone. Multiple actions must be undone or redone in sequence.

Deleting and Restoring Text with the Undo Button

1. Open Para 01.
2. Save the document with Save As and name it Ch 01, Ex 07.
3. Make the following changes to the document:
   a. Move the insertion point to the end of the document. Press the Backspace key until the last seven words of the document *(and type sizes that stress important information.)* are deleted. Be sure to delete the space before *and*.
   b. Undo the deletion by clicking the Undo button on the Standard toolbar.
   c. Redo the deletion by clicking the Redo button on the Standard toolbar.
   d. Key a period after the word *document* to end the sentence.
   e. Select the first sentence in the first paragraph and then delete it.

    f.   Select the second paragraph in the document and then delete it.

    g.   Undo the two deletions by completing the following steps:

        1)   Click the down-pointing triangle to the right of the Undo button.

        2)   Click the *second* Clear listed in the drop-down menu. (This will redisplay the first sentence in the first paragraph and the second paragraph. The first sentence will be selected.)

    h.   With the first sentence of the paragraph selected, press the Delete key.

4. Save the document again with the same name (Ch 01, Ex 07).

5. Print and then close Ch 01, Ex 07.

chapter summary

➤ Open Microsoft Word by clicking the Start button on the Taskbar, pointing to *Programs,* and then clicking *Microsoft Word*.

➤ The Title bar is the top line of the Word screen and displays the name of the current document. The Menu bar is the second line on the screen and contains a list of options that are used to customize a Word document.

➤ The Standard and Formatting toolbars display below the Menu bar and contain shortcuts for the most popular Word commands. Position the arrow pointer on a button on a toolbar and after one second a ScreenTip displays with the name of the button.

➤ The blinking vertical line is called the insertion point and indicates the position of the next character to be entered at the document screen. The underline symbol immediately below the insertion point is the end-of-document marker and indicates the end of the document.

➤ The mouse pointer displays on the screen as an I-beam called the I-beam pointer or as an arrow pointing up and to the left called the mouse pointer.

➤ The scroll bars appear as gray shaded bars along the right and toward the bottom of the document screen and are used to view various sections of a document.

➤ The Status bar appears as a gray bar below the horizontal scroll bar toward the bottom of the Word screen. It displays such information as the current location of the insertion point and whether certain modes are active.

➤ The Office Assistant is an on-screen Help feature that anticipates the type of help you need, as well as suggesting Help topics related to the work you are doing. The Assistant will also point out ways to perform tasks more easily and provide visual examples and step-by-step instructions for specific tasks.

➤ Word automatically wraps text to the next line as you key information. Press the Enter key only to end a paragraph, create a blank line, or end a short line.

➤ Word contains a feature named AutoCorrect that automatically corrects certain words as they are keyed.

➤ When keying text, the Spell It feature automatically inserts a wavy red line below words not contained in the Spelling dictionary, and the automatic grammar checker inserts a wavy green line below a sentence containing a grammatical error.

➤ Document names can contain a maximum of 255 characters, including the drive letter and folder names, and may include spaces. The following characters cannot be used when naming a document: / \ > < * ? " \ : ; and |.

➤ Drop-down menus and dialog boxes can be removed from the editing window with the mouse or the keyboard.

➤ When a document is saved on the disk using the Save or Save As options, the document remains in the document screen. To remove the document from the screen, click File and then Close or click the Close button located at the right side of the Menu bar.

➤ To print a document, open the document, and then click the Print button on the Standard toolbar or click File, Print, and then OK.

➤ Be sure to save all needed documents before exiting Word and Windows.

➤ In order to save on or to open documents from your data disk, the default folder should be changed. Change the default folder at the Open dialog box or the Save As dialog box.

➤ Open a document by displaying the Open dialog box and then double-clicking the desired document name.

➤ Click the New Blank Document button on the Standard toolbar to display a clear document screen.

➤ The display of toolbars can be turned on or off and toolbars can be moved to different locations on the screen.

➤ Word uses adaptive menus containing first-rank and second-rank options. Only the first-rank options are visible when the drop-down menu first displays. To display second-rank options, either click the down-pointing arrows at the bottom of the menu or pause on the menu for a few seconds. If you choose a second-rank option, it is promoted and becomes a first-rank option the next time the drop-down menu is displayed.

➤ The insertion point can be moved throughout the document without interfering with text by using the mouse, the keyboard, or the mouse combined with the keyboard.

➤ The insertion point can be moved by character, word, screen, or page, and from the first to the last character in a document.

➤ The horizontal and vertical scroll bars and the mouse can be used to scroll through a document. The scroll box indicates the location of the text in the document screen in relation to the remainder of the document.

➤ Click the Select Browse Object button located at the bottom of the vertical scroll bar to display options for browsing through a document.

➤ Switch to the Overtype mode if you want to key over something. When Overtype is on, the OVR mode button in the Status bar displays in black.

➤ Text can be deleted by character, word, line, several lines, or partial page using specific keys or by selecting text using the mouse or the keyboard.

➤ Save a previously saved document with a new name using the Save As command from the File drop-down menu.

➤ A specific amount of text can be selected using the mouse or the keyboard. That text can then be deleted or manipulated in other ways using Word functions.

➤ The selection bar can be used to select specific units of text such as a line. The selection bar is the space at the left side of the document screen between the left edge of the screen and the text.

➤ Use the Undo button on the Standard toolbar if you change your mind after keying, deleting, or formatting text and want to undo the deleting or formatting. Use the Redo button to redo something that had been undone with the Undo button.

commands review

Opening Word

1. Turn on the computer.
2. At the Windows 98 (or Windows 95) screen, position the mouse pointer on the Start button on the Taskbar (located at the bottom left side of the screen), and then click the left mouse button.
3. At the pop-up menu, point to Programs (you do not need to click the mouse button). This causes another menu to display to the right of the first pop-up menu.
4. Move the mouse pointer to *Microsoft Word* and then click the left mouse button.

Saving a Document

1. Click the Save button on the Standard toolbar or click File and then Save.
2. At the Save As dialog box, key the name of the document. (The document name displays in the File name text box.)
3. Click the Save button or press Enter.

Changing the Default Folder

1. Click the Open button on the Standard toolbar (the second button from the left) or click File and then Open.
2. At the Open dialog box, click the down-pointing triangle at the right side of the Look in text box.
3. From the drop-down list that displays, click *3½ Floppy (A:)*.
4. Click the Cancel button that displays in the lower right corner of the dialog box.

Closing a Document Using the Mouse

1. Click the Close button on the Menu bar or click File and then Close.

Opening a Document

1. Click the Open button on the Standard toolbar or click File and then Open.
2. At the Open dialog box, double-click the document name.

Printing a Document

1. Open the document.
2. Click the Print button on the Standard toolbar.
   or
1. Open the document.
2. Click File and then Print.
3. At the Print dialog box, click OK.

Exiting Word

1. Be sure all needed documents have been saved.
2. Click the Close button on the Title bar or click File and then Exit.

Exiting Windows

1. Click the Start button at the left side of the Taskbar.
2. At the pop-up menu, click Shut Down.
3. At the Shut Down Windows dialog box, make sure *Shut down* is selected, and then click Yes.

Scrolling Review

Changing the Display Using the Mouse and the Vertical Scroll Bar

Up one line	Click the up scroll triangle on the vertical scroll bar
Up several lines	Position the mouse pointer as above and then hold down left mouse button
Down one line	Click the down scroll triangle on the vertical scroll bar
Down several lines	Position the mouse pointer as above and then hold down left mouse button
Up one screen	Click with mouse pointer above the scroll box on the scroll bar
Down one screen	Click with mouse pointer below the scroll box on the scroll bar
To beginning of document	Position the mouse pointer on the scroll box, hold down left mouse button, drag the scroll box to the beginning of the scroll bar, and then release the mouse button
To end of document	Position the mouse pointer on the scroll box, hold down left mouse button, drag the scroll box to the end of the scroll bar, and then release the mouse button

Insertion Point Movement Review

Moving the Insertion Point Using the Mouse

To move to a specific location	Move mouse pointer to desired location and then click left mouse button
To move to the next page	Click the Next Page button
To move to the previous page	Click the Previous Page button
To move to a specific page	1. Click Edit and then Go To or double-click the page number at the left side of the Status bar.
	2. Key the page number.
	3. Click the Go To button or press Enter.
	4. Click the Close button.

Moving the Insertion Point Using the Keyboard

To move insertion point	*Press*
One character left	left arrow
One character right	right arrow
One line up	up arrow
One line down	down arrow
One word to the left	Ctrl + left arrow
One word to the right	Ctrl + right arrow
To end of line	End
To beginning of a line	Home
To beginning of current paragraph	Ctrl + up arrow
To beginning of previous paragraph	Ctrl + up arrow twice

To beginning of next paragraph	Ctrl + down arrow
Up one screen	Page Up
Down one screen	Page Down
To top of previous page	Ctrl + Page Up
To top of next page	Ctrl + Page Down
To beginning of document	Ctrl + Home
To end of document	Ctrl + End
To last location when document was closed	Shift + F5

Deletion Commands Review

To delete	Press
Character right of insertion point	Delete key
Character left of insertion point	Backspace key
Word before insertion point	Ctrl + Backspace
Word after insertion point	Ctrl + Delete

Selecting Text Review

Selecting Text Using the Mouse

To select text	Position I-beam pointer at the beginning of text to be selected, hold down left mouse button, drag the I-beam pointer to the end of text to be selected, and then release the mouse button

To select	Complete these steps
A word	Double-click the word
A line of text	Click in the selection bar to the left of line
Multiple lines of text	Drag in the selection bar to left of lines
A sentence	Hold down Ctrl key and then click anywhere in the sentence
A paragraph	Double-click in the selection bar next to paragraph or triple-click anywhere in the paragraph
Multiple paragraphs	Drag in the selection bar
An entire document	Triple-click in the selection bar
To cancel a selection	Click anywhere outside the selected text in the document screen

Selecting Text Using the Keyboard

To select	Press
One character to right	Shift + right arrow
One character to left	Shift + left arrow
To end of word	Ctrl + Shift + right arrow
To beginning of word	Ctrl + Shift + left arrow
To end of line	Shift + End
To beginning of line	Shift + Home

One line up	Shift + up arrow
One line down	Shift + down arrow
To beginning of paragraph	Ctrl + Shift + up arrow
To end of paragraph	Ctrl + Shift + down arrow
One screen up	Shift + Page Up
One screen down	Shift + Page Down
To end of document	Ctrl + Shift + End
To beginning of document	Ctrl + Shift + Home
Entire document	Ctrl + A or click Edit, Select All
To cancel a selection	Press any arrow key

Other Commands Review

Turn on Overtype	Double-click the OVR mode button on the Status bar, or press the Insert key
Undo	Click Undo button on the Standard toolbar
Redo	Click Redo button on the Standard toolbar
Save As	1. Click File and then Save As.
	2. At the Save As dialog box, key the document name.
	3. Click the Save button or press Enter.

thinking offline

Matching: In the space provided at the left, indicate the correct letter or letters that match each description.

- Ⓐ ButtonTip
- Ⓑ Fix It
- Ⓒ Formatting toolbar
- Ⓓ Horizontal scroll bar
- Ⓔ Menu bar
- Ⓕ Office Assistant
- Ⓖ Save As
- Ⓗ Scrolling
- Ⓘ Spell It
- Ⓙ Standard toolbar
- Ⓚ Status bar
- Ⓛ Title bar
- Ⓜ ScreenTip
- Ⓝ Vertical scroll bar

 1. This toolbar contains buttons for working with documents such as the Open button and the Save button.

 2. This toolbar contains buttons for formatting a document such as bold, italics, and underline.

 3. This displays below the horizontal scroll bar and displays the current location of the insertion point.

 4. This displays along the right side of the screen and is used to view various sections of a document.

_F_   5. This displays in the document screen and is an on-screen Help feature that anticipates the type of help you need as well as suggesting Help topics related to the work you are doing.

_H_   6. Doing this in a document changes the text displayed but does not move the insertion point.

_L_   7. This displays at the top of the Word screen and displays the name of the currently open document.

_M_   8. This appears after approximately one second when the mouse pointer is positioned on a button on a toolbar.

_G_   9. Use this option to save a previously created document with a new name.

_I_   10. This feature inserts a wavy red line below words not contained in the Spelling dictionary.

Completion: In the space provided at the right, indicate the correct term, command, or number.

1. This feature automatically corrects certain words as they are being keyed.   *Auto Correct*

2. This displays in the document screen as a blinking vertical line.   *Insertion Point*

3. This is the second line of the Word screen and contains a list of options that are used to customize a Word document.   *Menu Bar*

4. At a blank screen, click this button on the Standard toolbar to open a new blank document.   *New Blank Document*

5. Use this keyboard command to move the insertion point to the beginning of the previous page.   *Ctrl + Page Up*

6. When Overtype is on, this mode button displays in black on the Status bar.   *OVR*

7. Press this key on the keyboard to delete the character left of the insertion point.   *Backspace Key*

8. Complete these steps using the mouse to select one word.   *Double-Click the Word*

9. Use this keyboard command to select text to the end of the line.   *Shift + End*

10. If you click this button on the Standard toolbar, text you just keyed will be removed.   *Undo Button*

11. Use this keyboard command to move the insertion point to the end of the document.   *Control + End*

12. Use this keyboard command to select text to the end of the paragraph.   *Ctrl + Shift + down arrow*

13. To select various amounts of text using the mouse, you can click in this bar.   *Selection Bar*

Assessment 1

1. Open Windows and then open Word.
2. At the clear document screen, change the default folder to the drive where your disk is located and then double-click the *Chapter 01* folder. (Check with your instructor to determine if this step is necessary.)
3. At the clear document screen, key the text in figure 1.18. (Correct any errors highlighted by Spell It as they occur and remember to space once after end-of-sentence punctuation.)
4. Save the document and name it Ch 01, SA 01.
5. Print and then close Ch 01, SA 01.

figure

1.18   *Assessment 1*

In recent years, laptops and personal digital assistants have made computing away from the desk fairly common. In the future, such mobile computing will become ubiquitous. A specification for a Handheld Device Markup Language (HDML) for mobile computers with screens similar to those in cellular telephones has been proposed by the W3 Consortium. The W3 Consortium is the organization that develops new versions of the Hypertext Markup Language (HTML) used to create documents for the World Wide Web. HDML will make cellular phones smarter, allowing people to use wireless communications to read the day's news, check stock quotes, browse through catalogs, and place orders for goods and services.

Assessment 2

1. Open Para 03.
2. Save the document with Save As and name it Ch 01, SA 02.
3. Make the changes indicated by the proofreaders' marks in figure 1.19.
4. Save the document again with the same name (Ch 01, SA 02).
5. Print and then close Ch 01, SA 02.

figure 1.19   *Assessment 2*

Flyers are ~~typically~~ one of the least expensive forms of advertising. The ~~basic~~ ^{primary} goal of a flyer is to communicate a message at a glance, so the message should be brief and to the point. For the flyer to be effective, the basic layout and design should be free of clutter. ~~The flyer~~ and should not contain too much text or too many graphics. ~~Have the information arranged so it is easy to understand.~~

no ¶
When creating a flyer, use white space generously to set off an image or text. ~~Also,~~ consider directional flow in placing elements on a page. In a flyer, The left corner is usually read first. ~~Consider your audience when choosing type sizes. The older your audience, the larger the print might need to be.~~ Most important, always prepare a thumbnail sketch before beginning the project.

A graphics element, such as a watermark, can be very effective in a flyer. When using a watermark, try to find a graphic or text that matches the tone ~~or theme~~ of your message. The watermark can be used to add more ~~emphasis, color, and~~ excitement to a flyer.

Assessment 3

1. Open Para 04.
2. Save the document with Save As and name it Ch 01, SA 03.
3. Make the changes indicated by the proofreaders' marks in figure 1.20.
4. Save the document again with the same name (Ch 01, SA 03).
5. Print and then close Ch 01, SA 03.

figure

1.20   *Assessment 3*

for Windows

Word, ~~one of the best-selling word processing programs for microcomputers,~~ includes a wide variety of desktop publishing features. The ~~scope and~~ capabilities of these features

for Windows

have expanded with each new Word version. Some of the desktop publishing features include a ~~wide~~ variety of fonts and special symbols, drawing, charting, text design capabilities, graphic manipulation, templates, and much more.

no ¶

Design can be learned by studying ~~design~~ and ~~by~~ experiment**ing with design.** Collect and study designs that are attractive and visually interesting. Analyze what makes the design and layout unique and try using the same principles ~~or variations~~ in your publications. ¶ Take advantage of the special design and layout features that Word for Windows has to offer. Take the time to

an attractive publication

design. Layout and design is a lengthy process of revising, refining, and making adjustments. Start with small variations from the default formats to create designs that are attractive and visually interesting.

Assessment 4

1. At a clear document screen, compose a paragraph explaining when you would use the Save As command when saving a document and the advantages to Save As.
2. Save the document and name it Ch 01, SA 04.
3. Print and then close Ch 01, SA 04.

Chapter 02

Formatting Characters and Using Help

As you work with Word, you will learn a number of commands and procedures that affect how the document appears when printed. The appearance of a document in the document screen and how it looks when printed is called the *format*. Formatting can include such elements as bolding, italicizing, and underlining characters, and inserting special symbols. Microsoft Word contains an on-screen reference manual including information on features and commands for each program within the suite. In this chapter, you will learn to use the Help feature to display information about Word.

Formatting Characters

Formatting a document can include adding enhancements to characters such as bolding, underlining, and italicizing. A variety of formatting options is displayed in figure 2.1.

figure

2.1
Character Formatting

Formatting	Method
Uppercase letters	Press the Caps Lock key
Bold	Press Ctrl + B or click the Bold button on the Formatting toolbar
Underline	Press Ctrl + U or click the Underline button on the Formatting toolbar
Italics	Press Ctrl + I or click the Italic button on the Formatting toolbar

More than one type of character formatting can be applied to the same text. For example, you can bold and underline the same text as shown in figure 2.2. If formatting is applied to text, it can be removed by selecting the text and then clicking the appropriate button on the Formatting toolbar or pressing the shortcut command. For example, to remove underlining from text, you would select the text to which you want the underlining removed, and then click the Underline button on the Formatting toolbar or press Ctrl + U.

U

Underline

All character formatting can be removed from selected text with the shortcut command, Ctrl + spacebar. This removes *all* character formatting. For example, if bold and italics are applied to text, selecting the text and then pressing Ctrl + spacebar will remove both bold and italics.

(Before completing computer exercises, delete the Chapter 01 *folder on your disk. Next, copy the* Chapter 02 *folder from the CD that accompanies this textbook to your disk and then make* Chapter 02 *the active folder.)*

exercise

Applying Character Formatting to Text as It Is Keyed

1. At a clear document screen, key the document shown in figure 2.2 with the following specifications:
   a. While keying the document, bold the text shown bolded in the figure by completing the following steps:
      1) Click the Bold button on the Formatting toolbar or press Ctrl + B. (This turns on bold.)
      2) Key the text.
      3) Click the Bold button on the Formatting toolbar or press Ctrl + B. (This turns off bold.)
   b. While keying the document, underline the text shown underlined in the figure by completing the following steps:
      1) Click the Underline button on the Formatting toolbar or press Ctrl + U.
      2) Key the text.
      3) Click the Underline button on the Formatting toolbar or press Ctrl + U.

    c. While keying the document, italicize the text shown in italics in the figure by completing the following steps:
      1) Click the Italic button on the Formatting toolbar or press Ctrl + I.
      2) Key the text.
      3) Click the Italic button on the Formatting toolbar or press Ctrl + I.
2. Save the document and name it Ch 02, Ex 01a.
3. Print Ch 02, Ex 01a.
4. With the document still open, make the following changes:
    a. Remove underlining from the title by completing the following steps:
      1) Select the title *TECHNOTALK*.
      2) Click the Underline button on the Formatting toolbar.
    b. Add underlining to the bolded word *Byte* by completing the following steps:
      1) Select the word *Byte* (do not include the colon).
      2) Click the Underline button on the Formatting toolbar.
    c. Select and then underline each of the other bolded words that begin the remaining paragraphs (*Nibble, Stuff,* and *Zip*).
5. Save the document with Save As and name it Ch 02, Ex 01b.
6. Print and then close Ch 02, Ex 01b.

figure

2.2   *Exercise 1*

TECHNOTALK

Byte: An eight-bit binary number, as in 10011010. The word *byte* extends the vowel in *bit*. It is also a homophone of the present-tense form of the past-tense verb *bit*.

Nibble: A four-bit binary number, as in 1001 or 1010. The word *nibble* is an obvious play on the word *byte*.

Stuff: To compress a file using the SIT compression format.

Zip: To compress a file using ZIP compression format.

Changing Fonts

The default font used by Word is 10-point Times New Roman (or 12-point Times New Roman, if you followed the steps presented in chapter 1 on changing the default font). You may want to change this default to some other font for such reasons as changing the mood of a document, enhancing the visual appeal, and increasing the readability of the text. A font consists of three elements—typeface, type size, and type style.

Choosing a Typeface

A *typeface* is a set of characters with a common design and shape. (Word refers to typeface as *font*.) Typefaces may be decorative or plain and are either *monospaced* or *proportional*. A monospaced typeface allots the same amount of horizontal space for each character. Courier is an example of a monospaced typeface. Proportional typefaces allot a varying amount of space for each character. The space allotted is based on the width of the character. For example, the lowercase *i* will take up less space than the uppercase *M*.

Proportional typefaces are divided into two main categories: *serif* and *sans serif*. A serif is a small line at the end of a character stroke. Traditionally, a serif typeface is used with documents that are text intensive (documents that are mainly text) because the serifs help move the reader's eyes across the page. A sans serif typeface does not have serifs (*sans* is French for *without*). Sans serif typefaces are often used for headlines and advertisements that are not text intensive. Figure 2.3 shows examples of serif and sans serif typefaces.

As mentioned earlier in chapter 1, space once after end-of-sentence punctuation and after a colon when text is set in a proportional typeface. Proportional typeface is set closer together and extra white space at the end of a sentence or after a colon is not needed.

figure
2.3   *Serif and Sans Serif Typefaces*

Serif Typefaces	Sans Serif Typefaces
Bookman Old Style	*Arial*
Garamond	Eurostile
Goudy Old Style	**Haettenschweiler**
Modern No. 20	**Impact**
Rockwell	Lucida Sans
Times New Roman	Tahoma

Choosing a Type Size

Type size is divided into two categories: *pitch* and *point size*. Pitch is a measurement used for monospaced typefaces; it reflects the number of characters that can be printed in 1 horizontal inch. (For some printers, the pitch is referred to as *cpi*, or *characters per inch*. For example, the font Courier 10 cpi is the same as 10-pitch Courier.)

Proportional typefaces can be set in different sizes. The size of proportional type is measured vertically in units called *points*. A point is approximately 1/72 of an inch. The higher the point size, the larger the characters. Examples of different point sizes in the Arial typeface are shown in figure 2.4.

figure 2.4   *Different Point Sizes in Arial*

8-point Arial
12-point Arial
18-point Arial
24-point Arial

Choosing a Type Style

Within a typeface, characters may have a varying style. There are four main categories of type styles: normal (for some typefaces, this may be referred to as *light*, *black*, *regular*, or *roman*); bold, italic, and bold italic. Figure 2.5 illustrates the four main type styles in 12 points.

figure 2.5   *Four Main Type Styles*

Tahoma regular	Times New Roman regular
Tahoma bold	**Times New Roman bold**
Tahoma italic	*Times New Roman italic*
Tahoma bold italic	***Times New Roman bold italic***

The term *font* describes a particular typeface in a specific style and size. Some examples of fonts include *10-pitch Courier*, *10-point Arial*, *12-point Tahoma bold*, and *12-point Times New Roman bold italic*.

Using the Font Dialog Box

The fonts available display in the Font list box at the Font dialog box. To display the Font dialog box, shown in figure 2.6, click Format and then Font. You can also display the Font dialog box with a shortcut menu. To do this, position the I-beam pointer anywhere within the document screen, click the *right* mouse button, and then click the left mouse button on Font.

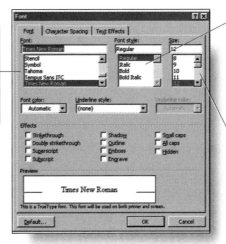

figure 2.6

Font Dialog Box

Choose a typeface in this list box. Use the scroll bar at the right side of the box to view various typefaces available.

Choose a type style in this list box. The options in the box may vary depending on the typeface selected.

Choose a type size in this list box; or, select the current measurement in the top box and then key the desired measurement.

The Font list box at the Font dialog box displays the typefaces (fonts) available with your printer. Figure 2.6 shows the typefaces available with a laser printer (the fonts displayed with your printer may vary from those shown). To select a typeface, select the desired typeface (font), and then click OK or press Enter. When different typefaces are selected, the Preview box at the bottom of the dialog box displays the appearance of the selected font.

The Size list box at the Font dialog box displays a variety of common type sizes. Decrease point size to make text smaller or increase point size to make text larger. To select a point size with the mouse, click the desired point size. To view more point sizes, click the down-pointing triangle in the Size scroll bar. You can also key a specific point size. To do this, select the number in the Size text box, and then key the desired point size.

The Font style list box displays the styles available with the selected typeface. As you select different typefaces at the Font dialog box, the list of styles changes in the Font style list box. Choose from a variety of type styles such as regular, bold, italic, or bold and italic.

exercise 2

Changing the Font at the Font Dialog Box

1. Open Para 04.
2. Save the document with Save As and name it Ch 02, Ex 02.
3. Change the typeface to 13-point Bookman Old Style italic by completing the following steps:
   a. Select the entire document. (*Hint: To select the entire document press Ctrl + A or click Edit, expand the drop-down menu, and then click Select All.*)

b. Display the Font dialog box by clicking Format and then Font.

c. At the Font dialog box, click the up-pointing triangle at the right side of the Font list box until Bookman Old Style displays, and then click Bookman Old Style. (If Bookman Old Style is not available, choose another serif typeface such as Galliard BT or Garamond.)

d. Change the Size option to 13 by selecting the *12* displayed in the Size list box and then keying **13**.

e. Click *Italic* in the Font style list box.

f. Click OK or press Enter.

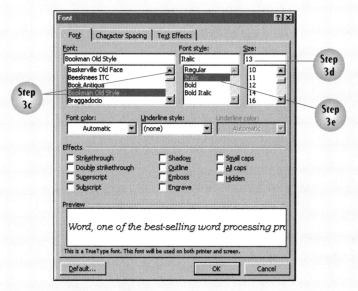

4. At the document screen, deselect the text by clicking anywhere in the document screen outside the selected text.

5. Save the document again with the same name (Ch 02, Ex 02).

6. Print and then close Ch 02, Ex 02.

In addition to using the Font dialog box to select a typeface, you can use the Font button on the Formatting toolbar. The Font button displays a font name followed by a down-pointing triangle. For example, if your default typeface is Times New Roman, that name displays in the Font button. If you click the down-pointing triangle at the right side of the Font button, a drop-down list displays. Click the desired typeface at this drop-down list.

Font

Font size can be changed with options from the Font Size button on the Formatting toolbar. The Font Size button contains the current point size followed by a down-pointing triangle. To change the type size with the Font Size button, click the down-pointing triangle at the right side of the Font Size button, and then click the desired size at the drop-down list.

Font Size

The Formatting toolbar also contains a Font Color button to change the color of selected text. Click the Font Color button and the selected text changes to the color that displays on the button (below the A). To choose a different color, click the down-pointing triangle at the right side of the button and then click the desired color at the palette of color choices.

Font Color

Changing the Font, Size, and Color Using Buttons on the Formatting Toolbar

1. Open Para 03.
2. Save the document with Save As and name it Ch 02, Ex 03.
3. Change the typeface to 14-point Arial and the color to Violet using buttons on the Formatting toolbar by completing the following steps:
   a. Select the entire document. *(Hint: To select the entire document press Ctrl + A or click Edit, expand the drop-down menu, and then click Select All.)*
   b. Click the down-pointing triangle at the right side of the Font button on the Formatting toolbar and then click *Arial* at the drop-down list. (You may need to scroll up the list to display *Arial*.)
   c. Click the down-pointing triangle at the right side of the Font Size button on the Formatting toolbar and then click *14* at the drop-down list.
   d. Change the font color to Violet by completing the following steps:
      1) Click the down-pointing triangle at the right side of the Font Color button (last button on the Formatting toolbar).
      2) At the palette of color choices that displays, click Violet (second color option from the right in the third row).
4. Deselect the text to see what it looks like set in 14-point Arial.
5. Save the document again with the same name (Ch 02, Ex 03).
6. Print and then close Ch 02, Ex 03.

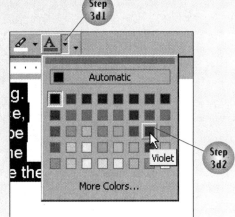

The Font dialog box contains a variety of underlining options. Click the down-pointing triangle at the right side of the Underline style option box and a drop-down palette of underlining styles displays containing options such as a double line, thick line, dashed line, etc.

Click the down-pointing triangle at the right side of the Font color text box and a palette choices displays. Position the arrow pointer on a color and after one second a yellow box displays with the color name. Use this option to change the color of selected text.

exercise 4

Changing the Font and Text Color and Underlining Text

1. Open Notice 02.
2. Save the document with Save As and name it Ch 02, Ex 04.
3. Change the font and text color by completing the following steps:
   a. Select the entire document.
   b. Display the Font dialog box.
   c. Change the font to 14-point Goudy Old Style bold. (If Goudy Old Style is not available, consider using another decorative serif typeface such as BernhardMod BT or Bookman Old Style.)
   d. With the Font dialog box still displayed, change the text color to Blue by clicking the down-pointing triangle at the right side of the Font color text box, and then clicking Blue (sixth color option from the left in the second row).
   e. Click OK or press Enter.
   f. Deselect the text.

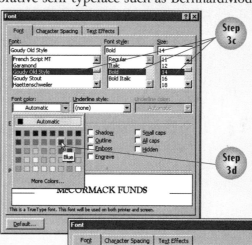

4. Double underline the text *Thursday, April 26, 2001* by completing the following steps:
   a. Select *Thursday, April 26, 2001*.
   b. Display the Font dialog box.
   c. Click the down-pointing triangle at the right side of the Underline style option box and then click the double-line option (see figure) at the drop-down list.
   d. Click OK to close the dialog box.
5. Apply a thick underline to the text *7:30 p.m.* by completing the following steps:
   a. Select *7:30 p.m.*
   b. Display the Font dialog box.
   c. Click the down-pointing triangle at the right side of the Underline style option box and then click the thick-line option (see figure) that displays below the double-line option.
   d. Click OK or press Enter.
   e. Deselect the text.
6. Save the document again with the same name (Ch 02, Ex 04).
7. Print and then close Ch 02, Ex 04.

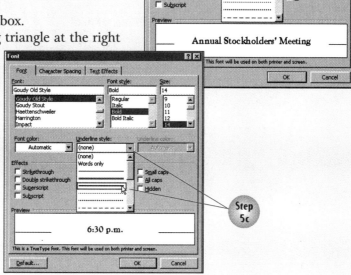

The Effects section of the Font dialog box contains a variety of options that can be used to create different character styles. For example, you can strikethrough text (which has a practical application for some legal documents in which deleted text must be retained in the document), or create superscript and subscript text. With the Hidden option from the Font dialog box, you can include such items as comments, personal messages, or questions in a document. These items can be displayed, printed, or hidden. The Small caps option lets you print small capital letters. This works for some printers, but not all. Additional effects include Double strikethrough, Shadow, Outline, Emboss, Engrave, and All caps.

Changing Text to Small Caps

1. Open Notice 02.
2. Save the document with Save As and name it Ch 02, Ex 05.
3. Select the entire document and then make the following changes:
    a. Display the Font dialog box and change the font to 18-point Modern No. 20 bold. (Do not close the dialog box. If Modern No. 20 is not available, consider using another decorative serif typeface such as Dauphin or BernhardMod BT.)
    b. With the Font dialog box still displayed, change the font color to Green.
    c. With the Font dialog box still displayed, click Small caps in the Effects section.
    d. Click OK or press Enter to close the Font dialog box.
4. Save the document again with the same name (Ch 02, Ex 05).
5. Print and then close Ch 02, Ex 05.

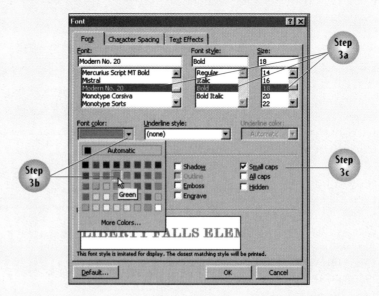

Superscript text is raised slightly above the text line and subscripted text is lowered slightly below the text line. Use the superscript effect for some mathematical equations such as four to the third power (written as 4^3) and use the subscript effect to create some chemical formulas such as H_2O. Create superscript text with the Superscript effect and subscript with the Subscript effect at the Font dialog box. Superscript text can also be created with the shortcut command, Ctrl + Shift + =; subscript text can be created with the shortcut command, Ctrl + =.

Applying Superscript Effect to Text and Changing the Font

1. At a clear document screen, key the text shown in figure 2.7 with the following specifications:
    a. Create the first superscript number in the document by completing the following steps:
        1) Key text to the point where the superscript number is to appear.
        2) Display the Font dialog box.
        3) At the Font dialog box, click the Superscript check box located in the Effects section (this inserts a check mark).
        4) Click OK to close the Font dialog box.
        5) Key the superscript number.
        6) Turn off Superscript by displaying the Font dialog box, clicking the Superscript check box (this removes the check mark), and then clicking OK to close the dialog box.
    b. Create the second superscript number in the document by completing the following steps:
        1) Key text to the point where the superscript number is to appear.
        2) Press Ctrl + Shift + =.
        3) Key the superscript number.
        4) Press Ctrl + Shift + =.
    c. Continue keying the document up to the first subscript number and then create the subscript number by completing the following steps:
        1) Press Ctrl + =.
        2) Key the subscript number.
        3) Press Ctrl + =.
    d. Finish keying the remainder of the document.
    e. After keying the document, select the entire document, and then change the font to 12-point Bookman Old Style (or a similar serif typeface such as New Century Schoolbook or Garamond).
2. Save the document and name it Ch 02, Ex 06.
3. Print and then close Ch 02, Ex 06.

figure

2.7

Exercise 6

What is the relationship between the indices C, D, and I, to both r^1 and r^2?

What is the improvement when $r^1 = .55$ and r^2 is nearly .79?

What is the main effect on the scores of X_1, X_2, and X_3?

Adjusting Character Spacing

Each typeface is designed with a specific amount of space between characters. This character spacing can be changed with options at the Font dialog box with the Character Spacing tab selected as shown in figure 2.8. To display this dialog box, click Format and then Font. At the Font dialog box, click the Character Spacing tab.

figure

2.8

Font Dialog Box with Character Spacing Tab Selected

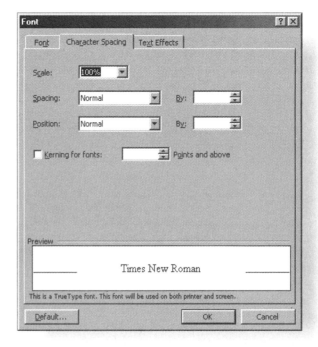

Choose the Scale option to stretch or compress text horizontally as a percentage of the current size. You can choose a percentage from 1 to 600. Expand or condense the spacing between characters with the Spacing option. Choose either the *Expanded* or *Condensed* option and then enter the desired percentage amount in the By text box. Raise or lower selected text in relation to the baseline with the Position option. Choose either the *Raised* or *Lowered* option and then enter the percentage amount in the By text box.

Kerning is a term that refers to the adjustment of spacing between certain character combinations. Kerning provides text with a more evenly spaced look and works only with TrueType or Adobe Type 1 fonts. Turn on automatic kerning by inserting a check mark in the Kerning for fonts check box. Specify the beginning point size that you want kerned in the Points and above text box.

Animating Text

Animation effects can be added to text at the Font dialog box with the Text Effects tab selected. To display this dialog box, shown in figure 2.9, click Format and then Font. At the Font dialog box click the Text Effects tab.

figure

2.9 Font Dialog Box with Text Effects Tab Selected

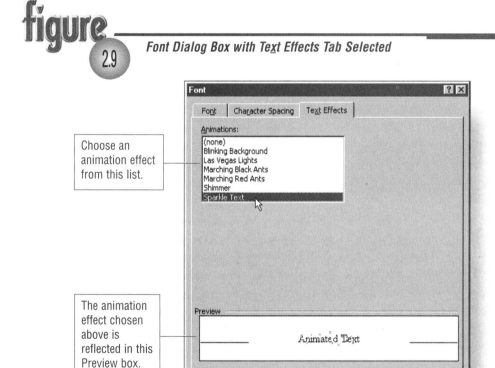

Choose an animation effect from this list.

The animation effect chosen above is reflected in this Preview box.

Animation effects can be added to text, such as a blinking background, a shimmer or sparkle. To add an animation effect, select the text, display the Font dialog box with the Text Effects tab selected, click the desired effect, and then close the Font dialog box. Animation effects added to text display in the screen but do not print.

exercise 7

Adjusting Character Spacing and Scaling, Turning on Kerning, and Animating Text

1. Open Notice 01.
2. Save the document with Save As and name it Ch 02, Ex 07.
3. Adjust character spacing and turn on kerning by completing the following steps:
   a. Select the entire document.
   b. Click Format and then Font.
   c. At the Font dialog box, click the Character Spacing tab.
   d. At the Font dialog box with the Character Spacing tab selected, click the down-pointing triangle at the right side of the Spacing option, and then click *Expanded* at the drop-down list. (This inserts *1 pt* in the By text box.)
   e. Click in the Kerning for fonts check box. (This inserts a check mark in the check box and also inserts *12* in the Points and above text box.)
   f. Click OK to close the dialog box.
   g. Deselect the text.

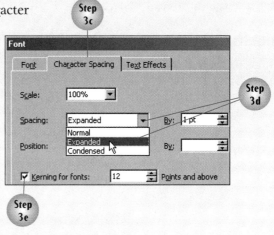

4. Save the document again with the same name (Ch 02, Ex 07).
5. Print Ch 02, Ex 07.
6. With Ch 02, Ex 07 still open, compress text horizontally by completing the following steps:
   a. Select the entire document.
   b. Click Format and then Font.
   c. At the Font dialog box, click the Character Spacing tab.
   d. At the Font dialog box with the Character Spacing tab selected, click the down-pointing triangle at the right side of the Spacing option, and then click *Normal* at the drop-down list.
   e. Select *100%* in the Scale option text box and then key **97**. (This compresses text to 97 percent of the original horizontal spacing.)
   f. Click OK to close the dialog box.
   g. Deselect the text.

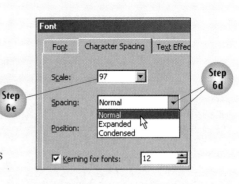

7. Add a sparkle background to the title of the
   document by completing the following steps:
   a. Select the title *EMERALD HEIGHTS
      ELEMENTARY SCHOOL CARNIVAL*.
   b. Click F̲ormat and then F̲ont.
   c. At the Font dialog box, click the Te̲xt
      Effects tab.
   d. Click the *Sparkle Text* option in the list
      box.
   e. Click OK to close the dialog box.
8. Save the document again with the same
   name (Ch 02, Ex 07).
9. Print and then close Ch 02, Ex 07.

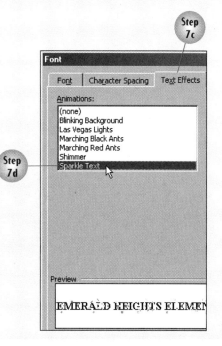

Inserting Symbols

Many of the typefaces (fonts) include special symbols such as bullets, publishing
symbols, and letters with special punctuation (such as É, ö, and ñ). To insert a
symbol, display the Symbol dialog box with the S̲ymbols tab selected as shown in
figure 2.10 by clicking I̲nsert and then S̲ymbol. At the Symbol dialog box, double-
click the desired symbol, and then click Close; or click the desired symbol, click
I̲nsert, and then click Close.

figure
2.10

Symbol Dialog Box with S̲ymbols Tab Selected

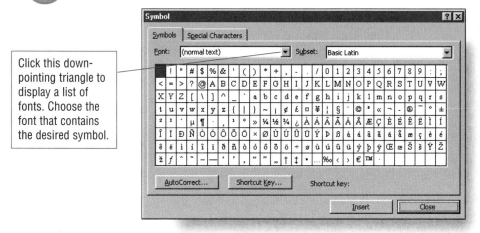

Changing the Font for Symbols

At the Symbol dialog box with the Symbols tab selected, you can change the font with the Font option. When you change the font, different symbols display in the dialog box. To change the font, display the Symbol dialog box with the Symbols tab selected, click the down-pointing triangle to the right of the Font text box, and then click the desired font at the drop-down list.

Before Completing Exercise 8

In exercise 8 and other exercises in this textbook, you will be required to create memos. Please refer to Appendix B at the end of this textbook for the correct placement and spacing of a traditional-style memo. Unless otherwise instructed by your teacher, use this format when creating memos. The initials of the person keying the memo usually appear at the end of the memo. In this textbook, the initials will appear in the exercises as XX. Key your initials where you see the XX. Identifying a document name is a good idea because it lets you find and open the document quickly and easily at a future date. In this textbook, the document name is keyed after the reference initials.

Note: The typist's initials are generally keyed in lowercase letters. Word's AutoCorrect feature, by default, automatically changes the first letter to an uppercase. For this reason, uppercase letters are used for the initials. (If you want to key initials in lowercase letters, consider turning off the Capitalize first letter of sentence option at the AutoCorrect dialog box. To display the AutoCorrect dialog box, click Tools and then AutoCorrect.)

Creating Special Symbols

(Note: In exercise 8, you will be using the Tab key to align text after the headings in a memo. The Tab key is located above the Caps Lock key at the left side of the keyboard.)

1. At a clear document screen, create the memo shown in figure 2.11 in the traditional memo format with the following specifications:
   a. Use Caps Lock to key the memo headings—*DATE, TO, FROM,* and *SUBJECT.* To align the information after *DATE:,* key **DATE:,** press the Tab key twice, and then key **June 7, 2001**. (Press the Tab key twice after TO: and once after FROM: and SUBJECT: to properly align the text.)
   b. Key the text in the memo to the point where the ë is to be inserted and then complete the following steps:
      1) Click Insert and then Symbol.
      2) At the Symbol dialog box with the Symbols tab selected, make sure *(normal text)* displays in the Font text box. (If not, click the down-pointing triangle at the right side of the Font text box, and then click *(normal text)*. This font displays at the beginning of the list.)
      3) Double-click the ë symbol (approximately the third symbol from the left in the seventh row).

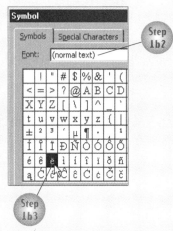

4) Click the Close button.

c. Key the text in the memo to the point where the degree (°) symbol is to be inserted and then complete the following steps:

1) Click Insert and then Symbol.

2) At the Symbol dialog box with the Symbols tab selected, make sure *(normal text)* displays in the Font text box, and then double-click the degree symbol (approximately the tenth symbol from the left in the fifth row).

3) Click the Close button.

4) Repeat these steps for the second occurrence of the degree symbol.

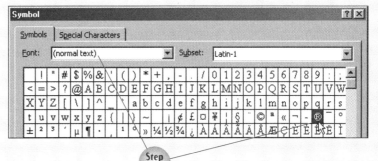

d. Key the text in the memo to the point where the ® symbol is to be inserted and then complete the following steps:

1) Click Insert and then Symbol.

2) At the Symbol dialog box with the Symbols tab selected, make sure *(normal text)* displays in the Font text box, and then double-click the ® symbol (approximately the third symbol from the right in the fourth row).

3) Click Close.

e. Key the text in the memo to the point where the globe symbol (🌏) is to be inserted and then complete the following steps:

1) Click Insert and then Symbol.

2) At the Symbol dialog box with the Symbols tab selected, click the down-pointing triangle at the right side of the Font text box, and then click *Webdings*. (You will need to scroll down the list to display *Webdings*.)

3) Double-click the 🌏 symbol (approximately the second symbol from the right in the bottom row).

4) Click Close.

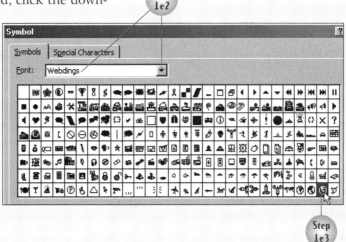

f. Key the text in the memo to the point where the airplane symbol (✈) is to be inserted and then complete the following steps:

1) Click Insert and then Symbol.
2) At the Symbol dialog box with the Symbols tab selected, make sure *Webdings* is selected in the Font text box.
3) Double-click the airplane symbol (approximately the fourteenth symbol from the left in the bottom row).
4) Click Close.

g. Key the remainder of the text in the memo.

2. Save the memo and name it Ch 02, Ex 08.
3. Print and then close Ch 02, Ex 08.

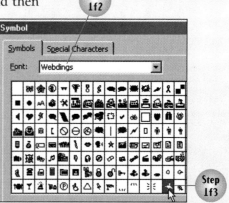

Step 1f2

Step 1f3

figure

2.11 *Exercise 8*

DATE: June 7, 2001

TO: Bill Lowe

FROM: Pauline Metcalf

SUBJECT: FEBRUARY NEWSLETTER

The layout for the February newsletter looks great! According to Sylvia Raphaël, the image on the second page can be rotated either 90° or 270°. What would you prefer? Sylvia plans to offer an informal workshop on some of the graphic capabilities of Microsoft® Word 2000. Contact either person for input into your training needs. In the International section of the newsletter, Sylvia wants to insert a graphic symbol such as a globe (🌐) or an airplane (✈). Which one do you like? Please let her know.

XX:Ch 02, Ex 08

Using Help

Word's Help feature is an on-screen reference manual containing information about all Word features and commands. Get help using the Office Assistant or turn off the Assistant and get help from the Microsoft Word Help dialog box.

Getting Help from the Office Assistant

The Office Assistant will provide information about specific topics. To get help using the Office Assistant, click the Office Assistant or click <u>H</u>elp and then Microsoft Word <u>H</u>elp. This causes a box to display above the Office Assistant as shown in figure 2.12. (If the Office Assistant is not visible, click the Microsoft Word Help button on the Standard toolbar or click <u>H</u>elp and then Show the <u>O</u>ffice Assistant.)

Microsoft
Word Help

Office Assistant Help Box

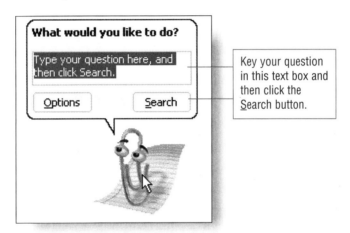

When the help box displays above the Office Assistant, the text *Type your question here, and then click Search.* displays in the text box below the question *What would you like to do?* This text is already selected, so key a question about a specific Word feature, and then click the <u>S</u>earch button. The Office Assistant will display a list of related topics. At this list, click the desired topic and information will display in a Microsoft Word Help dialog box. After reading the information, click the Close button located in the upper right corner of the dialog box (contains an X).

The Microsoft Word Help dialog box contains a toolbar with the buttons shown in figure 2.13. Click the Show button to expand the dialog box and display three tabs—<u>C</u>ontents, <u>A</u>nswer Wizard, <u>I</u>ndex. If you move to various help items, click the Back button to return to the previous window. The Forward button is dimmed until the Back button has been clicked. When the Forward button is active, click the button to move forward to a help item. Click the Print button to send the Help information to the printer. Click the Options button and a drop-down menu displays with many of the same features as the buttons. For example, there is a Show Tabs option that will expand the dialog box, and <u>B</u>ack and <u>F</u>orward options that do the same thing as the Back and Forward buttons. Additional options include <u>H</u>ome, <u>S</u>top, <u>R</u>efresh, <u>I</u>nternet Options, and <u>P</u>rint.

Show

Back

Forward

Print

Options

figure 2.13 Microsoft Word Help Dialog Box Toolbar Buttons

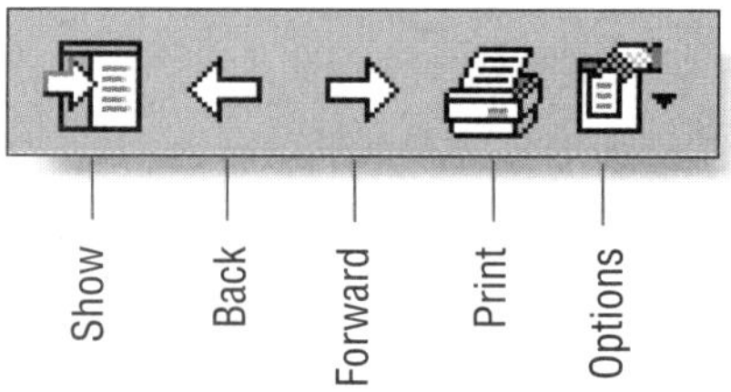

Show
Back
Forward
Print
Options

exercise 9

Using the Office Assistant to Learn about Selecting Text

1. At a clear document screen, use the Office Assistant to read information about selecting text by completing the following steps:
   a. Make sure the Office Assistant is visible. (If it is not, click Help and then Show the Office Assistant. Remove the yellow box above the Assistant by clicking in the document screen.)
   b. Click the Office Assistant.
   c. At the yellow box that displays above the Office Assistant, key **How do I select text?**
   d. Click the Search button.
   e. At the list that displays in the yellow box, click *Select text and graphics*. (When you position the arrow pointer on the topic, the pointer turns into a hand.)
   f. At the Microsoft Word Help dialog box, click *Select text and graphics by using the mouse* in the *What do you want to do?* section.
   g. Read the information about selecting using the mouse and then click the Print button on the dialog box toolbar.
   h. Click the Back button on the dialog box toolbar.
   i. Click *Select text and graphics by using the keyboard*.
   j. Read the information about selecting using the keyboard and then click the Print button on the dialog box toolbar.
   k. Click the Close button located in the upper right corner of the dialog box (contains an X).
2. Click in the document screen outside the Office Assistant yellow box. (This removes the yellow box.)

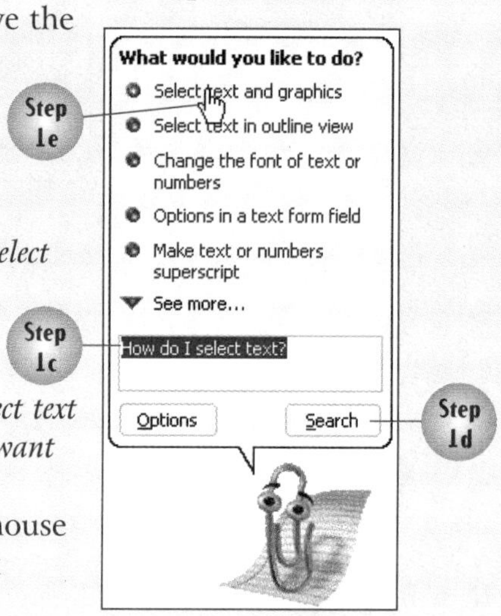

What would you like to do?
Select text and graphics
Select text in outline view
Change the font of text or numbers
Options in a text form field
Make text or numbers superscript
See more...
How do I select text?
Options
Search
Step 1e
Step 1c
Step 1d

Using the Expanded Microsoft Word Help Dialog Box

The Microsoft Word Help dialog box toolbar contains a Show button. Click the Show button and the dialog box expands as shown in figure 2.14. Three tabs display in the expanded dialog box—Contents, Answer Wizard, and Index.

figure
2.14

Expanded Microsoft Word Help Dialog Box

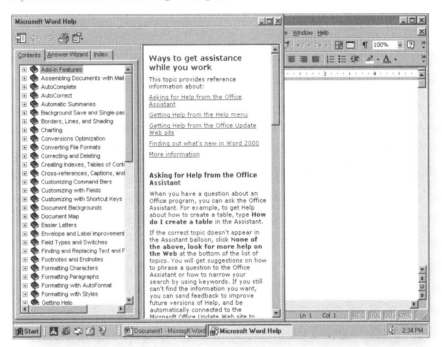

Select the Contents tab at the expanded Microsoft Word Help dialog box and a variety of categories display preceded by an icon of a closed book. Most of these categories contain additional categories. To display these additional categories, double-click a category. This causes the closed book icon to change to an open book icon and the additional categories to display below the selected category.

Click the Answer Wizard tab and a text box displays preceded by the question "What would you like to do?" Key your question in the text box and then click the Search button. This displays a list of categories in the Select topic to display list box. Click a topic in the list box, and information about the topic displays at the right side of the dialog box.

With the Index tab selected, enter a keyword in the Type keyword list box, and then click the Search button. Topics related to the keyword display in the Choose a topic list box. Click a topic in this list box and information about that topic displays at the right side of the dialog box. You can also scroll through the *Or choose keywords* list box to display the desired topic. The topics in this list box are alphabetized.

Hiding/Turning Off the Office Assistant

To hide the Office Assistant, click Help and then Hide the Office Assistant. Redisplay the Office Assistant by clicking the Microsoft Word Help button on the Standard toolbar or by clicking Help and then Show the Office Assistant.

The Office Assistant can also be turned off for the entire Word session. To do this, click the Office Assistant and then click the Options button that displays in the yellow box. At the Office Assistant dialog box that displays as shown in figure 2.15, click the Use the Office Assistant option to remove the check mark, and then click OK.

figure

2.15

Office Assistant Dialog Box

Remove this check mark to turn off the Office Assistant.

Office Assistant

Gallery | Options

☑ Use the Office Assistant

  ☑ Respond to F1 key   ☑ Move when in the way

  ☑ Help with wizards   ☑ Guess Help topics

  ☑ Display alerts   ☑ Make sounds

  ☐ Search for both product and programming help when programming

Show tips about

  ☑ Using features more effectively   ☐ Only show high priority tips

  ☑ Using the mouse more effectively ☐ Show the Tip of the Day at startup

  ☐ Keyboard shortcuts   [Reset my tips]

[OK] [Cancel]

exercise 10

Turning Off the Office Assistant and Using Help

1. At a clear document screen, turn off the Office Assistant by completing the following steps:
   a. Make sure the Office Assistant is visible.
   b. Click the Office Assistant.
   c. Click the Options button in the yellow box.
   d. At the Office Assistant dialog box, click the Use the Office Assistant option (this removes the check mark).
   e. Click OK to close the dialog box.
2. Use the Help feature with the Contents tab selected to find information on formatting characters by completing the following steps:
   a. Click Help on the Menu bar and then click Microsoft Word Help.
   b. At the Microsoft Word Help dialog box, click the Contents tab. (Skip this step if the Contents tab is already selected.)
   c. Double-click *Formatting* in the Contents list box. (This displays subcategories below *Formatting*.)
   d. Double-click *Formatting Characters* in the Contents list box. (This displays subcategories below *Formatting Characters*.)

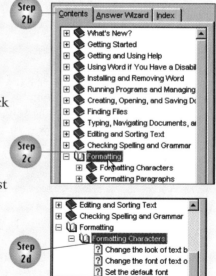

Step 2b

Contents | Answer Wizard | Index

⊞ 🔖 What's New?
⊞ 🔖 Getting Started
⊞ 🔖 Getting and Using Help
⊞ 🔖 Using Word if You Have a Disabil
⊞ 🔖 Installing and Removing Word
⊞ 🔖 Running Programs and Managing
⊞ 🔖 Creating, Opening, and Saving Do
⊞ 🔖 Finding Files
⊞ 🔖 Typing, Navigating Documents, a
⊞ 🔖 Editing and Sorting Text
⊞ 🔖 Checking Spelling and Grammar

Step 2c

⊟ 📖 Formatting
  ⊞ 🔖 Formatting Characters
  ⊞ 🔖 Formatting Paragraphs

⊞ 🔖 Editing and Sorting Text
⊞ 🔖 Checking Spelling and Grammar
⊟ 📖 Formatting
  ⊟ 📖 Formatting Characters

Step 2d

    ? Change the look of text b
    ? Change the font of text o
    ? Set the default font

e. Click a subcategory topic that interests you and then read the information about the subcategory that displays at the right side of the dialog.

f. Click several other subcategories that interest you and read the information about them.

3. Use the Help feature with the <u>A</u>nswer Wizard tab selected to search for information on saving a document by completing the following steps:

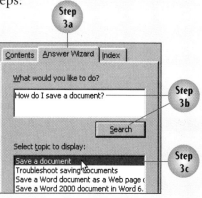

Step 3a

a. Click the <u>A</u>nswer Wizard tab.

b. Key **How do I save a document?** in the <u>W</u>hat would you like to do? text box and then click the <u>S</u>earch button.

c. Click *Save a document* in the Select <u>t</u>opic to display list box.

d. Click the *Save a new, unnamed document* topic that displays at the right side of the dialog box under the heading *Saving documents in Microsoft Word format*.

e. Read the information about saving a new, unnamed document that displays at the right side of the dialog box and then click the Back button.

f. Click the *Save an existing document* topic that displays at the right side of the dialog box under the heading *Saving documents in Microsoft Word format*.

g. Read the information about saving an existing document that displays at the right side of the dialog box.

4. Use the Help feature with the <u>I</u>ndex tab selected to search for information on printing by completing the following steps:

Step 4a

a. Click the <u>I</u>ndex tab.

b. Key **print** in the <u>T</u>ype keywords text box and then click the <u>S</u>earch button.

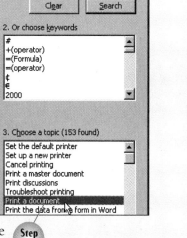

c. Click the topic *Print a document* that displays in the <u>C</u>hoose a topic list box.

d. Click the *Print a range of pages* topic that displays at the right side of the dialog box under the heading *What do you want to do?*.

e. Read the information and then click the Back button on the dialog box toolbar.

f. Click the *Print more than one copy at a time* topic that displays at the right side of the dialog box under the heading *What do you want to do?*.

g. Read the information that displays at the right side of the dialog box.

h. Click the Print button on the dialog box toolbar to print the information on print more than one copy.

5. Click the Close button that displays in the upper right corner of the dialog box (contains an X) to close the Microsoft Word Help dialog box.

Step 4c

6. Turn on the display of the Office Assistant by clicking <u>H</u>elp and then Show the <u>O</u>ffice Assistant.

Using Additional Help Features

Click the Help option on the Menu bar, expand the drop-down menu, and a variety of help features are available. You have already learned about the Microsoft Word Help option and the Hide the Office Assistant (or Show the Office Assistant) option. The drop-down menu contains a number of other options.

Choose the What's This option to point to a specific item and display information about that item. For example, to display information about a button on a toolbar, click Help and then What's This. This causes the mouse pointer to display with a question mark attached. Click a button on a toolbar and the name of the button along with information about the button displays in a yellow box. You can also use this option to display information on what formatting has been applied to specific text. To do this, click Help and then What's This. Click specific text in the document and a gray box displays containing information on paragraph formatting and font formatting.

Click Office on the Web from the Help drop-down menu and you are connected to the Microsoft Office Update Web site. From this site, you can get answers to the most frequently asked questions about Word. You can also get up-to-date tips, templates, clip art, and Help files.

If you have been a WordPerfect user and would like information on how to carry out a command in Word, click Help, expand the drop-down menu, and then click WordPerfect Help.

Word contains a self-repairing feature that will find and fix errors in Word. To run this feature, click Help, expand the drop-down menu, and then click Detect and Repair. This displays the Detect and Repair dialog box with a message telling you that during the process you may be asked to provide the installation source and exit or open applications. Click the Start button to begin the detect and repair process.

The last option at the Help drop-down menu, About Microsoft Word, displays information such as the release date, license number, and system information. You can also display information about Microsoft's technical support such as a listing of support telephone numbers.

exercise

Using What's This and Displaying System Information

1. At a clear document screen, use the What's This feature by completing the following steps:
   a. Click Help, expand the drop-down menu, and then click What's This. (This causes the mouse pointer to display with a question mark attached.)
   b. Click the Bold button on the Formatting toolbar. (This causes a yellow box to display with information on the Bold button.)
   c. Click in the document screen outside the yellow box. (This removes the box.)
   d. Click Help and then What's This.

e. Click the Select Browse Object button (displays toward the bottom of the vertical scroll bar). (This causes a yellow box to display with information on the Select Browse Object.)

f. Click in the document screen outside the yellow box. (This removes the box.)

2. Read information about Word by completing the following steps:

a. Click Help, expand the drop-down menu, and then click About Microsoft Word.

b. At the About Microsoft Word dialog box, click the System Info button that displays in the lower right corner of the dialog box.

c. At the Microsoft System Information dialog box, read the information, and then exit the dialog box by clicking File (on the dialog box menu bar) and then Exit.

d. At the About Microsoft Word dialog box, click the Tech Support button that displays in the lower right corner of the dialog box.

e. Read the information that displays in the Microsoft Word Help dialog box and then click the Close button that displays in the upper right corner of the dialog box (contains an X).

f. At the About Microsoft Word dialog box, click OK.

Using ScreenTips

Word includes a ScreenTips feature that is available in every dialog box and displays as a button containing a question mark. This button displays in the upper right corner of dialog boxes. To use the ScreenTips feature, click the ScreenTips button, and then click an item in the dialog box. Word will display an explanation about the particular item.

ScreenTips

Using ScreenTips

1. At a clear document screen, display information about specific items in the Font dialog box by completing the following steps:

a. Display the Font dialog box with the Font tab selected.

b. Click the ScreenTips button. (This button is located in the upper right corner of the dialog box and contains a question mark.)

c. Move the arrow pointer (displays with a question mark attached) to the Size option and then click the left mouse button. (This displays a yellow box containing information on font size.)

d. Click the ScreenTips button and then click the Font color option.

e. Close the Font dialog box.

2. Display the Font dialog box with the Character Spacing tab selected. Display information about specific options (you choose the options) by completing steps similar to those in step 1.

3. Close the Font dialog box.

chapter summary

➤ The appearance of a document in the document screen and how it looks when printed is called the format.

➤ Text can be bolded, italicized, and underlined with buttons on the Formatting toolbar or with shortcut commands. Do this as text is keyed or apply the features later by selecting the text and then choosing the desired feature.

➤ You can remove all character formatting from selected text by pressing Ctrl + spacebar.

➤ A font consists of three parts: typeface, type style, and type size.

➤ A typeface is a set of characters with a common design and shape. Typefaces are either monospaced, allotting the same amount of horizontal space to each character, or proportional, allotting a varying amount of space for each character.

➤ A type style is a variation of style within a certain typeface. There are four main kinds of type styles: normal, bold, italic, and bold italic.

➤ Type size is measured in pitch or point size. Pitch is the number of characters per inch—the higher the pitch, the smaller the characters. Point size is a vertical measurement—the higher the point size, the larger the characters.

➤ Change the font at the Font dialog box or use the Font button on the Formatting toolbar. Click the Font Size button on the Formatting toolbar to change the font size or click the Font Color button to change the text color.

➤ The Effects section of the Font dialog box contains a variety of options that can be used to create different character styles such as Strikethrough, Double strikethrough, Superscript, Subscript, Shadow, Outline, Emboss, Engrave, Small caps, All caps, and Hidden.

➤ Adjust character spacing and turn on kerning with options at the Font dialog box with the Character Spacing tab selected.

➤ Animate text in the screen with options at the Font dialog box with the Text Effects tab selected.

➤ Many of the typefaces (fonts) include special symbols such as bullets and publishing symbols. Insert a symbol in a document at the Symbols dialog box.

➤ Word's Help feature is an on-screen reference manual containing information about all Word features and commands.

➤ To get help from the Office Assistant, click the Assistant, key a question, and then click the Search button.

➤ Some Help information displays in the Microsoft Word Help dialog box. This dialog box contains a toolbar with the following buttons—Show, Back, Forward, Print, and Options.

➤ The expanded Microsoft Word Help dialog box displays with three tabs—Contents, Answer Wizard, and Index.

➤ Hide the Office Assistant by clicking Help and then Hide the Office Assistant. Redisplay the Office Assistant by clicking the Microsoft Word Help button on the Standard toolbar or by clicking Help and then Show the Office Assistant.

➤ Turn off the Office Assistant for the entire Word session by clicking the Office Assistant and then clicking the Options button. At the Office Assistant dialog box, click the Use the Office Assistant option to remove the check mark, and then click OK.

- Additional options from the <u>H</u>elp drop-down menu include What's <u>T</u>his, Office on the <u>W</u>eb, Word<u>P</u>erfect Help, Detect and <u>R</u>epair, and <u>A</u>bout Microsoft Word.
- Use the ScreenTips button in any dialog box to read information about specific items in the dialog box.

commands review

	Mouse	Keyboard
Bold	Click the Bold button on the Formatting toolbar	Ctrl + B
Italics	Click the Italic button on the Formatting toolbar	Ctrl + I
Underline	Click the Underline button on the Formatting toolbar	Ctrl + U
Remove all character formatting from selected text		Ctrl + spacebar
Display Font dialog box	Format, Font	Format, Font
Display Symbol dialog box	Insert, Symbol	Insert, Symbol
Display Microsoft Word Help dialog box	Click Office Assistant, key question, click Search button, and then click desired topic; or turn off Office Assistant and then click Help and then Microsoft Word Help	
Display Office Assistant dialog box	Click Office Assistant and then click Options button	

thinking offline

Matching: In the space provided at the left, indicate the correct letter <u>or letters</u> that match each description.

Ⓐ	Arial	Ⓔ	font	Ⓘ	sans serif	Ⓜ	Times New Roman
Ⓑ	monospaced	Ⓕ	pitch	Ⓙ	serif	Ⓝ	type size
Ⓒ	Garamond	Ⓖ	point	Ⓚ	subscript	Ⓞ	type style
Ⓓ	italic	Ⓗ	proportional	Ⓛ	superscript	Ⓟ	typeface

_i_ 1. This kind of typeface does not have a small line at the end of each character stroke.

_B_ 2. This term refers to a particular typeface in a specific style and size.

_H_ 3. This kind of typeface allots a varying amount of space for each character.

_K_ 4. This term refers to text that is lowered slightly below the regular line of text.

_G_ 5. With this type of measurement, the higher the number, the larger the characters.

ACM 6. These are examples of different typefaces.

_L_ 7. This term refers to text that is raised slightly above the regular line of text.

Completion: In the space provided at the right, indicate the correct term, symbol, or command.

1. Change the font of selected text with this button on the Formatting toolbar.

   Font Button

2. This is the shortcut command to bold text.

   Bold Button

3. This is the shortcut command to underline text.

   U Button

4. This keyboard command removes all character formatting from selected text.

   Ctrl + spacebar

5. Turn on kerning at the Font dialog box with this tab selected.

   Character Spacing

6. Add animation effects to text with options at the Font dialog box with this tab selected.

   Text Effects

7. Display the Office Assistant dialog box by clicking the Office Assistant and then clicking this button.

   Help

8. Click this button on the Microsoft Word Help dialog box toolbar to expand the dialog box.

   Options

9. Click this tab at the expanded Microsoft Word Help dialog box to display a variety of categories preceded by an icon of a closed book.

   Contents

10. In the space provided below, list the steps you would complete to insert the symbol ê into a document.

    Click Insert and then Symbol - Select the Symbols Tab (make sure normal text is displayed in Font text box) Double-Click the ê symbol - Click the Close Button

working hands-on

Assessment 1

1. At a clear document screen, key the document shown in figure 2.16. Bold, italicize, and underline the text as shown.
2. Save the document and name it Ch 02, SA 01.
3. Print and then close Ch 02, SA 01.

figure

Assessment 1

<u>Planning a Multimedia Work</u>

There are three common methods for organizing multimedia works. The methods include the following:

Sequential Page-based Multimedia: The work can be a sequence of pages or slides, appearing one after the other, that incorporate various elements such as text, sound, still graphics, and video.

Hypertext Page-based Multimedia: The work can be a set of pages containing links that the user can follow at will.

Movie-based Multimedia: The work can be a movie or series of movies that stop from time to time to enable the user to follow a link.

To plan a sequential page-based multimedia or movie-based multimedia, people usually prepare a *storyboard*, which consists of sketches of the pages or frames as they will appear in the final work. To plan hypertext page-based multimedia, people generally prepare a *tree diagram* showing the links between pages.

Assessment 2

1. Open Ch 02, SA 01.
2. Save the document with Save As and name it Ch 02, SA 02.
3. Make the following changes to the document:
   a. Select the entire document and then change to a serif typeface (other than Times New Roman).
   b. With the entire document still selected, display the Font dialog box with the Character Spacing tab selected, change the Spacing option to *Expanded* (by 1 pt), turn on kerning, and then close the dialog box.
   c. Remove the underlining from the title *Planning a Multimedia Work*.
   d. Removing the bolding from the headings *Sequential Page-based Multimedia*, *Hypertext Page-based Multimedia*, and *Movie-based Multimedia* and insert underlining instead. (Do not underline the colon [:] after each heading.)
4. Save the document again with the same name (Ch 02, SA 02).
5. Print and then close Ch 02, SA 02.

Assessment 3

1. Open Memo 01.
2. Save the memo with Save As and name it Ch 02, SA 03.
3. Make the following changes:
   a. Select the book title, *The ABC's of Business Communications*, remove the underlining, and then add italics.
   b. Select the book title, *Communications for the Business Office*, remove the underlining, and then add italics.

    c.   Select the book title, *Basics of Business Communications*, remove the underlining, and then add italics.

    d.   Select the book title, *Communicating with Style*, remove the underlining, and then add italics.

    e.   Select and bold the headings *DATE:*, *TO:*, *FROM:*, and *SUBJECT:*. (If necessary, realign the date, *October 26, 2001*, after *DATE:*.)

    f.   Insert your initials at the end of the document where you see the "XX." Change the document name after your initials from Memo 01 to Ch 02, SA 03.

    g.   Select the entire document and then change to a serif typeface (other than Times New Roman).

4. Save the document again with the same name (Ch 02, SA 03).
5. Print and then close Ch 02, SA 03.

Assessment 4

1. Open Notice 02.
2. Save the document with Save As and name it Ch 02, SA 04.
3. Make the following changes to the document:
    a.   Select the entire document.
    b.   Change the font to 16-point Bookman Old Style bold, the font color to Red, and apply the Shadow effect.
4. Save the document again with the same name (Ch 02, SA 04).
5. Print and then close Ch 02, SA 04.

Assessment 5

1. At a clear document screen, key the memo shown in figure 2.17 in a traditional-style memo format with the following specifications:
    a.   Italicize, superscript, and subscript text and insert special symbols as shown in the memo. (The symbols é and ñ are available at the Symbol dialog box with the *(normal text)* font selected.)
    b.   After keying the memo, select the entire memo, and then change the font to 12-point Century Schoolbook.
2. Save the memo and name it Ch 02, SA 05.
3. Print and then close Ch 02, SA 05.

figure

2.17   *Assessment 5*

DATE: February 12, 2001; TO: René MacDonald; FROM: Gerald Ibañez; SUBJECT: STATISTICAL ANALYSIS

I have been running an analysis on the areas mentioned in your February 2 memo. Completing the computations has brought up the following questions:

With smaller section ratios of r^1 and r^2 (.10 to .25)[1], what will be the yield increase?

What is the interaction effect on the scores of X_1, X_2, and X_3?

XX:Ch 02, SA 05

Chapter 03

Formatting Paragraphs

In Word, a paragraph is any amount of text followed by the press of the Enter key. In this chapter, you will learn to apply paragraph formatting to text such as changing text alignment, indenting text, applying formatting with Format Painter, inserting numbers and bullets, and changing line spacing.

Displaying Nonprinting Characters

A paragraph mark is inserted in a document each time the Enter key is pressed. By default, this paragraph mark is not visible. When changes are made to a paragraph, the formatting changes are inserted in the paragraph mark. If the paragraph mark is deleted, the formatting in the mark is eliminated and the text returns to the default.

When you begin formatting text by paragraph, displaying nonprinting characters can be useful. If you want to remove paragraph formatting from text, delete the paragraph mark. To display the paragraph mark and other nonprinting characters, click the Show/Hide ¶ button on the Standard toolbar, use a shortcut command, or choose options from the Options dialog box.

Show/Hide

To display nonprinting characters using the Standard toolbar, click the Show/Hide ¶ button. You can also display nonprinting characters by pressing Shift + Ctrl + *. Either of these methods causes nonprinting characters to display as shown in the document in figure 3.1.

figure
3.1

Document with Nonprinting Symbols Displayed

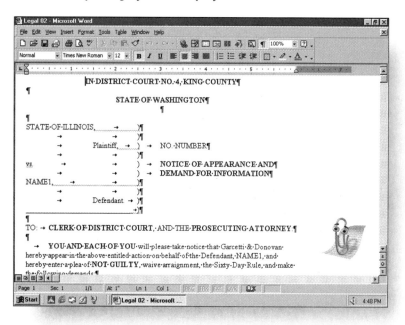

To turn off the display of nonprinting characters, click the Show/Hide ¶ button on the Standard toolbar or press Shift + Ctrl + *. The Show/Hide ¶ button on the Standard toolbar and Shift + Ctrl + * turn on the display of all nonprinting characters. To control which nonprinting characters display, use the Options dialog box shown in figure 3.2. To display this dialog box, click Tools and then Options. At the Options dialog box, make sure the View tab is selected.

figure
3.2

Options Dialog Box with View Tab Selected

Insert a check mark in the check box for the nonprinting characters you want displayed.

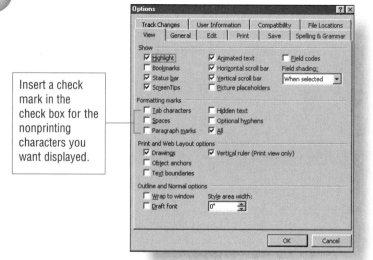

Chapter Three

Choose options from the Formatting marks section of the Options dialog box to determine what nonprinting symbols you want displayed in the document. Click the <u>A</u>ll option if you want all nonprinting characters displayed. After making changes to the Options dialog box, click OK or press Enter.

(Before completing computer exercises, delete the Chapter 02 *folder on your disk. Next, copy the* Chapter 03 *folder from the CD that accompanies this textbook to your disk and then make* Chapter 03 *the active folder.)*

Displaying Nonprinting Characters

1. Open Legal 01.
2. Turn on the display of nonprinting characters by clicking the Show/Hide ¶ button on the Standard toolbar.
3. Scroll through the document to see how the document appears with nonprinting characters displayed.
4. Position the insertion point at the beginning of the document and then turn off the display of nonprinting characters by clicking the Show/Hide ¶ button on the Standard toolbar.
5. Turn on the display of only tab and paragraph marks by completing the following steps:
    a. Click <u>T</u>ools and then <u>O</u>ptions.
    b. At the Options dialog box, make sure the View tab is selected.
    c. At the Options dialog box with the View tab selected, click <u>T</u>ab characters in the Formatting marks section (this inserts a check mark in the check box). **Step 5c**
    d. Click Paragraph <u>m</u>arks in the Formatting marks section (this inserts a check mark). **Step 5d**
    e. Click OK or press Enter.
6. Scroll through the document to see how the document appears with tab and paragraph marks visible.
7. Turn off the display of tab and paragraph marks by completing step 5.
8. Close Legal 01 without saving it.

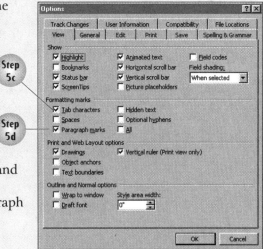

Changing Paragraph Alignment

By default, paragraphs in a Word document are aligned at the left margin and ragged at the right margin. This default alignment can be changed with buttons on the Formatting toolbar or with shortcut commands. Text in a paragraph can be aligned at the left margin, between margins, at the right margin, or at the left and right margins. Figure 3.3 illustrates the different paragraph alignments.

figure
3.3

Paragraph Alignments

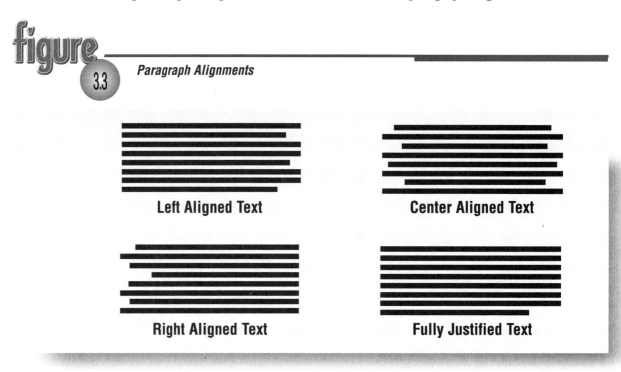

Left Aligned Text

Center Aligned Text

Right Aligned Text

Fully Justified Text

Use the buttons on the Formatting toolbar or the shortcut commands shown in figure 3.4 to change the alignment of text in paragraphs.

figure
3.4

Paragraph Alignment Buttons and Commands

To align text	Button	Shortcut command
at the left margin		Ctrl + L
between margins		Ctrl + E
at the right margin		Ctrl + R
at the left and right margins		Ctrl + J

You can change the alignment of text in paragraphs before you key the text or you can change the alignment of existing text. If you change the alignment before keying text, the alignment formatting is inserted in the paragraph mark. As you key text and press Enter, the paragraph formatting is continued. For example, if you press Ctrl + E to turn on center aligning, key text for the first paragraph, and then press Enter, the center alignment formatting is still active and the insertion point displays in the middle of the left and right margins.

Align Left

To return paragraph alignment to the default (left aligned), click the Align Left button on the Formatting toolbar or press Ctrl + L. You can also return all paragraph formatting to the default by pressing Ctrl + Q. This shortcut command returns all paragraph formatting (not just alignment) to the default settings.

To change the alignment of existing text in a paragraph, position the insertion point anywhere within the paragraph. The entire paragraph does not have to be selected. To change the alignment of several adjacent paragraphs in a document, select a portion of the first paragraph through a portion of the last paragraph. Only a portion of the first and last paragraphs needs to be selected.

If you want to apply paragraph formatting to several paragraphs that are not adjacent, you can use the Repeat key, F4, or the Repeat option from the Edit drop-down menu. For example, if you apply center alignment to a paragraph and then want to repeat it for another paragraph, position the insertion point anywhere in the other paragraph and then press F4. Or, click Edit and then Repeat Paragraph Alignment.

Changing Paragraph Alignment to Center

1. At a clear document screen, key the text shown in figure 3.5.
2. After keying the text, make the following changes:
    a. Select the entire document.
    b. Change the font to 14-point Tahoma bold. (If Tahoma is not available, choose a similar sans serif typeface such as Arial or Univers.)
    c. With the document still selected, press Ctrl + E to change the paragraph alignment to center.
3. Save the document and name it Ch 03, Ex 02.
4. Print and then close Ch 03, Ex 02.

Exercise 2

OT 250, BUSINESS COMMUNICATIONS

Monday through Friday

8:00 a.m. to 8:50 a.m.

Room 106

Changing Paragraph Alignment to Justified

1. Open Para 02.
2. Save the document with Save As and name it Ch 03, Ex 03.
3. Change the alignment of the text in paragraphs to justified by completing the following steps:
   a. Select the entire document.
   b. Click the Justify button on the Formatting toolbar.
4. Save the document again with the same name (Ch 03, Ex 03).
5. Print and then close Ch 03, Ex 03.

Changing Alignment at the Paragraph Dialog Box

Paragraph alignment can also be changed at the Paragraph dialog box shown in figure 3.6. To change the alignment of text in a paragraph, display the Paragraph dialog box by clicking Format and then Paragraph. At the Paragraph dialog box, click the down-pointing triangle at the right side of the Alignment text box. At the drop-down list that displays, click the desired alignment option, and then click OK or press Enter.

figure
3.6
Paragraph Dialog Box

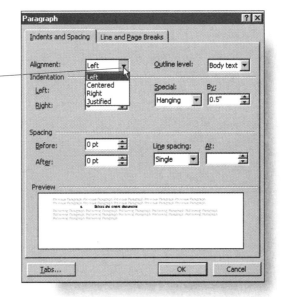

Change paragraph alignment by clicking this down-pointing triangle and then clicking the desired alignment at the drop-down list.

exercise

Changing Paragraph Alignment to Justified Using the Paragraph Dialog Box

1. Open Para 04.
2. Save the document with Save As and name it Ch 03, Ex 04.
3. Change the alignment of text in paragraphs to Justified using the Paragraph dialog box by completing the following steps:
    a. Select the entire document.
    b. Click Format and then Paragraph.
    c. At the Paragraph dialog box with the Indents and Spacing tab selected, click the down-pointing triangle at the right of the Alignment text box, and then click *Justified*.
    d. Click OK or press Enter.
    e. Deselect the text.
4. Save the document again with the same name (Ch 03, Ex 04).
5. Print and then close Ch 03, Ex 04.

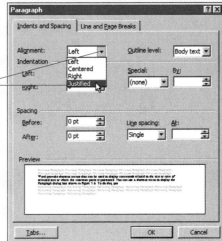

Using Shortcut Menus

Word provides shortcut menus that can be used to display commands related to the text or item of selected text or where the insertion point is positioned. You can use a shortcut menu to display the Paragraph dialog box shown in figure 3.6. To do this, position the insertion point in the text that you want formatted, click the *right* button on the mouse, and then click P̲aragraph at the shortcut menu.

Some keyboards include a Shortcut Menu key located in the bottom row of the keyboard (to the right of the spacebar—contains an image of a menu). When pressed, this key will display a shortcut menu with the P̲aragraph option.

Changing Paragraph Alignment to Right Using a Shortcut Menu

1. At a clear document screen, turn on the display of nonprinting characters.
2. Change the alignment of text to right by completing the following steps:
   a. Position the I-beam pointer anywhere in the document screen and then click the *right* mouse button.
   b. At the shortcut menu that displays, click P̲aragraph.
   c. At the Paragraph dialog box, change the Alignment to *Right*.
   d. Click OK or press Enter.
3. Key the first line of text shown in figure 3.7 and then press Enter.
4. Key the remaining lines of text. (Each time you press Enter, the formatting from the previous paragraph is carried to the next paragraph.)
5. Select the entire document, change the font to 14-point Tahoma bold, and then deselect the text.
6. Turn off the display of nonprinting characters.
7. Save the document and name it Ch 03, Ex 05.
8. Print and then close Ch 03, Ex 05.

Exercise 5

Coleman Development Corporation
3451 Classen Boulevard
Oklahoma City, OK 76341
(801) 555-4500

Spacing Before and After Paragraphs

Space can be added before and after a paragraph by pressing the Enter key. If you want more control over the spacing above or below paragraphs, use the B̲efore and/or Aft̲er options at the Paragraph dialog box with the I̲ndents and Spacing tab selected.

If spacing before or after a paragraph is added at the Paragraph dialog box, the spacing is part of the paragraph and will be moved, copied, or deleted with the paragraph. If a paragraph, such as a heading, contains spacing above it, and the paragraph falls at the top of a page, the spacing is ignored.

Spacing above or below paragraphs is added in points. For example, to add 9 points of spacing below selected paragraphs you would display the Paragraph dialog box with the Indents and Spacing tab selected, select the current measurement in the After text box, and then key **9**. You can also click the up-pointing or down-pointing triangles to increase or decrease the amount of spacing before or after paragraphs. With the shortcut command, Ctrl + 0 (zero), you can add 12 points of space before a paragraph.

Spacing before Paragraphs

1. Open Quiz.
2. Save the document with Save As and name it Ch 03, Ex 06.
3. Make the following changes to the document:
   a. Select the entire document and then change the font to 12-point Bookman Old Style (or a similar serif typeface).
   b. Select the title *CHAPTER QUIZ* and then change the font to 14-point Arial bold.
   c. Add 18 points of spacing before paragraphs by completing the following steps:
      1) Select from the sentence that begins *Industralization and colonization...*through the sentence that begins *What is the significance....*
      2) With the text selected, click Format and then Paragraph.
      3) At the Paragraph dialog box with the Indents and Spacing tab selected, click three times on the up-pointing triangle at the right side of the Before option (in the Spacing section). (This changes the measurement in the text box to *18 pt.*)
      4) Click OK to close the dialog box.
      5) Deselect the text.
4. Save the document again with the same name (Ch 03, Ex 06).
5. Print and then close Ch 03, Ex 06.

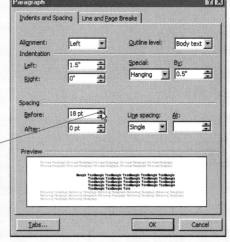

Indenting Text in Paragraphs

By now you are familiar with the word wrap feature of Word, which ends lines and wraps the insertion point to the next line. To indent text from the left margin, or the left and right margins, or to create numbered items, use indent buttons on the Formatting toolbar, shortcut commands, options from the Paragraph dialog box, markers on the Ruler, or the Alignment button on the Ruler. Indent markers and the Alignment button on the Ruler are identified in figure 3.8. Refer to figure 3.9 for methods for indenting text in a document.

Ruler and Indent Markers

Methods for Indenting Text

Indent	Methods for indenting
First line of paragraph	• Press the Tab key. • Display Paragraph dialog box, click down-pointing triangle to the right of the Special text box, click *First line*, and then click OK. • Drag the first line indent marker on the Ruler. • Click the Alignment button located at the left side of the Ruler until the First Line Indent button displays and then click on the Ruler at the desired location.
Text from left margin	• Click the Increase Indent button on the Formatting toolbar to increase indent or click the Decrease Indent button to decrease the indent. • Press Ctrl + M to increase indent or press Ctrl + Shift + M to decrease indent. • Display the Paragraph dialog box, key the desired indent measurement in the Left text box, and then click OK. • Drag the left indent marker on the Ruler.
Text from left and right margins	• Display the Paragraph dialog box, key the desired indent measurement in the Left text box and the Right text box, and then click OK. • Drag the left indent marker and the right indent marker on the Ruler.
All lines of text except the first (called a hanging indent)	• Press Ctrl + T. (Press Ctrl + Shift + T to remove hanging indent.)

- Display the Paragraph dialog box, click the down-pointing triangle to the right of the Special text box, click *Hanging*, and then click OK.
- Click the Alignment button located at the left side of the Ruler until the Hanging Indent button displays and then click on the Ruler at the desired location.

Indenting the First Line of Paragraphs Using the Alignment Button

1. Open Para 03.
2. Save the document with Save As and name it Ch 03, Ex 07.
3. Indent the first line of each paragraph 0.25 inch using the Alignment button on the Ruler by completing the following steps:
   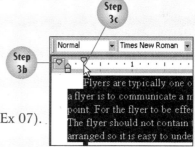
   a. Select the entire document.
   b. Click the Alignment button located at the left side of the Ruler until the First Line Indent button displays.
   c. Click on the 0.25-inch mark on the Ruler.
   d. Deselect the text.
4. Save the document again with the same name (Ch 03, Ex 07).
5. Print and then close Ch 03, Ex 07.

Indenting Text from the Left Margin

1. Open Memo 02.
2. Save the document with Save As and name it Ch 03, Ex 08.
3. Indent the second paragraph in the document (containing the book title) to the first tab setting by completing the following steps:
   a. Position the insertion point anywhere in the second paragraph.
   b. Press Ctrl + M.
4. Indent the third paragraph by completing the following steps:
   a. Position the insertion point anywhere in the third paragraph.
   b. Click the Increase Indent button on the Formatting toolbar.
5. Indent the fourth paragraph by completing the following steps:
   a. Position the insertion point anywhere in the fourth paragraph.
   b. Click Format and then Paragraph.

c. At the Paragraph dialog box, click the up-pointing triangle at the right side of the <u>L</u>eft text box until *0.5"* displays.

d. Click OK or press Enter.

6. Indent the fifth paragraph in the document by completing the following steps:

a. Make sure the Ruler is displayed. (If not, click <u>V</u>iew, expand the drop-down menu, and then click <u>R</u>uler.)

b. Position the insertion point anywhere in the fifth paragraph.

c. Position the mouse pointer on the Left Indent marker on the Ruler, hold down the left mouse button, drag the marker to the 0.5-inch mark on the Ruler, and then release the mouse button.

7. Save the document again with the same name (Ch 03, Ex 08).

8. Print and then close Ch 03, Ex 08.

exercise 9

Indenting Text from the Left and Right Margins

1. At a clear document screen, key the document shown in figure 3.10. Bold and center align the title as shown.

2. After keying the document, indent the third paragraph of the document from the left and right margins by completing the following steps:

a. Make sure the Ruler is displayed.

b. Position the insertion point anywhere in the third paragraph.

c. Position the mouse pointer on the Left Indent marker on the Ruler, hold down the left mouse button, drag the marker to the 0.5-inch mark on the Ruler, and then release the mouse button.

d. Position the mouse pointer on the Right Indent marker on the Ruler, hold down the left mouse button, drag the marker to the 5.5-inch mark on the Ruler, and then release the mouse button.

3. Indent the fifth paragraph in the document from the left and right margins by completing the following steps:

a. Position the insertion point anywhere within the fifth paragraph.

b. Click F<u>o</u>rmat and then <u>P</u>aragraph.

c. At the Paragraph dialog box, select the current measurement in the <u>L</u>eft text box, and then key **0.5**.

d. Select the current measurement in the <u>R</u>ight text box and then key **0.5**.

e. Click OK or press Enter.

4. Select all the paragraphs in the document (excluding the title), change the paragraph alignment to justified, and then deselect the text.

5. Save the document and name it Ch 03, Ex 09.

6. Print and then close Ch 03, Ex 09.

figure

3.10

Exercise 9

DESKTOP PUBLISHING

Desktop publishing is the use of a microcomputer-based system to produce publication materials that includes typeset or near-typeset quality text and graphics integrated on a page. These materials can include memos, correspondence, notices, flyers, posters, certificates, office forms, brochures, schedules, catalogues, reports, manuals, newsletters, newspapers, magazines, or books.

In her book, *Desktop Publishing Technology and Design*, Holly Yasui states:

What makes desktop publishing different from traditional publishing is that equipment small enough to fit on a person's desktop can provide all the resources needed to prepare and assemble pages.

In a later section of her book, Holly Yasui makes the following statement about desktop publishing technology:

In the graphic arts world, desktop publishing is considered a *prepress* technology, that is, the desktop publishing system itself is generally not used to produce the final multiple copies of a publication, but rather to produce masters for reproduction.

exercise 10

Creating Hanging Paragraphs

1. Open Bibliography.
2. Save the document with Save As and name it Ch 03, Ex 10.
3. Create a hanging indent for the first two paragraphs by completing the following steps:
    a. Select at least a portion of the first and second paragraphs.
    b. Press Ctrl + T.
4. Create a hanging indent for the third and fourth paragraphs by completing the following steps:
    a. Select at least a portion of the third and fourth paragraphs.
    b. Click Format and then Paragraph.
    c. At the Paragraph dialog box with the Indents and Spacing tab selected, click the down-pointing triangle at the right side of the Special text box (contains the word *(none)*).

d. At the drop-down menu that displays, click *Hanging*.
e. Click OK or press Enter.
5. Make the following changes to the document:
   a. Select the entire document.
   b. Change to a serif typeface other than Times New Roman.
   c. Change the paragraph alignment to justified.
   d. Deselect the text.
6. Save the document again with the same name (Ch 03, Ex 10).
7. Print and then close Ch 03, Ex 10.

Formatting with Format Painter

Format
Painter

The Standard toolbar contains a button that can be used to copy character formatting to different locations in the document. This button is called the Format Painter and displays on the Standard toolbar as a paintbrush. To use the Format Painter button, position the insertion point on a character containing the desired character formatting, click the Format Painter button, and then select text to which you want the character formatting applied. When you click the Format Painter button, the mouse I-beam pointer displays with a paintbrush attached. If you want to apply character formatting a single time, click the Format Painter button once. If, however, you want to apply the character formatting in more than one location in the document, double-click the Format Painter button. If you double-clicked the Format Painter button, turn off the feature by clicking the Format Painter button once.

exercise 11

Formatting Headings with the Format Painter

1. Open Report 01.
2. Save the document with Save As and name it Ch 03, Ex 11.
3. Make the following changes to the document:
   a. Select the entire document and then change the font to 12-point Garamond (or a similar serif typeface such as Bookman Old Style or New Century Schoolbook).
   b. Select the title *DESKTOP PUBLISHING* and then change the font to 16-point Arial bold.
   c. Select the heading *Defining Desktop Publishing* and then change the font to 14-point Arial bold.
   d. Use the Format Painter button and apply the 14-point Arial bold font to the other headings by completing the following steps:
      1) Position the insertion point on any character in the heading *Defining Desktop Publishing*.
      2) Double-click the Format Painter button on the Standard toolbar.
      3) Using the mouse, select the heading *Initiating the Desktop Publishing Process*. (You will need to scroll down the report to display this heading.)
      4) Using the mouse, select the heading *Planning the Publication*.
      5) Using the mouse, select the heading *Creating the Content*.

6) Click once on the Format Painter button on the Standard toolbar. (This turns off the feature.)

7) Deselect the heading.

4. Save the document again with the same name (Ch 03, Ex 11). (The formatting you apply to this document may create a page break in an undesirable location. You will learn how to control page breaks in chapter 4.)

5. Print and then close Ch 03, Ex 11.

Creating Numbered and Bulleted Paragraphs

If you key **1.**, press the spacebar, key a paragraph of text, and then press Enter, Word will indent the number approximately 0.25 inch and then hang indent the text in the paragraph approximately 0.5 inch from the left margin. Additionally, *2.* will be inserted 0.25 inch from the left margin at the beginning of the next paragraph. This is part of Word's AutoFormat feature. (If this feature is not activated, you can turn it on by clicking <u>T</u>ools and then <u>A</u>utoCorrect. At the AutoCorrect dialog box, click the AutoFormat As You Type tab. Click in the Automatic <u>n</u>umbered lists check box to insert a check mark and then click OK.) Continue keying numbered items and Word will insert the next number in the list. To turn off numbering, press the Enter key twice or click the Numbering button on the Formatting toolbar. (You can also remove all paragraph formatting from a paragraph, including automatic numbering, by pressing Ctrl + Q.)

Numbering

If you press Enter twice between numbered paragraphs, the automatic number is removed. To turn it back on, key the next number in the list (and the period) followed by a space, key the paragraph of text, and then press Enter. Word will automatically indent the number and hang indent the text.

Creating Numbered Paragraphs

(Note: In this exercise and other exercises in the text, you will be required to create business letters. Please refer to Appendix C at the end of this text for the correct placement and spacing of a block-style business letter.)

1. At a clear document screen, key the text shown in figure 3.11 in an appropriate business letter format. When keying the numbered paragraphs, complete the following steps:
   a. Key **1.** at the left margin and then press the spacebar.
   b. Key the paragraph of text and then press the Enter key twice.
   c. Key **2.** at the left margin and then press the spacebar.
   d. Key the paragraph of text and then press the Enter key twice.
   e. Key **3.** at the left margin and then press the spacebar.
   f. Key the paragraph of text and then press the Enter key twice.
   g. Key the remaining text of the document.
2. Save the letter and name it Ch 03, Ex 12.
3. Print and then close Ch 03, Ex 12.

figure 3.11   *Exercise 12*

January 3, 2001

Ms. Stephanie Branson
Coleman Development Corporation
3451 Classen Boulevard
Oklahoma City, OK 76341

Dear Ms. Branson:

The development summary for the Tahoma region was completed recently. It analyzes the economic and demographic outlook for the region for the next two decades. Three basic conclusions are reached in the summary:

1. Significant *quantitative* growth is headed in the direction of the Tahoma region, exceeding forecasts made in the recent past.

2. The growth that will be experienced in the Tahoma region has important *qualitative* potential, created by the types of jobs and personal income that will be added to the area's economic base.

3. To fully capture this qualitative potential, managers of the Tahoma region will need to utilize self-contained communities and other planned developments.

A community meeting has been planned for February 22, 2001, at 7:30 p.m. in the West Creek Community Center. Representatives from local cities are interested in the findings of the summary and will be attending this meeting.

Sincerely,

Dean Talmadge
Tahoma Regional Manager

XX:Ch 03, Ex 12

If you do not want automatic numbering in a document, turn off the feature at the AutoCorrect dialog box with the AutoFormat As You Type tab selected as shown in figure 3.12. To display this dialog box, click Tools and then AutoCorrect. At the AutoCorrect dialog box, click the AutoFormat As You Type tab. To turn off automatic numbering, remove the check mark from the option *Automatic numbered lists*.

AutoCorrect Dialog Box with AutoFormat As You Type Tab Selected

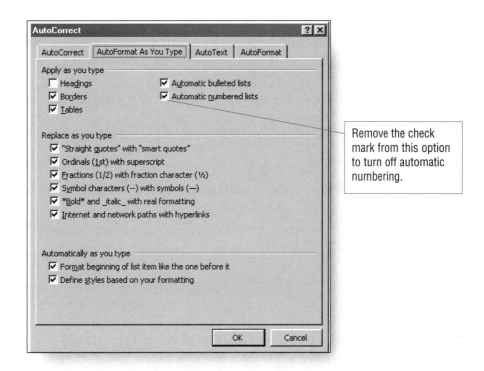

Remove the check mark from this option to turn off automatic numbering.

You can also automate the creation of numbered paragraphs with the Numbering button on the Formatting toolbar. To use this button, key the text (do not key the number) for each paragraph to be numbered, select the paragraphs to be numbered, and then click the Numbering button on the Formatting toolbar. Numbered paragraphs can be inserted or deleted from text.

Inserting Paragraph Numbering

1. Open Quiz.
2. Save the document with Save As and name it Ch 03, Ex 13.
3. Insert paragraph numbering before all paragraphs of text in the document (except the title) by completing the following steps:
   a. Select all paragraphs of text in the document (except the title).
   b. Click the Numbering button on the Formatting toolbar.
4. Add the paragraph shown in figure 3.13 between paragraphs 5 and 6 by completing the following steps:
   a. Position the insertion point immediately to the right of the question mark at the end of the fifth paragraph.
   b. Press Enter.
   c. Key the paragraph shown in figure 3.13
5. Delete the second question (paragraph) by completing the following steps:
   a. Select the text of the second paragraph (you will not be able to select the number).
   b. Press the Delete key.
6. Save the document again with the same name (Ch 03, Ex 13).
7. Print and then close Ch 03, Ex 13.

figure

3.13   *Exercise 13*

Cellular mobile telephone service was offered for the first time in the 1980s. What role will this technology most likely play in the future?

In addition to automatically numbering paragraphs, Word's AutoFormat feature will create bulleted paragraphs. (If this feature is not activated, you can turn it on by clicking Tools and then AutoCorrect. At the AutoCorrect dialog box, click the AutoFormat As You Type tab. Click in the Automatic bulleted lists check box to insert a check mark, and then click OK.)

Bullets

You can also create bulleted paragraphs with the Bullets button on the Formatting toolbar. Figure 3.14 shows an example of bulleted paragraphs. Bulleted lists with hanging indents are automatically created when a paragraph begins with the symbol *, >, or -. Key one of the symbols, press the spacebar, key text, and then press Enter. The AutoFormat feature inserts a bullet approximately 0.25 inch from the left margin and indents the text following the bullet another 0.25 inch. The type of bullet inserted depends on the type of character entered. For example, if you use the asterisk (*) symbol, a round bullet is inserted. An arrow bullet is inserted if the greater than symbol (>) is used.

84

figure
3.14

Bulleted Paragraphs

- This is a paragraph preceded by a bullet. A bullet is used to indicate a list of items or topics.

- This is another paragraph preceded by a bullet. Bulleted paragraphs can be easily created by keying certain symbols before the text or with the Bullets button on the Formatting toolbar.

The automatic bulleting feature, like the numbering feature, can be turned off at the AutoCorrect dialog box with the AutoFormat As You Type tab selected. To display this dialog box, shown in figure 3.12, click Tools and then AutoCorrect. At the AutoCorrect dialog box, click the AutoFormat As You Type tab. To turn off automatic bulleting, remove the check mark from the Automatic bulleted lists option.

exercise 14

Creating Bullets

1. At a clear document screen, key the text shown in figure 3.15. Bold and center the title in uppercase letters as indicated. Create the bulleted paragraphs by completing the following steps:
   a. With the insertion point positioned at the left margin of the first paragraph to contain a bullet, key the greater than symbol (>).
   b. Press the spacebar once.
   c. Key the text of the first bulleted paragraph *(What is the intent of the document?)*.
   d. Press the Enter key once and then continue keying the text after the bullets.
2. After keying the last bulleted paragraph, press the Enter key twice (this turns off bullets), and then key the last paragraph shown in figure 3.15.
3. Save the document and name it Ch 03, Ex 14.
4. Print and then close Ch 03, Ex 14.

figure

3.15

Exercise 14

DESIGNING A DOCUMENT

A well-planned and relevant design sets one document apart from another. Just as people may be judged by their appearance, a publication may be judged by its design. Design also helps organize ideas so the reader can find information quickly and easily. Whether you are creating a business flyer, letterhead, or newsletter, anything you create will look more attractive, more professional, and more convincing if you take a little extra time to design it. When designing a document, you need to consider many factors:

- ➤ What is the intent of the document?
- ➤ Who is the intended audience?
- ➤ What is the feeling the document is meant to elicit?
- ➤ What is the most important information and how can it be emphasized?
- ➤ What different types of information are to be presented and how can these elements be distinguished and kept internally consistent?
- ➤ How much space is available?
- ➤ How will the document be distributed?

Answering these questions will help you determine the design and layout of your communication.

Bulleted paragraphs can also be created with the Bullets button on the Formatting toolbar. To create bulleted paragraphs using the Bullets button, key the text (do not key the bullet) of the paragraphs, select the paragraphs, and then click the Bullets button on the Formatting toolbar.

exercise 15

Inserting Bullets Using the Bullets Button

1. Open Quiz.
2. Save the document with Save As and name it Ch 03, Ex 15.
3. Insert bullets before the quiz questions and increase spacing after the paragraphs by completing the following steps:
   a. Select the text in the document (excluding the title and the blank line below the title).

  b. Click the Bullets button on the Formatting toolbar.
  c. With the paragraphs still selected, display the Paragraph dialog box, change the After measurement to *24 pt*, and then close the dialog box.
  d. Click anywhere outside the selected text to deselect it.
 4. Save the document again with the same name (Ch 03, Ex 15).
 5. Print and then close Ch 03, Ex 15.

In addition to the Bullets button on the Formatting toolbar, you can also use options from the Bullets and Numbering dialog box to number paragraphs or insert bullets. To display this dialog box, click Format, expand the drop-down menu, and then click Bullets and Numbering. The Bullets and Numbering dialog box contains three tabs: Bulleted, Numbered, and Outline Numbered. Select the Bulleted tab, as shown in figure 3.16, if you want to insert bullets before selected paragraphs.

figure
3.16 *Bullets and Numbering Dialog Box with Bulleted Tab Selected*

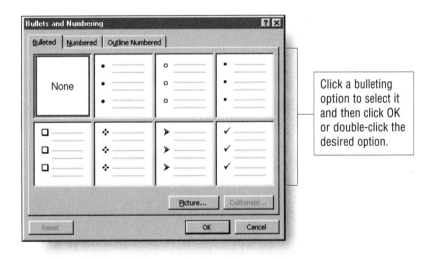

Click a bulleting option to select it and then click OK or double-click the desired option.

Select the Numbered tab if you want to insert numbers before selected paragraphs. When you click Numbered, the dialog box displays as shown in figure 3.17.

figure

3.17

*Bullets and Numbering Dialog Box with **N**umbered Tab Selected*

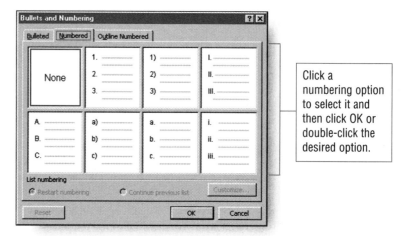

Click a numbering option to select it and then click OK or double-click the desired option.

At the Bullets and Numbering dialog box with the O**u**tline Numbered tab selected, as shown in figure 3.18, you can specify the type of numbering for paragraphs at the left margin, first tab, second tab, etc. (The options that display with *Heading 1*, *Heading 2*, or *Heading 3* are not available unless the text to be numbered has been formatted with a Heading style. You will learn more about styles in chapter 20.)

figure

3.18

*Bullets and Numbering Dialog Box with O**u**tline Numbered Tab Selected*

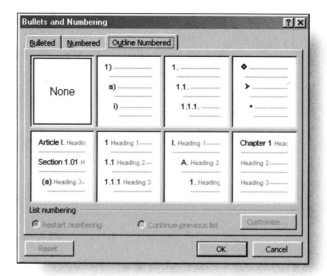

Numbering Paragraphs Using the Bullets and Numbering Dialog Box

1. Open List.
2. Save the document with Save As and name it Ch 03, Ex 16.
3. Number the paragraphs in the document using the Bullets and Numbering dialog box by completing the following steps:

   a. Select the paragraphs of text in the document (excluding the title and the blank lines below the title).

   Step 3c

   b. Click Format, expand the drop-down menu, and then click Bullets and Numbering.

   Step 3d

   c. At the Bullets and Numbering dialog box, click the Numbered tab.

   d. Click the second numbering option box in the top row.

   e. Click OK or press Enter.

4. Add *Annuity Contracts* between paragraphs 4 and 5 by completing the following steps:

   a. Position the insertion point immediately to the right of the *t* in *Role of Account*.

   b. Press Enter. (This moves the insertion point a double space below the previous paragraph.)

   c. Key **Annuity Contracts**.

5. Select and then delete *Investment Practices of the Account* (paragraph 2). (Delete any extra line spaces.)

6. Save the document again with the same name (Ch 03, Ex 16).

7. Print and then close Ch 03, Ex 16.

Creating an Outline Numbered List

1. Open Agenda.
2. Save the document with Save As and name it Ch 03, Ex 17.
3. Apply outline numbering to the document by completing the following steps:

   a. Select the paragraphs in the document *excluding* the title, subtitle, and blank lines below the subtitle.

   b. Click Format and then Bullets and Numbering.

c. At the Bullets and Numbering dialog box, click the O̲utline Numbered tab.

d. Click the second option from the left in the top row.

e. Click OK or press Enter to close the dialog box.

f. Deselect the text.

4. Save the document again with the same name (Ch 03, Ex 17).

5. Print Ch 03, Ex 17.

6. With the document still open, make the following changes:

a. Delete *Sponsors* in the Education section.

b. Move the insertion point immediately right of the last letter in *Personal Lines* (in the Sales and Marketing section), press the Enter key, and then key **Production Report**.

7. Select the entire document and then change to a serif typeface of your choosing (other than Times New Roman).

8. Save the document again with the same name (Ch 03, Ex 17).

9. Print and then close Ch 03, Ex 17.

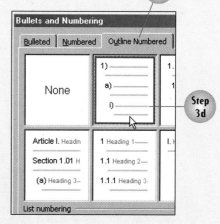

Creating Ordinals

Word's AutoFormat feature automatically formats ordinal numbers. For example, if you key **1st** and then press the spacebar, Word will correct it to *1ˢᵗ*. Word automatically changes the font size of the *st* and formats the letters as superscript text. This automatic feature will change other ordinal numbers such as 2ⁿᵈ, 3ʳᵈ, 4ᵗʰ, etc.

Keying a Document with Ordinals

1. At a clear document screen, key the text shown in figure 3.19. Let Word's AutoFormat feature insert the arrow bullets and automatically change the formatting of the ordinal numbers.

2. Save the document and name it Ch 03, Ex 18.

3. Print and then close Ch 03, Ex 18.

figure

3.19   *Exercise 18*

DATE: September 12, 2001

TO: Barry Langstrom

FROM: Mona Brown

SUBJECT: DEVELOPMENT CONTRACT

After reading the contract prepared by the Coleman Development Corporation, I would like to see the following changes made:

> ➤ Delete the 2nd paragraph in the 4th section.
> ➤ Add a paragraph between the 3rd and 4th paragraphs in the 5th section that fully describes the responsibilities of the development corporation.
> ➤ Remove the words *and others* in the 1st paragraph of the 6th section.

Please contact me after you have read the contract and the changes. I would like to submit the changes before the end of the month.

XX:Ch 03, Ex 18

Changing Line Spacing

By default, the word wrap feature single-spaces text. There may be occasions when you want to change to another spacing, such as line and a half or double. Line spacing can be changed with shortcut commands or options from the Paragraph dialog box. Figure 3.20 illustrates the shortcut commands to change line spacing.

figure
3.20 Line Spacing Shortcut Commands

Press	To change line spacing to
Ctrl + 1	single spacing
Ctrl + 2	double spacing
Ctrl + 5	1.5-line spacing

exercise 19

Changing Line Spacing

1. Open Para 02.
2. Save the document with Save As and name it Ch 03, Ex 19.
3. Change the line spacing for all paragraphs to 1.5-line spacing by completing the following steps:
   a. Select the entire document.
   b. Press Ctrl + 5.
4. Change the alignment of all paragraphs to justified. (Be sure to deselect the text.)
5. Save the document again with the same name (Ch 03, Ex 19).
6. Print and then close Ch 03, Ex 19.

Line spacing can also be changed at the Paragraph dialog box. At the Paragraph dialog box, you can change line spacing with the Line spacing option or the At option. If you click the down-pointing triangle at the right side of the Line spacing text box at the Paragraph dialog box, a drop-down list displays with a variety of spacing options. For example, to change the line spacing to double you would click *Double* at the drop-down list. You can key a specific line spacing measurement in the At text box at the Paragraph dialog box. For example, to change the line spacing to 1.75, key **1.75** in the At text box.

exercise 20

Changing Line Spacing at the Paragraph Dialog Box

1. Open Quiz.
2. Save the document with Save As and name it Ch 03, Ex 20.
3. Insert bullets before the test questions.
4. Change the line spacing to 1.75 using the Paragraph dialog box by completing the following steps:

a. Select the paragraphs in the document (excluding the title and the blank line below the title).
b. Click Format and then Paragraph.
c. At the Paragraph dialog box, make sure the Indents and Spacing tab is selected, click inside the At text box, and then key **1.75**. (This text box is located to the right of the Line spacing text box.)
d. Click OK or press Enter.
e. Deselect the text.

5. Save the document again with the same name (Ch 03, Ex 20).
6. Change the line spacing to double using a shortcut command by completing the following steps:
   a. Select the paragraphs in the document (excluding the title and the blank line below the title).
   b. Press Ctrl + 2.
   c. Deselect the text.
7. Save the document again with the same name (Ch 03, Ex 20).
8. Print and then close Ch 03, Ex 20.

Paragraph dialog box:

Indents and Spacing | Line and Page Breaks

Alignment: Left Outline level: Body text
Indentation
Left: 0" Special: (none) By:
Right: 0"

Spacing
Before: 0 pt Line spacing: At:
After: 0 pt Multiple 1.75

Preview

Tabs... OK Cancel

Step 4c

Repeating the Last Action

Use the Format Painter feature to copy character formatting to different locations in a document. If you want to apply other types of formatting to a document, such as paragraph formatting, consider using the Repeat command. To use the Repeat command, apply the desired formatting, move the insertion point to the next location where you want the formatting applied, click Edit, expand the drop-down menu, and then click Repeat; or press Ctrl + Y.

exercise 21

Formatting Using the Repeat Command

1. Open Report 01.
2. Save the document with Save As and name it Ch 03, Ex 21.
3. Make the following changes to the document:
   a. Select the entire document.
   b. Change the line spacing to single.
   c. Deselect the text.
   d. Bold the title *DESKTOP PUBLISHING* and the headings *Defining Desktop Publishing, Initiating the Desktop Publishing Process, Planning the Publication*, and *Creating the Content*.

4. Apply paragraph formatting and repeat the formatting by completing the following steps:
   a. Position the insertion point anywhere in the heading *Defining Desktop Publishing*.
   b. Click F_ormat and then _Paragraph.
   c. At the Paragraph dialog box, click twice on the up-pointing triangle at the right side of the _Before option (in the Spacing section). (This changes the measurement in the text box to *12 pt.*)
   d. Click once on the up-pointing triangle at the right side of the Aft_er option. (This changes the measurement in the text box to *6 pt.*)
   e. Click OK to close the Paragraph dialog box.
   f. Repeat the paragraph formatting for the second heading by completing the following steps:
      1) Position the insertion point anywhere in the heading *Initiating the Desktop Publishing Process*.
      2) Click _Edit, expand the drop-down menu, and then click _Repeat Paragraph Formatting.
   g. Repeat the paragraph formatting for the third heading by positioning the insertion point anywhere in the heading *Planning the Publication* and then pressing Ctrl + Y.
   h. Repeat the paragraph formatting for the fourth heading by positioning the insertion point anywhere in the heading *Creating the Content* and then pressing Ctrl + Y.
5. Save the document again with the same name (Ch 03, Ex 21).
6. Print and then close Ch 03, Ex 21.

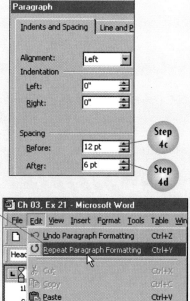

Step 4c

Step 4d

Step 4f2

chapter summary

➤ To turn on or off the display of nonprinting characters such as paragraph marks, click the Show/Hide ¶ button on the Standard toolbar. To control which nonprinting characters display, use the Options dialog box.

➤ In Word, a paragraph is any amount of text followed by a paragraph mark (a stroke of the Enter key). Word inserts into the paragraph mark any paragraph formatting that is turned on.

➤ To remove paragraph formatting from text, delete the paragraph mark or remove all paragraph formatting by pressing Ctrl + Q.

➤ By default, paragraphs in a Word document are aligned at the left margin and ragged at the right margin. This default alignment can be changed with buttons on the Formatting toolbar, at the Paragraph dialog box, or with shortcut commands for left, center, right, or fully aligned.

➤ If you want to apply paragraph formatting to several paragraphs that are not adjacent, you can use the Repeat key, F4, or the _Repeat option from the _Edit drop-down menu.

➤ The first line of text in a paragraph can be indented by pressing the Tab key, with an option from the Paragraph dialog box, or with the first-line indent marker on the Ruler.

➤ All lines of text in a paragraph can be indented to a tab or to a specific measurement from the left margin with an option from the Paragraph dialog box or the left indent marker on the Ruler.

➤ Text in paragraphs can be indented from the left and the right margins with options at the Paragraph dialog box or with the left and right indent markers on the Ruler.

➤ In a hanging paragraph, the first line of the paragraph remains at the left margin, while the remaining lines are indented to the first tab. Hanging paragraphs can be created with a shortcut command, with options from the Paragraph dialog box, with the hanging indent marker on the Ruler, or with the Hanging Indent button.

➤ Use the Format Painter button on the Standard toolbar to copy character formatting already applied to text to different locations in the document.

➤ Word's AutoFormat feature will automatically format numbered and bulleted lists as well as create ordinal numbers.

➤ Bulleted lists with hanging indents are automatically created when a paragraph begins with *, >, or -. The type of bullet inserted depends on the type of character entered.

➤ Paragraphs can be numbered with the Numbering button on the Formatting toolbar and bullets can be inserted before paragraphs with the Bullets button. Numbers or bullets can also be inserted with options at the Bullets and Numbering dialog box.

➤ Line spacing can be changed with shortcut commands or options from the Paragraph dialog box.

➤ Repeat the last action by clicking Edit, expanding the drop-down menu, and then clicking Repeat; or by pressing Ctrl + Y.

commands review

	Mouse	Keyboard
Turn on/off display of nonprinting characters	Click Show/Hide ¶ button on Standard toolbar	
Display Options dialog box	Tools, Options	Tools, Options
Align text at the left margin	Click Align Left button on Formatting toolbar	Ctrl + L
Align text between margins	Click Center button on Formatting toolbar	Ctrl + E
Align text at the right margin	Click Align Right button on Formatting toolbar	Ctrl + R
Align text at the left and right margins	Click Justify button on Formatting toolbar	Ctrl + J
Return all paragraph formatting to normal		Ctrl + Q
Repeat formatting command for several paragraphs	Position insertion point in paragraph, click Edit, Repeat Paragraph Alignment	F4
Paragraph dialog box	Format, Paragraph	Format, Paragraph
Indent first line of a paragraph	At the Paragraph dialog box, click Special, then *First line*; or drag first line indent marker on the Ruler to desired measurement	Tab key

Indent left margin of all lines of text in a paragraph or selected paragraphs	At the Paragraph dialog box, key indent measurement in the Left text box; or press Ctrl + M; or drag left indent marker on Ruler to desired measurement; or click Increase Indent button on Formatting toolbar	
Decrease indent of text in a paragraph	Decrease number in the Left text box at the Paragraph dialog box; or press Ctrl + Shift + M; or drag left indent marker on Ruler to desired measurement; or click Decrease Indent button on Formatting toolbar	
Indent left and right margins of paragraph	At the Paragraph dialog box, key indent measurement in the Left and Right text boxes; or drag left indent marker on Ruler to desired measurement, and then drag right indent marker to desired measurement	
Create a hanging paragraph	At the Paragraph dialog box, key the desired indent measurement in the Left text box, click Special, then *Hanging;* or drag hanging indent marker on Ruler to desired measurement	Ctrl + T
Create numbered/bulleted paragraphs	Select paragraphs, click Numbering or Bullets button on Formatting toolbar; or display the Bullets and Numbering dialog box	
Bullets and Numbering dialog box	Format, Bullets and Numbering	Format, Bullets and Numbering
Change to single spacing		Ctrl + 1
Change to double spacing		Ctrl + 2
Change to 1.5-line spacing		Ctrl + 5
Change line spacing at Paragraph dialog box	Click the up- or down-pointing triangle to the right of At box; key measurement in At box; or click Line Spacing	
Repeat the last action	Edit, expand drop-down menu, Repeat	Ctrl + Y

thinking offline

Completion: In the space provided at the right, indicate the correct term, symbol, or command.

1. Word inserts paragraph formatting into this mark.   *paragraph*

2. If the insertion point is positioned at the left margin, the insertion point is moved to this measurement from the left margin when you press the Tab key.   *0.5*

3. To turn on or off the display of nonprinting characters, click this button on the Standard toolbar.   *Show / Hide*

4. You can return all paragraph formatting to normal with this keyboard command.   *Ctrl + Q*

5. This is the default paragraph alignment.   *aligned at Left Ragged at right*

6. Click this button on the Formatting toolbar to align text at the right margin.

Right Alignment

7. To indent right and left margins in a paragraph, display this dialog box.

Format

8. Indent the left margin of a paragraph with this shortcut command.

Tab Key

9. In this kind of paragraph, the first line remains at the left margin and the remaining lines are indented to the first tab.

Hanging

10. The number, 2nd, is referred to as this.

Superscript

11. Automate the creation of bulleted paragraphs with the Bullets button on this toolbar.

Formatting Toolbar

12. The Bullets and Numbering dialog box contains three tabs: Bulleted, Numbered, and this.

Outline Numbered

13. At the Paragraph dialog box, change line spacing with the Line spacing option or this.

At

14. This is the default line spacing.

Single

15. This is the shortcut command to change line spacing to 2.

Ctrl + 2

16. This is the shortcut command to repeat the last action.

Ctrl + Y

17. In the space provided below, list the steps you would complete to format paragraphs in a document as hanging paragraphs.

At the Paragraph Dialog box, key the desired indent measurement in the Left text box, click special, then Hanging

18. In the space provided below, list the steps you would complete to change the line spacing to 1.25.

working hands-on

Assessment 1

1. Open Memo 01.
2. Save the document with Save As and name it Ch 03, SA 01.
3. Turn on the display of nonprinting characters.
4. Make the following changes to the memo:

a. Bold the headings *DATE:*, *TO:*, *FROM:*, and *SUBJECT:* (if necessary, realign the text after *DATE:*).

b. Change the paragraph alignment to justified for the three paragraphs in the body of the memo.

c. Change the line spacing to 1.5 for the three paragraphs in the body of the memo.

5. Turn off the display of the nonprinting characters.

6. Save the document again with the same name (Ch 03, SA 01).

7. Print and then close Ch 03, SA 01.

Assessment 2

1. At a clear document screen, key the memo shown in figure 3.21 with the following specifications:

a. Bold text as indicated.

b. Center text as indicated.

c. Change the alignment of paragraphs in the body of the memo to justified.

2. Save the memo and name it Ch 03, SA 02.

3. Print and then close Ch 03, SA 02.

figure

3.21   *Assessment 2*

DATE: March 15, 2001

TO: Administrative Support Staff

FROM: Sheila Arnold, Training and Education

SUBJECT: BUSINESS COMMUNICATIONS CLASSES

Plains Community College administrative support staff will have the opportunity to complete classes in written business documents. This training is designed for any support staff member who wishes to improve the grammar, punctuation, style, and clarity of his or her business documents.

The business communications classes will be held in Room 120 from 3:30 p.m. to 5:30 p.m. on the following days:

Monday, April 2
Wednesday, April 4
Tuesday, April 17
Thursday, April 19

The training sessions are limited to 15 employees. To register, please call Training and Education at extension 575.

XX:Ch 03, SA 02

Assessment 3

1. At a clear document screen, key the memo shown in figure 3.22. Indent the second paragraph in the body of the memo 0.5 inch from the left and right margins.
2. Save the memo and name it Ch 03, SA 03.
3. Print and then close Ch 03, SA 03.

figure

3.22

Assessment 3

DATE: December 5, 2001

TO: Richard Polk, College Relations

FROM: Christy Edmonds, OT Department

SUBJECT: BUSINESS COMMUNICATIONS COURSE

The business communications course, BUS 250, has been a great success this semester. Because of the interest in the course, we have decided to offer it again in the spring semester. Please include the following description for the course in the spring schedule:

> Students in Business Communications, BUS 250, will learn to recognize basic barriers to effective communication; plan and prepare oral communications; follow a process for preparing business documents; and evaluate and improve presentation skills.

I would like to see the course advertised not only in the spring schedule but also in the school newspaper. Would you help me write an advertisement for the newspaper? You can contact me at extension 405.

XX:Ch 03, SA 03

Assessment 4

1. At a clear document screen, create the document shown in figure 3.23 with the following specifications:
   a. Change the line spacing to double.
   b. Center, bold, and italicize text as indicated.
   c. Create hanging paragraphs as indicated.
   d. Change the alignment of paragraphs to justified.
2. Save the document and name it Ch 03, SA 04.
3. Print and then close Ch 03, SA 04.

figure

BIBLIOGRAPHY

Aiken, Charles A. (1996). *Oral Communications*, 3rd edition (pp. 24-33). Salt Lake City, UT:

Blue Ridge Publishing Company.

Florez, Lisa M. (1997). *Computerized Business Documents* (pp. 19-22). Boston, MA:

Northampton Publishers.

Greenfield, Noel E. (1998). *Complete Business Forms* (pp. 43-51). Philadelphia, PA:

Greenleaf Press.

Ketchum, Marilyn A. (1997). *Oral and Written Communications*, 2nd edition (pp. 38-42). New

Orleans, LA: Pontchartrain Publishing, Inc.

Assessment 5

1. Open Report 03.
2. Save the document with Save As and name it Ch 03, SA 05.
3. Make the following changes to the document:
    a. Select the entire document and then change to a serif font (other than Times New Roman) in 12-point size.
    b. Select the title *MODULE 1: DEFINING NEWSLETTER ELEMENTS* and then change the font to 14-point Tahoma bold (or a similar sans serif typeface).
    c. Use Format Painter to change the font to 14-point Tahoma bold for the other title *MODULE 2: PLANNING A NEWSLETTER*.
    d. Select the heading *Designing a Newsletter* and then change the font to 14-point Tahoma bold.
    e. Use Format Painter to change the font to 14-point Tahoma bold for the other two headings *Defining Basic Newsletter Elements* and *Defining the Purpose of a Newsletter* (located in module 2).
4. Save the document again with the same name (Ch 03, SA 05).
5. Print and then close Ch 03, SA 05.

Assessment 6

1. Open Memo 02.
2. Save the document with Save As and name it Ch 03, SA 06.
3. Make the following changes to the memo:
    a. Insert bullets before paragraphs two through five (the paragraphs containing the book titles).

b.   Change the alignment of paragraphs in the body of the memo to justified.
4.   Save the document again with the same name (Ch 03, SA 06).
5.   Print and then close Ch 03, SA 06.

Assessment 7

1.   Open Job Desc.
2.   Save the document with Save As and name it Ch 03, SA 07.
3.   Bold and center the title, *JOB DESCRIPTION*, and subtitle, *REGISTERED NURSE*.
4.   Select the text paragraphs in the document (except the title, subtitle, and blank line below the subtitle) and then make the following changes:
     a.   Change the alignment to justified.
     b.   Insert bullets at the beginning of each paragraph.
     c.   Increase the spacing after the selected paragraphs to *6 pt. (Hint: Do this with the After option at the Paragraph dialog box.)*
5.   Delete the fifth paragraph.
6.   Add the paragraph shown in figure 3.24 between the fourth and fifth paragraphs.
7.   Save the document again with the same name (Ch 03, SA 07).
8.   Print and then close Ch 03, SA 07.

figure
3.24   *Assessment 7*

Supervises, trains, and monitors licensed practical nurses and nurses aides.

Assessment 8

1.   At a clear document screen, create the document shown in figure 3.25.
2.   After keying the document, select the text in the document (except the title and blank line below the title), and then make the following changes:
     a.   Turn on numbering
     b.   Increase spacing after the selected paragraphs to *12 pt*.
3.   Save the document and name it Ch 03, SA 08.
4.   Print Ch 03, SA 08.
5.   Make the following changes to the document:
     a.   Delete *Binary format*.
     b.   Add *Decompression program* between the fourth and fifth paragraphs.
     c.   Add *Protocol* between the eleventh and twelfth paragraphs.
6.   Save the document again with the same name (Ch 03, SA 08).
7.   Print and then close Ch 03, SA 08.

figure

3.25

Assessment 8

INTERNET TERMINOLOGY

Applet
Binary format
Browser
Cable modem
Chat room
Domain
Extraction program
Home page
Information superhighway
Network-centric graphical user interface
Newsgroups
Search engine

Formatting Documents and Sections

Word assumes that you are using standard-sized paper, which is 8.5 inches wide and 11 inches long. By default, a Word document contains 1-inch top and bottom margins and 1.25-inch left and right margins. With the default top and bottom margins of 1 inch, a total of 9 inches of text will print on a page (1 inch for the top margin, 9 inches of printed text, and then 1 inch for the bottom margin). There are a variety of features that can affect how much text prints on a page such as page margins, widow/orphan control, and paper size.

Changing the View

As you create documents longer than one page, you will notice that when the insertion point nears 9.8 inches (or approximately line 45 [this number may vary]) a page break is inserted in the document. The page break is inserted at the next line (at the 10" measurement). The line below the page break is the beginning of the next page.

The display of the page break will vary depending on the view selected. By default, the Normal view is selected. At this view, a page break displays as a row of dots. If you change to the Print Layout view, a page break displays as an actual break in the page. Figure 4.1 shows an example of a page break in a document in the Normal view and another in the Print Layout view.

Page Break in Normal View

> publication project. This may be costly and time-consuming. With the use of desktop publishing software, one person may be performing all of the tasks necessary to complete a project, greatly reducing the costs of publishing documents. The two approaches have a
>
> great deal in common. Both approaches involve setting goals, planning and organizing content, analyzing layout and design, arranging design elements, typesetting, printing, and distributing the project.

Page Break in Print Layout View

> publication project. This may be costly and time-consuming. With the use of desktop publishing software, one person may be performing all of the tasks necessary to complete a project, greatly reducing the costs of publishing documents. The two approaches have a
>
> great deal in common. Both approaches involve setting goals, planning and organizing content, analyzing layout and design, arranging design elements, typesetting, printing, and distributing the project.

To change to the Print Layout view, click <u>V</u>iew and then <u>P</u>rint Layout or click the Print Layout View button at the left side of the horizontal scroll bar. (The Print Layout View button is the third button from the left side of the screen before the horizontal scroll bar.) To change back to the Normal view, click <u>V</u>iew and then <u>N</u>ormal or click the Normal View button at the left side of the horizontal scroll bar. (The Normal View button is the first button from the left.)

Print Layout View

Normal View

When you are working in a document containing more than one page of text, the Status bar displays the page where the insertion point is positioned and will also display the current page followed by the total number of pages in a document. For example, if the insertion point is positioned somewhere on page 3 of a 12-page document (with one section), the left side of the Status bar will display *Page 3 Sec 1 3/12*. The *3/12* indicates that the insertion point is positioned on page 3 in a document containing 12 pages.

Changing Margins

A Word document, by default, contains 1-inch top and bottom margins and 1.25-inch left and right margins. These default margins are displayed in the Page Setup dialog box shown in figure 4.2. To display the Page Setup dialog box, click <u>F</u>ile and then Page Set<u>u</u>p. You can also display the Page Setup dialog box by double-clicking on the gray area at the top of the Ruler. At the Page Setup dialog box, make sure the <u>M</u>argins tab is selected.

figure

4.2

Page Setup Dialog Box with <u>M</u>argins Tab Selected

Notice the default top, bottom, left, and right margin measurements.

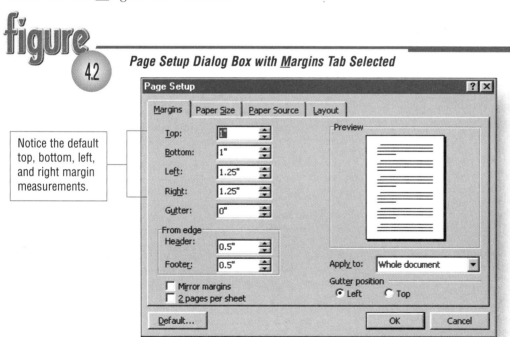

To change margins, select the current measurement in either the <u>T</u>op, <u>B</u>ottom, Le<u>f</u>t, or R<u>i</u>ght text box, and then key the new measurement for the margin. You can also increase a measurement by clicking the up-pointing triangle at the right side of the text box. Decrease a measurement by clicking the down-pointing triangle. As you make changes to the margin measurements at the Page Setup dialog box, the sample page in the Preview box illustrates the effects of the margins.

If you want the new margins to affect the entire document, position the insertion point anywhere within the document, and then make margin changes at the Page Setup dialog box. If you want margin changes to affect only a portion of the document, divide the document into sections. You will learn more about sections later in this chapter. You can also specify that margin changes affect the text in a document from the position of the insertion point to the end of the document. To do this, click the down-pointing triangle at the right side of the Apply to text box at the Page Setup dialog box. At the drop-down list that displays, click *This point forward*.

(Before completing computer exercises, delete the Chapter 03 *folder on your disk. Next, copy the* Chapter 04 *folder from the CD that accompanies this textbook to your disk and then make* Chapter 04 *the active folder.)*

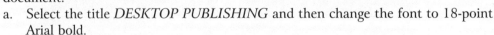

Changing Margins

1. Open Report 01.
2. Save the report with Save As and name it Ch 04, Ex 01.
3. Change the top margin to 1.5 inches and the left and right margins to 1 inch by completing the following steps:
   a. Click File and then Page Setup.
   b. At the Page Setup dialog box, make sure the Margins tab is selected.
   c. Click the up-pointing triangle after the Top option until *1.5"* displays in the Top text box.

   Step 3c

   d. Click the down-pointing triangle after the Left option until *1"* displays in the Left text box.

   Step 3d

   Step 3e

   e. Click the down-pointing triangle after the Right option until *1"* displays in the Right text box.
   f. Click OK to close the dialog box.
4. Make the following changes to the document:
   a. Select the title *DESKTOP PUBLISHING* and then change the font to 18-point Arial bold.
   b. Select the heading *Defining Desktop Publishing* and then change the font to 14-point Arial bold.
   c. Use Format Painter to change the formatting to 14-point Arial bold for the headings *Initiating the Desktop Publishing Process*, *Planning the Publication*, and *Creating the Content*.
5. Save the document again with the same name (Ch 04, Ex 01).
6. Print and then close Ch 04, Ex 01.

Changing Margins with the Ruler

You can change margins at the Page Setup dialog box as you did in exercise 1 or with the Ruler. At the Page Setup dialog box, you can enter specific margin measurements; at the Ruler, you can visually set margins.

At the Normal view, a horizontal ruler displays below the Formatting toolbar. You can change paragraph indents with this ruler in the Normal view but you cannot make changes to the left and right margins. If you want to make changes to the left, right, top, or bottom margins using rulers, change to the Print Layout view. At this view, the horizontal ruler displays below the Formatting toolbar and a vertical ruler displays along the left side of the screen. Figure 4.3 shows a document in the Print Layout view and identifies the horizontal and vertical rulers.

figure
4.3

Rulers in Print Layout View

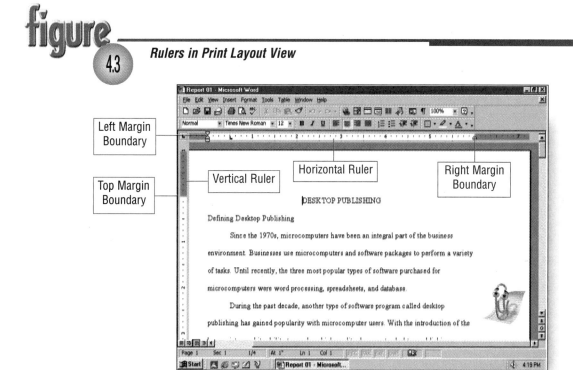

The horizontal and vertical rulers each contain a gray area and a white area. The gray area indicates the margin while the white area indicates the space between margins. The edge between the gray and white area is called the *margin boundary*.

To change margins using a ruler in the Print Layout view, position the mouse pointer on the margin boundary. This causes the mouse pointer to turn into a double-headed arrow. Hold down the left mouse button, drag the margin boundary to the desired location, and then release the mouse button.

exercise 2

Increasing Margins Using the Horizontal Ruler

1. Open Para 02.
2. Save the document with Save As and name it Ch 04, Ex 02.
3. Increase the left and right margins by approximately 0.5 inch, and increase the top margin to 2 inches using the Ruler by completing the following steps:
   a. Make sure the Ruler is displayed.
   b. Change the view to Print Layout by clicking <u>V</u>iew and then <u>P</u>rint Layout; or clicking the Print Layout View button at the left side of the horizontal scroll bar.
   c. Position the mouse pointer on the margin boundary at the left side of the horizontal ruler until the pointer turns into a double-headed arrow pointing left and right. (A yellow box containing *Left Margin* will display.)

   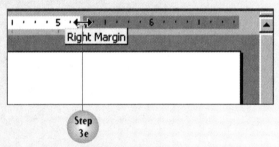

   d. Hold down the left mouse button, drag the margin boundary to the right approximately 0.5 inch, and then release the mouse button. (As you drag the margin boundary, a dashed vertical line appears in the document screen. Use this to help you position the left margin. When you drag the margin boundary, the entire horizontal ruler moves.)
   e. Position the mouse pointer on the margin boundary at the right side of the horizontal ruler until it turns into a double-headed arrow pointing left and right. (A yellow box containing *Right Margin* will display.) (If the margin boundary at the right side of the horizontal ruler is not visible, position the mouse pointer on the scroll box in the horizontal scroll bar, hold down the left mouse button, drag the scroll box to the right edge of the horizontal scroll bar, and then release the mouse button.)
   f. Hold down the left mouse button, drag the margin boundary to the left about 0.5 inch, and then release the mouse button. (When you drag the right margin boundary, the horizontal ruler is stationary and the margin boundary moves along it.)
   g. Position the mouse pointer on the top margin boundary on the vertical ruler until it turns into a double-headed arrow pointing up and down (and a yellow box containing *Top Margin* displays).
   h. Hold down the left mouse button, drag the top margin boundary down until the 2-inch gray mark displays at the top of the vertical ruler, and then release the mouse button.

   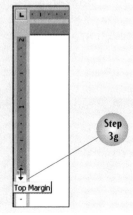

4. Change back to the Normal view by clicking <u>V</u>iew and then <u>N</u>ormal or clicking the Normal View button at the left side of the horizontal scroll bar.
5. Save the document again with the same name (Ch 04, Ex 02).
6. Print and then close Ch 04, Ex 02.

When you move the left margin boundary on the horizontal ruler or the top margin boundary on the vertical ruler, the entire ruler moves. If you want to move margin boundaries to a precise measurement, you can use the Alt key when dragging a margin boundary. If you position the mouse pointer on a margin boundary on the horizontal ruler, hold down the Alt key, and then hold down the left mouse button, the width of the text line displays in the horizontal ruler. If you position the mouse pointer on a margin boundary on the vertical ruler, hold down the Alt key and then hold down the left mouse button, the length of the top margin (or bottom margin) displays in the vertical ruler.

exercise 3

Changing Margins to Specific Measurements Using the Horizontal and Vertical Rulers

1. Open Legal 02.
2. Save the document with Save As and name it Ch 04, Ex 03.
3. Change the top margin to 1.5 inches and the left and right margins to 1 inch by completing the following steps:
   a. Change to the Print Layout view.
   b. Position the mouse pointer on the left margin boundary, hold down the Alt key and the left mouse button, drag the margin boundary to the left until *1"* appears in the gray area and *6.25"* appears in the white area on the horizontal ruler, then release the mouse button and then the Alt key.
   c. Position the mouse pointer on the right margin boundary until it turns into a double-headed arrow pointing left and right.
   d. Hold down the Alt key and the left mouse button, drag the right margin boundary to the right until *6.5"* displays in the white area and *1"* displays in the gray area on the horizontal ruler, then release the mouse button and then the Alt key.
   e. Position the mouse pointer on the top margin boundary on the vertical ruler until it turns into a double-headed arrow pointing up and down.
   f. Hold down the Alt key and the left mouse button, drag the top margin boundary down until *1.5"* displays in the gray area on the vertical ruler, then release the mouse button and then the Alt key.

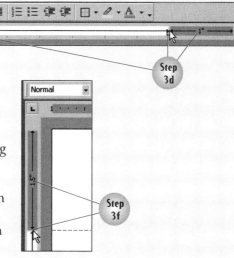

4. Change back to the Normal view.
5. Save the document again with the same name (Ch 04, Ex 03).
6. Print and then close Ch 04, Ex 03.

Creating Mirror Margins

The Page Setup dialog box contains the option Mirror margins. If this option is active (a check mark appears in the check box), the measurements for left and right margins are applied to odd-numbered pages and reversed for even-numbered pages. For example, if you change the left margin to 2.5 inches and the right margin to 1 inch, odd-numbered pages will have these margins but even-numbered pages will have a left margin of 1 inch and a right margin of 2.5 inches. When a check mark is inserted in the Mirror margins option, the Left option changes to Inside and the Right option changes to Outside.

Creating Mirror Margins

1. Open Report 01.
2. Save the document with Save As and name it Ch 04, Ex 04.
3. Make the following changes to the document:
   a. Select the title *DESKTOP PUBLISHING* and then change the font to 14-point Arial bold.
   b. Select the heading *Defining Desktop Publishing* and then change the font to 14-point Arial bold.
   c. Use Format Painter to apply 14-point Arial bold to the remaining headings: *Initiating the Desktop Publishing Process*, *Planning the Publication*, and *Creating the Content*.
   d. Change the left margin to 2 inches, the right margin to 1 inch, and create mirror margins by completing the following steps:
      1) Click File and then Page Setup.
      2) At the Page Setup dialog box with the Margins tab selected, change the left margin to 2 inches and the right margin to 1 inch.
      3) Click Mirror margins. (This inserts a check mark in the check box and changes the Left option to Inside and the Right option to Outside.)
      4) Click OK or press Enter.
4. Save the document again with the same name (Ch 04, Ex 04).
5. Print and then close Ch 04, Ex 04.

Adding a Gutter Margin

Use the Gutter option at the Page Setup dialog box to create gutter margins for bound material. The default setting for gutter margins is 0 inches. When creating a document that is to be bound and printed on both sides, such as a report or manual, change the gutter margin measurement to properly position text on the page. In addition, the Mirror margins option must be active.

For left-bound material to properly display on the page, change the gutter margins to approximately 0.5 inch, and turn on the Mirror margins option. When you make these changes, Word adds the 0.5 inch of extra margin to the right margin on even pages and to the left margin on odd pages. When the material is bound, even-numbered pages are generally located at the left and odd-numbered pages are generally located at the right. The 0.5-inch gutter margin allows room for the binding. If the material is to be bound at the top, choose the *Top* option in the Gutter position section of the Page Setup dialog box.

Changing Left, Right, and Gutter Margins

1. Open Report 02.
2. Save the document with Save As and name it Ch 04, Ex 05.
3. Make the following changes to the document:
   a. Select the entire document and then change the font to 12-point Century Schoolbook (or a similar serif typeface).
   b. Set the title *DESKTOP PUBLISHING DESIGN* in 14-point Arial bold as well as the headings *Designing a Document* and *Creating Focus*.
   c. Change the left and right margins to 1 inch and the gutter margin to 0.5 inch and turn on the Mirror margins option by completing the following steps:
      1) Click File and then Page Setup.
      2) At the Page Setup dialog box, make sure the Margins tab is selected, and then change the left and right margins to 1 inch.
      3) Click Mirror margins. (This inserts a check mark and changes the Left option to Inside and the Right option to Outside.)
      4) Click the up-pointing triangle at the right side of the Gutter option until *0.5"* displays.
      5) Click OK or press Enter.

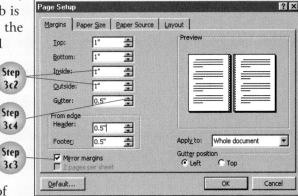

4. Save the document again with the same name (Ch 04, Ex 05).
5. Print and then close Ch 04, Ex 05.

Inserting a Section Break

By default, changes made to margins in a document are applied to all text in the document. If you want margin changes to apply to specific text in a document, select the text first. Text in a document can also be divided into sections. When a document is divided into sections, each section can be formatted separately. For example, different margin settings can be applied to each section in a document.

A section can insert a page break in a document or a continuous section can be created that does not insert a page break. To insert a continuous section break in a document, position the insertion point at the location in the document where you want the new section to begin, and then click Insert and then Break. At the Break dialog box shown in figure 4.4, click Continuous, and then click OK or press Enter.

Break Dialog Box

4.4

Click this option to insert a continuous section break.

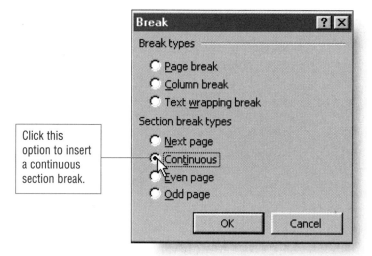

A section break displays in the Normal view as a double line of dots across the screen with the words *Section Break (Continuous)* inserted in the middle. In the Print Layout view, a section break does not display on the screen. However, the section number where the insertion point is located displays in the Status bar as *Sec* followed by the number.

To create a section break and begin a new page, position the insertion point at the location in the document where you want the new section to begin, click Insert, and then Break. At the Break dialog box, click Next page, and then click OK or press Enter.

In the Normal view, a section break that begins a new page displays as a double row of dots across the screen with the words *Section Break (Next Page)* inserted in the middle. In the Print Layout view, a section break that begins a new page displays as a new page.

At the Break dialog box, click <u>E</u>ven page if you want to insert a section break and begin the next page with an even number. Click <u>O</u>dd page if you want to insert a section break and begin the next page with an odd number. For example, if you position the insertion point somewhere in the middle of page 4 and then insert a section break with the <u>E</u>ven page option, a section break is inserted and the page below the section break is page 6.

If you change margins in a section of text, the Appl<u>y</u> to option at the Page Setup dialog box will have the default setting of *This section*.

Inserting Section Breaks

1. Open Quote.
2. Save the document with Save As and name it Ch 04, Ex 06.
3. Make the following changes to the document:
    a. Insert a section break between the first two paragraphs by completing the following steps:
        1) Position the insertion point on the blank line between the first and second paragraphs.
        2) Click <u>I</u>nsert and then <u>B</u>reak.
        3) At the Break dialog box, click Con<u>t</u>inuous in the Section break types section.
        4) Click OK or press Enter.
    b. Insert a section break between the second and third paragraphs by completing steps similar to those in step 3a.
    c. Insert a section break between the third and fourth paragraphs by completing steps similar to those in step 3a.
    d. Position the insertion point anywhere in the second paragraph and then change the left and right margins to 1.75 inches. (At the Page Setup dialog box, make sure the default setting at the Appl<u>y</u> to option is *This section*.)
    e. Position the insertion point anywhere in the fourth paragraph and then change the left and right margins to 1.75 inches. (At the Page Setup dialog box, make sure the default setting at the Appl<u>y</u> to option is *This section*.)
4. Change to Print Layout view to see how the document will appear when printed and then change back to Normal view.
5. Save the document again with the same name (Ch 04, Ex 06).
6. Print and then close Ch 04, Ex 06.

Affecting Text Flow

There are several options from the Paragraph dialog box with the Line and <u>P</u>age Breaks tab selected that will affect the position of page breaks within a document. With the Line and <u>P</u>age Breaks tab selected, the Paragraph dialog box displays as shown in figure 4.5.

Paragraph Dialog Box with Line and _P_age Breaks Tab Selected

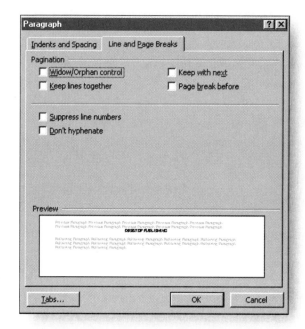

Turning Widow/Orphan Control On/Off

In a long document, you will want to avoid creating widows or orphans. A widow is the last line of a paragraph that appears at the top of a page. An orphan is the first line of a paragraph that appears at the bottom of a page.

In Word, widows and orphans are automatically prevented from appearing in text. Word accomplishes this by adjusting the page breaks in a document. Because of this, the last line of text on various pages will not always occur at the same line measurement or count. If you wish to turn off the widow and orphan control, display the Paragraph dialog box with the Line and _P_age Breaks tab selected, and then click _W_idow/Orphan control. This removes the check mark from the option.

Keeping a Paragraph of Text Together

Even with widow/orphan control on, Word may insert a page break in a document between text in a paragraph or several paragraphs that should stay together as a unit. The Paragraph dialog box with the Line and _P_age Breaks tab selected contains options to keep a paragraph, a group of paragraphs, or a group of lines together.

To keep a paragraph together, you can instruct Word not to insert a page break within a paragraph. This format instruction is stored in the paragraph mark, so as the paragraph is moved within the document, the format instruction moves with it. To tell Word not to insert a page break within a paragraph, display the Paragraph dialog box with the Line and _P_age Breaks tab selected, and then click _K_eep lines together. The same steps can be used to keep a group of consecutive paragraphs together. To do this, select the paragraphs first, display the Paragraph dialog box, and then click _K_eep lines together.

With the Keep with next option at the Paragraph dialog box, you can tell Word to keep the paragraph where the insertion point is located together with the next paragraph. If there is not enough room for the paragraph and the next paragraph, Word moves both paragraphs to the next page.

Use the Page break before option if you want a particular paragraph to print at the top of a page. Position the insertion point in the paragraph that you want to begin a new page, display the Paragraph dialog box with the Line and Page Breaks tab selected, and then click Page break before.

Keeping Text Together

(Note: Due to slight differences in how printers interpret line height, a page break may not display in the report after the heading Planning the Publication. *Before completing this exercise, check with your instructor to see if you need to make any minor changes to margins or font size for text and headings.)*

1. Open Report 01.
2. Save the document with Save As and name it Ch 04, Ex 07.
3. Make the following changes to the document:
    a. Change the top, left, and right margins to 1.5 inches.
    b. Select the title *DESKTOP PUBLISHING* and then change the font to 14-point Arial bold.
    c. Select the heading *Defining Desktop Publishing* and then change the font to 14-point Arial bold.
    d. Use Format Painter to apply 14-point Arial bold to the remaining headings: *Initiating the Desktop Publishing Process*, *Planning the Publication*, and *Creating the Content*.
4. Tell Word to keep the heading *Planning the Publication* and the paragraph that follows it together on the same page by completing the following steps:
    a. Position the insertion point on any character in the heading *Planning the Publication* (located at the bottom of page 2).
    b. Click Format and then Paragraph.
    c. At the Paragraph dialog box, click the Line and Page Breaks tab.
    d. Click in the Keep with next check box to insert a check mark.
    e. Click OK or press Enter.
5. Save the document again with the same name (Ch 04, Ex 07).
6. Print and then close Ch 04, Ex 07.

Inserting Hard Page Breaks

Word's default settings break each page after Line 9.8″ (approximately). Word automatically inserts page breaks in a document as you edit it. Since Word does this automatically, you may find that page breaks sometimes occur in undesirable locations. To remedy this, you can insert your own page break.

In the Normal view, the Word page break, called a *soft* page break, displays as a row of dots across the screen. In the Print Layout view, the page break displays as a gray bar between two pages. If you do not like where the soft page break is inserted in a document, you can insert your own page break. A page break that you insert in a document is called a *hard* page break. To insert a hard page break in a document, position the insertion point where you want the break to occur, and then click Insert and then Break. At the Break dialog box, make sure Page break is selected, and then click OK or press Enter. You can also insert a hard page break by positioning the insertion point where you want the break to occur in the document and then pressing Ctrl + Enter.

A hard page break displays in the Normal view as a line of dots with the words *Page Break* in the middle of the line. A hard page break displays in the same manner as a soft page break in the Print Layout view.

Soft page breaks automatically adjust if text is added to or deleted from a document. A hard page break does not adjust and is therefore less flexible than a soft page break. If you add or delete text from a document with a hard page break, check the break to determine whether it is still in a desirable location.

A hard page break can be deleted from a document. To delete a hard page break, position the insertion point on the page break, and then press the Delete key.

exercise 8

Inserting Hard Page Breaks

1. Open Report 01.
2. Save the document with Save As and name it Ch 04, Ex 08.
3. Make the following changes to the document:
   a. Select the title *DESKTOP PUBLISHING* and then change the font to 14-point Univers bold. (If your printer does not support Univers, choose a similar sans serif typeface, such as Arial.)
   b. Select the heading *Defining Desktop Publishing* and then change the font to 14-point Univers bold.
   c. Use the Format Painter to apply 14-point Univers bold to the remaining headings: *Initiating the Desktop Publishing Process*, *Planning the Publication*, and *Creating the Content*.
   d. Change the left and right margins to 1.5 inches.
4. Insert a hard page break at the beginning of the last paragraph on the first page by completing the following steps:
   a. Position the insertion point at the beginning of the last paragraph on the first page that begins *In traditional publishing, several people....*
   b. Click Insert and then Break.
   c. At the Break dialog box, make sure Page break is selected, and then click OK or press Enter.

5. Insert a hard page break at the beginning of the last paragraph on the third page by completing the following steps:
   a. Position the insertion point at the beginning of the last paragraph on the third page that begins *Collect examples of effective designs*.
   b. Press Ctrl + Enter.
6. Save the document again with the same name (Ch 04, Ex 08).
7. Print and then close Ch 04, Ex 08.

Changing Paper Size

Word assumes that you are printing on standard stationery—8.5 inches wide by 11 inches long. If you need to print text on different-sized stationery, change the paper size at the Page Setup dialog box with the Paper Size tab selected as shown in figure 4.6.

figure
4.6
Page Setup Dialog Box with Paper Size Tab Selected

Click this down-pointing triangle to display a list of paper sizes.

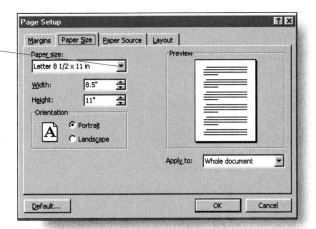

Word provides several predefined paper sizes. The number and type of paper sizes will vary depending on the selected printer. Use the predefined paper sizes if they are the necessary sizes. If the predefined sizes do not include what you need, create your own paper size with the Custom size option. If you choose the Custom size option at the Page Setup dialog box, you can enter the desired measurements for the width and height of the paper size.

Word provides two orientations for paper sizes—Portrait and Landscape. Figure 4.7 illustrates how text appears on the page in portrait and landscape orientations.

By default, the change in paper size will affect the entire document. At the Page Setup dialog box, the Apply to option has a default setting of *Whole document*. This can be changed to *This point forward*. At this setting, the paper size change will affect text from the current position of the insertion point to the end of the document.

figure

Portrait and Landscape Orientations

Landscape

Portrait

exercise 9

Changing Paper Size

1. Open Para 03.
2. Save the document with Save As and name it Ch 04, Ex 09.
3. Change the paper size to 5.5 inches by 8.5 inches by completing the following steps:
   a. Click File and then Page Setup.
   b. At the Page Setup dialog box, click the Paper Size tab. (Skip this step if the Paper Size tab is already selected.)
   c. Click the down-pointing triangle to the right of the Width text box until 5.5″ displays in the Width text box.
   d. Click the down-pointing triangle to the right of the Height text box until 8.5″ displays in the Height text box.
   e. Click OK or press Enter.
4. Select the entire document, change the font to 10-point Arial, and then deselect the text.
5. Save the document again with the same name (Ch 04, Ex 09).
6. Print and then close Ch 04, Ex 09.

Step 3c

Step 3d

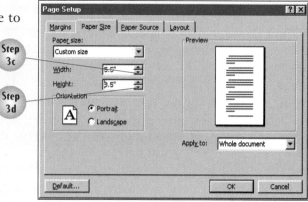

exercise 10

Changing to a Predesigned Paper Size

(Note: Check with your instructor before completing this exercise. Your printer may not be capable of printing on legal-sized stationery.)

1. Open Report 03.
2. Save the document with Save As and name it Ch 04, Ex 10.
3. Change the paper size to Legal by completing the following steps:
   a. Click File and then Page Setup.
   b. At the Page Setup dialog box click the Paper Size tab. (Skip this step if the Paper Size tab is already selected.)
   c. Click the down-pointing triangle at the right of the Paper size option and then click *Legal 8.5 x 14 in* at the drop-down list. (This paper size may be listed as *Legal 8 1/2 x 14 in* or *US Legal*.)

   Step 3c

   d. Click OK or press Enter.
4. Insert a hard page break at the beginning of the line containing the title *MODULE 2: PLANNING A NEWSLETTER*.
5. Save the document again with the same name (Ch 04, Ex 10).
6. Print and then close Ch 04, Ex 10. (Check with your instructor before printing to see if your printer is capable of printing legal-sized documents.)

Page Setup dialog box:
Margins | Paper Size | Paper Source | Layout
Paper size: Letter 8 1/2 x 11 in
- Letter 8 1/2 x 11 in
- Legal 8 1/2 x 14 in
- Executive 7 1/4 x 10 1/2 in
- A4 210 x 297 mm
- Envelope #10 4 1/8 x 9 1/2 in

Portrait / Landscape
Preview
Apply to: Whole document
Default... | OK | Cancel

exercise 11

Changing to Landscape Orientation

1. Open Para 05.
2. Save the document with Save As and name it Ch 04, Ex 11.
3. Change margins and page orientation by completing the following steps:
   a. Display the Page Setup dialog box with the Margins tab selected.
   b. Change the left and right margins to 1.5 inches.
   c. Click the Paper Size tab.
   d. At the Page Setup dialog box with the Paper Size tab selected, click Landscape in the Orientation section.
   e. Click OK to close the dialog box.
4. Save the document again with the same name (Ch 04, Ex 11).
5. Print and then close Ch 04, Ex 11.

Vertically Centering Text on the Page

Text in a Word document is aligned at the top of the page by default. You can change this alignment with the <u>V</u>ertical alignment option at the Page Setup dialog box with the <u>L</u>ayout tab selected as shown in figure 4.8.

Page Setup Dialog Box with <u>L</u>ayout Tab Selected

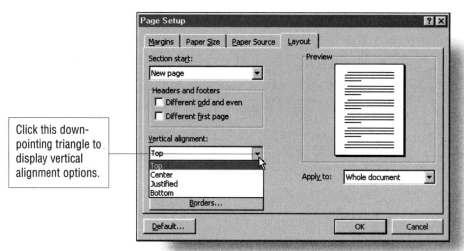

Click this down-pointing triangle to display vertical alignment options.

The <u>V</u>ertical alignment option from the Page Setup dialog box contains four choices—Top, Center, Justified, and Bottom. The default setting is Top, which aligns text at the top of the page. Choose Center if you want text centered vertically on the page. The Justified option will align text between the top and the bottom margins. The Center option positions text in the middle of the page vertically, while the Justified option adds space between paragraphs of text (not within) to fill the page from the top to bottom margins. If you center or justify text, the text does not display centered or justified on the screen in the Normal view but it does display centered or justified in the Print Layout view. Choose the Bottom option to align text in the document vertically along the bottom of the page.

Vertically Centering Text

1. Open Notice 02.
2. Save the document with Save As and name it Ch 04, Ex 12.
3. Select the text in the document and then change the font to 24-point Goudy Old Style. (If this typeface is not available, choose a similar decorative typeface such as Bookman Old Style.)
4. Center the text between the top and bottom margins by completing the following steps:

a. Delete the blank lines at the bottom of the document.
b. Click File and then Page Setup.
c. At the Page Setup dialog box, click the Layout tab. (Skip this step if the Layout tab is already selected.)
d. Click the down-pointing triangle at the right of the Vertical alignment text box and then click *Center* at the drop-down list.
e. Click OK or press Enter.

5. Save the document again with the same name (Ch 04, Ex 12).

6. Print and then close Ch 04, Ex 12.

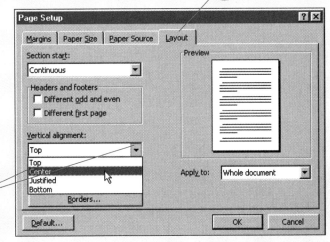

Step 4c

Step 4d

Changing Paper Size and Justifying Text between Top and Bottom Margins

1. Open Para 04.
2. Save the document with Save As and name it Ch 04, Ex 13.
3. Make the following changes to the document:
   a. Display the Page Setup dialog box with the Paper Size tab selected.
   b. Change the Width to 5.5 inches and the Height to 8.5 inches.
   c. Click the Layout tab.
   d. At the Page Setup dialog box with the Layout tab selected, click the down-pointing triangle at the right of the Vertical alignment text box and then click *Justified* at the drop-down list.
   e. Click OK or press Enter to close the dialog box.
   f. Press Ctrl + End to move the insertion point to the end of the document and then press the Backspace key twice.

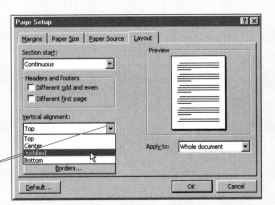

Step 3d

4. Save the document again with the same name (Ch 04, Ex 13).
5. Print and then close Ch 04, Ex 13.

Previewing a Document

Before printing a document, viewing the document may be useful. Word's Print Preview feature displays the document on the screen as it will appear when printed. With this feature, you can view a partial page, single page, multiple pages, or zoom in on a particular area of a page.

Print Preview

To view a document, click File and then Print Preview; or click the Print Preview button on the Standard toolbar. (The Print Preview button is the sixth button from the left on the Standard toolbar.) When Print Preview is displayed, the page where the insertion point is located is displayed in the screen. Figure 4.9 shows a document in Print Preview.

figure 4.9

Document in Print Preview

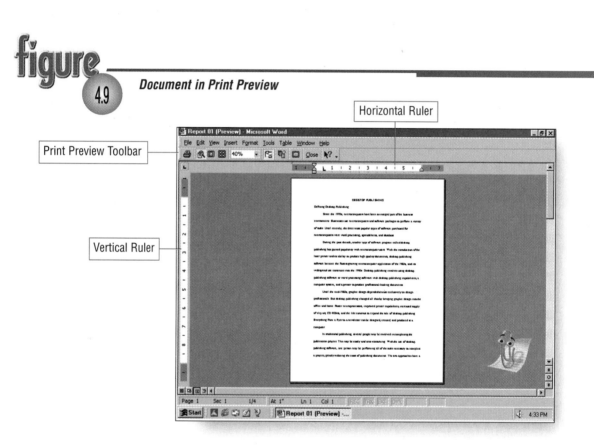

The toolbar along the top of the screen in Print Preview is the Print Preview toolbar. With buttons on this toolbar, you can change the display of the document, send a document to the printer, and turn the display of the Ruler on or off. Figure 4.10 shows the buttons on the Print Preview toolbar and what each button will perform.

figure 4.10

Print Preview Toolbar Buttons

Click this button	Named	To do this
Print button	Print	Send the current document to the printer.
Magnifier button	Magnifier	Toggle the mouse pointer between a magnifying glass, which is used to view the document, and the normal mouse pointer, which is used to edit the document.
One Page button	One Page	Display individual pages in the document.
Multiple Pages button	Multiple Pages	Display multiple pages in the document (up to 18 pages).
42%	Zoom	Change viewing by percentage option or to Page Width, Whole Page, or Two Pages.
View Ruler button	View Ruler	Turn the display of the Ruler on or off.
Shrink to Fit button	Shrink to Fit	Try to "shrink" the contents of the last page in the document onto the previous page if there is only a small amount of text on the last page.
Full Screen button	Full Screen	Toggle the screen display between the normal display and full screen display, which removes everything from the Print Preview screen except the document and the Print Preview toolbar.
Close	Close Preview	Close Print Preview and return to document screen.
Context Sensitive Help button	Context Sensitive Help	Display context-sensitive help.

While in Print Preview, you can move through a document using the insertion point movement keys, the horizontal and vertical scroll bars, and/or the Page Up and Page Down keys.

exercise 14

Viewing a Document with Print Preview

1. Open Report 04.
2. View the document by completing the following steps:
   a. Click the Print Preview button on the Standard toolbar.
   b. Click the Multiple Pages button on the Print Preview toolbar. (This causes a grid to appear immediately below the button.)
   c. Position the mouse pointer in the upper left portion of the grid, drag the mouse down and to the right until the message at the bottom of the grid displays as *2 x 2 Pages*, and then click the left mouse button.
   d. Click the Full Screen button on the Print Preview toolbar. (This displays only the pages in the document and the Print Preview toolbar.)
   e. Click the Full Screen button again to restore the screen display.
   f. Click the One Page button on the Print Preview toolbar.
   g. Click the down-pointing triangle at the right of the Zoom button and then click *50%* at the drop-down list.
   h. Click the down-pointing triangle at the right of the Zoom button and then click *75%* at the drop-down list.
   i. Click the One Page button on the Print Preview toolbar.
   j. Click the Close button on the Print Preview toolbar.
3. Close Report 04.

Step 2b

Step 2c   Step 2d

Step 2f

Full Screen

One Page

Editing in Print Preview

Print Preview is used to view a document before printing, but it can also be used to edit a document. To edit a document in Print Preview, you would complete the following steps:

Magnifier

1. In Print Preview, make sure the Magnifier button on the Print Preview toolbar is active. (If the Magnifier button is active, it displays with a lighter gray background than the other buttons. By default, the Magnifier button is active when you first display Print Preview.)
2. Position the mouse pointer (displays as a magnifying glass) in the part of the document you want to edit and then click the left button. This changes the display to 100% magnification.
3. Click the Magnifier button to turn it off. This returns the mouse pointer to normal.
4. Edit the document in the normal manner.
5. Click the Magnifier button and then click the document. This returns the display of the document to the previous magnification.

In Print Preview you can change the top, bottom, left, and right margins using the rulers. In Print Preview, a horizontal ruler displays above the document and a vertical ruler displays at the left side of the document. If these rulers are not visible, clicking the View Ruler button on the Print Preview toolbar will display them.

View Ruler

Use the horizontal and vertical rulers to change margins in the same manner as you used the horizontal and vertical rulers in the normal document screen. The horizontal ruler contains a left and right margin boundary and the vertical ruler contains a top and bottom margin boundary. To change a margin, position the mouse pointer on the margin boundary until it turns into a double-headed arrow, and then drag the margin boundary to the desired position.

Editing a Document in Print Preview

1. Open Notice 01.
2. Save the document with Save As and name it Ch 04, Ex 15.
3. Display Print Preview and make changes to the document by completing the following steps:
    a. Click the Print Preview button on the Standard toolbar.
    b. Position the mouse pointer (displays as a magnifying glass) in the first paragraph of text in the document and then click the left button. This changes the display to 100% magnification.
    c. Click the Magnifier button to turn it off. This returns the mouse pointer to normal.
    d. Make the following edits to text in the first paragraph of the document:
        1) Change *6:00* to *6:30*.
        2) Change *9:30* to *10:00*.
        3) Change *Mike Shelton* to *Maggie Hayes*.
    e. Make the following edits to the text in the third paragraph of the document:
        1) Add *hamburgers,* after the words *Hot dogs,*.
        2) Change *9:00* to *9:30*.
    f. Click the Magnifier button and then click the document. This returns the display of the document to the previous magnification.
    g. Make sure the rulers are displayed. (If they are not displayed, click the View Ruler button on the Print Preview toolbar.)
    h. Make the following changes to the left, right, and top margins:
        1) Drag the left margin boundary to the right on the horizontal ruler until the 2-inch mark displays in the gray area.
        2) Drag the right margin boundary to the left on the horizontal ruler to the 4.5-inch mark in the white area.
        3) Drag the top margin boundary down on the vertical ruler until the 3-inch mark displays in the gray area.
    i. Click Close to close Print Preview.
4. Save the document again with the same name (Ch 04, Ex 15).
5. Print and then close Ch 04, Ex 15.

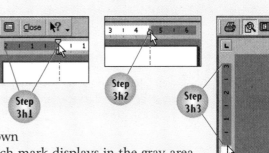

Changing the Document Zoom

Zoom

In the previous section of this chapter you learned about the Zoom button on the Print Preview toolbar. With this button, you can change the percentage of display in Print Preview or change the display to Page Width, Whole Page, or Two Pages. The Zoom button changes the display of the document in Print Preview. You can also change the display of text at the document screen (not Print Preview) with the Zoom button on the Standard toolbar or with the Zoom option from the View drop-down menu. If you click the down-pointing triangle at the right side of the Zoom button on the Standard toolbar, the drop-down list shown in figure 4.11 displays.

figure
4.11

Zoom Drop-Down List

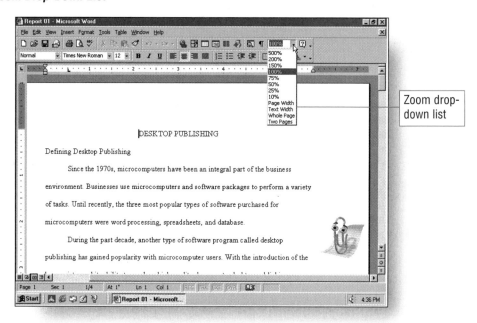

Zoom drop-down list

Click one of the percentage options to change the display to that percentage. Click the Page Width option and the screen display will change so that you can view text from the left to the right margins. When you make a change at the Zoom drop-down list, that change stays in effect for the document until you change to another option.

You can change the display of text at the document screen with options from the Zoom drop-down list and also at the Zoom dialog box shown in figure 4.12. To display the Zoom dialog box, click View, expand the drop-down menu, and then click Zoom.

4.12

Zoom Dialog Box

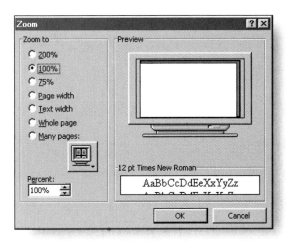

At the Zoom option dialog box you can change the display to 200%, 100%, or 75%. You can also change the display to Page width. The Whole page and Many pages options are dimmed if the view is Normal. If the view is changed to Print Layout, the Whole page and Many pages options are available. To specify a percentage measurement, use the Percent option. Changes made at the Zoom dialog box stay in effect for the document until another change is made.

exercise 16

Changing the Display of Text Using Zoom

1. Open Report 03.
2. Change the display by completing the following steps:
    a. Click the down-pointing triangle at the right side of the Zoom button on the Standard toolbar and then click *50%* at the drop-down list.
    b. Click the down-pointing triangle at the right side of the Zoom button on the Standard toolbar and then click *Page Width* at the drop-down list.
    c. Click View and then Zoom.
    d. At the Zoom dialog box, click 200%.
    e. Click OK or press Enter.
    f. Click View and then Print Layout.
    g. Click View and then Zoom.
    h. At the Zoom dialog box, click Whole page.
    i. Click OK or press Enter.
    j. Click the down-pointing triangle at the right side of the Zoom button on the Standard toolbar and then click *100%* at the drop-down list.
3. Close Report 03.

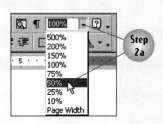

Step 2a

Using the Click and Type Feature

In chapter 3, you learned to change paragraph alignment with buttons on the Formatting toolbar, shortcut commands, or options at the Paragraph dialog box. Another method for changing paragraph alignment is to use the *click and type* feature. Before using this feature, you must change to the Print Layout view.

In Print Layout view, hover the mouse pointer between the left and right margins (at approximately the 3-inch mark on the Ruler). After a few seconds, four short horizontal lines display below the I-beam pointer. These horizontal lines represent center alignment. Double-click the mouse button and the insertion point is moved to the center of the margins and the Center button on the Formatting toolbar is activated.

You can change to right alignment in a similar manner. Hover the mouse pointer near the right margin and after a few seconds horizontal lines display at the left side of the I-beam pointer. These horizontal lines represent right alignment and are similar in appearance to the lines on the Align Right button on the Formatting toolbar. With the right alignment lines displayed at the left side of the I-beam pointer, double-click the left mouse button. To change to left alignment, hover the mouse pointer near the left margin. When horizontal lines display representing left alignment, double-click the left mouse button.

If the alignment lines are not displayed near the I-beam pointer and you double-click the left mouse button, a left tab is set at the position of the insertion point. You will learn about tabs in chapter 7. If you want to change the alignment and not set a tab, be sure the alignment lines display near the I-beam pointer before double-clicking the mouse button.

Using Click and Type to Align Text

1. At a clear document screen, create the document shown in figure 4.13 by completing the following steps:
   a. Change to the Print Layout view by clicking <u>V</u>iew and then <u>P</u>rint Layout.
   b. Position the I-beam pointer between the left and right margins at about the 3-inch mark on the horizontal ruler and the 2½-inch mark on the vertical ruler.
   c. When the center alignment lines display below the I-beam pointer, double-click the left mouse button.
   d. Key the centered text shown in figure 4.13.
   e. After keying the centered text, change to right alignment by completing the following steps:
      1) Position the I-beam pointer near the right margin at approximately the 4-inch mark on the vertical ruler until the right alignment lines display at the left side of the I-beam pointer. (You may need to scroll down the document to display the 4-inch mark on the vertical ruler.)
      2) Double-click the left mouse button.
   f. Key the right aligned text shown in figure 4.13.
2. Make the following changes to the document:
   a. Select the centered text and then change the font to 14-point Arial bold and the line spacing to 2.

b. Select the right aligned text and then change the font to 8-point Arial bold.
c. Deselect the text.
3. Save the document and name it Ch 04, Ex 17.
4. Print and then close Ch 04, Ex 17.

Exercise 17

MICROSOFT WORD 2000 TRAINING
Designing Publication Documents
Wednesday, March 14, 2001
Technology Center
8:30 a.m. – 3:00 p.m.

Sponsored by
Design Technologies

chapter summary

➤ By default, a Word document contains 1.25-inch left and right margins and 1-inch top and bottom margins.

➤ Word inserts a page break at approximately 10 inches from the top of each page. With the default 1-inch top and bottom margins, this allows a total of 9 inches to be printed on a standard page. The page break displays as a row of dots in Normal view and as an actual break in the page in Print Layout.

➤ Margin settings can be changed visually on the horizontal and vertical rulers that display in the Print Layout view.

➤ Mirror margins can be created at the Page Setup dialog box. With this option, the measurements for left and right margins are applied to odd-numbered pages and reversed for even-numbered pages.

➤ For left-bound material to properly display on the page, change the gutter margins at the Page Setup dialog box from the default 0 inches to approximately 0.5 inch and also select the Mirror margins option. Choose the *Top* option in the Gutter position section of the Page Setup dialog box if the material is to be bound at the top.

➤ Formatting is generally applied to an entire document or to selected text. A document can also be divided into sections to which separate formatting can be applied.

➤ In Word, widows and orphans are automatically prevented from appearing in text. Turn off this feature at the Paragraph dialog box with the Line and Page Breaks tab selected.

➤ The Paragraph dialog box with the Line and Page Breaks tab selected contains options to keep a paragraph, a group of paragraphs, or a group of lines together.

➤ The page break that Word inserts automatically is a soft page break. A page break that you insert is a hard page break.

➤ To print text on a paper size that is different from the default of 8.5 by 11 inches, display the Page Setup dialog box with the Paper Size tab selected.

➤ The Vertical alignment option at the Page Setup dialog box contains three choices—Top, Center, and Justified.

➤ With Word's Print Preview feature, you can view a partial page, single page, multiple pages, or zoom in on a particular area of a page. With buttons on the Print Preview toolbar at the top of the Print Preview screen, you can change the display of the document, send a document to the printer, and turn the display of the rulers on or off.

➤ In addition to viewing how a document will look when printed, you can edit a document while in Print Preview. You can also change the margins while in Print Preview by using the rulers.

➤ The Zoom button changes the display of the document in Print Preview. You can also change the display of text at the document screen with the Zoom button on the Standard toolbar or with the Zoom option from the View drop-down menu.

➤ Text can be centered, right aligned, and left aligned using the click and type feature.

commands review

	Mouse	Keyboard
Print Layout view	View, Print Layout; or click Page Layout View button at left side of horizontal scroll bar	View, Print Layout
Normal view (default)	View, Normal; or click Normal View button at left side of horizontal scroll bar	View, Normal
Page Setup dialog box	File, Page Setup	File, Page Setup
Insert continuous section break	Insert, Break, Continuous	Insert, Break, Continuous
Insert section break and begin new page	Insert, Break, Next page	Insert, Break, Next page
Paragraph dialog box	Format, Paragraph	Format, Paragraph
Insert a hard page break	Insert, Break, Page break	Ctrl + Enter
Print Preview	File, Print Preview; or click Print Preview button on the Standard toolbar	File, Print Preview
Change to center alignment	Hover I-beam pointer near center of margins until center alignment lines display below I-beam pointer, then double-click left mouse button	

Change to right alignment	Hover I-beam pointer near right margin until right alignment lines display at left side of I-beam pointer, then double-click left mouse button
Change to left alignment	Hover I-beam pointer near left margin until left alignment alignment lines display at right side of I-beam pointer, then double-click left mouse button

thinking offline

Matching: In the space provided at the left, indicate the correct letter that matches each description. Some choices may be used more than once.

Ⓐ	1 inch	Ⓕ	10 inches
Ⓑ	8.5 inches	Ⓖ	11 inches
Ⓒ	9 inches	Ⓗ	9.5 inches
Ⓓ	11.5 inches	Ⓘ	0 inches
Ⓔ	1.25 inches	Ⓙ	1.5 inches

_____ 1. Length of a standard piece of paper.

_____ 2. Default top margin.

_____ 3. Approximate number of vertical inches of text on a page.

_____ 4. Width of a standard piece of paper.

_____ 5. Default left margin.

_____ 6. Default right margin.

_____ 7. Default bottom margin.

_____ 8. Default gutter margin.

_____ 9. Approximate number of inches from the top of the page at which an automatic page break occurs on a page.

Completion: In the space provided at the right, indicate the correct term, symbol, or command.

1. A page break displays as a row of dots at this view. _____

2. Click this button located at the left side of the horizontal scroll bar to change to the Print Layout view. _____

3. Change margins in a document at this dialog box. _____

4. To move margin boundaries to a precise measurement, hold down this key while dragging the boundary. _____

5. Turn on/off the widow/orphan control at the Paragraph dialog box with this tab selected. _____

6. Press these keys on the keyboard to insert a hard page break in a document. _____

7. Word provides two orientations for paper sizes—Portrait and this. _____

8. The Vertical alignment option at the Page Setup dialog box contains four choices—Top, Center, Botttom, and this. _____

9. Click this button on the Standard toolbar to preview a document. _____

10. Click this button on the Standard toolbar to change the percentage of display. _____

working hands-on

Assessment 1

1. Open Report 02.
2. Save the document with Save As and name it Ch 04, SA 01.
3. Make the following changes to the document:
   a. Change the top, bottom, left, and right margins to 1.5 inches.
   b. Select the entire document and then change the font size to 13 points. (To change the size to 13 points, you will need to select the current size, and then key **13**.)
   c. Select the title *DESKTOP PUBLISHING DESIGN* and then change the font size to 16 points and turn on bold.
   d. Change the font size to 16 points and turn on bold for the headings *Designing a Document* and *Creating Focus*.
   e. Select the last three bulleted paragraphs in the first list of bulleted items. (These last three bulleted paragraphs should display at the bottom of the first page and the top of the second page.)
   f. Display the Paragraph dialog box with the Line and Page Breaks tab selected, click Keep with next, and then close the dialog box.
4. Check page breaks and, if necessary, make adjustments to page breaks.
5. Save the document again with the same name (Ch 04, SA 01).
6. Print and then close Ch 04, SA 01.

Assessment 2

1. Open Report 02.
2. Save the document with Save As and name it Ch 04, SA 02.
3. Make the following changes to the document:
   a. Display the Page Setup dialog box with the Margins tab selected, change the left margin to 2 inches, the right margin to 1 inch, click the Mirror margins option, and then close the dialog box.
   b. Select the entire document and then change the font to 12-point Garamond (or a similar serif typeface).
   c. Select the title *DESKTOP PUBLISHING DESIGN* and then change the font to 16-point Univers bold. (If your printer does not support Univers, choose a similar sans serif typeface.)
   d. Change the font to 16-point Univers bold for the headings *Designing a Document* and *Creating Focus*.
   e. Check the page breaks in the document and make changes, if needed.
4. Save the document again with the same name (Ch 04, SA 02).
5. Print and then close Ch 04, SA 02.

Assessment 3

1. Open Para 04.
2. Save the document with Save As and name it Ch 04, SA 03.
3. Make the following changes to the document:
   a. Change the paper size to 5.5 inches by 8.5 inches.
   b. Change the top and bottom margins to 1.5 inches and the left and right margins to 1 inch.
   c. Select the entire document, change the font to 10-point Arial, and then deselect the text.
   d. Change the vertical alignment of the text in the document to center.
4. Preview the document before printing.
5. Save the document again with the same name (Ch 04, SA 03).
6. Print and then close Ch 04, SA 03.

Assessment 4

1. At a clear document screen, key the text shown in figure 4.14. Center and bold the text as indicated.
2. Change the vertical alignment of the text in the document to justified.
3. Preview the document before printing.
4. Save the document and name it Ch 04, SA 04.
5. Print and then close Ch 04, SA 04.

 **figure**
4.14   *Assessment 4*

SUPERVISORY TECHNIQUES
by Charlie Fields
BUS 210
November 28, 2001

Chapter 05

Maintaining and Printing Documents

PERFORMANCE OBJECTIVES

Upon successful completion of chapter 5, you will be able to:
- Create a folder.
- Copy, move, rename, delete, and print documents.
- Display document properties.
- Create a shortcut to a document.
- Print specific pages in a document.
- Print multiple copies of a document.
- Print odd and/or even pages in a document.
- Create and print envelopes.
- Create and print labels.

Almost every company that conducts business maintains a filing system. The system may consist of documents, folders, and cabinets, or it may be a computerized filing system where information is stored on tapes and disks. Whatever type of filing system a business uses, daily maintenance of files is important to a company's operation. In this chapter, you will learn to maintain files (documents) in Word, including such activities as creating file folders and copying, moving, renaming, and printing documents.

In chapter 1, you learned to print a document with the Print button on the Standard toolbar or through the Print dialog box. By default, one copy of all pages of the currently open document is printed. In this chapter, you will learn to customize a print job with selections from the Print dialog box.

Maintaining Documents

Many file (document) management tasks can be completed at the Open dialog box (and some at the Save As dialog box). These tasks can include creating a subfolder; copying, moving, printing, and renaming documents; opening multiple documents; and opening a document as read-only. To display the Open dialog box, click the Open button on the Standard toolbar or click File and then Open. To display the Save As dialog box, click File and then Save As.

Creating a Folder

In Word, documents are grouped logically and placed in *folders*. A folder can be created within a folder. The main folder on a disk or drive is called the *root* folder. Additional folders can be created as a branch of this root folder. At the Open or Save As dialog boxes, documents display in the list box preceded by a document icon and a folder is preceded by a folder icon .

Create New Folder

Up One Level

Back

A new folder can be created with the Create New Folder button at the Open dialog box or Save As dialog box. To create a new folder, click the Create New Folder button (located on the dialog box toolbar). At the New Folder dialog box shown in figure 5.1, key a name for the folder, and then click OK or press Enter. The new folder becomes the active folder. If you want to make the previous folder the active folder, click the Up One Level button on the dialog box toolbar. Clicking this button changes to the folder that was up one level from the current folder. After clicking the Up One Level button, the Back button becomes active. Click this button and the previously active folder becomes active again.

A folder name can contain a maximum of 255 characters. Numbers, spaces, and symbols can be used in the folder name, except those symbols explained in chapter 1 in the *Naming a Document* section.

(Before completing computer exercises, delete the Chapter 04 *folder on your disk. Next, copy the* Chapter 05 *folder from the CD that accompanies this textbook to your disk and then make* Chapter 05 *the active folder.)*

figure

5.1

New Folder Dialog Box

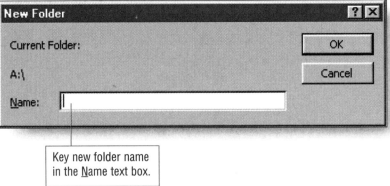

Key new folder name in the Name text box.

exercise

Creating a Folder

1. Create a folder named *Memos* on your disk by completing the following steps:
   a. Display the Open dialog box and open the *Chapter 05* folder on your disk.
   b. Click the Create New Folder button (located on the dialog box toolbar).
   c. At the New Folder dialog box, key **Memos**.
   d. Click OK or press Enter. (The *Memos* folder is now the active folder.)
   e. Change back to the *Chapter 05* folder by clicking the Up One Level button on the dialog box toolbar.
2. Click the Cancel button to close the Open dialog box.

Selecting Documents

Document management tasks can be completed on one document or selected documents. For example, you can move one document to a different folder, or you can select several documents and move them at one time. Selected documents can be deleted, copied, moved, or printed.

To select one document, display the Open dialog box, and then click the desired document. To select several adjacent documents (documents displayed next to each other), using the mouse, you would complete the following steps:

1. Display the Open dialog box.
2. Click the first document to make it active.
3. Position the mouse pointer on the last document to be selected, hold down the Shift key, and then click the left mouse button.

You can also select documents that are not adjacent in the Open dialog box. To do this with the mouse, you would complete the following steps:

1. Display the Open dialog box.
2. Click the first document you want selected.
3. Hold down the Ctrl key.
4. Click each document you want selected.
5. When all desired documents are selected, release the Ctrl key.

When the Open dialog box is displayed, the first document in the Look in list box is automatically selected. Before selecting documents to be copied, deselect the first document (unless this first document is to be included with the other selected documents). To deselect the first document, position the mouse pointer anywhere in a clear portion of the Look in list box (not on a document name), and then click the left mouse button.

Deleting Documents and Folders

At some point, you may want to delete certain documents from your data disk or any other disk or folder in which you may be working. If you use Word on a regular basis, you should establish a system for deleting documents. The system you choose depends on the work you are doing and the amount of folder or disk space available. To delete a document, display the Open or Save As dialog box, select the document, and then click the Delete button on the dialog box toolbar. At the dialog box asking you to confirm the deletion, click Yes.

Delete

You can also delete a document by displaying the Open dialog box, selecting the document to be deleted, clicking the Tools button on the dialog box toolbar, and then clicking Delete at the drop-down menu.

Tools

Another method for deleting a document is to display the Open dialog box, right-click the document to be deleted, and then click Delete at the shortcut menu.

Deleting a Document

1. Delete a document by completing the following steps:
   a. Display the Open dialog box with the *Chapter 05* folder active.
   b. Click *Para 05* to select it.
   c. Click the Delete button on the dialog box toolbar.
   d. At the question asking if you want to delete the selected document, click <u>Y</u>es.
2. Close the Open dialog box.

Deleting Selected Documents

1. Delete selected documents by completing the following steps:
   a. Display the Open dialog box with the *Chapter 05* folder active.
   b. Click *Notice 02*.
   c. Hold down the Shift key and then click *Notice 04*.
   d. Click the Too<u>l</u>s button on the dialog box toolbar.
   e. At the drop-down menu that displays, click <u>D</u>elete.

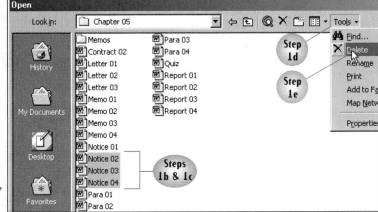

   f. At the question asking if you are sure you want to delete the items, click <u>Y</u>es.
   g. At the message asking if you want to delete the read-only file, click the Yes to <u>A</u>ll button.
2. Close the Open dialog box.

A folder and all its contents can be deleted at the Open or Save As dialog box. Delete a folder and its contents in the same manner as deleting a document or selected documents.

Deleting to the Recycle Bin

Documents deleted from your data disk are deleted permanently. (There are recovery programs, however, that will help you recover deleted text. If you accidentally delete a document or documents from a disk, do not do anything more with the disk until you can run a recovery program.) Documents deleted from the hard drive are automatically sent to the Windows Recycle Bin. If you accidentally delete a document to the Recycle Bin, it can be easily restored. To free space on the drive, empty the Recycle Bin on a periodic basis. Restoring a document from or emptying the contents of the Recycle Bin is done at the Windows 98 (or 95) desktop (not in Word). To empty the Recycle Bin, you would complete the following steps:

1. Display the Windows 98 (or 95) desktop. (If you are just beginning, turn on the computer, and Windows 98 [or 95] will open. If you are currently working in Word, click the Minimize button at the right side of the Title bar. The Minimize button contains the single underline symbol [_]. Be sure to click the Minimize button on the Title bar and not the one just below it on the Menu bar.)
2. At the Windows 98 (or 95) desktop, double-click the *Recycle Bin* icon (located at the left side of the desktop).
3. At the Recycle Bin dialog box, click File and then Empty Recycle Bin.
4. At the question asking if you are sure you want to empty the Recycle Bin, click Yes.

If you want to empty only specific documents from the Recycle Bin, hold down the Ctrl key while clicking the documents to be emptied. Position the mouse pointer on one of the selected documents, click the *right* mouse button, and then click the left mouse button on Delete. At the question asking if you want to delete the selected documents, click Yes.

A document or selected documents can also be restored from the Recycle Bin. To do this, you would complete the following steps:

1. At the Windows 98 (or 95) desktop, double-click the *Recycle Bin* icon.
2. At the Recycle Bin dialog box, click the document to be restored. (If you are restoring more than one document, hold down the Ctrl key while clicking the desired documents.)
3. Click File and then Restore.

At the Recycle Bin dialog box, you can also restore a document by positioning the mouse pointer on the document to be restored, clicking the *right* mouse button, and then clicking the left mouse button on Restore.

If you minimized the Word program by clicking the Minimize button, you can maximize (display the Word screen) the Word program at the desktop by clicking the Microsoft Word - (document name) button located on the Taskbar (at the bottom of the screen).

Copying Files

In previous chapters, you have been opening a document from your disk and saving it with a new name on the same disk. This process makes an exact copy of the document, leaving the original on the disk. You have been copying documents and saving the new document in the same folder as the original document. You can also copy a document into another folder and use the document's original name or give it a different name, or select documents at the Open dialog box and copy them to the same folder or into a different folder. To copy a document into another folder, you would complete the following steps:

1. Open the document you want to copy.
2. Display the Save As dialog box.
3. At the Save As dialog box, change to the desired folder. To do this, click the down-pointing triangle to the right of the Save in text box, and then click the desired folder at the drop-down menu.
4. Click the Save button in the lower right corner of the dialog box.

Saving a Copy of an Open Document

1. Open Memo 01.
2. Save the document with Save As and name it Books. (Make sure *Chapter 05* is the active folder.)
3. Save a copy of the Books document in the *Memos* folder created in exercise 1 by completing the following steps: (If your system does not contain this folder, check with your instructor to determine if there is another folder you can use.)
   a. With Books still open, display the Save As dialog box.
   b. At the Save As dialog box, change to the *Memos* folder. To do this, double-click *Memos* at the beginning of the list box (folders are listed before documents).
   c. Click the Save button located in the lower right corner of the dialog box.
4. Close Books.
5. Change the folder back to the *Chapter 05* folder by completing the following steps:
   a. Display the Open dialog box.
   b. Click the Up One Level button on the dialog box toolbar.
   c. Click Cancel to close the Open dialog box.

A document can be copied to another folder without opening the document first. To do this, use the Copy and Paste options from a shortcut menu at the Open (or Save As) dialog box.

Copying a Document at the Open Dialog Box

1. Copy Memo 02 to the *Memos* folder by completing the following steps:
   a. Display the Open dialog box with the *Chapter 05* folder active.
   b. Position the mouse pointer on Memo 02, click the *right* mouse button, and then click <u>C</u>opy at the shortcut menu.
   c. Change to the *Memos* folder by double-clicking *Memos* at the beginning of the list box.
   d. Position the mouse pointer in any white area (not on a document name) in the list box, click the *right* mouse button, and then click <u>P</u>aste at the shortcut menu.
2. Change back to the Chapter 05 folder by clicking the Up One Level button located on the dialog box toolbar.
3. Close the Open dialog box.

A document or selected documents can be copied into the same folder. When you do this, Word names the document(s) "Copy of xxx" (where xxx is the current document name). You can copy one document or selected documents into the same folder.

Copying Selected Documents into the Same Folder

1. Copy documents into the same folder by completing the following steps:
   a. Display the Open dialog box with the *Chapter 05* folder active.
   b. Select *Para 01*, *Para 02*, and *Para 03*. (To do this, click *Para 01*, hold down the Shift key, and then click *Para 03*.)
   c. Position the mouse pointer on one of the selected documents, click the *right* mouse button, and then click <u>C</u>opy at the shortcut menu.
   d. Position the mouse pointer in any white area in the list box, click the *right* mouse button, and then click <u>P</u>aste at the shortcut menu. (In a few moments, Word will redisplay the Open dialog box with the following documents added: Copy of Para 01, Copy of Para 02, and Copy of Para 03.)
2. Close the Open dialog box.

exercise 7

Copying Selected Documents into a Different Folder

1. Copy several documents to the *Memos* folder by completing the following steps:
   a. Display the Open dialog box with the *Chapter 05* folder active.
   b. Select *Memo 01*, *Memo 03*, and *Memo 04* by completing the following steps:
      1) Click once on *Memo 01*. (This selects the document.)
      2) Hold down the Ctrl key, click *Memo 03*, click *Memo 04*, and then release the Ctrl key.
   c. Position the mouse pointer on one of the selected documents, click the *right* mouse button, and then click Copy at the shortcut menu.
   d. Double-click the folder named *Memos*. (This folder is located at the beginning of the list box.)
   e. When the *Memos* folder is displayed, position the mouse pointer in any white area in the list box, click the *right* mouse button, and then click Paste at the shortcut menu.
   f. Click the Up One Level button to change back to the *Chapter 05* folder.
2. Close the Open dialog box by clicking the Cancel button.

Sending Documents to a Different Drive or Folder

With the Copy and Paste options from the shortcut menu at the Open or Save As dialog box, you can copy documents to another folder or drive. With the Send To option, you can quickly send a copy of a document to another drive or folder. To use this option, position the mouse pointer on the document you want copied, click the *right* mouse button, position the mouse pointer on Send To (this causes a side menu to display), and then click the desired drive or folder.

Cutting and Pasting a Document

A document can be removed from one folder or disk and inserted in another folder or on a disk using the Cut and Paste options from the shortcut menu at the Open dialog box. To do this you would display the Open dialog box, position the mouse pointer on the document to be removed (cut), click the *right* mouse button, and then click Cut at the shortcut menu. Change to the desired folder, position the mouse pointer in a white area in the list box, click the *right* mouse button, and then click Paste at the shortcut menu.

Cutting and Pasting a Document

1. Save and move a document into a different folder by completing the following steps:
   a. Open Memo 04.
   b. Save the document with Save As and name it Emp Survey.
   c. Close Emp Survey.
   d. Move Emp Survey to the *Memos* folder by completing the following steps:
      1) Display the Open dialog box with the *Chapter 05* folder active.
      2) Position the mouse pointer on Emp Survey, click the *right* mouse button, and then click Cut at the shortcut menu.
      3) Double-click *Memos* to make it the active folder.
      4) Position the mouse pointer in the white area in the list box, click the *right* mouse button, and then click Paste at the shortcut menu.
   e. Click the Up One Level button to make *Chapter 05* the active folder.
2. Close the Open dialog box.

Renaming Documents

At the Open dialog box, use the Rename option from the Tools drop-down menu to give a document a different name. The Rename option changes the name of the document and keeps it in the same folder. To use Rename, display the Open dialog box, click once on the document to be renamed, and then click the Tools button on the dialog box toolbar. This causes a black border to surround the document name and the name to be selected. Key the desired name and then press Enter.

You can also rename a document by right-clicking the document name at the Open dialog box and then clicking Rename at the shortcut menu. Key the desired name for the document and then press the Enter key.

Renaming a Document

1. Rename a document located in the *Memos* folder by completing the following steps:
   a. Display the Open dialog box with *Chapter 05* the active folder.
   b. Double-click *Memos* to make it the active folder.
   c. Click *Memo 01* to select it.
   d. Click the Tools button on the dialog box toolbar.
   e. At the drop-down menu that displays, click Rename.
   f. Key **Nguyen** and then press the Enter key. (Depending on your system setup, you may need to key **Nguyen.doc**.)
   g. At the message asking if you want to change the name of the read-only file, click Yes.
   h. Complete steps similar to those in 1b through 1g to rename Memo 02 to St. Claire (or St. Claire.doc).
   i. Click the Up One Level button.
2. Close the Open dialog box.

Deleting a Folder and Its Contents

As you learned earlier in this chapter, a document or selected documents can be deleted. In addition to documents, a folder (and all its contents) can be deleted. Delete a folder in the same manner as a document is deleted.

Deleting a Folder and Its Contents

1. Delete the *Memos* folder and its contents by completing the following steps:
    a. Display the Open dialog box with *Chapter 05* the active folder.
    b. Click once on the *Memos* folder to select it.
    c. Click the Delete button on the dialog box toolbar.
    d. At the question asking if you want to remove the folder and its contents, click <u>Y</u>es.
    e. At the message asking if you are sure you want to delete the read-only file, click the Yes to <u>A</u>ll button.
2. Close the Open dialog box.

Opening Documents

A document or selected documents can be opened at the Open dialog box. To open one document, display the Open dialog box, and then double-click the document. You can also open a document by positioning the mouse pointer on the desired document, clicking the *right* mouse button, and then clicking <u>O</u>pen at the shortcut menu. To open more than one document, select the documents in the Open dialog box and then click the <u>O</u>pen button; or, position the mouse pointer on one of the selected documents, click the *right* mouse button, and then click <u>O</u>pen at the shortcut menu.

Closing Documents

If more than one document is open, all open documents can be closed at the same time. To do this, hold down the Shift key, click <u>F</u>ile and then <u>C</u>lose All. Holding down the Shift key before clicking <u>F</u>ile causes the <u>C</u>lose option to change to <u>C</u>lose All.

Opening and Closing Several Documents

1. Open several documents by completing the following steps:
    a. Display the Open dialog box with *Chapter 05* the active folder.
    b. Select *Memo 01*, *Memo 02*, *Memo 03*, and *Memo 04*.
    c. Position the mouse pointer on one of the selected documents, click the *right* mouse button, and then click the left mouse button on <u>O</u>pen.
2. Close the open documents by completing the following steps:
    a. Hold down the Shift key.
    b. Click <u>F</u>ile and then <u>C</u>lose All.

Opening Read-Only Documents

A document can be opened that is read-only. With a read-only document, you can make changes to the document but you cannot save those changes with the same name. Word protects the original document and does not allow you to save the changes to the document with the same name. You can, however, open a document as read-only, make changes to it, and then save the document with a different name.

The documents in the folders you copy from the CD are read-only documents. To open a document as read-only, display the Open dialog box, position the mouse pointer on the desired document, click the *right* mouse button, and then click the left mouse button on Open Read-Only. With a read-only document displayed, clicking the Save button, or clicking File and then Save, causes the Save As dialog box to display where you can key a new name for the document.

Opening a Read-Only Document

1. Open a document and save it with a new name by completing the following steps:
    a. Display the Open dialog box with Chapter 05 the active folder.
    b. Open Notice 01.
    c. Save the document with Save As and name it Carnival.
    d. Close Carnival.
2. Open Carnival as a read-only document by completing the following steps:
    a. Display the Open dialog box with *Chapter 05* the active folder.
    b. Position the mouse pointer on Carnival, click the *right* mouse button, and then click the left mouse button on Open Read-Only.
3. With Carnival open, make the following changes:
    a. Change *EMERALD HEIGHTS* (in the title) to *LIBERTY FALLS*.
    b. Change *Emerald Heights* (in the first paragraph) to *Liberty Falls*.
    c. Change *April 6* (in the first and the fourth paragraphs) to *May 11*.
    d. Change *6:00* (in the first paragraph) to *6:30*.
    e. Change *Mike Shelton* (in the first paragraph) to *Christine Long*.
4. Save the document by completing the following steps:
    a. Click the Save button on the Standard toolbar.
    b. At the Save As dialog box, key **Ch 05, Ex 12**, and then press Enter.
5. Print and then close Ch 05, Ex 12.

Protecting Documents

If you create a document containing sensitive, restricted, or private information, consider protecting the document with a password. Word provides a variety of methods for protecting documents. In the previous section, you learned to open a document as read-only. A read-only document is protected from being edited and then saved. You can also protect a document from being modified or from being opened by other users by requiring a password.

Protect a document from being modified or opened without a password by opening the document and then displaying the Save As dialog box. At the Save As dialog box, click the Tools button on the dialog box toolbar, and then click General Options at the drop-down list. This displays the Save dialog box shown in figure 5.2. If you want to protect a document from being modified, key a password in the Password to modify text box and then press Enter. This displays the Confirm Password dialog box. At this dialog box, key the same password again and then press Enter. Follow the same basic steps to protect a document from being opened except key a password in the Password to open text box. A password can contain up to 15 characters, can include spaces, and is case sensitive.

figure
5.2

Save Dialog Box

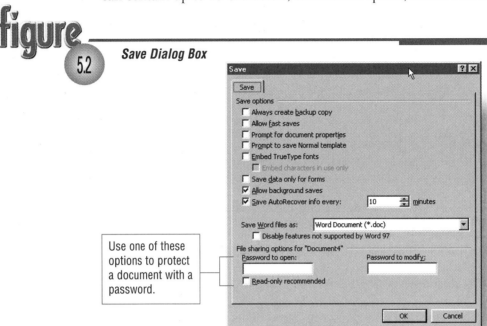

Use one of these options to protect a document with a password.

exercise
13

Protecting a Document with a Password

1. Open Contract 02.
2. Save the document with Save As and name it Ch 05, Ex 13.
3. Protect the document with a password by completing the following steps:
    a. Click File and then Save As.
    b. At the Save As dialog box, click the Tools button on the dialog box toolbar, and then click General Options at the drop-down list.
    c. At the Save dialog box, click in the Password to open text box, and then key your first name. (If it is longer than 15 characters, abbreviate it. You will not see your name—instead Word inserts asterisks.)
    d. After keying your name, press Enter.
    e. At the Confirm Password dialog box, key your name again (be sure to key it exactly as you did at the Save dialog box—including upper- or lowercase letters), and then press Enter.
    f. At the Save As dialog box, click the Save button.
4. Close Ch 05, Ex 13.
5. Open Ch 05, Ex 13, keying your password when prompted.
6. Close Ch 05, Ex 13.

Displaying Document Properties

Word will provide specific details about a document with the Properties option from the Open or Save As dialog boxes shortcut menus. To display information about a document, display the Open dialog box (or Save As dialog box), and then select the desired document. Click the Tools button on the dialog box toolbar and then click *Properties* at the drop-down menu. You can also display document properties by positioning the mouse pointer on the desired document, clicking the *right* mouse button, and then clicking the left button on Properties. This displays a Properties dialog box similar to the one shown in figure 5.3.

Properties Dialog Box

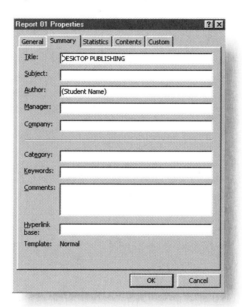

By default (this may vary), the Summary tab is selected and fields such as title, subject, author, keywords, and commands display. Some of these fields may contain information while others are blank. You can key specific information in each of these fields to describe the document. To move the insertion point to the next field, press the Tab key. To move the insertion point to the previous field, press Shift + Tab. Key information in the fields desired and then click OK to close the Properties dialog box.

Other tabs can be selected at the Properties dialog box to view additional information about the document. If you click the General tab, information about the document type, size, and location displays. Click the Statistics tab to view information such as the number of pages, paragraphs, lines, words, characters, and bytes included in the document. You can view the document without bringing it to the document screen by clicking the Contents tab. This displays a portion of the document in a viewing window. Click the Custom tab if you want to customize the properties of a document.

exercise 14

Displaying Document Properties

1. Display information about Report 01 by completing the following steps:
   a. Display the Open dialog box with *Chapter 05* the active folder.
   b. Click once on *Report 01* to select it.
   c. Click the Tools button on the dialog box toolbar and then click Properties at the drop-down menu.
   d. Read the information displayed in the Properties dialog box and then click the General tab.
   e. Read the information displayed with the General tab selected and then click the Statistics tab.
   f. Read the information displayed with the Statistics tab selected and then click the Contents tab.
   g. Read the information displayed with the Contents tab selected.
   h. Click the Cancel button to remove the Properties dialog box.
2. At the Open dialog box, display the Properties dialog box for the document named Report 02.
3. Display information for the document named Report 03.
4. Close the Open dialog box.

In exercise 14, you displayed document properties for a document by clicking the Tools button on the dialog box toolbar and then clicking Properties at the drop-down menu. Another method for displaying document properties is to open the document, click File, expand the drop-down menu, and then click Properties. Move the insertion point to different text boxes in the document properties dialog box by clicking in the desired text box. You can also move to the next text box by pressing the Tab key or move to the previous text box by pressing Shift + Tab.

exercise 15

Adding Information to the Document Properties Dialog Box

1. Open Report 03.
2. Save the document with Save As and name it Ch 05, Ex 15.
3. Add information to the document properties dialog box by completing the following steps:
   a. Click File, expand the drop-down menu, and then click Properties.
   b. At the Ch 05, Ex 15 properties dialog box, make sure the Summary tab is selected, and then key the following text in the specified text box:

Subject	=	**Newsletter Design**
Category	=	**Newsletters**
Keywords	=	**newsletter, design**
Comments	=	**This document contains information on designing a newsletter, identifying the purpose of a newsletter, and basic newsletter elements.**

c. Click OK to close the Ch 05, Ex 15 properties dialog box.
4. Save the document again with the same name (Ch 05, Ex 15).
5. Close Ch 05, Ex 15. (Later in this chapter, you will learn how to print the document properties. You will print the document properties for Ch 05, Ex 15 in exercise 21.)

Changing Views

When the Open dialog box or Save As dialog box is displayed, the list of documents in the active folder is displayed. This display can be changed with options from the Views drop-down menu. Click the down-pointing triangle at the right side of the Views button on the dialog box toolbar and a drop-down menu displays with the following options: List, Details, Properties, Preview, and Arrange Icons.

Views

By default, the List option is active, which displays folders and documents alphabetized by name. Choose the Details option to display additional information about folders and documents such as the size, type, and modification date. Select a document and then choose the Properties option and information about the document displays to the right of the list box. This information includes the title, author, and revision date of the document along with information such as the number of pages, words, and characters in the document. Choose the Preview option to display a portion of the currently selected document in a window to the right of the list box. This option is helpful if you are searching for a specific document and cannot remember the name of the document.

By default, the list of documents displays in alphabetic order by name. With the Arrange Icons option, you can arrange documents by type, size, or date. To use this option, click the down-pointing triangle at the right side of the Views button on the dialog box toolbar, point to Arrange Icons, and then choose the desired option from the side menu that displays.

The Open and Save As dialog boxes contain buttons for displaying specific folders or locations. Click the History button located to the left of the list box to display a list of the most recently opened documents or folders. Click the My Documents button to display the *My Documents* folder documents or click the Desktop button to display desktop folders and shortcuts. Display any Web folders by clicking the Web Folders button.

Adding Folders to the Favorites List

If you open documents within a specific folder on a regular basis, consider adding the folder to the Favorites list. To do this, select the desired folder, click the down-pointing triangle at the right side of the Tools button on the dialog box toolbar, and then click Add to Favorites at the drop-down menu. Once a folder has been added to the Favorites list, click the Favorites button located at the left side of the list box. This displays the folder and any other folders that have been added to the Favorites list.

exercise 16

Changing the View and Adding a Favorites Folder at the Open Dialog Box

1. Display the Open dialog box with *Chapter 05* the active folder.
2. Change the view at the Open dialog box by completing the following steps:
   a. Click the down-pointing triangle at the right side of the Views button on the dialog box toolbar.
   b. At the drop-down menu that displays, click Details.
   c. Scroll through the list of documents and view the information on the size and type of the document and the last modification date.

3. Display document properties for specific documents by completing the following steps:
   a. At the Open dialog box, click once on the document *Memo 01*.
   b. Click the down-pointing triangle at the right side of the Views button on the dialog box toolbar.
   c. At the drop-down menu that displays, click Properties.
   d. Read the properties information for Memo 01.
   e. Click *Memo 02* in the list box and then read the properties information for the document.
4. Preview documents by completing the following steps:
   a. At the Open dialog box, click once on *Report 01* to select it.
   b. Click the down-pointing triangle at the right side of the Views button on the dialog box toolbar and then click Preview at the drop-down menu.
   c. Click *Report 02* to preview a portion of the document in the viewing window.
5. Return the display of documents back to list by completing the following steps:
   a. At the Open dialog box, click the down-pointing triangle at the right side of the Views button on the dialog box toolbar.
   b. At the drop-down menu that displays, click List.
6. Create a folder and then add it to the Favorites list by completing the following steps:
   a. At the Open dialog box, create a folder named *Reports*.
   b. Click the Up One Level button.
   c. Add the *Reports* folder to the Favorites list by completing the following steps:
      1) Click once on the *Reports* folder to select it.
      2) Click the Tools button on the dialog box toolbar.
      3) At the drop-down menu that displays, click Add to Favorites.
   d. Change to the *My Documents* folder by clicking the My Documents button located at the left side of the list box.
   e. Change to the *Reports* folder by completing the following steps:
      1) Click the Favorites button located at the left side of the list box.
      2) In the list of folders, double-click *Reports*. (This folder is empty.)
7. Click the Up One Level button to display the *Chapter 05* folder and then delete the *Reports* folder.

8. With the Open dialog box still displayed, remove the *Reports* folder from the Favorites list by completing the following steps:
   a. Click the Favorites button located at the left side of the list box.
   b. Click once on *Reports* in the list box to select it.
   c. Click the Delete button on the dialog box toolbar.
   d. At the question asking if you are sure you want to delete the folder, click <u>Y</u>es.
9. Close the Open dialog box.

Creating Shortcuts

When working with a disk or in a drive where many folders and folders within folders have been created, the Create <u>S</u>hortcut option from the Open or Save As dialog boxes shortcut menus can be very useful. With the Create <u>S</u>hortcut option, you create a shortcut document name that "points" to the original document. This shortcut name does not contain the original document—it is simply a marker that lets you quickly open the document.

For example, suppose you have a disk in drive A with the following folders: *Contracts*, *Insurance*, and *Liability*. *Liability* is a folder within *Insurance*, which is a folder within *Contracts*. You have saved a document named *Auto Insurance* in the *Liability* folder. You use this document on a consistent basis and would like to open the document without always having to change to the *Liability* folder. To do this, you can create a shortcut document name that displays in the main folder for drive A. A shortcut document name is created in the folder where the original document is located and then cut and pasted to a different folder. Exercise 17 covers the steps to create and then cut and paste a shortcut document name.

exercise 17

Creating a Folder, Then Creating a Shortcut Document Name

1. Display the Open dialog box with *Chapter 05* the active folder and then make the following changes:
   a. Create a folder named *Tests*.
   b. Click the Up One Level button.
   c. Copy the document named Quiz to the *Tests* folder.
   d. With the *Tests* folder the active folder, rename Quiz to Telecommunications Test. (At the message asking if you are sure you want to change the name of the read-only file, click <u>Y</u>es. Depending on your system setup, you may need to add the file extension .doc to the document name.)
   e. Create a shortcut document name in the *Chapter 05* folder that "points" to the original document by completing the following steps:
      1) Position the mouse pointer on Telecommunications Test and then click the right mouse button.
      2) At the shortcut menu, click Create <u>S</u>hortcut. (This inserts the name Shortcut to Telecommunications Test in the Tests folder.)
      3) Position the mouse pointer on Shortcut to Telecommunications Test and then click the right mouse button.

      4) At the shortcut menu, click Cut.

      5) Click the Up One Level button to return to the *Chapter 05* folder.

      6) Position the mouse pointer in the white area in the Open dialog box list box and then click the *right* mouse button.

      7) At the shortcut menu, click Paste.

2. Click the Cancel button to close the Open dialog box.

3. Display the Open dialog box with *Chapter 05* the active folder and then open Telecommunications Test by double-clicking *Shortcut to Telecommunications Test*. (This opens the original document that is located in the Tests folder.)

4. Close Telecommunications Test.

5. Display the Open dialog box with *Chapter 05* the active folder, delete the *Tests* folder and all its contents, and then delete the Shortcut to Telecommunications Test document.

6. Close the Open dialog box.

Printing Documents

Up to this point, you have opened a document and then printed it. At the Open dialog box, you can use the Print option from the Tools drop-down menu or the Print option from the shortcut menu to print a document or several documents without opening them.

Printing Documents

1. Display the Open dialog box with *Chapter 05* the active folder.

2. Select *Para 01*, *Para 02*, and *Para 03*.

3. Click the Tools button on the dialog box toolbar.

4. At the drop-down menu that displays, click Print.

      In chapter 1, you learned to print the document displayed in the document screen at the Print dialog box. By default, one copy of all pages of the currently open document is printed. With options at the Print dialog box, you can specify the number of copies to print and also specific pages for printing. To display the Print dialog box shown in figure 5.4, click File and then Print.

figure
5.4

Print Dialog Box

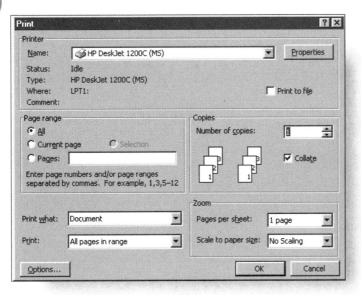

Selecting Printers

The name of the selected printer displays in the <u>N</u>ame text box in the Printer section of the Print dialog box. If more than one printer was selected when Microsoft Office was installed, you can select another printer at the Print dialog box. To display a list of installed printers, click the down-pointing triangle to the right of the <u>N</u>ame text box. Select the desired printer from the drop-down list by clicking the printer name.

Each printer has a set of properties that can be viewed by clicking the <u>P</u>roperties button at the Print dialog box. The options at the Properties dialog box will vary with each printer. At the Properties dialog box, you are able to set such options as paper size, layout, orientation, paper source, and print quality. If a color printer is selected, color options can also be set.

If you want to cancel the current print job, double-click the *Print Status* icon on the Status bar (located at the right side). Depending on how much of the document has been sent to the printer, this may or may not stop the printing of the entire document.

Printing Specific Text or Pages

The Page range section of the Print dialog box contains settings you can use to specify the amount of text you want printed. At the default setting of <u>A</u>ll, all pages of the current document are printed. Choose the Curr<u>e</u>nt page option to print the page where the insertion point is located. If you want to select and then print a portion of the document, choose the Selectio<u>n</u> option at the Print dialog box. This prints only the text that has been selected in the current document. (This option is dimmed unless text is selected in the document.)

With the Pages option, you can identify a specific page, multiple pages, and/or a range of pages. If you want specific multiple pages printed, use a comma (,) to indicate *and* and use a hyphen (-) to indicate *through*. For example, to print pages 2 and 5, you would key **2,5** in the Pages text box. To print pages 6 through 10, you would key **6-10**.

Printing Specific Pages

1. Open Report 01.
2. Print pages 1 and 4 of the report by completing the following steps:
   a. Display the Print dialog box by clicking <u>F</u>ile and then <u>P</u>rint.
   b. At the Print dialog box, click Pages.
   c. Key **1,4** in the Pages text box.
   d. Click OK or press Enter.
3. Close Report 01.

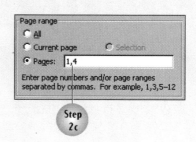

Step 2c

Printing Multiple Copies

If you want to print more than one copy of a document, use the Number of <u>c</u>opies option from the Print dialog box. To print more copies of the document, increase the number in the Number of <u>c</u>opies text box.

If you print several copies of a document containing multiple pages, Word prints the pages in the document collated. For example, if you print two copies of a three-page document, pages 1, 2, and 3 are printed, and then the pages are printed a second time. Printing pages collated is helpful but takes more printing time. To speed up the printing time, you can tell Word <u>not</u> to print the pages collated. However, time is required to manually arrange the pages into sets. To do this, remove the check mark from the Colla<u>t</u>e option at the Print dialog box. With the check mark removed, Word will print all copies of the first page, then all copies of the second page, and so on.

Printing Multiple Copies of a Document

1. Open Memo 01.
2. Print three copies of the document by completing the following steps:
   a. Display the Print dialog box.
   b. Key **3**. (The insertion point is automatically positioned in the Number of <u>c</u>opies text box when the Print dialog box displays.)
   c. Click OK or press Enter.
3. Close Memo 01.

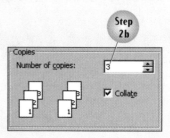

Step 2b

Printing Specific Parts of a Document

By default, Word prints the document currently displayed in the document screen. With Print _what_ options you can print various parts of a document. If you click the down-pointing triangle after the Print _what_ text box, a drop-down list displays with the options _Document_, _Document properties_, _Comments_, _Styles_, _AutoText entries_, and _Key assignments_. As you learn about these options, you can print these sections by clicking the desired option.

Printing Document Properties

1. Open Ch 05, Ex 15.
2. Print only the document properties by completing the following steps:
   a. Click File and then Print.
   b. At the Print dialog box, click the down-pointing triangle at the right side of the Print _what_ list box, and then click _Document properties_ at the drop-down list.

   c. Click OK.
3. Close Ch 05, Ex 15.

Printing Odd and/or Even Pages

If you are printing on both sides of the paper, the Odd pages and Even pages selections from the Print option are useful. For example, you can print all odd pages in the document, turn the pages over, and then print all even pages on the back side. To print odd or even pages, display the Print dialog box. At the Print dialog box, click the down-pointing triangle at the right side of the Print text box, and then click _Odd pages_ or _Even pages_.

Printing Odd-Numbered Pages

1. Open Report 03.
2. Print only odd-numbered pages by completing the following steps:
   a. Display the Print dialog box.
   b. At the Print dialog box, click the down-pointing triangle at the right side of the Print text box, and then click _Odd pages_ at the drop-down list.

   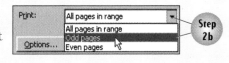

   c. Click OK or press Enter.
3. Close Report 03.

Changing Print Options

Clicking the Options button at the Print dialog box causes the Print dialog box with the Print tab selected to display as shown in figure 5.5.

figure
5.5

Print Dialog Box with Print Tab Selected

With the selections from the Printing options section, you can print the document in draft, reverse the print order (last pages first, etc.), and update fields and links. With the Include with document options, you can identify what additional information or text you wanted printed with the document, such as the document properties information, comments, or hidden text.

exercise

Printing a Document in Reverse Order

1. Open Report 04.
2. Print this document in reverse order by completing the following steps:
   a. Display the Print dialog box.
   b. Click the Options button.
   c. At the Print dialog box with the Print tab selected, click Reverse print order. (This inserts a check mark in the check box.)
   d. Click OK or press Enter.
   e. At the Print dialog box, click OK or press Enter.

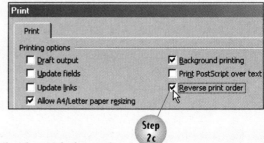

Step 2c

3. After the document is printed, remove the check mark from the Reverse print order check box by completing the following steps:

     a. Display the Print dialog box.
     b. Click the Options button.
     c. At the Print dialog box with the Print tab selected, click Reverse print order. (This removes the check mark from the check box.)
     d. Click OK or press Enter.
     e. At the Print dialog box, click Close.
  4. Close Report 04.

Printing Envelopes

With Word's envelope feature you can create and print an envelope. You can use the delivery address in the current document or enter the delivery address and return address at the Envelopes and Labels dialog box.

Creating an Envelope at a Clear Document Screen

To create an envelope at a clear document screen using the envelope feature, display the Envelopes and Labels dialog box shown in figure 5.6 by clicking Tools, and then Envelopes and Labels. At the Envelopes and Labels dialog box with the Envelopes tab selected, key the delivery address. (When the Envelopes and Labels dialog box displays, the insertion point is automatically positioned in the Delivery address text box.) Press the Enter key to end each line in the address. Click in the Return address text box, and then key the return address. Press the Enter key to end each line in the address. Click the Print button to print the envelope or click the Add to Document button to insert the envelope delivery address and return address in the current document screen formatted for an envelope. Word uses 12-point Arial for the delivery address and 10-point Arial for the return address.

figure

5.6 *Envelopes and Labels Dialog Box with Envelopes Tab Selected*

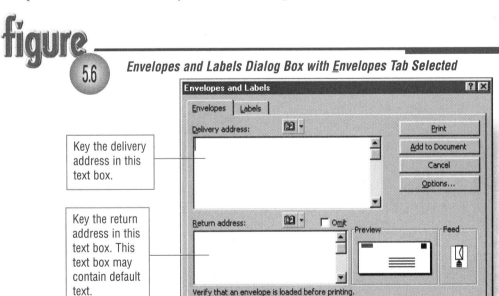

If you entered a return address before printing the envelope, Word will display the question *"Do you want to save the new return address as the default return address?"* At this question, click Yes if you want the current return address available for future envelopes. Click No if you do not want the current return address used as the default.

When you send the envelope text to the printer, you may be prompted to insert the envelope in the printer. This depends on the printer you are using.

If a default return address displays in the <u>R</u>eturn address section of the dialog box, you can tell Word to omit the return address when printing the envelope by clicking the O<u>m</u>it check box.

The Envelopes and Labels dialog box contains a Preview sample box and a Feed sample box. The Preview sample box shows how the envelope will appear when printed and the Feed sample box shows how the envelope will be inserted into the printer.

Printing an Envelope

1. At a clear document screen, create an envelope that prints the delivery address and return address shown in figure 5.7 by completing the following steps:
   a. Click <u>T</u>ools and then <u>E</u>nvelopes and Labels.
   b. At the Envelopes and Labels dialog box with the <u>E</u>nvelopes tab selected, key the delivery address shown in figure 5.7 (the one containing the name *Mrs. Roseanne Moore*). (Press the Enter key to end each line in the name and address.)
   c. Click in the <u>R</u>eturn address text box.
   d. Key the return address shown in figure 5.7 (the one containing the name *Mr. Thomas Aniston*). (Press the Enter key to end each line in the name and address.)
   e. Click the <u>A</u>dd to Document button.
   f. At the message, *Do you want to save the new return address as the default return address?*, click <u>N</u>o.
2. Save the document and name it Ch 05, Ex 24.
3. Print and then close Ch 05, Ex 24.

Exercise 24

Mr. Thomas Aniston
1210 South Alameda
Santa Fe, NM 77342

                            Mrs. Roseanne Moore
                            321 Aurora Boulevard
                            Santa Fe, NM 78329

Creating an Envelope with an Existing Document

If you open the Envelopes and Labels dialog box in a document containing a name and address, the name and address are automatically inserted in the Delivery address section of the dialog box. To do this, open a document containing a name and address, and then display the Envelopes and Labels dialog box.

In exercise 24, you added the envelope to the current document. At the Envelopes and Labels dialog box, you can send the envelope directly to the printer without inserting it in the document. To do this, click the Print button instead of the Add to Document button. When you click the Print button, the envelope is sent directly to the printer (but not the text in the document).

Creating an Envelope in an Existing Document

1. Open Letter 01.
2. Create and print an envelope for the document by completing the following steps:
   a. Click Tools and then Envelopes and Labels.
   b. At the Envelopes and Labels dialog box with the Envelopes tab selected, make sure the delivery address displays properly in the Delivery address section.
   c. If any text displays in the Return address section, insert a check mark in the Omit check box, which is located to the right of the Return address option. (This tells Word not to print the return address on the envelope.)
   d. Click the Print button.
3. Close Letter 01 without saving the changes.

Changing Envelope Options

If you click the Options button at the Envelopes and Labels dialog box, the Envelope Options dialog box with the Envelope Options tab selected displays as shown in figure 5.8.

Envelope Options Dialog Box with Envelope Options Tab Selected

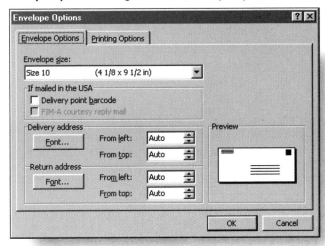

Word provides a variety of envelope sizes from which you can choose. To view the list of envelope sizes, click the down-pointing triangle at the right side of the Envelope size text box. You can include a delivery point bar code for the delivery address at the Envelope Options dialog box. The bar code is a machine-readable representation of the Zip Code and speeds mail sorting, increases the accuracy of delivery, and reduces postage costs.

To create a delivery point bar code for the delivery address, click Delivery point barcode at the Envelope Options dialog box. Word automatically converts the Zip Code displayed in the Delivery address section of the Envelopes and Labels dialog box into vertical lines that create the bar code.

The Envelope Options dialog box also contains a FIM-A courtesy reply mail option. This option is dimmed unless the Delivery point barcode option is selected. A FIM (Facing Identification Mark) identifies the front (face) of the envelope during presorting. A courtesy reply envelope is provided as a service to the recipient and is preprinted with the sender's name and address. To add a FIM to an envelope, click the FIM-A courtesy reply mail option at the Envelope Options dialog box.

The delivery address and the return address will print with the default font. If you want to change the delivery address font, click the Font button at the Envelope Options dialog box. This displays the Envelope Address dialog box with the Font tab selected. The options at the Envelope Address dialog box with the Font tab selected are the same as the options available at the Font dialog box. At this dialog box, choose the desired font and then click OK or press Enter. This returns you to the Envelope Options dialog box.

To change the font for the return address, click the Font button at the Envelope Options dialog box. This displays the Envelope Address dialog box with the Font tab selected. Choose the desired font at this dialog box and then click OK or press Enter.

Word automatically determines the location of the delivery and return addresses from the top and left edges of the envelope. If you want to control where the delivery address is printed on the envelope, enter the desired measurement in the From left text box at the Envelope Options dialog box. Enter the desired top measurement in the From top text box. Enter the desired measurements in the From left and From top text boxes for the return address.

The Preview box at the Envelope Options dialog box displays how the envelope will appear when printed. The Preview box changes as changes are made to the dialog box.

If you click the Printing Options tab at the Envelope Options dialog box, the dialog box displays as shown in figure 5.9.

figure

5.9 Envelope Options Dialog Box with Printing Options Tab Selected

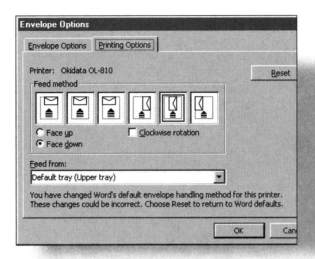

Word determines the feed method for envelopes and the feed form. If this method does not work for your printer, choose the correct feed method and feed form at the Envelope Options dialog box with the Printing Options tab selected. Feed methods are visually displayed at the dialog box. You can also determine if the envelope is fed into the printer face up or face down.

exercise

Creating an Envelope with a Delivery Point Bar Code and a FIM

1. Open Letter 03.
2. Save the document with Save As and name it Ch 05, Ex 26.
3. Select the entire letter, change the font to 12-point Bookman Old Style (or a similar serif typeface such as Century Schoolbook or Garamond), and then deselect the letter.
4. Create an envelope for the letter, add a delivery point bar code and a FIM to the envelope, and change the font of the delivery address by completing the following steps:
   a. Click Tools and then Envelopes and Labels.
   b. At the Envelopes and Labels dialog box with the Envelopes tab selected, delete any text that may display in the Return address text box. (If there is a check mark in the Omit check box, click Omit to remove the check mark, and then delete any text in the Return address text box.)
   c. Click the Options button.
   d. At the Envelope Options dialog box, click the Envelope Options tab.

e. At the Envelope Options dialog box with the Envelope Options tab selected, click Delivery point barcode. (This inserts a check mark in the check box.)
f. Click FIM-A courtesy reply mail.
g. Click the Font button (immediately below Delivery address).
h. At the Envelope Address dialog box with the Font tab selected, click *Bookman Old Style* (or the serif typeface name you chose in step 3) in the Font list box. (You will need to scroll up the list box to display this font.)
i. Make sure *12* displays in the Size list box.
j. Click OK or press Enter.
k. At the Envelope Options dialog box, click OK or press Enter.
l. At the Envelopes and Labels dialog box, click the Add to Document button.

5. Save the document again with the same name (Ch 05, Ex 26).
6. Print and then close Ch 05, Ex 26.

Printing Labels

Use Word's labels feature to print text on mailing labels, file labels, disk labels, or other types of labels. Word includes a variety of predefined labels that can be purchased at an office supply store. To create a sheet of mailing labels with the same name and address using the default options, click Tools and then Envelopes and Labels. At the Envelopes and Labels dialog box, click the Labels tab. At the Envelopes and Labels dialog box with the Labels tab selected, as displayed in figure 5.10, key the desired address in the Address text box. Click the New Document button to insert the mailing label in a new document or click the Print button to send the mailing label directly to the printer.

figure

5.10   *Envelopes and Labels Dialog Box with Labels Tab Selected*

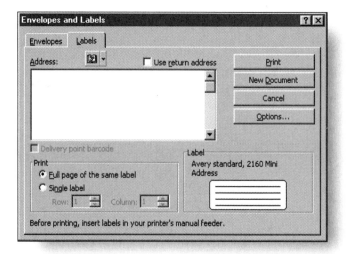

If you open the Envelopes and Labels dialog box (with the Labels tab selected) in a document containing a name and address, the name and address are automatically inserted in the Address section of the dialog box. To enter different names in each of the mailing labels, you would start at a clear document screen, and then click Tools and then Envelopes and Labels. At the Envelopes and Labels dialog box, click the Labels tab, and then click the New Document button. When you click the New Document button, the Envelopes and Labels dialog box is removed from the screen and the document screen displays with label forms. The insertion point is positioned in the first label form. Key the name and address in this label and then press the Tab key to move the insertion point to the next label. Pressing Shift + Tab will move the insertion point to the preceding label.

Creating Mailing Labels

1. Open Letter 02.
2. Create mailing labels with the delivery address by completing the following steps:
   a. Click Tools and then Envelopes and Labels.
   b. At the Envelopes and Labels dialog box, click the Labels tab.
   c. Make sure the delivery address displays properly in the Address section.
   d. Click the New Document button.
3. Save the mailing label document and name it Ch 05, Ex 27.
4. Print and then close Ch 05, Ex 27.
5. Close Letter 02.

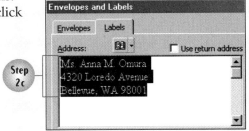

Changing Label Options

If you click the Options button at the Envelopes and Labels dialog box with the Labels tab selected, the Label Options dialog box shown in figure 5.11 displays.

5.11 **Label Options Dialog Box**

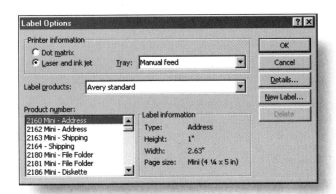

In the Printer information section of the dialog box, the type of printer you are using is displayed. If you are using a laser printer, you can specify where labels are located. The default setting depends on the selected printer.

The Label products option lets you choose from options such as Avery standard, Avery A4 and A5 sizes, Formtec, Pimaco, Zweckform, and Other. This list will vary depending on the selected printer. The list of labels in the Product number list box will change depending on what label product you select.

To select a different label product number, click the desired label in the Product number list box. When you select a label, information about that label is displayed in the Label information section of the Label Options dialog box including the type, height, width, and paper size. When you select a label, Word automatically determines label margins. If, however, you want to customize these default settings, click the Details button at the Label Options dialog box.

exercise 28

Creating Customized Mailing Labels

1. At a clear document screen, create mailing labels by completing the following steps:
   a. Click Tools and then Envelopes and Labels.
   b. Make sure the Labels tab is selected. (If not, click Labels.)
   c. Click the Options button.
   d. At the Label Options dialog box, make sure *Avery standard* displays in the Label products text box.
   e. Click the down-pointing triangle at the right side of the Product number list box until *5662 - Address* is visible and then click *5662 - Address*.
   f. Click OK or press Enter.
   g. At the Envelopes and Labels dialog box, click the New Document button.
   h. At the document screen, key the first name and address shown in figure 5.12 in the first label.
   i. Press Tab to move the insertion point to the next label and then key the second name and address shown in figure 5.12. Continue in this manner until all names and addresses have been keyed.
2. Save the document and name it Ch 05, Ex 28.
3. Print and then close Ch 05, Ex 28.
4. At the clear document screen, close the document screen.

Step 1d

Step 1e

Exercise 28

Ms. Barbara Peralt
9832 Meander Way
Harrisburg, PA 34201

Mr. Paul Tsukamoto
12032 North 32nd Street
Hershey, PA 32102

Mrs. Darlene Emerson
10293 Margate Drive
Carlisle, PA 34102

Mr. and Mrs. Marc Cross
7543 160th Street East
Harrisburg, PA 34095

Sending a Word Document by E-mail

Computers within a company can be connected by a private network referred to
as an "intranet." With an intranet, employees within a company can send a Word
document by e-mail. To send a Word document by e-mail, you will need to have
Outlook available on your system. System configurations can be quite varied and
you may find that your screen does not exactly match what you see in the figure
in this section. Steps in exercise 29 may need to be modified to accommodate
your system.

To send a document by e-mail, open the document in Word, and then click
the E-mail button on the Standard toolbar. (You can also click File, point to Send
To, and then click Mail Recipient.) This displays the e-mail header below the
Formatting toolbar as shown in figure 5.13. When the e-mail header displays,
Outlook is automatically opened.

E-mail Header

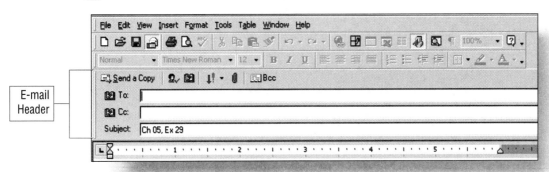

At the e-mail header, fill in the recipient information and then click the <u>S</u>end a Copy button. Word sends a copy of the document to the recipient and closes the e-mail header. The original document remains open for editing. When the document is saved, the e-mail information is saved with the document.

The e-mail header contains buttons you can use to customize the e-mail message. Buttons are available for sending a copy of a document, selecting a name from an address book, establishing a priority level, and specifying delivery options.

In exercise 29 you will send the e-mail to your instructor. If your system is networked and your computer is not part of an intranet system, skip step 3d (clicking the <u>S</u>end a Copy button).

Creating and Printing an Outlook e-mail Message

(Note: Before completing this exercise, check to see if you can send e-mail messages. If you cannot, consider completing all the steps in the exercise except step 3d.)

1. Open Contract 02.
2. Save the document with Save As and name it Ch 05, Ex 29.
3. Send Ch 05, Ex 29 by e-mail by completing the following steps:
    a. Click the E-mail button on the Standard toolbar.
    b. At the e-mail header, key your instructor's name in the To text box. (Depending on how the system is configured, you may need to key your instructor's e-mail address.)
    c. Click the down-pointing triangle at the right side of the Set Priority button and then click <u>H</u>igh Priority at the drop-down list.
    d. Click the <u>S</u>end a Copy button.
    e. If necessary, click the E-mail button on the Standard toolbar to turn off the display of the e-mail header.
4. Save the document again with the same name (Ch 05, Ex 29).
5. Close the Ch 05, Ex 29 document.

chapter summary

➤ Word documents are grouped logically into folders. A new folder can be created at the Open dialog box or the Save As dialog box.

➤ One document or several documents can be selected at the Open dialog box. A document or selected documents can be copied, moved, renamed, deleted, printed, or opened.

➤ A copy of a document can be made by opening the document and then saving it with a different name. A document can also be copied with the Copy option from the Open dialog box shortcut menu. A document or selected documents can be copied to the same folder or to a different folder. If a document is copied to the same folder, Word adds *Copy of* before the document name.

➤ Use the Cut and Paste options from the Open dialog box shortcut menu to move a document from one folder to another.

➤ Use the Rename option from the Open dialog box Tools drop-down menu or the shortcut menu to give a document a different name.

➤ Documents and/or folders can be deleted with the Delete button on the Open or Save As dialog box toolbar or the Delete option from the shortcut menu. Documents deleted from the hard drive are sent to the Windows Recycle Bin. Documents can be emptied or recovered from the Recycle Bin at the Windows desktop.

➤ Several documents can be opened at one time at the Open dialog box. All open documents can be closed at the same time by holding down the Shift key, clicking File, and then clicking Close All.

➤ A document can be opened as read-only. A read-only document must be saved with a different name from the original.

➤ You can protect a document from being opened by other users or from being modified by requiring a password.

➤ Display document properties information about a document or add information to the document properties by clicking the Properties option from the Open dialog box shortcut menu. You can also display document properties by clicking File and then Properties.

➤ Additional information about documents can be displayed at the Open or Save As dialog box by choosing different options from the Views button on the dialog box toolbar. In addition to a list of documents, information such as the type and size of the document can be displayed; information about the properties of each document can be displayed; and a portion of each document can be displayed to the right of the list box.

➤ A shortcut document name can be created in a different folder than the original document that "points" to the original document. This shortcut name does not contain the original document; it is simply a marker that lets you quickly open the document.

➤ A document or selected documents can be printed at the Open dialog box.

➤ Use options at the Print dialog box to customize a print job.

➤ To cancel a print job, double-click the *Print Status* icon on the Status bar (located at the far right side).

➤ The Page range section of the Print dialog box contains settings you can use to specify the amount of text you want printed. With the Pages option, you can identify a specific page for printing, multiple pages, and/or a range of pages. You can also specify a section to be printed or pages within a section for printing.

➤ You can select text and then print only the selected text.

➤ Use the Number of copies option at the Print dialog box to print more than one copy of a document.

➤ Print various parts of a document with the Print what options at the Print dialog box.

➤ The Odd pages and Even pages selections from the Print option are useful if you are printing on both sides of the paper.

➤ With Word's envelope feature you can create and print an envelope at the Envelopes and Labels dialog box.

➤ If you open the Envelopes and Labels dialog box in a document containing a name and address, that information is automatically inserted in the Delivery address section of the dialog box.

➤ You can include a delivery point bar code for the delivery address at the Envelope Options dialog box.

➤ These additional options are available at the Envelope Options dialog box: Envelope size, FIM-A courtesy reply mail, delivery and return address fonts, and options to change the top and left measurements for the delivery and return addresses.

➤ Use Word's labels feature to print text on mailing labels, file labels, disk labels, or other types of labels.

➤ These additional options are available at the Label Options dialog box: Printer information, Label products (to choose the type of label), and Details (to change label margins).

➤ When computers are connected by an intranet, a Word document can be sent by e-mail. Click the E-mail button on the Standard toolbar to display the e-mail header.

commands review

	Mouse/Keyboard
Open dialog box	File, Open; or click the Open button on Standard toolbar
Save As dialog box	File, Save As
Close all open documents	Hold Shift key, click File, Close All
Display document properties	File, Properties
Print dialog box	File, Print
Envelopes and Labels dialog box	Tools, Envelopes and Labels
Display e-mail header	Click E-mail button on Standard toolbar; or click File, point to Send To, then click Mail Recipient

thinking offline

Completion: In the space provided at the right, indicate the correct term, symbol, or command.

1. A new folder can be created with this button at the Open or Save As dialog box.

2. Click this button at the Open or Save As dialog box to change to the folder that is up one level from the current folder.

3. To select documents at the Open dialog box that are not adjacent using the mouse, hold down this key while clicking the desired documents.

4. A document can be copied to another folder without opening the document using the <u>C</u>opy option and this option from the Open dialog box shortcut menu.

5. To close all open documents at once, hold down this key, click <u>F</u>ile, and then <u>C</u>lose All.

6. When a document or selected documents are deleted from the hard drive, the documents are sent to this bin.

7. When specifying a range of pages to be printed, this character indicates *and*.

8. When specifying a range of pages to be printed, this character indicates *through*.

9. To print pages 1 through 4 in a document, key this in the Pages text box at the Print dialog box.

10. Key this in the Pages text box at the Print dialog box to print pages 2, 4, and 6 through 12.

11. To display the Envelopes and Labels dialog box, click this option on the Menu bar, and then click <u>E</u>nvelopes and Labels.

12. If you open the Envelopes and Labels dialog box in a document containing a name and address, the name and address are automatically inserted in this section of the dialog box.

13. Include this bar code on an envelope to speed mail sorting, increase the accuracy of delivery, and reduce postage costs.

14. The letters FIM in FIM-A courtesy reply mail stand for this.

15. Click the E-mail button on this toolbar to display the e-mail header.

16. In the space provided, list the steps you would complete to create a folder named *Finances*.

_____

_____

_____

17. In the space provided, list the steps you would complete to open several consecutive documents at one time.

_____

_____

_____

working hands-on

Assessment 1

1. Display the Open dialog box and then create a new folder named *Letters*.
2. Copy (be sure to use the Copy option and not the Cut option) all documents beginning with *Letter* into the *Letters* folder.
3. With the *Letters* folder as the active folder, rename the following documents:
   a. Rename Letter 01 to Donovan.
   b. Rename Letter 02 to Omura.
4. Make *Chapter 05* the active folder.
5. Close the Open dialog box.

Assessment 2

1. Display the Open dialog box with *Chapter 05* the active folder and then complete the following steps:
   a. Delete the documents named *Copy of Para 01*, *Copy of Para 02*, and *Copy of Para 03*.
   b. Delete the *Letters* folder and all documents contained within it.
2. Close the Open dialog box.

Assessment 3

1. Display the Open dialog box and then find the total number of words in the following documents:
   a. Contract 02
   b. Report 03
2. With the Open dialog box still displayed, change to the Details view and then determine the size (in kilobytes) of the following documents:
   a. Memo 01
   b. Letter 01
   c. Report 01
3. Change back to the List view.
4. Open Report 01.
5. Print only the document properties for Report 01.
6. Close Report 01.

Assessment 4

1. Open Report 02.
2. Print two copies of page 2, displaying the Print dialog box only once.
3. Close Report 02.

Assessment 5

1. Open Report 03.
2. Save the document with Save As and name it Ch 05, SA 05.
3. Make the following changes to the document:
   a. Change the top and bottom margins to 1.5 inches.
   b. Bold the two titles and all the headings in the document.
4. Save the document again with the same name (Ch 05, SA 05).
5. Print pages 2 through 4 of the report.
6. Close Ch 05, SA 05.

Assessment 6

1. At a clear document screen, create an envelope that prints the delivery address and return address shown in figure 5.14. Include the delivery point bar code and the FIM. Add the envelope to the document.
2. Save the envelope document and name it Ch 05, SA 06.
3. Print and then close Ch 05, SA 06.

Assessment 6

Ms. Gina McCammon
2003 Rydale Drive
Boston, MA 20192

Mr. Matthew Williams
5554 Kensington Place
Boston, MA 20843

Assessment 7

1. Open Letter 03.
2. Create mailing labels with the delivery address.
3. Save the labels as a new document and name it Ch 05, SA 07.
4. Print and then close Ch 05, SA 07.
5. Close Letter 03.

Performance *Unit One*

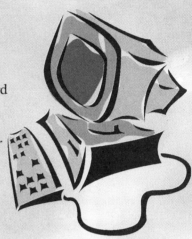

Unit 01 PA

Assessments

PREPARING AND MANAGING DOCUMENTS

DEMONSTRATING YOUR SKILLS

In this unit, you have learned to create, edit, format, save, and print Word documents, and manage documents on disk.

(Before completing unit assessments, delete the Chapter 05 *folder on your disk. Next, copy the* Unit 01 *folder from the CD that accompanies this textbook to your disk and then make* Unit 01 *the active folder.)*

Assessment 1

1. At a clear document screen, key the text shown in figure U1.1.
2. Save the document and name it Unit 1, PA 01.
3. Print and then close Unit 1, PA 01.

GLOSSARY

Application: A piece of software, such as a word processing or spreadsheet program, used to perform specialized functions.

Baud rate: The number of times per second that a modem adjusts its signal frequency, sometimes improperly used to refer to transmission speed, which is properly measured in bits per second or bps.

Cache memory: A holding area in which the data and instructions most recently called from RAM by the processor are temporarily stored in order to speed up processing.

Debug: To find and fix a problem in a piece of hardware or software.

Encryption: The process of translating a file into a form that cannot easily be read by another without a key for decoding it.

Figure U1.1 • Assessment 1

Assessment 2

1. Open Unit 1, PA 01.
2. Save the document with Save As and name it Unit 1, PA 02.
3. Make the following changes to the document:
   a. Change the top, left, and right margins to 1.5 inches.
   b. Select the paragraphs that begin with bolded words, change the paragraph alignment to justified, and then insert numbering.
   c. Select the entire document and then change the font to 12-point Century Schoolbook (or a similar serif typeface).
4. Save the document again with the same name (Unit 1, PA 02).
5. Print and then close Unit 1, PA 02.

Assessment 3

1. At a clear document screen, key the text shown in figure U1.2 with the following specifications:
   a. Change the font to 20-point Tahoma bold and the color to dark blue.
   b. Animate the title *Networking Training* with an animation effect of your choosing. (The animation effect will not print.)
   c. Change the line spacing to 1.5 for the entire document.
   d. Center the text vertically on the page.
2. Save the document and name it Unit 1, PA 03.
3. Print and then close Unit 1, PA 03.

Networking Training
Thursday, June 14, 2001
Corporate Headquarters
Conference Room A
8:30 a.m. - 4:30 p.m.

Figure U1.2 • Assessment 3

Assessment 4

1. At a clear document screen, key the document (but not the bullets) shown in figure U1.3.
2. After keying the document, complete the following steps:
   a. Insert the bullets before the paragraphs of text as shown in figure U1.3.
   b. Select the entire document and then change the font to a serif typeface other than Times New Roman.
   c. Set the title *COMPUTER SPEED* in 14-point Arial bold.
   d. Select the first sentence of each bulleted item and then turn on bold.
   e. Change the alignment to justified for all paragraphs in the document except the title.
3. Save the document and name it Unit 1, PA 04.
4. Print and then close Unit 1, PA 04.

COMPUTER SPEED

One of the most frustrating of all computer experiences is waiting for the machine to load a program, save a file, or execute a command. Therefore, speed is important. Some factors that affect how quickly a computer runs include:

- Processor design. Generally speaking, newer processors are faster than older ones.

- Clock speed. Every personal computer has an internal clock that synchronizes events within the computer, in effect turning the processor on and off very rapidly, at speeds measured in megahertz, or millions of cycles per second. The higher the megahertz speed, the faster the computer.

- Presence and size of cache memory. Cache memory can speed up processing by reducing the number of calls that the processor makes to RAM.

- RAM size. The amount of RAM in a computer should be sufficient to accommodate the operating system, one or more open application programs, and files of whatever size with which the user commonly works.

Figure U1.3 • Assessment 4

Assessment 5

1. Open Letter 04.
2. Save the document with Save As and name it Unit 1, PA 05.
3. Create an envelope for the letter that includes the delivery point bar code and the FIM and add the envelope to the document.
4. Save the document again with the same name (Unit 1, PA 05).
5. Print only the envelope.
6. Close Unit 1, PA 05.

Assessment 6

1. Open Letter 04.
2. Create mailing labels with the delivery address. (You determine the type of mailing labels.)
3. Save the labels as a new document and name it Unit 1, PA 06.
4. Print and then close Unit 1, PA 06.
5. Close Letter 04 without saving the changes.

Assessment 7

1. At a clear document screen, create the document shown in figure U1.4 with the following specifications:
   a. Center, bold, and italicize the text as indicated.
   b. Use the automatic bullet feature to create the arrow bullets. *(Hint: To create the arrow bullet, key >, press the spacebar once, and then key the text following the bullet.)*
   c. After keying the document, change the left and right margins to 1.5 inches.
2. Save the document and name it Unit 1, PA 07.
3. Print Unit 1, PA 07.
4. Select the bulleted paragraphs and change to numbers (use the Numbering button on the Formatting toolbar).
5. Save the document again with the same name (Unit 1, PA 07).
6. Print and then close Unit 1, PA 07.

E-MAIL

A common use of the Internet, one that is transforming business and personal life, is *e-mail*, which is the transmission of messages, with or without attached files, over a network. E-mail has many advantages over traditional mail:

➤ It can be sent at any time.
➤ It is almost instantaneous, arriving at its destination in less than thirty minutes, even if that destination is across the globe.
➤ It costs much less than overnight or second-day delivery and does not involve long-distance telephone charges, as faxing does.
➤ It requires no special postage or handling.

For years, businesses have used e-mail over internal networks for communication among employees. Today, e-mail via the Internet is widely used for communication between connected individuals, businesses, and organizations.

Figure U1.4 • Assessment 7

Assessment 8

1. Open Report 04.
2. Save the document with Save As and name it Unit 1, PA 08.
3. Make the following changes to the document:
    a. Change the top margin to 1.5 inches, the left and right margins to 1 inch, turn on Mirror margins, and change the gutter margin to 0.5 inch.
    b. Select the entire document and then change to a serif typeface (other than Times New Roman) in 12-point size.
    c. Set the two titles, *MODULE 3: DESIGNING A NEWSLETTER* and *MODULE 4: CREATING NEWSLETTER LAYOUT*, in 14-point Arial bold.
    d. Set the heading *Applying Desktop Publishing Guidelines* in 14-point Arial bold.
    e. Use Format Painter to set the remaining headings (*Choosing Paper Size and Type, Choosing Paper Weight,* and *Creating Margins for Newsletters*) in 14-point Arial bold.
    f. Insert a page break at the title *MODULE 4: CREATING NEWSLETTER LAYOUT.*
4. Check page breaks in the document and, if necessary, adjust the page breaks.
5. Save the document again with the same name (Unit 1, PA 08).
6. Print and then close Unit 1, PA 08.

Assessment 9

1. Open Quiz.
2. Save the document with Save As and name it Unit 1, PA 09.
3. Make the following changes to the document:
   a. Delete the blank line after the title.
   b. Delete the blank lines at the end of the document.
   c. Select the entire document and then change to a serif typeface (other than Times New Roman) in 12-point size.
   d. Set the title *CHAPTER QUIZ* in 14-point size.
   e. Select the paragraphs of text (other than the title) and insert automatic numbering.
   f. Deselect the text and then change the vertical alignment of the document to *Justified*.
   g. Change to the Print Layout view and then change the Zoom to *Whole Page*.
   h. Change the Zoom back to *100%* and then change back to Normal view.
4. Save the document again with the same name (Unit 1, PA 09).
5. Print Unit 1, PA 09.
6. With Unit 1, PA 09 still open, change the page orientation to Landscape.
7. Save the document again with the same name (Unit 1, PA 09).
8. Print and then close Unit 1, PA 09.

CREATING ORIGINAL DOCUMENTS

The following activities give you the opportunity to practice your writing skills along with demonstrating an understanding of some of the important Word features you have mastered in this unit. Follow the steps explained below to improve your writing skills.

The Writing Process

Plan Gather ideas, select which information to include, and choose the order in which to present the information.

Checkpoints
- What is the purpose?
- Who is the audience and what do you want them to do?
- What information do the readers need to reach your intended conclusion?

Write   Following the information plan and keeping the reader in mind, draft the document using clear, direct sentences that say what you mean.

> **Checkpoints**
> - What are the subpoints for each main thought?
> - What is the simplest way to state the key ideas and supporting information?
> - How can you connect paragraphs so the reader moves smoothly from one idea to the next?

Revise   Improve what is written by changing, deleting, rearranging, or adding words, sentences, and paragraphs.

> **Checkpoints**
> - Is the meaning clear?
> - Do the ideas follow a logical order?
> - Have you included any unnecessary information?
> - Have you built your sentences around strong nouns and verbs?

Edit   Check spelling, sentence construction, word use, punctuation, and capitalization.

> **Checkpoints**
> - Can you spot any redundancies or cliches?
> - Can you reduce any phrases to an effective word (for example, change *the fact that* to *because*)?
> - Have you used commas only where there is a strong reason for doing so?
> - Did you proofread the document for errors that your spell checker cannot identify?

Publish   Prepare a final copy that could be reproduced and shared with others.

> **Checkpoints**
> - Which design elements—for example, bolding and different fonts—would help highlight important ideas or sections?
> - Would charts or other graphics help clarify meaning?

Use correct grammar, appropriate word choices, and clear sentence constructions.

Assessment 10

Situation: You are the public relations officer for the Coleman Development Corporation and are responsible for preparing an announcement with the following information:

- Stephanie Branson has been appointed president by the Board of Trustees.
- She has 25 years of experience in the land management field and has spent the past 10 years as president of Lancaster, Inc.

- The selection process began over six months ago and included several interviews and visitations to Lancaster by several board members.
- An open house is planned for August 16, 2001, from 1:30 to 5:00 p.m. in the corporation's conference room.

Include a title for the announcement. Name the announcement Unit 1, PA 10. Print and then close Unit 1, PA 10.

Assessment 11

Situation: You are an employee with the Washington County Department of Emergency Management. Prepare a letter to Vicki Fortino, superintendent of Bakersville School District, thanking her for the inquiry about earthquake preparedness. In the letter, talk about the importance of earthquake preparedness for all schools. Tell her that a basic earthquake survival kit includes the following items:

Water (two quarts to one gallon per person per day)
First-aid kit and first-aid books
Food (packaged, canned, no-cook, baby food, and foods for special diets)
Can opener (nonelectric)
Blankets or sleeping bags
Portable radio, flashlight, spare batteries
Essential medicines and glasses
Fire extinguisher (A-B-C type)
Food and water for pets
Cash or currency

Send the letter to:

Vicki Fortino, Superintendent
Bakersville School District
6600 Northside Drive
Bakersville, OR 99702

Use your own name in the complimentary close. (Since you are writing the letter, you do not need to include typist's initials at the end of the document—just the document name.) When the letter is completed, create an envelope for the letter and add it to the document. Save the completed document and name it Unit 1, PA 11. Print and then close Unit 1, PA 11.

Unit two

FORMATTING AND ENHANCING DOCUMENTS

MICROSOFT® WORD 2000

MOUS SKILLS—UNIT TWO

Chapter 06

Using Writing Tools

PERFORMANCE OBJECTIVES

Upon successful completion of chapter 6, you will be able to:

- Complete a spelling check on text in a document.
- Improve the grammar of text in a document using the grammar checker.
- Add words to and delete words from the AutoCorrect dialog box.
- Display synonyms and antonyms for specific words using the Thesaurus.
- Display information about a document such as the number of pages, words, characters, paragraphs, and lines.
- Find specific text or formatting in a document.
- Find specific text or formatting in a document and replace it with other text or formatting.

Word 2000 includes writing tools to help create a thoughtful and well-written document. One of these writing tools, a spelling checker, finds misspelled words and offers replacement words. It also finds duplicate words and irregular capitalizations. A grammar checker finds grammar and style errors in documents and provides possible corrections. Another tool, the Thesaurus, provides a list of synonyms, antonyms, and related words for a particular word. Use the Find and Replace feature to find specific text or formatting and replace it with other text or formatting.

Checking the Spelling and Grammar of a Document

Two tools for creating thoughtful and well-written documents include a spelling checker and a grammar checker. The spelling checker finds misspelled words and offers replacement words. It also finds duplicate words and irregular capitalizations. When you spell check a document, the spelling checker compares the words in your document with the words in its dictionary. If a match is found, the word is passed over. If there is no match for the word, the spelling checker will stop and select:

- a misspelled word when the misspelling does not match another word that exists in the dictionary
- typographical errors such as transposed letters
- double word occurrences (such as *and and*)
- irregular capitalization
- some proper names
- jargon and some technical terms

A small number of words in the spelling checker dictionary are proper names. You will find that many proper names will not appear in this dictionary. The spelling checker will not find a match for these proper names and will select the words for correction. The spelling checker may not stop, however, at all proper names. For example, the spelling checker would assume the first name *June* is spelled correctly and pass over it because *June* would appear in its dictionary as a month.

The grammar checker will search a document for errors in grammar, style, punctuation, and word usage. The spelling checker and the grammar checker can help you create a well-written document but do not replace the need for proofreading.

Before checking the spelling or grammar of a document, save the document currently displayed or open a document. You would complete the following steps to check a document for spelling and grammar errors:

Spelling and Grammar

1. Click the Spelling and Grammar button on the Standard toolbar or click Tools and then Spelling and Grammar.
2. If a spelling error is detected, the misspelled word is selected and a Spelling and Grammar dialog box, similar to the one shown in figure 6.1, displays. The sentence containing the misspelled word is displayed in the Not in Dictionary: text box. If a grammatical error is detected, the sentence containing the error is selected and the Spelling and Grammar dialog box, similar to the one shown in figure 6.2, displays.
3. If a misspelled word is selected, replace the word with the correct spelling, tell Word to ignore it and continue checking the document, or add the word to a custom dictionary. If a sentence containing a grammatical error is selected, the grammar checker displays the sentence in the top text box in the Spelling and Grammar dialog box. Choose to ignore or change errors found by the grammar checker.
4. When the spelling and grammar check is completed, the message *The spelling and grammar check is complete* displays. Click anywhere in the document screen outside the message box to remove the box.

figure 6.1

Spelling and Grammar Dialog Box with Spelling Error Selected

The spelling checker stops at this misspelled word and offers this suggestion.

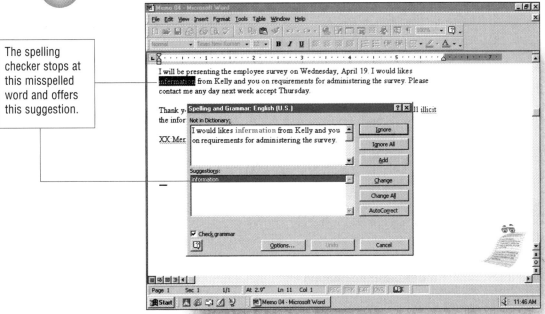

figure 6.2

Spelling and Grammar Dialog Box with Grammar Error Selected

The grammar checker selects this sentence and offers this suggestion to correct the grammar.

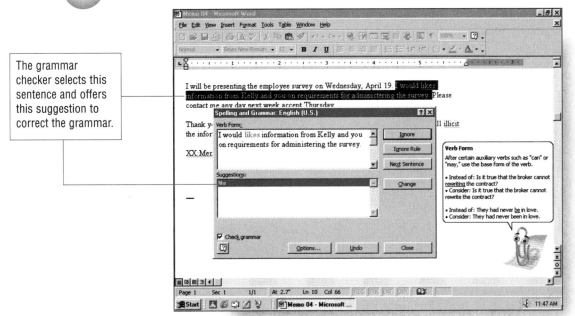

Spell Checking a Document

When a word is selected during a spelling and grammar check, you need to determine if the word should be corrected or if it should be ignored. Word provides buttons at the right side and bottom of the Spelling and Grammar dialog box to make decisions. The buttons and their functions are explained in figure 6.3.

figure
6.3

Spelling and Grammar Dialog Box Buttons

Button	Action
Ignore	Click the Ignore button to skip the current misspelled word.
Ignore All	Click the Ignore All button to skip all occurrences of the misspelled word in the document.
Add	Along with the spelling checker dictionary, a custom dictionary is available. Click the Add button if you want to add the selected word to the custom dictionary.
Change	Replace the selected word with the word in the Suggestions list box by clicking the Change button. (If you want to replace the selected word with one of the other words displayed in the Suggestions list box, double-click the desired word.)
Change All	If you want to correct the current word and the same word in other locations in the document, click the Change All button.
AutoCorrect	Misspelled words and the correct spelling can be added to the AutoCorrect list. When the spelling checker stops at a misspelled word, make sure the proper spelling is selected in the Suggestions list box, and then click the AutoCorrect button.
Undo	When the Spelling and Grammar dialog box first displays, the Undo button is dimmed. Once a spelling or grammar change is made, the Undo button becomes active. Click this button if you want to reverse the most recent spelling and grammar action.

By default, a spelling and grammar check are both completed on a document. If you want to check only the spelling in a document and not the grammar, remove the check mark from the Check grammar check box located in the lower left corner of the Spelling and Grammar dialog box.

Using Drop-Down Menus

As you learned in unit 1, Word 2000 contains adaptive menus. In chapters in unit 1, instructions were included for expanding drop-down menus. Beginning with this unit and continuing through the remainder of this textbook, the "expand the drop-down menu" instruction will not be included. If you cannot find a menu option, expand the drop-down menu. You might also consider turning off the adaptive menu feature. To do this, refer to the "Expanding Drop-Down Menus" section in chapter 1.

Spell Checking a Document

1. Open Memo 03.
2. Save the document with Save As and name it Ch 06, Ex 01.
3. Perform a spelling check by completing the following steps:
    a. Click the Spelling and Grammar button on the Standard toolbar (the seventh button from the left).
    b. The spelling checker selects the name *Drennan*. If the grammar checker is on, turn it off by clicking in the Chec_k_ grammar check box (located in the lower left corner of the dialog box) to remove the check mark. *Drennan* is a proper name, so click the _I_gnore button to tell the spelling checker to leave the name as written.
    c. The spelling checker selects the name *Takamura*. This is a proper name, so click the _I_gnore button to tell the spelling checker to leave the name as written.
    d. The spelling checker selects *infermation*. The proper spelling is selected in the Suggestions list box, so click the _C_hange button.
    e. The spelling checker selects *PIeces*. The proper capitalization is selected in the Suggestions list box, so click the _C_hange button.
    f. The spelling checker selects *colected*. The proper spelling is selected in the Suggestions list box, so click the _C_hange button.
    g. The spelling checker selects *fom*. Click the proper spelling *(from)* in the Suggestions list box, and then click the _C_hange button.
    h. The spelling checker selects *the*, which is a duplicate word. Click the _D_elete button to delete the selected *the*.
    i. The spelling checker selects *XX:Memo*. Click the _I_gnore button to leave this as written.
    j. At the message *The spelling check is complete*, click in the document screen outside this message to remove the message. (If the Office Assistant is turned off, click OK to close the message box.)
4. Save the document again with the same name (Ch 06, Ex 01).
5. Print and then close Ch 06, Ex 01.

Changing Spelling Options

Click the _O_ptions button at the Spelling and Grammar dialog box, and the Spelling & Grammar dialog box displays as shown in figure 6.4.

figure
6.4

Spelling & Grammar Dialog Box

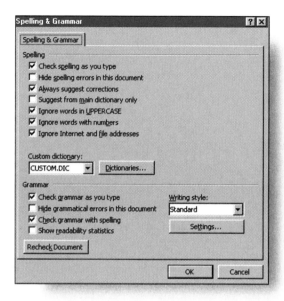

Figure 6.5 describes the options available in the Spelling section of the Spelling & Grammar dialog box. (The Grammar options are explained in the "Checking the Grammar and Style of a Document" section of this chapter.)

figure
6.5

Spelling Options at the Spelling & Grammar Dialog Box

Choose this option	And Word will
Check spelling as you type	check words in a document as they are being keyed by inserting a wavy red line below words not contained in the spelling dictionary.
Hide spelling errors	remove the wavy red line below words not contained in the spelling dictionary.
Always suggest corrections	always suggest corrections. Make this option inactive if you do not want suggestions (spelling checker will work faster).

Suggest from <u>m</u>ain	provide suggestions only from the main dictionary, not dictionary only from any custom dictionaries.
Ignore words in <u>UPPERCASE</u>	ignore words in all uppercase letters.
Ignore words with num<u>b</u>ers	ignore words that include numbers.
Ignore Internet and <u>f</u>ile addresses	ignore Internet addresses (such as http://www.companyname.com), file names, and electronic mail addresses.

At the Spelling & Grammar dialog box, you can also create or edit a custom dictionary. Custom dictionaries can be created for specialized terms or a specific profession. Refer to the Help feature for more information on custom dictionaries.

You can also display the Spelling & Grammar dialog box by clicking <u>T</u>ools and then <u>O</u>ptions. At the Options dialog box, click the Spelling & Grammar tab.

Editing While Spell Checking

When spell checking a document, you can temporarily leave the Spelling and Grammar dialog box, make corrections in the document, and then resume spell checking. For example, suppose while spell checking you notice a sentence that you want to change. To correct the sentence, move the I-beam pointer to the location in the sentence where the change is to occur, click the left mouse button, and then make changes to the sentence. To resume spell checking, click the Re<u>s</u>ume button, which was formerly the <u>I</u>gnore button.

Spell Checking a Document with Words in Uppercase and with Numbers

1. Open Letter 01.
2. Save the letter with Save As and name it Ch 06, Ex 02.
3. Review spell checking options by completing the following steps:
   a. Click <u>T</u>ools and then <u>O</u>ptions.
   b. At the Options dialog box, click the Spelling & Grammar tab.

c. Make sure there is a check mark in the Ignore words in UPPERCASE check box. (If there is no check mark, click in the check box before Ignore words in UPPERCASE to insert one.)

d. Make sure there is a check mark in the Ignore words with numbers check box. (If there is no check mark, click in the check box before Ignore words with numbers to insert one.)

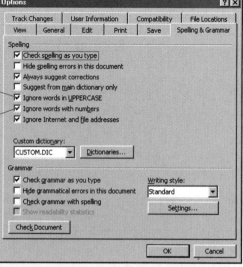

Step 3c

Step 3d

e. Click OK or press Enter to close the dialog box.

4. Perform a spelling check by completing the following steps:

a. Click the Spelling and Grammar button on the Standard toolbar.

b. The spelling checker selects the name *Garcetti*. If necessary, turn off the grammar checker by clicking in the Check grammar check box (located in the lower left corner of the dialog box) to remove the check mark. *Garcetti* is a proper name, so click the Ignore button to tell the spelling checker to leave the name as written.

c. The spelling checker selects *atached*. The proper spelling is selected in the Suggestions list box, so click the Change button.

d. The spelling checker selects *reprasenting*. The proper spelling is selected in the Suggestions list box, so click the Change button.

e. The spelling checker selects *correspondances*. The proper spelling is selected in the Suggestions list box, so click the Change button.

Step 4f

f. The spelling checker selects *suld* and does not offer the correct spelling (which is *should*). To correct the word in the Not in Dictionary: text box, move the insertion point immediately left of the *u* in *suld*, key *ho*, and then click the Change button.

g. The spelling checker selects *Streat*. The proper spelling is selected in the Suggestions list box, so click the Change button.

h. The spelling checker selects *XX:Letter*. Click the Ignore button to leave this as written.

i. When the spell check is completed, click outside the message box to remove it. (If the Office Assistant is turned off, click OK to close the message box.)

5. Save the document again with the same name (Ch 06, Ex 02).

6. Print and then close Ch 06, Ex 02.

Checking the Grammar and Style of a Document

Word includes a grammar checking feature that you can use to search a document for grammar, style, punctuation, and word usage. Like the spelling checker, the grammar checker does not find every error in a document and may stop at correct phrases. The grammar checker can help you create a well-written document but does not replace the need for proofreading.

To complete a grammar check (as well as a spelling check) on a document, click the Spelling and Grammar button on the Standard toolbar or click Tools and then Spelling and Grammar. The grammar checker selects the first sentence with a grammatical error and displays the sentence in the top text box in the dialog box. The grammar rule that is violated is displayed above the text box and information about the grammar rule displays. Choose to ignore or change errors found by the grammar checker. When the grammar checker is done, the open document is displayed in the screen. The changes made during the check are inserted in the document. You can save the document with the same name, overwriting the original; or, you can save the document with a different name, retaining the original.

By default, a spelling check is completed on a document during a grammar check. If a word is found in the document that does not match a word in the spelling dictionary, the word is selected and the sentence containing the error is displayed in the Not in Dictionary: text box. Make spelling corrections at the Spelling and Grammar dialog box as described earlier in this chapter.

If a grammar error is detected while completing a grammar and spelling check, the Spelling and Grammar dialog box displays as shown earlier in this chapter in figure 6.2. In figure 6.2 the grammar checker selected the sentence, *I would likes information from Kelly and you on requirements for administering the survey.*, and displayed *like* in the Suggestions list box.

Making Changes

When an error is detected during a grammar check, replacement word or words may be displayed in the Suggestions list box. If you agree with the suggested change, click the Change button. If the grammar checker does not offer a replacement word or words, you can temporarily leave the grammar checker and edit the text. To do this, position the I-beam pointer in the document screen (outside the Spelling and Grammar dialog box), and then click the left mouse button. Edit the text in the document and then click the Resume button (previously the Ignore button). When you click the Resume button, the grammar (and spell) checking is resumed at the location of the insertion point after you edited the document.

In some situations, the grammar checker will insert a sentence containing a grammatical error in the Spelling and Grammar dialog box. You can edit this sentence as needed and then click the Next Sentence button to resume grammar checking.

Ignoring Text

At times, the grammar checker will select text that you want left as written. Click the Ignore button to tell the grammar checker to ignore the selected text and move to the next error.

The grammar checker checks a document for a variety of grammar and style errors. In some situations, you may want the grammar checker to ignore a particular grammar or style rule. To do this, click the Ignore Rule button the first time the grammar checker displays text breaking the particular grammar or style rule you want ignored.

If the grammar checker selects a sentence in a document containing a grammar or style error and you want that sentence left as written, click the Next Sentence button. This tells the grammar checker to leave the current sentence unchanged and move to the next sentence.

Checking Grammar in a Document

1. Open Memo 04.
2. Save the document with Save As and name it Ch 06, Ex 03.
3. Perform a grammar check by completing the following steps:
   a. Click the Spelling and Grammar button on the Standard toolbar.
   b. The spelling checker selects the name *Rodan*. Make sure there is a check mark in the Check grammar check box located in this lower left corner of the dialog box. (If there is no check mark, click the option.) *Rodan* is a proper name, so click the Ignore button to tell the spelling checker to leave the name as written.
   c. The grammar checker selects the sentence *I would likes information from Kelly and you on requirements for administering the survey.* and displays *like* in the Suggestions list box. Information displays on Verb Form. Read this information and then click the Change button.
   d. The grammar checker selects the sentence *I feel confident that it will illicit the information needed to determines employee requirements.* and displays *elicit* in the Suggestions list box. Information displays on Commonly Confused Words. Read this information and then click the Change button.
   e. The grammar checker selects the same sentence again: *I feel confident that it will elicit the information needed to determines employee requirements.* and displays *determine* in the Suggestions list box. Information displays on Verb Form. Read this information and then click the Change button.
   f. The grammar checker selects *XX:Memo 04* and information displays on Spacing. Read this information and then click the Ignore button.
   g. At the message box telling you that the spelling and grammar check is completed, click in the document screen outside this box to remove the box. (If the grammer checker is turned off, click OK to close the message box.)
4. Save the document again with the same name (Ch 06, Ex 03).
5. Print and then close Ch 06, Ex 03.

Changing Grammar Checking Options

If you click the Options button in the Spelling and Grammar dialog box, the
Spelling & Grammar dialog box displays as shown earlier in figure 6.4. You can
also display this dialog box by clicking Tools and then Options. At the Options
dialog box, click the Spelling & Grammar tab. The options in the Spelling section
were discussed earlier in this chapter. Additional options display in the Grammar
section. Figure 6.6 identifies the check box options in the dialog box and what
will occur if the option is active.

6.6 *Grammar Options*

Make this option active	*To do this*
Check grammar as you type	Check grammar automatically and mark errors with wavy green line as you key text.
Hide grammatical errors in this document	Hide the wavy green line under possible grammatical errors in the document.
Check grammar with spelling	Check both spelling and grammar in a document. (Remove the check mark from this option if you want to check spelling in a document but not grammar.)
Show readability statistics	Display readability statistics about the document when grammar checking is completed.

If you make the Show readability statistics option active (insert a check
mark), readability statistics about the document will display when grammar
checking is completed. Most of the readability information is self-explanatory.
The last two statistics, however, are described in figure 6.7.

figure

6.7 *Readability Statistics*

Flesch Reading Ease	The Flesch reading ease is based on the average number of syllables per word and the average number of words per sentence. The higher the score, the greater the number of people who will be able to understand the text in the document. Standard writing generally scores in the 60-70 range.
Flesch-Kincaid Grade Level	This is based on the average number of syllables per word and the average number of words per sentence. The score indicates a grade level. Standard writing is generally written at the seventh or eighth grade level.

Changing Writing Style

At the Spelling & Grammar dialog box (as well as the Options dialog box with the Spelling & Grammar tab selected), you can specify a writing style. The default writing style is *Standard*. This can be changed to *Casual, Formal, Technical,* or *Custom*. Choose the writing style that matches the document you are checking. For example, if you are checking a scientific document, change the writing style to *Technical*. If you are checking a short story, consider changing the writing style to *Casual*. To change the writing style, click the down-pointing triangle at the right of the Writing style text box, and then click the desired style at the drop-down list.

exercise 4

Changing Grammar Checking Options, Then Grammar Checking a Document

1. Open Para 02.
2. Save the document with Save As and name it Ch 06, Ex 04.
3. Change grammar checking options by completing the following steps:
   a. Click Tools and then Options.
   b. At the Options dialog box, click the Spelling & Grammar tab.

c. At the Options dialog box with the Spelling & Grammar tab selected, click the Show readability statistics. (This inserts a check mark in the option.)

d. Click the down-pointing triangle at the right of the Writing style text box and then click *Formal* at the drop-down list.

e. Click OK to close the dialog box.

4. Complete a grammar check on the document by completing the following steps:

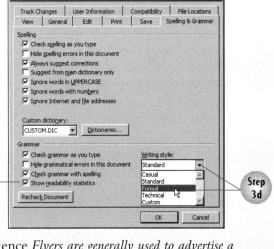

Step 3c

Step 3d

a. Click the Spelling and Grammar button on the Standard toolbar.

b. The grammar checker selects the sentence *Flyers are generally used to advertise a product or service that is available for a limited amount of time.* and displays information on Passive Voice.

c. Read the information on Passive Voice and then edit the sentence by deleting the words *are*, *used*, and *to* (located in the dialog box) so that the sentence reads *Flyers generally advertise a product or service that is available for a limited amount of time.*

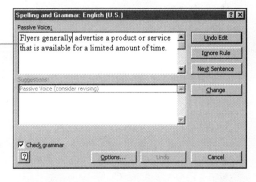

Step 4c

d. Click the Next Sentence button to continue grammar checking.

e. The grammar checker selects the sentence *As you can see, this form of advertising is used by just about anyone.* and displays information on Passive Voice.

f. Edit the sentence in the dialog box so it reads *As you can see, many people use this form of advertising.*

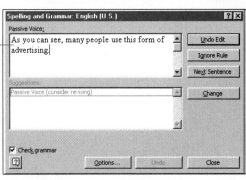

Step 4f

g. Click the Next Sentence button to continue grammar checking.

h. The grammar checker selects the sentence *A flyer with a large, color headline is an eye-catching way to announce an event or present important information.* and displays information on Number Agreement. Read this information and then click the Ignore button to leave the sentence as written.

i. The grammar checker displays the Readability Statistics dialog box for the document. Read the statistics and then click OK to close the dialog box.

5. Change the checking options back to the default by completing the following steps:

a. Click Tools and then Options.

b. At the Options dialog box, click the Spelling & Grammar tab.

    c.   At the Options dialog box with the Spelling & Grammar tab selected, click the Show <u>r</u>eadability statistics. (This removes the check mark from the check box.)

    d.   Click the down-pointing triangle at the right of the <u>W</u>riting style text box and then click *Standard* at the drop-down list.

    e.   Click OK to close the dialog box.

6. Save the document again with the same name (Ch 06, Ex 04).

7. Print and then close Ch 06, Ex 04.

Customizing AutoCorrect

Earlier in this chapter, you learned that a selected word can be added to AutoCorrect during a spelling check. You can add, delete, or change words at the AutoCorrect dialog box. To display the AutoCorrect dialog box with the AutoCorrect tab selected as shown in figure 6.8, click <u>T</u>ools and then <u>A</u>utoCorrect.

AutoCorrect Dialog Box with AutoCorrect Tab Selected

If you key the text shown in the first column of this list box and then press the spacebar, it is replaced by the text shown in the second column.

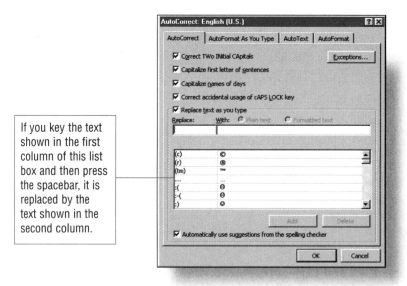

Several options display at the beginning of the AutoCorrect dialog box. If a check mark appears in the check box before the option, the option is active. Figure 6.9 describes what will occur if the option is active.

figure

6.9 *AutoCorrect Options*

If this option is active	Word will
Correct TWo INitial CApitals	change the second capital to a lowercase letter.
Capitalize first letter of sentences	capitalize the first letter of a word beginning a sentence.
Capitalize names of days	capitalize the first letter of days of the week.
Correct accidental use of cAPS LOCK key	correct instances in which the Caps Lock key is used incorrectly.
Replace text as you type	replace misspelled word with correct spelling as displayed in the list box at the bottom of the AutoCorrect dialog box.

Adding a Word to AutoCorrect

Commonly misspelled words or typographical errors can be added to AutoCorrect. For example, if you consistently key *oopen* instead of *open*, you can add *oopen* to AutoCorrect and tell it to correct it as *open*. To do this, you would display the AutoCorrect dialog box, key **oopen** in the Replace text box, key **open** in the With text box, and then click the Add button. The next time you key **oopen** and then press the spacebar, AutoCorrect changes it to *open*.

Deleting a Word from AutoCorrect

A word that is contained in AutoCorrect can be deleted. To delete a word, display the AutoCorrect dialog box, click the desired word in the list box (you may need to click the down-pointing triangle to display the desired word), and then click the Delete button.

exercise 5

Adding Text to and Deleting Text from AutoCorrect

1. At a clear document screen, add words to AutoCorrect by completing the following steps:

    a. Click <u>T</u>ools and then <u>A</u>utoCorrect.

    b. At the AutoCorrect dialog box with the AutoCorrect tab selected, make sure the insertion point is positioned in the <u>R</u>eplace text box. If not, click in the <u>R</u>eplace text box.

    c. Key **dtp**.

    d. Press the Tab key (this moves the insertion point to the <u>W</u>ith text box) and then key **desktop publishing**.

    e. Click the <u>A</u>dd button. (This adds *dtp* and *desktop publishing* to the AutoCorrect and also selects *dtp* in the <u>R</u>eplace text box.)

    f. Key **particuler** in the <u>R</u>eplace text box. (When you begin keying *particuler*, *dtp* is automatically deleted.)

    g. Press the Tab key and then key **particular**.

    h. Click the <u>A</u>dd button.

    i. With the insertion point positioned in the <u>R</u>eplace text box, key **populer**.

    j. Press the Tab key and then key **popular**.

    k. Click the <u>A</u>dd button.

    l. With the insertion point positioned in the <u>R</u>eplace text box, key **tf**.

    m. Press the Tab key and then key **typeface**.

    n. Click the <u>A</u>dd button.

    o. Click OK or press Enter.

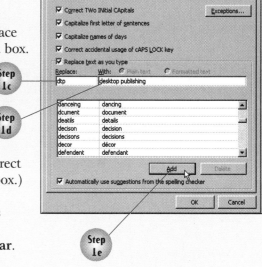

Step 1c

Step 1d

Step 1e

2. Key the text shown in figure 6.10. (Key the text exactly as shown. AutoCorrect will correct words as you key.)

3. Save the document and name it Ch 06, Ex 05.

4. Print Ch 06, Ex 05.

5. Delete the words you added to AutoCorrect by completing the following steps:

    a. Click <u>T</u>ools and then <u>A</u>utoCorrect.

    b. At the AutoCorrect dialog box, click *dtp* in the list box. (You will need to scroll down the list box to display *dtp*. To do this, consider dragging the scroll box on the vertical scroll bar at the right side of the list box until *dtp* is visible, and then click *dtp*.)

    c. Click the <u>D</u>elete button.

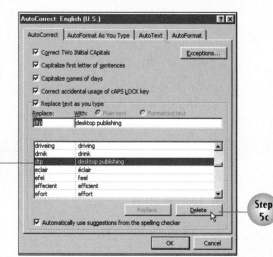

Step 5b

Step 5c

d.   Click the *particuler* option in the list box.
   e.   Click the <u>D</u>elete button.
   f.   Click the *populer* option in the list box.
   g.   Click the <u>D</u>elete button.
   h.   Click the *tf* option in the list box.
   i.   Click the <u>D</u>elete button.
   j.   Click OK or press Enter.
6.   Close Ch 06, Ex 05.

Exercise 5

CHOOSING A TYPEFACE

A tf is a set of characters with a common general design and shape. One of teh most
important considerations in establishing a particuler mood or feeling in a document is the
tf. For example, a decorative tf may be chosen for invitations or menus, while a simple
block-style tf may be chosen for headlines or reports. Choose a tf that reflects the
contents, your audience expectations, and the image you want to project.

There are many typefaces adn new designs are created on a regular basis. The most
populer tf for typewriters is Courier. There are a variety of typefaces populer with dtp
programs including Arial, Bookman, Century Schoolbook, Garamond, Helvetica, and
Times New Roman.

Using the Thesaurus

Word offers a Thesaurus program that can be used to find synonyms, antonyms,
and related words for a particular word. Synonyms are words that have the same
or nearly the same meaning. When using the Thesaurus, Word may display
antonyms for some words. Antonyms are words with opposite meanings. With the
Thesaurus, you can improve the clarity of business documents.

    To use the Thesaurus, position the insertion point next to any character in the
word for which you want to find a synonym or antonym, click <u>T</u>ools, point to
<u>L</u>anguage, and then click <u>T</u>hesaurus. At the Thesaurus dialog box shown in figure
6.11, select the desired synonym (or antonym) in the <u>M</u>eanings list box, and then
click the <u>R</u>eplace button.

figure 6.11

Thesaurus Dialog Box

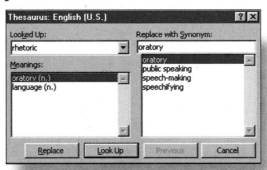

At the Thesaurus dialog box, a list of words displays in the Meanings list box. Depending on the word you are looking up, the words in the Meanings list box may display followed by *(n.)* for *noun*, *(adj.)* for *adjective*, or *(adv.)* for *adverb*. You might also see the words *Antonym* and *Related Words*. The first word in the Meanings list box is selected by default, and synonyms for that word are displayed in the Replace with Synonym list box. The Replace with Synonyms list box may also display an antonym for a word. An antonym displays with *(Antonym)* following the word.

You can view synonyms in the Replace with Synonym list box for the words shown in the Meanings list box by clicking the desired word.

exercise 6

Finding Synonyms Using Thesaurus

1. At a clear document screen, look up synonyms for the word *rhetoric* by completing the following steps:
   a. Key **rhetoric**.
   b. With the insertion point positioned in the word or immediately after the word, click Tools, point to Language, and then click Thesaurus.
   c. After viewing the synonyms for *rhetoric*, close the Thesaurus dialog box by clicking the Cancel button.
2. Look up synonyms for the word *subtle* by completing steps similar to those in 1.
3. Look up synonyms for the word *insipid* by completing steps similar to those in 1.
4. Close the document without saving it.

Using Buttons

Use the buttons at the bottom of the Thesaurus dialog box to replace a word, look up a different word, or display the previous word. The buttons and their functions are explained in figure 6.12.

figure

6.12

Thesaurus Dialog Box Buttons

Button	Action
Replace	Click the <u>R</u>eplace button to replace the word in the document with the word displayed in the Replace with <u>S</u>ynonym list box.
Look Up	Look up synonyms for words displayed in either the <u>M</u>eanings list box or the Replace with <u>S</u>ynonym list box by clicking the word for which you want to look up synonyms and then clicking the <u>L</u>ook Up button. Or, double-click the word for which you want synonyms displayed.
Cancel	Click the Cancel button to remove the Thesaurus dialog box from the document screen without making a change.
Previous	Click the <u>P</u>revious button to display the previous word looked up.

Displaying Synonyms Using a Shortcut Menu

Another method for displaying synonyms for a word is to use a shortcut menu. To do this, position the mouse pointer on the word and then click the *right* mouse button. At the shortcut menu that displays, point to S<u>y</u>nonyms, and then click the desired synonym at the side menu. Figure 6.13 shows synonyms in the shortcut menu side menu for the word *prospective*. Click the <u>T</u>hesaurus option at the bottom of the side menu to display the Thesaurus dialog box.

figure

6.13

Shortcut Menu Synonym Side Menu

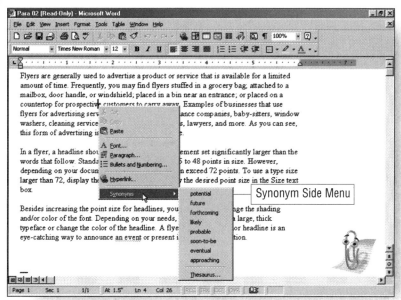

exercise 7

Changing Words Using Thesaurus

1. Open Memo 01.
2. Save the memo with Save As and name it Ch 06, Ex 07.
3. Change the word *excellent* in the first paragraph to *outstanding* using Thesaurus by completing the following steps:
    a. Position the insertion point in the word *excellent*.
    b. Display the Thesaurus dialog box.
    c. At the Thesaurus dialog box, make sure *outstanding* is displayed in the Replace with Synonyms list box, and then click the Replace button.
4. Follow similar steps to change *retail* in the third paragraph to *sell*.
5. Change *approximately* in the third paragraph using a shortcut menu by completing the following steps:
    a. Position the mouse pointer on the word *approximately* located in the first sentence of the third paragraph.
    b. Click the *right* mouse button.
    c. At the shortcut menu that displays, point to Synonyms, and then click *about* at the side menu.
6. Save the memo again with the same name (Ch 06, Ex 07).
7. Print and then close Ch 06, Ex 07.

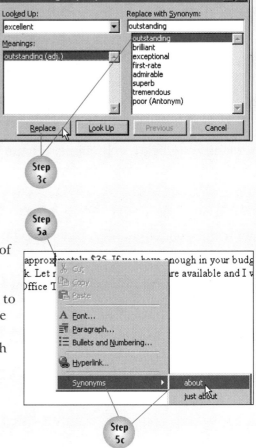

Step 3c

Step 5a

Step 5c

Displaying Word Count

With the Word Count option from the Tools menu, the number of pages, words, characters, paragraphs, and lines in a document can be displayed. To use this option, open the document for which you want the word count displayed, and then click Tools and then Word Count. This displays a Word Count dialog box similar to the one shown in figure 6.14. Figure 6.14 shows statistics for the Report 01 document. After reading the information displayed in the Word Count dialog box, click the Close button or press Enter.

figure
6.14

Word Count Dialog Box

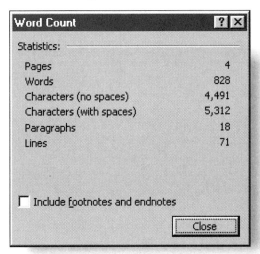

Displaying Word Count

1. Open Report 01.
2. Display a word count for the document by completing the following steps:
   a. Click Tools and then Word Count.
   b. After reading the statistics in the Word Count dialog box, click the Close button.
3. Close Report 01 without saving changes.
4. Open Report 03.
5. Display the word count for the document by completing step 2.
6. Close Report 03 without saving changes.

Finding Text

If you compose many documents at the keyboard, the Find and Replace feature can be helpful in locating words or phrases that are overused within a document. For example, if you overuse the phrase *I feel that...* in a document, you can find every occurrence of the phrase, and then decide to leave it in the document or edit it. The Find and Replace feature can also be used to move quickly to a specific location in a document. This is particularly useful in long documents if you want to position the insertion point at a specific location within a page.

To find specific text or formatting in a document, click Edit and then Find. This displays the Find and Replace dialog box with the Find tab selected as shown in figure 6.15. Enter the characters for which you are searching in the Find what text box. You can enter up to 256 characters in this text box. Click the Find Next button and Word searches for and selects the first occurrence of the text in the document. Make corrections to the text if needed and then search for the next occurrence by clicking the Find Next button again. Click the Cancel button to close the Find and Replace dialog box.

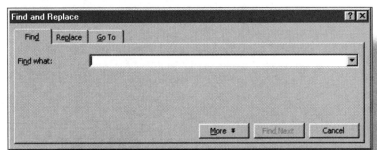

figure
6.15
Find and Replace Dialog Box with Find Tab Selected

exercise 9

Finding Words

1. Open Report 01.
2. Find every occurrence of *desktop publishing* in the document by completing the following steps:
   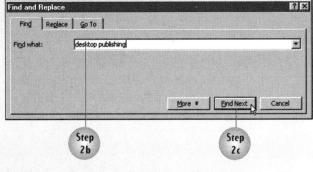
   a. With the insertion point positioned at the beginning of the document, click Edit and then Find.
   b. At the Find and Replace dialog box with the Find tab selected, key **desktop publishing** in the Find what text box.
   c. Click the Find Next button.
   d. Word searches for and selects the first occurrence of *desktop publishing*.
   e. Search for the next occurrence of *desktop publishing* by clicking the Find Next button again.
   f. Continue clicking the Find Next button until the message *Word has finished searching the document* displays. (If the Office Assistant is turned off, click OK to remove the message.)
   g. Click the Cancel button to close the Find and Replace dialog box.
3. Close Report 01.

   The next time you open the Find and Replace dialog box, you can display a list of text for which you have searched by clicking the down-pointing triangle after the Find what text box. For example, if you searched for *type size* and then performed another search for *type style*, the third time you open the Find and Replace dialog box, clicking the down-pointing triangle after the Find what text box will display a drop-down list with *type style* and *type size*. Click text from this drop-down list if you want to perform a search on that text.

Choosing Find Check Box Options

The Find and Replace dialog box contains a variety of check boxes with options you can choose for completing a search. To display these options, click the <u>M</u>ore button located at the bottom of the dialog box. This causes the Find and Replace dialog box to expand as shown in figure 6.16. Each option and what will occur if it is selected is described in figure 6.17.

Expanded Find and Replace Dialog Box

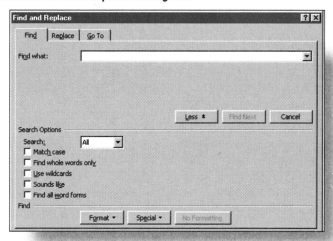

Options at the Find and Replace Dialog Box with the Fin<u>d</u> Tab Selected

Choose this option	*To do this*
Mat<u>c</u>h case	Exactly match the case of the search text. For example, if you search for *Book* and select the Mat<u>c</u>h case option, Word will stop at *Book* but not *book* or *BOOK*.
Find whole words onl<u>y</u>	Find a whole word, not a part of a word. For example, if you search for *her* and *did not* select Find whole words only, Word would stop at *there*, *here*, *hers*, etc.
<u>U</u>se wildcards	Search for wildcards, special characters, or special search operators.
Sounds li<u>k</u>e	Match words that sound alike but are spelled differently, such as *know* and *no*.
Find all <u>w</u>ord forms	Find all forms of the word entered in the Fi<u>n</u>d what text box. For example, if you enter *hold*, Word will stop at *held* and *holding*.

To remove the display of options toward the bottom of the Find and Replace dialog box, click the Less button. (The Less button was previously the More button.)

Choosing a Find Direction

The Search: option at the Find and Replace dialog box has a default setting of *All*. At this setting, Word will search the entire document. This can be changed to Up or Down. Choose *Up* and Word will search the document from the insertion point to the beginning of the document. Choose *Down* and Word will search the document from the insertion point to the end of the document.

exercise

Finding Whole Words and Word Forms

1. Open Para 05.
2. Find every occurrence of the word *publishing* that exactly matches the case by completing the following steps:
   a. Make sure the insertion point is positioned at the beginning of the document.
   b. Click Edit and then Find.
   c. At the Find and Replace dialog box with the Find tab selected, key **publishing** in the Find what text box.
   d. Click the More button located at the bottom of the dialog box.
   e. Click the Match case option. (This inserts a check mark in the check box.)
   f. Click the Find whole words only option. (This inserts a check mark in the check box.)
   g. Click the Find Next button.
   h. Word searches for and selects the first occurrence of *publishing* (that exactly matches the case).
   i. Search for the next occurrence of *publishing* by clicking the Find Next button.
   j. Continue clicking the Find Next button until the message *Word has finished searching the document* displays. (If the Office Assistant is turned off, click OK to remove the message.)
   k. Click the Cancel button to close the Find and Replace dialog box.
3. Find every occurrence of the word *produce* and all its word forms by completing the following steps:
   a. Make sure the insertion point is positioned at the beginning of the document.
   b. Click Edit and then Find.

Step 2c

Step 2e

Step 2f

Step 2g

c. At the Find and Replace dialog box with the Find tab selected, key **produce** in the Find what text box.
d. Click the Find all word forms option. (If this option if not visible, click the More button.)
e. Click the Find Next button.
f. Word searches for and selects the first occurrence of *produce* (or a word form of *produce*).
g. Search for the next occurrence of *produce* (or a word form of *produce*) by clicking the Find Next button.
h. Continue clicking the Find Next button until the message *Word has finished searching the document* displays. (If the Office Assistant is turned off, click OK to remove the message.)
i. Remove the check mark from the Find all word forms option.
j. Click the Less button to turn off the display of the options toward the bottom of the dialog box.
k. Click the Cancel button to close the Find and Replace dialog box.
4. Close Para 05.

Finding Formatting

You can search a document for some character and paragraph formatting. For example, you can search for bold characters, characters set in a specific font, as well as some paragraph formatting such as indents and spacing. To search for specific formatting, display the Find and Replace dialog box with the Find tab selected, and then click the Format button. (If this button is not visible, click the More button.) At the pop-up list that displays, click the type of formatting for which you are searching (such as *Font* or *Paragraph*). At the specific formatting dialog box that displays, identify the formatting, and then close the dialog box. The formatting for which you are searching displays below the Find what text box.

The text and/or formatting that you searched for previously remains in the Find what text box. The next time you perform a search, the text you key in the Find what text box will replace the existing text. This does not, however, remove formatting. To remove previous formatting, click the No Formatting button that displays at the bottom of the expanded Find and Replace dialog box.

Finding Formatting

1. Open Survey 01.
2. Find all text set in bold by completing the following steps:

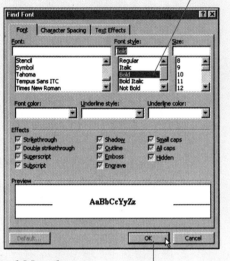

Step 2g

a. Make sure the insertion point is positioned at the beginning of the document, click Edit and then Find.
b. With the insertion point positioned in the Find what text box, press the Delete key. (This deletes any text that displays in the text box.)
c. Click the More button. (This expands the dialog box and displays additional options.)
d. If the Find all word forms option contains a check mark, click the option to remove the check mark.
e. Click the Format button.
f. At the pop-up list that displays, click *Font*.
g. At the Find Font dialog box, click *Bold* in the Font style list box.
h. Click OK or press Enter to close the Find Font dialog box.

Step 2h

i. At the Find and Replace dialog box, click the Find Next button.
j. Continue clicking the Find Next button until the message *Word has finished searching the document* displays. (If the Office Assistant is turned off, click OK to remove the message.)
k. Click the No Formatting button.
l. Click the Less button to turn off the display of the additional options.
m. Click the Cancel button to close the Find and Replace dialog box.
3. Close Survey 01.

Finding and Replacing Text

With Word's Find and Replace feature, you can look for specific characters or formatting and replace with other characters or formatting. With the Find and Replace feature, you can:

- Use abbreviations for common phrases when entering text and then replace the abbreviations with the actual text later.
- Set up standard documents with generic names and replace them with other names to make personalized documents.
- Find and replace formatting.

To use Find and Replace, click Edit and then Replace. This displays the Find and Replace dialog box with the Replace tab selected as shown in figure 6.18.

figure
6.18

Find and Replace Dialog Box with the Replace Tab Selected

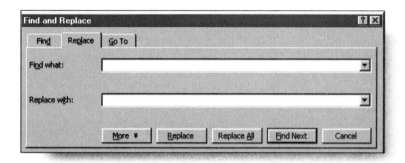

Enter the characters and/or formatting for which you are searching in the Find what text box. Press the Tab key to move the insertion point to the Replace with text box and then key the replacement text or insert the replacement formatting. You can also move the insertion point to the Replace with text box by clicking inside the text box.

The Find and Replace dialog box contains several command buttons. Click the Find Next button to tell Word to find the next occurrence of the characters and/or formatting. Click the Replace button to replace the characters or formatting and find the next occurrence. If you know that you want all occurrences of the characters or formatting in the Find what text box replaced with the characters or formatting in the Replace with text box, click the Replace All button. This replaces every occurrence from the location of the insertion point to the beginning or end of the document (depending on the search direction). Click the Cancel button to close the Find and Replace dialog box.

Finding and Replacing Text

1. Open Legal 01.
2. Save the document with Save As and name it Ch 06, Ex 12.
3. Find all occurrences of *NAME1* and replace with *ROSLYN C. KERR* by completing the following steps:
   a. With the insertion point positioned at the beginning of the document, click Edit and then Replace.

b. At the Find and Replace dialog box with the Replace tab selected, if *Format: Font: Bold* displays below the Find what text box, click the <u>M</u>ore button, click the No Formatting button, and then click the <u>L</u>ess button. (This removes the bold formatting from exercise 11.)

c. With the insertion point positioned inside the Find what text box, key **NAME1**.

d. Press the Tab key to move the insertion point to the Replace with text box.

e. Key **ROSLYN C. KERR**.

f. Click the Replace <u>A</u>ll button.

g. When all replacements are made, the message *Word has completed its search of the document and has made 5 replacements* displays. (If the Office Assistant is turned off, click OK to remove the message.) (Do not close the Find and Replace dialog box.)

4. With the Find and Replace dialog box still open, complete steps similar to those in 3d through 3g to find all occurrences of *NAME2* and replace with *JULIA C. RAINEY*.

5. With the Find and Replace dialog box still open, complete steps similar to those in 3d through 3g to find the one occurrence of *NUMBER* and replace with *C-9811*.

6. Close the Find and Replace dialog box.

7. Save the document again with the same name (Ch 06, Ex 12).

8. Print and then close Ch 06, Ex 12.

In exercise 12, Word made all replacements without getting confirmation from you. If you want to confirm each replacement before it is made, click the <u>F</u>ind Next button to move to the first occurrence of the word. To replace the word, click the <u>R</u>eplace button. To leave the word as written, click the <u>F</u>ind Next button.

The next time you open the Find and Replace dialog box, you can display a list of text entered in the Replace with text box. To do this, click the down-pointing triangle after the Replace with text box, and then click the desired text at the drop-down list. This inserts it in the Replace with text box.

exercise 13

Finding and Replacing Specific Text

1. Open Report 04.

2. Save the document with Save As and name it Ch 06, Ex 13.

3. Find some of the occurrences of *paper* and replace with *stationery* by completing the following steps:

a. With the insertion point positioned at the beginning of the document, click <u>E</u>dit and then <u>R</u>eplace.

b. At the Find and Replace dialog box, key **paper** in the Find what text box.
c. Press the Tab key (this moves the insertion point to the Replace with text box) and then key **stationery**.
d. Click the Find Next button. (If the Find and Replace dialog box is in the way of viewing the text in the document, move

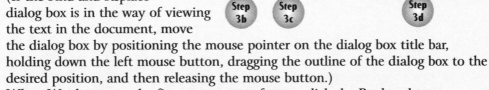

the dialog box by positioning the mouse pointer on the dialog box title bar, holding down the left mouse button, dragging the outline of the dialog box to the desired position, and then releasing the mouse button.)
e. When Word stops at the first occurrence of *paper*, click the Replace button.
f. Continue clicking the Replace button when Word stops at an occurrence of *paper*, except when *paper* falls after *8.5-by-11-inch* and when Word selects *papers*. At these occurrences, click the Find Next button.
g. When the find and replace is completed, click the Close button to close the Find and Replace dialog box.
4. Save the document again with the same name (Ch 06, Ex 13).
5. Print and then close Ch 06, Ex 13.

Choosing Find Check Box Options

If you click the <u>M</u>ore button at the Find and Replace dialog box with the Replace tab selected, the same options display as those in the Find and Replace dialog box with the Fin<u>d</u> tab selected. Refer to figure 6.17 for an explanation of the options. If you click the Find all <u>w</u>ord forms option, you can find all forms of a word and replace it with the correct form. For example, in exercise 14 you will search for all word forms of *produce* and replace with *create*. This means that Word will replace *produce* with *create*, *producing* with *creating*, and *produced* with *created*.

Finding and Replacing Word Forms

1. Open Para 05.
2. Save the document with Save As and name it Ch 06, Ex 14.
3. Find all forms of the word *produce* and replace it with forms of *create* by completing the following steps:
   a. Make sure the insertion point is positioned at the beginning of the document.
   b. Click <u>E</u>dit and then R<u>e</u>place.

c. At the Find and Replace dialog box with the Replace tab selected, key **produce** in the Find what text box.
d. Press the Tab key and then key **create** in the Replace with text box.
e. Click the More button.
f. Click the Find all word forms option. (This inserts a check mark in the check box.)
g. Click the Replace All button.
h. At the message, *Replace All is not recommended with Find All Word Forms. Continue with Replace All?*, click OK.
i. When the find and replace is completed, click the Find all word forms option to remove the check mark.
j. Click the Less button.
k. Click the Close button to close the Find and Replace dialog box.
4. Save the document again with the same name (Ch 06, Ex 14).
5. Print and then close Ch 06, Ex 14.

Finding and Replacing Formatting

With Word's Find and Replace feature, you can search for specific formatting or characters containing specific formatting and replace it with other characters or formatting. For example, you can search for the text *Type Style* set in 14-point Arial and replace it with the text *Type Style* set in 18-point Times New Roman.

exercise 15

Finding and Replacing Fonts

1. Open Survey 01.
2. Save the document with Save As and name it Ch 06, Ex 15.
3. Make the following changes to the document:
   a. Change the top and bottom margins to 0.75 inch and the left and right margins to 1 inch.
   b. Change the font for the entire document to 12-point Bookman Old Style (or a similar serif typeface such as Century Schoolbook or Garamond).
   c. Select the title, *TEACHER DEVELOPMENT TOPICS*, and the subtitle, *Activities within Your Classroom*, and then change the font to 16-point Arial bold.

d. Select *Directions:* (be sure to include the colon) in the first paragraph and then change the font to 14-point Arial bold. Use Format Painter to change the font to 14-point Arial bold for the following:

> *Classroom Presentations:*
> *Expertise in Your Discipline:*
> *Information Technology:*
> *Thinking Skills:*
> *Active Listening:*

4. Save the document again with the same name (Ch 06, Ex 15).
5. Print Ch 06, Ex 15.
6. With Ch 06, Ex 15 still open, find text set in 16-point Arial bold and replace it with text set in 14-point Bookman Old Style bold (or the typeface you chose in step 3b) by completing the following steps:

a. Move the insertion point to the beginning of the document and then display the Find and Replace dialog box.

b. At the Find and Replace dialog box, click the More button. (If there is a check mark in the Find all word forms check box, click the option to remove the mark.)

c. With the insertion point positioned in the Find what text box (make sure there is no text in the text box), click the Format button located at the bottom of the dialog box and then click *Font* at the pop-up list.

d. At the Find Font dialog box, click *Arial* in the Font list box, click *Bold* in the Font style list box, and then click *16* in the Size list box.

e. Click OK or press Enter to close the Find Font dialog box.

f. At the Find and Replace dialog box, click inside the Replace with text box. (Make sure there is no text in the text box.)

g. Click the Format button located at the bottom of the dialog box and then click *Font* at the pop-up list.

h. At the Find Font dialog box, click *Bookman Old Style* in the Font list box (or the typeface you chose in step 3b), click *Bold* in the Font style list box, and then click *14* in the Size list box.

i. Click OK or press Enter to close the Find Font dialog box.

j. At the Find and Replace dialog box, click the Replace All button.

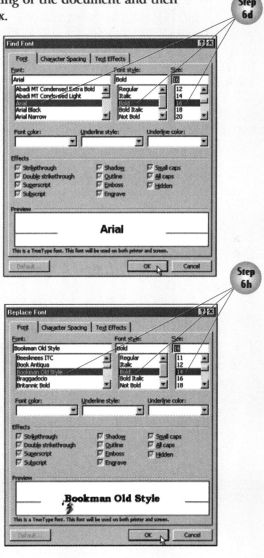

Step 6d

Step 6h

7. With the Find and Replace dialog box still open, find all text set in 14-point Arial bold and replace it with text set in 12-point Bookman Old Style bold by completing the following steps:
    a. Click inside the Find what text box at the Find and Replace dialog box.
    b. Click the No Formatting button located at the bottom of the dialog box.
    c. With the insertion point still positioned in the Find what text box, click the Format button located at the bottom of the dialog box and then click *Font* at the pop-up list.
    d. At the Find Font dialog box, click *Arial* in the Font list box, click *Bold* in the Font style list box, and then click *14* in the Size list box.
    e. Click OK or press Enter to close the Find Font dialog box.
    f. At the Find and Replace dialog box, click inside the Replace with text box.
    g. Click the No Formatting button located at the bottom of the dialog box.
    h. Click the Format button located at the bottom of the dialog box and then click *Font* at the pop-up list.
    i. At the Find Font dialog box, click *Bookman Old Style* (or the typeface you chose in step 3b) in the Font list box, click *Bold* in the Font style list box, and then click *12* in the Size list box.
    j. Click OK or press Enter to close the dialog box.
    k. At the Find and Replace dialog box, click the Replace All button.
    l. When the find and replace is completed (if the Office Assistant is turned off, click OK to remove the message), click the Less button to turn off the display of the additional options.
    m. Close the Find and Replace dialog box.
8. Save the document again with the same name (Ch 06, Ex 15).
9. Print and then close Ch 06, Ex 15.

Navigating in a Document Using Go To

As you learned, you can use the Find and Replace dialog box to find specific text or formatting in a document, or to find and replace specific text or formatting. You can also use the Find and Replace dialog box with the Go To tab selected, as shown in figure 6.19, to find or go to a specific location or item. To display this dialog box, display the Find and Replace dialog box and then click the Go To tab; or, click Edit and then click Go To; or, press Ctrl + G.

figure

6.19

Find and Replace Dialog Box with Go To Tab Selected

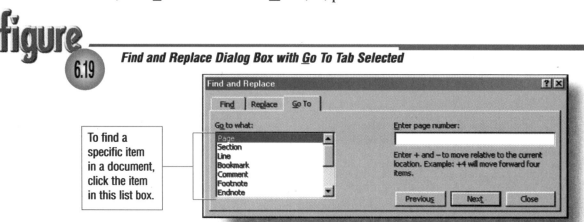

To find a specific item in a document such as a page or line, click the desired item in the Go to what list box, and then click the Go To button.

Navigating in a Document Using Go To

1. Open Report 03.
2. Insert a section break that begins a new page at the title *MODULE 2: PLANNING A NEWSLETTER*.
3. Position the insertion point at the beginning of the document and then move the insertion point to specific locations in the document by completing the following steps:
   a. Click Edit and then click Go To.
   b. At the Find and Replace dialog box with the Go To tab selected, click *Line* in the Go to what list box.
   c. Click in the Enter line number text box and then key **10**.
   d. Click the Go To button. (This moves the insertion point to line 10 on the first page of the document—check the Status bar.)

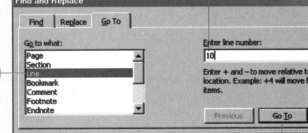

   e. At the Find and Replace dialog box with the Go To tab selected, click *Page* in the Go to what list box.
   f. Click in the Enter page number text box and then key **2**.
   g. Click the Go To button. (This moves the insertion point to the beginning of page 2.
   h. At the Find and Replace dialog box with the Go To tab selected, click *Section* in the Go to what list box.
   i. Click in the Enter section number list box and then key **2**.
   j. Click the Go To button. (This moves the insertion point to the beginning of the second section.)
   k. Click the Close button to close the Find and Replace dialog box.
4. Close Report 03 without saving the changes.

chapter summary

➤ Word includes a spelling and grammar checker.

➤ The spelling checker matches the words in your document with the words in its dictionary. If a match is not found, the word is selected and possible corrections are suggested.

➤ While the spelling checker is at work, these buttons are available: Ignore and Ignore All, Change and Change All, Add, or AutoCorrect. Several other options are available at the Options dialog box.

➤ When checking the spelling and/or grammar in a document, you can temporarily leave the Spelling and Grammar dialog box, make corrections in the document, and then resume checking.

➤ With the grammar checker, you can search a document for correct grammar, style, punctuation, and word usage.

➤ While the grammar checker is at work, these buttons are available: Ignore, Ignore All, Next Sentence, and Change.

➤ When a grammar error is detected, information displays about the specific error.

➤ Words can be added to AutoCorrect during a spelling check as well as at the AutoCorrect dialog box.

➤ Use the Thesaurus to find synonyms and antonyms for words in your document.

➤ While the Thesaurus is at work, these buttons are available: Replace, Look Up, Cancel, and Previous.

➤ Display the number of pages, words, characters, paragraphs, and lines in a document with the Word Count option from the Tools drop-down menu.

➤ Use the Find feature to quickly locate specific words, phrases, or formatting. Once located, these items can then be edited or deleted.

➤ When you open the Find and Replace dialog box, you can display a list of text for which you previously have searched by clicking the down-pointing triangle at the right of the Find what text box.

➤ The Find and Replace dialog box contains a variety of check boxes with options for completing a search, such as Match case, Find whole words only, Use wildcards, Sounds like, and Find all word forms.

➤ You can search a document for some character and paragraph formatting such as bold characters, specific fonts, indents, and spacing.

➤ With Word's Find and Replace feature, you can look for text or formatting and replace with other text or formatting.

➤ The Find and Replace dialog box contains buttons such as Find Next, Replace, Replace All, and Cancel. With these buttons you can choose to skip an occurrence of the search item, replace it, or replace all occurrences at once.

➤ The next time you open the Find and Replace dialog box, you can display a list of text you have entered in the Replace with text box.

➤ Navigate through a document with options at the Find and Replace dialog box with the Go To tab selected.

commands review

Mouse/Keyboard

Spelling and Grammar dialog box	Click Spelling and Grammar button on Standard toolbar; or click Tools, Spelling and Grammar
Options dialog box	Tools, Options
AutoCorrect dialog box	Tools, AutoCorrect
Thesaurus dialog box	Tools, Language, Thesaurus
Word Count dialog box	Tools, Word Count
Find and Replace dialog box	Edit, Find with Find tab selected
Find and Replace dialog box with Replace tab selected	Edit, Replace
Find and Replace dialog box with Go To tab selected	Edit, Go To; or press Ctrl + G

thinking offline

Completion: In the space provided at the right, indicate the correct term, symbol, or command.

1. Display the Spelling and Grammar dialog box by clicking the Spelling and Grammar button on this toolbar.

2. This is the default writing style that the grammar checker uses when checking grammar in a document.

3. When choosing a writing style for checking a document, the options available are Standard, Casual, Technical, *Custom, and this.

4. Use this program to find synonyms for a word.

5. Click this option at the Tools drop-down menu to display information about the document such as the number of pages, words, characters, paragraphs, and lines.

6. To display the AutoCorrect dialog box with the AutoCorrect tab selected, click this option on the Menu bar and then click AutoCorrect.

7. This term refers to words with similar meanings.

8. Click this option from the Edit drop-down menu to display the Find and Replace dialog box with the Replace tab selected.

9. If you want to replace every occurrence of what you are searching for in a document, click this button at the Find and Replace dialog box.

10. Click this button at the Find and Replace dialog box if you do not want to replace an occurrence with the replace text.

_____

11. Click this option at the Find and Replace dialog box if you are searching for a word and all its forms.

_____

12. In the space provided below, write the steps you would complete to find all occurrences of the word *remove* and all its word forms and replace it with *delete* and all its word forms.

_____

_____

_____

working hands-on

Assessment 1

1. Open Summary 01.
2. Save the document with Save As and name it Ch 06, SA 01.
3. Complete a spell check on the document. (The words *duplexing* and *codecs* are spelled correctly.)
4. After completing the spell check, insert bullets before each paragraph (except the title).
5. Save the document again with the same name (Ch 06, SA 01).
6. Print and then close Ch 06, SA 01.

Assessment 2

1. Open Letter 02.
2. Save the document with Save As and name it Ch 06, SA 02.
3. Complete a spelling and grammar check on the document.
4. After the spelling and grammar check is completed, proofread the letter and make necessary changes. (There are mistakes that the spelling and grammar checker will not select.)
5. Save the document again with the same name (Ch 06, SA 02).
6. Print and then close Ch 06, SA 02.

Assessment 3

1. Open Letter 03.
2. Save the document with Save As and name it Ch 06, SA 03.
3. Change the grammar check option to *Formal* and then complete a spelling and grammar check. (Proper names are spelled correctly; leave passive sentences as written.)
4. After completing the grammar check, proofread the letter and make necessary changes. (There are mistakes in the letter that the grammar checker will not select.)

5. Change the grammar check option back to *Standard*.
6. Save the document again with the same name (Ch 06, SA 03).
7. Print and then close Ch 06, SA 03.

Assessment 4

1. Open Para 02.
2. Save the document with Save As and name it Ch 06, SA 04.
3. Use Thesaurus to make the following changes:
   a. Change *prospective* in the first paragraph to *future*.
   b. Change *significantly* in the second paragraph to *considerably*.
   c. Change *desired* in the second paragraph to *preferred*.
   d. Change *way* in the third paragraph to *method*.
4. Save the document again with the same name (Ch 06, SA 04).
5. Print and then close Ch 06, SA 04.

Assessment 5

1. Open Para 05.
2. Save the document with Save As and name it Ch 06, SA 05.
3. This document overuses the words *producing* and *produce*, as well as *newsletters* and *designing*. Use Thesaurus to make changes to some of the occurrences of *producing*, *produce*, and *designing*. Also, consider rewriting some of the sentences to reduce the number of times *newsletters* appears in the document.
4. Save the document again with the same name (Ch 06, SA 05).
5. Print and then close Ch 06, SA 05.

Assessment 6

1. Open Contract 02.
2. Save the document with Save As and name it Ch 06, SA 06.
3. Make the following changes to the document:
   a. Find all occurrences of *REINBERG MANUFACTURING* and replace with *COLEMAN CORPORATION*.
   b. Find all occurrences of *RM* and replace with *CC*.
   c. Find all occurrences of *LABOR WORKER'S UNION* and replace with *INDUSTRIAL WORKER'S UNION*.
   d. Find all occurrences of *LWU* and replace with *IWU*.
4. Save the document again with the same name (Ch 06, SA 06).
5. Print and then close Ch 06, SA 06.

Assessment 7

1. Open Mortgage.
2. Save the document with Save As and name it Ch 06, SA 07.
3. Make the following changes to the document:
   a. Insert the title *MORTGAGE CONTRACT* centered at the beginning of the document. Separate the title from the first paragraph of text in the document by a blank line.
   b. Select the title and then change the font to 18-point Tahoma bold.
   c. Select the heading *Delinquency:* (be sure to include the colon [:]) and then change the font to 14-point Tahoma bold italic.

d. Use Format Painter to change the font for the remaining headings in the document to 14-point Tahoma bold italic.
4. Save the document again with the same name (Ch 06, SA 07).
5. Print Ch 06, SA 07.
6. With the document still open, make the following changes:
    a. Search for 18-point Tahoma bold formatting and replace with 16-point Arial bold formatting.
    b. Search for 14-point Tahoma bold italic formatting and replace with 13-point Arial bold formatting.
7. Save the document again with the same name (Ch 06, SA 07).
8. Print and then close Ch 06, SA 07.

Chapter 07

Manipulating Tabs

PERFORMANCE OBJECTIVES

Upon completion of chapter 7, you will be able to:
- Set left, right, center, decimal, and bar tabs on the Ruler or at the Tabs dialog box.
- Move, clear, and delete tabs from the Ruler.
- Set leader tabs.
- Reset default tabs.
- Visually align columns of text.

When you work with a document, Word offers a variety of default settings such as margins and line spacing. One of these defaults is left tabs set every 0.5 inch. In some situations, these default tab settings are appropriate; in others, you may want to create your own tab settings. Tabs can be set on the Ruler or at the Tabs dialog box.

Manipulating Tabs on the Ruler

The Ruler can be used, together with the mouse, to set, move, and/or delete tabs. The Ruler displays below the Formatting toolbar as shown in figure 7.1. (If the Ruler is not displayed, click View and then Ruler.

figure

7.1 *Ruler*

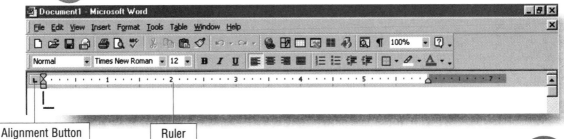

Alignment Button   Ruler

The Ruler displays left tabs set every 0.5 inch. These default tabs are indicated by tiny vertical lines along the bottom of the Ruler. With a left tab, text aligns at the left edge of the tab. The other types of tabs that can be set on the Ruler are center, right, decimal, and bar.

Alignment

The small button at the left side of the Ruler is called the Alignment button. Each time you click the Alignment button, a different tab or paragraph alignment symbol displays. Figure 7.2 shows the tab alignment symbols and what type of tab each will set.

figure
7.2
Tab Alignment Symbols

L	=	left tab
⊥	=	center tab
⌐	=	right tab
⊥·	=	decimal tab
I	=	bar tab

The columns displayed in figure 7.3 show text aligned at different tabs. The text in the first column in figure 7.3 was keyed at a left tab. The second column of text was keyed at a center tab, the third column at a right tab, and the fourth column at a decimal tab. (Refer to figure 7.8 for an example of a bar tab.)

figure
7.3
Types of Tabs

Mathews	British Columbia	Victoria	34.565
Angleton	Saskatchewan	Regina	2,314.0888
Carras	Alberta	Edmonton	368.9

Setting Tabs

To set a left tab on the Ruler, make sure the left alignment symbol (**L**) displays in the Alignment button. Position the mouse pointer just below the tick mark (the marks on the Ruler) where you want the tab symbol to appear, and then click the left mouse button. When you set a tab on the Ruler, any default tabs to the left are automatically deleted by Word.

Set a center, right, decimal, or bar tab on the Ruler in a similar manner. Before setting a tab on the Ruler, click the Alignment button at the left side of the Ruler until the appropriate tab symbol displays, and then set the tab. If you change the tab symbol on the Alignment button, the symbol remains until you change it again or you exit Word. If you exit and then reenter Word, the tab symbol returns to the default of left tab.

You can set the tabs first and then key text or key text at the default tab settings and then set tabs. If you set tabs and then key text, the tab formatting is inserted in the paragraph mark. As you press the Enter key, the paragraph mark is copied down to the next line and the tab formatting is carried with the paragraph mark.

Turning on the display of nonprinting characters is useful when creating tabbed text. With nonprinting characters turned on, the paragraph mark that contains the tab formatting displays. Also, when the Tab key is pressed, a right-pointing arrow displays in the document screen. To turn on the display of nonprinting characters, click the Show/Hide ¶ button on the Standard toolbar or press Shift + Ctrl + *.

Setting Left Tabs on the Ruler

1. At a clear document screen, key the document shown in figure 7.4 by completing the following steps:
   a. Key the heading **TRAINING DEPARTMENT**, centered and bolded.
   b. Press Enter twice.
   c. Return the paragraph alignment back to left and turn off bold.
   d. Set left tabs at the 1-inch mark and the 3.5-inch mark on the Ruler by completing the following steps:
      1) Click the Show/Hide ¶ button on the Standard toolbar to turn on the display of nonprinting characters.
      2) Make sure the Ruler is displayed. (If the Ruler is not displayed, click View and then Ruler.)
      3) Make sure the left tab symbol displays on the Alignment button at the left side of the Ruler.
      4) Position the mouse pointer below the 1-inch mark on the Ruler and then click the left mouse button.

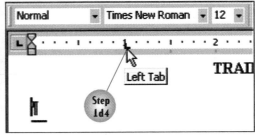

5) Position the mouse pointer below the 3.5-inch mark on the Ruler and then click the left mouse button.

e. Key the text in columns as shown in figure 7.4. Press the Tab key before keying each column entry. (Make sure you press Tab before keying the text in the first column as well as the second column.)

f. Click the Show/Hide ¶ button on the Standard toolbar to turn off the display of nonprinting characters.

2. Save the document and name it Ch 07, Ex 01.

3. Print and then close Ch 07, Ex 01.

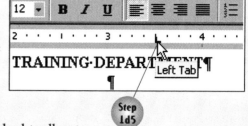

Exercise 1

TRAINING DEPARTMENT

Robert Ludlow	Director
Jessie Mundell	Trainer Supervisor
Rose Paolino	Trainer Specialist
Dale Barlow	Trainer Specialist
Marion Cummings	Administrative Assistant
Alfred King	Administrative Assistant

Inserting a New Line

When you press the Enter key, the insertion point is moved down to the next line and a paragraph mark is inserted in the document. Paragraph formatting is stored in this paragraph mark. For example, if you make changes to tab settings, these changes are inserted in the paragraph mark. In some situations, you may want to start a new line but not a new paragraph. To do this, press Shift + Enter. Word inserts a line break symbol (visible when nonprinting characters have been turned on) and moves the insertion point to the next line.

If you change tab settings and then create columns of text using the New Line command, Shift + Enter, the tab formatting is stored in the paragraph mark at the end of the columns. If you want to make changes to the tab settings for text in the columns, position the insertion point anywhere within the columns (all the text in the columns does not have to be selected), and then make the changes.

If you set tabs for existing text, you must press the Tab key before keying each column entry. After the text is keyed, select the lines of text you want to be formatted with the new tab settings, and then set the tabs on the Ruler.

Setting Tabs at a Specific Measurement

If you want to set a tab at a specific measurement on the Ruler, hold down the Alt key, position the mouse pointer at the desired position, and then hold down the left mouse button. This displays two measurements on the Ruler. The first measurement displays the location of the mouse pointer on the Ruler in relation to the left margin. The second measurement is the distance from the location of the mouse pointer on the Ruler to the right margin. With the left mouse button held down, position the tab symbol at the desired location, then release the mouse button and then the Alt key.

Setting Left and Center Tabs on the Ruler

1. At a clear document screen, key the document shown in figure 7.5 by completing the following steps:
    a. Key the heading **TRAINING SCHEDULE AND COSTS**, centered and bolded.
    b. Press Enter three times.
    c. Return the paragraph alignment back to left and turn off bold.
    d. Set a left tab at the 0.5-inch mark, a center tab at the 3.5-inch mark, and a right tab at the 5.5-inch mark by completing the following steps:
        1) Click the Show/Hide ¶ button on the Standard toolbar to turn on the display of nonprinting characters.
        2) Make sure the Ruler is displayed and then make sure the left tab symbol displays on the Alignment button.
        3) Position the mouse pointer below the 0.5-inch mark on the Ruler, then hold down the Alt key and then the left mouse button. Make sure the first measurement on the Ruler displays as *0.5"*, then release the mouse button and then the Alt key.
        4) Position the mouse pointer on the Alignment button at the left side of the Ruler and then click the left mouse button until the center tab symbol ⊥ displays.
        5) Position the mouse pointer below the 3.5-inch mark on the Ruler, then hold down the Alt key and then the left mouse button. Make sure the first measurement on the Ruler displays as *3.5"*, then release the mouse button and then the Alt key.

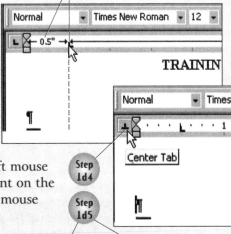

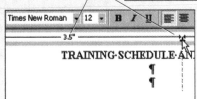

6) Position the mouse pointer on the Alignment button at the left side of the Ruler and then click the left mouse button until the right tab symbol ⌐ displays.

7) Position the mouse pointer below the 5.5-inch mark on the Ruler, then hold down the Alt key and then the left mouse button. Make sure the first measurement on the Ruler displays as *5.5"*, then release the mouse button and then the Alt key.

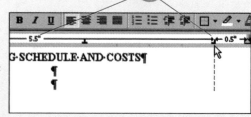

e. Key the text in columns as shown in figure 7.5. Press the Tab key before keying each column entry and press Shift + Enter twice after keying the text in the third column. (This moves the insertion point a double space below the text and inserts the New Line command. *Note: You **must** use the New Line command, Shift + Enter, to move the insertion point to the next line in the columnar text because you will be using this document again in exercise 3.*)

2. Save the document and name it Ch 07, Ex 02.
3. Print and then close Ch 07, Ex 02.

figure 7.5 — Exercise 2

TRAINING SCHEDULE AND COSTS

Supervision	October 15	$125
Document Preparation	October 30	150
Accessing the Internet	November 4	140
Ethics in Business	November 24	95

Moving Tabs

After a tab has been set on the Ruler, it can be moved to a new location. To move a single tab, position the mouse pointer on the tab symbol on the Ruler, hold down the left mouse button, drag the symbol to the new location on the Ruler, and then release the mouse button.

Moving Tabs on the Ruler

1. Open Ch 07, Ex 02.
2. Save the document with Save As and name it Ch 07, Ex 03.
3. Move the text in columns by completing the following steps:
   a. Position the insertion point on any character in the first column of text.
   b. Position the mouse pointer on the left tab symbol on the Ruler, drag the symbol to the 1-inch mark, and then release the left mouse button.
   c. Position the mouse pointer on the right tab symbol on the Ruler, drag the symbol to the 5-inch mark, and then release the left mouse button.
4. Save the document again with the same name (Ch 07, Ex 03).
5. Print and then close Ch 07, Ex 03.

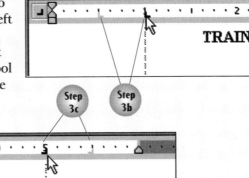

Deleting Tabs

A tab can be removed from the Ruler. To do this, position the mouse pointer on the tab symbol you want deleted, hold down the left mouse button, drag the symbol down into the document screen, and then release the mouse button.

Moving and Deleting Tabs on the Ruler

1. Open Tab 01.
2. Save the document with Save As and name it Ch 07, Ex 04.
3. Move the tab settings so the columns are more balanced by completing the following steps:
   a. Position the insertion point anywhere in the first column entry *Human Resources*.
   b. Position the mouse pointer on the left tab symbol at the 0.5-inch mark, hold down the left mouse button, drag the left tab symbol to the 1.25-inch mark on the Ruler, and then release the mouse button. *(Hint: Use the Alt key to help you precisely position the tab symbol.)*

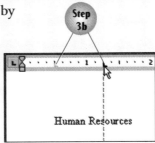

c. Position the mouse pointer on the decimal tab symbol at the 3.5-inch mark, hold down the left mouse button, drag the decimal tab symbol into the document screen, and then release the mouse button. (This deletes the tab and merges the second column of text with the first column.)

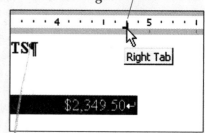

d. Click the Alignment button at the left side of the Ruler until the right tab symbol displays.
e. Position the mouse pointer on the 4.75-inch mark on the Ruler and then click the left mouse button. *(Hint: Use the Alt key to help you precisely position the tab symbol.)*
f. Deselect the text.
4. Save the document again with the same name (Ch 07, Ex 04).
5. Print and then close Ch 07, Ex 04.

Manipulating Tabs at the Tabs Dialog Box

Use the Tabs dialog box shown in figure 7.6 to set tabs at a specific measurement. You can also use the Tabs dialog box to set tabs with preceding leaders and clear one tab or all tabs. To display the Tabs dialog box, click Format and then Tabs.

Tabs Dialog Box

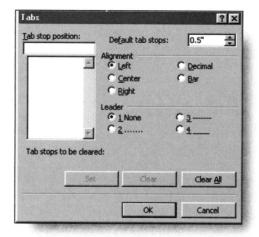

Clearing Tabs

At the Tabs dialog box, you can clear an individual tab or all tabs. To clear all tabs, click the Clear All button. To clear an individual tab, specify the tab position, and then click the Clear button.

Setting Tabs

At the Tabs dialog box, you can set a left, right, center, decimal, or bar tab. (For an example of a bar tab, refer to figure 7.8.) You can also set tabs with preceding leaders. To change the type of tab at the Tabs dialog box, display the dialog box, and then click the desired tab in the Alignment section.

The Tab stop position option at the Tabs dialog box is used to identify the specific measurement where the tab is to be set. To set a tab, click the desired tab alignment, click in the Tab stop position text box, and then key the desired measurement.

Setting Left Tabs at the Tabs Dialog Box

1. At a clear document screen, key the document shown in figure 7.7 by completing the following steps:
    a. Key the headings in the memo and the first paragraph, and then center and bold the title **OCTOBER ACTIVITIES**. (Be sure to return the paragraph alignment back to left and turn off bold.)
    b. With the insertion point a double space below the title, *OCTOBER ACTIVITIES*, use the Tabs dialog box to set a left tab at the 1-inch mark and the 2.2-inch mark by completing the following steps:
        1) Click Format and then Tabs.
        2) At the Tabs dialog box, click the Clear All button.
        3) Make sure Left is selected in the Alignment section of the dialog box. (If not, click Left in the Alignment section.)
        4) Key 1. (The insertion point should automatically be positioned in the Tab stop position text box. If not, click in the Tab stop position text box.)
        5) Click Set.
        6) Key 2.2 (in the Tab stop position text box).
        7) Click Set.
        8) Click OK or press Enter.

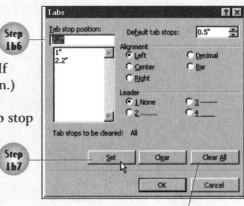

    c. Key the text in columns as shown in figure 7.7. Press the Tab key before keying each column entry. (Make sure you press Tab before keying the text in the first column as well as the second column.)
2. Key the remaining text in the memo.
3. Save the memo and name it Ch 07, Ex 05.
4. Print and then close Ch 07, Ex 05.

figure

7.7 *Exercise 5*

DATE: September 6, 2001

TO: Louise Drennan, Editor

FROM: Denise Quincy

SUBJECT: OCTOBER NEWSLETTER

A variety of exciting activities are planned for October. Please include the following information in the October newsletter.

OCTOBER ACTIVITIES

October 1	Back-to-school luncheon for teachers
October 9	Skating party
October 16	Open house
October 23	Walk-a-thon (fund raiser)
October 25	Fall performance

The Activities Committee is busy planning the school carnival. If the final schedule for the carnival is ready before the publication date of the October newsletter, I will fax it to you.

XX:Ch 07, Ex 05

exercise

6

Setting Left and Vertical Tabs at the Tabs Dialog Box

1. At a clear document screen, key the document shown in figure 7.8 by completing the following steps:
   a. Key the title, **MONROE FAST PITCH SOFTBALL**, bolded and centered, and then press the Enter key twice.
   b. Key the subtitle, **At-home Games for the Chargers**, bolded and centered, and then press the Enter key three times. (Be sure to return the paragraph alignment to left and turn off bold.)

c. Display the Tabs dialog box and then set left tabs and vertical bar tabs by completing the following steps:
   1) Click Format and then Tabs.
   2) At the Tabs dialog box, click the Clear All button.
   3) Make sure Left is selected in the Alignment section of the dialog box. (If not, click Left.)
   4) Key 1.25. (The insertion point should automatically be positioned in the Tab stop position text box. If not, click in the Tab stop position text box.)
   5) Click Set.
   6) Key 2.75.
   7) Click Set.
   8) Key 4.25.
   9) Click Set.
   10) Key 2.25.
   11) Click Bar.
   12) Click Set.
   13) Key 3.75.
   14) Click Set.
   15) Click OK or press Enter.

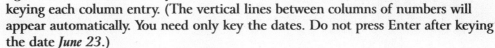

d. Key the text in columns as shown in figure 7.8. Press the Tab key before keying each column entry. (The vertical lines between columns of numbers will appear automatically. You need only key the dates. Do not press Enter after keying the date *June 23*.)

2. Save the document and name it Ch 07, Ex 06.
3. Print and then close Ch 07, Ex 06.

figure

7.8 **Exercise 6**

MONROE FAST PITCH SOFTBALL

At-home Games for the Chargers

April 7	May 5	June 3
April 14	May 12	June 10
April 21	May 20	June 16
April 28	May 27	June 23

Setting Leader Tabs

Tabs can be set with leaders. Leaders are useful in a table of contents or other material where you want to direct the reader's eyes across the page. Figure 7.9 shows an example of leaders. The text in the first column was keyed at a left tab and the text in the second column was keyed at a right tab with leaders.

figure

7.9

Leader Tabs

British Columbia...Victoria
Alberta...Edmonton
Saskatchewan..Regina
Manitoba...Winnipeg
Ontario...Toronto
Quebec ....Quebec

Leaders can be periods (.), hyphens (-), or underlines (_). To add leaders to a tab, click the type of leader desired in the Leader section of the Tabs dialog box.

exercise 7

Setting a Left Tab and a Right Tab with Dot Leaders

1. At a clear document screen, create the document shown in figure 7.10 by completing the following steps:
   a. Change the font to 12-point Tahoma. (If your printer does not support Tahoma, choose a similar sans serif typeface such as Univers.)
   b. Center and bold the title **TABLE OF CONTENTS**.
   c. Press Enter three times. (Be sure to return the alignment of the paragraph back to left and turn off bold.)
   d. Set a left tab and a right tab with dot leaders by completing the following steps:
      1) Click Format and then Tabs.
      2) At the Tabs dialog box, click the Clear All button.
      3) Make sure Left is selected in the Alignment section of the dialog box. (If not, click Left.)
      4) Make sure the insertion point is positioned in the Tab stop position text box and then key 1.
      5) Click Set.
      6) Key 5.
      7) Click Right in the Alignment section of the dialog box.
      8) Click 2....... in the Leader section of the dialog box.
      9) Click Set.
      10) Click OK or press Enter.

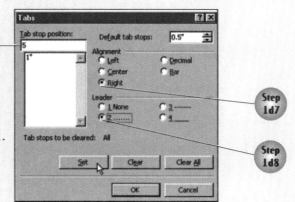

e.   Key the text in columns as shown in figure 7.10. Press the Tab key before keying
     each column entry.
2.   Save the document and name it Ch 07, Ex 07.
3.   Print and then close Ch 07, Ex 07.

Exercise 7

TABLE OF CONTENTS

Telecommunications Basics 2

Basic Transmission Technology 12

Voice Telecommunications 24

Data Telecommunications 36

Video Telecommunications 48

Voice, Data, and Video Integration 63

Setting a Left Tab and Right Tab with Leaders at the Tabs Dialog Box

1.   At a clear document screen, key the document shown in figure 7.11 by completing the
     following steps:
     a.   Key the letter through the first paragraph.
     b.   With the insertion point a double space below the first paragraph, set a left tab
          and a right tab with hyphen leaders by
          completing the following steps:

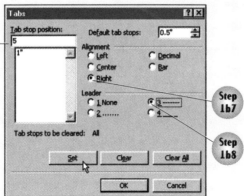

          1)   Click Format and then Tabs.
          2)   At the Tabs dialog box, click
               the Clear All button.
          3)   Make sure Left is selected in the
               Alignment section of the dialog box.
               (If not, click Left.)
          4)   Make sure the insertion point is
               positioned in the Tab stop position
               text box and then key 1.
          5)   Click Set.
          6)   Key 5.
          7)   Click Right in the Alignment section of the dialog box.
          8)   Click 3 ------------- in the Leader section of the dialog box.

      9) Click <u>S</u>et.

      10) Click OK or press Enter.

  c. Key the text in columns as shown in figure 7.11. Press the Tab key before keying each column entry.

  d. After keying the column text, press the Enter key twice, and then key the remaining text of the letter.

2. Save the document and name it Ch 07, Ex 08.

3. Print and then close Ch 07, Ex 08.

figure

7.11

Exercise 8

November 7, 2001

Mr. and Mrs. Donald Sturgis
1519 South Fourth Avenue
Salem, OR 99023

Dear Mr. and Mrs. Sturgis:

Hotel reservations for your trip to the Hawaiian Islands have been finalized. As you requested, all hotel reservations have been made at Grand Palace hotels. Reservations have been confirmed for the following dates:

            Maui Grand Palace------------------------------------December 4-8
            Grand Palace Resort--------------------------------December 9-12
            Grand Palace Seaside----------------------------December 13-15
            Honolulu Grand Palace--------------------------December 16-18

Your airline reservations have not been confirmed. I am still waiting for a reduction in price. I have heard that airlines will be lowering their rates during the next two weeks. As soon as the airfare is reduced below $500, I will make your flight reservations.

Will you need a car while you are vacationing in Hawaii? Please let me know if you would like me to reserve a car for you at each island.

Sincerely,

Frank Truman

XX:Ch 07, Ex 08

Resetting Default Tab Settings

Word sets left tabs every 0.5 inch by default. If you set a tab on the Ruler or at the Tabs dialog box, any tabs to the left are automatically deleted. The interval between default tabs can be changed with the Default tab settings option at the Tabs dialog box. For example, if you want to set tabs every 1 inch, you would key 1 in the Default tab settings text box.

Visually Aligning Columns

Columns of text or data in a document are usually centered between the left and right margins to provide a balanced look. If you do not know the measurements for setting tabs for columns of text, try visually centering columns of text using the Ruler. To do this, you would follow these basic steps:

1. Display the Ruler.
2. Press the Tab key and then key the text for the first row.
3. Press the Tab key and then key the text for the second row. (Continue in this manner for any additional rows of text. Text may not align; this will be corrected in a later step.)
4. Select the text in the columns.
5. Make sure the correct tab alignment symbol is displayed at the left side of the Ruler, position the mouse pointer on the Ruler at the desired location for the first tab, and then click the left mouse button.
6. Set additional tabs on the Ruler as needed. Be sure to change to the proper tab alignment symbol before setting a tab.
7. With the text in columns still selected, drag each tab symbol on the Ruler until the text in the columns displays visually centered between the left and right margins.

Setting Left Tabs for Existing Text

1. At a clear document screen, key the document shown in figure 7.12 by completing the following steps:
   a. Key the title, **COLEMAN DEVELOPMENT CORPORATION**, centered and bolded.
   b. Press the Enter key three times. (Be sure to return the alignment of the paragraph back to left and turn off bold.)
   c. Press the Tab key and then key **President**.
   d. Press the Tab key and then key **Stephanie Branson**.
   e. Press the Enter key twice, press the Tab key, and then key **Vice President**.
   f. Press the Tab and then key **James Zenger**.
   g. Continue keying the remaining text in columns as shown in figure 7.12. Press Tab before each column entry. (The text in the second column will not align.)
   h. After all column text is keyed, select the text in the columns.

i. Make sure the left tab alignment symbol displays at the left side of the Ruler. Position the mouse pointer on the Ruler at approximately the 1-inch mark on the Ruler and then click the left mouse button.

j. Position the mouse pointer on the Ruler at approximately the 4-inch mark on the Ruler and then click the left mouse button.

k. If the columns of text do not look balanced, drag each left tab symbol to a more desirable location on the Ruler.

2. Save the document and name it Ch 07, Ex 09.

3. Print and then close Ch 07, Ex 09.

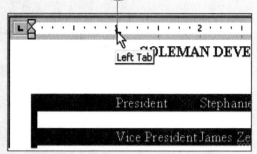

Step 1i

figure

7.12

Exercise 9

COLEMAN DEVELOPMENT CORPORATION

President	Stephanie Branson
Vice President	James Zenger
Manager of Land Development	Paul O'Shea
Director of Training	Robert Ludlow
Director of Finances	Pamela Sturman

Keying Column Headings

If the column heading is the longest line in the column, use the heading to determine tab settings. Column headings that are shorter than the column entries can be visually centered above the entries. To do this, key the column entries first, leaving blank lines above the columns for the headings. After the column entries have been keyed, move the insertion point above the columns, visually determine the center of the columns, and then key the headings.

Some businesses are accepting column headings aligned at the tab settings rather than centered. Keying column headings at the tab stop takes less time than centering headings.

exercise 10

Setting Left and Right Tabs for Existing Text

1. At a clear document screen, key the document shown in figure 7.13 by completing the following steps:
   a. Key the title, **SUPERVISION CLASS**, centered and bolded.
   b. Press the Enter key three times. (Be sure to return the alignment of the paragraph back to left.)
   c. Press the Tab key and then key **Name**.
   d. Press the Tab key and then key **#1**.
   e. Press the Tab key and then key **#2**.
   f. Press the Tab key, key **#3**, and then turn off bold.
   g. Press the Enter key twice, press the Tab key, and then key **Annie Long**.
   h. Press the Tab key and then key **78**.
   i. Press the Tab key and then key **80**.
   j. Press the Tab key and then key **84**.
   k. Press the Enter key and then continue keying the remaining text in columns as shown in figure 7.13. Press Tab before each column entry. (The text in the second, third, and fourth columns will not align.)
   l. After all column text is keyed, select the text in the columns (including the column headings).
   m. Make sure the left tab alignment symbol is displayed at the left side of the Ruler. Position the mouse pointer on the Ruler at approximately the 1-inch mark on the Ruler and then click the left mouse button.

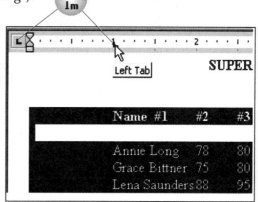

Step 1m

Left Tab

   n. Change to the right tab alignment symbol, position the mouse pointer on the Ruler at approximately the 3-inch mark on the Ruler, and then click the left mouse button.
   o. Set a right tab at the 4-inch mark and another at the 5-inch mark on the Ruler.
   p. If the columns of text do not look balanced, drag each tab symbol to a more desirable location on the Ruler.
2. Save the document and name it Ch 07, Ex 10.
3. Print and then close Ch 07, Ex 10.

figure
7.13

Exercise 10

SUPERVISION CLASS

Name	#1	#2	#3
Annie Long	78	80	84
Grace Bittner	75	80	78
Lena Saunders	88	95	93
Steven Quarles	68	73	70
Chris Yoshihara	100	94	97
Jeffrey Gehring	64	74	82
Christine Kirby	97	89	100
Marilee Metcalf	74	85	78
Alisa Shepherd	98	100	94

chapter summary

➤ By default, tabs are set every 0.5 inch. These settings can be changed on the Ruler or at the Tabs dialog box.

➤ Use the Alignment button located at the left side of the Ruler to select a left, right, center, decimal, or bar tab. When you set a tab on the Ruler, any tabs to the left are automatically deleted.

➤ You can set tabs before or after keying text. If you set them before, the tab formatting is inserted in the paragraph mark. As you press the Enter key, the tab formatting is copied to the next paragraph mark. If you set tabs after keying text, select the lines of text you want to be formatted with the new tabs, and then set the tabs on the Ruler or at the Tabs dialog box.

➤ Turning on the display of nonprinting characters, such as those for paragraphs and tabs, is useful when creating tabbed text.

➤ After a tab has been set on the Ruler, it can be moved or deleted using the mouse pointer.

➤ At the Tabs dialog box, you can set tabs at specific measurements, set tabs with preceding leaders, and clear one tab or all tabs.

➤ Preceding leaders can be periods, hyphens, or underlines.

➤ The 0.5-inch interval between default tabs can be changed with the Default tab settings option at the Tabs dialog box.

commands review

	Mouse	Keyboard
Display the Ruler	View, Ruler	View, Ruler
Display nonprinting characters	Click Show/Hide ¶ button on Standard toolbar	Shift + Ctrl + *
Tabs dialog box	Format, Tabs	Format, Tabs
New Line command		Shift + Enter

thinking offline

Completion: In the space provided at the right, indicate the correct term, symbol, or command.

1. By default, each tab is set apart from the other by this measurement.

2. These are the five types of tabs that can be set on the Ruler.

3. This is the default tab type.

4. Tabs can be set on the Ruler or here.

5. To remove all previous tabs, click this button at the Tabs dialog box.

6. Press these keys on the keyboard to insert a New Line command.

7. Click this button on the Standard toolbar to turn on the display of nonprinting characters.

8. This is the name for the line of periods that can run between columns of text.

9. Tab formatting is inserted in this symbol if you set tabs before keying text.

10. To display the Tabs dialog box, click this option on the Menu bar, and then click Tabs.

working hands-on

Assessment 1

1. At a clear document screen, change the font to 12-point Arial, and then key the document shown in figure 7.14. (Be sure to bold the title.) Before keying the text in columns, set left tabs at the 0.5-inch mark, the 3-inch mark, and the 4.5-inch mark on the Ruler.
2. Save the document and name it Ch 07, SA 01.
3. Print and then close Ch 07, SA 01.

figure
7.14 *Assessment 1*

FINANCIAL PLANNING WORKSHOPS

Estate Planning	02/06/01	6:30 - 8:30
Saving for College	02/13/01	7:00 - 8:30
Preparing for Retirement	03/07/01	6:00 - 8:00
High-Yield Investments	03/14/01	7:00 - 8:30

Assessment 2

1. At a clear document screen, key the memo shown in figure 7.15. Before keying the text in columns, display the Tabs dialog box, clear all tabs, and then set a left tab at the 1-inch mark, and right tabs at the 3-inch mark, the 4-inch mark, and the 5-inch mark.
2. After keying the memo, save the document and name it Ch 07, SA 02.
3. Print and then close Ch 07, SA 02.

figure

7.15

Assessment 2

DATE: November 21, 2001

TO: Louise Drennan, Editor

FROM: Vicki Fortino, Superintendent

SUBJECT: SCHOOL LEVY

With the recent passing of the school levy, I would like the following information presented in the next newsletter to help community members understand how levy dollars are utilized.

The operations levy will raise $6.3 million in 2002 and $6.9 million in 2003. The computer levy will raise $4 million over three years. The bus levy will raise $1 million over two years. The bond was approved by voters in 2000.

The following information shows the projected tax rates per $1,000 of assessed property value for 2002, 2003, and 2004.

	2002	2003	2004
Operations	$3.98	$3.95	$0.00
Computers	1.04	0.98	0.77
Bus	0.31	0.28	0.00
Bond	3.12	3.12	3.12

Money from the school bus levy will help purchase new school buses. These new buses will save taxpayers thousands of dollars through lower maintenance and fuel cost. The computer levy will purchase computers, printers, and related hardware and software for student use. Computers and communications technology are an essential part of ensuring that every student who graduates has the skills to compete in the job market. Every school in the district will receive equipment funded by the computer levy.

XX:Ch 07, SA 02

Assessment 3

1. At a clear document screen, key the document shown in figure 7.16 with the following specifications:
   a. Change the font to 12-point Century Schoolbook (or a similar serif typeface).
   b. Bold and center the title as shown.
   c. Before keying the text in columns, display the Tabs dialog box, and then set left tabs at the 1-inch mark and the 1.5-inch mark, and a right tab with dot leaders at the 5-inch mark.
2. Save the document and name it Ch 07, SA 03.
3. Print and then close Ch 07, SA 03.

figure 7.16   *Assessment 3*

TABLE OF CONTENTS

Assessment 4

1. Open Ch 07, SA 03 as a read-only document.
2. Select the text in columns and then move the tab symbols on the Ruler as follows:
   a. Move the left tab symbol at the 1-inch mark to the 0.5-inch mark.
   b. Move the left tab symbol at the 1.5-inch mark to the 1-inch mark.
   c. Move the right tab symbol at the 5-inch mark to the 5.5-inch mark.
3. Save the document with Save As and name it Ch 07, SA 04.
4. Print and then close Ch 07, SA 04.

Assessment 5

1. At a clear document screen, key the document shown in figure 7.17. You determine the tab settings for the text in columns. (Align the first column at a left tab and the second column at a right tab. Make sure you include the leaders.)
2. Save the document and name it Ch 07, SA 05.
3. Print and then close Ch 07, SA 05.

 **figure**
7.17

Assessment 5

LAND DEVELOPMENT DEPARTMENT

Paul O'Shea - Manager

Tamara Langston- - - - - - - - - - - - - - - - Assistant Manager

Daniel Roarke - - - - - - - - - - - - - Environmental Specialist

Jeanne Beeler - Legal Aide

Carl Wassal - - - - - - - - - - - - - - Administrative Assistant

Ching Ney - - - - - - - - - - - - - - - Administrative Assistant

Assessment 6

1. At a clear document screen, key the text shown in figure 7.18 in an appropriate business letter format. You determine the tab settings for the text in columns.
2. After keying the letter, save it and name it Ch 07, SA 06.
3. Print and then close Ch 07, SA 06.

figure
7.18   *Assessment 6*

October 10, 2001

Mr. and Mrs. George Sedgwick
2033 Regents Boulevard
Salem, OR 99022

Dear Mr. and Mrs. Sedgwick:

The travel experts at Travel Advantage have specially chosen the most exciting and inviting vacation destinations for you and your family. This month, we are offering a package travel plan to St. Thomas, a dazzling Caribbean island. At St. Thomas, you will be able to enjoy boating, swimming, sailing, wind surfing, scuba diving, golfing, and tennis. The St. Thomas package includes round-trip airfare, seven nights' hotel accommodations, and round-trip airport transfers. The prices for this exciting vacation vary depending on the city of departure. Sample prices are shown below.

	Regular	TA Price
Los Angeles	$1,320	$1,088
Dallas	1,220	930
Chicago	1,250	980
New York	1,040	880

This package offer includes a bonus of 2-for-1 pricing on sightseeing tours, a diving course at Bolongo Bay, and a full-day or half-day catamaran cruise. Call us now to make your reservations for beautiful St. Thomas. All prices are firm through the end of April. After that, prices may vary depending on hotel availability.

Sincerely,

Lisa Wellington
Travel Consultant

XX:Ch 07, SA 06

 **Chapter 08**

Manipulating Text within and between Documents

8

PERFORMANCE OBJECTIVES

Upon successful completion of chapter 8, you will be able to:

- Delete, move, copy, and paste selected text.
- Save selected text as a separate document.
- Insert a document into another document.
- Open and close multiple documents.
- Split a window.
- Arrange windows.
- Size and move windows.
- Cut and paste or cut and copy text between documents.

Some documents may need to be heavily revised, and these revisions may include deleting, moving, or copying blocks of text. This kind of editing is generally referred to as *cut and paste*. Cutting and pasting can be done within the same document, or text can be selected and then moved or copied to another document. Also, a document can be inserted into another document. This might be useful in a situation where you want to create a personalized document with standard text. You can open multiple documents and then cut and paste or copy and paste text between documents.

Working with Blocks of Text

When cutting and pasting, you work with blocks of text. A block of text is a portion of text that you have selected. (Chapter 1 explained the various methods for selecting text.) A block of text can be as small as one character or as large as an entire page or document. Once a block of text has been selected, it can be deleted, moved to a new location, or copied and placed in a certain location within a document. The last two operations involve using Word's Cut, Copy, and Paste features.

Deleting a Block of Text

Word offers different methods for deleting text from a document. To delete a single character, you can use either the Delete key or the Backspace key. To delete more than a single character, select the portion of text to be deleted, and then choose one of the following options:

Cut

- Press Delete.
- Click the Cut button on the Standard toolbar.
- Choose Edit and then Cut.

If you press the Delete key, the text is deleted permanently. (You can restore deleted text with the Undo Clear option from the Edit menu or with the Undo or Redo buttons on the Standard toolbar.) The Cut button on the Standard toolbar and the Cut option from the Edit drop-down menu will delete the selected text and insert it to the *Clipboard*. Word's Clipboard is a temporary area of memory. The Clipboard holds text while it is being moved or copied to a new location in the document or to a different document.

Delete selected text with the Delete key if you do not need it again. Use the other methods if you might want to insert deleted text in the current document or a different document.

exercise

Deleting Selected Text

1. Open Report 01.
2. Save the document with Save As and name it Ch 08, Ex 01.
3. Select and bold the title *DESKTOP PUBLISHING* and the headings *Defining Desktop Publishing, Initiating the Desktop Publishing Process, Planning the Publication,* and *Creating the Content.*
4. Delete the following text in the report:
   a. Delete the last sentence in the second paragraph in the *Defining Desktop Publishing* section (the sentence that begins *Desktop Publishing involves using desktop publishing software...*) by completing the following steps:
      1) Select the sentence.
      2) Press the Delete key.
   b. Delete the last sentence in the third paragraph in the *Defining Desktop Publishing* section (the sentence that begins *Everything from a flyer to a newsletter...*) by completing the following steps:
      1) Select the sentence.
      2) Click the Cut button on the Standard toolbar.

Step 4b2

Step 4b1

   c. Delete the second paragraph in the *Planning the Publication* section of the report.
5. Check page breaks in the document and, if necessary, adjust the page breaks.
6. Save the document again with the same name (Ch 08, Ex 01).
7. Print and then close Ch 08, Ex 01.

Moving Blocks of Text

Word offers a variety of methods for moving text. After you have selected a block of text, move text with buttons on the Standard toolbar or options from the Edit drop-down menu.

To move a block of selected text from one location to another using buttons on the Standard toolbar, you would complete the following steps:

1. Select the text.
2. Click the Cut button on the Standard toolbar.
3. Position the insertion point at the location where the selected text is to be inserted.
4. Click the Paste button on the Standard toolbar.

Paste

To move a block of selected text from one location to another using options from the Edit menu, you would complete the following steps:

1. Select the text.
2. Choose Edit and then Cut.
3. Position the insertion point at the location where the selected text is to be inserted.
4. Choose Edit and then Paste.

In addition to the methods just described, a block of selected text can also be moved with the mouse. There are two methods for moving text with the mouse. You can use the mouse to drag selected text to a new location or use a shortcut menu. To drag selected text to a new location, you would complete the following steps:

1. Select the text to be moved with the mouse.
2. Move the I-beam pointer inside the selected text until it becomes an arrow pointer.
3. Hold down the left mouse button, drag the arrow pointer (displays with a gray box attached) to the location where you want the selected text inserted, and then release the button.
4. Deselect the text.

When you hold down the left mouse button and drag the mouse, the arrow pointer displays with a small gray box attached. In addition, the insertion point displays as a grayed vertical bar. When the insertion point (grayed vertical bar) is located in the desired position, release the mouse button. The selected text is removed from its original position and inserted in the new location.

To move selected text with a shortcut menu, you would complete the following steps:

1. Select the text to be moved with the mouse.
2. Move the I-beam pointer inside the selected text until it becomes an arrow pointer.
3. Click the *right* mouse button.
4. At the shortcut menu that displays, click Cut.
5. Position the insertion point where the text is to be inserted.
6. Click the *right* mouse button to display the shortcut menu and then click Paste.

When selected text is cut from a document and inserted in the Clipboard, it stays in the Clipboard until other text is inserted in the Clipboard. For this reason, you can paste text from the Clipboard more than just once. For example, if you cut text to the Clipboard, you can paste this text in different locations within the document or other documents as many times as desired.

Moving Selected Text

1. Open Para 03.
2. Save the document with Save As and name it Ch 08, Ex 02.
3. Move the following text in the document:
   a. Move the second paragraph above the first paragraph by completing the following steps:
      1) Select the second paragraph including the blank line below the paragraph.
      2) Click the Cut button on the Standard toolbar.
      3) Position the insertion point at the beginning of the first paragraph.
      4) Click the Paste button on the Standard toolbar.

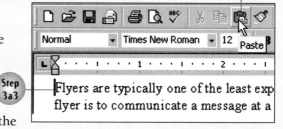

Step 3a4

Step 3a3

   b. Move the third paragraph above the second paragraph by completing the following steps:
      1) Select the third paragraph including the blank line below the paragraph.
      2) Click Edit and then Cut.
      3) Position the insertion point at the beginning of the second paragraph.
      4) Click Edit and then Paste.

Step 3c1

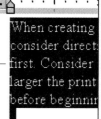

   c. Move the first paragraph to the end of the document using the mouse by completing the following steps:
      1) Using the mouse, select the first paragraph including the blank line below the paragraph.
      2) Move the I-beam pointer inside the selected text until it becomes an arrow pointer.
      3) Hold down the left mouse button, drag the arrow pointer (displays with a small gray box attached) a double space below the last paragraph (make sure the insertion point, which displays as a grayed vertical bar, is positioned a double space below the last paragraph), and then release the mouse button.
      4) Deselect the text.
4. Save the document again with the same name (Ch 08, Ex 02).
5. Print and then close Ch 08, Ex 02.

Step 3c3

Copying a Block of Text

Copying selected text can be useful in documents that contain repetitive portions of text. You can use this function to insert duplicate portions of text in a document instead of rekeying the text. After you have selected a block of text, copy the text with buttons on the Standard toolbar or options from the Edit drop-down menu.

To copy text with the buttons on the Standard toolbar, you would complete the following steps:

1. Select the text to be copied.
2. Click the Copy button on the Standard toolbar.
3. Move the insertion point to the location where the copied text is to be inserted.
4. Click the Paste button on the Standard toolbar.

Copy

To copy text with options from the Edit drop-down menu, you would complete the following steps:

1. Select the text to be copied.
2. Click Edit and then Copy.
3. Move the insertion point to the location where the copied text is to be inserted.
4. Click Edit and then Paste.

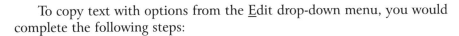
exercise 3

Copying Selected Text with Buttons on the Standard Toolbar

1. Open Block 01.
2. Save the document with Save As and name it Ch 08, Ex 03.
3. Select the entire document and then change the font to 14-point Tahoma bold.
4. Copy the text in the document to the end of the document by completing the following steps:
   a. Select the text in the document and include two blank lines below the text.
   b. Click the Copy button on the Standard toolbar.
   c. Move the insertion point to the end of the document.
   d. Click the Paste button on the Standard toolbar.
5. Copy the text again to the end of the document. To do this, position the insertion point at the end of the document and then click the Paste button on the Standard toolbar.
6. Save the document with the same name (Ch 08, Ex 03).
7. Print and then close Ch 08, Ex 03.

Step 4b

Copy

Training Departme

Director's Meetin

Thursday, October 11

exercise 4

Copying Selected Text Using the Mouse

1. Open Block 02.
2. Save the document with Save As and name it Ch 08, Ex 04.
3. Copy the text in the document using the mouse by completing the following steps:
   a. Select the text with the mouse. Include the two blank lines below the text.
   b. Move the I-beam pointer inside the selected text until it becomes an arrow pointer.
   c. Hold down the Ctrl key and then the left mouse button. Drag the arrow pointer (displays with a small gray box and a box with a plus symbol inside) to the end of the document immediately above the end-of-document marker (make sure the insertion point, which displays as a grayed vertical bar, is positioned immediately above the end-of-document marker), and then release the mouse button and then the Ctrl key.
   d. Deselect the text.
4. Select the entire document and then copy it to the end of the document. (You should have a total of four forms. Make sure all forms fit on one page. If the forms do not fit on one page, consider deleting any extra blank lines between forms.)
5. Save the document again with the same name (Ch 08, Ex 04).
6. Print and then close Ch 08, Ex 04.

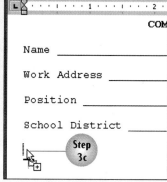

Collecting and Pasting Multiple Items

Word 2000 includes a new feature called *collecting and pasting* that you can use to collect up to 12 different items and then paste them in various locations. Display the Clipboard toolbar shown in figure 8.1 when you want to collect and paste items. Display this toolbar by right-clicking any currently displayed toolbar and then clicking Clipboard. You can also display the toolbar by clicking View, pointing to Toolbars, and then clicking Clipboard.

Clipboard Toolbar

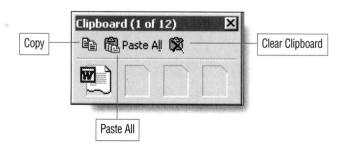

Select text or an object you want to copy and then click the Copy button on the Clipboard toolbar. Continue selecting text or items and clicking the Copy button. To insert an item, position the insertion point in the desired location and then click the button on the Clipboard representing the item. Position the insertion point on a button and a ScreenTip displays with information on the item. If the item is text, the first 50 characters display. When all desired items are inserted, click the Clear Clipboard button to remove any remaining items.

Clear Clipboard

Usually, if you cut or copy any two items consecutively, the Clipboard toolbar automatically displays. If you close the Clipboard toolbar three times in a row without clicking a button on the toolbar, the Clipboard toolbar will no longer appear automatically. To display the Clipboard toolbar, right-click any currently displayed toolbar, and then click *Clipboard*. You can also click <u>V</u>iew, point to <u>T</u>oolbars, and then click *Clipboard*. When you display the Clipboard toolbar and then click a button on the toolbar, the count is reset, and from that point on the Clipboard toolbar appears automatically again.

exercise 5

Collecting and Pasting Paragraphs of Text

1. Open Contract 02.
2. Display the Clipboard toolbar by right-clicking an existing toolbar and then clicking *Clipboard* at the drop-down list. (If there are any items in the Clipboard, click the Clear Clipboard button.)
3. Select paragraph 2 in the *TRANSFERS AND MOVING EXPENSES* section and then click the Copy button on the Clipboard toolbar.
4. Select and then copy each of the following paragraphs:
   a. Paragraph 4 in the *TRANSFERS AND MOVING EXPENSES* section.
   b. Paragraph 1 in the *SICK LEAVE* section.
   c. Paragraph 3 in the *SICK LEAVE* section.
   d. Paragraph 5 in the *SICK LEAVE* section.
5. Paste the paragraphs by completing the following steps:
   a. Click the New Blank Document button on the Standard toolbar.
   b. Key **CONTRACT NEGOTIATION ITEMS** centered and bolded.
   c. Press Enter twice, turn off bold, and return the paragraph alignment back to Left.
   d. Click the button on the Clipboard representing paragraph 2. (When the paragraph is inserted in the document, the paragraph number changes to 1.)
   e. Click the button on the Clipboard representing paragraph 4.
   f. Click the button on the Clipboard representing paragraph 3.
   g. Click the button on the Clipboard representing paragraph 5.

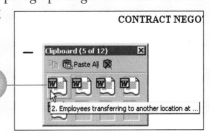

6. Click the Clear Clipboard button on the Clipboard toolbar.
7. Turn off the display of the Clipboard toolbar.
8. Select the numbered paragraphs and then click the Numbering button on the Formatting toolbar. (This properly renumbers the paragraphs.)
9. Save the document and name it Ch 08, Ex 05.
10. Print and then close Ch 08, Ex 05.
11. Close Contract 02 without saving the changes.

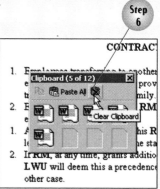

Working with Documents

Some documents may contain standard information—information that remains the same. For example, a legal document, such as a will, may contain text that is standard and appears in all wills. Repetitive text can be saved as a separate document and then inserted into an existing document whenever needed.

There are two methods that can be used for saving text into a separate document. The first is to save a document just as you have been doing. The other method is to select standard text within a document and save it as a separate document.

Saving Standard Text

If you know in advance what information or text is standard and will be used again, you can save it as a separate document. You should determine how to break down the information based on how it will be used. After deciding how to break down the information, key the text at a clear document screen, and then save it in the normal manner.

Saving Selected Text

When you create a document and then realize that a portion of the text in the document will be needed for future documents, you can save it as a separate document. To do this, you would copy the text, paste it into a new document screen, and then save it in the normal manner.

Inserting a Document

A document containing standard text can be inserted into an existing document with the File option from the Insert drop-down menu. To insert a standard document into an existing document, position the insertion point in the current document at the location where the standard text is to be inserted, then click Insert and then File. At the Insert File dialog box shown in figure 8.2, double-click the document name to be inserted.

figure
8.2

Insert File Dialog Box

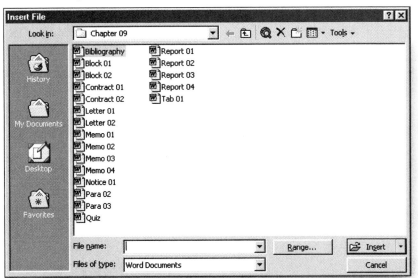

exercise 6

Saving Selected Text as a Separate Document

1. Open Memo 02.
2. Select the paragraphs containing book titles (the second through the fifth paragraphs) and then save them as a separate document named Textbooks by completing the following steps:
   a. Select the second through the fifth paragraphs (the paragraphs containing book titles).
   b. Click the Copy button on the Standard toolbar.
   c. Click the New Blank Document button on the Standard toolbar.
   d. At the clear document screen, click the Paste button on the Standard toolbar.
   e. Save the document and name it Textbooks.
   f. Close the Textbooks document.
3. Close Memo 02 without saving any changes.
4. At a clear document screen, key the memo headings and the first paragraph of the text shown in figure 8.3. Use an appropriate memo format. After keying the first paragraph, press Enter twice, and then insert the Textbooks document by completing the following steps:
   a. Click Insert and then File.
   b. At the Insert File dialog box, double-click *Textbooks*.
5. Move the insertion point a double space below the last paragraph and then key the last paragraph shown in figure 8.3. Include your initials and the document name a double space below the last line of the paragraph.

6. Select the second through the fifth paragraphs (the paragraphs containing book titles) and then insert bullets before the paragraphs. (Use the Bullets button on the Formatting toolbar.)
7. Save the memo and name it Ch 08, Ex 06.
8. Print and then close Ch 08, Ex 06.

Exercise 6

DATE: December 6, 2001; TO: All OT Staff; FROM: Christy Edmonds; SUBJECT: BUSINESS COMMUNICATIONS BOOKS

The library has recently purchased several reference books on business communications. These books are now available at the library. The books that are available include:

[Insert Textbooks document here.]

You may want to use these reference books for your business communications classes. Students may also want to use them for preparing documents or writing reports.

XX:Ch 08, Ex 06

Working with Windows

Word operates within the Windows environment created by the Windows 95 or 98 program. However, when working in Word, a *window* refers to the document screen. The Windows program creates an environment in which various software programs are used with menu bars, scroll bars, and icons to represent programs and files. With the Windows program, you can open several different software programs and move between them quickly. Similarly, using windows in Word, you can open several different documents and move between them quickly.

Opening Multiple Windows

With multiple documents open, you can move the insertion point between them. You can move or copy information between documents or compare the contents of several documents. The maximum number of documents (windows) that you can have open at one time depends on the memory of your computer system and the amount of text in each document. When you open a new window, it is placed on top of the original window. Once multiple windows are open, you can resize the windows to see all or a portion of them on the screen.

A document can be opened at the Open dialog box, or a blank document can be opened by clicking the New Blank Document button on the Standard toolbar. You can also open multiple documents at the same time at the Open dialog box (as learned in an earlier chapter).

When you are working in a document, the document fills the entire document screen. If you open another document without closing the first, the newly opened document will fill the document screen. The first document is still open, but it is covered by the new one.

When a document is open, a button displays on the Taskbar. This button represents the open document and contains a document icon and the document name. (Depending on the length of the document name and the size of the button, not all of the name may be visible.) Another method for determining what documents are open is to click the <u>W</u>indow option on the Menu bar. This displays a drop-down menu similar to the one shown in figure 8.4. (The number of documents and document names displayed at the bottom of the menu will vary.)

Window Drop-Down Menu

figure
8.4

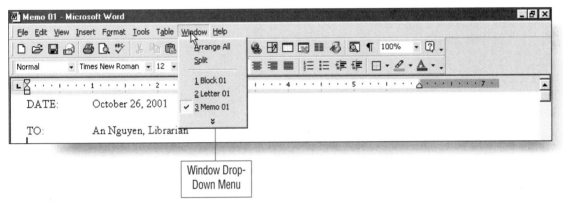

Window Drop-Down Menu

The open document names are displayed at the bottom of the menu. The document name with the check mark in front of it is the *active* document. The active document is the document containing the insertion point. To make one of the other documents active, click the document name. If you are using the keyboard, key the number shown in front of the desired document. When you change the active document, the Window menu is removed and the new active document is displayed. *(Note: Some virus protection software will let you open only one document at a time.)*

Closing Multiple Windows

All open documents can be closed at the same time. To do this, hold down the Shift key, and then click <u>F</u>ile on the Menu bar. This causes the <u>F</u>ile drop-down menu to display with the <u>C</u>lose All option (instead of the <u>C</u>lose option). Click the <u>C</u>lose All option and all open documents will be closed.

exercise 7

Opening and Closing Multiple Windows

(Note: If you are using Word on a network system that contains a virus checker, you may not be able to open multiple documents at once.)

1. Open several documents at the same time by completing the following steps:
   a. Display the Open dialog box.
   b. Click the document named Block 01.
   c. Hold down the Ctrl key, then click *Letter 01* and then *Memo 01*.
   d. Release the Ctrl key and then click the <u>O</u>pen button located in the bottom right corner of the dialog box.
2. Make Letter 01 the active document by clicking the button on the Taskbar containing the name Letter 01.
3. Make Block 01 the active document by clicking <u>W</u>indow and then <u>1</u>.
4. Close all open documents by completing the following steps:
   a. Hold down the Shift key.
   b. Click <u>F</u>ile on the Menu bar.
   c. Click <u>C</u>lose All.

Splitting a Window

With the <u>S</u>plit command from the <u>W</u>indow drop-down menu you can divide a window into two *panes*. This is helpful if you want to view different parts of the same document at one time. You may want to display an outline for a report in one pane, for example, and the portion of the report that you are editing in the other. The original window is split into two panes that extend horizontally across the screen.

A window can be split with the <u>S</u>plit option from the <u>W</u>indow drop-down menu or with the Split bar. To split the current document window using the <u>S</u>plit option, click <u>W</u>indow and then <u>S</u>plit. This causes a wide gray line to display in the middle of the screen and the mouse pointer to display as a double-headed arrow pointing up and down with a small double line between. Move this double-headed arrow pointer up or down, if desired, by dragging the mouse or by pressing the up and/or down arrow keys on the keyboard. When the double-headed arrow is positioned at the desired location in the document, click the left mouse button or press the Enter key.

You can also split the window with the split bar. The split bar is the small gray horizontal bar above the up scroll triangle on the vertical scroll bar as identified in figure 8.5.

figure

8.5

Split Bar

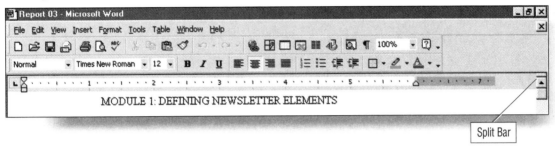

MODULE 1: DEFINING NEWSLETTER ELEMENTS

Split Bar

To split the window with the split bar, position the arrow pointer on the split bar until it turns into a short double line with an up- and down-pointing arrow. Hold down the left mouse button, drag the double-headed arrow into the document screen to the location where you want the window split, and then release the mouse button.

When a window is split, the insertion point is positioned in the bottom pane. To move the insertion point to the other pane with the mouse, position the I-beam pointer in the other pane, and then click the left mouse button. If you are using the keyboard, press F6 to move to the next pane. (You can also press Shift + F6, which is the Previous Pane command.) Figure 8.6 displays a document split into two windows.

figure

8.6

Split Window

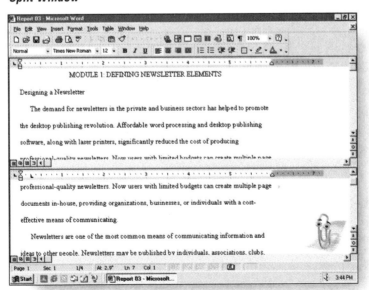

To remove the split line from the document, click <u>W</u>indow and then Remove Split. You can also remove the split with the mouse. To do this, position the arrow pointer on the split line until it turns into a short double line with an up- and down-pointing arrow. Hold down the left mouse button, drag the split line up to the top of the screen or down to the bottom of the screen, and then release the mouse button.

Moving Selected Text between Split Windows

1. Open Report 03.
2. Save the document with Save As and name it Ch 08, Ex 08.
3. Split the window by completing the following steps:
   a. Click <u>W</u>indow and then <u>S</u>plit.
   b. With the split line displayed in the middle of the document screen, click the left mouse button.
   c. With the insertion point positioned in the bottom pane, move the *MODULE 1: DEFINING NEWSLETTER ELEMENTS* section below the *MODULE 2: PLANNING A NEWSLETTER* section by completing the following steps:
      1) Select the *MODULE 1: DEFINING NEWSLETTER ELEMENTS* section from the title to right above *MODULE 2: PLANNING A NEWSLETTER*.
      2) Click the Cut button on the Standard toolbar.
      3) Position the arrow pointer at the end of the document in the top window pane and then click the left mouse button.
      4) Click the Paste button on the Standard toolbar.
      5) Change the number in the two titles to *MODULE 1: PLANNING A NEWSLETTER* and *MODULE 2: DEFINING NEWSLETTER ELEMENTS*.
4. Insert a section break that begins a new page above *MODULE 2: DEFINING NEWSLETTER ELEMENTS* by completing the following steps:
   a. Position the arrow pointer immediately left of the *M* in *MODULE 2: DEFINING NEWSLETTER ELEMENTS* in the bottom window pane and then click the left mouse button.
   b. Click <u>I</u>nsert and then <u>B</u>reak.
   c. At the Break dialog box, click <u>N</u>ext page.
   d. Click OK or press Enter.
5. Remove the split from the window by clicking <u>W</u>indow and then Remove Split.
6. Check page breaks in the document and, if necessary, make corrections to the page breaks.
7. Save the document again with the same name (Ch 08, Ex 08).
8. Print and then close Ch 08, Ex 08.

Arranging Windows

If you have more than one document open, you can use the <u>A</u>rrange All option from the <u>W</u>indow drop-down menu to view a portion of all open documents. To do this, choose <u>W</u>indow and then <u>A</u>rrange All. Figure 8.7 shows a document screen with three open documents that have been arranged.

figure
8.7

Arranged Documents

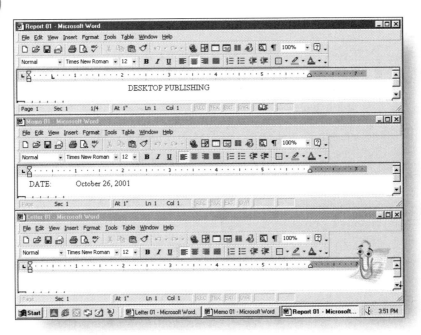

When open documents are arranged, a portion of each window displays on the screen. The title bar for each document displays along with the vertical and horizontal scroll bars.

exercise 9

Arranging Windows

1. Open the following documents: Letter 02, Memo 02, Para 02, and Report 02.
2. Arrange the windows by clicking <u>W</u>indow and then <u>A</u>rrange All.
3. Make Letter 02 the active document by positioning the arrow pointer on the title bar for Letter 02 and then clicking the left mouse button.
4. Close Letter 02.
5. Make Para 02 active and then close it.
6. Closing the remaining documents.
7. Click the Maximize button to maximize the window. (This button is located in the upper right corner of the active window. You will learn more about this button in the next section.)

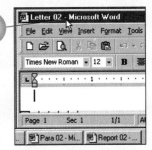

Step 3

Maximizing, Minimizing, and Restoring Documents

Maximize

Minimize

Restore

Use the Maximize and Minimize buttons in the upper right corner of the active document window to change the size of the window. The Maximize button is the button in the upper right corner of the active document immediately to the left of the Close button. (The Close button is the button containing the X.) The Minimize button is located immediately to the left of the Maximize button.

If you arrange all open documents and then click the Maximize button in the active document, the active document expands to fill the document screen. In addition, the Maximize button changes to the Restore button. To return the active document back to its size before it was maximized, click the Restore button. If you click the Minimize button in the active document, the document is reduced and a button displays on the Taskbar representing the document. To restore a document that has been minimized, click the button on the Taskbar representing the document.

In addition to using the Maximize, Minimize, Restore, and Close buttons for a document, you can also use a shortcut menu. To display the shortcut menu for a document, position the arrow pointer on the title bar of the document, and then click the right mouse button. This causes a shortcut menu to display with the options Restore, Move, Size, Minimize, Maximize, and Close. At this menu, click the desired option.

Maximizing, Minimizing, and Restoring Documents

1. Open Tab 01.
2. Maximize Tab 01 by clicking the Maximize button at the right side of the Title bar. (The Maximize button is the button at the right side of the Title bar, immediately left of the Close button.)
3. Open Memo 03.
4. Open Report 03.
5. Arrange the windows.
6. Make Memo 03 the active window.
7. Minimize Memo 03 using the mouse by clicking the Minimize button in the upper right corner of the active window.
8. Make Tab 01 the active document and then minimize Tab 01.
9. Restore Tab 01 by clicking the button on the Taskbar representing the document.
10. Restore Memo 03 by clicking the button on the Taskbar representing the document.
11. Make Report 03 the active document and then close it.
12. Close Memo 03.
13. Maximize Tab 01 by clicking the Maximize button at the right side of the Tab 01 Title bar.
14. Close Tab 01.

The size of documents that have been arranged can be increased or decreased using the mouse. To increase or decrease the size of the active document window vertically, move the mouse pointer to the double-line border at the right or left side of the window until it turns into a left- and right-pointing arrow. Hold down the left mouse button and then drag the border to the right or left. When the window is the desired size, release the mouse button.

To increase or decrease the size of the active window horizontally, move the mouse pointer to the double-line border at the top or bottom of the window until it turns into an up- and down-pointing arrow. Hold down the left mouse button and then drag the border up or down to increase or decrease the size. When the window is the desired size, release the mouse button.

Documents that have been arranged can also be moved. To move an arranged document, make sure it is the active document, position the arrow pointer on the Title bar, hold down the left mouse button, drag the outline of the document window to the desired location, and then release the mouse button.

Changing the Size of a Window Using the Mouse

1. Open Memo 04.
2. Open Report 01.
3. Arrange the windows.
4. Change the size of the Report 01 document window by completing the following steps:

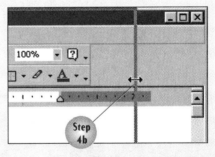

   a. Position the mouse pointer on the double-line border at the right side of the window until it turns into a left- and right-pointing arrow.
   b. Hold down the left mouse button, drag the border to the left approximately 1 inch, and then release the mouse button.
   c. Position the mouse pointer on the double-line border at the left side of the window until it turns into a left- and right-pointing arrow.

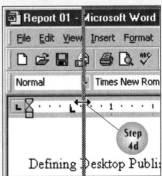

   d. Hold down the left mouse button, drag the border to the right approximately 1 inch, and then release the mouse button.
5. Make the same changes to Memo 04.
6. Close Memo 04.
7. Maximize Report 01 by clicking the Maximize button at the upper right side of the Report 01 window.
8. Close Report 01.

Cutting and Pasting Text between Documents

With several documents open, you can easily move, copy, and/or paste text from one document to another. To move, copy, and/or paste text between documents, use the cutting and pasting options you learned earlier in this chapter together with the information about windows in this chapter.

Copying Selected Text from One Open Document to Another

1. At a clear document screen, key the memo shown in figure 8.8 in an appropriate memo format. (Press the Enter key three times after keying the first paragraph and before you key the second paragraph.)
2. Save the memo and name it Ch 08, Ex 12.
3. With Ch 08, Ex 12 still open in the screen, open Memo 02.
4. With Memo 02 as the active document, copy the first three books listed in the memo by completing the following steps:
   a. Select the three paragraphs containing the first three book titles.
   b. Click the Copy button on the Standard toolbar.
   c. Deselect the text.
   d. Make Ch 08, Ex 12 the active document.
   e. Position the insertion point a double space below the first paragraph and then click the Paste button on the Standard toolbar.
5. Save the memo again with the same name (Ch 08, Ex 12).
6. Print and then close Ch 08, Ex 12.
7. Close Memo 02.

Exercise 12

DATE: November 15, 2001; TO: An Nguyen, Librarian; FROM: Marlene St. Claire, Assistant Librarian; SUBJECT: BUSINESS COMMUNICATIONS BOOKS

I found $80.50 in the library reference fund and $27.00 in the emergency fund. With these combined amounts, I was able to purchase the following books:

With funds that will become available January 1, we should be able to purchase the remaining two books.

XX:Ch 08, Ex 12

chapter summary

➤ Deleting, moving, or copying blocks of text within a document is generally referred to as *cutting and pasting*. A block of text can be as small as one character or as large as an entire page or document.

➤ When deleting a block of text, use the Delete key if you do not need that text again; use the Cut button on the Standard toolbar or the Cut option from the Edit drop-down menu if you might want to insert the deleted text in the current or a different document.

➤ Selected text can be copied in a document or a different document using the Copy and Paste buttons on the Standard toolbar or the Copy and Paste options from the Edit drop-down menu.

➤ With the collecting and pasting feature you can collect up to 12 different items and then paste them in various locations.

➤ Text that will be used repeatedly in one or more documents can be saved as a separate document. This text can be keyed and the document saved as usual, or the text can be selected within a document and saved as a separate document. This separate document can then be inserted into an existing document with the File option from the Insert drop-down menu.

➤ When working in Word 2000, a window refers to the document screen.

➤ You can open multiple documents and copy or move text between documents or compare the contents of several documents.

➤ A new (empty) window can be opened in several ways.

➤ Each document that is opened will fill the entire editing window. Move among the open documents by clicking the button on the Taskbar representing the document or by clicking Window on the Menu bar and then clicking the desired document name. The active document is the document containing the insertion point.

➤ With the Split command from the Window drop-down menu, you can divide a window into two panes. This enables you to view different parts of the same document at one time.

➤ Use the Arrange All option from the Window drop-down menu to view a portion of all open documents.

➤ Use the Maximize, Minimize, and Restore buttons in the upper right corner of the window to reduce or increase the size of the active window.

➤ The size of documents that have been arranged can be changed using the mouse. A document that has been arranged can also be moved using the mouse.

➤ With several documents open, you can easily move, copy, and/or paste text from one document to another.

commands review

	Mouse	Keyboard
Delete one character		Press Delete or Backspace
Delete selected text permanently		Press Delete
Delete selected text and insert it in the Clipboard	Edit, Cut; or click Cut button on Standard toolbar; or with I-beam pointer inside text block, click *right* mouse button, click Cut	Edit, Cut
Insert text from Clipboard to new location	Edit, Paste; or click Paste button on Standard toolbar; or click *right* mouse button, click Paste	Edit, Paste
Copy selected text	Edit, Copy, move insertion point to new location, then Edit, Paste; or click Copy button on Standard toolbar, then click Paste button at new location	Edit, Copy, then Edit, Paste
Display Clipboard toolbar	Right-click any currently displayed toolbar, then click Clipboard	View, Toolbars, Clipboard
Deselect text	Click left mouse button outside selected text	Press any arrow key
Save selected paragraph as separate document	Edit, Copy, or click Copy button on Standard toolbar; click the New Blank Document button on Standard toolbar; then click Edit, Paste, or click Paste button on Standard toolbar; then save in the normal manner	Edit, Copy; choose File, New, Enter; choose Edit, Paste, then save document in the normal manner
Insert document into another	With insertion point at the desired location for the standard text, click Insert, then File; double-click the desired document	With insertion point at the desired location for the standard text, choose Insert, then File; key document name; then press Enter
Split a window	Window, Split; or position arrow pointer on split box until it becomes an up- and down-pointing arrow, then hold down left mouse button, drag arrow down into document screen to desired location, and then release mouse button	Window, Split
Remove split window	Window, Remove Split	Window, Remove Split

Move insertion point to other window	Position I-beam pointer in pane, click left mouse button	F6
Arrange all open documents	Window, Arrange All	Window, Arrange All
Minimize a document	Click Minimize button at right side of Menu bar	
Maximize a document	Click Maximize button at right side of Menu bar	
Size an arranged document using the mouse	With arrow pointer on double-line border at right/left or top/bottom, hold down left mouse button, drag the border to increase or decrease window size	
Move an arranged document	Position arrow pointer in Title bar, hold down left mouse button, drag outline to desired position, then release mouse button	

thinking offline ··

Completion: In the space provided at the right, indicate the correct term, command, or number.

1. Press this button on the keyboard if you want to permanently delete selected text.

2. Click this button on the Standard toolbar to insert text currently located in the Clipboard at the location of the insertion point.

3. To copy selected text with the mouse, hold down this key while dragging selected text.

4. With the collecting and pasting feature you can collect up to this many different items and then paste them in various locations.

5. Do this to deselect text with the mouse.

6. To insert a document into another document, click File from this drop-down menu.

7. To close all open documents at the same time, hold down this key and then click File and then Close All.

8. To remove a split line from a document, click Remove Split from this drop-down menu.

9. Click this option from the Window drop-down menu to arrange all open documents.

10. Expand the active document to fill the document screen by clicking this button located in the upper right corner of the active document.

11. Click this button to shrink a document.

working hands-on

Assessment 1

1. Open Report 04.
2. Save the document with Save As and name it Ch 08, SA 01.
3. Make the following changes to the report:
   a. Select and then delete the last sentence in the first paragraph of the *Applying Desktop Publishing Guidelines* section.
   b. Select and then delete the last paragraph in the *Applying Desktop Publishing* section of the report (the paragraph that begins *If you decide to use color...*).
   c. Move the section titled *Creating Margins for Newsletters* above the section titled *Choosing Paper Size and Type*.
   d. Select the entire document and then change to a serif typeface other than Times New Roman.
   e. Check page breaks in the document and, if necessary, adjust the page breaks.
4. Save the document again with the same name (Ch 08, SA 01).
5. Print and then close Ch 08, SA 01.

Assessment 2

1. At a clear document screen, create the document shown in figure 8.9. Double-space between lines and triple-space after the last line in the document.
2. Make the following changes to the document:
   a. Change the font for the entire document to 14-point Goudy Old Style bold. (If this typeface is not available, choose a fancy or decorative typeface.)
   b. Select and then copy the text a triple space below the original text.
   c. Paste the text two more times. (There should be a total of four forms when you are done and they should fit on one page.)
3. Save the document and name it Ch 08, SA 02.
4. Print and then close Ch 08, SA 02.

 **figure**
8.9

Assessment 2

NEWS FLASH!!

EMERALD HEIGHTS ELEMENTARY SCHOOL

No School, Friday, November 2, 2001

Elementary Teacher Work Day!

Assessment 3

1. Open Contract 01.
2. Select the document and then click the Numbering button on the Formatting toolbar. (This inserts a number before each paragraph.)
3. Display the Clipboard toolbar, click the Clear Clipboard button to remove any items that may display in the toolbar, and then collect the following paragraphs:
   a. Select paragraph 3 and then click the Copy button on the Clipboard toolbar.
   b. Select paragraph 4 and then click the Copy button on the Clipboard toolbar.
   c. Select paragraph 5 and then click the Copy button on the Clipboard toolbar.
   d. Select paragraph 6 and then click the Copy button on the Clipboard toolbar.
   e. Select paragraph 7 and then click the Copy button on the Clipboard toolbar.
4. Click the New Blank Document button on the Standard toolbar.
5. At the clear document screen, complete the following steps:
   a. Key **AGREEMENT** centered and bolded.
   b. Press Enter twice, turn off bold, and return the paragraph alignment back to Left.
   c. Click the button on the Clipboard representing paragraph 4. (When the paragraph is inserted in the document, the paragraph number changes.)
   d. Click the button on the Clipboard representing paragraph 5.
   e. Click the button on the Clipboard representing paragraph 7.
   f. Click the button on the Clipboard representing paragraph 3.
   g. Click the button on the Clipboard representing paragraph 6.
6. Click the Clear Clipboard button on the Clipboard toolbar.
7. Turn off the display of the Clipboard toolbar.
8. Save the document and name it Ch 08, SA 03.
9. Print and then close Ch 08, SA 03.
10. Close Contract 01 without saving the changes.

Assessment 4

1. Open Bibliography, Letter 01, Notice 01, and Quiz.
2. Make Notice 01 the active document.
3. Make Bibliography the active document.
4. Arrange all the windows.
5. Make Quiz the active document and then minimize it.
6. Minimize the remaining documents.
7. Restore Bibliography by clicking the button on the Taskbar representing the document.
8. Restore Letter 01.
9. Restore Notice 01.
10. Restore Quiz.
11. Close Quiz.
12. Close Notice 01.
13. Close Letter 01.
14. Maximize Bibliography.
15. Close Bibliography.

Assessment 5

1. At a clear editing window, key the letter shown in figure 8.10 in an appropriate letter format through the first paragraph (to the location where the bolded message is displayed).
2. Save the letter and name it Ch 08, SA 05.
3. With Ch 08, SA 05 still open, open Contract 01.
4. Arrange the windows.

5. With Contract 01 the active document, copy the first paragraph a double space below the first paragraph in the letter in Ch 08, SA 05.
6. Key the third paragraph in the letter as shown in figure 8.10.
7. Make Contract 01 the active document and then copy the sixth paragraph a double space below the third paragraph in the letter in Ch 08, SA 05.
8. Make Contract 01 the active document and then close it.
9. Maximize Ch 08, SA 05.
10. Key the remaining text in the letter.
11. Save the letter again with the same name (Ch 08, SA 05).
12. Print and then close Ch 08, SA 05.

figure

8.10 *Assessment 5*

April 19, 2001

Mr. Dennis Wong, President
Industrial Workers Union
795 South 63rd Street
Oklahoma City, OK 76554

Dear Mr. Wong:

I received the draft of the purpose and scope for the agreement between the Coleman Development Corporation and the Industrial Workers Union. In the first section of the agreement, I recommend adding the following paragraph between the third and fourth paragraphs:

[Insert the first paragraph from Contract 01 here.]

Additionally, I recommend adding the following paragraph between the fifth and sixth paragraphs:

[Insert the sixth paragraph from Contract 01 here.]

The preliminary agreement looks good. I feel confident that we can complete these contract negotiations by the end of the month.

Sincerely,

Julian Carr
Attorney at Law

XX:Ch 08, SA 05

Chapter 09

Formatting with Special Features

PERFORMANCE OBJECTIVES

Upon successful completion of chapter 9, you will be able to:
- Automatically insert the date and time in a document.
- Highlight text in a document.
- Create documents using a Word template and a wizard.
- Format and edit text in newspaper columns.
- Apply styles.
- Create an outline-style numbered list.

In this chapter, you will learn to use a variety of Word features that can automate the creation of documents. You will learn to insert the date and/or time in a document automatically with shortcut commands or with options at the Date and Time dialog box; highlight specific points in a document using the Highlight feature; use templates to produce a variety of documents such as memos, letters, reports, invoices, and résumés; and use wizards to guide you through the creation of documents. You will also learn to enhance the visual appeal of documents by formatting text into newspaper columns and applying styles.

Inserting the Date and Time

The current date and/or time can be inserted in a document with options from the Date and Time dialog box shown in figure 9.1. To display this dialog box, click Insert and then Date and Time. The Date and Time dialog box contains a list of date and time options in the Available formats list box. Click the desired date or time format, then click OK or press Enter.

figure

9.1

Date and Time Dialog Box

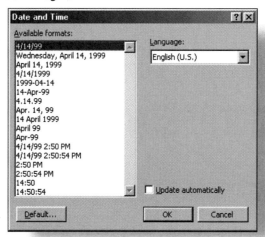

The date can also be inserted in a document with the shortcut command Alt + Shift + D. When you press Alt + Shift + D, the date is inserted in figures (such as 10/1/01). Press Alt + Shift + T to insert the current time in the document. The time is inserted in figures followed by AM or PM (such as 2:33 PM).

The date and/or time is inserted in the document as regular text. The date and/or time can also be inserted in a document as a field. If a date is inserted in a document as a field, the date is automatically updated if the document is opened on a different day. If the time is inserted as a field, the time is automatically updated when the document is opened again. To insert the date and/or time as a field, click the Update automatically check box that displays toward the bottom of the Date and Time dialog box.

exercise

Inserting the Date And Time

1. Open Memo 01.
2. Save the document with Save As and name it Ch 09, Ex 01.
3. Make the following changes to the memo:
   a. Delete the date *October 26, 2001* and then insert the current date by pressing Alt + Shift + D.
   b. Move the insertion point to the line below *XX:Memo 01* (located at the end of the memo) and then insert the current time by pressing Alt + Shift + T.
4. Print Ch 09, Ex 01.
5. Delete the current date you just inserted and then insert the current date in a different format by completing the following steps:
   a. Click Insert and then Date and Time.

b. At the Date and Time dialog box, click the fourth option in the Available formats list box.
   c. Click OK or press Enter.
6. Save the document again with the same name (Ch 09, Ex 01).
7. Print and then close Ch 09, Ex 01.

Highlighting Text

As people read information in books, magazines, periodicals, papers, etc., they may highlight important information with a highlighting pen. A highlighting pen creates a colored background through which the text can be read. This colored background draws the reader's eyes to the specific text.

Word provides a button on the Formatting toolbar that lets you highlight text in a document using the mouse. With this highlighting feature, you can select and highlight specific text in a document with a variety of colors.

To use this feature, click the Highlight button on the Formatting toolbar, and then select the desired text using the mouse. When the Highlight button is activated, the I-beam pointer displays with a pen attached. Continue selecting text you want highlighted and when completed, click once on the Highlight button to deactivate it.

Highlight

The default highlighting color is yellow. You can change this color by clicking the down-pointing triangle to the right of the Highlight button. From the drop-down list of colors that displays, click the desired color. This changes the color of the small rectangle below the pen on the Highlight button. If you are using a noncolor printer, highlighted text will print with a gray background. To remove highlighting from text, change the highlighting color to *None*, activate the Highlight button, and then select the highlighted text.

Highlighting Text in a Document

1. Open Report 01.
2. Save the document with Save As and name it Ch 09, Ex 02.
3. Change the highlighting color and then highlight text in the document by completing the following steps:

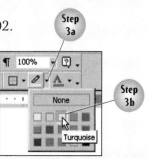
Step 3a

Step 3b

   a. Click the down-pointing triangle to the right of the Highlight button on the Formatting toolbar.
   b. From the drop-down list of colors, click the Turquoise color.
   c. Select the sentence, *Desktop publishing involves using desktop publishing software or word processing software with desktop publishing capabilities, a computer system, and a printer to produce professional-looking documents.*, that displays at the end of the second paragraph.
   d. Select the sentence, *With the use of desktop publishing software, one person may be performing all of the tasks necessary to complete a project, greatly reducing the costs of publishing documents.*, that displays in the fourth paragraph.

e. Select the sentence, *The beginning process of creating a publication involves two steps— planning the publication and creating the content.*, that displays in the first paragraph of the *Initiating the Desktop Publishing Process* section of the document.

f. Select the sentence, *During this stage, clearly identify the purpose of your communication.*, that displays in the first paragraph of the *Planning the Publication* section of the document.

g. Select the sentence, *Create a document that communicates the message clearly to your intended audience.*, that displays at the end of the first paragraph in the *Creating the Content* section of the document.

h. Select the sentence, *Clear and organized content combined with an attractive layout and design contribute to the effectiveness of your message.*, that displays at the end of the document.

i. Click the Highlight button to deactivate it.

4. Save the document again with the same name (Ch 09, Ex 02).
5. Print Ch 09, Ex 02.
6. Deselect text in the document by completing the following steps:

a. Click the down-pointing triangle to the right of the Highlight button on the Formatting toolbar.

b. From the drop-down list that displays, click *None*.

c. Select the sentence, *Desktop publishing involves using desktop publishing software or word processing software with desktop publishing capabilities, a computer system, and a printer to produce professional-looking documents.*, that displays at the end of the second paragraph.

d. Select the sentence, *During this stage, clearly identify the purpose of your communication.*, that displays in the first paragraph of the *Planning the Publication* section of the document.

e. Return the highlight color to yellow.

f. Click the Highlight button to deactivate it.

7. Save the document again with the same name (Ch 09, Ex 02).
8. Print and then close Ch 09, Ex 02.

Using Templates

Word has included a number of *template* documents that are formatted for specific uses. Each Word document is based on a template document with the *Normal* template the default. With Word templates, you can easily create a variety of documents, such as letters, memos, and awards, with specialized formatting. Along with templates, Word also includes *wizards*. Wizards are templates that do most of the work for you. *(Note: During a typical installation, not all templates may be installed. Before completing the template exercises, check to see if the templates described in figure 9.4 are available.)*

Templates and wizards are available at the New dialog box. To display this dialog box, shown in figure 9.2, click File and then New. The New dialog box contains several tabs for displaying a variety of templates and wizards. If the default tab, General, is selected as shown in figure 9.2, the Blank Document template displays. To view other templates and wizards, click a different tab at the top of the New dialog box. For example, if you click the Memos tab, the following templates and wizards display: Contemporary Memo, Elegant Memo, Memo Wizard, and Professional Memo.

figure
9.2

New Dialog Box

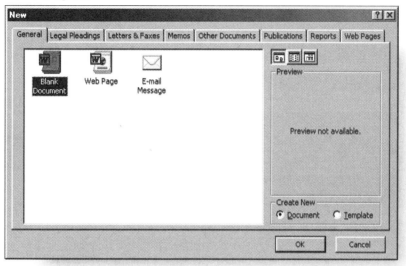

To create a document based on a different template, click the desired template, and then click OK. You can also double-click the desired template. If you click once on the desired template, a sample template displays in the Preview box at the right side of the dialog box. When you double-click a template, a template document is opened with certain formatting already applied. Specific information is then entered in the template document. After all information has been entered, the template document is saved in the normal manner. If, for example, you double-click *Contemporary Memo*, the template document shown in figure 9.3 displays (you see only a portion of the top of the memo).

figure
9.3

Contemporary Memo Template

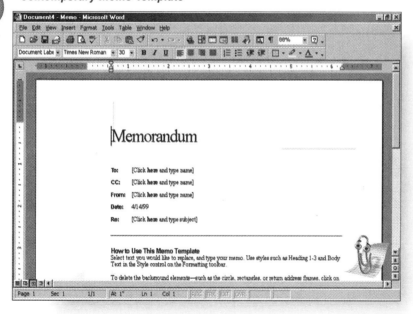

At the Contemporary Memo template, text in brackets identifies where specific information is to be entered. For example, text after *To:* displays as *[Click **here** and type name]*. The word *here* displays in bold. Position the I-beam pointer on the word *here*, and then click the left mouse button. This selects the bracketed text. Key the name of the person receiving the memo. When you begin keying the person's name, the selected bracketed text is automatically deleted. Continue in this manner to insert the appropriate text after the headings. Before keying the text for the body of the memo, select and then delete the existing text (below *Re:*).

Use other template documents in a similar manner. The formatting and text will vary for each template document. Figure 9.4 shows the template documents available with each tab at the New dialog box.

figure
9.4   **Template Documents**

Tab	Template
General	Blank Document
	Web Page
	E-mail Message
Legal Pleadings	Pleading Wizard
Letters & Faxes	Contemporary Fax
	Contemporary Letter
	Elegant Fax
	Elegant Letter
	Envelope Wizard
	Fax Wizard
	Letter Wizard
	Mailing Label Wizard
	Professional Fax
	Professional Letter
Memos	Contemporary Memo
	Elegant Memo
	Memo Wizard
	Professional Memo
Other Documents	Agenda Wizard
	Batch Conversion
	Calendar Wizard
	Contemporary Resume
	Elegant Resume
	Professional Resume
	Resume Wizard

Publications	Brochure
	Directory
	Manual
	Thesis
Reports	Contemporary Report
	Elegant Report
	Professional Report
Web Pages	Column with Contents
	Frequently Asked Questions
	Left-aligned Column
	Personal Web Page
	Right-aligned Column
	Simple Layout
	Table of Contents
	Web Page Wizard

exercise 3

Creating a Memo with a Memo Template

1. Use the Contemporary Memo template to create a memo by completing the following steps:
   a. Click File and then New.
   b. At the New dialog box, click the Memos tab.
   c. At the New dialog box with the Memos tab selected, double-click *Contemporary Memo*.

   d. At the Contemporary Memo template document, complete the following steps to key the text in the memo:
      1) Position the I-beam pointer on the word *here* in the bracketed text *[Click **here** and type name]* after *To:*, click the left mouse button, and then key **Stephanie Branson, President**.
      2) Position the I-beam pointer on the word *here* in the bracketed text *[Click **here** and type name]* after *CC:*, click the left mouse button, and then key **Brandon Kent, Vice President**.
      3) Position the I-beam pointer on the word *here* in the bracketed text *[Click **here** and type name]* after *From:*, click the left mouse button, and then key **Paul O'Shea, Development Manager**.
      4) Position the I-beam pointer on the word *here* in the bracketed text *[Click **here** and type subject]* after *Re:*, click the left mouse button, and then key **Tahoma Region Project**.

5) Select and then delete the text in the memo from *How To Use This Memo Template* to the end of the document.
6) Key the text shown in figure 9.5.
2. Save the memo and name it Ch 09, Ex 03.
3. Print and then close Ch 09, Ex 03. (This memo template will print with several graphics including horizontal and vertical lines as well as lightened images.)

Exercise 3

Anita Stratten, a city council member from West Creek, recently requested that a representative from Coleman Development Corporation attend the next city council meeting. Ms. Stratten indicated that the city council would like to hear more about the development proposed by Coleman.

The development proposal is almost completed. What do you think about the information being presented at the West Creek city council meeting next month? I could make the presentation or someone from my department. Please let me know if you feel a presentation to the community is appropriate at this time.

Using Wizards

Wizards are template documents that do most of the work for you. When you select a wizard template document, Word asks you questions and gives you choices about what type of formatting you want applied to the document. Follow the steps provided by the wizard to complete the document.

Creating a Letter Using a Wizard

1. Create a letter using the Letter Wizard by completing the following steps:
   a. Click <u>F</u>ile and then <u>N</u>ew.
   b. At the New dialog box, click the Letter & Faxes tab.
   c. At the New dialog box with the Letter & Faxes tab selected, double-click the *Letter Wizard* icon.
   d. At the message displayed by the Office Assistant, click the *Send one letter* option.
   e. At the Letter Wizard – Step 1 of 4 dialog box, complete the following steps:

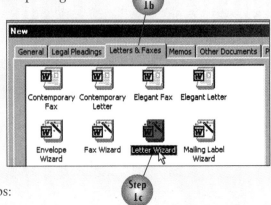

Step 1b

Step 1c

1) Click the down-pointing triangle at the right side of the Choose a page design option, and then click *Contemporary Letter* at the drop-down list.

2) Click the Next> button.

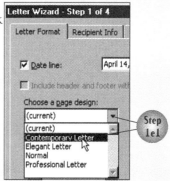

f. At the Letter Wizard – Step 2 of 4 dialog box, complete the following steps:

1) Key **Ms. Amanda Tolman** in the Recipient's name text box.

2) Press the Tab key. (This moves the insertion point to the Delivery address text box.)

3) Key **452 Angeline Road**.

4) Press Enter.

5) Key **Vancouver, WA 98612**.

6) Click the Business option located in the lower right corner of the dialog box.

7) Click the Next> button.

g. At the Letter Wizard – Step 3 of 4 dialog box, click the Next> button.

h. At the Letter Wizard – Step 4 of 4 dialog box, complete the following steps:

1) Select the text that currently displays in the Sender's name text box, and then key **Matthew Greer**.

2) Click in the Job title text box and then key **Investment Manager**.

3) Click in the Writer/typist's initials text box and then key your initials.

4) Click the Finish button.

i. At the Office Assistant message, click Cancel.

j. At the letter, insert a file for the body of the letter by completing the following steps:

1) Select the text *Type your letter here. To add, remove, or change letter elements, choose Letter Wizard from the Tools menu.* and then press the Delete key.

2) Click Insert and then File.

3) At the Insert File dialog box, make sure *Chapter 09* is the active folder, and then double-click *Letter 05*.

k. Move down the name and inside address by positioning the insertion point at the beginning of the name *Ms. Amanda Tolman* and then pressing the Enter key twice.

2. Save the letter and name it Ch 09, Ex 04.

3. Print and then close Ch 09, Ex 04.

Creating Newspaper Columns

When preparing a document containing text, an important point to consider is the readability of the document. Readability refers to the ease with which a person can read and understand groups of words. The line length of text in a document can enhance or detract from the readability of text. If the line length is too long, the reader may lose his or her place on the line and have a difficult time moving to the next line below. To improve the readability of some documents such as newsletters or reports, you may want to set the text in columns.

One common type of column is newspaper, which is commonly used for text in newspapers, newsletters, and magazines. Newspaper columns contain text that flows up and down in the document as shown in figure 9.6. When the first column on the page is filled with text, the insertion point moves to the top of the next column on the same page. When the last column on the page is filled with text, the insertion point moves to the beginning of the first column on the next page.

figure

9.6

Newspaper Columns

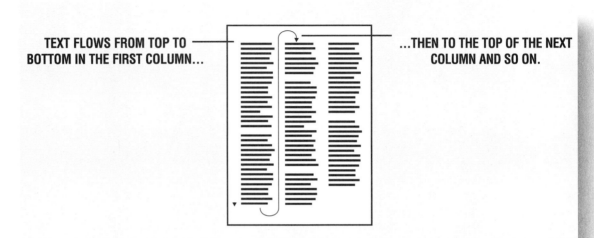

TEXT FLOWS FROM TOP TO BOTTOM IN THE FIRST COLUMN...

...THEN TO THE TOP OF THE NEXT COLUMN AND SO ON.

Columns

Newspaper columns can be created with the Columns button on the Standard toolbar or with options from the Columns dialog box. Columns of equal width are created with the Columns button on the Standard toolbar. To create columns of unequal width, use the Columns dialog box. The formatting for newspaper columns can be established before the text is keyed or it can be applied to existing text. Keying text first and then formatting it into newspaper columns is generally faster.

A document can include as many columns as there is room for on the page. Word determines how many columns can be included on the page based on the page width, the margin widths, and the size and spacing of the columns. Columns must be at least one-half inch in width.

Changes in columns affect the entire document or the section of the document in which the insertion point is positioned. If you want to create different numbers or styles of columns in a document, divide the document into sections.

There are three methods for inserting section breaks into a document. One method is to use the Break dialog box. (To display this dialog box, click Insert and then Break.) Another method is to use the Columns dialog box and specify that text is to be formatted into columns from the location of the insertion point forward in the document. The third method is to select the text first and then apply column formatting.

Creating Newspaper Columns with the Columns Button

To use the Columns button on the Standard toolbar, position the arrow pointer on the button and then hold down the left mouse button. This causes a grid to display as shown in figure 9.7. Drag the mouse down and to the right until the desired number of columns displays with a blue background on the Columns grid and then release the mouse button.

figure

9.7

Columns Grid

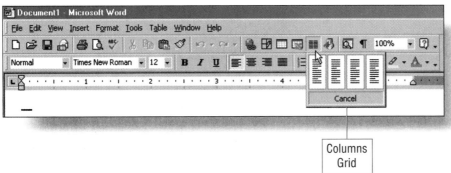

Columns
Grid

If a document contains a title and you want that title to span both columns, position the insertion point at the left margin where the first line of text that will begin the columns displays, then click <u>I</u>nsert and then <u>B</u>reak. This displays the Break dialog box. At the Break dialog box, click Con<u>t</u>inuous, and then click OK or press Enter.

In addition to the method just described, you could also format the text in a document into columns and not the title by selecting the text in the document (excluding the title), and then using the Columns button on the Standard toolbar to create the columns. A third method is explained in the next section on creating columns with options from the Columns dialog box.

In the Normal view, text will display in a single column at the left side of the document screen. If you want to view columns as they will appear when printed, change to the Print Layout view.

exercise

5

Formatting Text into Newspaper Columns Using the Columns Button

1. Open Report 01.
2. Save the document with Save As and name it Ch 09, Ex 05.
3. Change to the Print Layout view.
4. Select the title and then change the font to 14-point Times New Roman bold.
5. Select each of the following headings individually and then turn on bold:

    Defining Desktop Publishing
    Initiating the Desktop Publishing Process
    Planning the Publication
    Creating the Content

6. Select the text in the document from the beginning of the heading *Defining Desktop Publishing* to the end of the document (this is all text except the title and the blank line below the title). With the text selected, make the following changes:
    a. Change the font to 11-point Times New Roman.

b. Change the line spacing to single.
c. Display the Tabs dialog box and then set a left tab at 0.25 inch.
d. Format the text into two newspaper columns by positioning the arrow pointer on the Columns button on the Standard toolbar, holding down the left mouse button, dragging the mouse down and to the right until two columns display with a blue background on the Columns grid (and *2 Columns* displays below the grid), and then releasing the mouse button.

e. Deselect the text.
f. Insert six points of space after the heading *Defining Desktop Publishing*. *(Hint: Do this at the Paragraph dialog box with the Indents and Spacing tab selected.)*
g. Insert six points of space before and after the following headings:

> *Initiating the Desktop Publishing Process*
> *Planning the Publication*
> *Creating the Content*

7. Save the document again with the same name (Ch 09, Ex 05).
8. Print page 1 of the document.
9. Close Ch 09, Ex 05.

Creating Newspaper Columns with the Columns Dialog Box

The Columns dialog box can be used to create newspaper columns that are equal or unequal in width. To display the Columns dialog box shown in figure 9.8, click Format and then Columns.

Columns Dialog box

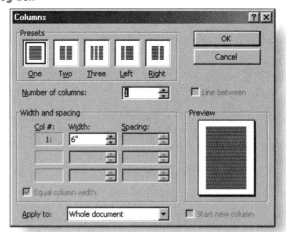

If you are creating columns of equal width, key the number of columns desired for the document in the Number of columns text box. You can also click the up-pointing triangle to the right of the Number of columns text box until the desired number displays.

You can also use options in the Presets section of the dialog box to specify the number of columns. By default, the One option is selected in the Presets section. Click the Two option if you want two columns of text in a document or click Three if you want three. If you click the Left option, the right column of text will be twice as wide as the left column of text. Click the Right option if you want the left column twice as wide. The options contain a Preview box showing what the columns will look like.

Word automatically determines column widths for the number of columns specified. By default, the Equal column width option contains a check mark. At this setting, column widths are the same. If you want to enter your own column widths or change the amount of space between columns, specify the number of columns desired and then click Equal column width to remove the check mark from the check box. When the check mark is removed, column measurements display in black below the Col #, Width, and Spacing options. To change the measurements of the columns, click the up- or down-pointing triangles to the right of the Width and Spacing options until the desired measurements display in the text box. If you are using the keyboard, press the Tab key until the column or spacing measurement you want to change is selected, and then key the new measurement.

The dialog box only has room to display measurements for three columns. If you specify more than three columns, a vertical scroll bar displays to the left of the column numbers. To view other column measurements, click the down-pointing triangle at the bottom of the scroll bar.

By default, columns are separated by 0.5 inch of space. The amount of space between columns can be increased or decreased with the Spacing option. At this option, you can key a new measurement for the amount of spacing between columns or you can click the up- or down-pointing triangle after the text box to increase or decrease the measurement.

By default, column formatting is applied to the whole document. With the Apply to option at the bottom of the Columns dialog box, you can change this from *Whole document* to *This point forward*. At the *This point forward* option, a section break is inserted and the column formatting is applied to text from the location of the insertion point to the end of the document or until other column formatting is encountered.

exercise 6

Formatting Text into Newspaper Columns Using the Columns Dialog Box

1. Open Report 02.
2. Save the document with Save As and name it Ch 09, Ex 06.
3. Select the entire document and then make the following changes:
   a. Change the font to 10-point Times New Roman.
   b. Change the line spacing to single.
   c. Display the Tabs dialog box and then set a left tab at 0.2 inch.
   d. Deselect the text.
   e. Move the insertion point to the end of the title *DESKTOP PUBLISHING DESIGN* and then press the Enter key.

f. Bold the title of the document as well as the two headings in the document.

4. Format the text (except the title) into three columns by completing the following steps:

   a. Position the insertion point at the left margin of the heading *Designing a Document*.

   b. Click Format and then Columns.

   c. At the Columns dialog box, click the Three option in the Presets section.

   d. Click the down-pointing triangle at the right side of the Apply to text box and then click *This point forward* at the drop-down list.

   e. Click OK or press Enter.

5. Save the document again with the same name (Ch 09, Ex 06).

6. Print page 1 of the document.

7. Close Ch 09, Ex 06.

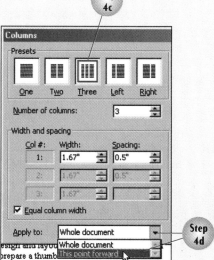

A line can be inserted between columns that sets off the columns and adds visual separation of the columns. To insert a line between columns, click the Line between option at the Columns dialog box. The line between columns is the length of the longest column in the section. The line can be seen in the Print Layout view or in Print Preview. With the Start new column option, you can specify where to begin a new column of text. The Start new column option is dimmed until the Apply to option is set at *This point forward*. When you enter column settings in the Columns dialog box, an example of how the columns will appear is shown in the Preview box in the lower right corner of the dialog box.

Formatting Text into Uneven Newspaper Columns with a Line Between

1. Open Report 03.

2. Copy a portion of the report into a new document and then save the new document by completing the following steps:

   a. Select the text in the *MODULE 1: DEFINING NEWSLETTER ELEMENTS* section of the report. (Select from the Module 1 title to just before the title *MODULE 2: PLANNING A NEWSLETTER.*)

   b. Click the Copy button on the Standard toolbar.

   c. Click the New Blank Document button on the Standard toolbar.

   d. At the clear document screen, click the Paste button on the Standard toolbar.

   e. Save the document and name it Ch 09, Ex 07.

   f. Make Report 03 the active document and then close it. (This will display Ch 09, Ex 07 in the document screen.)

3. With Ch 09, Ex 07 open, make the following changes:

   a. Select the entire document and then change the font to 11-point Times New Roman.

b. Set the title *MODULE 1: DEFINING NEWSLETTER ELEMENTS* in 14-point Arial bold.

c. Set the two headings *Designing a Newsletter* and *Defining Basic Newsletter Elements* in 10-point Arial bold.

d. Select the text from the beginning of the heading *Designing a Newsletter* to the end of the document and then change the line spacing to single.

e. Insert 6 points of space after the heading *Designing a Newsletter*.

f. Insert 6 points of space before and after the heading *Defining Basic Newsletter Elements*.

4. Format the text of the report into uneven columns with a line between by completing the following steps:

a. Change to the Print Layout view.

b. Position the insertion point at the left margin of the heading *Designing a Newsletter*.

c. Click Format and then Columns.

d. At the Columns dialog box, click the down-pointing triangle at the right side of the Apply to text box, and then click *This point forward* at the drop-down list.

e. Click Left in the Presets section of the Columns dialog box.

f. Click the Line between option (this inserts a check mark in the check box).

g. Click OK or press Enter.

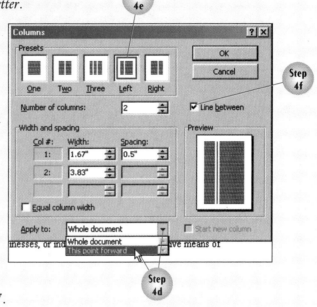

5. Save the document again with the same name (Ch 09, Ex 07).

6. Print and then close Ch 09, Ex 07.

Inserting a Column and/or Page Break

When formatting text into columns, Word automatically breaks the columns to fit the page. At times, column breaks may appear in an undesirable location. For example, a heading may appear at the bottom of the column, while the text after the heading begins at the top of the next column. You can insert a column break into a document to control where columns end and begin on the page.

To insert a column break, position the insertion point where you want the new column to begin, and then press Ctrl + Shift + Enter. You can also insert a column break by positioning the insertion point at the location where the new column is to begin, and then clicking Insert and then Break. At the Break dialog box, click Column break, and then click OK or press Enter.

If you insert a column break in the last column on a page, the column begins on the next page. If you want a column that is not the last column on the page to begin on the next page, insert a page break. To do this, press Ctrl + Enter. You can also insert a page break by positioning the insertion point at the location in the text where you want the new page to begin, then clicking Insert, and then Break. At the Break dialog box, click Page Break, and then click OK or press Enter.

exercise 8

Formatting Text into Newspaper Columns and Inserting a Column Break

1. Open Ch 09, Ex 07.
2. Save the document with Save As and name it Ch 09, Ex 08.
3. Make the following changes to the report:
   a. Select the entire document and then change the font to 12-point Garamond.
   b. Change the columns to two even columns by completing the following steps:
      1) Position the insertion point immediately left of the *D* in *Designing a Newsletter*.
      2) Click Format and then Columns.
      3) At the Columns dialog box, click Two in the Presets section.
      4) Click OK or press Enter to close the dialog box.

      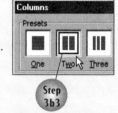

      Step 3b3

   c. Insert a column break at the heading *Defining Basic Newsletter Elements* by completing the following steps:
      1) Position the insertion point immediately left of the *D* in *Defining*. (This heading is located toward the bottom of the first column.)
      2) Click Insert and then Break.
      3) At the Break dialog box, click Column break.
      4) Click OK or press Enter.

      Step 3c3

      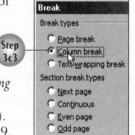

   d. Remove the 6 points of spacing before the heading *Defining Basic Newsletter Elements*.
4. Save the document again with the same name (Ch 09, Ex 08).
5. Print only the first page of Ch 09, Ex 08 and then close Ch 09, Ex 08.

Editing Text in Columns

To edit text formatted into columns, move the insertion point either within or between columns. Move the insertion point with the mouse or with the keyboard.

Moving the Insertion Point within Columns

To move the insertion point in a document using the mouse, position the arrow pointer where desired, and then click the left button. If you are using the keyboard, the insertion point movement keys—up, down, left, and right arrows—cause the insertion point to move in the direction indicated. If you press the up or down arrow key, the insertion point moves up or down within the column. If the insertion point is located on the last line of a column on a page, pressing the down arrow key will cause the insertion point to move to the beginning in the same column on the next page. If the insertion point is located on the beginning of a line of text in columns, pressing the up arrow key will cause the insertion point to move to the end of the same column on the previous page.

The left and right arrow keys move the insertion point in the direction indicated within the column. When the insertion point gets to the end of the line within the column, it moves down to the beginning of the next line within the same column.

Moving the Insertion Point between Columns

You can use the mouse or the keyboard to move the insertion point between columns. If you are using the mouse, position the mouse pointer where desired, and then click the left button. If you are using the keyboard, press Alt + up arrow to move the insertion point to the top of the previous column, or press Alt + down arrow to move the insertion point to the top of the next column.

Editing Text in Newspaper Columns

1. Open Ch 09, Ex 05.
2. Save the document with Save As and name it Ch 09, Ex 09.
3. Make the following changes to the report:
    a. Select the entire document and then change the font to 11-point Century Schoolbook.
    b. Select the title and then change the font to 16-point Univers bold. (If Univers is not available, choose a sans serif typeface such as Arial or Tahoma.)
    c. Set the following headings in 12-point Univers bold (do not use Format Painter because the paragraph before formatting will be removed):

    > *Defining Desktop Publishing*
    > *Initiating the Desktop Publishing Process*
    > *Planning the Publication*
    > *Creating the Content*

4. Save the document again with the same name (Ch 09, Ex 09).
5. Print only the first page of Ch 09, Ex 09.
6. Close Ch 09, Ex 09.

Removing Column Formatting

If a document contains text formatted into columns, the column formatting can be removed with the Columns button on the Standard toolbar or with the Columns dialog box. To remove column formatting using the Columns button, position the insertion point in the section containing columns, or select the text in columns. Click the Columns button on the Standard toolbar and then click the first column in the Columns grid.

To remove column formatting using the Columns dialog box, position the insertion point in the section containing columns, or select the text in columns, then click Format and then Columns. At the Columns dialog box, click One in the Presets section, and then click OK or press Enter.

Changing Column Width and Spacing

The width of and spacing between text formatted into columns can be changed with the column marker on the horizontal ruler. The horizontal ruler is displayed when the Print Layout view is selected. The horizontal ruler and the column marker are identified in figure 9.9.

Column Marker on the Horizontal Ruler

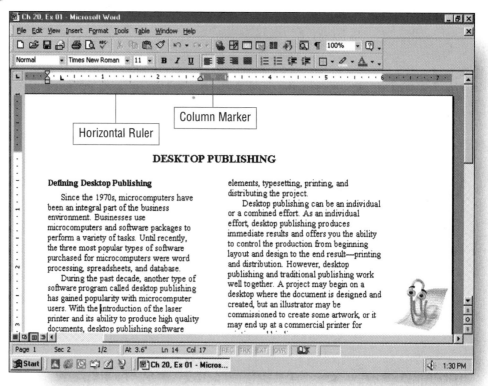

To change the width (and also the spacing) of columns of text in a document using the column marker on the horizontal ruler, position the arrow pointer on the left or right edge of the column marker on the horizontal ruler until it turns into a double-headed arrow pointing left and right. Hold down the left mouse button, drag the column marker to the left or right to make the column of text wider or thinner, and then release the mouse button. Hold down the Alt key while dragging the column marker and measurements display on the horizontal ruler. Measurements display for the columns as well as the space between columns.

If the columns are of equal width, changing the width of one column changes the width of all columns. If the columns are of unequal width, changing the width of a column only changes that column.

Changing Spacing between Newspaper Columns Using the Column Marker

1. Open Ch 09, Ex 09.
2. Save the document with Save As and name it Ch 09, Ex 10.
3. Make sure the view is Print Layout. (If not, click <u>V</u>iew and then <u>P</u>rint Layout.)
4. Position the insertion point anywhere in the heading *Defining Desktop Publishing* and then change the spacing between columns using the column marker on the horizontal ruler by completing the following steps:
   a. Position the arrow pointer at the left side of the column marker on the horizontal ruler until it turns into a double-headed arrow pointing left and right.
   b. Hold down the left mouse button and then the Alt key.
   c. Drag the mouse to the right until the measurement inside the column marker displays as *0.25″* (this number is hard to see) and the measurement at the left side of the ruler displays as *3″*.

   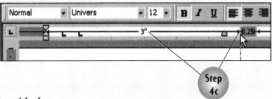

   d. Release the mouse button and then the Alt key.
5. Save the document again with the same name (Ch 09, Ex 10).
6. Print only the first page of Ch 09, Ex 10.
7. Close Ch 09, Ex 10.

Balancing Columns on a Page

In a document containing text formatted into columns, Word automatically lines up (balances) the last line of text at the bottom of each column, except the last page. Text in the first column of the last page may flow to the end of the page, while the text in the second column may end far short of the end of the page. Columns can be balanced by inserting a section break at the end of the text. To do this, position the insertion point at the end of the text in the last column of the section you want to balance, then click <u>I</u>nsert and then <u>B</u>reak. At the Break dialog box, click Con<u>t</u>inuous, and then click OK. Figure 9.10 shows the last page of a document containing unbalanced columns and a page where the columns have been balanced.

figure

9.10 *Unbalanced and Balanced Columns*

UNBALANCED COLUMNS **BALANCED COLUMNS**

exercise 11

Changing the Width and Balancing Newspaper Columns

1. Open Ch 09, Ex 06.
2. Save the document with Save As and name it Ch 09, Ex 11.
3. Make the following changes to the report:
   a. Change the width of the spacing between columns by completing the following steps:
      1) Move the insertion point to the beginning of the heading *Designing a Document*.
      2) Position the arrow pointer at the left side of the first column marker from the left on the horizontal ruler until it turns into a double-headed arrow pointing left and right.
      3) Hold down the left mouse button and then the Alt key.
      4) Drag the mouse to the right until the measurement inside the column marker displays as approximately *0.3"* and the measurement at the left side of the ruler displays as *1.8"*.

      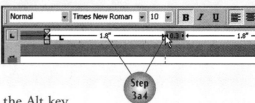

      5) Release the mouse button and then the Alt key.

b. Position the insertion point immediately right of the period at the end of the report and then insert a continuous break to balance the columns on the third page by completing the following steps:

1) Move the insertion point to the end of the document.
2) Click Insert and then Break.
3) At the Break dialog box, click Continuous.
4) Click OK or press Enter.

4. Save the document again with the same name (Ch 09, Ex 11).
5. Print and then close Ch 09, Ex 11.

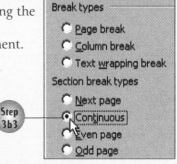

Applying Styles

A Word document, by default, is based on the Normal template document. Within a Normal template document, a Normal style is applied to text by default. This Normal style sets text in the default font, uses left alignment and single spacing, and turns on the Widow/Orphan control. In addition to this Normal style, other styles with specific formatting are available in a document based on the Normal template document. Other Word templates contain additional styles, which can be viewed at the Style dialog box.

Applying Styles with the Style Button

Style

The Style button on the Formatting toolbar offers one method for applying a style to text in a document. To apply a style, position the insertion point in the paragraph to which you want the style applied, or select the text, and then click the down-pointing triangle to the right of the Style button (the first button from the left). This causes a drop-down list to display as shown in figure 9.11. Click the desired style in the list to apply the style to the text in the document.

9.11 **Style Drop-Down List**

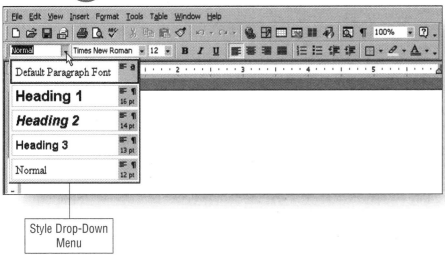

Style Drop-Down Menu

When you click a style in the drop-down list, the list is removed from the screen and the style is applied to the text. This formatting applied by the style will vary. For example, the *Heading 1* style applies the font 16-point Arial bold and the *Heading 2* style applies the font 14-point Arial bold italic. At the Style drop-down list, an icon with a brief visual presentation of the style displays at the right side of the drop-down list.

When a style is applied to text, the style name displays in the Style button on the Formatting toolbar. In addition, the font for the style displays in the Font button and the size for the style displays in the Font Size button.

Applying Predesigned Styles

1. Open Report 03.
2. Save the document with Save As and name it Ch 09, Ex 12.
3. Select the entire document, change the line spacing to single, and then deselect the document.
4. Apply the *Heading 1* style to the title by completing the following steps:
   a. Position the insertion point on any character in the title *MODULE 1: DEFINING NEWSLETTER ELEMENTS*.
   b. Click the down-pointing triangle at the right side of the Style button on the Formatting toolbar.
   c. At the drop-down list that displays, click *Heading 1*.
5. Apply the *Heading 2* style to the first heading by completing the following steps:
   a. Position the insertion point on any character in the heading *Designing a Newsletter*.
   b. Click the down-pointing triangle at the right side of the Style button on the Formatting toolbar.
   c. At the drop-down list that displays, click *Heading 2*.
6. Complete steps similar to those in 4 or 5 to apply the specified style to the following text:

Defining Basic Newsletter Elements	=	Heading 2
MODULE 2: PLANNING A NEWSLETTER	=	Heading 1
Defining the Purpose of a Newsletter	=	Heading 2

7. Save the document again with the same name (Ch 09, Ex 12).
8. Print and then close Ch 09, Ex 12.

Applying Styles at the Style Dialog Box

The Style drop-down list displays only a few styles. Word provides many more predesigned styles than this that you can use to format text in a document. You can display the list of styles available with Word at the Style dialog box, shown in figure 9.12. To display the Style dialog box, click F̲ormat and then S̲tyle.

figure

9.12

Style Dialog Box

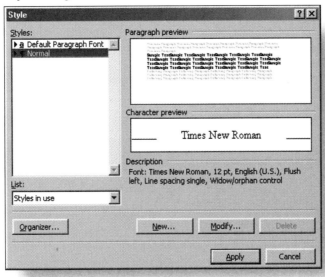

To display the entire list of styles provided by Word, click the down-pointing triangle at the right side of the List text box, and then click *All styles* at the drop-down list. When you click *All styles*, the list of styles in the Styles list box displays as shown in figure 9.13. The list is longer than the list box. In the Styles list box, paragraph styles are preceded by a paragraph mark (¶) and character styles are preceded by the symbol *a*.

figure

9.13

Style Dialog Box with All Styles Displayed

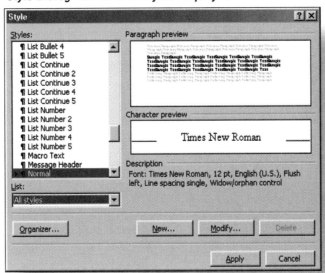

At the right side of the Style dialog box, the Paragraph preview box displays an example of how the selected style will format text. The Character preview box displays the font used to format text. A description of the style is displayed in the Description section of the dialog box.

To apply a style at the Style dialog box, position the insertion point within the paragraph of text to be formatted; or, if applying a character style, select the text, then click Format and then Style. At the Style dialog box, click the down-pointing triangle at the right side of the List text box, and then click *All styles*. Click the desired style in the list and then click the Apply button.

exercise 13

Formatting a Document with Styles

1. Open Report 02.
2. Save the document with Save As and name it Ch 09, Ex 13.
3. Make the following changes to the report:
   a. Select the entire document and then change the line spacing to single.
   b. Position the insertion point at the beginning of the heading *Designing a Document* and then press the Enter key once.
   c. Position the insertion point at the beginning of the heading *Creating Focus* and then press the Enter key once.
4. Format the title and headings in the report using styles by completing the following steps:

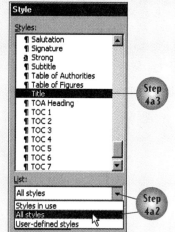

Step 4a3

Step 4a2

   a. Position the insertion point anywhere within the title *DESKTOP PUBLISHING DESIGN* and then apply the *Title* style by completing the following steps:
      1) Click Format and then Style.
      2) At the Style dialog box, click the down-pointing triangle to the right of the List text box, and then click *All styles*.
      3) Scroll down the list of styles in the Styles list box until *Title* is visible and then click *Title*.
      4) Click the Apply button.
   b. Position the insertion point anywhere within the heading *Designing a Document* and then apply the *Subtitle* style by completing steps similar to those in 4a.
   c. Position the insertion point anywhere within the heading *Creating Focus* and then apply the *Subtitle* style by completing steps similar to those in 4a.
5. Save the document again with the same name (Ch 09, Ex 13).
6. Print and then close Ch 09, Ex 13.

Creating an Outline Style Numbered List

In chapter 3, you learned how to apply numbering to selected text with options at the Bullets and Numbering dialog box. Certain options at the Bullets and Numbering dialog box with the Outline Numbered tab selected are available only when heading styles have been applied to text. In exercise 14, you will apply heading styles to text and then apply outline style numbering to the text.

exercise 14

Creating an Outline Style Numbered List

1. Open Agenda.
2. Save the document with Save As and name it Ch 09, Ex 14.
3. Make the following changes to the document:
   a. Delete the following text:

   > *First Quarter* (below *Income Report*)
   > *Second Quarter* (below *Income Report*)
   > *First Quarter* (below *Expense Report*)
   > *Second Quarter* (below *Expense Report*)

   b. Apply the *Heading 2* style to the following text:

   > *Sales and Marketing*
   > *Financial*
   > *Services and Procedures*
   > *Education*

   c. Apply the *Heading 3* style to the following text:

   > *Commercial Lines*
   > *Personal Lines*
   > *Year-end Production Report*
   > *Income Report*
   > *Expense Report*
   > *Accounts Receivable*
   > *Accounts Payable*
   > *Collections*
   > *Update*
   > *Sponsors*
   > *Seminars*
   > *Training*

   d. Apply outline style numbering by completing the following steps:
      1) Select the text from the beginning of *Sales and Marketing* to the end of the document.
      2) Click Format and then Bullets and Numbering.
      3) At the Bullets and Numbering dialog box, click the Outline Numbered tab.
      4) Click the third option from the left in the bottom row.
      5) Click OK to close the dialog box.
   e. Select the title *COMMERCIAL LINES DEPARTMENT* and the subtitle *MEETING AGENDA* and then change the font to 16-point Arial bold.
4. Save the document again with the same name (Ch 09, Ex 14).
5. Print and then close Ch 09, Ex 14.

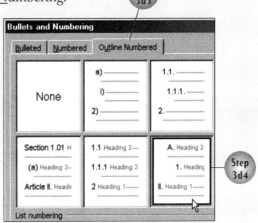

chapter summary

➤ The current date and/or time can be inserted in a document with options from the Date and Time dialog box or with shortcut commands.

➤ With the Highlight feature, you can highlight specific text in a document using the mouse. A variety of highlighting colors is available.

➤ With Word templates, you can easily create a variety of documents, such as letters, memos, and awards, with specialized formatting.

➤ Wizards are templates that do most of the work for you.

➤ The templates and wizards provided by Word are available at the New dialog box.

➤ Newspaper columns of equal width can be created with the Columns button on the Standard toolbar or with options from the Columns dialog box. To create columns of unequal width, use the Columns dialog box.

➤ Keying text first and then formatting it into newspaper columns is generally faster, but the formatting can be established before the text is keyed.

➤ By default, column formatting is applied to the whole document.

➤ In the Normal view, text will display in a single column at the left side of the document screen. Change to the Print Layout view to display columns as they will appear when printed.

➤ Options at the Columns dialog box let you change the spacing between columns, apply column formatting from the point of the insertion point forward, insert a line between columns, or start a new column.

➤ To move the insertion point in a document with columns using the mouse, position the arrow pointer where desired, and then click the left button. To move the insertion point with the keyboard, use the arrow keys.

➤ Column formatting can be removed with the Columns button on the Standard toolbar or at the Columns dialog box.

➤ The width of and spacing between text formatted into columns can be changed with the column marker on the horizontal ruler.

➤ Word automatically lines up (balances) the last line of text at the bottom of each column. The last page of columns can be balanced by inserting a section break at the end of the text.

➤ A Word document is based on the Normal template document; within this template document, a Normal style is applied to text. In addition to the Normal style, other styles with specific formatting are available in a document based on the Normal template document.

➤ Other Word templates contain additional styles, which can be viewed at the Style dialog box.

➤ Apply a style using the Style button on the Formatting toolbar or with options at the Style dialog box.

	Mouse	Keyboard
Insert date/time	Insert, Date and Time, click desired selection, click OK	Alt + Shift + D (for Date) Alt + Shift + T (for Time)
Activate Highlight feature	Click Highlight button on Formatting toolbar	
New dialog box	File, New	File, New
Display Columns dialog box	Format, Columns	Format, Columns
Insert a column break	Insert, Break, Column break	Ctrl + Shift + Enter
Insert a page break	Insert, Break, Page break	Ctrl + Enter
Insert a section break	Insert, Break, Continuous	Insert, Break, Continuous
Move insertion point between columns	Position mouse pointer where desired, click left button	Alt + up arrow (top of previous column) Alt + down arrow (top of next column)
Display Style dialog box	Format, Style	Format, Style

thinking offline

Completion: In the space provided at the right, indicate the correct term, command, or number.

1. This is the shortcut command to insert the current date.
2. The Highlight button is located on this toolbar.
3. Choose a template or wizard at this dialog box.
4. This is the minimum width for a column.
5. Change to this view to display columns as they will appear when printed.
6. The Columns button is located on this toolbar.
7. Click this option in the Presets section of the Columns dialog box to specify that the left column is to be twice as wide as the right column.
8. Create columns of unequal width here.
9. Columns are separated by this amount of space by default.
10. To insert a vertical line between columns, click this option at the Columns dialog box.
11. Insert this (or these) into a document to control where columns end and begin on the page.

12. Use this on the horizontal ruler to change the width of columns.

_____

13. To balance all columns on the last page of text, insert this at the end of the text.

_____

14. By default, a Word document is based on this template document.

_____

15. The predesigned styles based on the default template document are displayed by clicking this button on the Formatting toolbar.

_____

working hands-on

Assessment 1

1. Use the Contemporary Letter template (displays when the Letters & Faxes tab is selected at the New dialog box) to create a business letter. Select the text in brackets, delete it, and then key the information as shown below each bracketed item:

*[Click **here** and type return address]* (This text is located in the upper right corner of the template. You may want to change the percentage of display to a larger number to see the text.)
**1201 James Street
St. Louis, MO 62033**

Select ***Company Name Here*** and then key the following:
GOOD SAMARITAN HOSPITAL

*[Click **here** and type recipient's address]*
**Ms. Mariah Jackson
300 Blue Ridge Boulevard
Kansas City, MO 63009**

Select *Dear Sir or Madam:* and then key **Dear Ms. Jackson:**

Select the text *Type your letter here. For more details on modifying this letter template, double-click* ⊠ *. To return to this letter, use the Windows menu.*, and then key the following:

Thank you for the registered nurse job description. I will be including the additional job requirements listed in your letter. A committee spent several months designing a recruitment plan. A copy of that plan is attached. The plan is very thorough and will help us recruit highly qualified nurses. I will contact you after the eight registered nursing positions have been filled.

*[Click **here** and type your name]*
Victor Durham

*[Click **here** and type job title]*
Director of Nursing

*[Click **here** and type slogan]* (This is located at the bottom.)
Community health needs

2. After creating the letter, save it and name it Ch 09, SA 01.
3. Print and then close Ch 09, SA 01.

Assessment 2

1. Use a memo template of your choosing and compose a memo to your instructor describing three Word shortcut features you have learned up to this point.
2. When the memo is completed, save it and name it Ch 09, SA 02.
3. Print and then close Ch 09, SA 02.

Assessment 3

1. Open Report 02.
2. Save the document with Save As and name it Ch 09, SA 03.
3. Make the following changes to the report:
    a. Change the left and right margins to 1 inch.
    b. Select the text from the heading *Designing a Document* to the end of the document, change the line spacing to single, and then deselect the text.
    c. Set the title *DESKTOP PUBLISHING DESIGN* and the headings *Designing a Document* and *Creating Focus* in 14-point Times New Roman bold.
    d. Format the text from the heading *Designing a Document* to the end of the document into two newspaper columns.
    e. Move the insertion point to the end of the document (at the beginning of a blank line), insert the current date, press Enter, and then insert the current time.
4. Save the document again with the same name (Ch 09, SA 03).
5. Print and then close Ch 09, SA 03.

Assessment 4

1. Open Report 04.
2. Make the following changes to the document:
    a. Select the text (including the title) in module 3.
    b. Copy the selected text to a new document.
    c. Save this new document as Ch 09, SA 04.
    d. Make Report 04 the active document and then close Report 04.
3. With Ch 09, SA 04 the active document, make the following changes:
    a. Select the text from the heading *Applying Desktop Publishing Guidelines* to the end of the document and then make the following changes:
        1) Change the line spacing to single.
        2) Format the selected text into two evenly spaced newspaper columns with a line between.
    b. Deselect the text.
    c. Add 6 points of space after the heading *Applying Desktop Publishing Guidelines*.
    d. Change to the Print Layout view.
    e. Select the title *MODULE 3: DESIGNING A NEWSLETTER* and then change the font to 14-point Arial bold.
    f. Select the heading *Applying Desktop Publishing Guidelines* and then change the font to 10-point Arial bold.
    g. Position the insertion point after the last period at the end of the document and then insert a continuous section break.
4. Save the document again with the same name (Ch 09, SA 04).
5. Print and then close Ch 09, SA 04.

Assessment 5

1. Open Report 03.
2. Save the document with Save As and name it Ch 09, SA 05.
3. Select the entire document and then change to single line spacing.
4. Apply the specified styles to the following headings:

MODULE 1: DEFINING NEWSLETTER ELEMENTS	=	Heading 1
Designing a Newsletter	=	Heading 2
Defining Basic Newsletter Elements	=	Heading 2
MODULE 2: PLANNING A NEWSLETTER	=	Heading 1
Defining the Purpose of a Newsletter	=	Heading 2

5. Save the document again with the same name (Ch 09, SA 05).
6. Print and then close Ch 09, SA 05.

Assessment 6

1. Open Outline.
2. Save the document with Save As and name it Ch 09, SA 06.
3. Apply the following styles:
   a. Apply the *Heading 2* style to all lines of text that begin at the left margin.
   b. Apply the *Heading 3* style to all lines of text that begin at the first tab stop.
4. Apply outline style numbering by displaying the Bullets and Numbering dialog box with the Outline Numbered tab selected, clicking the third option from the left in the bottom row, and then clicking OK.
5. Save the document again with the same name (Ch 09, SA 06).

Chapter 10

Creating Headers and Footers in a Document

10

PERFORMANCE OBJECTIVES

Upon successful completion of chapter 10, you will be able to:

- Create a header and footer in a document.
- Format, edit, and delete a header or footer.
- Reposition a header or footer.
- Create a different header or footer on the first page of a document.
- Create a header or footer for odd pages and another for even pages.
- Create a header or footer for different sections in a document.
- Insert AutoText in a header or footer.
- Insert page numbering in a document.

In a Word document, text can be created that prints at the top of every page and/or the bottom of every page. Text can be printed on all pages, only even pages, only odd pages, or specific sections in a document. Also, page numbering can be inserted in a document.

Working with Headers and Footers

Text that appears at the top of every page is called a *header* and text that appears at the bottom of every page is referred to as a *footer*. Headers and footers are common in manuscripts, textbooks, reports, and other publications.

Creating a Header or Footer

Create a header or footer by clicking <u>V</u>iew and then <u>H</u>eader and Footer. Word automatically changes to the Print Layout view, dims the text in the document, inserts a pane where the header or footer is entered, and displays the Header and Footer toolbar. Figure 10.1 shows a document with a header pane and the Header and Footer toolbar displayed.

figure

10.1

Header Pane and Header and Footer Toolbar

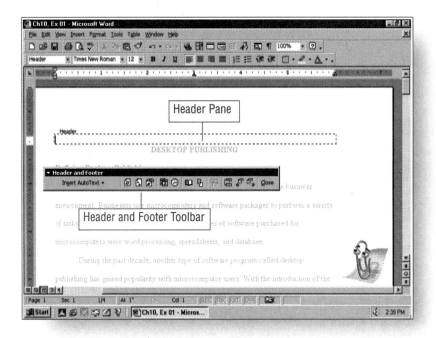

Switch Between
Header and Footer

By default, the insertion point is positioned in the header pane. In this pane, key the header text. If you are creating a footer, click the Switch Between Header and Footer button on the Header and Footer toolbar, and then key text in the footer pane.

Header and footer text can be formatted in the same manner as text in the document. For example, the font of header or footer text can be changed, character formatting such as bolding, italicizing, and underlining can be added, margins can be changed, and much more.

After keying the header or footer text, click the Close button on the Header and Footer toolbar. Clicking Close returns to the previous view. In the Normal view, a header or footer does not display in the screen. A header or footer will display dimmed in the Print Layout view. To view how a header and/or footer will print, click the Print Preview button on the Standard toolbar. By default, a header and/or footer prints on every page in the document. Later in this chapter you will learn how to create headers and footers for specific sections of a document.

exercise 1

Creating a Header

1. Open Report 01.
2. Save the document with Save As and name it Ch 10, Ex 01.
3. Bold the title *DESKTOP PUBLISHING* and the four headings: *Defining Desktop Publishing*, *Initiating the Desktop Publishing Process*, *Planning the Publication*, and *Creating the Content*.
4. Create the header *Desktop Publishing* that is bolded and prints at the left margin on every page by completing the following steps:

    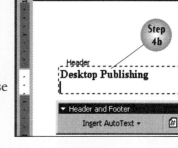

    a. Click <u>V</u>iew and then <u>H</u>eader and Footer.
    b. At the header pane, turn on bold, key **Desktop Publishing**, and then press enter. (If the Header and Footer toolbar is in the way, position the mouse pointer on any gray area on the toolbar or on the Title bar, hold down the left mouse button, drag the outline of the toolbar to a more desirable location, and then release the mouse button.)
    c. Click the <u>C</u>lose button on the Header and Footer toolbar.
5. Display Print Preview to see how the header will appear on each page when printed. (Press the Page Down key to view the second and third pages of the report.) After previewing the document, close Print Preview.
6. Check page breaks in the document and, if necessary, adjust the page breaks.
7. Save the document again with the same name (Ch 10, Ex 01).
8. Print and then close Ch 10, Ex 01.

(Note: Most printers cannot print to the edge of the page. If your header does not print in exercise 1, you may need to increase the distance from the edge of the page to the header. To increase this measurement, display the Page Setup dialog box by clicking <u>F</u>ile and then Page Setup. At the Page Setup dialog box, make sure the <u>M</u>argins tab is selected, and then increase the number for the He<u>a</u>der option as well as the Footer: option in the From edge section of the dialog box. The amount of increase depends on your printer.)

Creating a footer is similar to creating a header. To create a footer, switch to the footer pane by clicking the Switch Between Header and Footer button on the Header and Footer toolbar. Figure 10.2 displays the buttons on the Header and Footer toolbar, the name of each button, and what each button will perform.

figure

Header and Footer Toolbar Buttons

Click this button	Named	To do this
Insert AutoText ▾	Insert AutoText	Insert AutoText in header/footer.
	Insert Page Number	Insert page number in header/footer.
	Insert Number of Pages	Print the total number of pages in the active document.
	Format Page Number	Format the page numbers in the current section.
	Insert Date	Insert date in header/footer.
	Insert Time	Insert time in header/footer.
	Page Setup	Display Page Setup dialog box.
	Show/Hide Document Text	Turn on/off the display of document text.
	Same as Previous	Link/Unlink header/footer to or from previous section.
	Switch Between Header and Footer	Switch between the header pane and the footer pane.
	Show Previous	Show previous section's header/footer.
	Show Next	Show next section's header/footer.
Close	Close Header and Footer	Close header/footer pane.

When creating a header or footer, the main document text is displayed but dimmed. This dimmed text can be hidden while creating a header or footer by clicking the Show/Hide Document Text button on the Header and Footer toolbar. To redisplay the dimmed document text, click the button again.

Show/Hide
Document Text

Formatting a Header or Footer

Header or footer text does not take on the character formatting of the document. For example, if you change the font for the document text, header or footer text remains at the default font. However, margin changes made to the document text do affect header or footer text. If you want header or footer text character formatting to be the same as the document text, you must format header or footer text in the header or footer pane in the normal manner.

A header or footer contains three alignment settings. (These settings are designed to work with the default left and right margins of 1.25 inches. If changes are made to the margins, these settings may not operate as described.) If you want text aligned at the left margin, make sure the insertion point is positioned at the left side of the header or footer pane, and then key the text. To center text in the header or footer pane, press the Tab key. This moves the insertion point to a preset tab. From the left margin, pressing the Tab key twice will move the insertion point to the right margin of the header or footer pane. Text keyed at this tab will be right aligned.

Insert Page
Number

With buttons on the Header and Footer toolbar, you can insert page numbering and the date and/or time in a header or footer. To insert page numbering in a header or footer, display the header or footer pane and then click the Insert Page Number button on the Header and Footer toolbar. This inserts the number of the page where the insertion point is currently located. The correct page number will also appear on all other pages in the document. Click the Insert Date button on the Header and Footer toolbar to insert the current date in a header or footer, and click the Insert Time button to insert the current time in a header or footer.

Insert Date

Insert Time

Creating and Formatting a Footer

1. Open Report 02.
2. Save the document with Save As and name it Ch 10, Ex 02.
3. Select the entire document and then change the font to 12-point Century Schoolbook (or a similar serif typeface).
4. Bold the title *DESKTOP PUBLISHING DESIGN* and the two headings *Designing a Document* and *Creating Focus*.
5. Create the footer *Desktop Publishing Design* in 12-point Century Schoolbook bold that prints at the left margin of every page and *Page #* (where # represents the page number) in 12-point Century Schoolbook bold that prints at the right margin of every page by completing the following steps:
   a. Click <u>V</u>iew and then <u>H</u>eader and Footer.
   b. Click the Switch Between Header and Footer button on the Header and Footer toolbar. (This displays the footer pane.)

c. Change the font to 12-point Century Schoolbook bold (or the typeface you chose in step 3).
d. Key **Desktop Publishing Design**.
e. Press the Tab key twice.
f. Key **Page** and then press the spacebar once.
g. Click the Insert Page Number button on the Header and Footer toolbar.
h. Select the page number and then change the font to 12-point Century Schoolbook bold (or the typeface you chose in step 3).
i. Click the Close button on the Header and Footer toolbar.

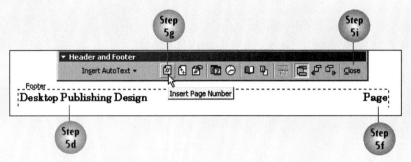

6. View the document in Print Preview.
7. Check page breaks in the document and, if necessary, adjust the page breaks.
8. Save the document again with the same name (Ch 10, Ex 02).
9. Print and then close Ch 10, Ex 02.

Inserting AutoText in a Header or Footer

Insert
AutoText

Click the Insert AutoText button on the Header and Footer toolbar and a drop-down list displays with a variety of options. Choose an option to automatically insert specific text. For example, choose the *Last printed* option and Word will insert the date the document was last printed; or, choose the *Filename and path* option and Word will insert the entire name and path.

exercise 3

Inserting AutoText in a Footer

1. Open Report 02.
2. Save the document with Save As and name it Ch 10, Ex 03.
3. Select the entire document and then change to a serif typeface other than Times New Roman.
4. Bold the title *DESKTOP PUBLISHING DESIGN* and the two headings *Designing a Document* and *Creating Focus*.
5. Create a header and footer with AutoText by completing the following steps:
    a. Click View and then Header and Footer.
    b. Click the Insert AutoText button on the Header and Footer toolbar and then click *Filename and path* at the drop-down list. After inserting the AutoText, press the Enter key.

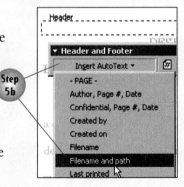

c. Select the header text and then change to the serif typeface you chose in step 3.
d. Click the Switch Between Header and Footer button on the Header and Footer toolbar. (This displays the footer pane.)
e. Click the Insert AutoText button on the Header and Footer toolbar and then click *Author, Page #, Date* at the drop-down list.

f. Select the footer text and then change to the serif typeface you chose in step 3.
g. Click the Close button on the Header and Footer toolbar.
6. View the document in Print Preview.
7. Check page breaks in the document and, if necessary, adjust the page breaks.
8. Save the document again with the same name (Ch 10, Ex 03).
9. Print and then close Ch 10, Ex 03.

Editing a Header or Footer

Changes can be made to a header or footer in a document. There are two methods you can use to display a header or footer for editing. You can display a header or footer for editing in the Print Layout view. To do this, open the document containing the header or footer to be edited, click View and then Print Layout; or click the Print Layout View button at the left side of the horizontal scroll bar. Double-click the dimmed header or footer you want to edit. Edit the header or footer as needed and then double-click the dimmed document text to make it active.

You can also display a header or footer for editing by clicking View and then Header and Footer. Click the Switch Between Header and Footer button (if you want to edit a footer), click the Show Next button or the Show Previous, if necessary, to display the header or footer you want to edit. When the proper header or footer pane is displayed, edit the header or footer as needed, and then click the Close button on the Header and Footer toolbar.

Show Next

Show Previous

Editing a Footer

1. Open Ch 10, Ex 02.
2. Save the document with Save As and name it Ch 10, Ex 04.
3. Change the top margin for the report to 1.5 inches and the left and right margins to 1 inch.
4. Edit the footer by completing the following steps:
a. Click View and then Header and Footer.
b. Click the Switch Between Header and Footer button on the Header and Footer toolbar. (This will display the footer pane containing the footer created in exercise 2.)

c. Delete *Desktop Publishing Design* from the footer pane. (Leave *Page #*, which is located toward the right margin.)

d. Key **Designing Documents** at the left margin in the footer pane.

e. Click the Close button on the Header and Footer toolbar.

5. View the document in Print Preview.

6. Check page breaks in the document and, if necessary, adjust the page breaks.

7. Save the document again with the same name (Ch 10, Ex 04).

8. Print and then close Ch 10, Ex 04.

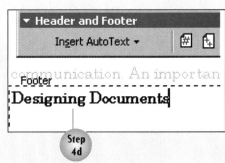

Step
4d

Deleting a Header or Footer

A header or footer can be deleted from a document by deleting it from the header or footer pane. To delete a header or footer, change to the Print Layout view, and then double-click the header or footer to be deleted. With the header or footer displayed in the header or footer pane, select the header or footer text, and then press the Delete key. Click the Close button on the Header and Footer toolbar to close the header or footer pane. (You can also close the header or footer pane by double-clicking the dimmed document text.)

A header or footer pane can also be displayed by clicking View and then Header and Footer. At the header pane, click the Switch Between Header and Footer, the Show Next, or the Show Previous buttons until the desired header or footer is displayed.

Deleting a Header and Creating a Footer

1. Open Ch 10, Ex 01.

2. Save the document with Save As and name it Ch 10, Ex 05.

3. Select the entire document and then change the font to 12-point Century Schoolbook (or a similar serif typeface).

4. Delete the header *Desktop Publishing* by completing the following steps:
    a. Change to the Print Layout view.
    b. Double-click the dimmed header.
    c. With the header displayed in the header pane, select the header text, and then press the Delete key.
    d. Close the header pane by double-clicking the dimmed document text.

5. Create a footer with AutoText by completing the following steps:
    a. Click View and then Header and Footer.
    b. Click the Switch Between Header and Footer button. (This displays the footer pane.)

c. Click the Insert AutoText button on the Header and Footer toolbar and then click *Page X of Y* at the drop-down list.

d. Select the footer text and then change to the serif typeface you chose in step 3 and turn on bold.

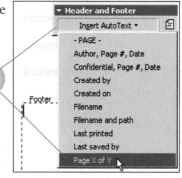

Step 5c

6. Change to the Normal view.
7. Check page breaks in the document and, if necessary, adjust the page breaks.
8. Save the document again with the same name (Ch 10, Ex 05).
9. Print and then close Ch 10, Ex 05. (You may want to preview the document before printing.)

Positioning a Header or Footer

Word inserts a header or footer 0.5 inch from the edge of the page. You can change this default position at the Page Setup dialog box. To change the distance from the edge of the paper, display the Header and Footer toolbar, and then click the Page Setup button. At the Page Setup dialog box with the Margins tab selected, click the up- or down-pointing triangle after Header (located in the From edge section) or after Footer until the desired measurement displays.

Page Setup

Positioning a Footer

1. Open Ch 10, Ex 05.
2. Save the document with Save As and name it Ch 10, Ex 06.
3. Change the top and bottom margins to 1.5 inches.
4. Change the position of the footer to 0.75 inch by completing the following steps:

Step 4d

a. Click View and then Header and Footer.
b. Click the Switch Between Header and Footer button to display the footer pane.
c. Click the Page Setup button on the Header and Footer toolbar.
d. At the Page Setup dialog box, click the Margins tab.
e. Select the *1"* measurement in the Footer: text box (located in the From edge section) and then key **0.75**.

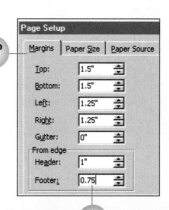

Step 4e

f. Click OK or press Enter.
g. Click the Close button on the Header and Footer toolbar.
5. Check page breaks in the document and, if necessary, make adjustments to the page breaks.
6. Save the document again with the same name (Ch 10, Ex 06).
7. Print and then close Ch 10, Ex 06. (You may want to preview the document before printing.)

Creating Different Headers/Footers in a Document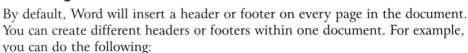

By default, Word will insert a header or footer on every page in the document. You can create different headers or footers within one document. For example, you can do the following:

- create a unique header or footer on the first page;
- omit a header or footer on the first page;
- create different headers or footers for odd and even pages; or
- create different headers or footers for sections in a document.

Creating a First Page Header/Footer

A different header or footer can be created on the first page of a document. To do this, position the insertion point anywhere in the first page, then click View and then Header and Footer. (If you are creating a footer, click the Switch Between Header and Footer button.) Click the Page Setup button on the Header and Footer toolbar. At the Page Setup dialog box, make sure the Layout tab is selected, click Different first page, and then click OK. Key the desired text for the first page header or footer text. Click the Show Next button on the Header and Footer toolbar. (This opens another header or footer pane.) Key the text for the other header or footer that will print on all but the first page and then click Close at the Header and Footer toolbar. After creating the headers or footers, preview the document to see how the headers or footers will display when printed.

You can follow similar steps to omit a header or footer on the first page. For example, to omit a header or footer on the first page, complete the same steps as listed above except do not key text when the first header or footer pane is opened.

Creating a Header That Prints on All Pages except the First Page

1. Open Report 02.
2. Save the document with Save As and name it Ch 10, Ex 07.
3. Bold the title and headings in the document.
4. Create the header *Desktop Publishing Design* that is bolded and prints at the right margin on all pages except the first page by completing the following steps:
   a. Position the insertion point anywhere in the first page.
   b. Click View and then Header and Footer.
   c. Click the Page Setup button on the Header and Footer toolbar.
   d. At the Page Setup dialog box, make sure the Layout tab is selected.
   e. Click Different first page. (This inserts a check mark in the check box.)
   f. Click OK or press Enter.
   g. With the header pane displayed, click the Show Next button on the Header and Footer toolbar. (This opens another header pane.)

h. Press the Tab key twice, turn on bold, key **Desktop Publishing Design**, and then press the Enter key.

i. Click the Close button on the Header and Footer toolbar.

5. Save the document again with the same name (Ch 10, Ex 07).

6. Print and then close Ch 10, Ex 07. (You may want to preview the document before printing.)

Step 4h

Desktop Publishing Design

Creating a Header/Footer for Odd/Even Pages

One header or footer can be printed on even pages and another printed on odd pages. This might be useful in a document that will be bound after printing. To create a different odd and even header or footer, click View and then Header and Footer. (If you are creating a footer, click the Switch Between Header and Footer button.) Click the Page Setup button and then click Different odd and even (this inserts a check mark) at the Page Setup dialog box. At the odd header or footer pane, key the desired text, and then click the Show Next button on the Header and Footer toolbar. At the even header or footer pane, key the desired text, and then click the Close button.

exercise 8

Creating a Footer for Odd Pages and Another for Even Pages

1. Open Report 02.

2. Save the document with Save As and name it Ch 10, Ex 08.

3. Change the font for the entire document to 12-point Century Schoolbook (or a similar serif typeface).

4. Create a footer that prints on all odd pages and another that prints on all even pages by completing the following steps:

a. Click View and then Header and Footer.

b. Click the Switch Between Header and Footer button. (This displays the footer pane.)

c. Click the Page Setup button.

d. At the Page Setup dialog box, make sure the Layout tab is selected.

e. Click Different odd and even. (Make sure there is no check mark in the Different first page option.)

f. Click OK or press Enter.

g. At the odd footer pane, click the Align Right button on the Formatting toolbar and then key **Desktop Publishing Design**.

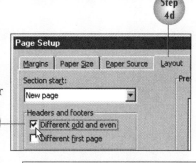

Step 4d

Step 4e

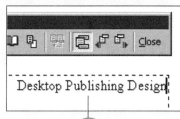

Desktop Publishing Design

Step 4g

h. Select the footer text, *Desktop Publishing Design,* and then change the font to 12-point Century Schoolbook bold (or the serif typeface you chose in step 3).

i. Click the Show Next button on the Header and Footer toolbar.

j. At the even footer pane, click the In<u>s</u>ert AutoText button, and then click *Filename and path* at the drop-down list.

k. Select the footer text and then change the font to 12-point Century Schoolbook bold (or the serif typeface you chose in step 3).

l. Click the <u>C</u>lose button on the Header and Footer toolbar.

5. Save the document again with the same name (Ch 10, Ex 08).

6. Print and then close Ch 10, Ex 08. (You may want to preview the document before printing.)

Creating a Header/Footer for Different Sections

In chapter 4, you learned how to create different sections in a document. A section can be created that begins a new page or a continuous section can be created. If you want different headers and/or footers for pages in a document, divide the document into sections.

For example, if a document contains several chapters, you can create a section for each chapter, and then create a different header or footer for each section. When dividing a document into sections by chapter, insert a section break that also begins a new page.

Same as Previous

When a header or footer is created for a specific section in a document, the header or footer can be created for all previous and next sections or just for next sections. If you want a header or footer to print on only those pages in a section and not the previous or next sections, you must deactivate the Same as Previous button. This tells Word not to print the header or footer on previous sections. Word will, however, print the header or footer on following sections. If you do not want the header or footer to print on following sections, create a blank header or footer at the next section. When creating a header or footer for a specific section in a document, preview the document to determine if the header or footer appears on the correct pages.

exercise 9

Creating Footers for Different Sections

1. Open Report 03.

2. Change the top margin to 1.5 inches.

3. Insert a section break that begins a new page at the line containing the module title *MODULE 2: PLANNING A NEWSLETTER.* (Be sure to insert a section break and not a page break.)

4. Create module and page numbering footers for the two modules by completing the following steps:
   a. Position the insertion point at the beginning of the document.
   b. Click View and then Header and Footer.
   c. Click the Switch Between Header and Footer button.
   d. At the footer pane, turn on bold, key **Module 1**, and then press the Tab key twice. (This moves the insertion point to the right margin.) Key **Page**, press the spacebar, key a hyphen (-), press the spacebar again, and then click the Insert Page Number button on the Header and Footer toolbar.
   e. Select and then bold the page number.
   f. Click the Show Next button.
   g. Click the Same as Previous button to deactivate it.
   h. Change *Module 1* to *Module 2* in the footer.
   i. Click the Close button on the Header and Footer toolbar.

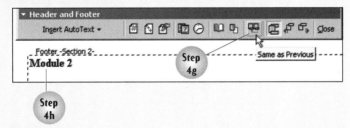

5. Check page breaks in the document and, if necessary, adjust the page breaks.
6. Save the document with Save As and name it Ch 10, Ex 09.
7. Print and then close Ch 10, Ex 09. (You may want to preview the document before printing.)

Inserting Page Numbering in a Document

Word, by default, does not print page numbers on a page. For documents such as memos and letters, this is appropriate. For longer documents, however, page numbers may be needed. Page numbers can be inserted in a header or footer or with options from the Page Numbers dialog box shown in figure 10.3. To display this dialog box, click Insert and then Page Numbers.

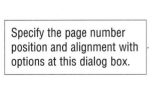 **Page Numbers Dialog Box**

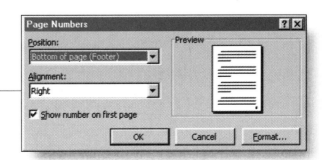

Specify the page number position and alignment with options at this dialog box.

The Position option at the Page Numbers dialog box contains two choices—Top of page (Header) and Bottom of page (Footer). With choices from the Alignment option, you can insert page numbering at the left margin, center of the page, right margin, at the inside margin (the margin closest to the binding in bound material), and at the outside margin (the margin furthest from the binding in bound material).

If you turn on page numbering in a document, the page number will appear on all pages in the document including the first page. If you do not want page numbering to appear on the first page, remove the check mark from the Show number on first page option at the Page Numbers dialog box.

Numbering Pages at the Bottom Right Margin

1. Open Report 02.
2. Save the document with Save As and name it Ch 10, Ex 10.
3. Change the top margin to 1.5 inches and the left and right margins to 1 inch.
4. Number pages at the bottom right margin of the page by completing the following steps:
   a. Click Insert and then Page Numbers.
   b. At the Page Numbers dialog box, make sure the Position option displays as Bottom of page (Footer). (If not, click the down-pointing triangle after the option, and then click *Bottom of page (Footer)*.)
   c. Make sure the Alignment option displays as *Right*. (If not, click the down-pointing triangle at the right of the Alignment text box, and then click *Right* at the drop-down list.)
   d. Click OK or press Enter.
5. Check page breaks in the document and, if necessary, adjust the page breaks.
6. Save the document again with the same name (Ch 10, Ex 10).
7. Print and then close Ch 10, Ex 10. (You may want to preview the document before printing.)

Step 4b

Step 4c

Page Numbers

Position:
Bottom of page (Footer)

Alignment:
Right

☑ Show number on first page

OK

Deleting Page Numbering

Page numbering in a document can be deleted in the same manner as deleting a header or footer. To delete page numbering in a document, click View and then Header and Footer. Display the header or footer pane containing the page numbering, select the page numbering, and then press the Delete key. Click the Close button on the Header and Footer toolbar.

Changing Page Numbering Format

At the Page Number Format dialog box shown in figure 10.4, you can change the numbering format, add chapter numbering, and specify where you want page numbering to begin and in what sections you want page numbering to appear. To display the Page Number Format dialog box, click the Format button at the Page Numbers dialog box.

figure
10.4

Page Number Format Dialog Box

> Specify the page number format with options at this dialog box.

Page Number Format

Number format: [1, 2, 3, ...]

☐ Include chapter number

Chapter starts with style [Heading 1]

Use separator: [- (hyphen)]

Examples: 1-1, 1-A

Page numbering

◉ Continue from previous section

○ Start at: [ ]

[OK] [Cancel]

Click the Number format option from the Page Number Format dialog box to change the numbering from Arabic numbers (1, 2, 3, etc.), to lowercase letters (a, b, c, etc.), uppercase letters (A, B, C, etc.), lowercase Roman numerals (i, ii, iii, etc.), or uppercase Roman numerals (I, II, III, etc.).

Chapter numbering can be included in a document. Word will number chapters in a document if the chapter heading is formatted with a heading style. You will learn about heading styles in a later chapter.

By default, page numbering begins with 1 and continues sequentially from 1 through all pages and sections in a document. You can change the beginning page number with the Start at option at the Page Number Format dialog box. You can change the beginning page number at the beginning of the document or change the page number at the beginning of a section.

exercise 11

Numbering Pages with Roman Numerals at the Outside Margins

1. Open Report 03.
2. Save the document with Save As and name it Ch 10, Ex 11.
3. Turn on page numbering, change the page numbering to outside margins, use lowercase Roman numerals, and change the beginning number to 3 by completing the following steps:
   a. Click Insert and then Page Numbers.
   b. At the Page Numbers dialog box, change the Alignment to *Outside*.
   c. Click the Format button.

d. At the Page Number Format dialog box, click the down-pointing triangle at the right of the Number format text box and then click *i, ii, iii, ...* at the drop-down list.
e. Click Start at and then key **3**.
f. Click OK or press Enter to close the Page Number Format dialog box.
g. Click OK or press Enter to close the Page Numbers dialog box.

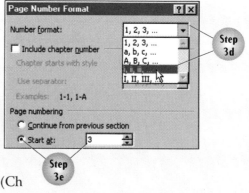

4. Check page breaks in the document and, if necessary, adjust the page breaks.
5. Save the document again with the same name (Ch 10, Ex 11).
6. Print and then close Ch 10, Ex 11. (You may want to preview the document before printing.)

chapter summary

➤ Text that appears at the top of every page is called a header; text that appears at the bottom of every page is called a footer.

➤ When you click <u>V</u>iew and then <u>H</u>eader and Footer, Word automatically changes to the Print Layout view, dims the text in the document, inserts a pane where the header or footer is entered, and also displays the Header and Footer toolbar.

➤ To create a footer, switch to the footer pane by clicking the Switch Between Header and Footer button on the Header and Footer toolbar.

➤ A header or footer does not display in the Normal view but will display dimmed in the Print Layout view. To see how the header or footer will print, display Print Preview.

➤ Header or footer text does not take on any character formatting applied to the document. If you want header or footer text character formatting to be the same as the document text, format that text in the header or footer pane in the normal manner.

➤ A header or footer contains three alignment settings: left, center, and right. Press the Tab key to move the insertion point to the center alignment setting and then press the Tab key again to move the insertion point to the right alignment setting.

➤ With buttons on the Header and Footer toolbar, you can insert page numbering and the date and/or time in a header or footer.

➤ You can edit a header or footer in the Print Layout view or in the header or footer pane.

➤ A header or footer can be deleted at the header or footer pane. In the Print Layout view, double-click the header or footer. With the header or footer pane displayed, select the text, and then press the Delete key.

➤ Word inserts a header or footer 0.5 inch from the edge of the page. A header or footer can be repositioned at the Page Setup dialog box.

➤ You can create more than one header or footer in a document.

➤ Insert page numbering in a document in a header or footer or with options from the Page Numbers dialog box.

➤ Format page numbers with options at the Page Number Format dialog box.

commands review

	Mouse	Keyboard
Create a Header or Footer	View, Header and Footer	View, Header and Footer
Print Preview	File, Print Preview; or click the Print Preview button on the Standard toolbar	File, Print Preview
Page Numbers dialog box	Insert, Page Numbers	Insert, Page Numbers

thinking offline

Completion: In the space provided, indicate the correct term, command, or number needed to complete the sentence.

1. After clicking View and then Header and Footer, the insertion point is automatically positioned in the _____ pane.

2. To create a footer, click the _____ button on the Header and Footer toolbar.

3. Headers/footers can be created for different pages in a document, and they can also be created for different _____ in a document.

4. If the header you wish to edit is not visible in the header or footer pane, click the _____ button or the _____ button on the Header and Footer toolbar.

5. Click the _____ button on the Standard toolbar to see how headers and footers will look on the page when printed.

6. Create footers on odd and even pages at the _____ dialog box.

7. Page numbers do not display in the _____ view.

8. Delete page numbers in a document by first displaying the _____.

9. Display the Page Numbers dialog box by clicking _____ and then Page Numbers.

10. Change the beginning page number with the _____ option at the Page Number Format dialog box.

working hands-on

Assessment 1

1. Open Report 02.
2. Make the following changes to the document:
   a. Select the entire document and then change the font to 13-point Garamond (or a similar serif typeface).
   b. Select the title *DESKTOP PUBLISHING DESIGN* and then change the font to 14-point Arial bold.
   c. Select the heading *Designing a Document* and then change the font to 12-point Arial bold.
   d. Use the Format Painter to change the font to 12-point Arial bold for the heading *Creating Focus*.
   e. Create the footer *Desktop Publishing Design* that is set in 12-point Arial bold and prints at the center of the footer pane.
3. Check page breaks in the document and, if necessary, adjust the page breaks.
4. Save the document with Save As and name it Ch 10, SA 01.
5. Print and then close Ch 10, SA 01. (You may want to preview the document before printing.)

Assessment 2

1. Open Ch 10, SA 01.
2. Save the document with Save As and name it Ch 10, SA 02.
3. Make the following changes to the document:
   a. Delete the footer in the document.
   b. Create a footer that prints the filename and path, is set in 12-point Arial bold, and prints at the right margin on all odd pages.
   c. Create the footer *Desktop Publishing* that is set in 12-point Arial bold and prints at the left margin on all even pages.
4. Save the document again with the same name (Ch 10, SA 02).
5. Print and then close Ch 10, SA 02. (You may want to preview the document before printing.)

Assessment 3

1. Open Report 04.
2. Make the following changes to the document:
   a. Select the entire document and then change the font to 12-point Century Schoolbook (or a similar serif typeface).
   b. Select the title *MODULE 3: DESIGNING A NEWSLETTER* and then change the font to 12-point Arial bold.
   c. Change the font to 12-point Arial bold for the following title and headings:

Applying Desktop Publishing Guidelines
MODULE 4: CREATING NEWSLETTER LAYOUT
Choosing Paper Size and Type
Choosing Paper Weight
Creating Margins for Newsletters

    d.   Insert a section break that begins a new page at the beginning of the line containing the title *MODULE 4: CREATING NEWSLETTER LAYOUT*. (Be sure to insert a section break and not a page break.)

    e.   Create the footer *Module 3: Designing a Newsletter*, which is set in 12-point Arial bold, is centered, and prints in the first section (the module 3 section).

    f.   Create the footer *Module 4: Creating Newsletter Layout*, which is set in 12-point Arial bold, is centered, and prints in the second section (the module 4 section).

3. Check page breaks in the document and, if necessary, adjust the page breaks.

4. Save the document with Save As and name it Ch 10, SA 03.

5. Print and then close Ch 10, SA 03. (You may want to preview the document before printing.)

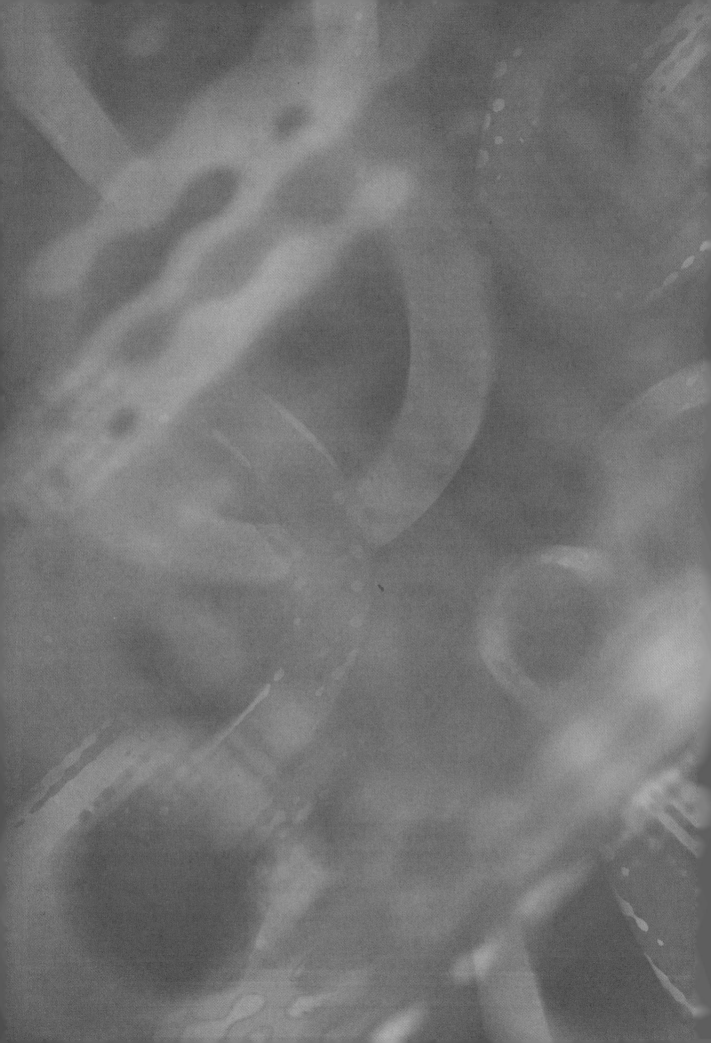

Chapter 11

Creating Footnotes and Endnotes

PERFORMANCE OBJECTIVES

Upon successful completion of chapter 11, you will be able to:

- Create footnotes and endnotes.
- View and edit footnotes and endnotes.
- Move, copy, and delete footnotes and endnotes.
- Customize footnote and endnote settings.
- Convert footnotes to endnotes and endnotes to footnotes.

A research paper or report contains information from a variety of sources. To give credit to those sources, a footnote can be inserted in the document. A *footnote* is an explanatory note or reference that is printed at the bottom of the page where it is referenced. An *endnote* is also an explanatory note or reference, but it prints at the end of the document.

Two steps are involved when creating a footnote or endnote. First, the note reference number is inserted in the document at the location where the note is referred to. The second step for creating a footnote or endnote is to key the note entry text.

Creating Footnotes and Endnotes

Footnotes and endnotes are created in a similar manner. To create a footnote in a document, you would complete the following steps:

1. Position the insertion point at the location in the document where the reference number is to appear.
2. Click Insert and then Footnote.
3. At the Footnote and Endnote dialog box shown in figure 11.1, make sure Footnote is selected, and then click OK or press Enter.
4. At the footnote pane shown in figure 11.2, key the footnote entry text.
5. Click the Close button or press Alt + Shift + C to close the footnote pane.

Footnote and Endnote Dialog Box

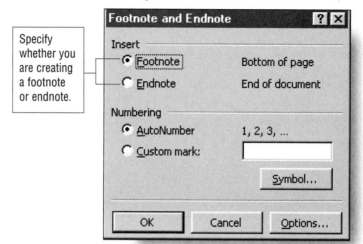

Specify whether you are creating a footnote or endnote.

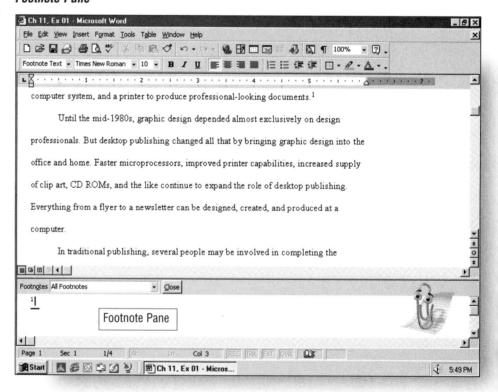

Footnote Pane

Footnote Pane

You can also create a footnote by pressing Alt + Ctrl + F. This displays the footnote pane. Key the footnote text and then click <u>C</u>lose or press Alt + Shift + C to close the footnote pane. When creating footnotes, Word numbers footnotes with Arabic numbers (1, 2, 3, etc.).

If you press the Enter key after keying the footnote entry text, footnotes will be separated by a blank line (double space). If you do not want footnote text separated by a blank line, do not press the Enter key after keying the footnote entry text.

Creating Footnotes

1. Open Report 01.
2. Save the document with Save As and name it Ch 11, Ex 01.
3. Make the following changes to the document:
   a. Select the title *DESKTOP PUBLISHING* and then change the font to 14-point Arial bold.
   b. Select the heading *Defining Desktop Publishing* and then change the font to 14-point Arial bold.
   c. Use Format Painter to apply 14-point Arial bold to the remaining headings: *Initiating the Desktop Publishing Process*, *Planning the Publication*, and *Creating the Content*.
4. Create the first footnote shown in figure 11.3 at the end of the second paragraph in the *Defining Desktop Publishing* section by completing the following steps:
   a. Position the insertion point at the end of the second paragraph in the *Defining Desktop Publishing* section.
   b. Click <u>I</u>nsert and then Foot<u>n</u>ote.
   c. At the Footnote and Endnote dialog box, make sure <u>F</u>ootnote is selected, and then click OK or press Enter.
   d. At the footnote pane, key the first footnote shown in figure 11.3. Press the Enter key once after keying the footnote text (this will separate the first footnote from the second footnote by a blank line).

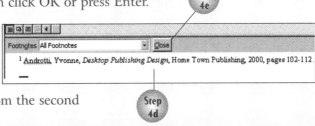

   e. Click the <u>C</u>lose button to close the footnote pane.
5. Move the insertion point to the end of the fourth paragraph in the *Defining Desktop Publishing* section and then create the second footnote shown in figure 11.3 by completing steps similar to those in 4.
6. Move the insertion point to the end of the only paragraph in the *Initiating the Desktop Publishing Process* section and then create the third footnote shown in figure 11.3 by completing steps similar to those in 4.
7. Move the insertion point to the end of the last paragraph in the *Planning the Publication* section and then create the fourth footnote shown in figure 11.3.
8. Move the insertion point to the end of the last paragraph in the *Creating the Content* section (the last paragraph in the document) and then create the fifth footnote shown in figure 11.3.
9. Check page breaks in the document and, if necessary, adjust the page breaks.
10. Save the document again with the same name (Ch 11, Ex 01).
11. Print and then close Ch 11, Ex 01.

Exercise 1

Androtti, Yvonne, *Desktop Publishing Design*, Home Town Publishing, 2000, pages 102-112.

Bolle, Lynette and Jonathon Steadman, "Designing with Style," *Design Technologies*, January/February 1999, pages 22-24.

Doucette, Wayne, "Beginning the DTP Process," *Desktop Designs*, November 1999, pages 31-34.

Elstrom, Lisa, *Desktop Publishing Technologies*, Lilly-Harris Publishers, 2000, pages 88-94.

Busching, Wallace, "Designing a Newsletter," *Business Computing*, April 1999, pages 15-22.

Create an endnote in a similar manner as a footnote. At the Footnote and Endnote dialog box, click Endnote, and then click OK or press Enter. At the endnote pane, key the endnote entry text, and then click the Close button or press Alt + Shift + C. When creating endnotes, Word numbers endnotes with lowercase Roman numerals (i, ii, iii, etc.). The endnote numbering method will display after AutoNumber at the Footnote and Endnote dialog box. Later in this chapter, you will learn how to change the numbering method. Press the Enter key after keying the endnote entry text if you want the endnote separated from the next endnote by a blank line (double space).

Footnotes and endnotes can be formatted in the normal manner. The note reference number and the note entry number print in the default font at 8-point size. The note entry text prints in the default font size. The note reference and the note entry text can be formatted, if desired, to match the formatting of the document text.

Printing Footnotes and Endnotes

When a document containing footnotes is printed, Word automatically reduces the number of text lines on a page by the number of lines in the footnote plus two lines for spacing between the text and the footnote. If there is not enough room on the page, the footnote number and footnote entry text are taken to the next page. Word separates the footnotes from the text with a 2-inch separator line that begins at the left margin.

When endnotes are created in a document, Word prints all endnote references at the end of the document separated from the text by a 2-inch separator line.

Creating Endnotes

1. Open Report 02.
2. Save the document with Save As and name it Ch 11, Ex 02.
3. Make the following changes to the document:
   a. Select the entire document and then change the font to 12-point Century Schoolbook (or a similar serif typeface).
   b. Select the title *DESKTOP PUBLISHING DESIGN* and then change the font to 14-point Century Schoolbook bold.
   c. Apply 14-point Century Schoolbook bold to the headings *Designing a Document* and *Creating Focus*.
4. Create the first endnote shown in figure 11.4 at the end of the last paragraph in the *Designing a Document* section by completing the following steps:
   a. Position the insertion point at the end of the last paragraph in the *Designing a Document* section.
   b. Click Insert and then Footnote.
   c. At the Footnote and Endnote dialog box, click Endnote.
   d. Click OK or press Enter.
   e. At the endnote pane, key the first endnote shown in figure 11.4. Press the Enter key once after keying the endnote text.
   f. Click the Close button to close the endnote pane.

   Step 4f   Step 4e

   Endnotes | All Endnotes | ▼ | Close
   i Voller, Anthony, *Desktop Publishing Theory and Design*, Robison Publishing House, 1999, pages 82-91.

5. Move the insertion point to the end of the first paragraph below the two bulleted paragraphs in the *Creating Focus* section and then create the second endnote shown in figure 11.4 by completing steps similar to those in 4.
6. Move the insertion point to the last paragraph in the document and then create the third endnote shown in figure 11.4 by completing steps similar to those in 4.
7. Check page breaks in the document and, if necessary, adjust the page breaks.
8. Save the document again with the same name (Ch 11, Ex 02).
9. Print and then close Ch 11, Ex 02. (You may want to preview the document before printing.)

figure
11.4   *Exercise 2*

Voller, Anthony, *Desktop Publishing Theory and Design*, Robison Publishing House, 1999, pages 82-91.

Rubiano, Lee and Eleanor Bolton, "Choosing the Right Typeface," *Designing Publications*, December 2001, pages 20-23.

Klein, Leland, "Focusing in on Your Document," *System Technologies*, March/April 2000, pages 9-12.

Viewing and Editing Footnotes and Endnotes

To edit existing footnote or endnote entry text, display the footnote or endnote text or the pane. There are several methods you can use for displaying the footnote or endnote text or pane. In the Normal view, the footnote or endnote text does not display. To display footnotes or endnotes, change to the Print Layout view. Footnotes will display at the bottom of the page where they are referenced and endnotes will display at the end of the document. Footnotes or endnotes can be edited in the normal manner in the Print Layout view.

Display a footnote or endnote pane by choosing <u>V</u>iew and then <u>F</u>ootnotes. (The <u>F</u>ootnotes option is dimmed unless an open document contains footnotes or endnotes.) If the document contains footnotes, the footnote pane is opened. If the document contains endnotes, the endnote pane is opened. If the document contains both footnotes and endnotes, you can switch between the panes by choosing All Footnotes or All Endnotes from the view text box at the top of the footnote or endnote pane. To do this, click the down-pointing triangle at the right side of the view text box at the top of the pane, and then click *All Footnotes* or *All Endnotes*.

You can display a footnote or endnote pane in the Normal view with the split bar. The split bar is the small gray bar located immediately above the up-pointing triangle at the top of the vertical scroll bar. To view a footnote or endnote pane, position the mouse pointer on the split bar until it turns into a double line with an up- and down-pointing arrow. Hold down the Shift key and the left mouse button, drag the split bar down to somewhere in the middle of the document screen, then release the mouse button and then the Shift key. The document displays in the upper portion of the split window and the footnote or endnote displays in the lower portion of the split window. To close a footnote or endnote pane, you can click the <u>C</u>lose button, press Alt + Shift + C, drag the split bar back up to the top of the screen, or double-click the split bar.

Another method for opening a footnote or endnote pane is to double-click the footnote or endnote reference number in the document text. You can close a footnote or endnote pane by double-clicking the number before the footnote or endnote entry text in the pane.

With the footnote or endnote pane visible, you can move the insertion point between the pane and the document. To do this with the mouse, click in the document text or click in the footnote or endnote pane. If you are using the keyboard, press F6 to move the insertion point to the next pane or press Shift + F6 to move to the previous pane.

exercise 3

Editing Footnotes

1. Open Ch 11, Ex 01.
2. Save the document with Save As and name it Ch 11, Ex 03.
3. Edit the footnotes by completing the following steps:
   a. Change to the Print Layout view.
   b. Move the insertion point to the bottom of the second page until the second footnote is visible.
   c. Make the following changes to the second footnote:
      1) Change *January/February* to *May/June*.
      2) Change *22-24* to *31-33*.
   d. Move the insertion point to the bottom of the third page until the fourth footnote is visible and then make the following changes to the fourth footnote:
      1) Change *Lilly-Harris Publishers* to *Gray Mountain Press*.
      2) Change *2000* to *2001*.
   e. Change back to the Normal view.
4. Save the document again with the same name (Ch 11, Ex 03).
5. Print and then close Ch 11, Ex 03.

exercise 4

Editing Endnotes

1. Open Ch 11, Ex 02.
2. Save the document with Save As and name it Ch 11, Ex 04.
3. Display the endnote pane and then change the font of the endnotes by completing the following steps:
   a. Click View and then Footnotes.
   b. At the endnote pane, select all endnote entry text and endnote numbers, and then change the font to 12-point Century Schoolbook.
   c. Click the Close button to close the endnote pane.
4. Save the document again with the same name (Ch 11, Ex 04).
5. Print and then close Ch 11, Ex 04. (You may want to preview the document before printing.)

Finding Footnotes or Endnotes

In a document containing footnotes or endnotes, you can move the insertion point to a particular footnote or endnote at the Find and Replace dialog box with the Go To tab selected. To display this dialog box, click Edit and then Go To, or press Ctrl + G. You can also display the Find and Replace dialog box with the Go To tab selected by double-clicking the numbers on the Status bar that display the current page where the insertion point is positioned, a forward slash (/), and then the total number of pages in the document.

At the Find and Replace dialog box with the Go To tab selected, click *Footnote* in the Go to what list box. Click in the Enter footnote number text box, key the desired footnote number, and then click the Go To button. When the insertion point is positioned on the desired footnote or endnote reference number, click the Close button in the Find and Replace dialog box.

In the Print Layout view, you can move the insertion point to a particular footnote or endnote reference number in the document text or to an entry number in a footnote or endnote pane. To move the insertion point to a specific entry number in a footnote pane, position the insertion point on the reference number in the document text, and then double-click the left mouse button. To move the insertion point to a specific reference number in the text document, double-click the entry text number in the footnote or endnote pane.

Displaying and Editing a Footnote

1. Open Ch 11, Ex 01.
2. Save the document with Save As and name it Ch 11, Ex 05.
3. Go to footnote number 3 and then edit the footnote by completing the following steps:
   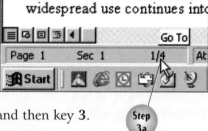
   a. Double-click the numbers *1/4* toward the left side of the Status bar.
   b. At the Find and Replace dialog box with the Go To tab selected, click *Footnote* in the Go to what list box.
   c. Click inside the Enter footnote number text box and then key **3**.
   d. Click the Go To button.

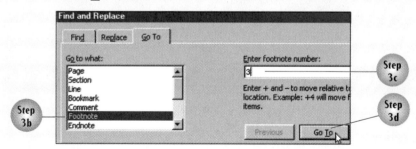

   e.   When the insertion point is positioned on the footnote reference number 3, click the Close button to close the Find and Replace dialog box.

   f.   With the insertion point still positioned on the footnote reference number, double-click the mouse button. (This displays the footnote pane.)

   g.   Make the following changes to the third footnote:

       1) Change the name from *Doucette, Wayne* to *Matheson, Felicia*.

       2) Change the page numbers from *31-34* to *47-50*.

   h.   Click the Close button to close the footnote pane.

4. Save the document again with the same name (Ch 11, Ex 05).

5. Print only the page where footnote 3 is located.

6. Close Ch 11, Ex 05.

Moving, Copying, or Deleting Footnotes or Endnotes

Footnote or endnote reference numbers can be moved, copied, or deleted in a document. If a footnote or endnote reference number is moved, copied, or deleted, all footnotes or endnotes remaining in the document are automatically renumbered. To move a footnote or endnote in a document, select the reference mark of the footnote or endnote that you want moved, and then click Edit and then Cut; or click the Cut button on the Standard toolbar. Position the insertion point at the location where you want the footnote or endnote reference inserted and then click Edit and then Paste; or click the Paste button on the Standard toolbar. You can also move a reference number to a different location in the document by selecting the reference number and then dragging it to the desired location.

To copy a reference number, complete similar steps except click Edit and then Copy or click the Copy button on the Standard toolbar. A reference number can also be copied to a different location in the document by selecting the reference number, holding down the Ctrl key, dragging the reference number to the desired location, and then releasing the mouse key and then the Ctrl key.

To delete a footnote or endnote from a document, select the reference number, and then press the Delete key or the Backspace key. When the reference number is deleted, the entry text is also deleted.

Editing and Deleting Footnotes

1. Open Ch 11, Ex 01.
2. Save the document with Save As and name it Ch 11, Ex 06.
3. Select the entire document, change the font to 12-point Century Schoolbook, and then deselect the document.
4. Display the footnote pane and then change the font to 12-point Century Schoolbook by completing the following steps:
   a. Click View and then Footnotes.
   b. At the footnote pane, select all footnote entry text and footnote numbers, and then change the font to 12-point Century Schoolbook.
   c. Click the Close button to close the footnote pane.
5. Delete the fourth footnote by completing the following steps:
   a. Move the insertion point to the fourth footnote reference number in the document text.
   b. Select the fourth footnote reference number and then press the Delete key or the Backspace key.
6. Move the third footnote reference number from the end of the only paragraph in *Initiating the Desktop Publishing Process* section to the end of the second paragraph in the *Planning the Publication* section by completing the following steps:

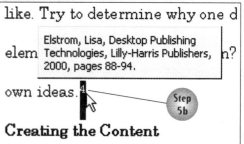

   a. Move the insertion point to the third footnote reference number.
   b. Select the third footnote reference number.
   c. Click the Cut button on the Standard toolbar.
   d. Position the insertion point at the end of the second paragraph in the *Planning the Publication* section.
   e. Click the Paste button on the Standard toolbar.
7. Check page breaks in the document and, if necessary, adjust the page breaks.
8. Save the document again with the same name (Ch 11, Ex 06).
9. Print and then close Ch 11, Ex 06.

Customizing Footnote or Endnote Settings

Footnotes or endnotes contain default settings. These default settings can be changed with options from the footnote or endnote pane or with options from the Note Options dialog box. When a footnote or endnote pane is visible, a view text box displays at the upper left corner of the pane. If you click the down-pointing triangle at the right side of this text box, a drop-down menu displays as shown in figure 11.5. (The options will change depending on whether a footnote or endnote pane is open.)

figure

11.5   *Footnote Pane Text Box Drop-Down Menu*

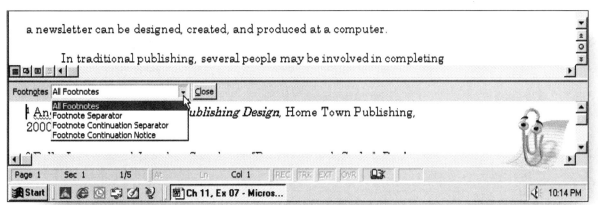

By default, Word inserts a 2-inch separator line that begins at the left margin and separates footnotes or endnotes from document text. Choose the *Footnote Separator* option to customize this line. When you click *Footnote Separator*, the pane display changes and shows the default separator line. Edit this line as desired. For example, you can delete it, change the position of the line, or lengthen or shorten the line. After customizing the line, click the C̲lose button. Click the R̲eset button if you want to reset the separator line back to the default. Complete similar steps to customize the endnote separator line.

If a footnote or endnote continues onto more than one page, Word inserts a continuation separator line between the note and the document text. This continuation separator line prints from the left to the right margin. Choose the *Footnote Continuation Separator* option if you want to customize the footnote continuation separator line. After customizing the line, click the C̲lose button to close the pane. Complete similar steps to customize a continuation separator line for endnotes.

If a footnote or endnote is continued on the next page, you can add text indicating that the note is continued on the next page. To do this, click the *Footnote Continuation Notice* option at the drop-down list, key the text you want to indicate that the note is continued, and then click the C̲lose button. Complete similar steps to add continuation text to endnotes.

With options from the Note Options dialog box with the All F̲ootnotes tab selected, shown in figure 11.6, you can further customize footnotes. To display this dialog box, click I̲nsert and then Foot̲note. At the Footnote and Endnote dialog box, click the O̲ptions button. The Note Options dialog box will display in a similar manner if the All E̲ndnotes tab is selected.

figure
11.6

Note Options Dialog Box with All Footnotes Tab Selected

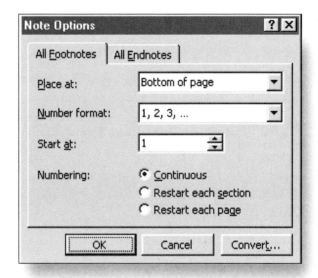

With the Place at option you can specify whether footnotes are printed at the bottom of the page or beneath text. By default, Word prints footnotes at the bottom of the page even if the text does not fill the entire page. Choose the *Beneath text* option from Place at if you want the footnote to print below the last line of text on the page.

The Place at option in the Note Options dialog box with the All Endnotes tab selected contains the choices *End of document* or *End of section*. At the default setting of *End of document*, endnotes print at the end of the document. Change this to *End of section* if you want endnotes to print at the end of the section in the document.

Word numbers footnotes with Arabic numbers and endnotes with lowercase Roman numerals. Change this default numbering with the Number format option at the Note Options dialog box. You can choose Arabic numbers, lowercase letters, uppercase letters, lowercase Roman numerals, uppercase Roman numerals, or special symbols.

Footnotes or endnotes are numbered sequentially beginning with 1. Use the Start at option from the Note Options dialog box if you want to change the beginning footnote or endnote number.

Word numbers footnotes or endnotes sequentially from the beginning to the end of a document. With options from the Numbering section of the Note Options dialog box you can change this to Restart each section, which restarts numbering at the beginning of each section, or Restart each page, which restarts numbering at the beginning of each page. (The Restart each page option is not available if the All Endnotes tab is selected.)

Footnotes or endnotes can be numbered with a symbol. To do this, click the Custom mark option at the Footnote and Endnote dialog box. To specify a symbol, click the Symbol button. At the Symbol dialog box that displays, click the desired symbol, and then click OK or press Enter. This inserts the selected symbol in the Custom mark text box. Continue creating the footnote or endnote in the normal manner.

Customizing Footnotes

1. Open Ch 11, Ex 06.
2. Save the document with Save As and name it Ch 11, Ex 07.
3. Customize the footnotes by completing the following steps:
    a. Click View and then Footnotes.
    b. At the footnote pane, click the down-pointing triangle to the right of the view text box, and then click *Footnote Separator*.
    c. At the footnote separator pane, click the Center button on the Formatting toolbar. (This centers the separator line between the left and right margins.)
    d. Click the Close button to close the separator pane.
    e. Click Insert and then Footnote.
    f. At the Footnote and Endnote dialog box, click the Options button.
    g. At the Note Options dialog box, make sure the All Footnotes tab is selected.
    h. Click the down-pointing triangle at the right of the Place at text box and then click *Beneath text* at the drop-down list.
    i. Click the up-pointing triangle after the Start at option until 5 displays in the text box.
    j. Click OK or press Enter to close the Note Options dialog box.
    k. Click the Close button to close the Footnote and Endnote dialog box.
4. Check page breaks in the document and, if necessary, adjust the page breaks.
5. Save the document again with the same name (Ch 11, Ex 07).
6. Print and then close Ch 11, Ex 07.

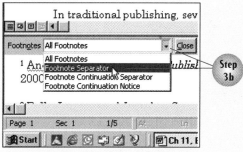

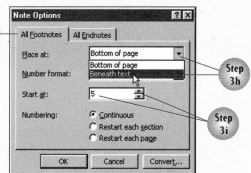

Converting Footnotes and Endnotes

Word provides an option at the Note Options dialog box that lets you convert footnotes to endnotes or endnotes to footnotes. To use this option, display the Note Options dialog box, and then click the Convert button. At the Convert Notes dialog box shown in figure 11.7, specify whether you want to convert footnotes to endnotes or endnotes to footnotes, and then click OK. Close the Note Options dialog box and then the Footnote and Endnote dialog box.

Convert Notes Dialog Box

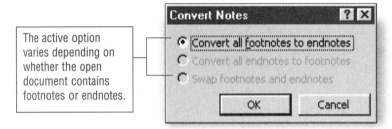

The active option varies depending on whether the open document contains footnotes or endnotes.

All footnotes and endnotes or individual footnotes or endnotes can be converted. To convert an individual endnote or footnote, click View and then Footnotes. Select the footnote or endnote to be converted. Position the insertion point in the footnote or endnote pane, and then click the *right* mouse button. At the shortcut menu that displays, click Convert to Footnote or Convert to Endnote. Click the Close button to close the footnote or endnote pane.

Converting Footnotes to Endnotes

1. Open Ch 11, Ex 06.
2. Save the document with Save As and name it Ch 11, Ex 08.
3. Convert the footnotes to endnotes by completing the following steps:
   a. Click Insert and then Footnote.
   b. At the Footnote and Endnote dialog box, click the Options button.
   c. At the Note Options dialog box, click the Convert button.
   d. At the Convert Notes dialog box, the Convert all footnotes to endnotes option is already selected so click OK to close the Convert Notes dialog box.
   e. Click OK or press Enter to close the Note Options dialog box.
   f. Click the Close button to close the Footnote and Endnote dialog box.
4. Check page breaks in the document and, if necessary, adjust the page breaks.
5. Save the document again with the same name (Ch 11, Ex 08).
6. Print and then close Ch 11, Ex 08.

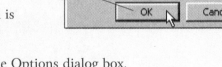

chapter summary

➤ Footnotes and endnotes are explanatory notes or references. Footnotes are printed at the bottom of the page; endnotes are printed at the end of the document.

➤ The first step in creating a footnote/endnote is to insert the note reference number at the location in the document where the note is referred. The second step is to key the note entry text.

➤ The footnote/endnote text is keyed at the footnote or endnote pane.

➤ By default, footnotes are numbered with Arabic numbers; endnotes are numbered with lowercase Roman numerals.

➤ The note reference number and the note entry text can be formatted to match the formatting of the document text.

➤ When printing a document containing footnotes, Word reduces the number of text lines on a page by the number of lines in the footnote plus two lines. Word separates footnotes and endnotes from the text with a 2-inch separator line.

➤ Footnotes and endnotes can be viewed and edited in the Print Layout view. Several methods can be used to edit at the footnote/endnote pane.

➤ You can use the Find and Replace dialog box with the Go To tab selected to move the insertion point to a particular footnote or endnote.

➤ Several methods can be used to move or copy a reference number within a document. If a footnote or endnote reference number is moved, copied, or deleted, all other footnotes/endnotes are automatically renumbered.

➤ To delete a footnote or endnote, select the reference number, and then press the Delete key or the Backspace key.

➤ The footnote or endnote default settings can be changed with options from the footnote or endnote pane or from the Note Options dialog box. Customizing changes can be made to the separator line, the footnote location, and the reference numbers.

➤ Footnotes can be converted to endnotes, or endnotes converted to footnotes, at the Convert Notes dialog box.

commands review

	Mouse	Keyboard
Footnote and Endnote dialog box	Insert, Footnote	Insert, Footnote
Create a footnote at the footnote pane	Insert, Footnote, Footnote	Alt + Ctrl + F
Create an endnote at the endnote pane	Insert, Footnote, Endnote	Insert, Footnote, Endnote
Close footnote or endnote pane	Close	Alt + Shift + C

Edit the footnote	View, Footnotes; or with mouse pointer on split bar, hold down Shift key and left mouse button, drag to middle of screen, release; or double-click reference number	Alt + Ctrl + F
Edit the endnote	View, Footnotes; or with mouse pointer on split bar, hold down Shift key and left mouse button, drag to middle of screen, release; or double-click reference number	View, Footnotes
Note Options dialog box	At the Footnote and Endnote dialog box, click Options	At the Footnote and Endnote dialog box, choose Options
Convert Notes dialog box	At the Footnote and Endnote dialog box, click Options, then click Convert	At the Footnote and Endnote dialog box, choose Options, then choose Convert

thinking offline

Completion: In the space provided, indicate the correct term, command, or number.

1. To display the Footnote and Endnote dialog box, first click this option on the Menu bar.

2. The footnote entry text is keyed here.

3. This is the keyboard command to access the footnote pane.

4. Word numbers footnotes with this type of number.

5. Word numbers endnotes with this type of number.

6. Display the Find and Replace dialog box with this tab selected to locate a specific footnote or endnote.

7. One way to begin moving a reference number to another location is by selecting the reference mark and then clicking this option on the Menu bar.

8. One way to copy a reference number to a different location is to select the number, hold down this key, and then drag the number to the desired location.

9. If you want footnotes to begin with a number other than 1, display this dialog box.

10. Footnotes or endnotes can be easily edited in this view.

11. By default, Word separates footnotes from text in the document by this.

12. Convert footnotes to endnotes at this dialog box.

working hands-on

1. Open Report 04.
2. Save the document with Save As and name it Ch 11, SA 01.
3. Make the following changes to the report:
   a. Insert a section break that begins a new page at the line containing the title *MODULE 4: CREATING A NEWSLETTER LAYOUT.*
   b. Number each page except the first page at the upper right corner of the page.
   c. Create the first footnote shown in figure 11.8 at the end of the first paragraph in the *Applying Desktop Publishing Guidelines* section of the report.
   d. Create the second footnote shown in figure 11.8 at the end of the third paragraph in the *Applying Desktop Publishing Guidelines* section of the report.
   e. Create the third footnote shown in figure 11.8 at the end of the last paragraph in the *Applying Desktop Publishing Guidelines* section of the report (middle of the second page).
   f. Create the fourth footnote shown in figure 11.8 at the end of the only paragraph in the *Choosing Paper Size and Type* section of the report.
   g. Create the fifth footnote shown in figure 11.8 at the end of the only paragraph in the *Choosing Paper Weight* section of the report.
4. Check page breaks in the document and, if necessary, adjust the page breaks.
5. Save the document again with the same name (Ch 11, SA 01).
6. Print and then close Ch 11, SA 01.

 figure

11.8   *Assessment 1*

Habermann, James, "Designing a Newsletter," *Desktop Designs*, January/February 2001, pages 23-29.

Pilante, Shirley G., "Adding Pizzazz to Your Newsletter," *Desktop Publisher*, September 2000, pages 32-39.

Maddock, Arlita G., "Guidelines for a Better Newsletter," *Business Computing*, June 2000, pages 9-14.

Alverso, Monica, "Paper Styles for Newsletters," *Design Technologies*, March 14, 1999, pages 45-51.

Alverso, Monica, "Paper Styles for Newsletters," *Design Technologies*, March 14, 1999, pages 52-53.

Assessment 2

1. Open Ch 11, SA 01.
2. Save the document with Save As and name it Ch 11, SA 02.
3. Make the following changes to the report:
   a. Select the entire document and then change the font to 12-point Century Schoolbook.
   b. Display the footnote pane, select all the footnotes, and then change the font to 12-point Century Schoolbook.
   c. Move the first footnote (the one after the first paragraph in the *Applying Desktop Publishing Guidelines* section) to the end of the fourth paragraph in the *Applying Desktop Publishing Guidelines* section.
   d. Delete the third footnote.
   e. Center the footnote separator line between the left and right margins.
4. Check page breaks in the document and, if necessary, adjust the page breaks.
5. Save the document again with the same name (Ch 11, SA 02).
6. Print and then close Ch 11, SA 02.

Assessment 3

1. Open Ch 11, SA 01.
2. Save the document with Save As and name it Ch 11, SA 03.
3. Make the following changes to the report:
   a. Change the font to 13-point Garamond for the document text and the footnotes.
   b. Convert the footnotes to endnotes.
   c. Make sure the endnotes are numbered with Arabic numbers. If they are not, change the numbering format to Arabic numbers.
4. Check page breaks in the document and, if necessary, adjust the page breaks.
5. Save the document again with the same name (Ch 11, SA 03).
6. Print and then close Ch 11, SA 03.

Unit 2 PA

FORMATTING AND ENHANCING DOCUMENTS

DEMONSTRATING YOUR SKILLS

In this unit, you have learned to enhance documents with writing tools such as Spelling, Thesaurus, and Grammar; produce business documents with customized features such as AutoText, columns, styles, and templates; and create multiple-page documents with elements such as headers, footers, page numbering, footnotes, and endnotes.

Assessment **one** 1

1. Open Document 01.
2. Save the document with Save As and name it Unit 2, PA 01.
3. Make the following changes to the document:
   a. Complete a spelling check and a grammar check on the document. (You determine what to edit and what to leave as written.)
   b. Select the document and then change the font to 12-point Century Schoolbook (or a similar serif typeface).
   c. Set the title in 14-point Century Schoolbook bold.
   d. Select the paragraphs in the body of the document (excluding the title) and then indent the first line of each paragraph 0.5 inch and change the paragraph alignment to justified.
   e. Proofread the document. (There are errors that are not selected by the spelling or grammar checker.)
4. Save the document again with the same name (Unit 2, PA 01).
5. Print and then close Unit 2, PA 01.

Assessment **two** 2

1. Open Document 02.
2. Save the document with Save As and name it Unit 2, PA 02.
3. Make the following changes to the letter:
   a. Complete a spelling check. (Proper names are spelled correctly.)
   b. Use the thesaurus to find appropriate synonyms for the following words:

1) *growth* in the first paragraph.
2) *best* in the first paragraph.
3) *many* in the last paragraph.

c. Select the entire document and then change the font to 12-point Century Schoolbook (or a similar serif typeface). (Make sure the letter fits on one page. If it does not, consider deleting a few blank lines before the date, or a few blank lines between the date and the inside address.)

4. Save the document again with the same name (Unit 2, PA 02).
5. Print and then close Unit 2, PA 02.

Assessment 3

1. At a clear document screen, create the document shown in figure U2.1 with the following specifications:
   a. Change the font to 12-point Garamond (or a similar typeface).
   b. Bold and center text as indicated in the figure.
   c. You determine the tab stops for the text in columns.
2. Save the document and name it Unit 2, PA 03.
3. Print and then close Unit 2, PA 03.

MANORWOOD SCHOOL DISTRICT

Enrollment Comparisons

School	1999	2000
Meeker Senior High	1,160	1,033
Rollings Senior High	890	993
Lakeview Middle School	690	587
Oakridge Middle School	681	801
Cedar Middle School	702	745
Stewart Elementary	521	498
Overman Elementary	386	404
Grant Elementary	478	512
Curtiss Elementary	403	455

Figure U2.1 • Assessment 3

Assessment 4

1. At a clear document screen, create the document shown in figure U2.2 with the following specifications:
   a. Bold and center text as indicated in the figure.
   b. You determine the tab stops for the text in columns.
2. Save the document and name it Unit 2, PA 04.
3. Print and then close Unit 2, PA 04.

TECHNOLOGY SEMINAR

Computers and Creativity . . . . Lincoln Room
Multimedia Software . . . . Washington Room
Computers in Science . . . . Jefferson Room
Software for Every Business Need . . . . Roosevelt Room
High-Width Band Networking . . . . Monroe Room
The Changing Nature of the Internet . . . . Kennedy Room
Computers and Privacy . . . . Truman Room

Figure U2.2 • Assessment 4

Assessment 5

1. Open Report 01.
2. Save the document with Save As and name it Unit 2, PA 05.
3. Make the following changes to the report:
   a. Select the entire document and then change the font to 12-point Century Schoolbook.
   b. Set the title and headings in 14-point Arial bold.
   c. Number the pages, except the first page, at the upper right margin.
   d. Create the footer *DESKTOP PUBLISHING* that prints centered at the bottom of every page and is set in 12-point Arial bold.
4. Check the page breaks in the document and, if necessary, adjust the page breaks.
5. Save the document again with the same name (Unit 2, PA 05).
6. Print and then close Unit 2, PA 05.

Assessment 6

1. Open Report 04.
2. Save the document with Save As and name it Unit 2, PA 06.
3. Make the following changes to the document:
   a. Select the entire document and then change the font to 12-point Rockwell. (If Rockwell is not available, choose a similar serif typeface such as Century Schoolbook.)
   b. Change the left and right margins to 1 inch.
   c. Insert a section break that begins a new page at the line containing the title *MODULE 4: CREATING NEWSLETTER LAYOUT*. (Be sure to insert a section break and not a page break.)
   d. Create the footer *Module 3: Designing a Newsletter* that prints at the left margin and *Page - #* that prints at the right margin on each page in the first section and is set in 12-point Rockwell bold.
   e. Create the footer *Module 4: Creating Newsletter Layout* that prints at the left margin and *Page - #* that prints at the right margin on each page in the second section and is set in 12-point Rockwell bold.
4. Check the page breaks in the document and, if necessary, adjust the page breaks.
5. Save the document again with the same name (Unit 2, PA 06).
6. Print and then close Unit 2, PA 06.

Assessment 7

1. Open Unit 2, PA 06.
2. Save the document with Save As and name it Unit 2, PA 07.
3. Make the following changes to the document:
   a. Delete the footer in the first section.
   b. Delete the footer in the second section.
   c. Create the header *Page - #* that prints at the top right margin on every page except the first page and is set in 12-point Rockwell bold.
   d. Create the first footnote shown in figure U2.3 at the end of the first paragraph in the *Applying Desktop Publishing Guidelines* section of the report.
   e. Create the second footnote shown in figure U2.3 at the end of the third paragraph in the *Applying Desktop Publishing Guidelines* section of the report.
   f. Create the third footnote shown in figure U2.3 at the end of the last paragraph in the *Applying Desktop Publishing Guidelines* section of the report.
   g. Create the fourth footnote shown in figure U2.3 at the end of the only paragraph in the *Choosing Paper Weight* section of the report.
   h. Display the footnote pane, select all the footnotes, and then change the font to 12-point Rockwell.
4. Check page breaks in the document and, if necessary, adjust the page breaks.
5. Save the document again with the same name (Unit 2, PA 07).
6. Print and then close Unit 2, PA 07.

Fellers, Laurie, *Desktop Publishing Design*, Cornwall & Lewis Publishing, 2000, pages 67-72.

Moriarity, Joel, "Adding Emphasis to Documents," *Desktop Publishing*, August 2001, pages 3-6.

Wong, Chun Man, *Desktop Publishing with Style*, Monroe-Ackerman Publishing, 1999, pages 87-93.

Jaquez, Andre, *Desktop Publishing Tips and Tricks*, Aurora Publishing House, 2000, pages 103-106.

Figure U2.3 • Assessment 7

Assessment 8 eight

1. Open Unit 2, PA 07.
2. Save the document with Save As and name it Unit 2, PA 08.
3. Make the following changes to the report:
   a. Convert the footnotes to endnotes.
   b. Make sure the endnotes numbering method is Arabic numbers.
   c. Edit endnote number 3 and change the publication year from *1999* to *2000* and change the pages from *87-93* to *61-68*.
4. Save the report again with the same name (Unit 2, PA 08).
5. Check the page breaks in the document and, if necessary, adjust the page breaks.
6. Print and then close Unit 2, PA 08.

Assessment 9 nine

1. Open Mortgage.
2. Complete the following steps:
   a. Select the first paragraph, copy it to a new document, save it and name it Mort 01, and then close Mort 01.
   b. Select the second paragraph, copy it to a new document, save it and name it Mort 02, and then close Mort 02.
   c. Select the third paragraph, copy it to a new document, save it and name it Mort 03, and then close Mort 03.
   d. Select the fourth paragraph, copy it to a new document, save it and name it Mort 04, and then close Mort 04.
   e. Select the fifth paragraph, copy it to a new document, save it and name it Mort 05, and then close Mort 05.
   f. Select the sixth paragraph, copy it to a new document, save it and name it Mort 06, and then close Mort 06.
   g. Select the seventh paragraph, copy it to a new document, save it and name it Mort 07, and then close Mort 07.
3. Close Mortgage.

4. At a clear document screen, create the document shown in figure U2.4. Insert the documents as indicated by the bracketed items.
5. Make the following changes to the document:
   a. Change the top and bottom margins to 1.5 inches.
   b. Number pages at the bottom center of the two pages.
6. Check the page break in the document and make sure it displays in a desirable position. (If not, insert your own page break.)
7. Save the document and name it Unit 2, PA 09.
8. Print and then close Unit 2, PA 09.

CONTRACT AND SECURITY AGREEMENT

BETWEEN

KEYSTONE MORTGAGE AND

DOUGLAS J. RICH AND PHYLLIS S. RICH

This contract is made this _____ day of _____, 2001, between KEYSTONE MORTGAGE, Seller, and DOUGLAS J. RICH and PHYLLIS S. RICH, Buyers. Having been quoted a cash price and a credit price and having chosen to pay the credit price, the Buyers agree to buy and Seller agrees to sell, subject to all the terms of this contract, the land parcel located at 432 Royal Oaks Drive, Reno, NV 89334.

[Insert Mort 03 here.]

[Insert Mort 01 here.]

[Insert Mort 02 here.]

[Insert Mort 05 here.]

[Insert Mort 07 here.]

[Insert Mort 04 here.]

[Insert Mort 06 here.]

_____
LEANNE S. TRENARY, President
KEYSTONE MORTGAGE

_____
DOUGLAS J. RICH, Buyer

_____
PHYLLIS S. RICH, Buyer

Figure U2.4 • Assessment 9

1. Open Unit 2, PA 09.
2. Save the document with Save As and name it Unit 2, PA 10.
3. Make the following changes to the document:
   a. Double-space the paragraphs within the body of the contract.
   b. Indent the first line of each paragraph.
   c. Delete the blank lines between paragraphs. (There should only be a double-space between all text in the body of the contract.)
   d. Delete the page numbering.
   e. Create a footer that prints on every page, is bolded, and contains *CONTRACT* at the left margin and *Page* followed by the page number at the right margin.
   f. Complete the following find and replaces:
      1) Find DOUGLAS J. RICH and replace with JOHN T. SHEAHAN.
      2) Find PHYLLIS S. RICH and replace with KIRSTEN C. SHEAHAN.
4. Save the document again with the same name (Unit 2, PA 10).
5. Print and then close Unit 2, PA 10.

CREATING ORIGINAL DOCUMENTS

The following activities give you the opportunity to practice your writing skills along with demonstrating an understanding of some of the important Word features you have mastered in this unit. When composing the documents, use correct grammar, appropriate word choices, and clear sentence construction.

Situation: You are the administrative assistant for Linda Shing, superintendent of the Kentwood School District. She has asked you to compose a memo to all elementary school principals telling them that an accreditation team will visit their school on the following days and times:

Oak Ridge Elementary	January 12	1:30 p.m.
Madison Creek Elementary	January 14	9:30 a.m.
Bell Valley Elementary	February 9	2:00 p.m.
South Bend Elementary	February 17	9:00 a.m.
Myers Heights Elementary	March 3	1:30 p.m.

When composing the memo, set the school names, days, and times in balanced columns. Save the memo and name it Unit 2, PA 11. Print and then close Unit 2, PA 11.

Assessment twelve 12

Situation: You are responsible for formatting the report in the document named Report 05. This report will be left bound and should include page numbers and headers and/or footers. Change to a serif typeface (other than Times New Roman) for the body of the report and a sans serif typeface for the title and headings. Correct the spelling in the document. Save the formatted report and name it Unit 2, PA 12. Print and then close Unit 2, PA 12.

Assessment thirteen 13

Create an appropriate title page for the report formatted in assessment 12. Include your name as the author of the report. Save the title page and name it Unit 2, PA 13. Print and then close Unit 2, PA 13.

Unit three

CUSTOMIZING DOCUMENTS AND ADDING VISUAL APPEAL

MICROSOFT® WORD 2000

MOUS SKILLS—UNIT THREE

Coding No.	SKILL	Pages
W2000.2	**Working with paragraphs**	
W2000.2.4	Apply borders and shading to paragraphs	431-437
W2000.3	**Working with documents**	
W2000.3.3	Use Web Page Preview	542
W2000.4	**Managing files**	
W2000.4.5	Create a new document using a wizard	548-552
W2000.4.6	Save as Web page	540-542
W2000.4.8	Create hyperlinks	547-548
W2000.5	**Using tables**	
W2000.5.1	Create and format tables	380-390
W2000.5.2	Add borders and shading to tables	390-396
W2000.5.3	Revise tables (insert and delete rows and columns, change cell formats)	404-407
W2000.5.4	Modify table structure (merge cells, change height and width)	397-402, 408-409
W2000.5.5	Rotate text in a table	412, 416-417
W2000.6	**Working with pictures and charts**	
W2000.6.1	Use the drawing toolbar	471-493
W2000.6.2	Insert graphics into a document (Word Art, clip art, images)	443-451, 493-510
W2000E.1	**Working with paragraphs**	
W2000E.1.1	Apply paragraph and section shading	433-437
W2000E.2	**Working with documents**	
W2000E.2.1	Create and modify page borders	440-443
W2000E.2.2	Format first page differently than subsequent pages	440-442
W2000E.2.5	Create watermarks	452-453
W2000E.3	**Using tables**	
W2000E.3.2	Perform calculations in a table	417-422
W2000E.4	**Working with pictures and charts**	
W2000E.4.2	Delete and position graphics	444, 448, 454-458
W2000E.5	**Using mail merge**	
W2000E.5.1	Create main document	353-354
W2000E.5.2	Create data source	347-352
W2000E.5.4	Merge main document and data source	355-358
W2000E.5.5	Generate labels	365-366
W2000E.5.6	Merge a document using alternate data sources	368-370
W2000E.6	**Using advanced features**	
W2000E.6.6	Use advanced text alignment features with graphics	487-489

Chapter 12

Merging Documents

P E R F O R M A N C E   O B J E C T I V E S

Upon successful completion of chapter 12, you will be able to:

- **Create a data source.**
- **Create a main document.**
- **Merge a data source and a main document to create personalized documents.**
- **Edit a data source.**
- **Create envelopes during a merge.**
- **Create an envelope main document and merge it with a data source.**
- **Create a label main document and merge it with a data source.**
- **Create a list main document and merge it with a data source.**
- **Input text during a merge.**

Word includes a mail merge feature that you can use to create letters and envelopes and much more, all with personalized information. There are two documents that need to be created for merging. One document, which Word calls the *data source*, contains the variable information. The second document contains the standard text along with identifiers showing where variable information (information that changes) is to be inserted. Word refers to this as the *main document*. After these documents are created, they are merged to produce personalized documents such as letters and envelopes.

A data source is a document that contains variable information about customers, clients, companies, etc. This may include such information as names, addresses, telephone numbers, and products. The person creating the data source determines the variable information included. When creating a data source, consider present and future needs.

Creating a Data Source with Mail Merge Helper

Generally, a merge takes two documents—the *data source* and the *main document.* These documents can be created in any order, but you might find creating the data source first and then the main document the more logical procedure.

The data source contains the variable information that will be inserted in the main document. Before creating a data source, determine what type of correspondence you will be creating and the type of information you will need to insert in the correspondence. Word provides predetermined field names that can be used when creating the data source. Use these field names if they represent the data you are creating.

Variable information in a data source is saved as a *record*. A record contains all the information for one unit (for example, a person, family, customer, client, or business). A series of fields makes one record, and a series of records makes a data source.

Word's Mail Merge Helper feature can be used to create a data source. For example, suppose the customer service manager of Lifetime Annuity Association wants to introduce a new sales representative to all customers in the Phoenix, Arizona, area. The manager determines that a personal letter should be sent to all customers in the greater Phoenix area. Figure 12.1 shows one way this letter can be written.

The date, body of the letter, and the complimentary close are standard. The variable information—information that will change with each letter—is the name, job title, company name, address, city, state, Zip Code, and salutation.

figure
12.1   *Sample Letter*

February 20, 2001

(Name)
(Job Title)
(Company)
(Address)
(City, State Zip)

Dear (Name):

At Lifetime Annuity Association, we are committed to providing insurance and financial planning services for employees of our customers. To provide continuing service to you, a new customer representative has been hired. The new customer representative, Mr. Raymond Miller, began his employment with Lifetime Annuity Association on February 1. He comes to our company with over 10 years' experience in the employee benefits and insurance industry.

Mr. Miller will be in the Phoenix area during the third week of March. He would like to schedule a time for a visit to your company, and will be contacting you by telephone next week.

Sincerely,

Evelyn Colwell, Manager
Customer Service Department

Before creating the letter as a main document, the data source is created. This document includes the variable information for each customer of Lifetime Annuity Association. In exercise 1, you will use the Mail Merge Helper to create a data source containing the customers of Lifetime Annuity Association who will receive the form letter.

Creating a Data Source

1. At a clear document screen create a data source named Customer data source containing the information shown in figure 12.2 by completing the following steps:
    a. Click Tools and then Mail Merge.
    b. At the Mail Merge Helper dialog box shown in figure 12.3, click the Create button (located below Main document).
    c. At the drop-down list that displays, click Form Letters.
    d. At the dialog box asking if you want to use the active document or a new document window, click the Active Window button.
    e. Click the Get Data button and then click Create Data Source at the drop-down list.
    f. At the Create Data Source dialog box shown in figure 12.4, the fields provided by Word are shown in the Field names in header row list box. These fields are needed for the data source except *Country* and *HomePhone*. Scroll down the Field names in header row list box until *Country* is visible, click *Country*, and then click the Remove Field Name button.
    g. With *HomePhone* selected in the Field names in header row list box, click the Remove Field Name button.
    h. Click OK.
    i. At the Save As dialog box, key **Customer data source**, and then click Save or press Enter.
    j. At the dialog box containing the warning that the data source contains no data, click the Edit Data Source button. This displays the Data Form dialog box shown in figure 12.5.
    k. At the Data Form dialog box, key the title, **Mrs.**, of the first customer shown in figure 12.2, and then press the Enter key or the Tab key.
    l. Continue keying the information in figure 12.2 for the customer, *Mrs. Sara Kerrick*, in the appropriate fields. Press the Enter key or the Tab key to move to the next field or press Shift + Tab to move to the preceding field.

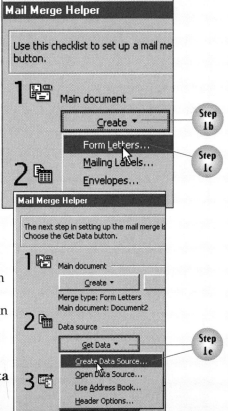

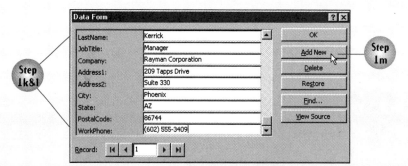

Step
1k&l

Step
1m

m. After entering all the information for *Mrs. Sara Kerrick*, click the Add New button. (You can also press Enter after keying the work phone.) This saves the information and displays a blank Data Form dialog box. Continue keying the information for each person in this manner until all records shown in figure 12.2 have been created.

n. After creating the last record for the data source, click the View Source button.

o. At the data source document, click the Save button on the Standard toolbar.

2. Print and then close Customer data source.

3. Close the clear document screen without saving the changes.

figure
12.2

Exercise 1

Title	=	**Mrs.**
FirstName	=	**Sara**
LastName	=	**Kerrick**
JobTitle	=	**Manager**
Company	=	**Rayman Corporation**
Address1	=	**209 Tapps Drive**
Address2	=	**Suite 330**
City	=	**Phoenix**
State	=	**AZ**
PostalCode	=	**86744**
WorkPhone	=	**(602) 555-3409**
Title	=	**Mr.**
FirstName	=	**Gerald**
LastName	=	**Jorgenson**
JobTitle	=	**Director**
Company	=	**Baxter Manufacturing**
Address1	=	**1203 North 24th Street**
Address2	=	(leave this blank)
City	=	**Phoenix**

State	=	**AZ**
PostalCode	=	**86342**
WorkPhone	=	**(602) 555-9800**
Title	=	**Ms.**
FirstName	=	**Linda**
LastName	=	**White**
JobTitle	=	**Assistant Manager**
Company	=	**Broadway Builders**
Address1	=	**8700 Broadway Avenue**
Address2	=	(leave this blank)
City	=	**Phoenix**
State	=	**AZ**
PostalCode	=	**86745**
WorkPhone	=	**(602) 555-3344**

Mail Merge Helper Dialog Box

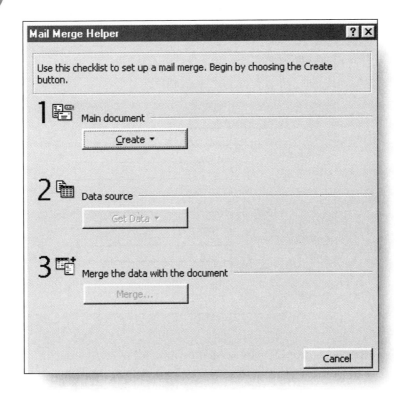

figure

12.4

Create Data Source Dialog Box

Create Data Source   ? X

A mail merge data source is composed of rows of data. The first row is called the header row. Each of the columns in the header row begins with a field name.

Word provides commonly used field names in the list below. You can add or remove field names to customize the header row.

Field name:

[   ]

Add Field Name >>

Remove Field Name

Field names in header row:

Title
FirstName
LastName
JobTitle
Company
Address1
Address2

Move ↑ ↓

Use these fields provided by Word. Remove fields you do not need and/or add your own fields.

MS Query...   OK   Cancel

figure

12.5

Data Form Dialog Box

Key text in the specified field. Press the Tab key to move to the next field or press Shift + Tab to move to the previous field.

Data Form   ? X

Title: [   ]
FirstName: [   ]
LastName: [   ]
JobTitle: [   ]
Company: [   ]
Address1: [   ]
Address2: [   ]
City: [   ]
State: [   ]

OK
Add New
Delete
Restore
Find...
View Source

Record: |◄ ◄ [1] ► ►|

In the printed Customer data source data source document, the first row of the table is called the *header row* and identifies the names of the fields. These field names are important in identifying where variable information will be inserted in a main document. Text in the table may wrap within a cell. The text will be inserted properly, however, in the main document. Some fields in a data source may not contain text. For example, in the second and third records in the Customer data source data source, there is no data for the *Address2* data field.

Creating the Main Document

When you have determined the fields and field names and created the data source, the next step is to create the main document. When the main document is completed and the fields have been inserted in the proper locations, it will look similar to the letter shown in figure 12.6. To create the main document shown in figure 12.6, complete exercise 2.

Notice that in figure 12.6 there is a space between the fields. Spaces are inserted between fields as if there was text and then when the variable information is inserted, it is spaced correctly. This is also true for punctuation. Insert punctuation in a main document as you would a normal document. For example, key the comma immediately after the «City» field in the address and key a colon (:) immediately after the «LastName» field in the salutation. The «Title» and «LastName» fields are used more than once in the main document in figure 12.6. Fields can be used in a main document as often as needed.

exercise

Creating a Main Document

1. At a clear document screen, create the main document shown in figure 12.6 and name it Customer main doc by completing the following steps:
   a. Click Tools and then Mail Merge.
   b. At the Mail Merge Helper dialog box, click the Create button (located below Main document), and then click Form Letters at the drop-down list.
   c. At the question asking if you want to use the active document window or a new document, click the Active Window button.
   d. At the Mail Merge Helper dialog box, click the Get Data button (located below Data source) and then click Open Data Source at the drop-down list.
   e. At the Open Data Source dialog box, double-click *Customer data source* in the list box.
   f. At the Microsoft Word dialog box telling you that Word found no fields in your main document, click the Edit Main Document button.
   g. At the clear document screen with the Mail Merge toolbar displayed above the Ruler, key the date at the beginning of the letter shown in figure 12.6, press the Enter key five times, and then insert the first field by completing the following steps:
      1) Click the Insert Merge Field button on the Mail Merge toolbar (first button from the left).
      2) Click *Title* at the drop-down menu.

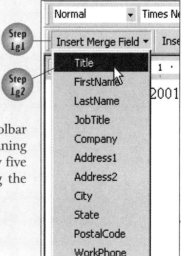

h. Press the spacebar once and then insert the *FirstName* data field by completing steps similar to those in 1g. Continue in this manner until all data fields have been entered as shown in figure 12.6. (Be sure to press the Enter key to end a text line as shown in the figure. Also, be sure to key the comma after the «City» field.)

i. Key the remaining text in the main document, proofread the document, and then click the Save button on the Standard toolbar.

j. At the Save As dialog box, key **Customer main doc**, and then click Save or press Enter.

2. Print and then close Customer main doc.

figure
12.6   *Exercise 2*

February 20, 2001

«Title» «FirstName» «LastName»
«JobTitle»
«Company»
«Address1»
«Address2»
«City», «State» «PostalCode»

Dear «Title» «Last Name»:

At Lifetime Annuity Association, we are committed to providing insurance and financial planning services for employees of our customers. To provide continuing service to you, a new customer representative has been hired. The new customer representative, Mr. Raymond Miller, began his employment with Lifetime Annuity Association on February 1. He comes to our company with over 10 years' experience in the employee benefits and insurance industry.

Mr. Miller will be in the Phoenix area during the third week of March. He would like to schedule a time for a visit to your company, and will be contacting you by telephone next week.

Sincerely,

Evelyn Colwell, Manager
Customer Service Department

XX:Customer main doc

Merging Files

Once the data source and the main document have been created and saved, they can be merged. Merged documents can be saved in a new document or they can be sent directly to the printer. There are several ways to merge a data source with a main document. A main document and a data source can be merged with buttons on the Mail Merge toolbar or options at the Merge dialog box.

When a main document is open, the Mail Merge toolbar shown in figure 12.7 displays below the Formatting toolbar and above the Ruler. Figure 12.7 identifies each button on the Mail Merge toolbar.

Buttons on the Mail Merge Toolbar

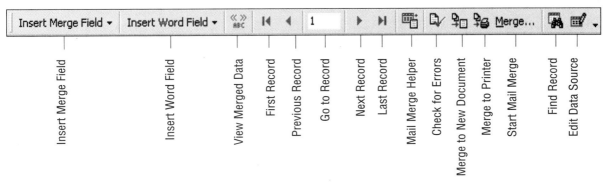

Merging to a New Document

To merge a main document with a data source to a new document using a button on the Mail Merge toolbar, open the main document, and then click the Merge to New Document button. During a merge, if a field contains no data, Word removes the blank line. For example, in the data source shown in figure 12.2, two records do not contain data for *Address2*. Instead of printing a line with no data, Word removes the blank line. At the Merge dialog box shown in figure 12.8, the <u>D</u>on't print blank lines when data fields are empty option is selected. If you do not want the blank line removed, click the <u>P</u>rint blank lines when data fields are empty option. To display the Merge dialog box, click the Start Mail Merge button on the Mail Merge toolbar.

Merge to New
Document

Start Mail
Merge

figure

12.8 *Merge Dialog Box*

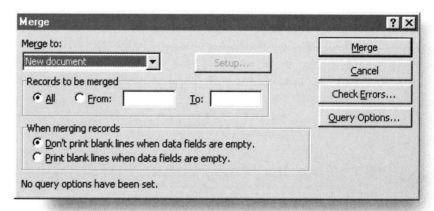

exercise 3

Merging Documents

1. Merge Customer main doc with Customer data source by completing the following steps:
   a. Open Customer main doc.
   b. Click the Merge to New Document button on the Mail Merge toolbar.
   c. When the main document is merged with the data source, save the document and name it Ch 12, Ex 03.
2. Print and then close Ch 12, Ex 03.
3. Close Customer main doc without saving the changes.

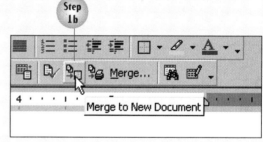

Step 1b

Merge to New Document

Merging to the Printer

Merge to Printer

In the steps in the preceding section, the records in the data source are merged with the main document and then inserted in a new document. You can also merge the records in a data source with a main document and send the merged documents directly to the printer. To do this, open the main document, and then click the Merge to Printer button on the Mail Merge toolbar.

Viewing Merged Records in the Main Document

When the main document is open, the data fields, such as «Title» and «FirstName», display in the document as shown in figure 12.6. With buttons on the Mail Merge toolbar, you can view the main document with the fields merged with the data source.

Click the View Merged Data button on the Mail Merge toolbar to view the main document merged with the first record in the data source. After viewing the main document merged with a record in the data source, click the View Merged Data button again to return the display to fields. When the View Merged Data button is active, it displays with a lighter gray background than the other buttons on the Mail Merge toolbar.

If you click the View Merged Data button, Word displays the main document merged with the first record in the data source. If you want to see the main document merged with the next record in the data source, click the Next Record button on the Mail Merge toolbar.

Click the First Record button to view the document merged with the first record in the data source or click the Last Record button to view the document merged with the last record in the data source. If you want to view the document merged with a specific record in the data source and you know the number of the record, key that number in the Go to Record box on the Mail Merge toolbar.

View Merged
Data

Next Record

First Record

Last Record

Creating a Main Document with a Data Source Attached

1. At a clear document screen, create the letter shown in figure 12.9 and attach it to the Customer data source document by completing the following steps:
   a. Click Tools and then Mail Merge.
   b. At the Mail Merge Helper dialog box, click the Create button (located below Main document), and then click Form Letters at the drop-down list.
   c. At the question asking if you want to use the active document window or a new document, click the Active Window button.
   d. At the Mail Merge Helper dialog box, click the Get Data button (located below Data source), and then click Open Data Source at the drop-down list.
   e. At the Open Data Source dialog box, double-click *Customer data source* in the list box.
   f. At the Microsoft Word dialog box telling you that Word found no fields in your main document, click the Edit Main Document button.
   g. At the clear document screen with the Mail Merge toolbar displayed above the Ruler, key the letter shown in figure 12.9. Insert the fields as indicated. (Use the Insert Merge Field button to do this.)
   h. After keying the entire main document, click the Save button on the Standard toolbar.
   i. At the Save As dialog box, key **Customer ltr2 main doc**, and then click Save or press Enter.

2. Position the insertion point at the beginning of the document and then click the View Merged Data button on the Mail Merge toolbar to view the main document merged with the first record in the data source.

3. Click the Next Record button on the Mail Merge toolbar to view the main document merged with the second record in the data source.
4. Click the Last Record button on the Mail Merge toolbar to view the main document merged with the last record in the data source.
5. Click the View Merged Data button on the Mail Merge toolbar. (This redisplays the main document with the fields.)
6. Print and then close Customer ltr2 main doc without saving the changes.

figure

12.9

Exercise 4

(current date)

‹‹Title›› ‹‹FirstName›› ‹‹LastName››
‹‹Address1››
‹‹City››, ‹‹State›› ‹‹PostalCode››

Dear ‹‹Title›› ‹‹LastName››:

A few weeks ago, we shared with you the exciting news that you are preapproved for the First Choice credit card. This card offers you the ability to earn one MilesPlus mile for every purchase dollar you charge.

Now is the time to take us up on this incredible offer. Just accept your preapproved First Choice credit card and we will credit your MilesPlus account with 5,000 bonus miles after your First Choice account has been opened.

All you need to do to accept your First Choice credit card is to mail your enclosed Acceptance Form in the postage-paid envelope provided or you can call our toll-free number, 1-800-555-8900. In addition to the miles you will earn, you will also enjoy cash advances available 24 hours a day, traveler's message service, and toll-free customer service.

Sincerely,

Walter Chamberlin
Marketing Manager

XX:Customer ltr2 main doc

Attachment

Checking for Errors

For a merge to operate smoothly, no errors can occur in the main document or the data source. Word includes a helpful feature you can use to check for errors in the main and data source documents. This provides you with the opportunity to correct errors before completing the merge.

To correct errors, open a main document, and then click the Check for Errors button on the Mail Merge toolbar. When you click the Check for Errors button, the Checking and Reporting Errors dialog box shown in figure 12.10 displays.

Check for Errors

12.10   *Checking and Reporting Errors Dialog Box*

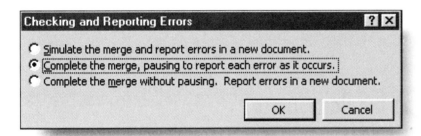

The Checking and Reporting Errors dialog box contains three options. You can tell Word to simulate the merge and then report errors in a new document; complete the merge, pausing to report each error as it occurs; or complete the merge without pausing and then report errors in a new document.

If you are going to merge a main document with a data source containing a large number of records and you expect there may be errors, click the Simulate the merge and report errors in a new document option. The steps to check will vary depending on the options you choose. Consider the following guidelines and you will reduce or eliminate errors in the merge:

- Field names must be unique, begin with a letter, and contain no spaces. (If you let Word choose the field names for you when creating the data source, this will not be a problem.)
- Field names must be in one row at the beginning of the data source.
- Each field (column) must have a field name.

exercise 5

Checking for Errors in a Main Document

1. Open Customer ltr2 main doc.
2. Check for errors in the main document and data source document by completing the following steps:
   a. Click the Check for Errors button on the Mail Merge toolbar.
   b. At the Checking and Reporting Errors dialog box, make sure Complete the merge, pausing to report each error as it occurs is selected, and then click OK or press Enter.
   c. If Word finds any errors, make the necessary corrections. If no errors are found, the main document is merged with the data source and the merged document is displayed in the document screen.
3. Save the merged document and name it Ch 12, Ex 05.
4. Print and then close Ch 12, Ex 05.
5. Close Customer ltr2 main doc without saving the changes.

Editing the Data Source

Edit Data Source

With the main document displayed, you can edit records in a data source with the Edit Data Source button on the Mail Merge toolbar. When you click the Edit Data Source button, Word displays the Data Form dialog box containing the information for the record number displayed in the Go to Record box on the Mail Merge toolbar.

With the Data Form dialog box displayed, make changes to the text in the record as required. Press the Tab key to move to the next field or press Shift + Tab to move to the previous field. Use the arrow buttons at the bottom left side of the Data Form dialog box to display the first record, next record, previous record, or last record in the data source.

To delete a record from the data source, display the desired record and then click the Delete button. If you edit a record and then decide you want to return the record to its original state before editing, click the Restore button.

If you want to make edits to the data source, click the View Source button. This displays the data source document in the table format. When the data source is displayed, the Database toolbar displays below the Formatting toolbar and above the Ruler. Figure 12.11 identifies the buttons on the Database toolbar and what you can perform with each button.

figure

12.11   *Buttons on the Database Toolbar*

Click this button	Named	To do this
	Data Form	Display the Data Form dialog box where you can add or delete records or edit existing records.
	Manage Fields	Display the Manage Fields dialog box where you can add, remove, or rename field names in the header row.
	Add New Record	Add a new record at the location of the insertion point in the table.
	Delete Record	Remove a record at the location of the insertion point in the table.
	Sort Ascending	Sort the records in the table in ascending order on the current field.
	Sort Descending	Sort the records in the table in descending order on the current field.
	Insert Database	Display the Database dialog box where you can insert a file containing a database.
	Update Field	Update fields in the document.
	Find Record	Display the Find in Field dialog box where you can search for a specific record.
	Mail Merge Main Document	Open the main document attached to the current data source.

With the buttons on the Database toolbar as described in figure 12.11, you can easily manage the data source document. If you want to add or remove field names from the header row in the data source, display the Manage Fields dialog box shown in figure 12.12 by clicking the Manage Fields button on the Database toolbar.

Manage Fields

figure
12.12
Manage Fields Dialog Box

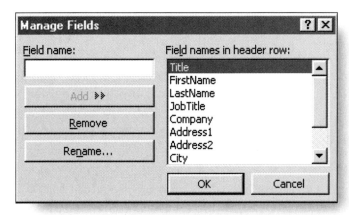

At the Manage Fields dialog box, you can add a data field to the data source and remove or rename a data field. To add a data field, key the new data field name in the Field name text box, and then click the Add button. Word adds the new field name to the end of the list in the Field names in header row list box and adds a new column at the right side of the table in the data source document. Key information in the cells in the new column as needed.

exercise

Editing a Data Source Document

1. Edit the Customer data source document by completing the following steps:
    a. Open Customer main doc.
    b. Click the Edit Data Source button on the Mail Merge toolbar.
    c. At the Data Form dialog box, click once on the button containing the right-pointing triangle immediately right of the Record text box. (This displays the second record in the data source containing the name *Gerald Jorgenson*.)

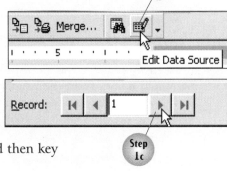

    d. Press the Tab key until *1203 North 24th Street* is selected, and then key **4133 Monta Vista**.
    e. Press the Tab key until *Phoenix* is selected and then key **Scottsdale**.
    f. Press the Tab key until *86342* is selected and then key **87332**.
    g. Click the View Source button (located at the right side of the Data Form dialog box). (This displays the data source document.)

h. At the data source document, click the Add New Record button on the Database toolbar.

Step 1h

i. With the insertion point positioned in the first cell of the new row, key the text after *Title*, and then press the Tab key. Continue keying the text as indicated below:

Title	=	Mrs.
FirstName	=	Barbara
LastName	=	Houston
JobTitle	=	Director
Company	=	CR Electrical
Address1	=	7903 South 122nd
Address2	=	Building C
City	=	Scottsdale
State	=	AZ
PostalCode	=	87923
WorkPhone	=	(602) 555-5050

j. Save the data source document with the same name (Customer data source).
k. Close Customer data source.
l. Click the Merge to New Document button on the Mail Merge toolbar.
2. Save the merged document and name it Ch 12, Ex 06.
3. Print and then close Ch 12, Ex 06.
4. Close Customer main doc and save the changes.

Merging Envelopes

If you create a letter as a main document and then merge it with a data source, more than likely you will need an envelope properly addressed in which to send the letters. An envelope can be created that contains data fields that are then merged with a data source. In this way, you can quickly prepare envelopes. In exercise 7 you will prepare envelopes for the customers in the data source document named Customer data source.

Creating an Envelope Main Document

1. At a clear document screen, create a main document for envelopes with the Customer data source document attached by completing the following steps:
    a. Click Tools and then Mail Merge.
    b. At the Mail Merge Helper dialog box, click the Create button (located below Main document) and then click Envelopes at the drop-down list.
    c. At the question asking if you want to use the active document window or a new document, click the Active Window button.
    d. At the Mail Merge Helper dialog box, click the Get Data button (located below Data source), and then click Open Data Source at the drop-down list.

e. At the Open Data Source dialog box, double-click *Customer data source* in the list box.
f. At the Microsoft Word dialog box telling you that Word needs to set up your main document, click the Set Up Main Document button.

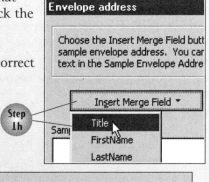

g. At the Envelope Options dialog box with the Envelope Options tab selected, make sure the correct envelope size is displayed, and then click OK.
h. At the Envelope address dialog box, click the Insert Merge Field button, and then click *Title* from the drop-down list. (This inserts «Title» in the Sample envelope address section of the dialog box.)
i. Continue choosing fields from the Insert Merge Field drop-down list as shown in figure 12.13.

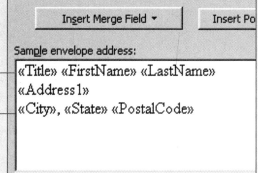

j. When all fields have been entered in the Sample envelope address section of the dialog box as shown in figure 12.13, click OK to close the Envelope address dialog box.
k. At the Mail Merge Helper dialog box, click the Merge button.
l. At the Merge dialog box, make sure *New document* displays in the Merge to text box, and then click the Merge button.

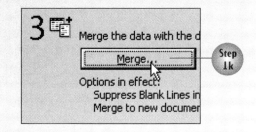

2. Save the merged document and name it Ch 12, Ex 07.
3. Print and then close Ch 12, Ex 07.
4. At the envelope main document, save it and name it Env main doc.
5. Close Env main doc.

figure

12.13   *Exercise 7*

‹‹Title›› ‹‹FirstName›› ‹‹LastName››
‹‹Address1››
‹‹City››, ‹‹State›› ‹‹PostalCode››

When you click the Merge button at the Merge dialog box, the records in the data source are merged with the envelope and then the merged envelopes are inserted in a document. Print this document in the normal manner. If you want to send the merged envelopes directly to the printer, change the Merge to option at the Merge dialog box to Printer, and then click the Merge button.

If you want to save the merged envelopes, save the document in the normal manner, and then close it. This displays the envelope main document. If you think you will need this envelope main document in the future, save it.

At the Envelope address dialog box, you can also identify a FIM for the envelope. To do this, click the Insert Postal Bar Code button. At the Insert Postal Bar Code dialog box, specify the *PostalCode* field in the Merge field with ZIP code text box, and then click FIM-A courtesy reply mail.

Merging Mailing Labels

Mailing labels can be created for records in a data source in much the same way that you create envelopes. Complete steps similar to those for creating envelopes for records in a data source. By default, records in a data source are merged with a mailing label, and then the merged labels are inserted in the document screen. Print a mailing label document in the normal manner. If you want to send merged labels directly to the printer, change the Merge to option at the Merge dialog box to Printer, and then click the Merge button.

If you want to save merged labels, save the document in the normal manner, and then close it. This displays the label main document. If you think you will need this label main document in the future, save it.

exercise

8

Creating Mailing Labels

1. At a clear document screen, create mailing labels for Avery 5163 shipping labels using the records in the Customer data source document by completing the following steps:
   a. Click Tools and then Mail Merge.
   b. At the Mail Merge Helper dialog box, click the Create button (located below Main document), and then click Mailing Labels at the drop-down list.
   c. At the question asking if you want to use the active document window or a new document, click the Active Window button.
   d. At the Mail Merge Helper dialog box, click the Get Data button (located below Data source), and then click Open Data Source at the drop-down list.
   e. At the Open Data Source dialog box, double-click *Customer data source* in the list box.
   f. At the Microsoft Word dialog box telling you that Word needs to set up your main document, click the Set Up Main Document button.
   g. At the Label Options dialog box, scroll down the Product number list box until *5163 - Shipping* is visible, and then click it.

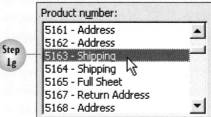

Step 1g

Product number:

5161 - Address
5162 - Address
5163 - Shipping
5164 - Shipping
5165 - Full Sheet
5167 - Return Address
5168 - Address

h. Click OK to close the Labels Options dialog box.
i. At the Create Labels dialog box, click the Insert Merge Field button, and then click *Title* at the drop-down list. (This inserts «Title» in the Sample label box.)
j. Continue choosing fields from the Insert Merge Field drop-down list as shown in figure 12.14.
k. Add a delivery point bar code to the label by completing the following steps:

Step 1j

Sample label:

«Title» «FirstName» «LastName»
«JobTitle»
«Company»
«Address 1»
«Address2»
«City», «State» «PostalCode»

   1) Click the Insert Postal Bar Code button.
   2) At the Insert Postal Bar Code dialog box, click the down-pointing triangle at the right side of the Merge field with ZIP code text box, scroll down the list until *PostalCode* is visible, and then click it.
   3) Click OK to close the Insert Postal Bar Code dialog box.

Insert Postal Bar Code   ? X

Merge field with ZIP code:

Address1
Address2
City
State
PostalCode
WorkPhone

OK   Cancel

Step 1k2

l. At the Create Labels dialog box, click OK.
m. At the Mail Merge Helper dialog box, click the Merge button.
n. At the Merge dialog box, make sure New document displays in the Merge to text box, and then click the Merge button.

2. Save the merged document and name it Ch 12, Ex 08.
3. Print and then close Ch 12, Ex 08.
4. At the labels main document, save it and name it Cust Label main doc.
5. Close Cust Label main doc.

figure

12.14

Exercise 8

«Title» «FirstName» «LastName»
«JobTitle»
«Company»
«Address1»
«Address2»
«City», «State» «PostalCode»

Creating Lists with Merge

When merging form letters, envelopes, or mailing labels, a new form is created for each record. For example, if there are eight records in the data source that is merged with a form letter, eight letters are created. If there are twenty records in a data source that is merged with a mailing label, twenty labels are created. In some situations, you may want merged information to remain on the same page. This is useful, for example, when creating a list such as a directory or address list.

A merge document can be created that inserts records on the same page by using the Catalog option from the Create drop-down list at the Mail Merge Helper dialog box. For example, suppose you want to create a list of the employees in a company by name, department, and extension. The first step is to create the data source using the Mail Merge Helper. In this example, the data source contains three fields: *Name*, *Department*, and *Extension*. After the data source is created, the next step is to create the main document and link it to the data source. In exercise 9, you will create a main document and link it to a data source to create a list.

Creating a List with Text from a Data Source Document

1. At a clear document screen, create a list containing the name, company name, and title for the customers in the Customer data source data source by completing the following steps:
   a. Click Tools and then Mail Merge.
   b. At the Mail Merge Helper dialog box, click the Create button (located below Main document), and then click Catalog at the drop-down list.
   c. At the question asking if you want to use the active document window or a new document, click the Active Window button.
   d. At the Mail Merge Helper dialog box, click the Get Data button (located below Data source) and then click Open Data Source at the drop-down list.
   e. At the Open Data Source dialog box, double-click *Customer data source* in the list box.
   f. At the Microsoft Word dialog box telling you that Word found no fields in your main document, click the Edit Main Document button.

g. At the clear document screen, complete the following steps:
   1) Set left tabs at the 2-inch mark and the 4-inch mark on the Ruler.
   2) Insert the *FirstName* field at the left margin by clicking the Insert Merge Field button on the Mail Merge toolbar and then clicking *FirstName*.
   3) Press the spacebar and then insert the *LastName* field.
   4) Press the Tab key and then insert the *JobTitle* field.
   5) Press the Tab key and then insert the *Company* field.
   6) Press the Enter key twice.

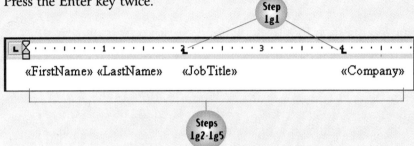

h. Click the Merge to New Document button on the Mail Merge toolbar.
2. At the merged document, complete the following steps:
   a. Position the insertion point at the beginning of the document.
   b. Press the Enter key three times.
   c. Move the insertion point back to the beginning of the document.
   d. Turn on bold and then key **Customer**.
   e. Press the Tab key and then key **Title**.
   f. Press the Tab key and then key **Company**.
3. Save the merged list document and name it Ch 12, Ex 09.
4. Print and then close Ch 12, Ex 09.
5. Save the list main document and name it Cust List main doc.
6. Close Cust List main doc.

Inputting Text During a Merge

Word's Merge feature contains a large number of Word fields that can be inserted in a main document. In this chapter, you will learn about the *Fill-in* field that is used for information that is input at the keyboard during a merge. For more information on the other Word fields, please refer to the on-screen help.

Situations may arise in which you do not need to keep all variable information in a data source. For example, there may be variable information that changes on a regular basis such as a customer's monthly balance, a product price, etc. Word lets you input variable information into a document during the merge using the keyboard. A Fill-in field is inserted in a main document by clicking the Insert Word Field button on the Mail Merge toolbar and then clicking Fill-in at the drop-down list. A document can contain any number of Fill-in fields.

Insert Word Field ▾

Insert Word Field

To insert a Fill-in field, open a main document, and position the insertion point at the location in the document where you want the field to display. Click the Insert Word Field button on the Mail Merge toolbar and then click Fill-in at the drop-down list that displays. At the Insert Word Field: Fill-in dialog box shown in figure 12.15, key a short message indicating what should be entered at the keyboard, and then click OK. At the Microsoft Word dialog box with the message you entered displayed in the upper left corner, key text you want to display in the document, and then click OK. When the Fill-in field or fields are added, save the main document in the normal manner.

figure

12.15

Insert Word Field: Fill-in Dialog Box

Key a short message in this text box indicating what should be entered at the keyboard.

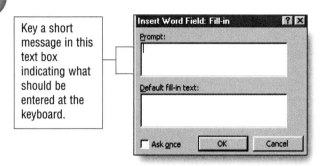

To merge the main document with the data source, click the Merge to New Document button on the Mail Merge toolbar or the Merge to Printer button. When Word merges the main document with the first record in the data source, the Microsoft Word dialog box displays with the message you entered displayed in the upper left corner. Key the required information for the first record in the data source and then click the OK button. If you are using the keyboard, key the required information, press the Tab key to make the OK button active, and then press Enter.

Word displays the dialog box again. Key the required information for the second record in the data source, and then click OK or press the Tab key and then press Enter. Continue in this manner until the required information has been entered for each record in the data source. Word then completes the merge.

exercise

Adding Fill-in Fields to a Document

1. Edit the Customer ltr2 main doc main document so it includes Fill-in fields by completing the following steps:
   a. Open Customer ltr2 main doc.
   b. Change the third paragraph in the letter to the paragraph shown in figure 12.16. Insert the first Fill-in field (displays in the paragraph in parentheses) by completing the following steps:
      1) Click the Insert Word Field button on the Mail Merge toolbar.
      2) At the drop-down menu that displays, click Fill-in.

Step 1b1

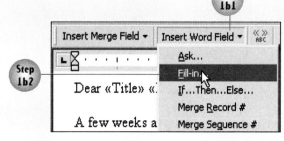

Step 1b2

3) At the Insert Word Field: Fill-in dialog box, key **Insert rep name** in the Prompt text box.
4) Click OK.
5) At the Microsoft Word dialog box with *Insert rep name* displayed in the upper left corner, key **(representative's name)**, and then click OK.

c. Complete steps similar to those in 1b to insert the second Fill-in field except key **Insert phone number** in the Prompt text box at the Insert Word Field: Fill-in dialog box and key **(phone number)** at the Microsoft Word dialog box.

2. When the paragraph is completed, save the document with Save As and name it Customer ltr3 main doc.

3. Merge the main document with the data source by completing the following steps:
   a. Click the Merge to New Document button on the Mail Merge toolbar.
   b. When Word merges the main document with the first record, a dialog box displays with the message *Insert rep name*. At this dialog box, key **Charles Noland**, and then click OK.
   c. At the dialog box with the message *Insert phone number*, key **(206) 555-3443**, and then click OK.
   d. At the dialog box with the message *Insert rep name*, key **Denise Nickel** (over *Charles Noland*), and then click OK.
   e. At the dialog box with the message *Insert phone number*, key **(206) 555-3430** (over the previous number), and then click OK.
   f. At the dialog box with the message *Insert rep name*, key **Andrew Christie** (over *Denise Nickel*), and then click OK.
   g. At the dialog box with the message *Insert phone number*, key **(206) 555-3456** (over the previous number), and then click OK.
   h. At the dialog box with the message *Insert rep name*, key **Nicole Gelmann** (over *Andrew Christie*), and then click OK.
   i. At the dialog box with the message *Insert phone number*, key **(206) 555-3422** (over the previous number), and then click OK.

4. Save the merged document and name it Ch 12, Ex 10.
5. Print and then close Ch 12, Ex 10.
6. Close Customer ltr3 main doc and save the changes.

Insert Word Field: Fill-in

Prompt:

Insert rep name

Step 1b3

Microsoft Word

Insert rep name

Step 1b5

(representative's name)

Microsoft Word

Insert rep name

Step 3b

Charles Noland

figure

12.16   *Exercise 10*

All you need to do to accept your First Choice card is to mail your enclosed Acceptance Form in the postage-paid envelope provided or call our service representative, **(representative's name)**, at **(phone number)**. In addition to the miles you will earn, you will also enjoy cash advances available 24 hours a day, traveler's message service, and toll-free customer service.

chapter summary

➤ Word includes a mail merge feature that you can use to create letters and envelopes and much more, all with personalized information.

➤ Two different documents are usually required for merging. The *data source* document contains the variable information. The *main document* contains the standard text along with identifiers showing where variable information is to be inserted.

➤ Use Word's Mail Merge Helper to assist you in creating the data source. At the Mail Merge Helper, Word provides predetermined field names that can be used when creating the data source.

➤ Variable information in a data source is saved as a *record*. A record contains all the information for one unit. A series of fields makes one record, and a series of records makes a data source.

➤ After determining what information you want in the main document, you need to determine what fields from the data source you will need and where they should be inserted in the main document.

➤ When creating a main document, you need to identify what data source will be used for the variable information. This is done at the Mail Merge Helper dialog box.

➤ Once the data source and the main document have been created and saved, they can be merged. Merged documents can be saved in a new document or sent directly to the printer.

➤ When the main document is open, you can use buttons on the Mail Merge toolbar to view how the document will look after merging with the first record, the next record, the last record, or a specific record from the data source.

➤ With the Check for Errors button on the Mail Merge toolbar, you can check the data source and the main document for errors before merging.

➤ With the Edit Data Source button on the Mail Merge toolbar, you can edit records in a data source. With buttons on the Database toolbar, you can easily manage the data source document.

➤ An envelope can be created that contains data fields that are then merged with a data source. Mailing labels can be created for records in a data source in much the same way.

➤ A merge document can be created that inserts records on the same page by using the Catalog option from the Create drop-down list at the Mail Merge Helper dialog box.

➤ Word lets you input variable information with the keyboard into a document during the merge. This Fill-in field is inserted in a main document by clicking the Insert Word Field button on the Mail Merge toolbar, and then clicking Fill-in at the drop-down list.

commands review

	Mouse/Keyboard
Display Mail Merge Helper dialog box	Tools, Mail Merge

thinking offline

Fill in the Blank: In the space provided, indicate the correct term, command, or number.

1. At the _____ dialog box, predetermined fields are provided by Word.

2. The first row of a data source table is called a _____ and identifies the names of the fields.

3. Before creating the main document, determine what information will remain the same and what information will _____.

4. When creating a main document, you need to identify what _____ will be used for the variable information.

5. The data source and the main document can be merged to a new document or to the _____.

6. A series of fields makes a _____.

7. Click the _____ button on the Mail Merge toolbar to view the main document merged with the first record in the data source.

8. With the main document displayed, you can edit records in a data source with the _____ button on the Mail Merge toolbar.

9. To begin creating envelopes for the names and addresses in a source document, click _____ at the Mail Merge Helper dialog box.

10. So that merged information remains on the same page, click the _____ option at the Create drop-down list at the Mail Merge Helper dialog box.

11. A field used for information that is input at the keyboard during a merge is called a(n) _____ field.

working hands-on

Assessment 1

1. Look at the letter in figure 12.18 and the information in figure 12.17. Determine the fields you need for the main document and the data source. Create the data source and name it Self-Study data source. Create the main document shown in figure 12.18, and then merge it with Self-Study data source to a new document.
2. Save the merged document and name it Ch 12, SA 01.
3. Print and then close Ch 12, SA 01.
4. Save the main document and name it Self-Study Ltr main doc.
5. Close Self-Study Ltr main doc.

figure

12.17 *Assessment 1*

Mr. and Mrs. Charles Vuong
10421 Fifth Avenue
Petersburg, ND 76322

Ms. Julie Combs
309 Fawcett Drive
Petersburg, ND 76322

Mr. John Stahl
4707 North Oakes
Apartment 4C
Petersburg, ND 76322

Mr. and Mrs. Darrell Wren
21883 South 43rd
Petersburg, ND 76322

Mrs. Rhonda Visell
5404 North Foster
Apartment 206
Petersburg, ND 76322

figure 12.18 **Assessment 1**

(current date)

Name
Address
City, State Zip

Dear (Name):

The results of the parent self-study are attached. As you read through the information, you will find there are several areas that will become a focus for change. Your input was extremely valuable and is being used to develop our student learning improvement plan and to apply for a legislative student learning improvement grant.

A concern that was mentioned repeatedly in the survey was the lack of computers. The reason new schools have access to the networking system and computers is that it is built into the entire new school package that is impacted by state matching funds. One of the levy components is computer technology to bring existing schools in line with the technology currently experienced in new buildings. We hope that the voter registration drive currently under way will impact the number of voters going to the polls in November.

Thank you for your input and for being an integral partner with us in your child(ren)'s education. If you would like to discuss the results further or have additional comments, please give me a call.

Sincerely,

Kathryn Rosell, Principal
Stewart Elementary School

XX:Self-Study Ltr main doc

Attachment

Assessment 2

1. Look at the letter in figure 12.20 and the information in figure 12.19. Determine the fields you need for the main document and the data source. Create the data source and name it MP Cust data source. Create the main document shown in figure 12.20 and then merge it with MP Cust data source to a new document.
2. Save the merged document and name it Ch 12, SA 02.
3. Print and then close Ch 12, SA 02.
4. Save the main document and name it MP Cust main doc.
5. Close MP Cust main doc.

figure
12.19   *Assessment 2*

Mr. and Mrs. Dennis Haynes
1810 23rd Avenue
Seattle, WA 98221

Ms. Deborah Burke
17420 Vander Road
Federal Way, WA 98045

Mr. Kevin Jergens
10605 Lakeside Drive
Seattle, WA 98188

Mr. and Mrs. Lloyd Rienhart
818 Vista Drive
Redmond, WA 98013

Dr. Janice Crivello
8905 West 50th Street
Seattle, WA 98041

(current date)

Name
Address
City, State Zip

Dear (Name):

We would like to introduce you to a great way to earn free travel to Alaska, Hawaii,
Europe, and Asia, and hundreds of other places. Because you are a valued MilesPlus
member, (Name), you have been preapproved for the First Choice credit card with a credit
line of $3,000. This is the only credit card that offers you the ability to earn one
MilesPlus mile for every purchase dollar you charge.

You can use your First Choice card for all kinds of purchases at over 10 million locations
throughout the world. Every purchase you make brings you closer to your next free flight
to Seaview Airlines destinations. You can also enjoy a 30-day, interest-free grace period
on your purchases when you pay your previous balance in full by the due date.

Take advantage of this special opportunity to earn more miles and fantastic free travel by
accepting your preapproved First Choice card today.

Sincerely,

Walter Chamberlin
Marketing Manager

XX:MP Cust main doc

Assessment 3

1. Open MP Cust main doc.
2. Click the Edit Data Source button on the Mail Merge toolbar and then make the following changes:
   a. Delete the fourth record in the data source.
   b. Make the following changes in the third record in the data source:
      1) Change the address from *10605 Lakeside Drive* to *3402 North 45th*.
      2) Change the city from *Seattle* to *Bellevue*.
      3) Change the Zip code from *98188* to *98065*.
   c. Add a new record with the following information:

      Ms. Megan Soltis
      10234 South Issaquah Road
      Bellevue, WA 98047

3. Close the Data Form.
4. At the MP Cust main doc document, click the Merge to New Document button on the Mail Merge toolbar.
5. Save the merged document and name it Ch 12, SA 03.
6. Print and then close Ch 12, SA 03.
7. Save MP Cust main doc.
8. Close MP Cust main doc saving the changes to MP Cust data source.

Assessment 4

1. Create an envelope main document for the records in the MP Cust data source data source.
2. Merge the envelope main document with MP Cust data source to a new document.
3. Save the merged document and name it Ch 12, SA 04.
4. Print and then close Ch 12, SA 04.
5. Save the envelope main document and name it MP Cust Env main doc.
6. Close MP Cust Env main doc.

Assessment 5

1. Create a mailing label main document for the records in the Self-Study data source data source. (Use the 5163 - Shipping mailing labels.)
2. Merge the mailing labels main document with the Self-Study data source data source to a new document.
3. Save the merged document and name it Ch 12, SA 05.
4. Print and then close Ch 12, SA 05.
5. Save the label main document and name it Self-Study Labels main doc.
6. Close Self-Study Labels main doc.

Assessment 6

1. Open MP Cust main doc.
2. Change the third paragraph in the letter MP Cust main doc so it reads as shown in figure 12.21. Include the Fill-in field as shown in parentheses in figure 12.21. (Key the message **Insert customer number** at the Insert Word Field: Fill-in dialog box.)
3. Save the edited main document with Save As and name it MP Cust2 main doc.
4. Merge the records to a new document. At the dialog boxes asking for the customer number, key the following:

Record 1	=	MP-875
Record 2	=	MP-231
Record 3	=	MP-110
Record 4	=	MP-877
Record 5	=	MP-234

5. Save the merged document and name it Ch 12, SA 06.
6. Print and then close Ch 12, SA 06.
7. Close MP Cust2 main doc, saving the changes.

figure

12.21   *Assessment 6*

We have assigned you customer number (**customer's number**). To accept this special offer, call our toll-free number at 1-800-555-3440 and tell the representative your customer number. It's as simple as that! You will have your new card within a few days!

Creating and Formatting Tables

PERFORMANCE OBJECTIVES

Upon successful completion of chapter 13, you will be able to:

- Create a table.
- Enter and edit text within cells in a table.
- Delete a table.
- Format a table by adding borders and shading, changing column width, aligning text within cells, inserting and deleting columns and rows, and merging and splitting cells.
- Apply formatting to a table with one of Word's predesigned AutoFormats.
- Create and format a table using buttons on the Tables and Borders toolbar.
- Perform calculations on values in a table.

With Word's Tables feature, you can create data in columns and rows. This data can consist of text, values, and formulas. The Tables feature can create columns of data in a manner similar to a spreadsheet. Many basic spreadsheet functions, such as inserting values, totaling numbers, and inserting formulas, can be performed in a Word table. In this chapter, you will learn how to create a table and use basic spreadsheet features.

With a Word table, a form can be created that contains boxes of information called *cells*. A cell is the intersection between a row and a column. A cell can contain text, characters, numbers, data, graphics, or formulas. Data within a cell can be formatted to display left, right, or center aligned, and can include character formatting such as bold, italics, and underlining. The formatting choices available with the Tables feature are quite extensive and allow flexibility in creating a variety of tables.

Creating a Table

Insert Table

A table can be created with the Insert Table button on the Standard toolbar or the Table option from the Menu bar. To create a table with the Insert Table button, position the mouse pointer on the Insert Table button on the Standard toolbar, and then hold down the left mouse button. This causes a grid to appear as shown in figure 13.1. Move the mouse pointer down and to the right until the correct number of rows and columns displays below the grid and then release the mouse button. As you move the mouse pointer in the grid, selected columns and rows are highlighted, and the number of rows and columns displays below the grid.

Table Grid

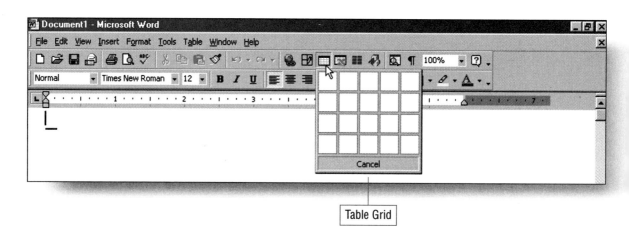

Table Grid

A table can also be created with options at the Insert Table dialog box shown in figure 13.2. Display the Insert Table dialog box by clicking Table, pointing to Insert, and then clicking Table. At the Insert Table dialog box, key the desired number of columns in the Number of columns text box. Press the Tab key or click in the Number of rows text box. Key the desired number of rows and then click OK or press Enter. A table is inserted in the document at the location of the insertion point.

figure

13.2 *Insert Table Dialog Box*

At this dialog box, specify the desired number of columns and rows for the table.

Figure 13.3 shows an example of a table with four columns and three rows. Various parts of the table are identified in figure 13.3 such as gridlines, move table column markers, end-of-cell markers, and the end-of-row markers. In a table, nonprinting characters identify the end of a cell and the end of a row. To view these characters, click the Show/Hide ¶ button on the Standard toolbar. The end-of-cell marker displays inside each cell and the end-of-row marker displays at the end of a row of cells.

figure

13.3

Table

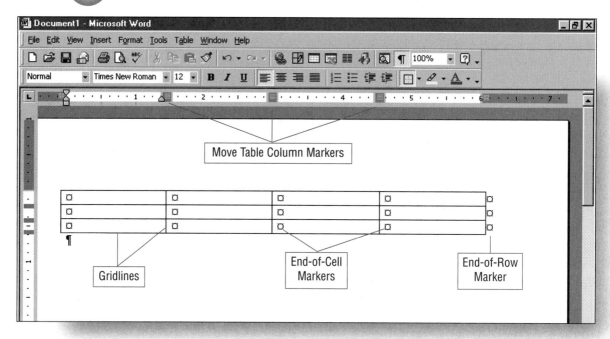

When a table is created, the insertion point is located in the cell in the upper left corner of the table. Cells in a table contain a cell designation. Columns in a table are lettered from left to right, beginning with A. Rows in a table are numbered from top to bottom beginning with 1. The cell in the upper left corner of the table is cell A1. The cell to the right of A1 is B1, the cell to the right of B1 is C1, and so on. The cells below A1 are A2, A3, A4, and so on. Some cell designations are shown in figure 13.4.

figure

13.4

Cell Designations

A1	B1	C1	D1
A2	B2	C2	D2
A3	B3	C3	D3

If the Ruler is displayed at the top of the document screen, move table column markers display on the Ruler. These markers represent the end of a column and are useful in changing the width of columns. Figure 13.3 identifies move table column markers.

Entering Text in Cells

With the insertion point positioned in a cell, key or edit text. Move the insertion point to other cells with the mouse by clicking in the desired cell. If you are using the keyboard, press the Tab key to move the insertion point to the next cell or press Shift + Tab to move the insertion point to the previous cell.

If the text you key does not fit on one line, it wraps to the next line within the same cell. Or, if you press Enter within a cell, the insertion point is moved to the next line within the same cell. The cell vertically lengthens to accommodate the text, and all cells in that row also lengthen. Pressing the Tab key in a table causes the insertion point to move to the next cell in the table. If you want to move the insertion point to a tab within a cell, press Ctrl + Tab.

If the insertion point is located in the last cell of the table and you press the Tab key, Word adds another row to the table. To avoid this situation, make sure you do not press the Tab key after entering text in the last cell, or immediately click the Undo button on the Standard toolbar. You can insert a page break within a table by pressing Ctrl + Enter. The page break is inserted between rows, not within.

When all information has been entered in the cells, move the insertion point below the table and, if necessary, continue keying the document, or save the document in the normal manner.

Moving the Insertion Point within a Table

To move the insertion point to different cells within the table using the mouse, click in the desired cell. To move the insertion point to different cells within the table using the keyboard, refer to the information shown in figure 13.5.

figure
13.5
Insertion Point Movement within a Table

To move the insertion point	Press
to next cell	Tab
to preceding cell	Shift + Tab
forward one character	right arrow key
backward one character	left arrow key
to previous row	up arrow key
to next row	down arrow key
to first cell in the row	Alt + Home (or Alt + 7 on numeric keypad*)
to last cell in the row	Alt + End (or Alt + 1 on numeric keypad*)
to top cell in the column	Alt + Page Up (or Alt + 9 on numeric keypad*)
to bottom cell in the column	Alt + Page Down (or Alt + 3 on numeric keypad*)

Num Lock must be off.

exercise 1

Creating a Table with the Insert Table Button

1. At a clear document screen, create the document shown in figure 13.6 by completing the following steps:
   a. Change the paragraph alignment to center and turn on bold.
   b. Key **COLEMAN DEVELOPMENT CORPORATION**.
   c. Press Enter twice.
   d. Key **Human Resources Department**.
   e. Press Enter three times.
   f. Turn off bold and then change the paragraph alignment to left.
   g. Create the table by completing the following steps:
      1) Position the mouse pointer on the Insert Table button on the Standard toolbar.
      2) Hold down the left mouse button. (This causes a grid to appear.)
      3) Move the mouse pointer down and to the right until the number below the grid displays as *6 x 2* and then release the mouse button.
   h. Key the text in the cells as indicated in figure 13.6. Press the Tab key to move to the next cell or press Shift + Tab to move to the preceding cell. (If you accidentally press the Enter key within a cell, immediately press the Backspace key. Do not press the Tab key after keying the text in the last cell. If you do, another row is inserted in the table. If this happens, immediately click the Undo button on the Standard toolbar.)
2. Save the table and name it Ch 13, Ex 01.
3. Print and then close Ch 13, Ex 01.

Step 1g1

Step 1g3

6 x 2 Table

figure

13.6   *Exercise 1*

COLEMAN DEVELOPMENT CORPORATION

Human Resources Department

Stephanie Branson	President
Brandon Kent	Vice President
Nicole Clark	Director
Jack Takagawa	Assistant Director
Darryl Ellis	Trainer
Lynette Lagasi	Trainer

Creating a Table at the Insert Table Dialog Box

1. At a clear document screen, create the table shown in figure 13.7 by completing the following steps:
   a. Change the paragraph alignment to center and turn on bold.
   b. Key **COLEMAN DEVELOPMENT CORPORATION**.
   c. Press Enter twice.
   d. Key **Executive Officers**.
   e. Press Enter three times.
   f. Turn off bold and change the paragraph alignment to left.
   g. Create the table by completing the following steps:
      1) Click Table, point to Insert, and then click Table.
      2) At the Insert Table dialog box, key **3** in the Number of columns text box. (The insertion point is automatically positioned in this text box.)
      3) Press the Tab key (this moves the insertion point to the Number of rows option) and then key **5**.
      4) Click OK or press Enter.

   Insert Table   ? ✕

   Table size
   Number of columns: 3
   Number of rows: 5

   Step 1g2

   Step 1g3

   h. Key the text in the cells as indicated in figure 13.7. Press the Tab key to move to the next cell or press Shift + Tab to move to the preceding cell. To create the text in the third column, press Ctrl + Tab, and then key the text. (This moves the insertion point to a tab within the cell.)
2. Save the table and name it Ch 13, Ex 02.
3. Print and then close Ch 13, Ex 02.

13.7   *Exercise 2*

COLEMAN DEVELOPMENT CORPORATION

Executive Officers

Chief Executive Officer	Mandy Armstead	#1034
President	Stephanie Branson	#1046
Vice President	Conrad Wheeler	#3092
Vice President	Selene Resnick	#3441
Vice President	Aurora Madsen	#2190

Selecting Cells

A table can be formatted in special ways. For example, the alignment of text in cells or rows can be changed or character formatting can be added. To identify the cells that are to be affected by the formatting, the specific cells need to be selected.

Selecting in a Table with the Mouse

The mouse pointer can be used to select a cell, row, column, or an entire table. The left edge of each cell, between the left column border and the end-of-cell marker or first character in the cell, is called the *cell selection bar*. When the mouse pointer is positioned in the cell selection bar, it turns into a black arrow pointing up and to the right (instead of the left). To select a particular cell, position the mouse pointer in the cell selection bar at the left edge of the cell until it turns into a black arrow pointing up and to the right, as shown in figure 13.8, and then click the left mouse button.

figure
13.8   *Cell Selection Bar*

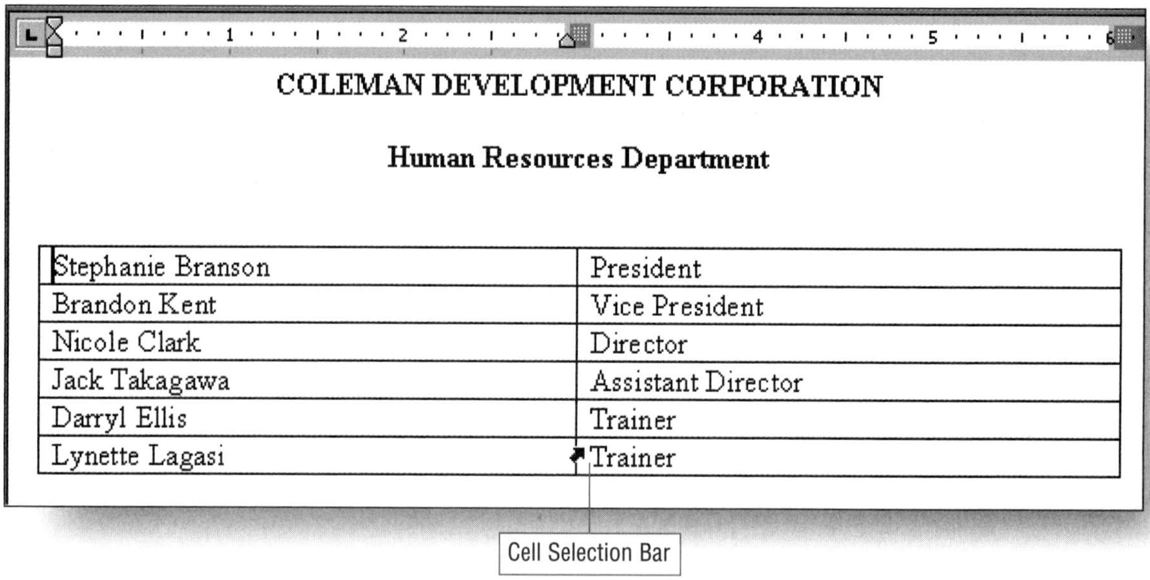

COLEMAN DEVELOPMENT CORPORATION	
Human Resources Department	
Stephanie Branson	President
Brandon Kent	Vice President
Nicole Clark	Director
Jack Takagawa	Assistant Director
Darryl Ellis	Trainer
Lynette Lagasi	Trainer

Cell Selection Bar

Each row in a table contains a row selection bar, which is the space just to the left of the left edge of the table. Figure 13.9 shows the mouse pointer in the row selection bar. When the mouse pointer is positioned in the row selection bar, the mouse pointer turns into an arrow pointing up and to the right.

To select a row, position the mouse pointer in the row selection bar at the left edge of the table until it turns into an arrow pointing up and to the right, and then click the left mouse button. You can also select a row by positioning the mouse pointer in the cell selection bar of any cell in the row and then double-clicking the left mouse button.

figure

13.9

Row Selection Bar

COLEMAN DEVELOPMENT CORPORATION

Human Resources Department

Stephanie Branson	President
Brandon Kent	Vice President
Nicole Clark	Director
Jack Takagawa	Assistant Director
Darryl Ellis	Trainer
Lynette Lagasi	Trainer

Row Selection Bar

To select a column, position the mouse pointer on the uppermost horizontal gridline of the table in the appropriate column until the pointer turns into a short, downward-pointing arrow. Click the left mouse button to select the column.

Once you have selected a particular cell, row, or column, hold down the Shift key; position the mouse pointer in another cell, row, or column; and then click the left mouse button. This selects all cells in the table from the location of the first selected cell, row, or column, to the location of the mouse pointer.

Cells in a table can also be selected by positioning the mouse pointer in the first cell to be selected, holding down the left mouse button, dragging the mouse pointer to the last cell to be selected, and then releasing the mouse button.

To select all cells within a table using the mouse, position the mouse pointer in any cell in the table, hold down the Alt key, and then double-click the left mouse button. You can also position the mouse pointer in the row selection bar at the left edge of the table until it turns into an arrow pointing up and to the right, hold down the left mouse button, drag down to select all rows in the table, and then release the left mouse button.

If you want to select only a portion of text within a cell (rather than the entire cell), position the mouse pointer at the beginning of the text, and then hold down the left mouse button as you drag the mouse across the text. When a cell is selected, the entire cell is changed to black. When text within cells is selected, only those lines containing text are selected.

Selecting and Formatting Cells in a Table

1. Open Ch 13, Ex 01.
2. Save the document with Save As and name it Ch 13, Ex 03.
3. Select and then bold the text in the cells in the first column using the mouse by completing the following steps:
   a. Position the mouse pointer on the uppermost horizontal gridline of the first column in the table until it turns into a short, downward-pointing arrow.
   b. Click the left mouse button.
   c. Click the Bold button on the Standard toolbar.
4. Select and then italicize the text in the cells in the second column by completing steps similar to those in 3a through 3c.
5. Save the document again with the same name (Ch 13, Ex 03).
6. Print and then close Ch 13, Ex 03.

Table figure showing:

COLEMAN DEVELOPME...

Steps 3a & 3b

Human Resources

Stephanie Branson	Pr
Brandon Kent	Vi
Nicole Clark	Di
Jack Takagawa	A:
Darryl Ellis	Tr
Lynette Lagasi	Tr

Selecting in a Table with the Keyboard

The keyboard can be used to select specific cells within a table. Figure 13.10 displays the commands for selecting specific amounts of a table.

figure

13.10 *Selecting in a Table with the Keyboard*

To select	Press
the next cell's contents	Tab
the preceding cell's contents	Shift + Tab
the entire table	Alt + 5 (on numeric keypad with Num Lock off)
adjacent cells	Hold Shift key, then press an arrow key repeatedly
a column	Position insertion point in top cell of column, hold down the Shift key, then press down arrow key until column is selected

If you want to select only text within cells, rather than the entire cell, press F8 to turn on the Extend mode, and then move the insertion point with an arrow key. When a cell is selected, the entire cell is changed to black. When text within a cell is selected, only those lines containing text are selected.

Selecting Cells with the Table Drop-Down Menu

A row or column of cells or all cells in a table can be selected with options from the Table drop-down menu. For example, to select a row of cells in a table, position the insertion point in any cell in the row, click Table, point to Select, and then click Row.

To select cells in a column, position the insertion point in any cell in the column, click Table, point to Select, and then click Column. To select all cells in the table, position the insertion point in any cell in the table, click Table, point to Select, and then click Table.

Selecting and Formatting Cells Using the Keyboard and the Table Drop-Down Menu

1. Open Ch 13, Ex 02.
2. Save the document with Save As and name it Ch 13, Ex 04.
3. Select and then bold the text in the cells in the first column using the keyboard by completing the following steps:
   a. Position the insertion point in the first cell of the first column (cell A1).
   b. Hold down the Shift key and then press the down arrow key four times. (This selects all cells in the first column.)
   c. Press Ctrl + B.
4. Select and then bold the text in the cells in the second column using the Table drop-down menu by completing the following steps:
   a. Position the insertion point in any cell in the second column.
   b. Click Table, point to Select, and then click Column.
   c. Click the Bold button on the Standard toolbar.

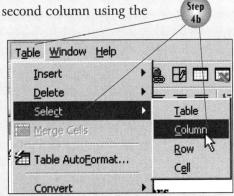

5. Select and then italicize the text in the cells in the third column by completing steps similar to those in 3 or 4.
6. Save the document again with the same name (Ch 13, Ex 04).
7. Print and then close Ch 13, Ex 04.

Deleting a Table

All text in cells within a table can be deleted, leaving the table gridlines, or all text and the gridlines can be deleted. To delete the text, leaving the gridlines, select the table, and then press the Delete key. If just the table is selected, the text in each cell is deleted leaving the gridlines. To delete the text in cells and the gridlines, click Table, point to Delete, and then click Table.

Copying and Deleting a Table

1. Open Ch 13, Ex 02.
2. Save the document with Save As and name it Ch 13, Ex 05.
3. Make the following changes to the document:
   a. Select and then delete the title *COLEMAN DEVELOPMENT CORPORATION*, and the subtitle *Executive Officers*.
   b. Move the insertion point below the table and then press the Enter key three times.
   c. Select the table by completing the following steps:
      1) Position the insertion point in any cell in the table.
      2) Click Table, point to Select, and then click Table.
   d. With the table selected, click the Copy button on the Standard toolbar.
   e. Move the insertion point to the end of the document and then click the Paste button on the Standard toolbar. (This inserts a copy of the table at the end of the document.)
   f. Select and then delete the first table in the document by completing the following steps:
      1) Position the insertion point in any cell in the table.
      2) Click Table, point to Delete, and then click Table.
4. Save the document again with the same name (Ch 13, Ex 05).
5. Print and then close Ch 13, Ex 05.

Formatting a Table

A table that has been created with Word's Tables feature can be formatted in a variety of ways. For example, borders and shading can be added to cells; rows and columns can be inserted or deleted; cells can be split or merged; and the alignment of the table can be changed.

Adding Borders

The gridlines creating a table can be customized with border options. Borders can be added to a selected cell(s) or an entire table with options at the Borders and Shading dialog box shown in figure 13.11. To display this dialog box, click Format and then Borders and Shading.

figure

13.11 *Borders and Shading Dialog Box with Borders Tab Selected*

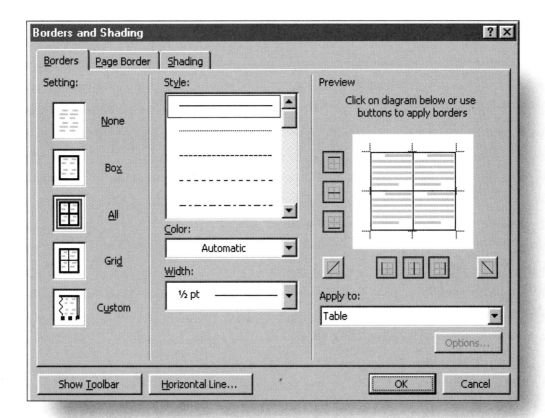

If you want a border option to apply to a specific cell, select the cell first, and then display the Borders and Shading dialog box. The Borders and Shading Apply to option will display with *Cell* in the text box. If the insertion point is positioned in a table (with no cell selected) or if the entire table is selected, changes made at the Borders and Shading dialog box will affect the entire table and the Apply to option will display with *Table*. Figure 13.12 describes the options available at the Borders and Shading dialog box.

figure

13.12 *Options at the Borders and Shading Dialog Box with Borders Tab Selected*

Choose this option	To do this
None	Remove all borders from selected cell(s) or table
Box	Insert a box border around the selected cell(s) or table
All	Insert a box border around and between selected cell(s) or table and apply preset shadow formatting to border
Grid	Insert a box border around selected cell(s) or table and apply preset 3-D border formatting, making the border look like a "window"
Custom	Create a custom border using options in the Preview diagram
Style	Choose a border style
Color	Choose a border color
Width	Specify the width of the border
Preview diagram	Click the sides of the Preview diagram to add or remove the currently selected settings
Apply to	Specify to what the border and shading should be applied
Options	Set additional margin and position settings (only available when Apply to is set at *Paragraph* or when Page Border tab is selected)

Chapter Thirteen

exercise 6

Formatting a Table with Border Lines around and between Cells

1. Open Ch 13, Ex 02.
2. Save the document with Save As and name it Ch 13, Ex 06.
3. Format the table so it displays as shown in figure 13.13 by completing the following steps:
   a. Position the insertion point in any cell in the table. (Make sure no text or cell is selected.)
   b. Click Format and then Borders and Shading.
   c. At the Borders and Shading dialog box with the Borders tab selected, click the None option in the Setting section. (This removes all borders from the Preview diagram.)
   d. Click the Custom option.
   e. Scroll to the end of the line styles in the Style list box and then click the fourth option from the end of the list.
   f. Change the line color to teal by clicking the down-pointing triangle at the right side of the Color option and then clicking the Teal color at the color palette (fifth color from the left in the second row).
   g. Apply the border to the outside of the table by completing the following steps:
      1) Click the top button at the left side of the Preview diagram. (This inserts a teal shadow border at the top of the Preview diagram.)
      2) Click the third button from the top at the left side of the Preview diagram. (This inserts a teal shadow border at the bottom of the table.)
      3) Click the second button from the left at the bottom of the Preview diagram. (This inserts a teal shadow border at the left side of the table.)
      4) Click the fourth button from the left at the bottom of the Preview diagram. (This inserts a teal shadow border at the right side of the table.)

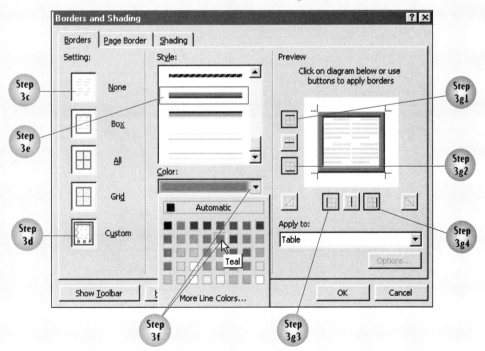

h. Add a single teal line between columns by completing the following steps:
   1) Scroll to the beginning of the line styles in the Style list box and then click the first line style (a single line).
   2) Change the line color to teal. (To do this, click the down-pointing triangle at the right of the Color option, and then click the Teal color at the color palette [fifth color from the left in the second row].)
   3) Click the third button from the left at the bottom of the Preview diagram. (This inserts a single teal line between columns.)
i. Click OK to close the Borders and Shading dialog box.
4. Save the document again with the same name (Ch 13, Ex 06).
5. Print and then close Ch 13, Ex 06.

figure

13.13   *Exercise 6*

COLEMAN DEVELOPMENT CORPORATION

Executive Officers

Chief Executive Officer	Mandy Armstead	#1034
President	Stephanie Branson	#1046
Vice President	Conrad Wheeler	#3092
Vice President	Selene Resnick	#3441
Vice President	Aurora Madsen	#2190

Adding Shading

To add visual appeal to a table, shading can be added to cells. Shading can be added to cells or selected cells with options at the Borders and Shading dialog box with the Shading tab selected as shown in figure 13.14. Figure 13.15 describes the options available at the Borders and Shading dialog box.

figure

13.14

Borders and Shading Dialog Box with Shading Tab Selected

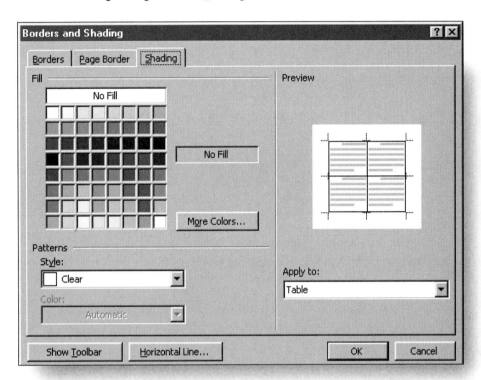

figure

13.15

Options at the Borders and Shading Dialog Box with Shading Tab Selected

Choose this option	To do this
Fill	Choose a fill color for selected cell(s) or entire table
Style	Choose a shading style to apply "over" fill color
Color	Choose a color for the lines and dots in the selected shading pattern
Preview diagram	Click the sides of the Preview diagram to add or remove the currently selected fill, style, and color
Apply to	Specify to what the border and shading should be applied

Adding a Border and Shading to a Table

1. Open Ch 13, Ex 02.
2. Save the document with Save As and name it Ch 13, Ex 07.
3. Add a border and shading to the table by completing the following steps:
   a. Move the insertion point to a cell within the table.
   b. Click Format and then Borders and Shading.
   c. At the Borders and Shading dialog box, make sure the Borders tab is selected.
   d. Choose a double-line style in the Style list box.
   e. Change the Color option to dark blue (sixth color from the left in the top row).
   f. Click the Box option located at the left side of the dialog box.
   g. Click the Shading tab.
   h. At the Borders and Shading dialog box with the Shading tab selected, click the Turquoise color in the Fill section. (Turquoise is the fifth color from the left in the second row from the bottom.)
   i. Click OK to close the dialog box.
4. Add a fill to the second column of cells by completing the following steps:
   a. Select cells B1 through B5.
   b. Click Format and then Borders and Shading.
   c. At the Borders and Shading dialog box, make sure the Shading tab is selected.
   d. At the Borders and Shading dialog box with the Shading tab selected, click the down-pointing triangle at the right side of the Style option, and then click 5% at the drop-down list.
   e. Click OK to close the Borders and Shading dialog box.
   f. Deselect the cells.
5. Save the document again with the same name (Ch 13, Ex 07).
6. Print and then close Ch 13, Ex 07.

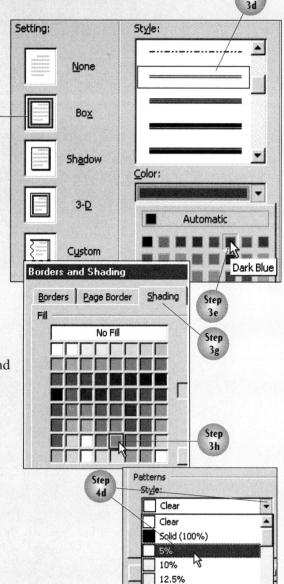

Changing Column Width

When a table is created, the columns are the same width. The width of the columns depends on the number of columns as well as the document margins. In some tables, you may want to change the width of certain columns to accommodate more or less text. You can change the width of columns using the mouse on the Ruler, in a table, or with options from the Table Properties dialog box.

Changing Column Width Using the Ruler

When the insertion point is positioned in a table, the column widths are displayed on the Ruler. These move table column markers are identified in figure 13.3. To change the column width using move table column markers on the Ruler, position the mouse pointer on a move table column marker until it turns into a left- and right-pointing arrow, hold down the left mouse button, and then drag the marker to make the column wider or narrower. (As you drag the marker, any move table column markers to the right are also moved.) When the move table column marker is in the desired position, release the mouse button.

If you want to see the column measurements as you drag a move table column marker, hold down the Alt key while dragging the marker. You can also view the column measurements by positioning the mouse pointer on a move table column marker, holding down the Alt key, and then holding down the left mouse button.

If you only want to move the move table column marker where the mouse pointer is positioned, hold down the Shift key, and then drag the marker on the Ruler. This does not change the overall size of the table. To change the column width of the column where the insertion point is positioned and all columns to the right, hold down the Ctrl key and the Shift key while you drag the move table column marker.

The first-line indent marker, the left indent marker, the right indent marker, and the hanging indent marker display on the Ruler for the column where the insertion point is positioned. These markers can be used to adjust the left or right column margins, indent the first line in a cell, or create a hanging indent. Changes made to the column margins affect only the column where the insertion point is positioned.

exercise 8

Creating a Table and Then Changing Column Width Using the Ruler

1. At a clear document screen, create the document shown in figure 13.16 by completing the following steps:
   a. Key the heading and first paragraph of the memo shown in figure 13.16.
   b. Create the table below the first paragraph by completing the following steps:
      1) Create a table with 3 columns and 7 rows (7 x 3).
      2) Change the width of the first column using the mouse by completing the following steps:

a) Make sure the Ruler is displayed.
b) Position the mouse pointer on the move table column marker between the 1-inch mark and the 3-inch mark on the Ruler until it turns into an arrow pointing left and right.
c) Hold down the Shift key and the Ctrl key, and then the left mouse button.
d) Drag the marker to the 3-inch mark, release the Shift key and the Ctrl key, and then release the mouse button.

| Normal | ▾ | Times New Roman | ▾ | 12 | ▾ | **B** | *I* | <u>U</u> | ≡ |

DATE: April 4, 2001

TO: Renée Williams   **Step 1b2d**

3) Key the text in the cells, bolding and centering the text as shown. Press Ctrl + Tab before keying the text in cells A2 through A7.
4) Add a double-line border around the table by completing the following steps:
a) With the insertion point positioned in any cell in the table, click Format and then Borders and Shading.
b) At the Borders and Shading dialog box, make sure the Borders tab is selected.
c) Scroll down the Style list box until the first double-line option displays and then click the first double-line option.
d) Click the Grid option that displays at the left side of the dialog box.
e) If necessary, change the Color option to Automatic.
f) Click OK to close the dialog box.

Step 1b4c

Step 1b4d

5) Add 10% fill to cells A1, B1, and C1 by completing the following steps:
a) Select cells A1, B1, and C1.
b) Click Format and then Borders and Shading.
c) At the Borders and Shading dialog box, click the Shading tab.
d) At the Borders and Shading dialog box with the Shading tab selected, click the down-pointing triangle at the right side of the Style option, and then click *10%* at the drop-down list.
e) Click OK to close the Borders and Shading dialog box.

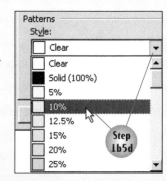

Step 1b5d

c. Position the insertion point below the table and then key the remaining text shown in figure 13.16.
2. Save the document and name it Ch 13, Ex 08.
3. Print and then close Ch 13, Ex 08.

figure

13.16 *Exercise 8*

DATE: April 4, 2001

TO: Renée Williams

FROM: Kyle McCleary

SUBJECT: DESKTOP PUBLISHING TRAINING

The deadline for signing up for the desktop publishing training was March 30. A total of six employees are registered for the training. The list of employees, employee number, and department is displayed in the table below.

Name	Employee #	Department
Gwenn Peterson	312-304-0098	Human Resources
Stanley Matias	123-293-5847	Human Resources
Deanne Merante	326-499-4834	Financial Planning
Karen Collier	654-300-6224	Sales
Michael Salas	231-392-8663	Sales
Anthony Bartels	654-332-3483	Support Services

Room 200 has been reserved for the training. Please let me know what special equipment you will need. There will be seven computers available in the room.

XX:Ch 13, Ex 08

Changing Column Width Using the Mouse

You can use the gridlines to change column widths within the table. To change column widths using the gridlines, position the mouse pointer on the gridline separating columns until the insertion point turns into left- and right-pointing arrows with a vertical double line between. Hold down the left mouse button, drag the gridline to the desired location, and then release the mouse button. Only the gridline where the insertion point is positioned is moved. If you want to change column widths for all columns to the right and increase the width of the table, hold down the Shift key while dragging the gridline. Hold down the Shift key and Ctrl key while dragging the gridline if you want to change the width of all columns to the right without changing the size of the table.

In a table containing text or other features, you can adjust the width of one column to accommodate the longest line of text in the column. To do this, position the mouse pointer on the right column gridline until it turns into left- and right-pointing arrows with a vertical double line between, and then double-click the left mouse button. To automatically size more than one column, select the columns first, and then double-click on a gridline.

Changing Column Width at the Table Properties Dialog Box

If you know the exact measurement for columns in a table, you can change column widths at the Table Properties dialog box with the Column tab selected as shown in figure 13.17. To display this dialog box, click Table and then Table Properties. At the Table Properties dialog box, click the Column tab. To change the column width, select the current measurement in the Preferred width text box, and then key the desired measurement. You can also click the up- or down-pointing triangle to increase or decrease the current measurement.

13.17   **Table Properties Dialog Box with Column Tab Selected**

Specify the desired column width at this dialog box.

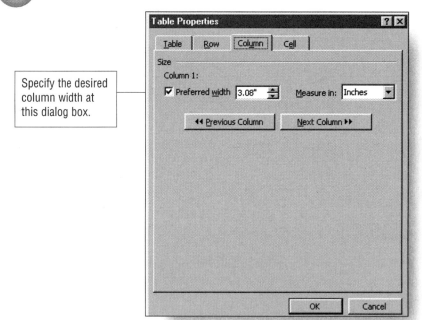

Changing Row Height

Change row height in a table in much the same manner as changing column width. You can change row height with an adjust table row marker on the vertical ruler, using a gridline, or with options at the Table Properties dialog box. To change row height using the vertical ruler, drag the adjust table row marker to the desired position on the ruler. To display the measurements on the ruler, hold down the Alt key while dragging the marker. To change row height using a gridline, drag the gridline to the desired position. Display row measurements by holding down the Alt key while dragging the gridline. Another method for adjusting row height is to display the Table Properties dialog box with the <u>R</u>ow tab selected. At this dialog box, click the <u>S</u>pecify height option, key the desired row measurement in the <u>S</u>pecify height text box, and then close the dialog box.

Changing Column Widths in a Table

1. Open Ch 13, Ex 02.
2. Save the document with Save As and name it Ch 13, Ex 09.
3. Change the width of the columns and add border lines and shading by completing the following steps:
   a. Position the mouse pointer on the gridline separating the first and second columns until the pointer turns into left- and right-pointing arrows with a vertical double line between.
   b. Hold down the left mouse button, drag the gridline to the left approximately 0.25 inch, and then release the mouse button. (Make sure the text in the first column does not wrap.)

Chief Executive Officer	Man
President	Stepl
Vice President	Con
Vice President	Sele
Vice President	Aurd

   Step 3b

   c. Position the mouse pointer on the gridline separating the second and third columns until the pointer turns into a left- and right-pointing arrow with a vertical double line between.
   d. Hold down the left mouse button, drag the gridline to the left approximately 0.75 inch, and then release the mouse button. (Make sure the text in the second column does not wrap.)

Mandy Armstead
Stephanie Branson
Conrad Wheeler
Selene Resnick
Aurora Madsen

   Step 3d

   e. Position the insertion point in the top cell in the third column.
   f. Click T<u>a</u>ble and then Table P<u>r</u>operties.
   g. At the Table Properties dialog box, click the Col<u>u</u>mn tab.
   h. At the Table Properties dialog box with the Col<u>u</u>mn tab selected, click the down-pointing triangle at the right side of the Preferred <u>w</u>idth text box until *1.6"* displays.
   i. Click OK or press Enter.
   j. Add the following to the table:

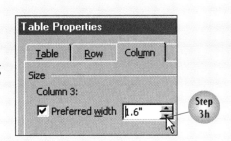

Step 3h

1) Add a thick/thin double-line border around the table.
2) Add a single line between the columns.
3) Add a light color fill to all cells in the table (you determine the color).
4. Change the height of the rows by completing the following steps:
   a. With the insertion point positioned in any cell in the table, click Table, point to Select, and then click Table.
   b. With the table selected, click Table and then Properties.
   c. At the Table Properties dialog box, click the Row tab.
   d. Click in the Specify height check box and then click the up-pointing triangle at the right side of the measurement box until 0.3″ displays.
   e. Click OK to close the dialog box.
   f. Deselect the table.
5. Save the document again with the same name (Ch 13, Ex 09).
6. Print and then close Ch 13, Ex 09. (The table will not be centered between the margins.)

Changing Cell Alignment

By default, text in cells aligns at the left side of the cell. Like normal text, this alignment can be changed to center, right, or justified. To change the alignment of text in cells, select the cells, and then click the desired alignment button on the Formatting toolbar. You can also change the alignment of text in selected cells with the Alignment option at the Paragraph dialog box with the Indents and Spacing tab selected or with a shortcut command. For example, to change the alignment of text to center in all cells in the second column of a table, you would select all cells in the second column, and then click the Center button on the Formatting toolbar.

exercise 10

Changing Cell Alignment in a Table

1. Open Ch 13, Ex 08.
2. Save the document with Save As and name it Ch 13, Ex 10.
3. Change the alignment of text in cells B2 through C7 to center by completing the following steps:
   a. Position the insertion point in cell B2 (the cell containing the number 312-304-0098).
   b. Hold down the Shift key, press the down arrow key five times, and then the right arrow key once. (This selects cells B2 through C7.)
   c. Click the Center button on the Formatting toolbar.
   d. Deselect the cells.
4. Save the document again with the same name (Ch 13, Ex 10).
5. Print and then close Ch 13, Ex 10.

Aligning the Table

By default, a table aligns at the left margin. This alignment can be changed with options at the Table Properties dialog box with the Table tab selected as shown in figure 13.18. To change the alignment, click the desired alignment option in the Alignment section of the dialog box.

figure

13.18 **Table Properties Dialog Box with Table Tab Selected**

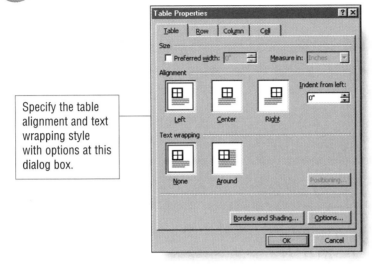

Specify the table alignment and text wrapping style with options at this dialog box.

exercise 11

Horizontally Aligning a Table

1. Open Ch 13, Ex 09.
2. Save the document with Save As and name it Ch 13, Ex 11.
3. Center the table horizontally by completing the following steps:
   a. Position the insertion point in any cell in the table.
   b. Click Table and then Table Properties.
   c. At the Table Properties dialog box, click the Table tab.
   d. At the Table Properties dialog box with the Table tab selected, click the Center option in the Alignment section.
   e. Click OK or press Enter.
4. Save the document again with the same name (Ch 13, Ex 11).
5. Print and then close Ch 13, Ex 11.

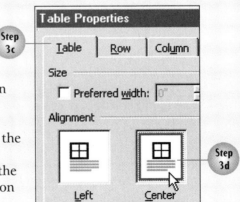

Step 3c

Step 3d

Inserting Rows

After a table has been created, rows can be added (inserted) to the table. There are several methods you can use to insert rows. You can use options from the Insert side menu to insert rows above or below the current row. To do this, position the insertion point in the row below where the row is to be inserted, click Table, point to Insert, and then click either Rows Above or Rows Below (depending on where you want the row inserted). If you want more than one row inserted, select the desired number of rows and then click Table, point to Insert, and choose Rows Above or Rows Below.

Insert Rows

You can also insert rows by selecting a row or several rows and then clicking the Insert Rows button on the Standard toolbar. The Insert Table button becomes the Insert Rows button on the Standard toolbar when a row or several rows are selected in a table.

Another method for inserting a row or several rows is to select a row (or rows) in a table, position the mouse pointer inside the selected row, click the *right* mouse button, and then click Insert Rows. Also, a row can be inserted at the end of the table by positioning the insertion point in the last cell in the table and then pressing the Tab key.

Inserting Rows in a Table

1. Open Ch 13, Ex 08.
2. Save the document with Save As and name it Ch 13, Ex 12.
3. Add two rows to the table by completing the following steps:
   a. Select the fourth and fifth row in the table.
   b. Click Table, point to Insert, and then click Rows Above.
   c. Deselect the rows.
   d. Position the insertion point in cell A4 (below *Stanley Matias*), press Ctrl + Tab, and then key **Richard Paige**.
   e. Key the following text in the specified cell:

B4	=	**412-335-2255**
C4	=	**Human Resources**
A5	=	**Cynthia Kohler**
B5	=	**566-345-2408**
C5	=	**Financial Planning**

4. Change the word *six* in the first paragraph to *eight*. Change the word *seven* in the last paragraph to *nine*.
5. Save the document again with the same name (Ch 13, Ex 12).
6. Print and then close Ch 13, Ex 12.

Inserting Columns

Columns can be inserted in a table in much the same way as rows. To insert a column, position the insertion point in a cell within the table, click Table, point to Insert, and then click Columns to the Left or Columns to the Right. If you want to insert more than one column, select the desired number of columns first.

Another method for inserting a column (or columns) is to select the column and then click the Insert Columns button on the Standard toolbar. The Insert Table button on the Standard toolbar becomes the Insert Columns button when a column or columns are selected.

A column or group of columns can also be inserted by selecting the column(s), clicking the *right* mouse button, and then clicking Insert Columns at the drop-down menu. Word inserts a column or columns to the left of the selected column or columns. If you want to add a column to the right side of the table, select all the end-of-row markers, and then click the Insert Columns button on the Standard toolbar.

Insert Columns

exercise 13

Inserting a Column in a Table

1. Open Ch 13, Ex 01.
2. Save the document with Save As and name it Ch 13, Ex 13.
3. Make the following changes to the table:
   a. Add a row to the table by completing the following steps:
      1) Position the insertion point in any cell in the first row.
      2) Click Table, point to Insert, and then click Rows Above.
      3) Position the insertion point in cell A1 (the first cell in the first row), change the alignment to center, turn on bold, and then key **Name**.
      4) Press the Tab key to move the insertion point to the next cell (cell B1), change the alignment to center, turn on bold, and then key **Title**.
   b. Add a column to the right side of the table by completing the following steps:
      1) Click the Show/Hide ¶ button on the Standard toolbar to turn on the display of nonprinting characters.
      2) Position the mouse pointer on the first end-of-row marker toward the top of the row at the far right side of the table until it turns into a small down-pointing arrow.
      3) Click the left mouse button. (This will select all of the end-of-row markers at the right side of the table.)

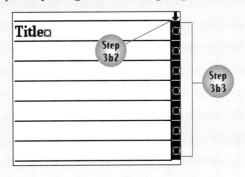

4) Click T<u>a</u>ble, point to <u>I</u>nsert, and then click Columns to the <u>L</u>eft.

5) Deselect the column.

c. Change the width of the first column to 1.5 inches by completing the following steps:

1) Position the insertion point in the first cell in the first column (cell A1).

2) Click T<u>a</u>ble and then Table P<u>r</u>operties.

3) At the Table Properties dialog box, click the Col<u>u</u>mn tab.

4) At the Table Properties dialog box with the Col<u>u</u>mn tab selected, click the down-pointing triangle at the right side of the Preferred <u>w</u>idth text box until *1.5"* displays.

5) Click OK or press Enter.

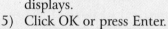

Table Properties

| T<u>a</u>ble | <u>R</u>ow | Col<u>u</u>mn |

Step 3c3

Size
Column 1:
☑ Preferred <u>w</u>idth 1.5"

Step 3c4

d. Position the insertion point in the first cell in the second column (cell B1) and then change the width of the column to 1.5 inches.

e. Position the insertion point in the first cell in the third column (cell C1) and then change the width of the column to 1 inch.

f. Select the cells in the last column (cells C1 through C7) and then change the alignment to center.

g. Key the following text in the specified cells:

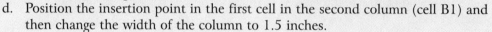

C1	=	Ext.
C2	=	1029
C3	=	2311
C4	=	3290
C5	=	2100
C6	=	1392
C7	=	2596

Title¤	Ext.¤	¤
President¤	1029¤	¤
Vice-President¤	2311¤	¤
Director¤	3290¤	¤
Assistant-Director¤	2100¤	¤
Trainer¤	1392¤	¤
Trainer¤	2596¤	¤

Step 3g

h. Click the Show/Hide ¶ button to turn off the display of nonprinting characters.

i. Center the table horizontally by completing the following steps:

1) Position the insertion point in any cell in the table.

2) Click T<u>a</u>ble and then Table P<u>r</u>operties.

3) At the Table Properties dialog box, click the <u>T</u>able tab.

4) At the Table Properties dialog box with the <u>T</u>able tab selected, click the <u>C</u>enter option in the Alignment section.

5) Click OK or press Enter.

4. Save the document again with the same name (Ch 13, Ex 13).

5. Print and then close Ch 13, Ex 13.

Deleting Cells, Rows, or Columns

Delete a column, row, or cell with options from the <u>D</u>elete side menu. For example, to delete a column, position the insertion point in any cell within the column, click T<u>a</u>ble, point to <u>D</u>elete, and then click <u>C</u>olumns. To delete a row, click T<u>a</u>ble, point to <u>D</u>elete, and then click <u>R</u>ows. To delete a specific cell, position the insertion point in the cell, click T<u>a</u>ble, point to <u>D</u>elete, and then click C<u>e</u>lls. This displays the Delete Cells dialog box shown in figure 13.19.

figure

13.19

Delete Cells Dialog Box

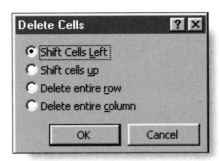

At the Delete Cells dialog box, the Shift Cells Left option is selected by default. At this option, cells will shift left after the cell (or selected cells) is deleted. Click the Shift cells up option if you want cells moved up after the cell (or selected cells) is deleted. Click Delete entire row to delete the row where the insertion point is positioned or click Delete entire column to delete the column where the insertion point is positioned.

The Delete Cells dialog box can also be displayed by positioning the mouse pointer in the table, clicking the *right* mouse button, and then clicking Delete Cells at the drop-down menu.

exercise 14

Deleting Rows and Columns in a Table

1. Open Ch 13, Ex 12.
2. Save the document with Save As and name it Ch 13, Ex 14.
3. Make the following changes to the table:
   a. Delete the bottom row in the table by completing the following steps:
      1) Position the insertion point in any cell in the bottom row.
      2) Click Table, point to Delete, and then click Rows.
   b. Delete the middle column by completing the following steps:
      1) Position the insertion point in any cell in the middle column.
      2) Click Table, point to Delete, and then click Columns.
   c. Center the table horizontally.
   d. Change the word *eight* in the first paragraph to *seven*. Change the word *nine* in the last paragraph to *eight*.
4. Save the document again with the same name (Ch 13, Ex 14).
5. Print and then close Ch 13, Ex 14.

Merging Cells

Cells can be merged with the Merge Cells option from the Table drop-down menu. To do this, select the cells to be merged, click Table, and then click Merge Cells.

Splitting Cells

Split a cell or a row or column of cells with options at the Split Cells dialog box shown in figure 13.20. To display this dialog box, position the insertion point in the cell to be split, click Table, and then click Split Cells. At the Split Cells dialog box, make sure the desired number of columns displays in the Number of columns text box, and then click OK or press Enter. To split an entire column or row of cells, select the column or row first, click Table, and then click Split Cells.

13.20   *Split Cells Dialog Box*

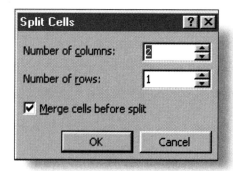

Creating a Table with Merged Cells

1. At a clear document screen, create the table shown in figure 13.21 by completing the following steps:
   a. Create a table with 3 columns and 10 rows (10 x 3).
   b. Change the width of the first column to 3 inches, the width of the second column to 2 inches, and the width of the third column to 1 inch. (The insertion point must be positioned in the top cell of the column before changing column width.)
   c. Merge the cells in the first row by completing the following steps:
      1) Select the first row.
      2) Click Table and then Merge Cells.
   d. Merge the cells in the second row by completing steps similar to those in step 1c.
   e. Select the entire table and then change the font to 12-point Arial bold.
   f. Key the text in the cells as shown in figure 13.21 center aligning the text as indicated.
   g. Add a double-line border around the outside of the table and a single-line border on the inside of the table by completing the following steps:

1) Position the insertion point in any cell in the table.
2) Click Format and then Borders and Shading.
3) At the Borders and Shading dialog box, make sure the Borders tab is selected.
4) Make sure the first line style (a single line) is selected in the Style list box.
5) Click the Grid option that displays at the left side of the dialog box.
6) Scroll down the line styles in the Style list box until the first double line displays and then click it.
7) Click OK or press Enter to close the Borders and Shading dialog box.
 h. Select the third row and then add 20% fill.
2. Save the document and name it Ch 13, Ex 15.
3. Print and then close Ch 13, Ex 15.

figure

13.21   *Exercise 15*

TRAINING AND EDUCATION DEPARTMENT		
Desktop Publishing Training		
Name	Department	Emp #

Formatting with AutoFormat

Formatting a table, such as adding borders or shading, aligning text in cells, changing fonts, etc., can take some time. Word has provided predesigned table formats that can quickly format your table for you. Table formats are contained in the Table AutoFormat dialog box shown in figure 13.22. To display this dialog box, position the insertion point in any cell in a table, click Table, and then click Table AutoFormat.

figure

13.22 **Table AutoFormat Dialog Box**

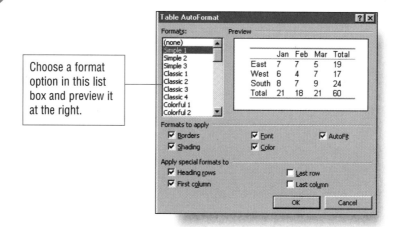

Choose a format option in this list box and preview it at the right.

Table formats are displayed in the Formats list box. Select a table format in the Formats list box and preview the appearance of the table in the Preview section. When previewing table formats, you can make some changes to the format by removing check marks from the options in the Formats to apply section of the dialog box. For example, if you like a format created by Word except for the shading, select the format in the Formats list box, and then click the Shading check box. This removes the check mark from the Shading check box and also removes the shading from the table shown in the Preview section.

If you want to apply the special formatting only to specific parts of the table, select the parts of the table you want the formatting applied to in the Apply special formats to section of the dialog box. For example, if you want the table formatting only applied to the first column in the table, insert a check mark in the First column option and remove the check marks from the other options.

exercise 16

Formatting a Table Using the Table AutoFormat Dialog Box

1. Open Ch 13, Ex 01.
2. Save the document with Save As and name it Ch 13, Ex 16.
3. Make the following changes to the table:
   a. Position the insertion point in any cell in the first row, click Table, point to Insert, and then click Rows Above.
   b. Key **Name** in the first cell in the first column (cell A1), centered and bolded.
   c. Key **Title** in the first cell in the second column (cell B1), centered and bolded.
   d. Automatically format the table by completing the following steps:
      1) Position the insertion point in any cell in the table.
      2) Click Table and then Table AutoFormat.

3) At the Table AutoFormat dialog box, click the down-pointing triangle to the right of the Forma_t_s list box until *Colorful 3* is visible, and then click *Colorful 3*.

4) Click OK or press Enter.

e. Center the table horizontally.

4. Save the document again with the same name (Ch 13, Ex 16).

5. Print and then close Ch 13, Ex 16.

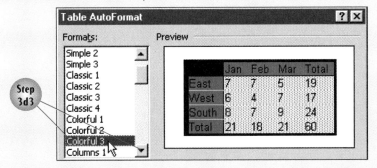

Creating a Table Using the Tables and Borders Toolbar

Word includes a Tables and Borders toolbar with options you can use to create a more free-form table. With buttons on the Tables and Borders toolbar, shown in figure 13.23, you can draw a table with specific borders as well as add shading and fill. To display this toolbar, click the Tables and Borders button on the Standard toolbar. Figure 13.24 identifies the buttons on the toolbar and the purpose of each.

Tables and Borders

figure

13.23   *Tables and Borders Toolbar*

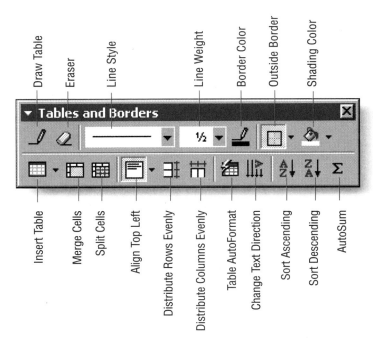

figure
13.24
Buttons on the Tables and Borders Toolbar

Click this button	Named	To do this
	Draw Table	Insert a table where you drag in the document
	Eraser	Erase border and/or cell lines
	Line Style	Specify the border line style
	Line Weight	Specify the thickness of the border line
	Border Color	Specify the border line color
	Outside Border	Add or remove border around selected text, paragraph, cells, or other object
	Shading Color	Add, modify, or remove fill color from selected object
	Insert Table	Display a pop-up menu with options to insert a table; insert a column, row, or cells; specify the fit of cell contents
	Merge Cells	Combine contents of selected adjacent cells into one cell
	Split Cells	Split selected cells in number of rows and columns specified
	Align Top Left	Display a palette of alignment options such as top center, top right, center left, center right, bottom left, bottom center, and bottom right
	Distribute Rows Evenly	Change selected rows or cells to equal row height
	Distribute Columns Evenly	Change selected columns or cells to equal column width
	Table AutoFormat	Apply predesigned formats to table or selected cells
	Change Text Direction	Orient selected text in a cell horizontally left or right

	Sort Ascending	Sort selected items alphabetically or numerically in ascending order
	Sort Descending	Sort selected items alphabetically or numerically in descending order
	AutoSum	Insert total of a column or row in cell

To create a table using buttons on the Tables and Borders toolbar, you would complete the following steps:

1. Turn on the display of the Tables and Borders toolbar by clicking the Tables and Borders button on the Standard toolbar. (The view is automatically changed to Print Layout.)
2. Position the mouse pointer (displays as a pencil) in the area of the editing window where you want the upper left corner of the table to display.
3. Hold down the left mouse button, drag the pencil pointer down and to the right until the outline displays the desired size of the table, and then release the mouse button. (This creates the border of the table.)
4. Use the pencil pointer to draw the row and column lines.
5. Click inside the cell where you want to key text.
6. Key the desired text. (When you key text, the pencil pointer turns into the normal mouse pointer.)

Many of the buttons on the Tables and Borders toolbar can be used to customize the table. For example, you can change the line style with Line Style options and then draw the desired portion of the table. Or, you can change the line style and then redraw lines in an existing table. Use options from the Shading Color button to add color to a cell or selected cells in a table.

Shading Color

exercise 17

Drawing a Table Using the Tables and Borders Toolbar

1. At a clear editing window, draw the table shown in figure 13.25 by completing the following steps:
   a. Key the title centered and bolded as shown in figure 13.25.
   b. Press the Enter key three times, turn off bold, and return the paragraph alignment to left.
   c. Turn on the display of the Tables and Borders toolbar by clicking the Tables and Borders button on the Standard toolbar.
   d. Position the mouse pointer (displays as a pencil) in the editing window and draw the table, row, and column lines as shown in figure 13.25. (To draw the lines, position the pencil in the desired location, hold down the left mouse button, draw the line, and then release the button. If you want to erase a line, click the Eraser button on the Tables and Borders toolbar and then drag across the line. To continue drawing the table, click the Draw Table button.)

e. Click the Draw Table button to deactivate it.
f. Change the vertical alignment of text in cells by completing the following steps:
   1) Select all cells in the table.
   2) Click the down-pointing triangle at the right side of the Align Top Left button located on the Tables and Borders toolbar.
   3) At the palette of alignment choices that displays, click the Align Center Left option (first option from the left in the second row).
g. With all cells in the table still selected, click the Distribute Rows Evenly button on the Tables and Borders toolbar.
h. Select all cells in the second and third columns and then click the Center button on the Formatting toolbar. (This button is located on the Formatting toolbar—not the Tables and Borders toolbar.)
i. Click in the first cell.
j. Key the text in the cells as shown in figure 13.25. (If text wraps in a cell, widen the column.)
2. Turn off the display of the Tables and Borders toolbar by clicking the Tables and Borders button on the Standard toolbar.
3. Save the document and name it Ch 13, Ex 17.
4. Print and then close Ch 13, Ex 17.

figure
13.25 *Exercise 17*

PROJECTED EXPENSES

Department	2000	2001
Support Services	$10,200	$11,355
Human Resources	$11,545	$12,800
Finance and Resource Management	$15,355	$16,433
Administration	$21,435	$24,700
Manufacturing and Production	$75,455	$81,600

exercise 18

Customizing a Table with the Tables and Borders Toolbar

1. Open Ch 13, Ex 17.
2. Save the document with Save As and name it Ch 13, Ex 18.
3. Customize the table by completing the following steps:
   a. Turn on the display of the Tables and Borders toolbar by clicking the Tables and Borders button on the Standard toolbar.
   b. Change the outside table border lines to double lines by completing the following steps:
      1) Click the down-pointing triangle at the right side of the Line Style button.
      2) At the drop-down list that displays, click the first double-line style.
      3) Position the pencil pointer in the upper left corner of the table, hold down the left mouse button, drag the pencil down the left side of the table until it reaches the bottom, and then release the mouse button. (This changes the single line to a double line.)
      4) Change the bottom border of the table to a double line by dragging the pencil across the bottom border. (Be sure to hold down the left mouse button as you drag.)
      5) Change the right border of the table to a double line by dragging the pencil along the right border.
      6) Change the top border of the table to a double line by dragging the pencil along the top border.
   c. Click the Draw Table button to deselect it.
   d. Add gray shading to cells by completing the following steps:

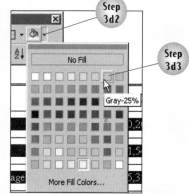

   1) Select cells A2 through C6.
   2) Click the down-pointing triangle at the right side of the Shading Color button on the Tables and Borders toolbar.
   3) At the palette of color choices that displays, click the Gray-25% color (this is the second option from the *right* in the top row).
   e. Add light turquoise shading to cells by completing the following steps:
      1) Select cells A1, B1, and C1.
      2) Click the down-pointing arrow at the right side of the Shading Color button on the Tables and Borders toolbar.
      3) At the palette of color choices, click the Light Turquoise color (fifth color from the left in the bottom row).

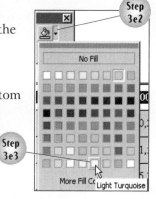

4. Save the document again with the same name (Ch 13, Ex 18).
5. Print and then close Ch 13, Ex 18.

exercise 19

Inserting a Column and Changing Text Direction

1. Open Ch 13, Ex 17.
2. Save the document with Save As and name it Ch 13, Ex 19.
3. Customize the table so it appears as shown in figure 13.26 by completing the following steps:
   a. Delete the title *PROJECTED EXPENSES*.
   b. Click in the first cell.
   c. Click T_able, point to _Insert, and then click Columns to the _Left. (This inserts a column at the left side of the table.)
   d. Change the width of the first and second columns by completing the following steps:
      1) Position the mouse pointer on the gridline that separates the first and second column until the pointer turns into left- and right-pointing arrows with a vertical double line between.
      2) Hold down the left mouse button, drag to the left approximately 0.75 inch, and then release the mouse button.
   e. Merge the cells in the first column by completing the following steps:
      1) Display the Tables and Borders toolbar.
      2) Click the Draw Table button to deactivate it.
      3) Select the first column.
      4) Click the Merge Cells button on the Tables and Borders toolbar.
   f. Key the text in the first cell as shown in figure 13.26 by completing the following steps:
      1) Make sure the insertion point is positioned in the first cell.
      2) Change the text direction by clicking twice on the Change Text Direction button on the Tables and Borders toolbar.
      3) Click the Center button on the Formatting toolbar.
      4) Change the font to 18-point Times New Roman bold.
      5) Key **Projected Expenses**.

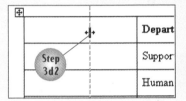

4. Save the document again with the same name (Ch 13, Ex 19).
5. Print and then close Ch 13, Ex 19.

figure

Exercise 19

Projected Expenses	Department	2000	2001
	Support Services	$10,200	$11,355
	Human Resources	$11,545	$12,800
	Finance and Resource Management	$15,355	$16,433
	Administration	$21,435	$24,700
	Manufacturing and Production	$75,455	$81,600

Performing Calculations

Numbers in a table can be calculated. Numbers can be added, subtracted, multiplied, and divided. In addition, you can calculate averages, percentages, and minimum and maximum values. Calculations can be performed in a Word table; however, for complex calculations, use a Microsoft Excel worksheet.

To perform a calculation in a table, position the insertion point in the cell where you want the result of the calculation to display. This cell should be empty. By default, Word assumes that you want to calculate the sum of cells immediately above or to the left of the cell where the insertion point is positioned. This default calculation can be changed.

As an example of how to calculate sums, you would complete the following steps to calculate the sum of cells in C2 through C5 and insert the result of the calculation in cell C6:

1. Position the insertion point in cell C6.
2. Click Table and then Formula.
3. At the Formula dialog box shown in figure 13.27, the calculation =SUM(ABOVE) displays in the Formula text box. This is the desired formula to calculate the sum.
4. Click OK or press Enter.

figure

13.27 *Formula Dialog Box*

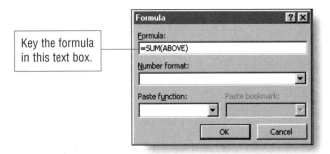

Key the formula in this text box.

Word adds the numbers in cells C2 through C5 and then inserts the result of this calculation in cell C6. To perform other types of calculations such as subtraction, multiplication, and division, the formula displayed in the Formula text box at the Formula dialog box must be changed. You can use an arithmetic sign to write a formula. For example, the formula A2-A3 (A2 minus A3) can be inserted in cell A4, which tells Word to insert the difference of A2 and A3 in cell A4. If changes are made to the numbers in cells A2 and A3, the value in A4 can be recalculated.

Four basic operators can be used when writing formulas: the plus sign (+) for addition, the minus sign (hyphen) for subtraction, the asterisk (*) for multiplication, and the forward slash (/) for division. If there are two or more operators in a calculation, Word calculates from left to right. If you want to change the order of calculation, use parentheses around the part of the calculation to be performed first.

In the default formula, the SUM part of the formula is called a *function*. Word provides other functions you can use to write a formula. These functions are available with the Paste function option at the Formula dialog box. For example, you can use the AVERAGE function to average numbers in cells. Examples of how formulas can be written are shown in figure 13.28.

The numbering format can be specified at the Formula dialog box. For example, if you are calculating money amounts, you can specify that the calculated numbers display with two numbers following the decimal point. To specify the numbering format, display the Formula dialog box, and then click the down-pointing triangle to the right of the Number format option. Click the desired formatting at the drop-down list that displays.

figure
13.28

Example Formulas

Cell E4 is the total price of items.
Cell B4 contains the quantity of items, and cell D4 contains the unit price. The formula for cell E4 is **=B4*D4**. (This formula multiplies the quantity of items in cell B4 by the unit price in cell D4.)

Cell D3 is the percentage of increase of sales from the previous year.
Cell B3 contains the amount of sales for the previous year, and cell C3 contains the amount of sales for the current year. The formula for cell D3 is **=(C3-B3)/C3*100**. (This formula subtracts the amount of sales last year from the amount of sales this year. The remaining amount is divided by the amount of sales this year and then multiplied by 100 to display the product as a percentage.)

Cell E1 is the average of test scores.
Cells A1 through D1 contain test scores. The formula to calculate the average score is **=(A1+B1+C1+D1)/4**. (This formula adds the scores from cells A1 through D1 and then divides that sum by 4.) You can also enter the formula as **=AVERAGE(LEFT)**. The AVERAGE function tells Word to average all entries left of cell E1.

exercise 20

Calculating Net Profit

1. At a clear document screen, create the document shown in figure 13.29 by completing the following steps:
   a. Press the Enter key once.
   b. Create a table with 4 columns and 6 rows (6 x 4).
   c. Select the first row and then merge the cells.
   d. Position the insertion point in the first row, press the Enter key once, change the alignment to center, turn on bold, key **COLEMAN CORPORATION**, and then press Enter once.
   e. Select the second row in the table and then click the Bold and the Center buttons on the Formatting toolbar.
   f. Select cells A3 through A6 and then change the alignment to center.
   g. Select cells B3 through D6 and then change the alignment to right.
   h. Key the text in the cells as shown in figure 13.29.
   i. Add border lines and shading to the table as shown in figure 13.29.

j. Insert a formula in cell D3 by completing the following steps:
    1) Position the insertion point in cell D3 (the cell below *Net Profit*).
    2) Click Table and then Formula.
    3) At the Formula dialog box, delete the formula in the Formula text box.
    4) Key **=B3-C3** in the Formula text box.
    5) Click the down-pointing triangle at the right side of the Number format text box and then click the third option from the top of the drop-down list.
    6) Click OK or press Enter.

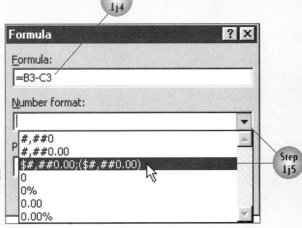

k. Insert the formula **=B4-C4** in cell D4 by completing steps similar to those in step 1j, except click the second option at the Number format drop-down list.

l. Insert the formula **=B5-C5** in cell D5 by completing steps similar to those in step 1j, except click the second option at the Number format drop-down list.

m. Insert the formula **=B6-C6** in cell D6 by completing steps similar to those in step 1j, except click the second option at the Number format drop-down list.

2. Save the document and name it Ch 13, Ex 20.
3. Print and then close Ch 13, Ex 20.

figure
13.29 *Exercise 20*

COLEMAN CORPORATION			
Year	Income	Expenses	Net Profit
1997	$4,390,130.20	$3,104,530.45	
1998	4,560,439.86	3,239,478.10	
1999	4,687,390.33	3,669,092.20	
2000	5,001,058.75	3,945,230.68	

exercise 21

Averaging Test Scores

1. Open Table 01.
2. Save the document with Save As and name it Ch 13, Ex 21.
3. Insert a formula in cell F3 to average test scores by completing the following steps:
   a. Position the insertion point in cell F3 (the cell below *Ave.*).
   b. Click T<u>a</u>ble and then F<u>o</u>rmula.
   c. Delete the formula in the <u>F</u>ormula text box *except* the equals sign.
   d. With the insertion point positioned immediately after the equals sign, click the down-pointing triangle to the right of the Paste f<u>u</u>nction text box.
   e. At the drop-down list that displays, click *AVERAGE*.
   f. With the insertion point positioned between the left and right parentheses, key **left**.
   g. Click the down-pointing triangle to the right of the <u>N</u>umber format text box and then click the fifth option from the top *(0%)* at the drop-down list.
   h. Click OK or press Enter.

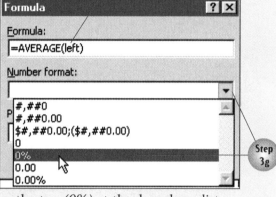

4. Position the insertion point in cell F4 and then press F4 (this is the Repeat command).
5. Position the insertion point in cell F5 and then press F4.
6. Position the insertion point in cell F6 and then press F4.
7. Position the insertion point in cell F7 and then press F4.
8. Position the insertion point in cell F8 and then press F4.
9. Save the document again with the same name (Ch 13, Ex 21).
10. Print and then close Ch 13, Ex 21.

If changes are made to numbers in cells that are part of a formula, select the result of the calculation, and then press the F9 function key. This recalculates the formula and inserts the new result of the calculation in the cell. You can also recalculate by completing the following steps:

1. Select the number in the cell containing the formula.
2. Click T<u>a</u>ble and then F<u>o</u>rmula.
3. At the Formula dialog box, click OK or press Enter.

exercise 22

Recalculating Test Scores

1. Open Ch 13, Ex 21.
2. Save the document with Save As and name it Ch 13, Ex 22.
3. Make the following changes to the table:
    a. Change the number in cell C3 from 81 to 85.
    b. Change the number in cell D5 from 90 to 96.
    c. Change the number in cell D8 from 87 to 95.
    d. Position the mouse pointer in cell F3, click the left mouse button (this inserts a gray background around the numbers in the cell), and then press F9. (Pressing F9 recalculates the average.)
    e. Click the number in cell F5 and then press F9.
    f. Click the number in cell F8 and then press F9.
4. Save the document again with the same name (Ch 13, Ex 22).
5. Print and then close Ch 13, Ex 22.

chapter summary

➤ Word's Tables feature can be used to create columns and rows of information. A cell is the intersection between a row and a column.

➤ A table can contain text, characters, numbers, data, graphics, or formulas. It can be extensively formatted and can include calculations.

➤ A table can be created with the Insert Table button on the Standard toolbar or at the Insert Table dialog box.

➤ Columns in a table are lettered from left to right beginning with A. Rows are numbered from top to bottom beginning with 1.

➤ The lines that form the cells of the table are called gridlines.

➤ With the insertion point positioned in a cell, key or edit text as you would normal text.

➤ To move the insertion point to different cells within the table using the mouse, position the mouse pointer in the desired cell, and then click the left button.

➤ To move the insertion point to different cells within the table using the keyboard, refer to the information shown in figure 13.5 in this chapter.

➤ Position the mouse pointer on the cell selection bar, the row selection bar, or the top gridline of a column to select a cell, row, or column.

➤ To use the keyboard to select specific cells within a table, refer to the information shown in figure 13.10 in this chapter.

➤ A row or column of cells or all cells in a table can be selected with options from the Table drop-down menu.

➤ All text in cells within a table can be deleted, leaving the table gridlines, or all text and the gridlines can be deleted.

- Borders and shading can be added to cells; rows and columns can be inserted or deleted; cells can be split or merged; and the alignment of the table can be changed.
- Column width can be changed using the mouse on the Ruler, in a table, or at the Table Properties dialog box with the Column tab selected.
- After a table has been created, various methods can be used to add rows and/or columns.
- Specific cells in a table or rows or columns in a table can be deleted.
- Word has provided predesigned table formats in the Table AutoFormat dialog box that can quickly format your table.
- Use buttons on the Tables and Borders toolbar to create and customize a table. Click the Tables and Borders button on the Standard toolbar to turn on the display of the Tables and Borders toolbar.
- Numbers in a table can be calculated by inserting a formula in a cell at the Formula dialog box.

commands review

	Mouse/Keyboard
Create table with Insert Table Button	With mouse pointer on Insert Table button on Standard toolbar, hold down left mouse button, move mouse pointer down and right until desired table size displays, then release button
Display Insert Table dialog box	Click Table, point to Insert, then click Table
Move insertion point to next cell	Press the Tab key
Move insertion point to previous cell	Press Shift + Tab
Insert tab within a cell	Press Ctrl + Tab
Insert page break within a table	Press Ctrl + Enter
Select a row, column, or all cells with Table drop-down menu	Position insertion point, click Table, point to Select, then click Table, Column, Row, or Cell
Delete text only from table	Select table, then press the Delete key
Delete table	Click Table, point to Delete, then click Table
Display Table Properties dialog box	Click Table and then Table Properties
Delete cells, rows, or columns	Click Table, point to Delete, then click Columns, Rows, or Cells
Display Table AutoFormat dialog box	With insertion point in a cell, click Table, then Table AutoFormat
Turn on/off display of Tables and Borders toolbar	Click Tables and Borders button on Standard toolbar
Display Formula dialog box	Click Table and then Formula

thinking offline

Completion: In the space provided at the right, indicate the correct term, command, or number.

1. Use this button on the Standard toolbar to create a table. _____

2. This is another name for the lines that form the cells of the table. _____

3. The end-of-row marker displays only when this button is active on the Standard toolbar. _____

4. The move table column markers display here. _____

5. Use this keyboard command to move the insertion point to the previous cell. _____

6. Use this keyboard command to insert a tab within a cell. _____

7. This is the name given to the space just to the left of the left edge of a table. _____

8. To add shading to a cell or selected cells, display this dialog box. _____

9. Change the width of columns at this dialog box with the Column tab selected. _____

10. Text in cells aligns at this side of the cell by default. _____

11. One method for inserting rows in a table is to select a row, position the mouse pointer inside the selected row, click the right mouse button, and then click this. _____

12. Choose this option at the Delete Cells dialog box if you want cells moved up after selected cells are deleted. _____

13. To merge cells A1 and B1, select A1 and B1, and then click this option at the Table drop-down menu. _____

14. To divide one cell into two columns, click this at the Table drop-down menu. _____

15. Choose predesigned table formats at this dialog box. _____

16. Click this button on the Tables and Borders toolbar to add, modify, or remove fill color from selected objects. _____

17. Click this button on the Tables and Borders toolbar to change the border line style. _____

18. This is the operator for multiplication that is used when writing formulas in a table. _____

19. This is the formula to add cells D2, D3, and D4, and then divide the total by 5. _____

20. This is the formula to multiply A1 by B1. _____

working hands-on

Assessment 1

1. At a clear document screen, create the table shown in figure 13.30. Bold and center the text as shown.
2. Save the document and name it Ch 13, SA 01.
3. Print and then close Ch 13, SA 01.

figure

13.30   *Assessment 1*

Name	Title	Department
Stanley McPherson	Vice President	Administrative Services
Chad Lowell	Director	Resource Management
Katherine Lewandowski	Director	Marketing and Sales
Anna Keibler	Assistant Director	Marketing and Sales
Kim Millerton	Administrative Assistant	Resource Management

Assessment 2

1. At a clear document screen, create the memo shown in figure 13.31 by completing the following steps:
   a. Key the headings and the first paragraph of the memo.
   b. With the insertion point a double space below the memo, create a table with 3 columns and 5 rows (5 x 3).
   c. Change the width of the first column to 2.25 inches, the width of the middle column to 1.5 inches, and the width of the third column to 2.25 inches.
   d. Select the cells in the second column and then change the alignment to center.
   e. Select the cells in the third column and then change the alignment to right.
   f. Key the text in the cells as shown in figure 13.31.
   g. After completing the table, position the insertion point a double space below the table, and then key the rest of the memo.
2. Save the document and name it Ch 13, SA 02.
3. Print and then close Ch 13, SA 02.

figure

13.31 *Assessment 2*

DATE: September 19, 2001

TO: Shawn O'Connell

FROM: David Olmsted

SUBJECT: SEPTEMBER NEWSLETTER

The following information needs to be included in the October newsletter under the heading, *Newsletter Resources.*

Superintendent	Linda Shing	Administrative Services
Assistant Superintendent	Rodney Valenzuela	Administrative Services
Curriculum Specialist	Sarah Brennan	District Headquarters
Newsletter Editor	David Olmsted	Shoreline Junior High School
Newsletter Assistant Editor	Christine Long	Oak Ridge Elementary School

Please include how employees can submit articles or items of interest to be published in the newsletter.

XX:Ch 13, SA 02

Assessment 3

1. At a clear document screen, create the table shown in figure 13.32 with the following specifications:
    a. Press the Enter key once and then create a table with 3 columns and 10 rows (10 x 3).
    b. Change the width of the first column to 2 inches, the width of the second column to 3 inches, and the width of the third column to 1 inch. (The insertion point must be positioned in the top cell in the column before changing column width.)
    c. Merge the cells in the first row (cells A1, B1, and C1).
    d. Key the text in the cells as indicated. Bold and center text as shown. Before keying the text in the first cell, press the Enter key once. After keying the text in the cell centered and bolded, press the Enter key once.
    e. Add border lines and shading to the table as shown in figure 13.32.
2. Save the document and name it Ch 13, SA 03.
3. Print and then close Ch 13, SA 03.

figure

13.32   *Assessment 3*

KENTWOOD SCHOOL DISTRICT		
Name	**School**	**Phone**
Devon Holleman	Kentwood High School	555-4555
Tina Pascual-Anderson	Mountain View Junior High School	555-1322
Mitchell Langford	Shoreline Junior High School	555-8770
Blaine Dowler	Emerald Heights Elementary School	555-4435
Tara Sandifer	Oak Ridge Elementary School	555-6644
Keith Gunter	Madison Creek Elementary School	555-5360
Corey Merritt	Bell Valley Elementary School	555-2287
Alfredo Marcoe	South Bend Elementary School	555-5667

Assessment 4

1. At a clear document screen, create the table shown in figure 13.33 with the
    following specifications:
    a. Create a table with 4 columns and 11 rows (11 x 4).
    b. With the insertion point positioned in the table, drag the move table column
        marker on the Ruler between the 1-inch mark and the 2-inch mark to the 4-
        inch mark on the Ruler.
    c. Merge the cells in the first row.
    d. Merge the cells in the second row.
    e. Select the first two rows in the table and then change the alignment to center.
    f. Select cells B3 through D11 and then change the alignment to center.
    g. Select the first two rows in the table and then change the font to 14-point
        Times New Roman bold.
    h. Select the cells in the third row and then change the font to 12-point Times
        New Roman bold.
    i. Select the remaining cells in the table and then change the font to 10-point
        Times New Roman and insert a left tab stop at the 0.25-inch mark on the
        Ruler.
    j. Key the text in the cells as indicated in the figure 13.33. Press Ctrl + Tab after
        the numbers to indent the insertion point.
    k. Add border lines as indicated in figure 13.33.
2. Save the document and name it Ch 13, SA 04.
3. Print and then close Ch 13, SA 04.

figure
13.33 *Assessment 4*

KENTWOOD SCHOOL DISTRICT			
Technology Study Question #6			
How will technology change your work environment?	**H.S.**	**J.H.S.**	**E.S.**
1. Improved access to centralized database.	1	2	2
2. Telephone lines for voice and data use in classroom.	3	2	1
3. Increased student access to information.	4	3	2
4. Better communication among peers.	4	4	3
5. Develop and implement a technology classroom model.	5	2	4
6. Technology to meet individual learning styles.	4	4	3
7. Elimination of textbook as primary delivery system.	5	2	3
8. Developing buildings as community learning/resource centers.	6	4	5

Assessment 5

1. At a clear document screen, create the document shown in figure 13.34 by completing the following steps:
   a. Key the headings and the first paragraph of the memo shown in figure 13.34.
   b. With the insertion point a double space below the first paragraph of the memo, create a table with 4 columns and 5 rows.
   c. Select the cells in the first row and then change the alignment to center.
   d. Select cells B2 through D5 and then change the alignment to right.
   e. Key the text in the cells as indicated. (Do not apply any special formatting to the text. This will be done with Table AutoFormat.)
   f. Position the insertion point in any cell in the table and then apply the List 8 formatting at the Table AutoFormat dialog box.
   g. Center the table horizontally.
   h. Position the insertion point in cell D2 and then insert the formula =C2-B2 and change the numbering format to two numbers after the decimal.
   i. Position the insertion point in cell D3 and then insert the formula =C3-B3 and change the numbering format to two numbers after the decimal.
   j. Position the insertion point in cell D4 and then insert the formula =C4-B4 and change the numbering format to two numbers after the decimal.
   k. Position the insertion point in cell D5 and then insert the formula =C5-B5 and change the numbering format to two numbers after the decimal.
2. After completing the table, move the insertion point a double space below the table and then key the rest of the memo.
3. Save the document and name it Ch 13, SA 05.
4. Print and then close Ch 13, SA 05.

figure

13.34 *Assessment 5*

DATE: June 5, 2001

TO: Corey Merritt, Principal

FROM: Ted Klein, PTO Treasurer

SUBJECT: FUND-RAISING EVENTS FOR 2000-2001

During the 2000-2001 school year, the Bell Valley Elementary School PTO sponsored
four major fund-raising events. These fund-raising events were very successful due to the
time donated by parents, teachers, staff, and children of Bell Valley Elementary School.
The following table shows the costs and profits for each event.

Event	Costs	Revenue	Net Profit
Walk-a-thon	$2,130.50	$7,340.35	
Fall Carnival	1,459.18	2,004.50	
T-Shirt Sales	2,340.00	3,120.80	
Rummage Sale	250.30	695.00	

As you can see from the table, the walk-a-thon generated the most profit. This was the
fourth year we have sponsored a walk-a-thon and each year the profits nearly double. The
rummage sale raised the least amount of money and seemed to require the most time
from PTO members and volunteers. At our next PTO meeting, we will discuss whether or
not to sponsor a rummage sale next year.

XX:Ch 13, SA 05

Assessment 6

1. At a clear document screen, create the table shown in figure 13.35 by completing
   the following steps:
   a. Press the Enter key and then create a table with 4 columns and 8 rows (8 x 4).
   b. Drag the move table column marker between the 1-inch mark and the 2-inch
      mark to the 2-inch mark on the Ruler.
   c. Merge the cells in the first row.
   d. Select the first two rows and then change the alignment to center and change
      the font to 14-point Century Gothic bold.
   e. Select cells B3 through D8 and then change the alignment to right.
   f. Select cells A3 through D8 and then change the font to 12-point Century
      Gothic.

g. Key the text in the cells as shown in figure 13.35. (Press Ctrl + Tab before keying the states in the first column.)

h. Insert the formula **=C3-B3** in cell D3 and change the number format to two decimals with a dollar sign. Insert the appropriate formula in cells D4, D5, D6, D7, and D8 to subtract Last Year numbers from This Year numbers. (Change the number format to two decimals without a dollar sign.)

i. Insert border lines and shading as shown in figure 13.35.

2. Save the document and name it Ch 13, SA 06.

3. Print and then close Ch 13, SA 06.

13.35 **Assessment 6**

MARIN CORPORATION			
Sales in Selected States			
State	**Last Year**	**This Year**	**Difference**
Washington	$1,304,293.90	$1,540,394.23	
Oregon	1,450,340.24	1,550,345.98	
Idaho	990,435.33	998,320.45	
California	3,340,288.45	3,445,230.50	
Nevada	1,032,483.78	1,224,889.34	
Texas	2,553,294.50	2,654,340.08	

Chapter 14

Adding Borders and Inserting Clip Art

PERFORMANCE OBJECTIVES

Upon successful completion of chapter 14, you will be able to:

- Add borders to paragraphs of text with options from the Borders button on the Formatting toolbar.
- Add borders and shading to paragraphs of text and to pages with options at the Borders and Shading dialog box.
- Add a border line to a footer.
- Insert, size, and move clip art images in a document.
- Create a watermark.
- Format clip art images.
- Download images from the Microsoft Clip Gallery.
- Create and format text boxes.

Microsoft Word 2000 contains a variety of features that help you enhance the visual appeal of a document. In this chapter, you will learn to add a border to a paragraph, selected paragraphs, or pages in a document, and add color and shading to a border. You will also learn to enhance a document by inserting a clip art image and downloading images from the Microsoft Clip Gallery.

Adding Borders with the Borders Button

Every paragraph you create in Word contains an invisible frame. A border that appears around this frame can be added to a paragraph. A border can be added to specific sides of the paragraph or to all sides. The type of border line and thickness of the line can be customized. In addition, you can add shading and fill to the border.

When a border is added to a paragraph of text, the border expands and contracts as text is inserted or deleted from the paragraph. You can create a border around a single paragraph or a border around selected paragraphs.

Creating a Border

Border

One method for creating a border is to use options from the Border button on the Formatting toolbar. The name of the button changes depending on the border choice that was previously selected at the button drop-down palette. When Word is first opened, the button name displays as Outside Border. Click the down-pointing triangle at the right side of the button and a palette of border choices displays as shown in figure 14.1.

Border Button Palette

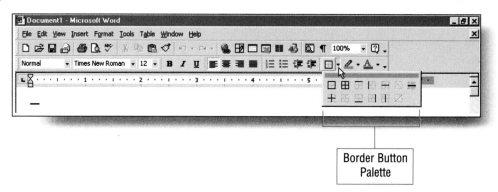

Border Button Palette

Click the option that will insert the desired border. For example, to insert a border at the bottom of the paragraph, click the Bottom Border option (third option from the left in the bottom row). Clicking an option will add the border to the paragraph where the insertion point is located. To add a border to more than one paragraph, select the paragraphs first and then click the desired option.

Adding Borders to Paragraphs of Text

1. Open Para 02.
2. Save the document with Save As and name it Ch 14, Ex 01.
3. Create a border around the first paragraph by completing the following steps:
    a. Position the insertion point anywhere in the first paragraph.
    b. Position the mouse pointer on the Border button on the Formatting toolbar and wait for the ScreenTip to display. Make sure the ScreenTip displays as Outside Border and then click the button. (If this is not the name for the button, click the down-pointing triangle at the right side of the button and then click the Outside Border option [first option in the top row].)

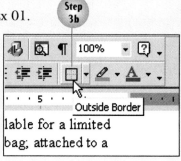

Step 3b

4. Complete steps similar to those in 3 to add a border to the second paragraph.
5. Complete steps similar to those in 3 to add a border to the third paragraph.
6. Save the document again with the same name (Ch 14, Ex 01).
7. Print Ch 14, Ex 01.
8. With the document still open, remove the borders by completing the following steps:

    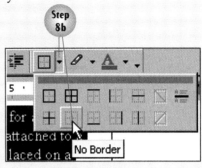

    a. Select the three paragraphs in the document. (You do not have to select all the text in the first and last paragraphs, just a portion.)
    b. Click the down-pointing triangle at the right side of the Border button on the Formatting toolbar and then click the No Border option (second option from the left in the bottom row). (This removes the borders from the three paragraphs.)
    c. Deselect the text.
9. Add a border around and between the paragraphs by completing the following steps:

    a. Select from the middle of the first paragraph to somewhere in the middle of the third paragraph.
    b. Click the down-pointing triangle at the right side of the Border button and then click the All Borders option (second option from the left in the top row).
    c. Deselect the text.
10. Save the document again with the same name (Ch 14, Ex 01).
11. Print and then close Ch 14, Ex 01.

Adding Borders and Shading

As you learned in the previous section, borders can be added to a paragraph or selected paragraphs with options from the Border button on the Formatting toolbar. If you want to customize the line creating the border or add shading, use options from the Borders and Shading dialog box. To display this dialog box, shown in figure 14.2, click Format and then Borders and Shading.

figure

14.2 **Borders and Shading Dialog Box with the Borders Tab Selected**

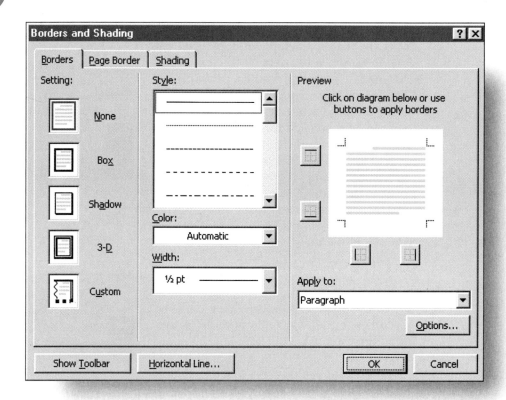

The buttons in the Setting section of the dialog box contain a visual display of line options. For example, click the Box button to insert a border around the paragraph (or selected paragraphs). Click the 3-D button to insert a border with a shadow, creating a three-dimensional look.

With the options in the Style list box, you can change the line style by clicking the desired style in the list box. The default line color is black. This can be changed to a different color by clicking the down-pointing triangle at the right side of the Color text box and then clicking the desired color at the drop-down list. If the desired color is not visible, scroll down the list. The default line width is ½ point. The line width can be changed by clicking the down-pointing triangle at the right side of the Width text box and then clicking the desired width at the pop-up list.

The diagram in the Preview section offers another method for inserting border lines. Specify where you want a border line to appear by clicking the desired location on the diagram. For example, if you want to insert a border at the bottom of the paragraph (or selected paragraphs), click the bottom portion of the diagram in the Preview section. This adds a border line to the diagram. You can also click a button in the Preview section that displays the desired border. For example, to add a border at the right side of the paragraph (or selected paragraphs), click the button that displays at the bottom of the diagram at the right side.

The Apply to option has a setting of *Paragraph*. This specifies to what the border and shading will apply. Click the Options button and options display for setting the desired distance between the edge of the border and the text.

Adding a Customized Border to a Document

1. Open Notice 02.
2. Save the document with Save As and name it Ch 14, Ex 02.
3. Make the following changes to the document:
    a. With the insertion point at the beginning of the document, press the Enter key twice.
    b. Select the entire document and then change the font to 18-point Mistral bold and the text color to Dark Red. (If Mistral is not available, choose a fancy, decorative typeface.)
    c. With the entire document still selected, add a dark blue shadow border by completing the following steps:
        1) Click Format and then Borders and Shading.
        2) At the Borders and Shading dialog box with the Borders tab selected, click the Shadow button.
        3) Click the down-pointing triangle at the right side of the Width text box and then click the *6 pt* line at the pop-up list.
        4) Click the down-pointing triangle at the right side of the Color text box and then click the Dark Blue color at the drop-down list.
        5) Click OK or press Enter.
4. Deselect the text and then save the document again with the same name (Ch 14, Ex 02).
5. Print and then close Ch 14, Ex 02.

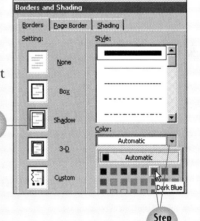

Adding Shading

With choices from the Borders and Shading dialog box with the Shading tab selected, shown in figure 14.3, you can add shading to the border around text. Fill color choices display in the upper left corner of the dialog box. To add a fill, click the desired color in this section. If you want to add a pattern, click the down-pointing triangle at the right side of the Style text box and then click the desired pattern at the drop-down list. If a pattern is added inside a border, the color of the pattern can be changed with the Color option. Click the down-pointing triangle at the right side of the Color text box and then click the desired color at the drop-down list.

The Preview area of the Borders and Shading dialog box with the Shading tab selected displays how the border shading and/or pattern will display.

figure
14.3

Borders and Shading Dialog Box with Shading Tab Selected

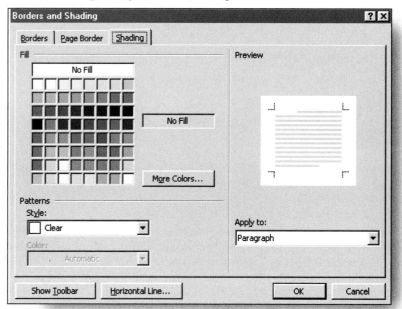

exercise 3

Adding Borders and Shading to Paragraphs of Text

1. Open Para 03.
2. Save the document with Save As and name it Ch 14, Ex 03.
3. Create a border around all the paragraphs in the document that is 3 points thick and contains 5% shading by completing the following steps:
   a. Select all paragraphs in the document (except the last two blank lines).
   b. Click Format and then Borders and Shading.
   c. At the Borders and Shading dialog box with the Borders tab selected, click the Box button located at the left side of the dialog box.
   d. Click the down-pointing triangle at the right side of the Width text box and then click *3 pt* at the pop-up list.
   e. Make sure that *Automatic* is selected in the Color text box. If not, click the down-pointing triangle at the right side of the Color text box and then click *Automatic* at the drop-down list. (This option is located at the beginning of the list.)
   f. Click the Shading tab.
   g. Click the light turquoise color in the Fill section of the dialog box.
   h. Click the down-pointing triangle at the right side of the Style list box and then click *5%* at the drop-down list.

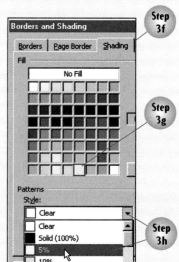

    i.   Click OK to close the dialog box.
4. Deselect the text and then save the document again with the same name (Ch 14, Ex 03).
5. Print and then close Ch 14, Ex 03.

Adding a Border and Shading to a Document

1. Open Notice 03.
2. Save the document with Save As and name it Ch 14, Ex 04.
3. Make the following changes to the document:
   a. With the insertion point positioned at the beginning of the document, press the Enter key twice.
   b. Select the entire document and then change the paragraph alignment to centered.
   c. With the entire document still selected, add a border and shading by completing the following steps:

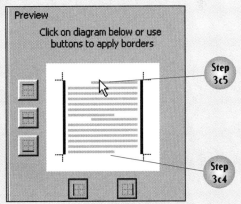

   1) Click Format and then Borders and Shading.
   2) At the Borders and Shading dialog box with the Borders tab selected, click the Box button located at the left side of the dialog box.
   3) Click the down-pointing triangle at the right side of the Width text box and then click 2¼ pt at the pop-up list.
   4) Click the bottom line of the diagram in the Preview section. (This removes the line.)
   5) Click the top line of the diagram in the Preview section. (This removes the line.)
   6) Click the Shading tab.
   7) At the Borders and Shading dialog box with the Shading tab selected, click the first color in the bottom row in the Fill section (this is a rose color).
   8) Click OK to close the dialog box.

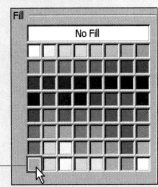

4. Deselect the text and then save the document again with the same name (Ch 14, Ex 04).
5. Print and then close Ch 14, Ex 04.

Word's border feature can be used to add lines in headers and/or footers. For example, you can add a line below text in a header or add a line above text in a footer. This line acts as a graphics element that adds visual appeal to a document.

Adding a Footer and Border Line to a Document

1. Open Report 02.
2. Save the document with Save As and name it Ch 14, Ex 05.
3. Create a footer that prints on every page of the document and contains a border line by completing the following steps:
   a. Click <u>V</u>iew and then <u>H</u>eader and Footer.
   b. At the header pane, click the Switch Between Header and Footer button on the Header and Footer toolbar.
   c. At the footer pane, turn on bold, and then key **Desktop Publishing** at the left margin.
   d. Press the Tab key twice.
   e. Key **Page** and then press the spacebar.
   f. Click the Insert Page Number button on the Header and Footer toolbar.
   g. Select the number 1, turn on bold, and then deselect the text.
   h. Click F<u>o</u>rmat and then <u>B</u>orders and Shading.
   i. At the Borders and Shading dialog box with the <u>B</u>orders tab selected, click the down-pointing triangle at the right side of the St<u>y</u>le list box until the first thick/thin double line displays and then click the thick/thin double line.
   j. Check the diagram in the Preview section of the dialog box. Click each side to remove the border line except the top border.
   k. Click OK to close the dialog box.
   l. Click the <u>C</u>lose button to close the Header and Footer toolbar.
4. Check the page breaks in the report and, if necessary, adjust the page breaks.
5. Save the document again with the same name (Ch 14, Ex 05).
6. Print and then close Ch 14, Ex 05.

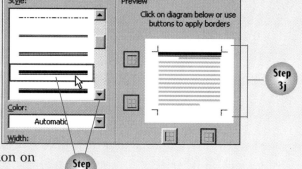

Inserting Horizontal Lines

In exercise 5, you inserted a thick/thin double line in a footer. Word also includes a horizontal line feature that inserts a graphic horizontal line in a document. To display the Horizontal Line dialog box shown in figure 14.4, display the Borders and Shading dialog box with any tab selected, and then click the <u>H</u>orizontal Line button located at the bottom of the dialog box.

figure
14.4 *Horizontal Line Dialog Box*

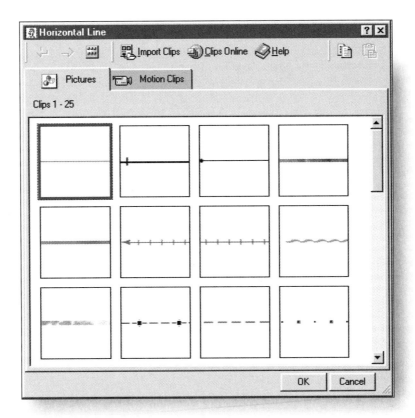

Insert a horizontal line into a document by clicking the desired line option and then clicking the Insert clip button that displays in a callout side menu. The Insert clip button displays at the top of the callout side menu. The Preview clip button displays in the callout side menu below the Insert clip button. Click this button to view how the horizontal line will display in the document.

Insert Clip

Preview Clip

exercise 6

Inserting Horizontal Lines in a Document

1. Open Notice 02.
2. Save the document with Save As and name it Ch 14, Ex 06.
3. Make the following changes to the document:
   a. Select the entire document, change the font to 14-point Goudy Old Style bold, and then deselect the document.
   b. Move the insertion point to the beginning of the document and then press Enter three times.
   c. Move the insertion point back to the beginning of the document and then insert a graphic horizontal line by completing the following steps:
      1) Click Format and then Borders and Shading.
      2) At the Borders and Shading dialog box, click the Horizontal Line button located at the bottom of the dialog box.
      3) At the Horizontal Line dialog box, click the last horizontal line option in the second row (see figure at right), and then click the Insert clip button at the callout side menu.
   d. Move the insertion point a triple space below the last line of text in the document and then insert the same graphic horizontal line as the one inserted in step 3c.
4. Save the document again with the same name (Ch 14, Ex 06).
5. Print and then close Ch 14, Ex 06.

Step 3c3

Adding Page Borders

The borders you have created have been included in a paragraph of text or selected paragraphs. Word also includes a page border feature that will insert a border around an entire page rather than just a paragraph. To insert a page border in a document, display the Borders and Shading dialog box and then click the Page Border tab. This displays the dialog box as shown in figure 14.5.

The options at the Borders and Shading dialog box with the Page Border tab selected are basically the same as those for paragraph borders. The difference is that the border is inserted around the page rather than the paragraph of text.

Specify on what page you want the page border to print with the Apply to option at the Borders and Shading dialog box with the Page Border tab selected. Click the down-pointing triangle at the right side of the Apply to option and then choose one of the following options: *Whole document, This section, This Section – First page only,* and *This Section – All except first page*

figure
14.5
Borders and Shading Dialog Box with _Page Border_ Tab Selected

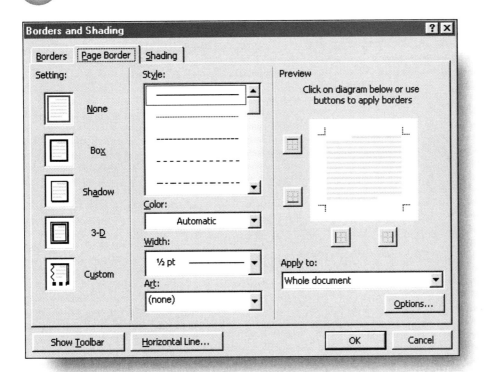

exercise 7

Inserting a Page Border in a Document

1. Open Report 02.
2. Save the document with Save As and name it Ch 14, Ex 07.
3. Make the following changes to the document:
   a. Select the entire document and then change the font to 12-point Garamond (or a similar serif typeface).
   b. Bold the following title and headings in the document:

   DESKTOP PUBLISHING DESIGN
   Designing a Document
   Creating Focus

4. Add a border to only the first page in the document by completing the following steps:
   a. With the insertion point positioned at the beginning of the document, click Format and then Borders and Shading.
   b. At the Borders and Shading dialog box, click the Page Border tab.
   c. Click the Box button in the Setting section.
   d. Scroll down the list of line styles in the Style list box until the end of the list displays and then click the third line from the end.
   e. Click the down-pointing triangle at the right side of the Apply to option and then click *This Section – First page only* at the drop-down list.
   f. Click OK to close the dialog box.
5. Save the document again with the same name (Ch 14, Ex 07).
6. Print and then close Ch 14, Ex 07.

The Borders and Shading dialog box with the Page Border tab selected offers an option for inserting on the page a border containing an image. To display the images available, click the down-pointing triangle at the right side of the Art text box and then scroll down the list. Click the desired image; this image is used to create the border around the page.

exercise 8

Inserting a Page Border Containing Balloons

1. Open Notice 01.
2. Save the document with Save As and name it Ch 14, Ex 08.
3. Make the following changes to the document:
   a. Select the entire document and then change to a decorative font of your choosing.
   b. Center the text vertically on the page by completing the following steps:
      1) Click File and then Page Setup.
      2) At the Page Setup dialog box, click the Layout tab.
      3) At the Page Setup dialog box with the Layout tab selected, click the down-pointing triangle at the right side of the Vertical alignment text box, and then click *Center* at the drop-down list.
      4) Click OK to close the Page Setup dialog box.

4. Add a decorative border to the document by completing the following steps:
   a. Display the Borders and Shading dialog box.
   b. At the Borders and Shading dialog box, click the Page Border tab.
   c. Click the Bo_x button in the Setting section.
   d. Click the down-pointing triangle at the right side of the A_rt text box.
   e. At the drop-down list that displays, scroll down the list until balloons display, and then click the balloons.
   f. Click OK to close the dialog box.
5. Save the document again with the same name (Ch 14, Ex 08).
6. Print and then close Ch 14, Ex 08.

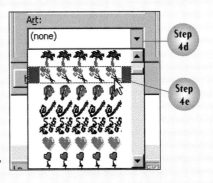

Step 4d

Step 4e

Adding Clip Art to Documents

Word 2000 includes a gallery of clip art images that can be inserted in a document. To insert a clip art image, click Insert, point to Picture, and then click Clip Art. This displays the Insert ClipArt dialog box with the Pictures tab selected as shown in figure 14.6.

Insert ClipArt Dialog Box with Pictures Tab Selected

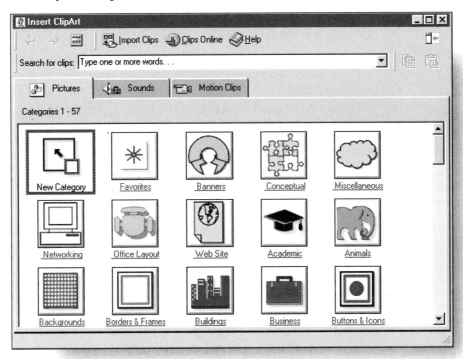

Insert Clip Art

Another method for displaying the Insert ClipArt dialog box is to click the Insert Clip Art button on the Drawing toolbar. To display the Drawing toolbar, position the mouse pointer on the Standard or Formatting toolbar, click the *right* mouse button, and then click Drawing at the drop-down list. You can also display clip art categories and images by clicking Insert and then Object. At the Object dialog box with the Create New tab selected, double-click *Microsoft Clip Gallery* in the list box. This displays the Microsoft Clip Gallery that contains the same options as the Insert ClipArt dialog box.

At the Insert ClipArt dialog box with the Pictures tab selected, click a category in the category list box. This displays a list of clip art available for the category. To insert a clip art image in the document, click the desired clip art, and then click the Insert clip button at the top of the callout side menu that displays. Remove the Insert ClipArt dialog box from the screen by clicking the Close button (contains an X) located in the upper right corner of the dialog box.

Back

All Categories

Maneuver through categories and clip art at the Insert ClipArt dialog box using buttons on the toolbar that displays at the top of the dialog box. For example, click the Back button to display clip art for the previously selected category. To redisplay all categories, click the All Categories button.

Add clip to Favorites or other category

Find similar clips

When you click a clip art image, a callout side menu displays containing several buttons. Click the Insert clip button to insert the image in the document. Click the Preview clip button to view how the clip art image will display in the document. If you want to add a clip art image to the Favorites category or to any other category, click the Add clip to Favorites or other category button. This expands the side menu and displays an option for entering the desired category. The side menu will continue to display expanded until you click the button again. Clicking the Find similar clips button on the callout side menu causes the side menu to expand and display with options for finding clips with similar styles, colors, shapes, and keywords. The side menu will remain expanded until you click the button again.

Sizing a Clip Art Image

Once a clip art image is inserted in a document, it can be sized using the sizing handles that display around a selected clip art image. To change the size of a clip art image, click in the image to select it, and then position the mouse pointer on a sizing handle until the pointer turns into a double-headed arrow. Hold down the left mouse button, drag the sizing handle in or out to decrease or increase the size of the image, and then release the mouse button.

Use the middle sizing handles at the left or right side of the image to make the image wider or thinner. Use the middle sizing handles at the top or bottom of the image to make the image taller or shorter. Use the sizing handles at the corners of the image to change both the width and height at the same time.

When sizing a clip art image, consider using the horizontal and vertical rulers that display in the Print Layout view. To deselect an image, click anywhere in the document outside the image.

exercise 9

Viewing Clip Art Images and Then Inserting and Sizing an Image in a Document

1. At a clear document screen, insert and then size a clip art image by completing the following steps:
   a. Change to the Print Layout view.
   b. Click <u>I</u>nsert, point to <u>P</u>icture, and then click <u>C</u>lip Art.
   c. At the Insert ClipArt dialog box (see figure 14.6), click the *Academic* category in the category list box (contains an image of a graduation cap).

   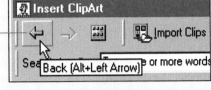

   d. Scroll through the list of academic clip art images.
   e. Click the Back button located at the left side of the Insert ClipArt dialog box.
   f. Scroll down the list of categories and then click the *Home & Family* category (contains an image of a house with people inside).

   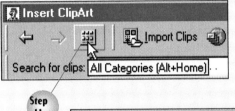

   g. Scroll through the list of home and family clip art images.
   h. Click the All Categories button located on the Insert ClipArt dialog box toolbar.

   i. Click the *Animals* category in the category list box (contains an image of an elephant).
   j. Click once on the bird clip art. (If this image is not available, click another animal of your choosing.)
   k. At the callout side menu, click the Insert clip button (top button).
   l. Click the close button (contains an X) that displays in the upper right corner of the dialog box.
   m. Decrease the size of the bird image by completing the following steps:
      1) Click the image to select it (black sizing handles display around the image).
      2) If necessary, click the down scroll triangle on the vertical scroll bar until the bottom sizing handles display.
      3) Position the mouse pointer on the bottom right sizing handle until the pointer turns into a diagonally pointing two-headed arrow.

4) Hold down the left mouse button, drag up and to the left until the size of the image is approximately 2 inches in width by 2.25 inches in height (use the horizontal and vertical rulers as visual aids), and then release the left mouse button.

5) Deselect the image.

2. Save the document and name it Ch 14, Ex 09.

3. Print and then close Ch 14, Ex 09.

Formatting Clip Art Images with Buttons on the Picture Toolbar

Clip art images inserted in a document can be formatted in a variety of ways. Formatting might include adding fill color and border lines, increasing or decreasing the brightness or contrast, choosing a wrapping style, and cropping the image. A variety of methods are available for changing the formatting of a clip art image. You can format an image with buttons on the Picture toolbar or options at the Format Picture dialog box.

To display the Picture toolbar, click a clip art image. This displays the Picture toolbar shown in figure 14.7. The buttons on the Picture toolbar are described in figure 14.8. (If the Picture toolbar does not display when you click a clip art image, position the mouse pointer on the image, click the *right* mouse button, and then click Show Picture Toolbar.)

14.7   *Picture Toolbar*

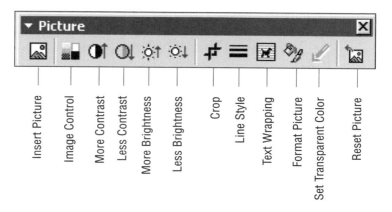

figure
14.8 — Picture Toolbar Buttons

Click this button	Named	To do this
![Insert Picture icon]	Insert Picture	Display the Insert Picture dialog box with a list of subfolders containing additional images.
![Image Control icon]	Image Control	Display a drop-down list with options for controlling how the image displays. Options include <u>A</u>utomatic, <u>G</u>rayscale, <u>B</u>lack & White, and <u>W</u>atermark.
![More Contrast icon]	More Contrast	Increase contrast of the image.
![Less Contrast icon]	Less Contrast	Decrease contrast of the image.
![More Brightness icon]	More Brightness	Increase brightness of the image.
![Less Brightness icon]	Less Brightness	Decrease brightness of the image.
![Crop icon]	Crop	Crop image so only a specific portion of the image is visible.
![Line Style icon]	Line Style	Insert a border around the image and specify the border line style.
![Text Wrapping icon]	Text Wrapping	Specify how text will wrap around or through the image. Choices include <u>S</u>quare, <u>T</u>ight, Th<u>r</u>ough, <u>N</u>one, T<u>o</u>p and Bottom, and <u>E</u>dit Wrap Points.
![Format Picture icon]	Format Picture	Display Format Picture dialog box with options for formatting the image. Tabs in the dialog box include Colors and Lines, Size, Position, Wrapping, and Picture.
![Set Transparent Color icon]	Set Transparent Color	This button is not active. (When an image contains a transparent area, the background color or texture of the page shows through the image. Set transparent color in Microsoft Photo Editor.)
![Reset Picture icon]	Reset Picture	Reset picture to its original size, position, and color.

Moving a Clip Art Image

Text
Wrapping

To move a clip art image in a document you must first choose a text wrapping option. To do this, select the image, click the Text Wrapping button on the Picture toolbar, and then click a wrapping option. This changes the sizing handles that display around the selected image from black to white. With white sizing handles displayed, position the mouse pointer inside the image until the pointer turns into a four-headed arrow. Hold down the left mouse button, drag the image to the desired position, and then release the mouse button.

Inserting, Moving, and Customizing a Clip Art Image

1. At a clear document screen, insert, move, and then size a clip art image by completing the following steps:
   a. Change to the Print Layout view.
   b. Display the Drawing toolbar by positioning the mouse pointer on the Standard or Formatting toolbar, clicking the *right* mouse button, and then clicking Drawing at the drop-down list.
   c. Click the Insert Clip Art button on the Drawing toolbar.
   d. At the Insert ClipArt dialog box, click the *Academic* category in the category list box (contains an image of a graduation cap).
   e. Click once on the books clip art. (If this image is not available, click another academic image of your choosing.)
   f. At the callout side menu, click the Insert clip button (top button).
   g. Click the Close button (contains an X) that displays in the upper right corner of the dialog box.

   Step 1e

   Insert clip

   Step 1f

   h. Customize the image of the books using buttons on the Picture toolbar by completing the following steps:
      1) Click the image to select it (black sizing handles display around the image).
      2) Click eight times on the More Contrast button on the Picture toolbar. (This increases the contrast of the colors used in the image.)
      3) Click twice on the More Brightness button on the Picture toolbar.
   i. Change the size of the image by completing the following steps:
      1) Scroll down the page until the bottom of the book image displays.
      2) Position the mouse pointer on the black sizing handle that displays in the lower right corner until a diagonally pointed, two-headed arrow displays.
      3) Hold down the left mouse button, drag into the image to decrease the size until it measures approximately 3.5 inches in width and 3 inches in height, and then release the mouse button. (Use the horizontal and vertical rulers to help you approximate the size.)

j. Move the image by completing the following steps:

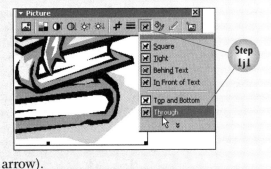

Step 1j1

1) With the image still selected, click the Text Wrapping button on the Picture toolbar, and then click Through at the drop-down list. (This changes the sizing handles from black to white.)
2) Position the mouse pointer inside the image (displays as a four-headed arrow).
3) Hold down the left mouse button, drag the outline of the image so it is centered horizontally between the left and right margins, and then release the mouse button.

k. Add a border line to the image by clicking the Line Style button on the Picture toolbar and then clicking the first *3 pt* option that displays at the drop-down list.

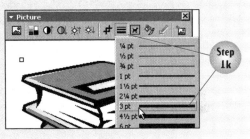

Step 1k

l. Click outside the clip art image to deselect it.

2. Save the document and name it Ch 14, Ex 10.
3. Print and then close Ch 14, Ex 10.

exercise 11

Inserting, Sizing, and Customizing a Clip Art Image

1. At a clear document screen, create the letterhead shown in figure 14.9 by completing the following steps:
   a. Change to the Print Layout view.
   b. Change the font to 36-point Brittanic Bold. (If Britannic Bold is not available, choose a typeface similar to the one shown in figure 14.9.)
   c. Key the company name *Movie Madness* and then press Enter.
   d. Change the font size to 18 points and then key the remaining text in the location indicated in figure 14.9 (the street address, city, state, Zip, and Web site address).
   e. Move the insertion point to the beginning of the document.
   f. Insert the image by completing the following steps:
      1) Make sure the Drawing toolbar is displayed. (If the Drawing toolbar is not displayed, position the mouse pointer on the Standard or Formatting toolbar, click the *right* mouse button, and then click Drawing at the drop-down list.)
      2) Click the Insert Clip Art button on the Drawing toolbar.
      3) At the Insert ClipArt dialog box, click the _Entertainment_ category in the category list box (contains an image of a microphone).
      4) Click once on the image of a movie projector (see figure 14.9).
      5) At the callout side menu that displays, click the Insert clip button (top button).
      6) Click the Close button that displays in the upper right corner of the dialog box.

g. Size the image by completing the following steps:
   1) Click once on the clip art image to select it (black sizing handles display).
   2) Position the mouse pointer on the black sizing handle that displays in the lower right corner until a diagonally pointed, two-headed arrow displays.
   3) Hold down the left mouse button, drag into the image to decrease the size until it measures approximately two inches by two inches, and then release the mouse button. (Use the horizontal and vertical rulers to help you approximate the size.)
h. Change the text wrapping of the clip art image and move the image by completing the following steps:
   1) With the clip art image selected (black sizing handles display around the image), click the Text Wrapping button on the Picture toolbar.
   2) At the drop-down list that displays, click Through.
   3) Position the mouse pointer (displays as a four-headed arrow) inside the clip art image, hold down the left mouse button, drag the image to the right margin at approximately the same horizontal position as the company name (see figure 14.9), and then release the mouse button.
2. Save the document and name it Ch 14, Ex 11.
3. Print and then close Ch 14, Ex 11.

14.9   *Exercise 11*

Movie Madness
1204 Ridgeway Avenue
Richmond, VA 24365
(804) 555-8880
www.mmadness.com

Searching for Clip Art Images

At the Insert ClipArt dialog box, you can search for a clip art image related to a specific topic or subject. To do this, display the Insert ClipArt dialog box, click in the Search for clips text box, key the topic or subject, and then press Enter. Word searches through the clip art images and then displays those images that match the topic or subject.

Cropping and Adding a Border to a Clip Art Image

1. At a clear document screen, insert a clip art image in a document, add a border to the image, crop the image, and then move the image by completing the following steps:

   Step 1c

   a. Change to the Print Layout view.
   b. Click Insert, point to Picture, and then click Clip Art.
   c. At the Insert ClipArt dialog box, click in the Search for clips text box, key **flags**, and then press Enter.
   d. Click once on the image shown at the right and then click the Insert clip button.
   e. Click the Close button that displays in the upper right corner of the dialog box.
   f. Click once on the image to select it.
   g. Make sure the Picture toolbar is displayed. (If it is not, position the mouse pointer in the image, click the *right* mouse button, and then click Show Picture Toolbar.)
   h. Crop the image so just the flag displays by completing the following steps:

      Step 1d   Step 1h1

      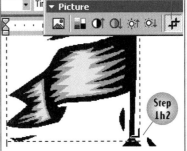

      1) Click the Crop button on the Picture toolbar.
      2) Position the mouse pointer on the bottom right sizing handle (the mouse pointer turns into a crop tool, which is a black square with overlapping lines), hold down the left mouse button, drag into the image to isolate the flag as shown at the right, and then release the mouse button.

         Step 1h2

      3) If necessary, drag other sizing handles (make sure the mouse pointer turns into the crop tool) until only the flag appears in the image border. (This may take some practice. If you are not satisfied with the result, click the Reset Picture button on the Picture toolbar and then try again.)
      4) With the flag isolated, click the Crop button on the Picture toolbar to turn it off.

   i. Increase the size of the clip art image so it is approximately 3 inches by 3 inches.
   j. Click the Text Wrapping button on the Picture toolbar and then click Through at the drop-down list. (This changes the sizing handles from black to white.)
   k. Move the image so it is centered horizontally between the left and right margins.

      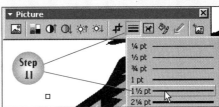

   l. Add a border line to the image by clicking the Line Style button on the Picture toolbar and then clicking the *1½ pt* option at the drop-down list.

      Step 1l

   m. Click outside the image to deselect it.

2. Save the image and name it Ch 14, Ex 12.
3. Print and then close Ch 14, Ex 12.

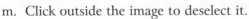

Creating a Watermark

An interesting effect can be created in a document with a watermark. A *watermark* is a lightened image that displays in a document. Text can be inserted in front of the watermark creating a document with a foreground and a background. The foreground is the text and the background is the watermark image. Figure 14.10 shows an example of a watermark you will be creating in exercise 13. The image of the leaves is the watermark and creates the background, and the text of the notice displays in front of the watermark and creates the foreground.

Watermark Example

MEEKER HIGH SCHOOL

Fall Performance

Performing Arts Center

Tuesday, October 16, 2001

7:00 p.m.

A Word document contains three levels: the text layer, a layer above the text, and a layer behind. The text layer is the one in which you generally work in a document. An object created with buttons on the Drawing toolbar can be drawn in a document containing text. By default, the object will display above the text layer, covering the text. If you want the object and the text in the document to display, move the object behind the text. You can do this with the Behind Text option from the Text Wrapping button on the Picture toolbar. Creating a watermark involves using the Image Control button on the Picture toolbar along with the Text Wrapping button.

Image Control

exercise 13

Creating a Watermark in a Document

1. Open Notice 04.
2. Save the document with Save As and name it Ch 14, Ex 13.
3. Make the following changes to the document:

   a. Select the entire document and then change the font to 18-point Goudy Old Style bold (or a similar decorative typeface).

   b. Deselect the text.

   c. Move the insertion point to the beginning of the document.

   d. Display the Insert ClipArt dialog box.

   e. At the Insert ClipArt dialog box, click in the Search for clips text box, key **leaves**, and then press Enter.

   f. When the images display, click the image of leaves shown in figure 14.10 and then click the Insert clip button.

   g. Close the Insert ClipArt dialog box.

   h. Click once on the image to select it.

   i. Decrease the size of the image by dragging the bottom right sizing handle to approximately the 3.75-inch mark on the horizontal ruler and the 3-inch mark on the vertical ruler.

   j. Click the Image Control button on the Picture toolbar and then click <u>W</u>atermark at the drop-down list that displays. (If the Picture toolbar is not displayed, display it by positioning the mouse pointer on the image, clicking the *right* mouse button, and then clicking Show Pictu<u>r</u>e Toolbar.)

   k. Click the Text Wrapping button on the Picture toolbar and then click Behin<u>d</u> Text at the drop-down list.

   l. With the watermark image still selected, drag it to the right so it is better centered beneath the text as shown in figure 14.10.

   m. Click outside the image to deselect it.

4. Save the document again with the same name (Ch 14, Ex 13).

5. Print and then close Ch 14, Ex 13.

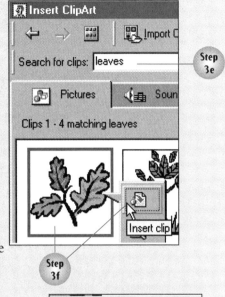

Step 3e

Step 3f

Step 3j

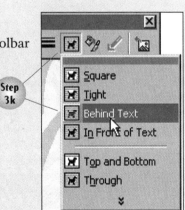

Step 3k

Formatting Clip Art Images at the Format Picture Dialog Box

Format Picture

With buttons on the Picture toolbar you can customize a clip art image. The same options on the Picture toolbar are also available at the Format Picture dialog box along with additional options. To display the Format Picture dialog box, select a clip art image, and then click the Format Picture button on the Picture toolbar. You can also display the Format Picture dialog box by selecting a clip art image and then clicking Format and then Picture.

The Format Picture dialog box displays with a variety of tabs. When you first display the Format Picture dialog box, more than likely, the Picture tab will be selected as shown in figure 14.11. With options from this dialog box, you can use specific measurements to crop an image and change the color, brightness, and contrast of an image. These same options are available with buttons on the Picture toolbar.

Format Picture Dialog Box with Picture Tab Selected

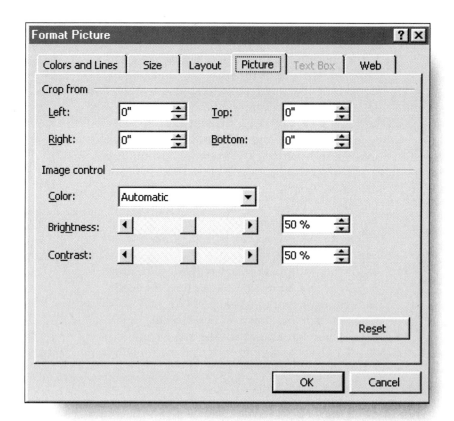

If you click the Colors and Lines tab on the Format Picture dialog box, the dialog box displays as shown in figure 14.12. A clip art image is inserted inside a border. This border is not visible by default. A fill can be added inside the border of the clip art image with the Color option in the Fill section. Add a border line to the image with choices from the Color options in the Line section. When you choose a border line color, the Dashed, Style, and Weight options become available. Use these options to further customize the border line.

14.12 **Format Picture Dialog Box with Colors and Lines Tab Selected**

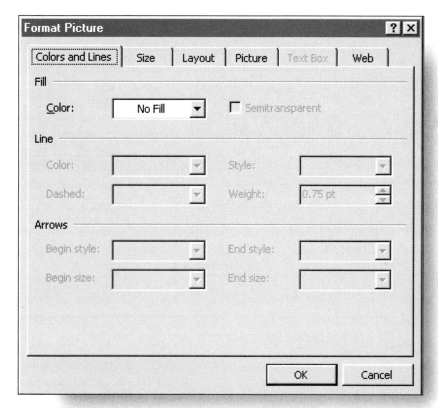

Click the Size tab at the Format Picture dialog box and the dialog box displays as shown in figure 14.13. At this dialog box, you can specify the height and width of the image as well as specify a percentage of scale for the height and width of the image.

figure

14.13

Format Picture Dialog Box with Size Tab Selected

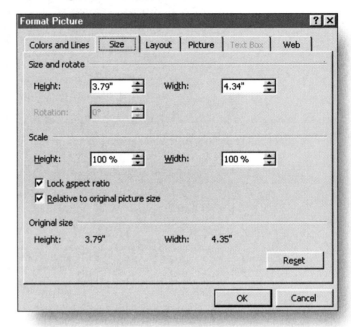

Click the Layout tab and the dialog box displays as shown in figure 14.14 with options for choosing a wrapping style and a horizontal alignment. The wrapping style options are similar to those available from the Text Wrapping button on the Picture toolbar. Choose an option in the Horizontal alignment section to specify where the clip art image aligns.

figure

14.14

Format Picture Dialog Box with Layout Tab Selected

Click the Advanced button located at the bottom of the Format Picture dialog box with the Layout tab selected and the Advanced Layout dialog box with the Picture Position tab selected displays as shown in figure 14.15. With options at this dialog box, you can specify the horizontal and vertical positioning of a clip art image on the page.

14.15 *Advanced Layout Dialog Box with Picture Position Tab Selected*

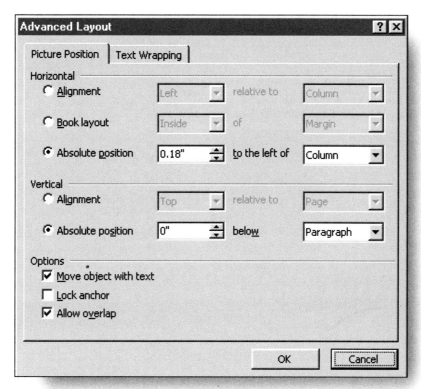

Click the Text Wrapping tab at the Advanced Layout dialog box and additional wrapping options display as shown in figure 14.16. At this dialog box, specify the wrapping style, which side of the image you want text wrapped, and the distance from text.

figure
14.16
Advanced Layout Dialog Box with Text Wrapping Tab Selected

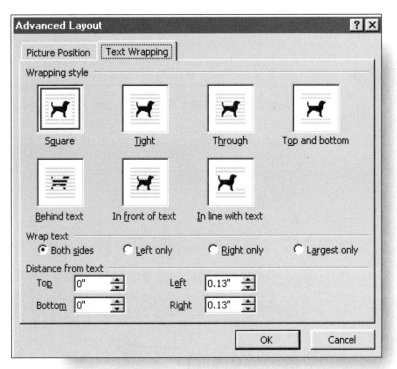

exercise 14

Formatting a Clip Art Image at the Format Picture Dialog Box

1. Open Para 04.
2. Save the document with Save As and name it Ch 14, Ex 14.
3. Select the entire document and then change the font to 13-point Garamond. (If this typeface is not available, choose a similar serif typeface such as Century Schoolbook.)
4. Deselect the text and then move the insertion point to the beginning of the document.
5. Insert a clip art image of a computer in the document as shown in figure 14.17 by completing the following steps:
   a. Change to the Print Layout view.
   b. Click Insert, point to Picture, and then click Clip Art.
   c. At the Insert ClipArt dialog box, click in the Search for clips text box, key **computer**, and then press Enter.
   d. Click once on the computer image shown in figure 14.17. (If this image is not available, choose another computer image.)
   e. At the callout side menu that displays, click the Insert clip button.

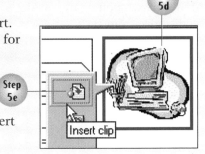

f. Click the Close button that displays in the upper right corner of the dialog box.

g. Click once on the image to select it.

h. Change the wrapping style, add a border, and change the size of the image by completing the following steps:

1) With the image selected, click the Text Wrapping button on the Picture toolbar and then click Through at the drop-down list. (This changes the sizing handles from black to white.)

2) With the image still selected, click the Format Picture button on the Picture toolbar.

3) At the Format Picture dialog box, click the Colors and Lines tab.

4) Click the down-pointing triangle at the right side of the Color text box in the Line section and then click the Black color option (first option in the top row).

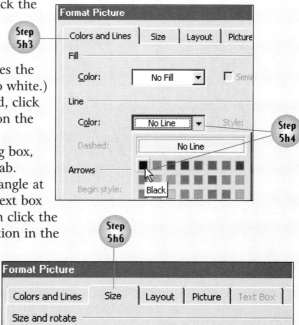

5) Click the up-pointing triangle at the right side of the Weight text box until *1 pt* displays in the text box.

6) Click the Size tab located at the top of the dialog box.

7) Select the current measurement in the Height text box and then key **1**.

8) Select the current measurement in the Width text box and then key **2**.

9) Click the Layout tab.

10) Click the Left option in the Horizontal alignment section of the dialog box.

11) Click OK to close the Format Picture dialog box.

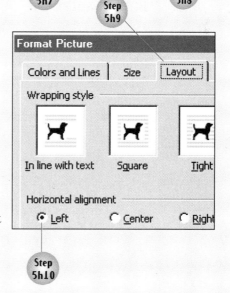

6. At the document screen, click outside the image to deselect it. (Make sure the computer image displays at the left margin next to the first paragraph of text. If the image appears to be out of alignment, select the image, and then drag it to a more desirable location.)

7. Save the document again with the same name (Ch 14, Ex 14).

8. Print and then close Ch 14, Ex 14.

figure

14.17 *Exercise 14*

Word, one of the best-selling word processing programs for microcomputers, includes a wide variety of desktop publishing features. The scope and capabilities of these features have expanded with each new Word version. Some of the desktop publishing features include a wide variety of fonts and special symbols, drawing, charting, text design capabilities, graphic manipulation, templates, and much more.

Design can be learned by studying design and by experimentation. Collect and study designs that are attractive and visually interesting. Analyze what makes the design and layout unique and try using the same principles or variations in your publications. Take advantage of the special design and layout features that Word for Windows has to offer. Take the time to design. Layout and design is a lengthy process of revising, refining, and making adjustments. Start with small variations from the default formats to create designs that are attractive and visually interesting.

Downloading Clip Art

(Note: The following steps and the steps in exercise 15 assume that Microsoft Internet Explorer is your default browser. If this is not your default browser, steps may need to be modified. Please check with your instructor.)

The Microsoft Web site offers a clip gallery with hundreds of clip art images you can download. To display the Microsoft Clip Gallery, you must have access to the Internet. (You will learn more about the Internet in chapter 16.) To download a clip art image, you would complete these basic steps:

Clips Online

1. Make sure you are connected to the Internet.
2. Display the Insert ClipArt dialog box.
3. At the Insert ClipArt dialog box, click the Clips Online button that displays toward the top of the dialog box.
4. At the message telling you to click OK to browse additional clips from a special Web page, click the OK button.
5. At the End-User License Agreement page, read the agreement, and then click the Accept button if you accept the terms of the agreement.
6. At the Microsoft Clip Gallery shown in figure 14.18 (your screen may vary), search for the desired image.
7. Download the desired image by clicking the download button that displays below the image.
8. Close the Insert ClipArt dialog box.
9. Close Microsoft Internet Explorer.

figure

14.18

Microsoft Clip Gallery

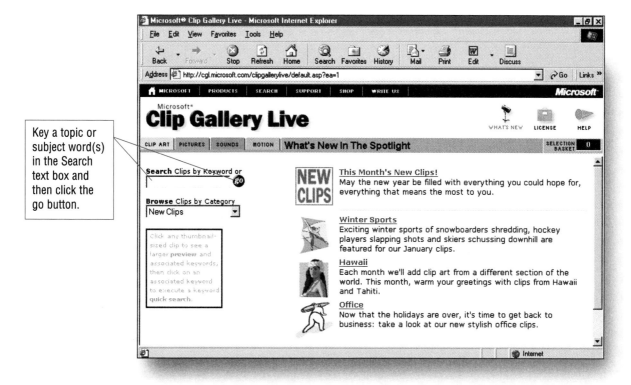

Key a topic or subject word(s) in the Search text box and then click the go button.

A downloaded clip is usually inserted in the Downloaded Clips category. To insert a downloaded clip art, display the Insert ClipArt dialog box, display the Downloaded Clips category, click the desired image, and then click the Insert clip button.

Deleting Downloaded Clip Art

Delete a clip art image from the Insert ClipArt dialog box by right-clicking the image and then clicking the Delete option from the shortcut menu. At the message telling you to click OK to delete the clip from all Clip Gallery categories, click the OK button.

Downloading a Clip Art Image from the Microsoft Clip Gallery

(Check with your instructor before completing this exercise to determine if you can download clip art with your system configuration.)

1. Open Notice 02.
2. Save the document with Save As and name it Ch 14, Ex 15.
3. Select the entire document, change the font to 18-point Goudy Old Style bold (or a similar serif typeface), and then deselect the document.
4. Download the umbrella clip shown in figure 14.19 from the Microsoft Clip Gallery by completing the following steps:
   a. Make sure you are connected to the Internet.
   b. Display the Insert ClipArt dialog box.
   c. At the Insert ClipArt dialog box, click the Clips Online button.
   d. At the message telling you to click OK to browse additional clips from a special Web page, click the OK button.
   e. At the End-User License Agreement page, read the agreement, and then click the Accept button if you accept the terms of the agreement.
   f. At the Microsoft Clip Gallery (see figure 14.18), click in the Search text box and then key **umbrella**.
   g. Click the **go** button that displays at the right side of the Search text box.
   h. When the umbrella clip images display, click the umbrella image shown in figure 14.19. (If this image is not available, choose a similar umbrella image.)
   i. Click the download button that displays immediately below the image (contains a small down-pointing red arrow).
   j. At the Insert ClipArt dialog box with the umbrella image displayed, click the Close button.
   k. Click File and then Close to close the Microsoft Internet Explorer.
5. Insert the umbrella clip art image into the document and change it to a watermark as shown in figure 14.19 by completing the following steps:
   a. Display the Insert ClipArt dialog box.
   b. At the Insert ClipArt dialog box, click the Downloaded Clips category.
   c. Click the umbrella image and then click the Insert clip button.
   d. Close the Insert ClipArt dialog box.
   e. Click the Image Control button on the Picture toolbar and then click Watermark at the drop-down menu.
   f. Click once on the Less Brightness button on the Picture toolbar.

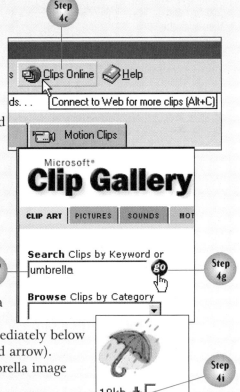

g. Click the Text Wrapping button on the Picture toolbar and then click Behind Text at the drop-down menu.

h. Move the image so it is positioned behind the text as shown in figure 14.19.

i. Deselect the image.

6. Save the document again with the same name (Ch 14, Ex 15).

7. Print Ch 14, Ex 15.

8. Delete the downloaded clip by completing the following steps:

a. Display the Insert ClipArt dialog box.

b. At the ClipArt dialog box, click the Downloaded Clips category.

c. Right-click the umbrella image you downloaded and then click Delete at the shortcut menu.

d. At the message telling you to click OK to delete the clip from all Clip Gallery categories, click the OK button.

e. Close the Insert ClipArt dialog box.

9. Close Ch 14, Ex 15.

14.19 *Exercise 15*

LIBERTY FALLS ELEMENTARY SCHOOL

Spring Performance

Performing Arts Center

Thursday, April 23, 2000

7:30 p.m.

Inserting a Text Box

A text box can be drawn in a document and then text can be keyed in the box. To insert a text box in a document, click Insert and then Text Box. This changes the I-beam pointer to crosshairs. Position the crosshairs in the document, hold down the left mouse button, drag the crosshairs until the box is the desired size, and then release the mouse button. The insertion point is positioned inside the text box. Key the desired text and then click outside the text box to deselect it.

A text box can be sized, moved, and formatted in the same manner as a clip art image. To format a text box, select the box, then click Format and then Text Box. This displays the Format Text Box dialog box that contains the same tabs and options as the Format Picture dialog box.

exercise 16

Inserting and Formatting a Text Box

1. Open Para 03.
2. Save the document with Save As and name it Ch 14, Ex 16.
3. Change to the Print Layout view.
4. Make the following changes to the document:
   a. Join all the paragraphs so there is only one paragraph in the document.
   b. Select the entire document and then change the font to 13-point Goudy Old Style. (If this typeface is not available, choose a similar typeface.)
   c. Deselect the text.
5. Insert a text box in the middle of the paragraph by completing the following steps:
   a. Click Insert and then Text Box.
   b. Using the horizontal and vertical rulers, draw a text box with these specifications:
      1) The box should span from the 1.5-inch mark on the horizontal ruler to the 4.5-inch mark on the horizontal ruler.
      2) The box should begin at approximately the 1-inch mark on the vertical ruler and extend down approximately two-thirds of an inch.

> Flyers are typically one of the least expensive forms of advertising. a flyer is to communicate a message at a glance, so the message sh to the p **Step** For the flyer to be effective, the basic layout and des of clutter **5b** e flyer should not contain too much text or too man the information area white space generous placing elements on audience when choo might need to be. Me beginning the project in a flyer. When using a watermark, try to find a graphic or text th tone or theme of your message. The watermark can be used to ad color, and excitement to a flyer.

   c. With the insertion point positioned inside the text box, make the following changes:
      1) Click the Center button on the Formatting toolbar.
      2) Change the font to 14-point Arial bold.
      3) Key **Flyers are one of the least expensive forms of advertising**.

d. With the text box still selected, wrap the text around the box by completing the following steps:

1) Click Format and then Text Box.
2) At the Format Text Box dialog box, click the Layout tab.
3) Click the Tight option in the Wrapping style section.
4) Click OK to close the dialog box.

Step 5d2

Step 5d3

Format Text Box

Colors and Lines | Size | Layout | Pictu

Wrapping style

In line with text   Square   Tight

e. Check to see if the text box is positioned approximately in the middle of the paragraph. If it is not, drag the box to a more desirable location.
f. Deselect the text box.

6. Save the document again with the same name (Ch 14, Ex 16).
7. Print and then close Ch 14, Ex 16.

chapter summary

➤ Every paragraph created in Word contains an invisible frame. A border that appears around this frame can be added to a paragraph.

➤ Options from the Border button on the Formatting toolbar can be used to insert borders around a paragraph or selected paragraphs.

➤ Use options at the Borders and Shading dialog box with the Borders tab selected to add a customized border to a paragraph or selected paragraphs.

➤ Use options at the Borders and Shading dialog box with the Shading tab selected to add shading or a pattern to a paragraph of text or selected paragraphs.

➤ Add a page border to a document at the Borders and Shading dialog box with the Page Border tab selected.

➤ Clip art images are available at the Insert ClipArt dialog box and are grouped by categories. Click a category in the category list box to display specific clip art images.

➤ Maneuver through categories and clip art at the Insert ClipArt dialog box using buttons on the toolbar. Click the Back button to display clip art for the previously selected category or click the All Categories to redisplay all categories.

➤ Use the sizing handles around a selected clip art image to size the image.

➤ Choose a text wrapping style and the black sizing handles around a selected clip art image change to white sizing handles.

➤ Move a clip art image by selecting the image with white sizing handles and then use the mouse to drag the image to the desired position.

➤ The Picture toolbar contains buttons for formatting a clip art image.

➤ A watermark is a lightened image that displays in a document, generally behind text. Create a watermark with options from the Image Control button and the Text Wrapping button on the Picture toolbar.

➤ Additional formatting options are available at the Format Picture dialog box.

➤ The Microsoft Web site offers a clip gallery with hundreds of clip art images you can download. To display the Microsoft Clip Gallery, make sure you are connected to the Internet, and then click the Clips Online button that displays toward the top of the Insert ClipArt dialog box.

➤ With the Text Box option from the Insert drop-down menu, a text box can be drawn in a document. The formatting options available for a clip art image are also available for a text box.

commands review

	Mouse/Keyboard
Display Borders and Shading dialog box	Format, Borders and Shading
Display Insert ClipArt dialog box	Insert, Picture, Clip Art
Display Microsoft Clip Gallery	Insert, Object, double-click Microsoft Clip Gallery
Display Drawing toolbar	Position mouse pointer on Standard or Formatting toolbar, click the right mouse button, and then click Drawing at the drop-down list
Display the on-line Microsoft Clip Gallery	Click the Clips Online button in the Insert ClipArt dialog box
Create a text box	Insert, Text Box

thinking offline

Completion: In the space provided at the right, indicate the correct term, command, or number.

1. The Border button is located on this toolbar.

2. Click this option on the Menu bar and then click Borders and Shading to display the Borders and Shading dialog box.

3. Click this button, located in the Setting section of the Borders and Shading dialog box, to add a border to paragraphs that has a three-dimensional look.

4. A diagram displays in this section of the Borders and Shading dialog box that displays how the border will appear in the document.

5. Click this tab at the Borders and Shading dialog box to display options for adding a page border to a document.

6. Use the sizing handles positioned at this location in a selected clip art image to change both the width and height at the same time.   _____

7. Use buttons on this toolbar to customize a clip art image.   _____

8. This term refers to a lightened image that displays in a document.   _____

9. Specify the width and height of a clip art image at the Format Picture dialog box with this tab selected.   _____

10. Click this button at the Insert ClipArt dialog box to display the on-line Microsoft Clip Gallery.   _____

11. To insert a text box in a document, click this option on the Menu bar and then click Te**x**t Box.   _____

12. In the space provided below, write the steps you would complete to insert into a document a clip art image of a computer disk.

_____

_____

_____

working hands-on

Assessment 1

1. Open Report 03.
2. Save the document with Save As and name it Ch 14, SA 01.
3. Make the following changes to the document:
   a. Select the entire document and then set it in a serif typeface of your choosing (other than Times New Roman).
   b. Set the title and headings in the report in a bold sans serif typeface of your choosing.
   c. Create a header with these specifications:
      1) Create the header so it prints on all pages except the first page.
      2) Include the text *Newsletter Elements* that prints at the left margin of the header and *Page #* (where the proper page number is inserted) that prints at the right margin.
      3) Insert a border of your choosing at the bottom of the header text.
4. Save the document again with the same name (Ch 14, SA 01).
5. Print and then close Ch 14, SA 01.

Assessment 2

1. Open Survey 01.
2. Save the document with Save As and name it Ch 14, SA 02.
3. Make the following changes to the document:
   a. Change the left and right margins to 1 inch.
   b. Select the title and the subtitle and then change the font to 14-point Times New Roman bold.
   c. Select the first numbered paragraph and the four lettered paragraphs below it.
   d. Display the Borders and Shading dialog box with the <u>B</u>orders tab selected, click the Bo<u>x</u> button at the left side of the dialog box, change the <u>W</u>idth option to ¾ pt, and then close the dialog box. (A border will display around the paragraphs and between the numbered paragraph and the lettered paragraphs.)
   e. Select the second numbered paragraph and the four lettered paragraphs below it and add the same border line as that in step 3d.
   f. Select the third numbered paragraph and the four lettered paragraphs below it and add the same border line as that in step 3d.
   g. Select the fourth numbered paragraph and the four lettered paragraphs below it and add the same border line as that in step 3d.
   h. Select the fifth numbered paragraph and the four lettered paragraphs below it and add the same border line as that in step 3d.
   i. Make sure the document fits on one page. (If not, decrease the top and/or bottom margins until the text fits on one page.)
4. Save the document again with the same name (Ch 14, SA 02).
5. Print and then close Ch 14, SA 02.

Assessment 3

1. Open Notice 02.
2. Save the document with Save As and name it Ch 14, SA 03.
3. Make the following changes to the document:
   a. Set the text in the document in a decorative font of your choosing. (You also determine the font size and font color.)
   b. Center the text vertically on the page.
   c. Insert a page border using one of the images available in the A<u>r</u>t drop-down list.
4. Save the document again with the same name (Ch 14, SA 03).
5. Print and then close Ch 14, SA 03.

Assessment 4

1. At a clear document screen, create the letterhead shown in figure 14.20 with the following specifications:
   a. Insert the clip art image shown in the figure. (Look for this clip art in the *Academic* category. If this image is not available, choose a different image.)
   b. Change the width of the image to approximately 2 inches and the height to approximately 1.75 inches.
   c. Click the Text Wrapping button on the Picture toolbar and then click <u>S</u>quare at the drop-down list.

d. Key the text right aligned as shown in figure 14.20. Set the company name in 20-point Goudy Old Style bold, the address and telephone number in 18-point Goudy Old Style bold, and the Web site address in 14-point Goudy Old Style bold.
2. Save the document and name it Ch 14, SA 04.
3. Print and then close Ch 14, SA 04.

Assessment 4

THE BOOKWORM
3410 Cascade Drive
Portland, OR 97044
(509) 555-3411
www.emcp.bookworm.com

Assessment 5

1. Open Notice 03.
2. Save the document with Save As and name it Ch 14, SA 05.
3. Make the following changes to the document:
    a. Change the font for all text in the document to a serif typeface and type size of your choosing.
    b. Center all the text in the document.
    c. Make sure you are connected to the Internet, go to the Microsoft Clip Gallery site (do this through the Insert ClipArt dialog box), and then download a clip art image related to *jazz* or *saxophone.* (You determine the image you want to download. Find something appropriate for the text in the notice.)
    d. Insert the downloaded clip art image into Ch 14, SA 05 as a watermark. (You determine the size and position of the watermark as well as the brightness and contrast. Make sure the text is legible above the watermark.)
4. Save the document again with the same name (Ch 14, SA 05).
5. Print and then close Ch 14, SA 05.

Assessment 6

1. At a clear document screen, create an announcement that contains the following information:
   a. Include the following text:

      SULLIVAN TRAVELS
      782 North 23rd Street
      Portland, Maine 01232
      Open House
      Thursday, April 5, 2001
      9:00 a.m. - 8:30 p.m.
      Stop by and check out our new offices!
      Sign up for a drawing for a free cruise!

   b. Set the above text in a decorative typeface and type size of your choosing. Add any additional text you desire.
   c. Include a decorative page border.
   d. Insert at least one clip art image or picture (related to travel) and position it in an appealing location on the page.
2. Save the document and name it Ch 14, SA 06.
3. Print and then close Ch 14, SA 06.

Chapter 15

Using Microsoft Draw and WordArt

PERFORMANCE OBJECTIVES

Upon successful completion of chapter 15, you will be able to:

- Draw shapes, create autoshapes, and create text boxes using buttons on the Drawing toolbar.
- Select, delete, move, copy, and size drawn objects.
- Customize a drawn object by adding fill color and shading, changing the line color and style, and adding shadow and 3-D effects.
- Flip an object.
- Add callouts.
- Modify text with WordArt.
- Size and move a WordArt text box.
- Change the font and font size of WordArt text.
- Customize WordArt text with buttons on the WordArt toolbar.
- Customize WordArt with buttons on the Drawing toolbar.

In chapter 14, you learned about the Insert Clip Art button on the Drawing toolbar. This toolbar contains a variety of other buttons you can use to draw and customize objects. With various buttons, you can draw freehand, draw shapes and objects, and create text boxes. Word provides a supplementary application named WordArt that you can use to create text in a variety of shapes and alignments, and to add 3-D effects.

Drawing Shapes and Lines

With buttons on the Drawing toolbar, you can draw a variety of shapes such as circles, squares, rectangles, ovals, as well as straight lines, free-form lines, lines with arrowheads, and much more. To display the Drawing toolbar, shown in figure 15.1, click the Drawing button on the Standard toolbar; or, position the mouse pointer on the Standard or Formatting toolbar, click the *right* mouse button, and then click *Drawing* at the drop-down list. A description of each button is provided in figure 15.2. As soon as you click a button on the Drawing toolbar, Word switches to the Print Layout view.

Drawing

figure

15.1

Drawing Toolbar

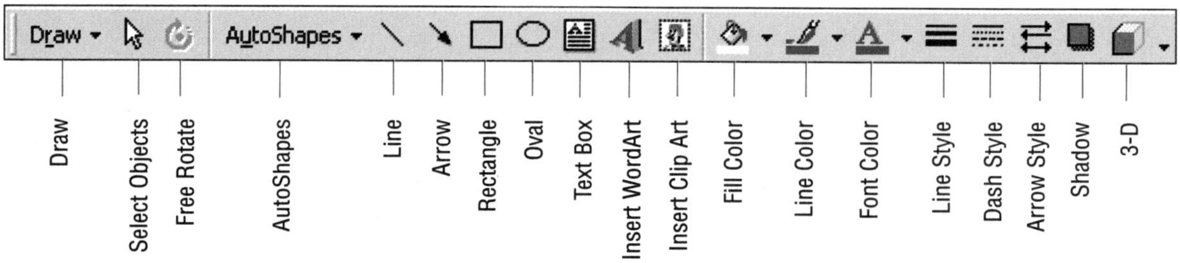

Draw ▾   ⤢   ↻   AutoShapes ▾   ＼   ↘   □   ○   📰   📐   🖼   ◇ ▾   ✏ ▾   **A** ▾   ▬   ▭   ⇄   ▪   ⬢ ▾

Draw | Select Objects | Free Rotate | AutoShapes | Line | Arrow | Rectangle | Oval | Text Box | Insert WordArt | Insert Clip Art | Fill Color | Line Color | Font Color | Line Style | Dash Style | Arrow Style | Shadow | 3-D

figure

15.2

Drawing Toolbar Buttons

Click this button	Named	To do this
Draw ▾	D<u>r</u>aw	Display a pop-up menu with options for grouping and positioning drawings.
⤢	Select Objects	Select text or objects.
↻	Free Rotate	Rotate selected object to any degree by dragging a corner of the object in the desired direction.
AutoShapes ▾	A<u>u</u>toShapes	Display a palette of shapes that can be drawn in a document. (To draw a shape circumscribed within a perfect square, hold down the Shift key while drawing the shape.)
＼	Line	Draw a line in a document.
↘	Arrow	Insert a line with an arrowhead. (To draw at 15-degree angles, hold down the Shift key.)
□	Rectangle	Draw a rectangle in a document. (To draw a perfect square, hold down the Shift key while drawing the shape.)
○	Oval	Draw an oval in a document. (To draw a perfect circle, hold down the Shift key while drawing the shape.)
📰	Text Box	Draw a box for text entry.

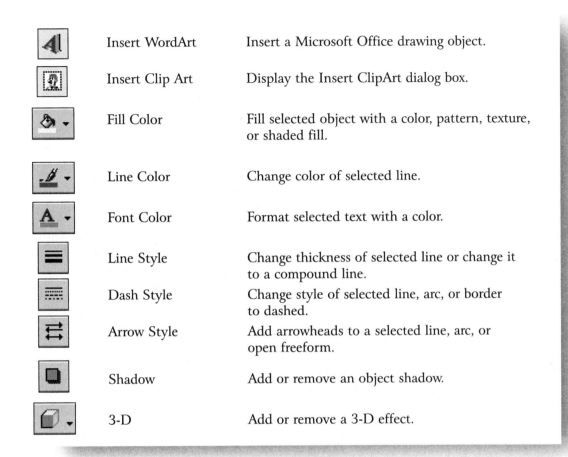

Insert WordArt	Insert a Microsoft Office drawing object.
Insert Clip Art	Display the Insert ClipArt dialog box.
Fill Color	Fill selected object with a color, pattern, texture, or shaded fill.
Line Color	Change color of selected line.
Font Color	Format selected text with a color.
Line Style	Change thickness of selected line or change it to a compound line.
Dash Style	Change style of selected line, arc, or border to dashed.
Arrow Style	Add arrowheads to a selected line, arc, or open freeform.
Shadow	Add or remove an object shadow.
3-D	Add or remove a 3-D effect.

With some of the buttons on the Drawing toolbar, you can draw a shape. If you draw a shape with the Line button or the Arrow button, the shape you draw is considered a *line drawing*. If you draw a shape with the Rectangle or Oval button, the shape you draw is considered an *enclosed object*. Later in this chapter you will learn how to add fill color to an enclosed object.

Line

If you want to draw the same shape more than once, double-click the shape button on the Drawing toolbar. After drawing the shapes, click the button again to deactivate it.

Arrow

Use the Rectangle button on the Drawing toolbar to draw a square or rectangle in a document. If you want to draw a square, hold down the Shift key while drawing the shape. The Shift key keeps all sides of the drawn object equal. Use the Oval button to draw a circle or an oval object. To draw a circle, hold down the Shift key while drawing the object.

Rectangle

Oval

Drawing a Circle and a Square

1. At a clear document screen, draw a circle and a square by completing the following steps:
   a. Display the Drawing toolbar by clicking the Drawing button on the Standard toolbar. (Skip this step if the Drawing toolbar is already displayed.)
   b. Click the Oval button on the Drawing toolbar.
   c. Position the crosshairs in the document screen toward the left side.
   d. Hold down the Shift key and the left mouse button, drag the mouse down and to the right until the outline image displays as approximately a 2-inch circle, then release the mouse button and then the Shift key.
   e. Click the Rectangle button on the Drawing toolbar.
   f. Position the crosshairs in the document screen toward the right side.
   g. Hold down the Shift key and the left mouse button, drag the mouse down and to the right until the outline image displays as approximately a 2-inch square, then release the mouse button and then the Shift key.
2. Save the document and name it Ch 15, Ex 01.
3. Print and then close Ch 15, Ex 01.

With the Line button, you can draw a line in the document screen. To do this, click the Line button on the Drawing toolbar. Position the crosshairs where you want to begin the line, hold down the left mouse button, drag the line to the location where you want the line to end, and then release the mouse button.

You can add as many lines as desired in the document screen by repeating the steps above. For example, you can draw a triangle by drawing three lines. If you want to draw more than one line, double-click the Line button. This makes the button active. After drawing all the necessary lines, click the Line button again to deactivate it.

Creating a Line with the Arrow Button

1. At a clear document screen, create the document shown in figure 15.3 by completing the following steps:
   a. Make sure the Drawing toolbar is displayed.
   b. Change the font to 24-point Copperplate Gothic Bold (or a similar decorative typeface).
   c. Click the Center button on the Formatting toolbar.
   d. Key **Mainline Manufacturing**. (The Copperplate Gothic Bold typeface uses small caps for lowercase letters.)
   e. Press the Enter key.

f.   Click the Arrow button on the Drawing toolbar.
g.   Draw the line as shown in figure 15.3. (The line will
     display with an arrow on one end. This will be
     changed in the next step. Hold down the Shift key
     to draw a straight line.)
h.   With the line still selected (a white sizing handle
     displays at each end), click the Arrow Style button
     on the Drawing toolbar.
i.   At the pop-up list that displays, click the second
     option from the bottom of the list (Arrow Style 10).
j.   Click outside the line to deselect it and display the
     arrow style.
2. Save the completed document and name it Ch
    15, Ex 02.
3. Print and then close Ch 15, Ex 02.

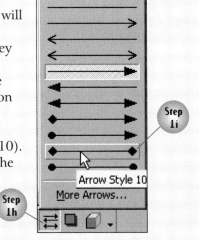

Step
1i

Step
1h

Exercise 2

MAINLINE MANUFACTURING

Creating Autoshapes

With options from the AutoShapes button, you can choose from a variety of
predesigned shapes. Click the AutoShapes button and a pop-up menu displays.
Point to the desired menu option and a side menu displays. This side menu will
offer autoshape choices for the selected option. For example, if you point to the
Basic Shapes option, a number of shapes such as a circle, square, triangle, box,
stop sign, etc., display at the right side of the pop-up menu. Click the desired
shape and the mouse pointer turns into crosshairs. Position the crosshairs in the
document screen, hold down the left mouse button, drag to create the shape, and
then release the button.

AutoShapes ▾

AutoShapes

exercise 3

Writing Your Name

1. At a clear document screen, write your first name by completing the following steps:
   a. Make sure the Drawing toolbar is displayed.
   b. Click the AutoShapes button on the Drawing toolbar, point to Lines, and then click the Scribble button. (The Scribble button is the last button in the bottom row. Position the mouse pointer on this button and *Scribble* displays after one second in a yellow box.)

   c. Position the mouse pointer in the document screen, hold down the left mouse button, and then move the mouse pointer (a pencil) in the necessary directions to draw your first name. When you release the mouse button, white sizing handles display around your name. If you need to continue drawing your name (for example, to cross a "T"), select the Scribble button again. (If you are not satisfied with the results, make sure white sizing handles display around your name and then press the Delete key. Draw your name again.)
2. Save the document and name it Ch 15, Ex 03.
3. Print and then close Ch 15, Ex 03.

exercise 4

Creating Stars

1. At a clear document screen, create a variety of stars by completing the following steps:
   a. Make sure the Drawing toolbar is displayed.
   b. Click the AutoShapes button on the Drawing toolbar, point to Stars and Banners, and then click the 8-Point Star button (first button from the left in the second row from the top).

   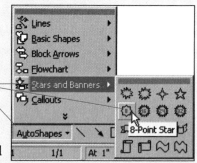

   c. Position the crosshairs in the document screen, hold down the left mouse button, drag the crosshairs to create the star, and then release the mouse button.
   d. The star displays with a small yellow box inside. This box is referred to as an *adjustment handle*. Position the mouse pointer on the adjustment handle, hold down the left mouse button, drag about halfway into the star, and then release the mouse button. (This causes the points of the star to drag into the star.)

   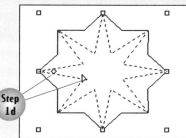

e. Click the A<u>u</u>toShapes button on the Drawing toolbar, point to <u>S</u>tars and Banners, and then click the 16-Point Star button (second button from the left in the second row from the top).
f. Position the crosshairs in the document screen, hold down the left mouse button, drag the crosshairs to create the star, and then release the mouse button.
g. Use the adjustment handle to drag the points of the star into the star.
h. Experiment with a few other star and/or banner buttons.
2. Save the document and name it Ch 15, Ex 04.
3. Print and then close Ch 15, Ex 04.

Creating a Text Box

With the Text Box button on the Drawing toolbar, you can create a box and then insert text inside the box. Text inside a box can be formatted in the normal manner. For example, you can change the font, alignment, or indent of the text.

Text Box

To create a text box, click the Text Box button, position the crosshairs in the document screen where you want the text to appear, hold down the left mouse button, drag to create the box, and then release the mouse button. This causes a box to appear in the drawing area similar to the one shown in figure 15.4. Key the text in the box. If the text you key fills more than the first line in the box, the text wraps to the next line. (The box, however, will not increase in size. If you need more room in the text box, select the box, and then use the sizing handles to make it bigger.)

figure

15.4

Text Box

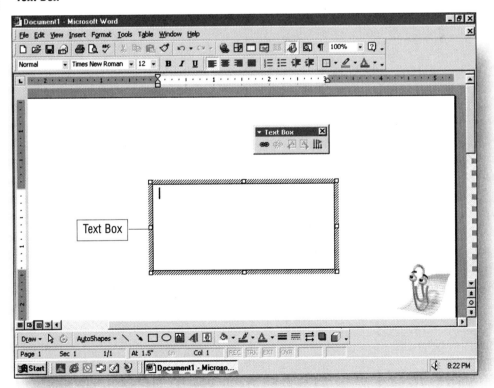

Creating an Oval and Then Keying Text Inside

1. At a clear document screen, create an oval shape, and then create a text box inside the oval with the words *Linda Shing* and *Superintendent* by completing the following steps:
   a. Make sure the Drawing toolbar is displayed and then click the Oval button.
   b. Position the crosshairs in the document screen (approximately below the 1.5-inch mark on the horizontal ruler), hold down the left mouse button, drag the mouse down and to the right until you have drawn an oval that is approximately 3 inches wide and 2 inches tall, and then release the mouse button.
   c. Click the Text Box button.
   d. Draw a text box inside the oval shape from the left side to the right side that is approximately 1 inch tall.
   e. Click the Center button on the Formatting toolbar.
   f. Press the Enter key once.
   g. Key **Linda Shing** in the text box and then press Enter.
   h. Key **Superintendent**. (The name and title should be centered in the oval. If not, insert or delete hard returns until the text appears centered.)
2. Save the document and name it Ch 15, Ex 05.
3. Print and then close Ch 15, Ex 05.

Changing Objects

Shapes drawn using tools on the Drawing toolbar are referred to as objects. An object can be customized in a variety of ways. For example, an object can be selected and then moved, copied, or deleted; or the size of the object can be changed.

Selecting an Object

After an object has been created in a document, you may decide to make changes or delete the object. To do this, the object must be selected. To select an enclosed object, position the mouse pointer anywhere inside the object (the mouse pointer displays with a four-headed arrow attached) and then click the left mouse button. To select a line, position the mouse pointer on the line until the pointer turns into an arrow with a four-headed arrow attached, and then click the left mouse button. When an object is selected, it displays surrounded by white sizing handles. Once an object is selected, it can be edited, such as changing the fill and the line, it can be moved, or it can be deleted.

If a document screen contains more than one object, you can select several objects at once using the Select Objects button on the Drawing toolbar. To do this, click the Select Objects button, position the crosshairs in the upper left corner of the area containing the objects, hold down the left mouse button, drag the outline to the lower right corner of the area containing the objects, and then release the mouse button. You can also select more than one object by holding down the Shift key as you click each object.

Select Objects

Each object in the selected area displays surrounded by white sizing handles. Objects in the selected area are connected. For example, if you move one of the objects in the selected area, the other objects move relatively.

Deleting an Object

An object you have drawn can be deleted from the document screen. To do this, select the object, and then press the Delete key.

Moving an Object

An object can be moved to a different location in this document. To do this with an enclosed object, position the mouse pointer inside the object (mouse pointer displays with a four-headed arrow attached), hold down the left mouse button, drag the outline of the object to the new location, and then release the mouse button. If you selected more than one object, moving one of the objects will also move the other objects. To move a line, select the line, and then position the mouse pointer on the line until it turns into an arrow with a four-headed arrow attached. Hold down the left mouse button, drag the outline of the line to the desired location, and then release the mouse button.

You can move a selected object with the keyboard by pressing one of the arrow keys. For example, to move an object down the screen, select the object, and then press the down arrow key.

Copying an Object

Moving an object removes the object from its original position and inserts it into a new location. If you want the object to stay in its original location and an exact copy to be inserted in a new location, use the Ctrl key while dragging the object.

Creating Organizational Boxes in Draw

1. At a clear document screen, create the organizational boxes shown in figure 15.5 by completing the following steps:
   a. With the Drawing toolbar displayed, click the Text Box button.
   b. Draw a text box from approximately the 2-inch mark on the horizontal ruler to the 4-inch mark on the horizontal ruler. Make the box about 1 inch in height.
   c. Press Enter to move the insertion point down one line inside the text box.
   d. Click the Center button on the Formatting toolbar.
   e. Key **Blaine Dowler**.

f.   Press Enter and then key **Principal**.
g.   Position the mouse pointer at the bottom of the text box until it turns into an arrow with a four-headed arrow attached.
h.   Hold down the Ctrl key and the left mouse button (this causes the four-headed arrow to change to a plus symbol), drag the outline of the text box down and to the left as shown in figure 15.5, and then release the left mouse button. (Do not release the Ctrl key.)
i.   With the Ctrl key still down, and the mouse pointer displayed with the plus symbol attached, hold down the left mouse button, drag the outline of the text box to the right as shown in figure 15.5, release the mouse button, and then release the Ctrl key.
j.   After copying the text box, key the names and titles shown in figure 15.5 in the second and third text boxes over the name *Blaine Dowler* and title *Principal*.
2.   Save the document and name it Ch 15, Ex 06.
3.   Print and then close Ch 15, Ex 06.

Exercise 6

| Blaine Dowler |
| Principal |

| Jennifer Dean | | Lewis Kennedy |
| Assistant Principal | | Assistant Principal |

Sizing an Object

With the sizing handles that appear around an object when it is selected, the size of the object can be changed. To change the size of the object, select it, and then position the mouse pointer on a sizing handle until it turns into a double-headed arrow. Hold down the left mouse button, drag the outline of the shape toward or away from the center of the object until it is the desired size, and then release the mouse button.

Creating and Sizing a Text Box

1. At a clear document screen, create a text box, key text in the box, and then size the box by completing the following steps:
   a. With the Drawing toolbar displayed, click the Text Box button, and then draw a text box in the document screen that is approximately 2 inches wide and 2.5 inches tall.
   b. With the insertion point inside the text box, change the font to 14-point Arial bold.
   c. Click the Center button on the Formatting toolbar.
   d. Key **COLEMAN DEVELOPMENT CORPORATION** (this will wrap).
   e. Press the Enter key.
   f. Key **3451 Classen Boulevard** (this will also wrap).
   g. Press Enter.
   h. Key **Oklahoma City, OK 76341**.
   i. Press Enter.
   j. Key **(801) 555-4500**.
   k. With the text box selected, use the white sizing handles around the text box to make the box wider until the company name displays on one line and you can see all of the text. Make the text box shorter so there is little space between the text and the bottom line of the box.
   l. Drag the text box to the middle of the document screen.
2. Save the document and name it Ch 15, Ex 07.
3. Print and then close Ch 15, Ex 07.

Step 1a-1j

> **COLEMAN
> DEVELOPMENT
> CORPORATION
> 3451 Classen
> Boulevard
> Oklahoma City, OK
> 76341
> (801) 555-4500**

Step 1k

> **COLEMAN DEVELOPMENT
> CORPORATION
> 3451 Classen Boulevard
> Oklahoma City, OK 76341
> (801) 555-4500**

Customizing Objects

With buttons on the Drawing toolbar, you can add fill color or pattern to an enclosed object, change thickness and color of the line that draws the object, and change the position of the object.

Adding Fill Shading or Color

Use the Fill Color button on the Drawing toolbar to add shading or color to an enclosed object such as a shape or a text box. To add shading or color, select the object, and then click the Fill Color button. This will fill the object with the fill color displayed on the Fill Color button. If you want to choose a different color, select the object, and then click the down-pointing triangle at the right side of the Fill Color button. This causes a palette of color choices to display. At this palette click the desired fill color.

Fill Color

The Fill Color palette also includes two options—More Fill Colors and Fill Effects. Click the More Fill Colors option and the Colors dialog box shown in figure 15.6 displays. At this dialog box, click the desired color in the Colors section, and then click OK.

figure

15.6   *Colors Dialog Box*

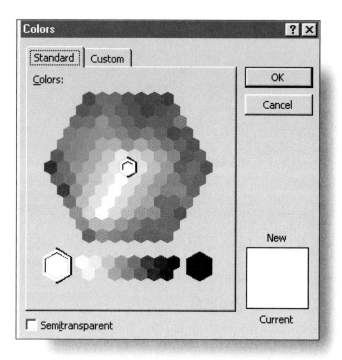

Click the other option at the Fill Color palette, Fill Effects, and the Fill Effects dialog box shown in figure 15.7 displays. At this dialog box, you can specify the number of colors, a shading style, and a shading variant. Make the desired choices at this dialog box and then click OK.

figure
15.7
Fill Effects Dialog Box

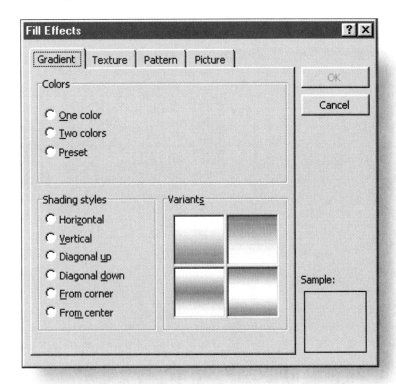

Changing Line Color

A line, shape, or text box is drawn with a black line. The color of this line can be changed with the Line Color button on the Drawing toolbar. Select an object and then click the Line Color button and the line color of the selected object changes to the color displayed on the button. If you want to choose a different color, select the object and then click the down-pointing triangle at the right side of the Line Color button. This causes a palette of color choices to display. At this palette, click the desired color.

The Line Color palette also includes two options—More Line Colors and Patterned Lines. Click the More Line Colors option and the Colors dialog box shown in figure 15.6 displays. Click the Patterned Lines option and the Patterned Lines dialog box shown in figure 15.8 displays. Choose a pattern and a foreground and/or or background color for the object at this dialog box.

Line Color

figure
15.8 *Patterned Lines Dialog Box*

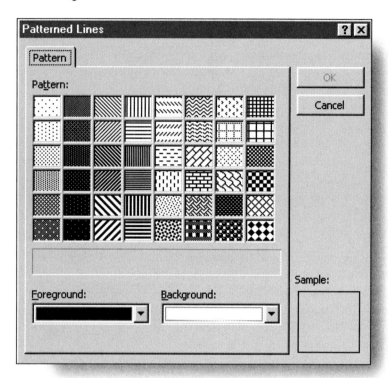

In some situations, you may want to remove the line around an object. For example, you may want to remove the lines of a text box after text has been added to it. To remove lines, select the object, click the down-pointing triangle at the right side of the Line Color button, and then click *No Line* at the pop-up menu.

exercise 8

Changing Fill Color

1. Open Ch 15, Ex 05.
2. Save the document with Save As and name it Ch 15, Ex 08.
3. Change the fill color of the oval shape by completing the following steps:
   a. Select the oval shape by positioning the mouse pointer on the line that forms the oval until it turns into an arrow with a four-headed arrow attached and then clicking the left mouse button.
   b. Click the down-pointing triangle at the right side of the Fill Color button on the Drawing toolbar.

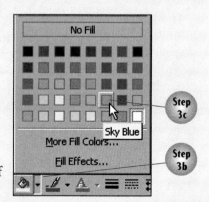

Step 3c

Step 3b

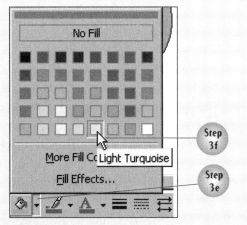

c. At the palette that displays, click the Sky Blue color (the sixth color from the left in the second row from the bottom).
d. Select the text box.
e. Click the down-pointing triangle at the right side of the Fill Color button on the Drawing toolbar.
f. At the palette that displays, click the Light Turquoise color (the fifth color from the left in the bottom row).
g. Deselect the text box.
4. Save the document again with the same name (Ch 15, Ex 08).
5. Print and then close Ch 15, Ex 08.

Changing Line Style

By default, Word draws shapes and text boxes with a thin black line. This line can be changed to a thicker line, a broken line, or a line with a mouse pointer. To change the line style, click the Line Style button, then click the desired line style at the pop-up menu that displays. Click the More Lines option at the pop-up menu and the Format AutoShape dialog box displays with the Colors and Lines tab selected. This dialog box contains the same options as the Format Picture dialog box.

Click the Dash Style button if you want to draw an object with a dashed line. Clicking this button causes a pop-up list to display containing dashed line options.

Line Style

Dash Style

Changing Line Style and Color

1. Open Ch 15, Ex 06.
2. Save the document with Save As and name it Ch 15, Ex 09.
3. Change the line style and color of the top box by completing the following steps:
   a. Position the I-beam pointer on one of the lines of the text box containing the name *Blaine Dowler* until it turns into an arrow with a four-headed arrow attached and then double-click the left mouse button. (This displays the Format Text Box dialog box.)
   b. At the Format Text Box dialog box, click the Colors and Lines tab.
   c. Click the down-pointing triangle to the right of the Color option in the Fill section and then click the Red color (first color from the left in the third row).
   d. Select the current point size measurement in the Weight text box and then key **4**.

e. Click OK or press Enter to close the Format Text Box dialog box.
4. Complete steps similar to those in 3 to change the line style and color for the text box at the left (containing the name *Jennifer Dean*).
5. Complete steps similar to those in 3 to change the line style and color for the text box at the right (containing the name *Lewis Kennedy*).
6. Save the document again with the same name (Ch 15, Ex 09).
7. Print and then close Ch 15, Ex 09.

Adding Shadow and 3-D Effects

Shadow

Click the Shadow button on the Drawing toolbar and a palette of shadow options displays. Click the desired option or click the Shadow Settings option and a Shadow Settings toolbar displays. This toolbar contains buttons for turning shadows off or on and buttons for nudging the shadow up, down, left, or right.

3-D

If you want to add a three-dimensional look to an object, select the object, and then click the 3-D button on the Drawing toolbar. This displays a palette of three-dimensional choices as well as a 3-D Settings option. Click this option and the 3-D Settings toolbar displays. This toolbar contains buttons for turning 3-D on or off and changing the tilt, depth, direction, and light source.

exercise 10

Adding Shadow and 3-D Effects to an Object

1. At a clear document screen, create a shape and add shadow and then 3-D effects to the shape by completing the following steps:
    a. With the Drawing toolbar displayed, click the Rectangle button.
    b. Draw a rectangle in the document (you determine the size).
    c. With the rectangle selected, add a fill color of your choosing.
    d. With the rectangle still selected, click the Shadow button on the Drawing toolbar, and then click a shadow option (you determine the shadow).
    e. Experiment with a few other shadow options. Click the Shadow Settings option and then experiment with buttons on the Shadow Settings toolbar. When done using the toolbar, click the Close button located in the upper right corner of the toolbar to turn it off.
    f. Save the document and name it Ch 15, Ex 10.
    g. Print Ch 15, Ex 10.
    h. Remove the Shadow effect from the rectangle. To do this, select the rectangle, click the Shadow button, and then click *No Shadow*.
    i. With the rectangle still selected, add a 3-D effect to the rectangle by clicking the 3-D button on the Drawing toolbar, and then clicking a 3-D option (you determine the option).

j. Experiment with a few other 3-D options. Click the 3-D Settings option and then experiment with buttons on the 3-D Settings toolbar. When you are finished using the toolbar, click the Close button located in the upper right corner of the toolbar to turn it off.
2. Save the document again with the same name (Ch 15, Ex 10).
3. Print and then close Ch 15, Ex 10.

Aligning Graphic Elements

Graphic elements such as clip art images, autoshapes, text boxes, and shapes can be aligned and distributed in a document. Distribute and align graphic elements with the Draw button on the Drawing toolbar. To align and distribute graphic elements, select the elements, click the Draw button on the Drawing toolbar, and then point to Align or Distribute. This causes a side menu to display with alignment and distribution options. Choose the desired alignment and distribution option from this list.

To identify the graphic elements you want to align and/or distribute, click the Select Objects button on the Drawing toolbar and then draw a border around the elements. Another method for selecting elements is to click the first element, hold down the Shift key, and then click any other elements you want aligned.

Creating a Certificate with Aligned AutoShapes

1. Create the certificate shown in figure 15.9 by completing the following steps:
    a. At a clear document screen, change the page orientation to Landscape by completing the following steps:
        1) Click File and then Page Setup.
        2) At the Page Setup Dialog box, click the Paper Size tab.
        3) At the Page Setup dialog box with the Paper Size tab selected, click the Landscape option in the Orientation section.
        4) Click OK to close the dialog box.
    b. Change the top, bottom, left, and right margins to 0.75 inch.
    c. Insert the page border shown in figure 15.9 by completing the following steps:
        1) Click Format and then Borders and Shading.
        2) At the Borders and Shading dialog box, click the Page Borders tab.

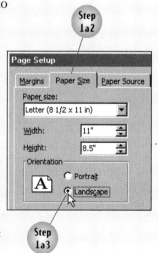

Step 1a2

Step 1a3

3) At the Borders and Shading dialog box with the <u>P</u>age Borders tab selected, click the down-pointing triangle at the right side of the A<u>r</u>t list box and then click the stars (shown at the right and in figure 15.9) at the drop-down list.

4) Click the up-pointing triangle at the right side of the <u>W</u>idth text box until *20 pt* displays in the text box.

5) Click OK to close the dialog box.

d. Create the text in the certificate as shown in figure 15.9 with the following specifications:

1) Set *Gold Star Service Award in* in 42-point Lucida Calligraphy bold with a Shado<u>w</u> effect. (Add the shadow effect by clicking the Shado<u>w</u> check box at the Font dialog box.) (If the Lucida Calligraphy typeface is not available, choose a similar decorative typeface.)

2) Set *Awarded to* in 18-point Lucida Calligraphy bold.

3) Set *Presented by* in 18-point Lucida Calligraphy bold.

4) Set *King County Outreach* in 22-point Lucida Calligraphy bold.

5) Set *June 1, 2001* in 18-point Lucida Calligraphy bold.

e. Create the star in the middle of the certificate with the following specifications:

1) Use the A<u>u</u>toShapes button on the Drawing toolbar to create the star.

2) Add light yellow fill to the star.

3) Draw a text box inside the star and then key *Chad Jeffries* inside the text box. Set *Chad Jeffries* in 22-point Lucida Calligraphy bold.

4) Add light yellow fill to the text box and remove the line around the text box.

f. Create and align the small stars toward the bottom of the certificate by completing the following steps:

1) Click the A<u>u</u>toShapes button on the Drawing toolbar, point to <u>S</u>tars and Banners, and then click 5-Point Star at the side menu.

2) Hold down the Shift key and then drag to create the first star. (If you are not happy with the size of the star, delete it, and then draw it again.)

3) Add light yellow fill to the star.

4) Copy the star by holding down the Ctrl key, dragging to the right, and then releasing the Ctrl key and the mouse button.

5) Copy the star four more times so the six stars are positioned as shown in figure 15.9.

6) Align the stars at the bottom by completing the following steps:

a) Click the Select Objects button on the Drawing toolbar.

b) Draw a border around all six stars. (When you select the stars you will also select text. The text will not affect the alignment of the stars.)

c) Click the D<u>r</u>aw button on the Drawing toolbar, point to <u>A</u>lign or Distribute, and then click Align <u>B</u>ottom.

7) Select the three stars at the left side of the certificate and then distribute the stars horizontally. (To do this, click the D<u>r</u>aw button on the Drawing toolbar, point to <u>A</u>lign or Distribute, and then click Distribute <u>H</u>orizontally.)

8) Select the three stars at the right side of the certificate, align the stars and then distribute the stars horizontally.

2. Save the completed certificate and name it Ch 15, Ex 11.

3. Print and then close Ch 15, Ex 11.

figure
15.9   *Exercise 11*

Flipping and Rotating an Object

A selected object can be rotated and flipped horizontally or vertically. To rotate or flip an object, select the object, click the Draw button on the Drawing toolbar, point to Rotate or Flip, and then click the desired rotation or flip option at the side menu that displays. A drawn object can be rotated, but a text box cannot.

Draw

Creating a Letterhead and Rotating an Arrow

1. At a clear document screen, create the letterhead shown in figure 15.10 by completing the following steps:
   a. Press Enter four times.
   b. Click the Center button on the Formatting toolbar.
   c. Change the font to 36-point Impact. (If Impact is not available, choose a similar typeface.)
   d. Key **Quick Time Printing**.
   e. Create the yellow arrow at the left side of the text by completing the following steps:

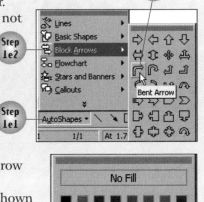

   1) Click the AutoShapes button on the Drawing toolbar.
   2) Point to Block Arrows. (This displays a side menu.)
   3) Click the first arrow from the left in the third row (the Bent Arrow).

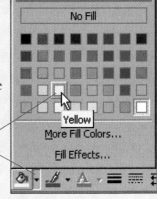

   4) Draw the arrow at the left side of the text as shown in figure 15.10. If you are not satisfied with the location of the arrow, drag it to the desired location. If you are not satisfied with the size of the arrow, use the sizing handles to increase or decrease the size.
   5) With the arrow still selected, add yellow fill. To do this, click the down-pointing triangle at the right side of the Fill Color button on the Drawing toolbar. At the palette of color choices that displays, click the Yellow color (third color from the left in the fourth row).
   f. With the yellow arrow still selected, copy it to the right side of the text. To do this, position the mouse pointer inside the arrow (displays with a four-headed arrow attached), then hold down the Ctrl key and then the left mouse button. Drag the arrow to the right side of the text, then release the mouse button and then the Ctrl key.
   g. Flip the arrow horizontally by completing the following steps:
   1) With the arrow at the right side of the text still selected, click the Draw button on the Drawing toolbar.
   2) At the pop-up menu that displays, point to Rotate or Flip.
   3) At the side menu that displays, click Flip Horizontal.
   h. If necessary, reposition the arrow so it displays as shown in figure 15.10.
2. Save the document and name it Ch 15, Ex 12.
3. Print and then close Ch 15, Ex 12.

figure

15.10 *Exercise 12*

Adding Callouts

Callouts are a useful tool for identifying parts of an illustration or picture. Many figures in this textbook include callouts identifying Word features. For example, figure 15.1 includes callouts identifying the buttons on the Drawing toolbar.

To create a callout, click the AutoShapes button, point to Callouts, and then click the desired callout design at the side menu that displays. Position the crosshairs at the location where you want the callout to point, hold down the left mouse button, drag to the location where callout text is to display, and then release the mouse button. (This inserts a text box in the document screen.) Key the callout text in the text box. Format text in a text box in the normal manner. The line that connects to the callout text box can be changed. For example, if you want the line to point in a slightly different direction, position the mouse pointer (with the four-headed arrow attached) on the callout line and then click the left mouse button. This causes yellow adjustment handles to display at each end of the line. Position the mouse pointer on one of the adjustment handles, hold down the left mouse button, drag the line in the desired direction, and then release the mouse button.

Inserting Pictures from a Disk

In chapter 14, you inserted clip art images in documents from the Insert ClipArt dialog box and you also downloaded clip art from the on-line Microsoft Clip Gallery. You can also insert clip art images from other sources such as a disk or folder. For example, in exercise 13 you will insert in a Word document a clip art image from the CD that accompanies this textbook.

To insert clip art from a different source, click Insert, point to Picture, and then click From File. This displays the Insert Picture dialog box. At this dialog box, change to the folder or drive containing the clip art. Click the desired clip art document name in the list box and then click the Insert button. (You can also just double-click the clip art document name.) Move, size, and/or format the clip art image in the same manner as clip art from the Microsoft Clip Gallery.

exercise 13

Adding Callouts to a Clip Art Image

1. At a clear document screen, create the document shown in figure 15.11 by completing the following steps:
   a. Change to the Print Layout view.
   b. Insert the CD that accompanies this textbook into the CD drive.
   c. Click Insert, point to Picture, and then click From File.
   d. At the Insert Picture dialog box, change to the drive where the CD is located.
   e. Double-click the *ClipArt* folder.
   f. Double-click *pc* in the list box.
   g. Click once on the image to select it.

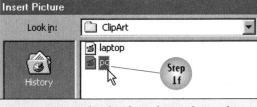

   h. Decrease the size of the image by dragging the bottom right sizing handle to approximately the 3-inch mark on the horizontal ruler and the 2.5-inch mark on the vertical ruler. (You will need to scroll down the screen to display the bottom right sizing handle.)
   i. With the image still selected, click the Text Wrapping button on the Picture toolbar, and then click Through at the drop-down list.
   j. With white sizing handles displayed around the computer image, drag the image to the middle of the screen.
   k. Add the callout for the monitor by completing the following steps:
      1) Click the AutoShapes button on the Drawing toolbar.
      2) At the pop-up menu that displays, point to Callouts.
      3) Click the second callout option from the left in the fourth row *(Line Callout 2 [No Border])*.
      4) Position the crosshairs on the left edge of the monitor, hold down the left mouse button, drag to the left (try to keep the line even), and then release the mouse button.
      5) With the insertion point inside the text box, change the font to 14-point Arial bold, click the Align Right button on the Formatting toolbar, and then key **Monitor**.
      6) Click outside the text box to deselect it.
   l. Complete steps similar to those in 1k to create the remaining callouts *(Keyboard, Mouse,* and *CPU)*. Do not click the Align Right button for *CPU* and *Mouse*. If the text *Keyboard* wraps within the callout text box, use a sizing handle to increase the size of the callout text box. You may want to decrease the size of the callout text for the box containing *CPU*.
2. Save the document and name it Ch 15, Ex 13.
3. Print and then close Ch 15, Ex 13.

492

15.11 *Exercise 13*

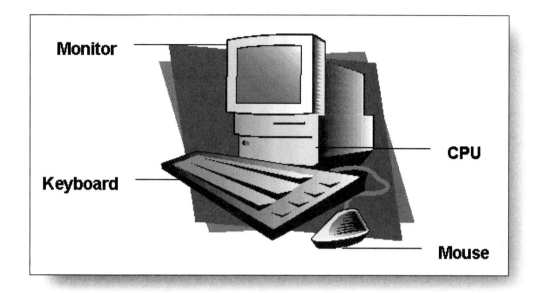

Monitor

CPU

Keyboard

Mouse

Using WordArt

With the WordArt application, you can distort or modify text to conform to a variety of shapes. This is useful for creating company logos and headings. With WordArt, you can change the font, style, and alignment of text. You can also use different fill patterns and colors, customize border lines, and add shadow and three-dimensional effects.

There are a variety of methods for displaying the WordArt Gallery shown in figure 15.12. You can click the Insert WordArt button on the Drawing toolbar; click Insert, point to Picture, and then WordArt; or click the Insert WordArt button on the WordArt toolbar shown in figure 15.13. To display the WordArt toolbar, click View, point to Toolbars, and then click WordArt; or, position the mouse pointer on a toolbar, click the *right* mouse button, and then click *WordArt* at the drop-down menu.

Insert
WordArt

figure

15.12

WordArt Gallery

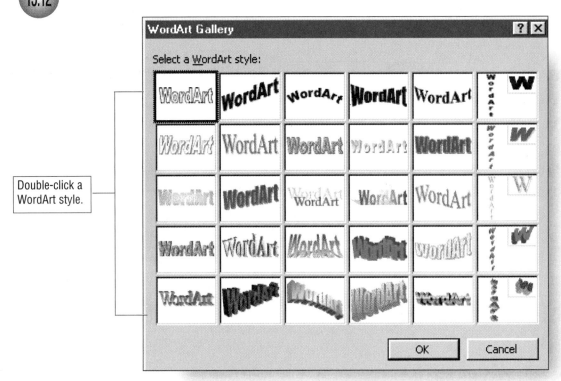

Double-click a
WordArt style.

figure

15.13

WordArt Toolbar

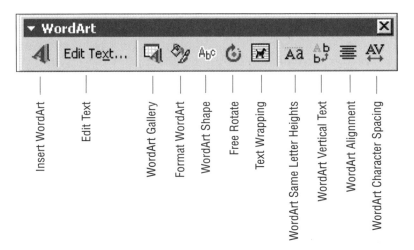

Insert WordArt

Edit Text

WordArt Gallery

Format WordArt

WordArt Shape

Free Rotate

Text Wrapping

WordArt Same Letter Heights

WordArt Vertical Text

WordArt Alignment

WordArt Character Spacing

Entering Text

Double-click a WordArt style at the WordArt Gallery and the Edit WordArt Text dialog box displays as shown in figure 15.14. At the Edit WordArt Text dialog box, the words *Your Text Here* are automatically selected in the Text box. Key the text in the text box and the original words are removed. Press the Enter key if you want to move the insertion point to the next line. After keying the desired text, click the OK button.

Edit WordArt Text Dialog Box

Key the desired WordArt text and apply a different font or size and then click OK.

exercise 14

Creating a Heading with WordArt

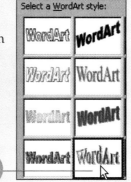

1. At a clear document screen, create the heading shown in figure 15.15 using WordArt by completing the following steps:
   a. At a clear document screen, press Enter seven times, and then move the insertion point back up to the first line.
   b. Display the Drawing toolbar.
   c. Click the Insert WordArt button on the Drawing toolbar.
   d. At the WordArt Gallery, double-click the second option from the left in the fourth row.
   e. At the Edit WordArt Text dialog box, key **Pacific Security Systems**.
   f. Click OK to close the dialog box.

Step 1d

g. Create the line below the company name by completing the following steps:
1) Click the Arrow button on the Drawing toolbar.
2) Draw a horizontal line as shown in figure 15.15.
3) With the horizontal line selected, change the arrow style by clicking the Arrow Style button on the Drawing toolbar, and then clicking the second option from the bottom (Arrow Style 10).
4) Increase the width of the line by clicking the Line Style button on the Drawing toolbar and then clicking the *3 pt* line at the pop-up menu.
5) Change the color of the horizontal line by clicking the down-pointing triangle at the right side of the Line Color button and then clicking the Blue-Gray color (second color option from the *right* in the second row from the top).

2. Deselect the line.
3. Save the document and name it Ch 15, Ex 14.
4. Print and then close Ch 15, Ex 14.

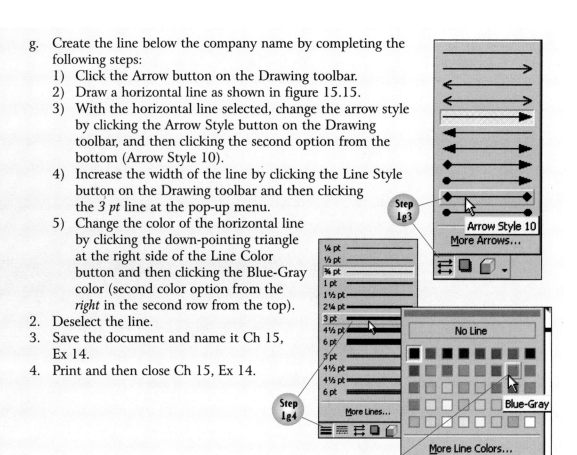

figure

15.15   *Exercise 14*

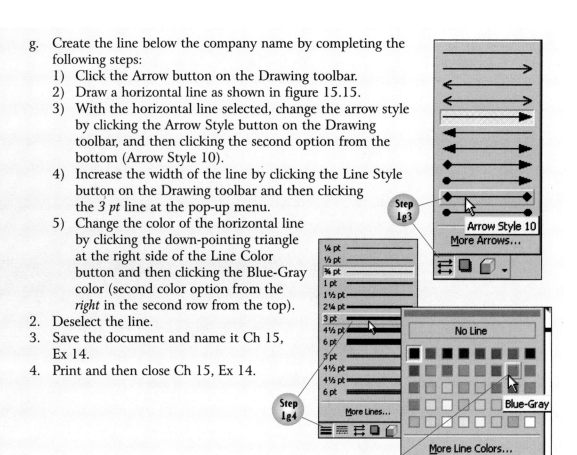

Sizing and Moving WordArt

When you click the OK button, the WordArt text is displayed in the document with the formatting you selected at the WordArt Gallery. The WordArt text is surrounded by white sizing handles and the WordArt toolbar displays near the text.

Use the white sizing handles to change the height and width of the WordArt text. Use the yellow diamond located at the bottom of the WordArt text to change the slant of the WordArt text. To do this, position the mouse pointer on the yellow diamond, hold down the left mouse button, drag to the left or right, and then release the mouse button. This moves the yellow diamond along the bottom of the WordArt and changes the slant of the text.

To move WordArt text, position the mouse pointer on any letter of the text until the mouse pointer displays with a four-headed arrow attached. Hold down the left mouse button, drag the outline of the WordArt text box to the desired position, and then release the mouse button.

When all changes have been made to the WordArt text, click outside the WordArt text box. This removes from the screen the white sizing handles, the yellow diamond, and the WordArt toolbar.

Creating, Moving, and Sizing WordArt Text

1. At a clear document screen, create, move, and size WordArt text by completing the following steps:
   a. Click the Insert WordArt button on the Drawing toolbar.
   b. At the WordArt Gallery, double-click the fourth option from the left in the third row.
   c. At the Edit WordArt Text dialog box, key **Marsdon Spring Festival**.
   d. Click OK to close the dialog box.
   e. Increase the size of the WordArt text by completing the following steps:
      1) Click the Zoom button on the Standard toolbar and then click *Whole Page* at the drop-down list.
      2) If the WordArt toolbar displays over the WordArt text, drag the toolbar out of the way. (To do this, position the mouse pointer on the blue title bar that displays at the top of the toolbar. Hold down the left mouse button, drag the toolbar to a more desirable position, and then release the mouse button.)
      3) Make the WordArt text twice as big by positioning the mouse pointer on the middle sizing handle at the bottom of the WordArt text box, drag down until the height of the box is approximately doubled, and then release the mouse button.

f. Position the mouse pointer (turns into a four-headed arrow) inside the WordArt text box, hold down the left mouse button, drag the text box so it is centered horizontally and vertically on the page, and then release the mouse button.
2. Click outside the WordArt text box to deselect it.
3. Save the document and name it Ch 15, Ex 15.
4. Print and then close Ch 15, Ex 15.

Changing the Font and Font Size

The font for WordArt text will vary depending on the choice you make at the WordArt Gallery. You can change the font at the Edit WordArt text dialog box with the Font option. To do this, click the down-pointing triangle at the right side of the Font text box. This causes a drop-down menu of font choices to display. Scroll through the list until the desired font is visible and then click the desired font.

The font size can be changed by clicking the down-pointing triangle at the right side of the Size text box. This causes a drop-down list of size options to display. Scroll through the list of sizes until the desired size is visible and then click the size.

The Edit WordArt Text dialog box contains Bold and Italic buttons. Click the Bold button to apply bold formatting to the WordArt text and click the Italic button to apply italic formatting.

Creating a Letterhead with WordArt

1. At a clear document screen, create the letterhead shown in figure 15.16 using WordArt by completing the following steps:
    a. At a clear document screen, make the following changes:
        1) Press Enter seven times.
        2) Move the insertion point back to the beginning of the document.
        3) Change the left and right margins to 1 inch.
    b. Click Insert, point to Picture, and then click WordArt.
    c. At the WordArt Gallery, double-click the fourth option from the left in the fourth row.

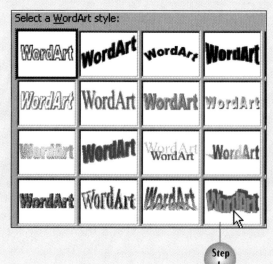

Step 1c

d. At the Edit WordArt Text dialog box, make the following changes:
1) Key **Blue Water Charters.**
2) Change the font to Britannic Bold and the size to 48 by completing the following steps:
   a) Click the down-pointing triangle at the right side of the Font text box.
   b) At the drop-down menu that displays, scroll up the list until *Britannic Bold* displays and then click it.
   c) Click the down-pointing triangle at the right side of the Size text box.
   d) At the drop-down menu that displays, scroll down the list until *48* displays and then click it.
3) Click the OK button to close the dialog box.
e. Position the mouse pointer below the WordArt text box and then click the left mouse button. (This removes the white sizing handles, the yellow diamond, and the WordArt toolbar.)
f. Create the border line shown in figure 15.16 by completing the following steps:
1) Make sure the insertion point is positioned immediately below the text *Blue Water Charters*.
2) Click Format and then Borders and Shading.
3) At the Borders and Shading dialog box with the Borders tab selected, scroll down the Style list box until the line shown in figure 15.16 displays (this is a thin/thick/thin line) and then click the line.

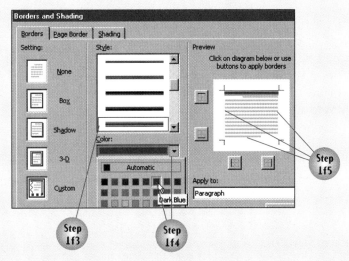

4) Click the down-pointing triangle at the right side of the Color list box and then click the Dark Blue color (sixth color option from the left in the top row).
5) At the Preview diagram at the right side of the dialog box, click the left, right, and bottom borders (this leaves the top border).
6) Click OK to close the dialog box.
g. Key the company slogan by completing the following steps:
1) Click the Center button on the Formatting toolbar.
2) Display the Font dialog box, change the font to 14-point Britannic Bold italic and the font color to Dark Blue (sixth color option from the left in the top row), and then click OK to close the dialog box.
3) Key **"Nature provides the water--we provide the fun!"**
2. Save the document and name it Ch 15, Ex 16.
3. Print and then close Ch 15, Ex 16.

figure
15.16
Exercise 16

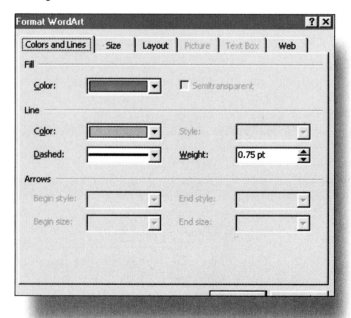

Customizing WordArt

WordArt Gallery

The WordArt toolbar contains buttons for customizing WordArt text. Figure 15.13 displays the WordArt toolbar with the buttons identified. Click the Insert WordArt button and the WordArt Gallery shown in figure 15.12 displays. You can also display this gallery by clicking the WordArt Gallery button on the WordArt toolbar. Click the Edit Text button and the Edit WordArt Text dialog box displays.

Edit Text

Customizing WordArt with Options at the Format WordArt Dialog Box

Format WordArt

WordArt text can be customized at the Format WordArt dialog box shown in figure 15.17. To display this dialog box, click the Format WordArt button on the WordArt toolbar.

figure
15.17

Format WordArt Dialog Box with Colors and Lines Tab Selected

Change the color of the WordArt text and the line creating the text at the Format WordArt dialog box with the Colors and Lines tab selected. Click the Size tab and the dialog box displays options for changing the size and rotation of the WordArt text as well as the scale of the text. To change the position of WordArt text, click the Position tab. At the Format WordArt dialog box with the Position tab selected, you can specify the horizontal and vertical position of the WordArt text. If you want to specify how text will wrap around WordArt text, click the Layout tab. This displays a dialog box with options for specifying the wrapping style of text and horizontal alignment of the WordArt. Click the Advanced button at the Format WordArt dialog box with the Layout tab selected and additional options display for choosing horizontal and vertical alignment and choosing a wrapping style.

Changing Shapes

The WordArt Gallery contains a variety of predesigned WordArt options. Formatting is already applied to these gallery choices. You can, however, customize the gallery choices with buttons on the WordArt toolbar. Use options from the WordArt Shape button to customize the shape of WordArt text. Click the WordArt Shape button on the WordArt toolbar and a palette of shape choices displays as shown in figure 15.18.

WordArt
Shape

figure

15.18   *WordArt Shape Palette*

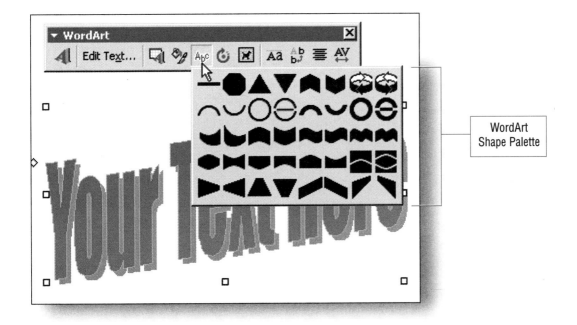

exercise 17

Creating, Shaping, and Sizing WordArt Text

1. At a clear document screen, create WordArt text, and then shape and size the text by completing the following steps:

   a. Click the Insert WordArt button on the Drawing toolbar.

   b. At the WordArt Gallery, double-click the fifth option from the left in the top row.

   c. At the Edit WordArt Text dialog box, key **Sierra Heights Engineering Services.** (Press the spacebar once after keying **Services.**)

   d. Click the OK button.

   e. Change the shape of the WordArt text by completing the following steps:

      1) Click the WordArt Shape button.

      2) At the palette of shape choices, click the third shape from the left in the second row (Circle [Curve]).

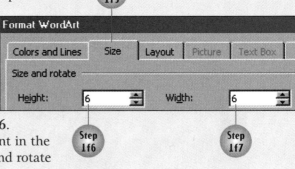

   f. Change the size and color of the WordArt text by completing the following steps:

      1) Click the Format WordArt button on the WordArt toolbar.

      2) At the Format WordArt dialog box, click the Colors and Lines tab.

      3) At the Format WordArt dialog box with the Colors and Lines tab selected, click the down-pointing triangle to the right of the Color box in the Fill section.

      4) At the color palette that displays, click the Sea Green color (fourth color option from the left in the third row).

      5) Click the Size tab.

      6) At the Format WordArt dialog box with the Size tab selected, select the current measurement in the Height text box (in the Size and rotate section), and then key **6.**

      7) Select the current measurement in the Width text box (in the Size and rotate section) and then key **6.**

      8) Click the Layout tab.

      9) At the Format WordArt dialog box with the Layout tab selected, click the Advanced button (located at the bottom of the dialog box).

10) At the Advanced Layout dialog box, click the Picture Position tab.

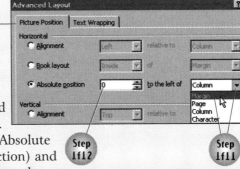

Step 1f10

11) At the Advanced Layout dialog box with the Picture Position tab selected, click the down-pointing triangle at the right side of the to the left of text box (in the Horizontal section—contains the word *Column*) and then click *Margin* at the drop-down list.

12) Select the current measurement in the Absolute position text box (in the Horizontal section) and then key **0**. (Be sure to key a zero and not the letter O.)

Step 1f12

Step 1f11

13) Click OK to close the Advanced Layout dialog box.
14) Click OK to close the Format WordArt dialog box.

g. Click outside the WordArt text (this deselects the WordArt text box).

2. Save the document and name it Ch 15, Ex 17.
3. Print and then close Ch 15, Ex 17.

Rotating WordArt Text

Click the Free Rotate button on the WordArt toolbar and small green circles display in each corner of the WordArt box. Use these rotation handles to rotate the WordArt text. To do this, position the mouse pointer on one of the small green circles until a circled arrow displays and the mouse pointer disappears. Hold down the left mouse button and the circled arrow changes to four arrows in a circle. With the left mouse button held down, drag the outline of the WordArt box to the desired rotation, and then release the mouse button.

Free Rotate

Changing Letter Height

By default, the height of WordArt uppercase letters will be greater than the height of lowercase letters. If you want all letters to have the same height, click the WordArt Same Letter Heights button on the WordArt toolbar.

WordArt Same
Letter Heights

Changing Vertical Alignment

WordArt text displays in a horizontal orientation. This can be changed to a vertical orientation by clicking the WordArt Vertical Text button on the WordArt toolbar.

WordArt
Vertical Text

Changing Text Alignment

Text in a WordArt text box is center aligned by default. With options from the WordArt Alignment button on the WordArt toolbar, this alignment can be changed. When you click the WordArt Alignment button, a drop-down list displays with the following options: Left Align, Center, Right Align, Word Justify, Letter Justify, and Stretch Justify.

WordArt
Alignment

Click the Left Align option if you want text aligned at the left side of the WordArt text box. Click Right Align to align text at the right side of the text box. Choose the Word Justify option to space the words to fit in the WordArt box. Use the Letter Justify option to space out the letters to fit in the WordArt box. Click the last option, Stretch Justify, to stretch letters to fit in the WordArt box.

Changing Character Spacing

WordArt Character Spacing

Click the WordArt Character Spacing button on the WordArt toolbar and a drop-down list displays with options for determining character spacing. By default, the Normal option is selected at the WordArt Character Spacing drop-down list. Choose one of the other options to either tighten up or loosen the spacing between characters. These options include Very Tight, Tight, Loose, Very Loose, and Custom.

Kerning is a term that refers to the decrease of space between specific letter pairs. By default, the Kern Character Pairs option is selected. If you do not want letter pairs kerned, remove the check mark from this option.

exercise 18

Creating and Then Customizing WordArt Text

1. At a clear document screen, create WordArt text, and then change the font, shape, and size of the text by completing the following steps:
   a. Click the Insert WordArt button on the Drawing toolbar.
   b. At the WordArt Gallery, double-click the second option from the left in the second row.

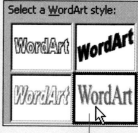

Select a WordArt style:

Step 1b

   c. At the Edit WordArt Text dialog box, make the following changes:
      1) Key **Now is the time**
      2) Press Enter and then key **to get out and**
      3) Press Enter and then key **vote!**
      4) Change the font to Braggadocio.
      5) Click the OK button to close the dialog box.
   d. Change the alignment, size, and position of the WordArt text by completing the following steps:

Step 1d1

      1) Click the WordArt Alignment button on the WordArt toolbar and then click Letter Justify at the drop-down list.

      2) Change the size and position of the WordArt by completing the following steps:
         a) Click the Format WordArt button on the WordArt toolbar.
         b) At the Format WordArt dialog box, click the Size tab.
         c) At the Format WordArt dialog box with the Size tab selected, select the current measurement in the Height text box (in the Size and rotate section), and then key **2.5**.
         d) Select the current measurement in the Width text box (in the Size and rotate section) and then key **6**.
         e) Click the Layout tab.
         f) At the Format WordArt dialog box with the Layout tab selected, click the Advanced button (located at the bottom of the dialog box).

g) At the Advanced Layout dialog box, click the Picture Position tab.

h) At the Advanced Layout dialog box with the Picture Position tab selected, click the down-pointing triangle at the right side of the to the left of text box (in the Horizontal section—contains the word *Column*) and then click *Margin* at the drop-down list.

i) Select the current measurement in the Absolute position text box (in the Horizontal section) and then key **0**. (Be sure to key a zero and not the letter O.)

j) Click OK to close the Advanced Layout dialog box.

k) Click OK to close the Format WordArt dialog box.

e. Click outside the WordArt text box to deselect it.

2. Save the document and name it Ch 15, Ex 18.

3. Print and then close Ch 15, Ex 18.

Customizing WordArt with Buttons on the Drawing Toolbar

Earlier in this chapter, you learned about the buttons on the Drawing toolbar (see figure 15.2). Buttons on this toolbar can also be used to customize WordArt text. For example, with buttons on the Drawing toolbar, you can change the letter color, line color, and line style, add a shadow, and add a three-dimensional effect.

Adding Fill Shading or Color

With the Fill Color button on the Drawing toolbar, shading or color can be added to WordArt text. Click the Fill Color button and the WordArt text will be filled with the color displayed on the button. If you want to choose a different color, click the down-pointing triangle at the right side of the Fill Color button, and then click the desired color at the color palette.

Fill Color

Creating and Then Customizing Gradient, Color, and Shading of WordArt Text

1. At a clear document screen, create the letterhead shown in figure 15.19 using WordArt by completing the following steps:

a. Click the Insert WordArt button on the Drawing toolbar.

b. At the WordArt Gallery, double-click the third option from the left in the top row.

c. At the Edit WordArt Text dialog box, key **North Air Adventures**, and then click OK to close the dialog box.

d. Click the WordArt Shape button on the WordArt toolbar.

e. Click the fifth shape from the left in the top row (Chevron Up).

Step 1b

Step 1e

Step 1d

f. Change the size and position of the WordArt by completing the following steps:
 1) Click the Format WordArt button on the WordArt toolbar.
 2) At the Format WordArt dialog box, click the Size tab.
 3) At the Format WordArt dialog box with the Size tab selected, select the current measurement in the Height text box (in the Size and rotate section), and then key 1.
 4) Select the current measurement in the Width text box (in the Size and rotate section) and then key 2.5.
 5) Click the Layout tab.
 6) At the Format WordArt dialog box with the Layout tab selected, click the Advanced button located at the bottom of the dialog box.
 7) At the Advanced Layout dialog box, click the Picture Position tab.
 8) At the Advanced Layout dialog box with the Picture Position tab selected, click the down-pointing triangle at the right side of the to the left of text box (in the Horizontal section—contains the word *Column*) and then click *Margin* at the drop-down list.

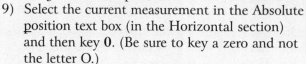

Step 1f9

Step 1f8

Step 1f10

 9) Select the current measurement in the Absolute position text box (in the Horizontal section) and then key 0. (Be sure to key a zero and not the letter O.)

Step 1f11

 10) Click the down-pointing triangle at the right side of the below text box (in the Vertical section—contains the word *Paragraph*) and then click *Margin* at the drop-down list.
 11) Select the current measurement in the Absolute position text box (in the Vertical section) and then key 0. (Be sure to key a zero and not the letter O.)
 12) Click OK to close the Advanced Layout dialog box.
 13) Click OK to close the Format WordArt dialog box.
g. Add a gradient and change colors by completing the following steps:
 1) Click the down-pointing triangle at the right side of the Fill Color button on the Drawing toolbar.

Step 1g3c

 2) At the palette of color choices, click Fill Effects located at the bottom of the palette.
 3) At the Fill Effects dialog box with the Gradient tab selected, make the following changes:

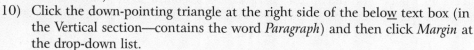

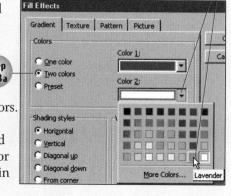

Step 1g3a

  a) Click in the circle preceding Two colors.
  b) Click the down-pointing triangle at the right side of the Color 1 box and then click the Plum color at the color palette (seventh color from the left in the fourth row).
  c) Click the down-pointing triangle at the right side of the Color 2 box and then click the Lavender color at the color palette (seventh color from the left in the fifth row).

4) Click OK to close the Fill Effects dialog box.

   h. Click outside the WordArt text to deselect it.

   i. Press Enter six times to move the insertion point below *North Air Adventures* and then create the border line by completing the following steps:

     1) Click F<u>o</u>rmat and then <u>B</u>orders and Shading.

     2) At the Borders and Shading dialog box with the <u>B</u>orders tab selected, click the line style shown in figure 15.19 in the St<u>y</u>le list box (third line option from the end of the line style list).

     3) Click the down-pointing triangle at the right side of the <u>C</u>olor box.

     4) At the drop-down list, scroll through the list until *Violet* is visible, and then click *Violet*.

     5) Click the left, right, and bottom side of the diagram in the Preview section. (This removes all border lines except the top border.)

     6) Click OK to close the dialog box.

2. Save the document and name it Ch 15, Ex 19.

3. Print and then close Ch 15, Ex 19.

Exercise 19

Changing Line Color and Style

Line Color

WordArt text is surrounded by a border line. The color of this line can be changed with the Line Color button on the Drawing toolbar. Click the Line Color button and the line color of the WordArt text changes to the color displayed on the button. To change a different color, click the down-pointing triangle at the right side of the Line Color button, and then click the desired color at the palette that displays.

Line Style

     The WordArt text line can be changed with options from the Line Style button on the Drawing toolbar. To change the line style, click the Line Style button, and then click the desired style at the pop-up menu.

Adding Shadow and 3-D Effects

Shadow

Click the Shadow button on the Drawing toolbar and a palette of shadow options displays. Click the desired option or click the Shadow Setting option and a Shadow Settings toolbar displays. This toolbar contains buttons for turning shadows off or on and buttons for nudging the shadow up, down, left, or right.

3-D

     If you want to add a three-dimensional look to an object, select the object, and then click the 3-D button on the Drawing toolbar. This displays a palette of three-dimensional choices as well as a 3-D Settings option. Click this option and the 3-D Settings toolbar displays. This toolbar contains buttons for turning 3-D on or off and changing the title, depth, direction, and light source.

exercise 20

Creating and Then Applying Pattern, Color, and Shading to WordArt Text

1. Create the WordArt text shown in figure 15.20 by completing the following steps:

Step 1b

   a. Click the Insert WordArt button on the Drawing toolbar.
   b. At the WordArt Gallery, double-click the third option from the left in the top row.
   c. At the Edit WordArt Text dialog box, key **Surfing the Internet**, and then click OK to close the dialog box.
   d. Click the WordArt Shape button on the WordArt toolbar and then click the second shape from the left in the fourth row (Deflate).

Step 1d

   e. Change the size and position of the WordArt by completing the following steps:
      1) Click the Format WordArt button on the WordArt toolbar.
      2) At the Format WordArt dialog box, click the Size tab.
      3) At the Format WordArt dialog box with the Size tab selected, select the current measurement in the Height text box (in the Size and rotate section), and then key **2**.
      4) Select the current measurement in Width text box (in the Size and rotate section) and then key **6**.

5) Click the Layout tab.
6) At the Format WordArt dialog box with the Layout tab selected, click the Advanced button (located at the bottom of the dialog box).

7) At the Advanced Layout dialog box, click the Picture Position tab.

8) At the Advanced Layout dialog box with the Picture Position tab selected, click the down-pointing triangle at the right side of the to the left of text box (in the Horizontal section—contains the word *Column*) and then click *Margin* at the drop-down list.

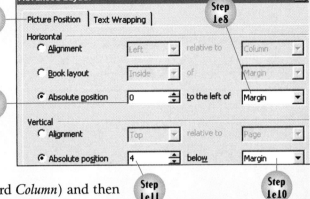

9) Select the current measurement in the Absolute position text box (in the Horizontal section) and then key **0**. (Be sure to key a zero and not the letter O.)

10) Click the down-pointing triangle at the right side of the below text box (in the Vertical section—contains the word *Paragraph*) and then click *Margin* at the drop-down list.

11) Select the current measurement in the Absolute position text box (in the Vertical section) and then key **4**.

12) Click OK to close the Advanced Layout dialog box.

13) Click OK to close the Format WordArt dialog box.

f. Add a pattern and change colors by completing the following steps:

1) Click the down-pointing triangle at the right side of the Fill Color button on the Drawing toolbar.

2) At the palette of color choices that displays, click Fill Effects located at the bottom of the palette.

3) At the Fill Effects dialog box, click the Pattern tab.

4) At the Fill Effects dialog box with the Pattern tab selected, make the following changes:

   a) Click the fourth pattern option from the left in the second row (Light horizontal).

   b) Click the down-pointing triangle at the right side of the Foreground box.

   c) At the color palette that displays, click the Turquoise color (fifth color from the left in the fourth row).

   d) Click the down-pointing triangle at the right side of the Background box.

   e) At the color palette that displays, click the Pink color (first color from the left in the fourth row).

5) Click OK to close the Fill Effects dialog box.

g. Add a shadow to the text by clicking the Shadow button on the Drawing toolbar and then clicking the second shadow option from the left in the fourth row (Shadow Style 14).

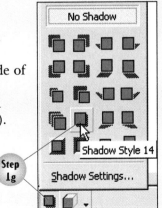

h. Click outside the WordArt text to deselect the WordArt box.
2. Save the document and name it Ch 15, Ex 20.
3. Print and then close Ch 15, Ex 20.

figure

15.20 *Exercise 20*

Surfing the Internet

chapter summary

➤ Create your own shapes and images with buttons on the Drawing toolbar.

➤ Display the Drawing toolbar by clicking the Drawing button on the Standard toolbar; or, by positioning the mouse pointer on the Standard or Formatting toolbar, clicking the *right* mouse button, and then clicking *Drawing* at the drop-down list.

➤ A shape drawn with the Line or Arrow buttons is considered a line drawing. A shape drawn with the Rectangle or Oval buttons is considered an enclosed object. Fill color can be added to enclosed objects.

➤ Click the Line button to draw a line in the document screen. To draw more than one line, double-click the Line button.

➤ A variety of predesigned shapes are available from the AutoShapes button on the Drawing toolbar.

➤ Create a text box by clicking the Text Box button on the Drawing toolbar and then drawing the box in the document screen.

➤ A text box can be drawn inside of a drawn shape.

➤ To select an enclosed object, position the mouse pointer anywhere inside the object and then click the left mouse button. To select a line, position the mouse pointer on the line until the pointer turns into an arrow with a four-headed arrow attached, and then click the left mouse button.

➤ To select several objects at once, click the Select Objects button, position the crosshairs in the upper left corner of the area containing the objects, hold down the left mouse button, drag the outline to the lower right corner of the area containing the objects, and then release the mouse button. You can also select more than one object by holding down the Shift key and then clicking each object.

➤ To delete an object, select it, and then press the Delete key.

➤ To move an object, select it, choose a wrapping style, and then drag the image to the desired location.

➤ To copy an object, select it, and then hold down the Ctrl key. Drag the outline of the object to the desired location, then release the mouse button and then the Ctrl key.

➤ Use the sizing handles that display around a selected object to increase or decrease the size of the object.

➤ Add fill color to an enclosed object with the Fill Color button on the Drawing toolbar.

➤ Change the line color with Line Color button on the Drawing toolbar.

➤ Change the line style with the Line Style, Dash Style, or Arrow Style buttons on the Drawing toolbar.

➤ Add a shadow effect to an object with options from the Shadow button on the Drawing toolbar.

➤ Add a three-dimensional effect to an object with options from the 3-D button on the Drawing toolbar.

➤ Align and distribute graphic elements by selecting the element and then clicking the Draw button on the Drawing toolbar, pointing to Align or Distribute, and then clicking the desired alignment or distribution.

➤ An object (but not a text box) can be flipped and rotated with options from the Draw button on the Drawing toolbar.

➤ Add a callout to an image with options from the AutoShapes button on the Drawing toolbar.

➤ With the WordArt application, you can distort or modify text to conform to a variety of shapes. With WordArt, you can change the font, size, and alignment of text. You can also add fill color, line color, change the line style, and add shadow and three-dimensional effects.

➤ Display the WordArt Gallery by clicking Insert, pointing to Picture, and then clicking WordArt or by clicking the Insert WordArt button on the Drawing or WordArt toolbar.

➤ Select an option at the WordArt Gallery by double-clicking the desired option.

➤ After choosing an option at the WordArt Gallery, the Edit WordArt Text dialog box displays. Key the desired WordArt text in this dialog box.

➤ Use the white sizing handles around WordArt text to change the size.

➤ Move WordArt text by positioning the arrow pointer on any letter until it displays with a four-headed arrow, hold down the left mouse button, move the outline of the WordArt box to the desired position, and then release the mouse button.

➤ Specify a font and font size for WordArt at the Edit WordArt Text dialog box.

➤ Create and customize WordArt with buttons on the Drawing toolbar and the WordArt toolbar.

commands review

Mouse/Keyboard

Display Drawing toolbar	Click Drawing button on Standard toolbar; or, position mouse pointer on Standard or Formatting toolbar, click the *right* mouse button, and then click *Drawing* at the drop-down list
Colors dialog box	Click down-pointing triangle at right side of Fill Color button and then click <u>M</u>ore Fill Colors
Fill Effects dialog box	Click down-pointing triangle at right side of Fill Color button and then click <u>F</u>ill Effects
Patterned Lines dialog box	Click down-pointing triangle at right side of Line Color button and then click <u>P</u>atterned Lines
Format Text Box dialog box	Double-click text box
Shadow Settings toolbar	Click the Shadow button and then click <u>S</u>hadow Settings
3-D Settings toolbar	Click the 3-D button and then click <u>3</u>-D Settings
Format AutoShape dialog box	Double-click autoshape
Display Align or Distribute side menu	Click D<u>r</u>aw button on Drawing toolbar and then point to Align or Distribute
WordArt Gallery	Click <u>I</u>nsert, point to <u>P</u>icture, click <u>W</u>ordArt; or click the Insert WordArt button on the Drawing or WordArt toolbar
Format WordArt dialog box	Click the Format WordArt button on WordArt toolbar
WordArt shape palette	Click the WordArt Shape button on WordArt toolbar
Drawing toolbar	Click Drawing button on Standard toolbar; or click <u>V</u>iew, point to <u>T</u>oolbars, click *Drawing;* or position arrow pointer on toolbar, click *right* mouse button, then click *Drawing*

thinking offline

Completion: In the space provided at the right, indicate the correct term, command, or number.

1. Choose a variety of predesigned shapes by first clicking this button on the Drawing toolbar.

2. To create a box and then insert text inside the box, begin by clicking this button on the Drawing toolbar.

3. To change the width and height of an object at the same time, use one of these sizing handles.

4. To draw a perfect circle, click the Oval button on the Drawing toolbar, hold down this key, and then draw the circle.

   _____

5. If you want to draw the same shape more than once, do this on the shape button on the Drawing toolbar.

   _____

6. This is a useful tool for identifying parts of an illustration or picture.

   _____

7. Click this button on the Drawing toolbar to display a variety of three-dimensional effects.

   _____

8. To select more than one object, hold down this key on the keyboard, and then click each object.

   _____

9. To copy a selected object, hold down this key on the keyboard while dragging the object.

   _____

10. A drawn object can be rotated or flipped, but not this type of box.

    _____

11. To display a list of callouts, click this button on the Drawing toolbar, and then point to Callouts.

    _____

12. Click the Insert WordArt button on the Drawing toolbar and this displays on the screen.

    _____

13. Key WordArt text at this dialog box.

    _____

14. Click this button on the WordArt toolbar to display a palette of shape options.

    _____

15. Click this button on the Drawing toolbar to change the color of WordArt text.

    _____

16. Change the color of the WordArt text and the line creating the text at this dialog box with the Colors and Lines tab selected.

    _____

17. In the space provided below, write the steps you would complete to draw a perfect square and then fill that square with red color. (Assume the Drawing toolbar is already displayed.)

    _____

    _____

    _____

18. In the space provided below, list the steps you would complete to change the text color to green and add a shadow to existing WordArt text.

    _____

    _____

    _____

working hands-on

Assessment 1

1. At a clear document screen, draw the square, circle, and rectangle shown in figure 15.21. After drawing the shapes, make the following changes:
   a. Select each shape, click the Line Style button on the Drawing toolbar, and then click the 2¼ pt option. (This makes the line thicker.)
   b. Add red fill to the square, yellow fill to the circle, and blue fill to the rectangle.
2. Save the document and name it Ch 15, SA 01.
3. Print and then close Ch 15, SA 01.

figure

15.21   *Assessment 1*

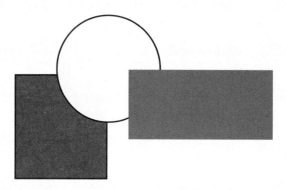

Assessment 2

1. At a clear document screen, create the organizational boxes shown in figure 15.22 with the following specifications:
   a. Key the title bolded and centered as shown in the figure.
   b. Press the Enter key three times and then create the first text box with the following specifications:
      1) Change the font to 12-point Arial bold.
      2) Key the text in the first box as shown in figure 15.22.
      3) Add pale blue fill to the text box.

c. After creating the first text box, copy the text box the number of times needed for the document. Change the title inside the boxes as shown in figure 15.22.

d. Select the title *DEPARTMENT OF TRAINING AND EDUCATION* and then change the font to 14-point Arial bold.

2. Save the document and name it Ch 15, SA 02.

3. Print and then close Ch 15, SA 02.

figure

15.22 *Assessment 2*

DEPARTMENT OF TRAINING AND EDUCATION

Director

Trainer

Trainer

Assistant

Assistant

Assessment 3

1. At a clear document screen, create the object shown in figure 15.23 with the following specifications:

a. Create the star with the 16-Point Star autoshape. Make the star approximately 5.5 inches wide and 4.5 inches tall. (Use the adjustment handle to drag in the points slightly.)

b. Add light yellow fill to the star.

c. Draw a text box inside the star.

d. Key the text shown inside the star in figure 15.23. Set the name *Taylor Ewing* in 28-point Impact bold. (If Impact is not available, choose a similar typeface.) Set the remaining text in 18-point Impact bold.

e. With the text box selected, remove the black line, and then add light yellow fill. (To remove the black line from the text box, click the down-pointing triangle at the right side of the Line Color button on the Drawing toolbar, and then click *No Line* at the palette of color choices.)

2. Save the document and name it Ch 15, SA 03.
3. Print and then close Ch 15, SA 03.

 **figure**

15.23 *Assessment 3*

Taylor Ewing
Employee
of the Month

Assessment 4

1. At a clear document screen, create the document shown in figure 15.24 with the following specifications:
   a. Create the first triangle with an autoshape from the Basic Shapes option.
   b. Copy the triangle to create a total of five triangles.
   c. Select and then flip vertically two of the triangles.
   d. Move the triangles so they are positioned as shown in figure 15.24.
   e. Add fill color to the triangles as shown in the figure.
2. Save the document and name it Ch 15, SA 04.
3. Print and then close Ch 15, SA 04.

figure

15.24   *Assessment 4*

Assessment 5

1. At a clear document screen, create the document shown in figure 15.25 with the following specifications:
   a. Insert the clip art image *laptop* from the ClipArt folder on the CD that accompanies this textbook.
   b. Change the size of the image to approximately 3 inches by 3 inches.
   c. Click the Text Wrapping button on the Picture toolbar and then click the Through option.
   d. Drag the selected image to the middle of the screen.
   e. Add the callouts shown in figure 15.25. (Set the callout text in 12-point Arial bold.)
2. Save the document and name it Ch 15, SA 05.
3. Print and then close Ch 15, SA 05.

figure

15.25   *Assessment 5*

Monitor

Keyboard

Touch Pad

Assessment 6

1. At a clear document screen, create the WordArt text and border line shown in figure 15.26 by completing the following steps:
   a. Press the Enter key eight times and then move the insertion point up to the first line.
   b. Display the WordArt Gallery.
   c. Double-click the third option from the left in the top row.
   d. At the Edit WordArt Text dialog box, key **Mountain**, press Enter, key **High School**, and then close the dialog box.
   e. Change the shape of the text to Triangle Up. *(Hint: Click the WordArt Shape button on the WordArt toolbar.)*
   f. Display the Format WordArt dialog box with the Size tab selected, change the height to *1.2* and the width to *2*, and then close the dialog box.
   g. Display the Format WordArt dialog box with the Layout tab selected, click Left in the Horizontal alignment section, and then close the dialog box.
   h. Deselect the WordArt text.
   i. Insert a thick/thin border below the company name as shown in figure 15.26. (Do this at the Borders and Shading dialog box.)
2. Save the document and name it Ch 15, SA 06.
3. Print and then close Ch 15, SA 06.

 **figure**

15.26 **Assessment 6**

Assessment 7

1. At a clear document screen, create the WordArt text shown in figure 15.27 with the following specifications (your text will appear much larger than what you see in figure 15.27):
   a. Display the WordArt Gallery.
   b. Double-click the fifth option from the left in the top row.
   c. At the Edit WordArt Text dialog box, complete the following steps:
      1) Key **Coleman Development Corporation** and then press Enter.
      2) Key **Forest Renovation** and then press Enter.
      3) Key **and Revitalization Project**.
      4) Change the font size to 28.
      5) Close the Edit WordArt Text dialog box.
   d. Change the shape of the text to a Button (Curve). *(Hint: Click the WordArt Shape button on the WordArt toolbar and then click the fourth option from the left in the second row.)*
   e. Display the Format WordArt dialog box with the Size tab selected, change the height and width to 6 inches, and then close the dialog box.
   f. Change the Fill Color to Green.
   g. Change the Zoom to Whole Page and then drag the WordArt text so it is centered horizontally and vertically on the page.
2. Save the document and name it Ch 15, SA 07.
3. Print and then close Ch 15, SA 07.

figure

15.27 *Assessment 7*

Assessment 8

1. At a clear document screen, create the text *Madison Creek Elementary School* as WordArt text that displays slanted across the entire page by completing the following steps:
   a. Display the WordArt Gallery.
   b. Double-click the second option from the left in the third row.
   c. At the Edit WordArt dialog box key **Madison Creek Elementary School**, and then close the dialog box.
   d. Change the shape of the text to a slant. *(Hint: Click the WordArt Shape button on the WordArt toolbar and then click the fifth shape from the left in the bottom row [Slant Up].)*
   e. Display the Fill Effects dialog box with the Pattern tab selected and then make the following changes:
      1) Click the third pattern option from the left in the bottom row (Wide upward diagonal).
      2) Change the foreground color to Dark Blue.
      3) Change the background color to Lavender.
      4) Close the dialog box.
   f. Click the down-pointing triangle at the right side of the Line Color button and then click the Dark Blue color.
   g. Display the Format WordArt dialog box with the Size tab selected, change the width to 6 inches, and then close the dialog box.
   h. Click the Shadow button on the Drawing toolbar and then click the second option from the left in the second row (Shadow Style 6).
2. Save the document and name it Ch 15, SA 08.
3. Print and then close Ch 15, SA 08.

Assessment 9

1. At a clear document screen, create the text *Spring Festival* as WordArt text. You determine the formatting of the text and include at least the following:
   a. Change the shape of the WordArt text.
   b. Add a pattern to the WordArt text.
   c. Change the foreground and background color of the WordArt text.
   d. Add a shadow or three-dimensional effect to the WordArt text.
2. Save the document and name it Ch 15, SA 09.
3. Print and then close Ch 15, SA 09.

Chapter 16

Exploring the Internet

PERFORMANCE OBJECTIVES

Upon successful completion of chapter 16, you will be able to:

- Browse the World Wide Web from within Word.
- Locate specific sites on the Web.
- Search for specific information on the Internet.
- Create and format a Web home page.
- Create hyperlinks.

Increasingly, businesses are accessing the Internet to conduct research, publish product or catalog information, communicate, and market products globally. In Microsoft Word 2000, you can jump to the Internet and browse the World Wide Web. You can also create a document in Word and then save it as a Web document with HyperText Markup Language (HTML) codes. HTML "tags" attached to information in a Web document enable the links and jumps between documents and data resources to operate. Information provided by the tags also instructs the browser software how to display text, images, animations, or sounds.

Understanding the Internet

The *Internet* is a network of computers connected around the world. In 1969, the U.S. Defense Department created a network to allow researchers at different sites to exchange information. The first network consisted of only four computers. Since then, the number of networks that have connected has grown exponentially, and it is no longer just a vehicle of information for researchers, but can be used by anyone with a modem attached to their computer.

Users access the Internet for several purposes: to communicate using e-mail, to subscribe to news groups, to transfer files, to socialize with other users around the globe in "chat" rooms, and largely to access virtually any kind of information imaginable.

To use the Internet, you generally need three things—an Internet Service Provider (ISP), a program to browse the Web (called a Web browser), and a search engine (used to locate specific data on the Internet).

A variety of Internet Service Providers are available. Local ISPs are available as well as commercial ISPs such as Microsoft Network®, America Online®, AT&T WorldNet Service®, and CompuServe®. To complete the exercises in this chapter, you will need access to the Internet through an ISP. Check with your instructor to determine the ISP used by your school to connect to the Internet.

Once you are connected to the Internet, you can access the *World Wide Web*. The World Wide Web is the most commonly used application on the Internet. The World Wide Web is a set of standards and protocols used to access information available on the Internet. The Internet is the physical network utilized to carry the data. To access the Web and maneuver within the Web, you need a software program called a *Web browser*. A Web browser allows you to move around the Internet by pointing and clicking with the mouse. A popular Web browser designed by Microsoft is the Microsoft Internet Explorer. The exercises in this chapter are created with the assumption that you will have Microsoft Internet Explorer available. If you will be using a different Web browser, some of the steps in the exercises may vary.

A phenomenal amount of information is available on the Internet. Searching through all that information to find the specific information you need can be an overwhelming task. Software programs, called *search engines*, have been created to help you search more quickly and easily for the desired information. There are many search engines available on the Internet, each offering the opportunity to search for specific information. As you use different search engines, you may find you prefer one over the others.

Browsing the World Wide Web

In this chapter, you will be completing several exercises and assessments that require you to search for locations and information on the World Wide Web. To do this, you will need the following:

1. A modem or network connection to a server with Internet access.
2. Browser software installed and configured. (This chapter will explore the World Wide Web using Microsoft Internet Explorer.)
3. An Internet Service Provider account.

A *modem* is a hardware device that allows data to be carried over telephone lines. The word "modem" is derived from MOdulator/DEModulator. The modem attached to your computer converts digital data into an analog signal that can be transferred over telephone lines. At the other end of the connection is another modem that converts the analog signal back to digital data for the receiving computer. There are internal and external modems available in a variety of speeds. Modem speed is measured in terms of the number of bits per second data is transferred. If you are using a computer connected to a network, the network server will route the data through its modem, or to another server with a modem.

An Internet Service Provider (ISP) sells access to the Internet. In order to provide this access, the ISP must have in place the hardware and software necessary to support access to the Internet, phone lines to accept the modem connections, and support staff to assist their customers. The ISP is responsible for configuring their computers, routers, and software to enable connectivity to every other individual and computer that make up the Internet.

Locating URLs on the Internet

We all know that we can dial a telephone number of a friend or relative in any country around the world and establish a connection within seconds. The global telephone system is an amazing network that functions because of a common set of protocols and standards that are agreed upon by each country. The Internet operates on the same principle. Computer protocols known as Transmission Control Protocol/Internet Protocol (TCP/IP) form the base of the Internet. Protocols are simply agreements on how various hardware and software should communicate with each other. The Internet Service Provider becomes the Domain Name Service (DNS), *the route to the Internet*. The DNS and IP determine how to route your computer to another location/computer on the Internet. Every computer directly linked to the Internet has a unique IP address.

This explanation has been overly simplified. The technical details on how computer A can "talk" to computer B do not directly involve a computer user any more than does picking up a phone in Vancouver, British Columbia, and dialing a number in San Diego, California.

Uniform Resource Locators, referred to as URLs, are the method used to identify locations on the Internet. The format of a URL is *http://server-name.path*. The first part of the URL, *http://*, identifies the protocol. The letters *http* stand for Hypertext Transfer Protocol, which is the protocol or language used to transfer data within the World Wide Web. The colon and slashes separate the protocol from the server name. The server name is the second component of the URL. For example, in the URL *http://www.microsoft.com*, the server name is identified as *microsoft*. The last part of the URL specifies the domain to which the server belongs. For example, *.com* refers to "commercial" and establishes that the URL is a commercial company. Other examples of domains include *.edu* for "educational," *.gov* for "government," and *.mil* for "military." Some examples of URLs are displayed in figure 16.1.

figure
16.1   *Sample URLs*

URL	Connects to
http://www.microsoft.com	Microsoft Corporation home page
http://www.emcp.com	EMC/Paradigm Publishing home page
http://lcweb.loc.gov	Library of Congress home page
http://pbs.org	Public Broadcasting Service home page
http://www.washington.edu	University of Washington home page
http://www.kodak.com	Eastman Kodak home page
http://www.alaska-air.com	Alaska Airlines home page

If you know the URL for a specific Web site and would like to visit that site, key the URL in the Address section of the Web toolbar. To display the Web toolbar, shown in figure 16.2, click View, point to Toolbars, and then click Web at the drop-down list. You can also display the Web toolbar by positioning the mouse pointer on a toolbar, clicking the *right* mouse button, and then clicking Web at the drop-down list.

Before keying a URL in the Address text box on the Web toolbar, make sure you are connected to the Internet through your Internet Service Provider. When keying a URL, you must key the address exactly as written, including any colons (:) or slashes (/).

When you key a URL in the Address section of the Web toolbar and then press Enter, your default Web browser is automatically activated. The home page for the specific URL displays on the screen in the Web browser. Figure 16.3 shows the Microsoft home page in the Internet Explorer Web browser. You will learn more about Internet Explorer later in this chapter.

When you are connected to a URL, the home page for the specific URL (Web site) displays. The home page is the starting point for viewing the Web site. At the home page, you can choose to "branch off" the home page to other pages within the Web site or jump to other Web sites. You do this with hyperlinks that are embedded in the home page. You will learn more about hyperlinks in the next section of this chapter. In exercise 1, you will be visiting some Web site home pages using URLs.

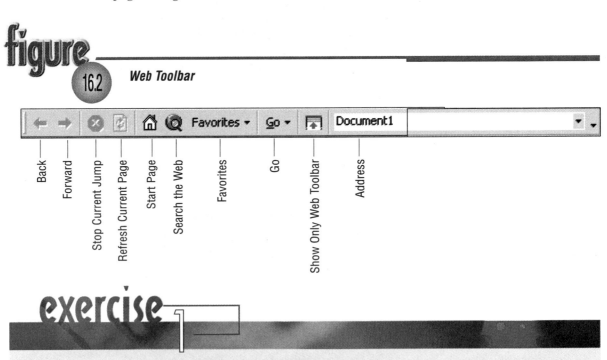

figure
16.2   *Web Toolbar*

exercise

Visiting Web Site Home Pages

1. Make sure you are connected to the Internet through an Internet Service Provider.
2. Explore several locations on the World Wide Web from within Word by completing the following steps:
   a. Display the Web toolbar by clicking View, pointing to Toolbars, and then clicking Web at the drop-down list.

b. Click in the Address text box located on the Web toolbar. (This will select the current document name in the text box.)

c. Display the home page for Microsoft by keying **http://www.microsoft.com** and then pressing Enter.

d. In a few moments, the Microsoft home page displays. The home page displays in your default Web browser similar to what is shown in figure 16.3. Home pages are updated frequently, so the Microsoft home page you are viewing will probably vary from what you see in figure 16.3. Scroll down the home page, reading the information about Microsoft.

Step 2c

e. After reading about Microsoft, view the Web site home page for *The New York Times* newspaper. To do this, click the current address located in the Address text box, key **http://www.nytimes.com** and then press Enter.

f. Read the information that displays about the newspaper.

3. After reading the information displayed on *The New York Times* home page, click File and then Close.

Step 2e

Microsoft Home Page

16.3

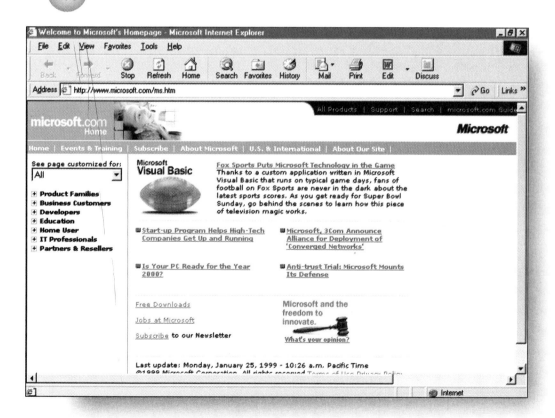

Using Hyperlinks

As you were viewing the Web site home pages for Microsoft and *The New York Times*, did you notice text that displayed in a different color and was also underlined? Text displayed in a different color and underlined indicates text that has been identified as a *hyperlink*. A hyperlink allows you to link or connect to another item. A hyperlink can display in a variety of ways. It can display as text in a different color and underlined or as headings or buttons. Move the mouse pointer to a hyperlink and the mouse pointer turns into a hand.

To use a hyperlink, position the mouse pointer on the desired hyperlink until the pointer turns into a hand, and then click the left mouse button. For example, when you displayed the Microsoft home page, you could have clicked the hyperlink *All Products* located at the top of the page to display information about Microsoft products. Most pages contain a variety of hyperlinks. Using these links, you can zero in on the exact information for which you are searching.

Back

Forward

The Web toolbar as well as the Internet Explorer Web browser contains a Back button (see figure 16.2) you can click to display the previous Web page. If you click the Back button and then would like to go back to the hyperlink, click the Forward button. Depending on your system configuration, Web pages may display in Microsoft Internet Explorer. Internet Explorer also contains a Back button and a Forward button. By clicking the Back button, you can back your way out of any hyperlinks and return to the default Web home page. In exercise 2, you will be exploring two sites on the World Wide Web and using hyperlinks to display specific information.

exercise 2

Visiting Web Sites and Using Hyperlinks

1. Make sure you are connected to the Internet through an Internet Service Provider.
2. Explore several sites on the World Wide Web by completing the following steps:
   a. At a clear document screen, make sure the Web toolbar displays.
   b. Click in the Address text box located on the Web toolbar.
   c. Key **http://www.time.com** and then press Enter.
   d. When the *Time Magazine* home page displays, click the hyperlink to the cover story by positioning the mouse pointer over an image or text that represents the cover story until the pointer turns into a hand and then clicking the left mouse button.
   e. When the cover story page displays, click the Print button on the Internet Explorer toolbar to print the page.
   f. Click the Back button to return to the *Time* home page.
   g. Click the current address located in the Address text box.
   h. Key **http://www.amazon.com** and then press Enter.

   i. When the Amazon.com home page displays, click the *BESTSELLERS* hyperlink. (This hyperlink is probably located toward the top of the Amazon.com page. If this hyperlink is not available, choose any other hyperlink that interests you.)
   j. When the bestseller page displays, print the page.
3. After printing the bestseller page, click <u>F</u>ile and then <u>C</u>lose.

Searching the Internet Using Internet Explorer

In the previous exercises, you jumped around the Web by keying URLs, which is a fast way to move from site to site. Often, however, you will access the Web to search for information and you will not know the URL that you want to visit.

Search engines are valuable tools to assist a user in locating information on a particular topic by simply keying a few words or a short phrase. There are many search engines available on the Internet such as Excite, Infoseek, Lycos, Yahoo, AltaVista, and HotBot. Each offers the opportunity to search for specific information. As you use different search engines, you may find you prefer one over the others.

Search the Web

To search for information on the Web, click the Search the Web button on the Web toolbar. This displays the Internet Explorer Search Setup page as shown in figure 16.4. As mentioned earlier in this chapter, Internet Explorer is a Web browser, which creates an environment in which you can search and display Web sites. Figure 16.4 identifies the features of the Internet Explorer program window and figure 16.5 describes the features.

figure
16.4
Internet Explorer Window

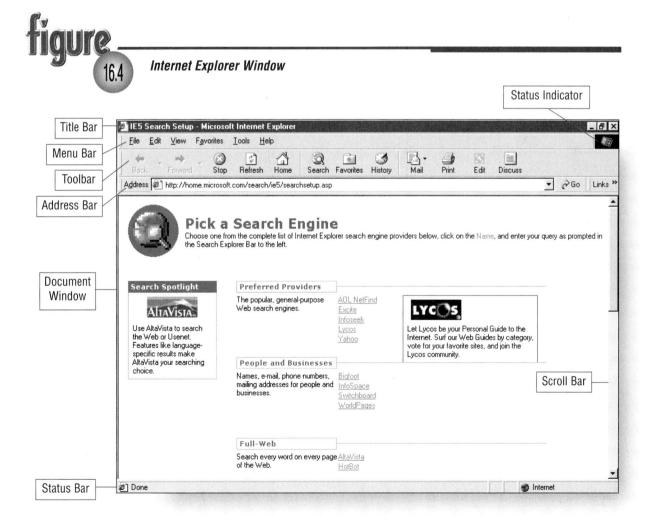

figure
16.5   *Internet Explorer Program Window Features*

Feature	Description
Title bar	Displays the name of the Web page followed by the name of the program—Microsoft Internet Explorer
Menu bar	Contains a list of options for using and customizing Internet Explorer
Toolbar	Contains buttons for commonly used features such as navigating, searching, printing, and formatting
Address bar	Displays the address of the current Web site page
Status indicator	Status indicator is the Microsoft logo; animates (moves) when a Web site is being loaded
Document window	Displays the contents of the current Web site
Scroll bar	Displays information in the current Web page
Status bar	Displays information about connection progress and the percentage of information that has been transferred

The Internet Explorer toolbar contains buttons for accessing a variety of commands. Figure 16.6 shows the buttons and describes each button.

figure
16.6   *Internet Explorer Toolbar Buttons*

Click this button	To do this
⇦ Back	Display previous Web page
⇨ Forward	Display next Web page
⊗ Stop	Stop loading a page

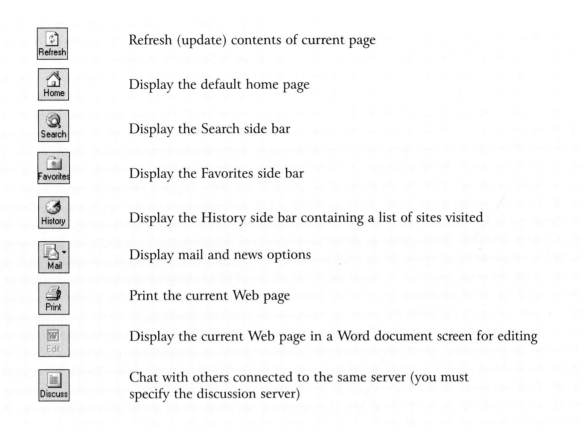

Refresh	Refresh (update) contents of current page
Home	Display the default home page
Search	Display the Search side bar
Favorites	Display the Favorites side bar
History	Display the History side bar containing a list of sites visited
Mail	Display mail and news options
Print	Print the current Web page
Edit	Display the current Web page in a Word document screen for editing
Discuss	Chat with others connected to the same server (you must specify the discussion server)

Searching for Specific Information on the Web

Click the Search the Web button on the Web toolbar and the Internet Explorer
Search Setup page displays as shown in figure 16.4. This page lists a variety of
search engines in different categories. (Web pages and search engines are
constantly changing, so you may discover that your Internet Explorer Search
Setup page may vary from what you see in figure 16.4. If that is the case, you
may need to modify some steps in the exercises in this chapter.) Click the desired
search engine name and a side bar displays. For example, click the AltaVista
search engine name and a side bar displays as shown in figure 16.7. Key specific
text in the white text box that displays toward the top of the AltaVista side bar
and then click the Search button. A list of sites displays in the AltaVista side bar
containing the specific text you entered in the white text box. Click a site listing
to jump to that site on the Web.

figure
16.7

AltaVista Side Bar

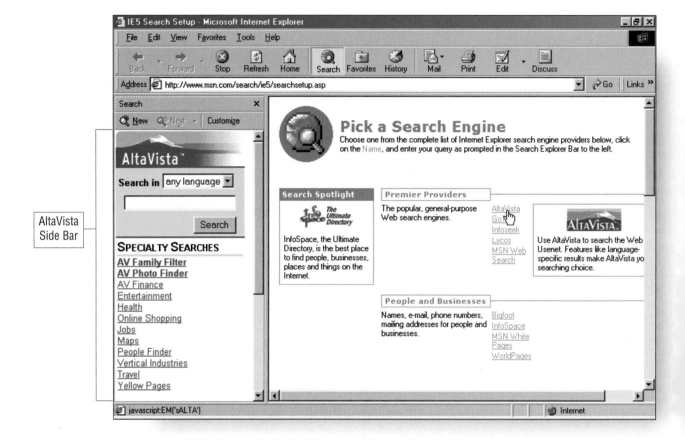

AltaVista Side Bar

As you gain experience searching the Web, you will develop methods to refine your search techniques and tools to limit the time spent browsing. Before you begin a research project, jot down your key words or phrases and think about ways to limit the sites that will be selected by being as specific as possible without restricting the search. As you will see in the next exercise, you can become overwhelmed with the number of sites that will be selected.

Using Search Engines to Locate Information on the Web

(Note: Web pages and search engines are changing constantly. If the instructions in this exercise do not match what you are viewing, you may need to substitute different steps than the ones instructed here.)

1. Jump to the World Wide Web from within Word and search for information on *lahars* (dense, viscous flows of volcanic debris) using the Excite search engine by completing these steps:
   a. At a clear document screen, make sure the Web toolbar displays, and then click the Search the Web button on the Web toolbar.
   b. At the Internet Explorer Search Setup page (like the one shown in figure 16.4), complete the following steps:
      1) Click *Excite* that displays in the *Full-Web* column.
      2) Click in the white text box (above the Search button) that displays toward the top of the Excite side bar (see figure 16.7).
      3) Key **lahars** in the text box.
      4) Click the Search button.
   c. In a few moments, the Excite search engine will return with the first 10 sites in the side bar that meet your search criteria. Click a site that interests you.
   d. Click the Print button on the Internet Explorer toolbar to print the Web page displayed.
   e. After printing the information, click the Back button on the Internet Explorer toolbar. (This displays the Search Setup page at the right side of the screen.)

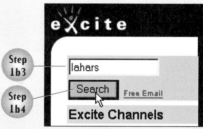

2. Search for information on the South African white shark using the Infoseek search engine by completing the following steps:
   a. Click *Infoseek* that displays in the *Premier Providers* column.
   b. Click in the white text box that displays toward the top of the Infoseek side bar. (You may need to scroll to see the white text box.)
   c. Key **South African white shark** in the text box and then press Enter.
   d. In a few moments, the Infoseek search engine will return with information that meets the search criteria. Scroll through the side bar and read the information presented by Infoseek.
   e. Click a site about the South African white shark that interests you.
   f. After viewing the site in the side bar, click the Search button on the Internet Explorer toolbar to remove the Search side bar.
3. Close Internet Explorer by clicking <u>F</u>ile on the Internet Explorer Menu bar and then clicking <u>C</u>lose at the drop-down menu.

Narrowing a Search

The Internet contains a phenomenal amount of information. Some searches can result in millions of "hits" (sites). Wading through all these sites can be very time consuming and counterproductive. Narrowing a search to very specific criteria can greatly reduce the number of hits for a search. For example, if you search for *physician-assisted suicide* using the Infoseek search engine, more than 500,000 sites may be found.

To reduce the number of documents found and to find only those documents containing very specific information, use *search operators.* Search operators may vary between search engines. Some operators may work within many engines, while others are specific to certain search engines. Some common search operators include symbols such as a quotation mark ("), a plus symbol (+), and a minus symbol (-). Figure 16.8 describes the operators and gives an explanation of each.

figure

16.8 *Search Operators*

Operator	Explanation
Plus (+)	Key a plus symbol directly in front of a word and only those documents containing the word will be found. Do not space after the symbol. If you are including more than one word, space between the first word and the next symbol or word. **Example:** Key **+baseball +rules** and only those documents containing both *baseball* and *rules* will be found.
Minus (-)	Key a minus symbol directly in front of a word that you do not want included in the search. This symbol is helpful in situations where you want to find a specific topic but want to narrow it by excluding certain parts of the topic. **Example:** Key **+whales -blue -killer** and the search engine will find those documents containing *whales* but <u>not</u> *blue* or *killer*.
Quotation Marks (")	If you enter terms for a search such as *University of Arizona*, a search engine will find documents containing any or all of the three words in any order. If you want only those documents found containing *University of Arizona* in this specific order, enclose the words in quotation marks. **Example:** Key **"University of Arizona"** and the search engine will find those documents containing the three words in the order specified between the quotation marks.

In addition to search operators, some search engines recognize Boolean operators when conducting a search. (Boolean operators are based on Boolean algebra [named after George Boole, an English mathematician], which is a mathematical system originally devised for the analysis of symbolic logic.) Boolean operators include AND, AND NOT, OR, and parentheses. Boolean operators must be keyed in all capital letters with a space on either side. Boolean operators are explained in figure 16.9.

figure 16.9 *Boolean Operators*

Operator	Explanation
AND	Find documents with words joined by AND. **Example:** Key **Disneyland AND California** and the search engine will find those documents containing both *Disneyland* and *California*.
OR	Find documents that contain at least one of the words joined by OR. **Example:** Key **volcanoes OR lahars** and the search engine will find those documents containing either *volcanoes* or *lahars*.
AND NOT	Find documents that contain the word before AND NOT but not the word after. **Example:** Key **bicycling AND NOT racing** and the search engine will find those documents containing the word *bicycling* but not the word *racing*.

Not all search engines use Boolean operators to limit searches. Each search engine should contain a Web page that explains how to conduct what is considered an advanced search. In exercise 4, you will be using two different search engines to find information and also print information on how to perform an advanced search with each of the two search engines.

exercise 4

Using Search Operators to Search for Specific Information on the Web

1. Jump to the World Wide Web from within Word and search for information on the *University of Michigan* using the Northern Light search engine by completing these steps:

   a. At a clear document screen, click the Search the Web button on the Web toolbar.

   b. At the Internet Explorer Search Setup page (like the one shown in figure 16.4), complete the following steps:

      1) Click *Northern Light* that displays in the *Full-Web* column.

      2) Click in the white text box that displays toward the top of the Northern Light side bar, key **University of Michigan**, and then press Enter.

   c. In a few moments, the Northern Light search engine will return with a list of sites that meets your search criteria. Write down the total number of sites found by Northern Light.

   d. Scroll down the side bar to see some of the sites that have been selected.

   e. Learn more about searching with Northern Light by completing the following steps:

      1) Click the *HELP* hyperlink that displays toward the top of the Northern Light side bar.

      2) Click the *Optimize Your Search* hyperlink that displays in the window at the right side of the screen. (You will need to scroll to the right to see this screen.)

      3) When the Optimize Your Search page displays, print the information by clicking the Print button on the Internet Explorer toolbar.

   f. Narrow the search by completing the following steps:

      1) Select the text *University of Michigan* that displays in the white text box located toward the top of the Northern Light side bar, key **"University of Michigan"** and then press Enter.

      2) When Northern Light returns with a list of sites, write down the total number of sites. Compare this number to the previous number. The number found with the search containing the quotation marks should be considerably lower than the search without the quotation marks.

   g. Click the Back button on the Internet Explorer toolbar until the Internet Explorer Search Setup page displays at the right side of the screen.

2. Find information on white sharks using the Excite search engine and then find information on white sharks, but not South African white sharks, by completing the following steps:

    a. At the Internet Explorer Search Setup page, click *Excite* in the *Full-Web* column.

    b. Click in the white text box that displays toward the top of the Excite side bar and then key **white sharks**.

    c. Click the Search button.

    d. When Excite returns with a list of sites, view the full screen by clicking the hyperlink *View Full Screen* that displays toward the bottom of the Excite side bar. (This displays additional information on Excite at the right side of the screen.)

    e. At the Excite full screen that displays at the right, look for the total number of hits for *white sharks* and then write down the number. (This number will probably display below *Web Results*.)

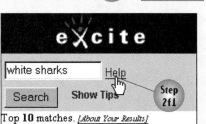

    f. Display information on advanced searches in Excite by completing the following steps:

        1) Click the *Help* hyperlink that displays at the right side of the white text box in the side bar.

        2) At the Excite help page that displays at the right side of the screen, click the *Advanced Search Tips* hyperlink.

        3) When the Advanced Search Tips page displays, click the Print button on the Internet Explorer toolbar.

        4) Read the information on advanced searches.

    g. Narrow the search to documents containing *white sharks* but <u>not</u> *South African* by completing the following steps:

        1) Select *white sharks* in the white text box that displays toward the top of the Excite side bar and then key **+white +sharks -South -African**.

        2) Click the *Search* button.

        3) When Excite returns with a list of sites, click the *View Full Screen* hyperlink located toward the bottom of the side bar. (This updates the information at the right side of the screen.)

        4) Look at the information that displays at the right side of the screen and then write down the total number of sites found. Compare this number to the previous number. The number found with the search containing the plus and minus symbols should be considerably lower than the search without the symbols.

    h. Click the Search button on the Internet Explorer toolbar to turn off the display of the Search side bar.

3. Click <u>F</u>ile and then <u>C</u>lose to close the Internet Explorer.

Each search engine Web site should contain information on how to narrow a search or conduct an advanced search. You may want to experiment with some of the other search engines to see if you can find information on how to conduct advanced searches within each.

Adding Favorite Sites to the Favorites List

Favorites

If you find a site that you would like to visit on a regular basis, that site can be added to a Favorites list. To do this, display the site, and then click the Favorites button on the Internet Explorer toolbar. This causes a side bar to display similar to the one shown in figure 16.10 (your folder names may vary).

Favorites Side Bar

To add a favorite site, click the Add button located at the top of the Favorites side bar. This displays the Add Favorite dialog box shown in figure 16.11. At this dialog box, make sure the information in the Name text box is correct (if not, select the text and then key your own information), and then click OK. The new site displays at the bottom of the list in the Favorites side bar. After a site has been added to the Favorites list, you can jump quickly to that site by clicking the Favorites button on the Internet Explorer toolbar and then clicking the site name at the Favorites side bar.

16.11 *Add Favorite Dialog Box*

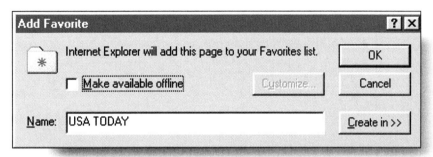

If you want to insert a favorites site into a folder, display the site, and then click the Add button. At the Add Favorite dialog box, click the Create in button located at the right side of the dialog box. This expands the dialog box and displays a list of folders. Click the folder into which you want the site listed and then click the OK button. To display the list of sites within a folder, click the folder name at the Favorites side bar. To turn off the display of sites within a folder, click the folder name again.

To delete a site from the Favorites side bar, position the mouse pointer on the site, click the *right* mouse button, and then click Delete at the pop-up menu that displays. At the Confirm File Delete dialog box, click the Yes button.

If you want to organize the list of favorite sites, click the Organize button located at the top of the Favorites side bar. This displays the Organize Favorites dialog box shown in figure 16.12. Use this dialog box to create a new folder, delete or rename a folder, or move a folder name up or down the Favorites list.

16.12 *Organize Favorites Dialog Box*

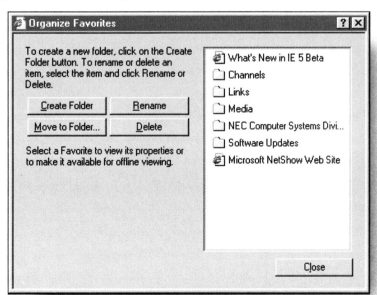

Displaying a List of Sites Visited

History

As you visit different Web sites, Internet Explorer keeps track of the sites. Click the History button on the Internet Explorer toolbar and a History side bar displays as shown in figure 16.13. This information can be useful for remembering Internet addresses previously visited and for monitoring Internet use. Close the History side bar by clicking the History button again or by clicking the Close button (contains an X) located in the upper right corner of the History side bar.

figure

16.13   *Internet Explorer History Side Bar*

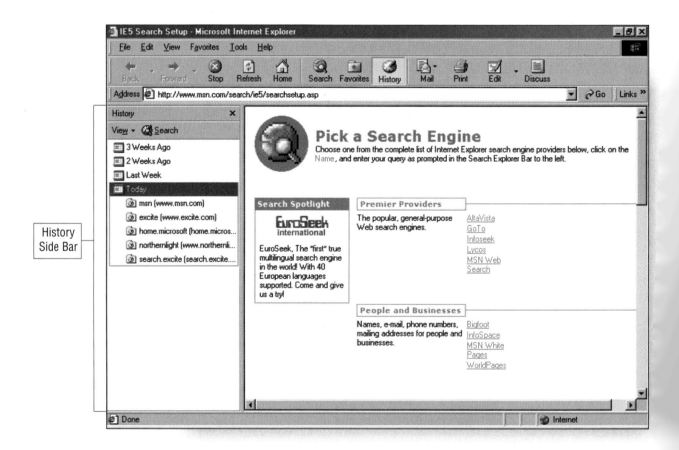

History
Side Bar

exercise 5

Exploring the Web, Adding Favorite Sites, and Displaying Sites Visited

1. Explore several locations on the World Wide Web from within Word using Internet Explorer and hyperlinks by completing the following steps:
   a. Click the Search the Web button on the Web toolbar.
   b. At the Internet Explorer Search Setup page, click in the Address text box. (This selects the current address.)
   c. Display the home page for *USA Today* by keying **http://www.usatoday.com** and then pressing Enter.
   d. Add the *USA Today* Web site to the Favorites list by completing the following steps:
      1) Click the Favorites button located on the Internet Explorer toolbar.
      2) At the Favorites side bar, click the Add button (displays toward the top of the side bar).
      3) At the Add Favorite dialog box, make sure *USA TODAY* displays in the Name text box, and then click OK.
      4) Click the Favorites button on the Internet Explorer toolbar to remove the Favorites side bar.

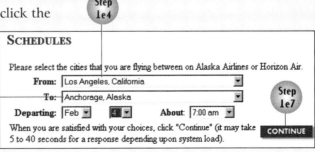

   e. Display the Alaska Airlines Web page, add it to the Favorites list, and then search for flight departure times from Los Angeles, California, to Anchorage, Alaska, by completing the following steps:
      1) Click in the Address text box to select the current URL, key **http://www.alaska-air.com**, and then press Enter.
      2) When the Alaska Airlines home page displays, add it to the Favorites list by completing steps similar to those in step 1d.
      3) At the Alaska Airlines home page, click the *Flight Schedules* hyperlink.
      4) At the schedule Web page, click the down-pointing triangle at the right side of the From text box, and then click *Los Angeles, California* at the drop-down list. (You will need to scroll down the list.)
      5) Make sure the To text box displays *Anchorage, Alaska*.
      6) Change the departing date from one week from today. (You will need to change the day and perhaps the month.)
      7) Click the CONTINUE button.

8) When the flight schedule page displays, click the Print button on the Internet Explorer toolbar.

f. Jump to the home page for *USA Today* by completing the following steps:
1) Click the Favorites button on the Internet Explorer toolbar to display the Favorites side bar.
2) At the Favorites side bar, click *USA TODAY*.
3) Click the Favorites button to turn off the display of the Favorites side bar.

g. Display a list of sites visited by completing the following steps:
1) Click the History button on the Internet Explorer toolbar. (Sites visited today display in the side bar.)
2) After viewing the sites visited, click the History button on the Internet Explorer toolbar to turn off the display of the History side bar.

h. Remove *Alaska Airlines* and *USA TODAY* from the Favorites side bar by completing the following steps:
1) Click the Favorites button on the Internet Explorer toolbar.
2) Right-click *Alaska Airlines* in the Favorites side bar and then click Delete at the drop-down menu.
3) At the Confirm File Delete dialog box, click Yes.
4) Right-click on *USA TODAY* in the Favorites side bar and then click Delete at the drop-down menu.
5) At the Confirm File Delete dialog box, click Yes.
6) Click the Favorites button on the Internet Explorer toolbar to turn off the display of the Favorites side bar.

2. Close Internet Explorer by clicking File and then Close.
3. If the Windows desktop displays, click the Microsoft Word button that displays on the Taskbar. (This will display the Word document screen.)

Step 1h2

Open
Create New Folder
Edit
Print

Make available offline

Send To

Cut
Copy

Delete
Rename

Properties

Creating a Web Page

Now that you have been "surfing the net," you have visited several Web site home pages and have an idea how a home page displays. Home pages are Web documents that describe a company, school, government, or individual and are created using a language called HyperText Markup Language (HTML). This is a language that Web browsers use to read hypertext documents. In the past, a person needed knowledge of HTML to design a Web page. Now a Web page can be created in Word and saved as a Web page or created with a Web Page Wizard.

Before creating a Web page, consider the information you want contained in the Web page. Carefully plan the layout of the information and where to position hyperlinks. Good Web page design is a key element to a successful Web page. Often a company will hire a professional Web page designer to create their home page. Before designing a Web page, you may want to visit a variety of Web pages and consider some of the following questions: What elements are included on the Web page? How are the elements distributed on the page? Is the information organized logically and is it easy to read? Is the Web page visually appealing? Evaluating Web pages on the Web will help you when designing your own.

To save a Word document as a Web page, click File and then Save as Web Page. At the Save As dialog box, key a name for the Web page document, and then press Enter or click the Save button (Word automatically changes the Save as type option to *Web Page*.)

Changing to the Web Layout View

When you save a document as a Web page, Word automatically changes to the Web Layout view. The Web Layout view displays a page as it will appear when published to the Web or an intranet. You can also change to the Web Layout view by clicking the Web Layout View button located at the left side of the horizontal scroll bar or by clicking View and then Web Layout.

Web Layout
View

Formatting a Web Page

Word provides themes and backgrounds that can be applied to documents. Themes and backgrounds are designed for viewing in a Word document, in an e-mail message, or on the Web. Backgrounds and some theme formatting do not print.

Applying a Theme to a Web Page

Some interesting and colorful formatting can be applied to a document with options at the Theme dialog box shown in figure 16.14. To display this dialog box, click Format and then Theme. Click a theme in the Choose a Theme list box and a preview displays at the right side. Click OK to close the dialog box and apply the theme to the document. (You can also double-click a theme at the Theme dialog box.)

When a theme is applied to a document, Word automatically changes to the Web Layout view. Theme formatting is designed for documents that will be published on the Web, on an intranet, or sent as an e-mail. Not all of the formatting applied by a theme will print.

figure

16.14 *Theme Dialog Box*

Click a theme in this list box and it is previewed at the right side of the dialog box.

Previewing a Document in Web Page Preview

When creating a Web page, you may want to preview it in your default Web browser. To do this, click File and then Web Page Preview. This displays the currently open document in the default Web browser and displays formatting supported by the browser.

Creating and Formatting a Web Page

1. Open Beltway Home Page.
2. Save the document as a Web page by completing the following steps:
   a. Click File and then Save as Web Page.
   b. Key **Beltway Web Page** and then press Enter.
3. Make the following formatting changes to the document:
   a. Select the company name, address, telephone number, and Web address; change the type size to 14 and turn on bold; and then deselect the text.
   b. Insert a horizontal line by completing the following steps:
      1) Position the insertion point on the blank line between the company Web address and the first paragraph of text in the body of the document.
      2) Click Format and then Borders and Shading.
      3) At the Borders and Shading dialog box, click the Horizontal Line button that displays at the bottom of the dialog box.
      4) At the Horizontal Line dialog box, click the option shown at the right and then click the Insert clip button.

      Step 3b4

   c. Apply the *Travel* theme by completing the following steps:
      1) Click Format and then Theme.
      2) Scroll through the list of themes in the Choose a Theme list box until *Travel* is visible and then click *Travel*.
      3) Click OK to close the dialog box.

      Step 3c2

   d. Select the entire document, change the font color to Lime Green, and then deselect the text. (You are changing the font color so the text will be visible when printed.)
4. Preview the document in Web Page Preview by completing the following steps:
   a. Click File and then Web Page Preview.
   b. If the Internet Explorer window display is small, click the Maximize button to enlarge the display.
   c. After viewing the document in the Web browser, click File and then Close.
5. Save the document again with the same name (Beltway Web Page).
6. Print and then close Beltway Web Page. (Not all of the theme formatting will print.)

Applying a Background to a Document

Apply a colorful background to a document by clicking Format and then Background. This causes a palette of color choices to display at the right side of the drop-down menu as shown in figure 16.15. Click the desired color or click the More Colors option to display the Colors dialog box.

Apply a background and the view is automatically changed to Web Layout. A background color does not display in the Normal or Print Layout views and will not print. Like a theme, background color is designed for formatting documents such as Web pages or e-mail messages that are viewed in the screen.

16.15 Background Side Menu

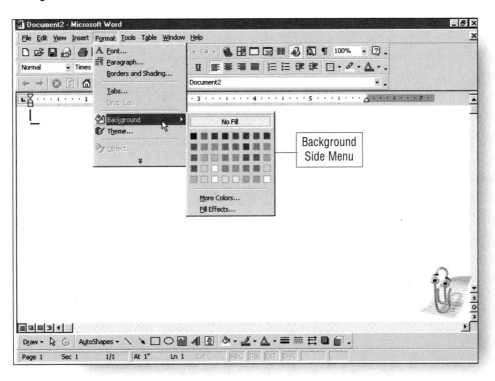

Click the Fill Effects option from the Background side menu and the Fill Effects dialog box displays as shown in figure 16.16. Use options from this dialog box to apply formatting such as a gradient, texture, and pattern.

figure

Fill Effects Dialog Box

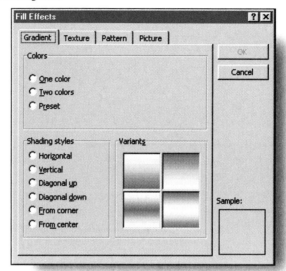

exercise 7

Applying a Background to a Web Page

1. Open Beltway Web Page. (If this document is not visible, change the Files of type option at the Open dialog box to *All Files*.)
2. Save the document with Save As and name it Beltway Background. (Make sure the Save as type option is *Web Page*.)
3. Change the background color of the Web page and add a gradient and texture by completing the following steps:

   Step 3a

   a. Click Format, point to Background, and then click the Sea Green color (fourth color from the left in the third row).

   b. Click Format, point to Background, and then click Fill Effects.

   c. At the Fill Effects dialog box with the Gradient tab selected, click From center in the Shading styles section.

   Step 3c

   d. Click OK to close the dialog box.
   e. Notice how the Web page displays.

4. Add a texture to the Web page by completing the following steps:
   a. Click Format, point to Background, and then click Fill Effects.

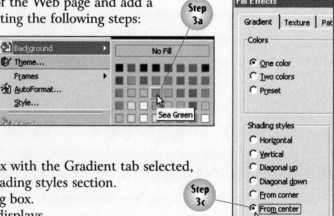

b. At the Fill Effects dialog box, click the Texture tab.
c. At the Fill Effects dialog box with the Texture tab selected, click the third texture option from the left in the bottom row (Purple mesh).
d. Click OK to close the dialog box.
e. Notice how the Web page displays.
5. Preview the Web page in Web Page Preview. (You may need to maximize the Internet Explorer window.) After viewing the document, close the Web browser.
6. Save the document again with the same name (Beltway Background).
7. Close Beltway Background. (Printing is optional—the texture does not print.)

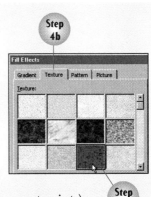

Formatting with Buttons on the Web Tools Toolbar

A Web page designer uses a variety of tools to prepare an appealing and successful Web page. Tools are available for formatting a Web page with buttons on the Web Tools toolbar shown in figure 16.17. Display the Web Tools toolbar by clicking View, pointing to Toolbars, and then clicking *Web Tools*. You can also display the Web Tools toolbar by right-clicking a currently displayed toolbar and then clicking *Web Tools* at the drop-down list. The shape of the toolbar shown in figure 16.17 has been changed to show the button names. The shape of your Web Tools toolbar will vary.

An interactive Web page, a page in which the viewer will provide input or answer questions, might include check boxes and option buttons. A Web page with a variety of options and choices might include drop-down boxes and list boxes. In exercise 8 you will be using two of the buttons on the Web Tools toolbar. As you continue to create and design Web pages, consider experimenting with other buttons on the Web Tools toolbar.

figure

16.17   Web Tools Toolbar Buttons

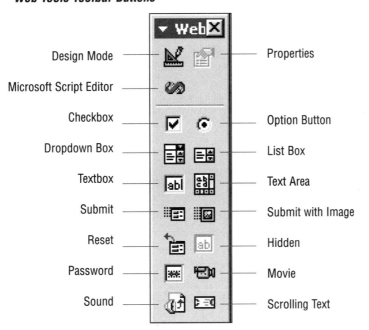

exercise 8

Inserting a Sound Clip and Scrolling Text to a Web Page

1. Open Beltway Web Page.
2. Save the document with Save As and name it Beltway Formatted.
3. Delete the horizontal line by clicking the line to select it and then pressing the Delete key.
4. Insert scrolling text in the Web page by completing the following steps:
   a. Display the Web Tools toolbar by clicking View, pointing to Toolbars, and then clicking Web Tools.
   b. Position the insertion point at the left margin on the blank line below the company Web address and then click the Center button on the Formatting toolbar.
   c. Click the Scrolling Text button on the Web Tools toolbar.

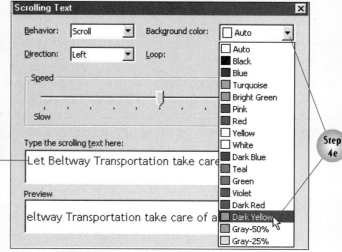

   d. At the Scrolling Text dialog box, select *Scrolling Text* that displays in the Type the scrolling text here text box and then key **Let Beltway Transportation take care of all your moving needs!**
   e. Click the down-pointing triangle at the right side of the Background color text box and then click *Dark Yellow* at the drop-down list.
   f. Click OK to close the Scrolling Text dialog box.
5. Add a sound clip to the Web page by completing the following steps:
   a. Click the Sound button on the Web Tools toolbar.
   b. At the Background Sound dialog box, click the Browse button.
   c. At the File Open dialog box (with the *Media* folder displayed), double-click *Canyon* in the list box.
   d. At the Background Sound dialog box, click the down-pointing triangle at the right side of the Loop text box, and then click *Infinite* at the drop-down list.

   e. Click OK to close the Background Sound dialog box.
6. Save the document again with the same name (Beltway Formatted).
7. Close the Web Tools toolbar.
8. Print and then close Beltway Formatted.

Creating Hyperlinks

The business Web sites you have visited, such as Microsoft and *USA Today*, have included hyperlinks to connect you to other pages or Web sites. You can create your own hyperlink in your Web page. To do this, select the text you want specified as the hyperlink, and then click the Insert Hyperlink button on the Standard toolbar. At the Insert Hyperlink dialog box shown in figure 16.18, key the Web site URL in the Type the file or Web page name text box, and then click OK.

Insert Hyperlink

16.18   **Insert Hyperlink Dialog Box**

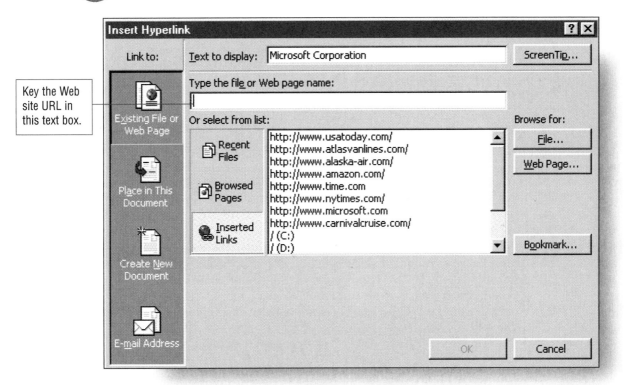

Another method for creating a hyperlink is to key the URL in a Word document. When you key the complete URL, Word automatically converts the URL to a hyperlink and changes the color of the URL. In exercise 9, you will be establishing hyperlinks from the Beltway Transportation Web page to moving company sites.

Creating Hyperlinks

1. Open Beltway Web Page.
2. Create a hyperlink so that clicking *Atlas Van Lines* displays the Atlas Van Lines Web page by completing the following steps:
   a. Select the text *Atlas Van Lines* that displays toward the end of the document (after a bullet).
   b. Click the Insert Hyperlink button on the Standard toolbar.
   c. At the Insert Hyperlink dialog box, key **http://www.atlasvanlines.com** in the Type the file or Web page name text box.
   d. Click OK. (This changes the color of the *Atlas Van Lines* text and also adds underlining to the text.)

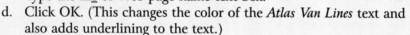

3. Complete steps similar to those in step 2 to create a hyperlink from *Bekins* to the URL *http://www.bekins.com*.
4. Complete steps similar to those in step 2 to create a hyperlink from *United Van Lines* to the URL *http://www.unitedvanlines.com*.
5. Click the Save button on the Standard toolbar to save the Web page with the hyperlinks added.
6. Jump to the hyperlink sites by completing the following steps:
   a. Click the hyperlink *Atlas Van Lines* that displays toward the end of the document.
   b. When the Atlas Van Lines Web page displays, scroll through the page, and then click on a hyperlink that interests you.
   c. After looking at this next page, click File and then Close.
   d. At the Beltway Web page document, click the hyperlink *Bekins*.
   e. After viewing the Bekins home page, click File and then Close.
   f. At the Beltway Web page document, click the hyperlink *United Van Lines*.
   g. After viewing the United Van Lines home page, click File and then Close.
7. Close the Beltway Web Page document.

Creating a Web Page Using the Web Page Wizard

Word provides a wizard that will help you prepare a Web page. To use the Wizard, click File and then New. At the New dialog box, click the Web Pages tab. At the New dialog box with the Web Pages tab selected, as shown in figure 16.19, double-click the *Web Page Wizard* icon. This displays the Web Page Wizard Start dialog box shown in figure 16.20. With the Web Page Wizard, you choose a title and location for the page, specify and organize pages, and choose a visual theme for the page.

figure
16.19   *New Dialog Box with Web Pages Tab Selected*

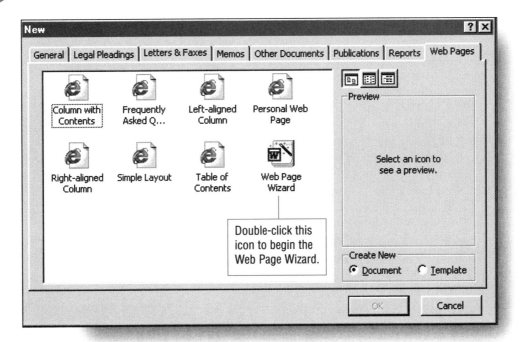

figure
16.20   *Web Page Wizard Start Dialog Box*

When using the Web Page Wizard, you will need to specify the location of the Web page document and related documents. In exercise 10, you will create a subfolder on your disk and then specify that subfolder as the location for the Web page documents.

Creating a Web Page Using the Web Page Wizard

1. Create a subfolder on your disk by completing the following steps:
   a. Display the Open dialog box.
   b. Make the *Chapter 16* folder on your disk the active folder.
   c. Click the Create New Folder button on the dialog box toolbar.
   d. At the New Folder dialog box, key **Web Pages** in the Name text box, and then click OK.
   e. Click the Cancel button to close the Open dialog box.
2. Create a Web page using the Web Page Wizard by completing the following steps:
   a. At a blank Word screen, click File and then New.
   b. At the New dialog box, click the Web Pages tab.
   c. At the New dialog box with the Web Pages tab selected, double-click the *Web Page Wizard* icon.
   d. At the Web Page Wizard Start dialog box, click the Next> button.
   e. At the Web Page Wizard Title and Location dialog box, key **Premium Produce** in the Web site title text box.

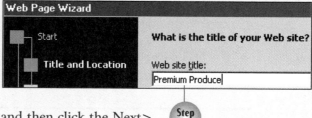

   f. Click the Next> button.
   g. At the Web Page Wizard Navigation dialog box, make sure Vertical frame is selected, and then click the Next> button.
   h. At the Web Page Wizard Add Pages dialog box, make the following changes:
      1) Click *Personal Web Page* in the Current pages in Web site list box and then click the Remove Page button.
      2) Click *Blank Page 2* in the Current pages in Web site list box and then click the Remove Page button.

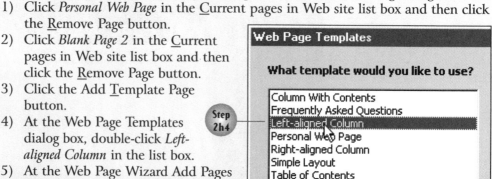

      3) Click the Add Template Page button.
      4) At the Web Page Templates dialog box, double-click *Left-aligned Column* in the list box.
      5) At the Web Page Wizard Add Pages dialog box, click the Next> button.
   i. At the Web Page Wizard Organize Pages dialog box, click the Move Up button (to move *Left-aligned Column* above *Blank Page 1*), and then click the Next> button.
   j. At the Web Page Wizard Visual Theme dialog box, choose a theme by completing the following steps:
      1) Click the Browse Themes button.

2) At the Theme dialog box, scroll down the list of themes in the Choose a Theme list box until *Nature* is visible and then click *Nature*.

3) Click OK to close the dialog box.

4) At the Web Page Wizard Visual Theme dialog box, click the Next> button.

k. At the Web Page Wizard Finish dialog box, click the Finish button. (If you are saving onto a disk, this may take some time.)

3. Format the Web page document by completing the following steps:

a. Turn off the display of the Frames toolbar by clicking the Close button (contains an X) that displays in the upper right corner of the toolbar.

b. Select the text *Main Heading Goes Here* and then key **Premium Produce**.

c. Select the text (below the picture) *Caption goes here.* and then key **Premium Produce--Premium Flavor**. (Key the two hyphens between *Produce* and *Premium* and AutoCorrect will change the two hyphens to a dash when you press the spacebar bar after keying *Premium*.)

d. Insert a file from the your disk by completing the following steps:

1) Select from the beginning of the text *Section Heading Goes Here* (the first occurrence of this text) to the end of the text in the document. (Make sure you do not select the picture or anything other than the text.)

2) With the text selected, press the Delete key.

3) Click Insert and then File.

4) At the Insert File dialog box, click the Up One Level button to make *Chapter 16* the active folder, and then double-click the document named Prem Pro Insert.

e. Insert a pricing table in the blank page by completing the following steps:

1) Click the *Blank Page 1* hyperlink that displays at the left side of the screen.

2) At the blank page 1 document, select the text *This Web Page Is Blank Page 1* and then press the Delete key.

3) Click Insert and then File.

4) At the Insert File dialog box, make sure *Chapter 16* is the active folder.

5) Double-click *Prem Pro Pricing* in the list box. (This inserts the table into the blank page 1 document.)

6) With the table inserted in the document, click the Save button on the Standard toolbar. (If you are saving onto a disk, this may take some time.)

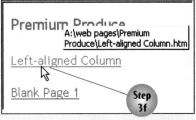

f. Return to the Premium Produce page by clicking the *Left-aligned Column* hyperlink that displays at the left side of the screen.

g. Change the hyperlink text by completing the following steps:

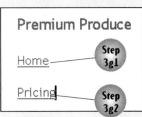

1) Select the *Left-aligned Column* hyperlink text and then key **Home**. (Make sure *Home* is underlined. If not, click the Undo button and try again.)

2) Select the *Blank Page 1* hyperlink text and then key **Pricing**. (Make sure *Pricing* is underlined. If not, click the Undo button and try again.)

h. Display the pricing table by clicking the *Pricing* hyperlink.

i. Return to the Premium Produce home page by clicking the *Home* hyperlink.

4. Save the Web document by clicking the Save button on the Standard toolbar. (This saves the document with the name of default.)

5. Print and then close the document.

The Web Page Wizard specifies a folder and subfolders for Web page files. This is because a Web page generally consists of a variety of items that are inserted in individual files. For example, each bullet image and clip art image or picture in a Web page is saved in a separate image file. Inserting all of these files into folders makes it easier for you to take this information to another location. For example, you can copy the contents of a Web page folder and all its subfolders to another computer or onto a disk.

During the Web Page Wizard steps, a vertical frame was chosen. A frame in a Web page helps you organize information and make it easily accessible. When a single Web page is divided into sections that can display separate Web pages, each section is referred to as a frame. In exercise 10, your Web page contained two frames—the section at the left containing the hyperlinks and the section at the right containing the company home page information.

Viewing the Web Pages Folder

1. Display the Open dialog box.
2. If necessary, change the File of type option to *All Files*.
3. Display the contents of the *Web Pages* folder by completing the following steps:
   a. Make the *Chapter 16* folder on your disk the active folder.
   b. Double-click the *Web Pages* folder.
   c. At the *Web Pages* folder, double-click the *Premium Produce* folder.
   d. At the *Premium Produce* folder, notice the documents saved in this folder by the Web Page Wizard.
   e. Double-click the folder *Blank Page 1_files*.
   f. Notice the documents saved in this folder by the Web Page Wizard and then click the Up One Level button.
   g. At the *Premium Produce* folder, double-click the *Left-aligned Column_files* folder. Notice the documents saved in this folder by the Web Page Wizard and then click the Up One Level button.
   h. Click the Up One Level two more times. (This returns you to the *Chapter 16* folder.)
4. Close the Open dialog box.

chapter summary

➤ The Internet is a network of computers connected around the world allowing exchange of information.

➤ Word provides the ability to jump to the Internet from the Word document screen.

➤ The World Wide Web is the most commonly used application on the Internet and is a set of standards and protocols used to access information available on the Internet.

➤ A software program used to access the Web is referred to as a Web browser.

➤ To locate information on the World Wide Web you need a modem, browser software, and an Internet Service Provider (ISP) account. An ISP sells access to the Internet.

- A modem is a hardware device that carries data over telephone lines.
- Uniform Resource Locators (URLs) are the method used to identify locations on the Web.
- A Web page can contain hyperlinks. Click a link to connect to another site, location, or page.
- Use a search engine such as Yahoo, Infoseek, or Excite to locate information on the Internet on a specific topic by keying a few words or a short phrase.
- Narrow a search by using search operators such as the plus symbol, minus symbol, quotation mark; or Boolean operators such as AND, OR, and AND NOT.
- Add a site that you visit regularly to the Favorites list at the Internet Explorer Favorites side bar. You can also delete and organize favorite sites at the Favorites side bar.
- Click the History button on the Internet Explorer toolbar to display the History side bar. This side bar displays sites visited for the current day as well as two previous days and three previous weeks.
- Home pages are Web documents that describe a company, school, government, or individual and are created using a language called HyperText Markup Language (HTML).
- A home page can be created in Word and saved as a Web page, or you can create a Web page using the Web Page Wizard.
- When a document is saved as a Web page, Word automatically changes to the Web Layout view.
- Apply a theme to a Web page with options at the Theme dialog box.
- Preview a document in the default Web browser by clicking File and then Web Page Preview.
- Apply a background color with options from the Background side menu.
- Apply a gradient, texture, or pattern to a Web page with options at the Fill Effects dialog box.
- Some theme formatting and background color, gradient, texture, and pattern do not print.
- The Web Tools toolbar contains buttons for customizing and designing a Web page.
- One method for creating a hyperlink is to select the text and then click the Insert Hyperlink button on the Standard toolbar. At the Insert Hyperlink dialog box, key the URL and then click OK.
- Start the Web Page Wizard by displaying the New dialog box, clicking the Web Pages tab, and then double-clicking the *Web Page Wizard* icon.

commands review

	Mouse
Display the Web toolbar	Click View, point to Toolbars, then click *Web;* or right-click any toolbar, then click *Web* at the drop-down menu
Display Internet Explorer Search Setup page	Click the Search the Web button on the Web toolbar
Display the Favorites side bar	Click the Favorites button on the Internet Explorer toolbar
Display the History side bar	Click the History button on the Internet Explorer toolbar

Change to the Web Layout view	Click the Web Layout View button at the left side of the horizontal scroll bar or click View and then Web Layout
Display the Theme dialog box	Click Format and then Theme
Web Page Preview	Click File and then Web Page Preview
Display the Background side menu	Click Format and then point to Background
Display Fill Effects dialog box	Click Format, point to Background, then click Fill Effects
Display Web Tools toolbar	Click View, point to Toolbars, then click *Web Tools;* or, right-click a toolbar and then click *Web Tools* at the drop-down list
Display the Insert Hyperlink dialog box	Click the Insert Hyperlink button on the Standard toolbar
Display the New dialog box	Click File and then New

Completion: In the space provided at the right, indicate the correct term or command.

1. List three reasons why users access the Internet.

2. The word "modem" is derived from this.

3. The letters ISP stand for this.

4. This is the method used to identify locations on the Internet.

5. To search for information on the Web using a search engine, click this button on the Web toolbar.

6. Click this in a home page to link to another page or location.

7. Click this button on the Internet Explorer toolbar to display the previous Web page or location.

8. List at least three search engines that can be used to search for specific information on the Internet.

9. Click this button on the Web toolbar to display the Internet Explorer Search Setup page.

10. Click this button on the Internet Explorer toolbar to display a side bar containing a list of sites visited in the current day, two previous days, or for three previous weeks.

11. A home page on the Web is created using this language.

12. When a document is saved as a Web page, the Web page displays in this view.

13. Use buttons on this toolbar to design and format a Web page. _____

14. Click <u>F</u>ile and then click this option at the drop-down menu to display the currently open document in the default Web browser. _____

15. Click this button on the Standard toolbar to add a hypertext link to selected text. _____

16. In the space provided, list the text and operators you would use to complete the following searches using the Excite search engine.

    a. Search for documents containing the words *better business bureau* in that sequence. _____

    b. Search for documents containing *travel* but not *international*. _____

    c. Search for documents containing *dolphins* or *porpoises*. _____

working hands-on ···

Assessment 1

1. Make sure you are connected to the Internet and then display the following sites:
   a. At a clear document screen, display the USA Today home page at *http://www.usatoday.com*.
   b. At the *USA Today* home page, find a section of the newspaper that interests you, find an article within that section, and then print the article.
   c. Display the Alaska Airlines home page at *http://www.alaska-air.com*.
   d. Search for flight departure times from Juneau, Alaska, to Orange County, California.
   e. Print the flight schedule.
   f. Display the United States Postal Services Web site at *http://www.usps.gov*.
   g. At the site, use hyperlinks to search for information on domestic postage rates, and then print the information.
2. Close Internet Explorer.

Assessment 2

1. Make sure you are connected to the Internet.
2. At a clear document screen, display the Web toolbar, and then click the Search the Web button on the Web toolbar.
3. At the Internet Explorer Search Setup page, complete the following searches:
   a. Use a search engine of your choosing to find information on bicycle racing.
   b. When the search engine displays a list of sites, scroll through the list, find a bicycle club that interests you, and then display the home page for the club.
   c. With the bicycle club home page displayed, print the page.
   d. Click the Back button until the Internet Explorer Search Setup page displays at the right side of the screen.
   e. Use a search engine of your choosing to find information on the Lincoln Memorial or other historic site.

    f.   When the search engine displays a list of sites, scroll through the list, find a site that interests you, and then display the home page.

    g.   With the home page displayed, print the page.

    h.   Click the Back button until the Internet Explorer Search Setup page displays at the right side of the screen.

    i.   Use a search engine of your choosing to find sites on kayaking in national parks.

    j.   When the search engine displays a list of sites, find a national park site that interests you, display the site, and then print the page.

    k.   Click the Back button until the Internet Explorer Search Setup page displays.

4.   Close Internet Explorer.

Assessment 3

1.   Open the Apex Home Page document.

2.   Make the following changes to the document:

    a.   Save the document as a Web page with the name Apex Web Page.

    b.   Make the following formatting changes to the document:

        1) Apply a theme of your choosing to the document.

        2) Increase the font size of the company name, Web address, address, and telephone number.

        3) Add a horizontal line somewhere in the document.

        4) Select *Apple Computer* and then create a hyperlink to *http://www.apple.com*.

        5) Select *Blizzard Entertainment* and then create a hyperlink to *http://www.blizzard.com*.

        6) Select *id Software* and then create a hyperlink to *http://www.idsoftware.com*.

        7) Select *Microsoft Corporation* and then create a hyperlink to *http://www.microsoft.com*.

        8) Make sure the text for the home page fits on one page. (If it does not, delete some blank lines.)

3.   Save the document again with the same name (Apex Web Page).

4.   Print and then close Apex Web Page.

Assessment 4

1.   Open Apex Web Page.

2.   Save the document with Save As and name it Apex Background.

3.   Make the following formatting changes to the document:

    a.   Apply a background color and gradient of your choosing.

    b.   Add the scrolling text *Apex Cyberware offers computer software at incredibly low prices!* somewhere in the document.

    c.   Add a sound clip to the document.

    d.   Preview the document in the default Web browser. (You may need to maximize the browser window.) After viewing the document, close the Web browser.

4.   Save the document again with the same name (Apex Background).

5.   Print and then close Apex Background.

Unit Three Performance Assessments

Unit 3 PA

CUSTOMIZING DOCUMENTS AND ADDING VISUAL APPEAL

DEMONSTRATING YOUR SKILLS

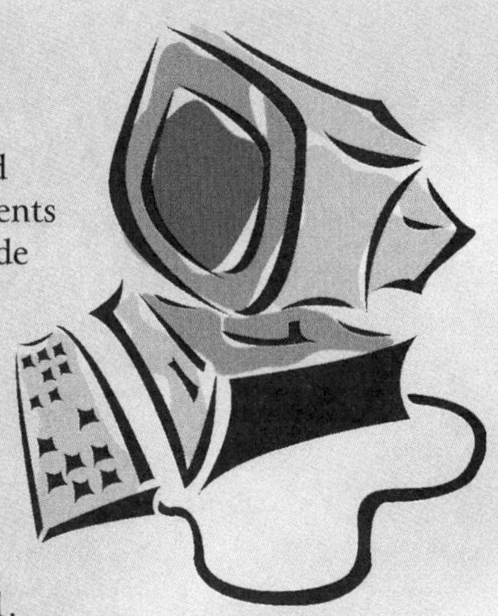

In this unit, you have learned to prepare form documents with personalized information; create and format tables; enhance the visual display of documents with borders, clip art, shapes, and WordArt text; and browse the World Wide Web, locate specific sites on the Web, create a Web home page, and create hyperlinks.

Assessment 1

1. Look at the letter in figure U3.2 and the information in figure U3.1. Determine the fields you need for the main document and the data source. Create the data source and name it Sound ds. Create a main document with the text shown in figure U3.2 (make sure it fits on one page), and then merge it with Sound ds.
2. Save the merged document and name it Unit 3, PA 01.
3. Print and then close Unit 3, PA 01.
4. Save the main document and name it Sound md.
5. Close Sound md.

Mrs. Antonio Mercado 3241 Court G Tampa, FL 33623	Ms. Kristina Vukovich 1120 South Monroe Tampa, FL 33655
Ms. Alexandria Remick 909 Wheeler South Tampa, FL 33620	Mr. Minh Vu 9302 Lawndale Southwest Tampa, FL 33623
Mr. Curtis Iverson 10139 93rd Court South Tampa, FL 33654	Mrs. Holly Bernard 8904 Emerson Road Tampa, FL 33620

Figure U3.1 • Assessment 1

December 10, 2001

Name
Address
City, State Zip

Dear (Name):

Sound Medical is switching hospital care in Tampa to St. Jude's Hospital beginning January 1, 2002. As mentioned in last month's letter, St. Jude's Hospital was selected because it meets our requirements for high-quality, customer-pleasing care that is also affordable and accessible. Our physicians look forward to caring for you in this new environment.

Over the past month, staff members at Sound Medical have been working to make this transition as smooth as possible. Surgeries planned after January 1 are being scheduled at St. Jude's Hospital. Mothers delivering babies any time after January 1 are receiving information about delivery room tours and prenatal classes available at St. Jude's. Your Sound Medical doctor will have privileges at St. Jude's and will continue to care for you if you need to be hospitalized.

You are a very important part of our patient family, (name), and we hope this information is helpful. If you have any additional questions or concerns, please call our hospital transition manager, Jeff Greenswald, at (813) 555-9886, between 8:00 a.m. and 4:30 p.m.

Sincerely,

Jody Tiemann
District Administrator

XX:Sound md

Figure U3.2 • Assessment 1

Assessment 2

1. Create a main document for envelopes that has the Sound ds data source document attached and then merge the envelope main document.
2. Save the merged document and name it Unit 3, PA 02.
3. Print and then close Unit 3, PA 02.
4. Close the envelope main document without saving the changes.

Assessment 3

1. At a clear document screen, create the table shown in figure U3.3. Include the lines and shading as shown in the figure.
2. Save the document and name it Unit 3, PA 03.
3. Print and then close Unit 3, PA 03.

COLEMAN DEVELOPMENT CORPORATION		
Community Development Committee Members		
Name	Company	Address

Figure U3.3 • Assessment 3

Assessment 4

1. At a clear document screen, create the table shown in figure U3.4. (The width of the first column is 2.6 inches and the width of the second and third columns is 1.7 inches. Include the lines and shading as shown in the figure.)
2. After creating the table, insert the formula =SUM(ABOVE) to calculate the amounts in the *First Half* column and the *Second Half* column.
3. Save the document and name it Unit 3, PA 04.
4. Print and then close Unit 3, PA 04.

COLEMAN DEVELOPMENT CORPORATION		
BALANCE SHEET		
Asset	First Half	Second Half
Bonds	$ 52,450,356.03	$ 53,340,559.00
Stocks	7,466,960.25	8,096,255.05
Mortgages	41,783,552.66	43,110,894.50
Real Estate	8,640,700.50	13,557,110.55
Long-Term Investments	1,155,220.24	1,098,452.85
Short-Term Investments	959,745.65	890,452.70
Other Assets	543,225.15	618,256.75
Total		

Figure U3.4 • Assessment 4

Assessment five 5

1. Open Notice 03.
2. Save the document with Save As and name it Unit 3, PA 05.
3. Make the following changes to the document:
   a. Horizontally and vertically center the text on the page.
   b. Select the text and then change to a decorative typeface in a larger point size and a different color.
   c. Insert a page border using one of the art images.
4. Save the document again with the same name (Unit 3, PA 05).
5. Print and then close Unit 3, PA 05.

Assessment six 6

1. At a clear document screen, create the document shown in figure U3.5 by completing the following steps:
   a. Change the font to 14-point Arial bold.
   b. Change the paragraph alignment to center.
   c. Key the text shown in figure U3.5.
   d. Insert the clip art image shown in the figure. (Search for this clip by keying **energy** in the Search for clips text box. If this clip art image is not available, choose a similar image.)
   e. Change the wrapping style of the clip art image to Square.

f. Format the clip art image so that the height is 2.3 inches and the width is 1.8 inches.

g. Drag the clip art image to the position shown in figure U3.5.

2. Save the document and name it Unit 3, PA 06.

3. Print and then close Unit 3, PA 06.

Exploring Alternative Energy Sources

Energy Conservation Organization

July 21, 2001

9:00 a.m. – 4:30 p.m.

Morton Community Center

Figure U3.5 • Assessment 6

Assessment 7

1. Open Unit 3, PA 06.

2. Save the document with Save As and name it Unit 3, PA 07.

3. Change the clip art image to a watermark that displays behind the text in the document.

4. Save the document again with the same name (Unit 3, PA 07).

5. Print and then close Unit 3, PA 07.

Assessment 8

1. At a clear document screen, create the letterhead shown in figure U3.6 with the following specifications:

a. Key the text right aligned as shown in figure U3.6.

b. Select the text and then change the font to 18-point Arial bold and the text color to Dark Blue.

c. Create the shapes shown using buttons on the Drawing toolbar. (Be sure to add the fill as shown in the shapes in figure U3.6.)

2. Save the document and name it Unit 3, PA 08.

3. Print and then close Unit 3, PA 08.

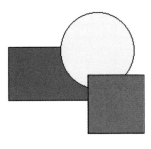

MODERN DESIGNS
2002 Hughes Road
Tucson, AZ 89322
(801) 555-7700

Figure U3.6 • Assessment 8

Assessment 9

1. At a clear document screen, create the document shown in figure U3.7 with the following specifications:
   a. Change the font to 16-point Bookman Old Style bold and the text color to Red and then press the Enter key six times.
   b. Key the text centered as shown in figure U3.7. Press the Enter key six times after keying the text.
   c. Click the AutoShapes button, point to Basic Shapes, and then click the heart shape.
   d. Draw a heart shape as shown in figure U3.7. Add red fill to the heart.
   e. Copy the heart as many times as needed to create the heart border around the text.
2. Save the document and name it Unit 3, PA 09.
3. Print and then close Unit 3, PA 09.

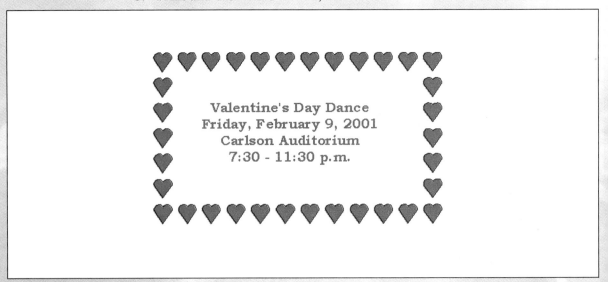

Valentine's Day Dance
Friday, February 9, 2001
Carlson Auditorium
7:30 - 11:30 p.m.

Figure U3.7 • Assessment 9

Assessment 10

1. At a clear document screen, use WordArt to create the flyer letterhead shown in figure U3.8 by completing the following steps:
   a. Press the Enter key seven times and then move the insertion back to the beginning of the document.
   b. Display the WordArt Gallery and then double-click the fifth option from the left in the fourth row.
   c. At the Edit WordArt Text dialog box, key **The Dupont Daily**, and then click OK.
   d. Make the following changes to the WordArt text:
      1) Change the shape to Arch Up (Curve).
      2) Change the height and width to 2 inches.
      3) Change the horizontal alignment to left.
      4) Display the Format WordArt dialog box with the Layout tab selected and then click the <u>A</u>dvanced button. At the Advanced Layout dialog box with the Picture Position tab selected, change the Absolute position measurement in the Vertical section to *0"*, and then close the dialog box. Click OK to close the Format WordArt dialog box.
   e. Deselect the WordArt text.
   f. Move the insertion point to the end of the document and then insert the border line shown in figure U3.8. *(Hint: Do this at the Borders and Shading dialog box.)*
2. Save the document and name it Unit 3, PA 10.
3. Print and then close Unit 3, PA 10.

Figure U3.8 • Assessment 10

Assessment 11

1. Make sure you are connected to the Internet.
2. Display the Web toolbar and then click the Search the Web button.
3. At the Internet Explorer program window, search for information on *mountain climbing*, specifically on *Mt. Everest*.
4. Scroll through the list of responses and jump to a site that interests you. Read the information on the home page and then print the home page. After printing the home page, jump to any other hyperlinks that interest you.
5. Explore other sites related to this topic.
6. Click the Back button until the Internet Explorer Search page displays.
7. Search for information on job opportunities, specifically in the technology field. (You determine the search engine and the search text.)
8. Scroll through the list of responses and jump to a site that interests you.
9. Print the site's home page.
10. Explore any other technology employment sites that interest you.
11. Close Internet Explorer.

Assessment 12

1. Make sure you are connected to the Internet.
2. Jump to the SAS Airlines home page at *http://www.sas.se*.
3. Find information on flight availability from Seattle, Washington, to Copenhagen, Denmark, for two weeks from today. *(Hint: At the SAS home page, look for a hyperlink to* Travel Service. *At the next page, look for a hyperlink to* Worldwide Timetable.*)*
4. When the timetable page displays, specify the city of departure (Seattle) and the city of arrival (Copenhagen) and the day and month of travel. When the information on departing flights displays, print the page.
5. Scroll to the bottom of the page on flights to Copenhagen and then enter information for the return. Set the return day from Copenhagen to Seattle for two weeks from the day of departure.
6. When the information on return flights displays, print the page.
7. Close Internet Explorer.

Assessment 13

1. Open WW Travel.
2. Save the document with Save As and name it Unit 3, PA 13.
3. Make the following changes to the document:
   a. Apply a theme of your choosing to the document.
   b. Turn on the display of the Web Tools toolbar.

c. Add the following scrolling text centered between the company Web site address and the first paragraph of text in the document: **World Wide Travel is offering a 20% discount on all cruises booked before the end of this month.**

d. Turn off the display of the Web Tools toolbar.

e. Select the text *Northwest Airlines* that displays in the paragraph of text below the bulleted items and insert a hyperlink to *http://www.nwa.com*.

4. Save the document again with the same name (Unit 3, PA 13).

5. Print and then close Unit 3, PA 13.

CREATING ORIGINAL DOCUMENTS

The following activities give you the opportunity to practice your writing skills along with demonstrating an understanding of some of the important Word features you have mastered in this unit. When composing the documents, use correct grammar, appropriate word choices, and clear sentence constructions.

Assessment 14

Situation: You are Shawn Wingard, volunteer coordinator for the Kentwood School District. Compose a letter to the new reading volunteers listed below thanking them for their interest in volunteering for the reading literacy program and invite them to an orientation on Thursday, October 11, 2001, from 7:00 to 8:30 p.m. During this orientation, volunteers will learn more about the reading program such as the goals of the program, the students who will be served by the program, the various reading levels within the program, the time commitment required of volunteers, and the materials needed for the program. Create a data source with the names and addresses below that is attached to the main document, which is the letter to the volunteers. You determine the names for the data source and the main document. After creating the data source and the main document, merge the data source with the main document. Save the merged document as Unit 3, PA 14. Print and then close Unit 3, PA 14.

Ms. Karen Lyons
9023 South 42nd Street
Kentwood, MI 48933

Mr. Bryan Hamilton
11023 12th Northeast
Kentwood, MI 48920

Mr. Richard Ulrich
453 Silverdale Road
Kentwood, MI 48930

Mrs. Lindsay Childers
8931 133rd Place Northwest
Kentwood, MI 48933

Mr. Juan Nunez
8329 Branchwood Drive
Kentwood, MI 48933

Ms. Lisa Taua
1129 Military Road South
Kentwood, MI 48930

Assessment 15

Situation: You are an administrative assistant in the Financial Planning Department at Coleman Development Corporation. You have been asked by your supervisor to prepare a table showing equipment expenditures for each department as shown below:

COLEMAN DEVELOPMENT CORPORATION

Equipment Expenditures

Department	Amount
Human Resources	$20,459.34
Research	98,490.80
Financial Planning	14,439.50
Support Services	10,340.00
Sales	21,492.80
Public Relations	32,400.00
Total Amount	(Calculate total)

Create a table with the data and insert a formula to calculate the total. Save this document and name it Unit 3, PA 15. Print and then close Unit 3, PA 15.

Assessment 16

Situation: You work for Video Express, a video rental store. You have been asked to design a letterhead for the store. When designing the letterhead, include an appropriate clip art image and a border along with the following information:

Video Express
3340 Walden Circle
Memphis, TN 74633
(615) 555-9005

Save the letterhead and name it Unit 3, PA 16. Print and then close Unit 3, PA 16.

Assessment 17

Create an announcement for Video Express telling customers that they will receive a liter of soda and a large bag of popcorn when they rent three or more videos at one time. This offer is good for the month of March. Include an appropriate clip art image in the announcement. Also, consider using WordArt on some of the text in the announcement. Save the announcement and name it Unit 3, PA 17. Print and then close Unit 3, PA 17.

Melina Tanner
235-3525

Unit four

ENHANCING THE PRESENTATION OF TEXT

MICROSOFT® WORD 2000

MOUS SKILLS—UNIT FOUR

Chapter 17

Formatting Documents with Special Features

PERFORMANCE OBJECTIVES

Upon successful completion of chapter 17, you will be able to:

- Hyphenate words in a document.
- Change the hyphenation options and hyphenation zones in a document.
- Add line numbering in a document.
- Insert bookmarks in a document.
- Add text to a document with the AutoText feature.
- Edit and delete an AutoText entry.
- Insert a nonbreaking space between words in a document.
- Find and replace special characters.
- Create a drop cap in a document.
- Customize toolbars.
- Create and edit an equation with the Microsoft Equation 3.0 equation editor.

In this chapter, you will learn about Word features that will help you format documents. The hyphenation feature hyphenates words at the end of lines, creating a less ragged margin. Add line numbering to documents such as legal documents. Insert bookmarks in specific locations in a document to help you find those locations later and insert cross-references to refer readers to another location in a document.

Use Word's AutoText feature to simplify inserting commonly used words, names, or phrases in a document. Increase the visual appeal of a document by adding drop caps to the document and by inserting nonbreaking spaces between words that are to be kept together as a unit. Use the find and replace feature to find special characters and nonprinting elements and replace with other special text. Word 2000 toolbars can be customized. For example, you add buttons to or remove buttons from a toolbar and move buttons and reset buttons on toolbars. With the Microsoft Equation 3.0 equation editor application, you can create mathematical equations with proper formatting.

Hyphenating Words

In some Word documents, especially documents with left and right margins wider than 1 inch, the right margin may appear quite ragged. If the paragraph alignment is changed to justified, the right margin will appear even, but there will be extra space added throughout the line. In these situations, hyphenating long words that fall at the end of the text line provides the document with a more balanced look.

Automatically Hyphenating Words

When using the hyphenation feature, you can tell Word to automatically hyphenate words in a document or you can manually insert hyphens. To automatically hyphenate words in a document, click Tools, point to Language, and then click Hyphenation. At the Hyphenation dialog box shown in figure 17.1, click Automatically hyphenate document, and then click OK or press Enter.

figure
17.1

Hyphenation Dialog Box

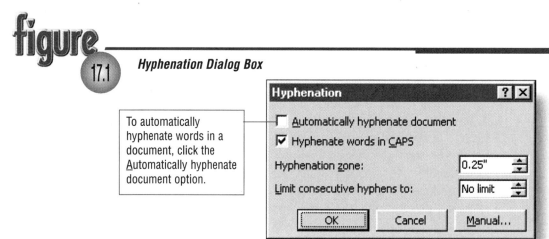

To automatically hyphenate words in a document, click the Automatically hyphenate document option.

After hyphens are inserted automatically in the document, scroll through the document and check to see if hyphens display in appropriate locations within the words. If, after hyphenating words in a document, you want to remove all hyphens, immediately click the Undo button on the Standard toolbar. This must be done immediately after hyphenating, since the Undo feature undoes only the last function.

Changing Hyphenation Options

By default, Word hyphenates words in all capital letters. If you do not want words in all capital letters hyphenated, remove the check mark from the Hyphenate words in CAPS option. With the Limit consecutive hyphens to option at the Hyphenation dialog box, you can limit the number of lines in a row that can end in hyphens. Generally, no more than two lines of text should display with a hyphen. To limit the hyphenation to two lines, click the up-pointing triangle at the right side of the Limit consecutive hyphens to option until 2 displays in the text box. You can also increase the number of lines by selecting the text that displays in the text box and then keying the desired number.

You can tell Word to ignore text in a paragraph or selected paragraphs when hyphenating. To do this, you would complete the following steps:

1. Position the insertion point in the paragraph or select the paragraphs where you do not want words hyphenated.
2. Click Format and then Paragraph.
3. At the Paragraph dialog box, click the Line and Page Breaks tab.
4. At the Paragraph dialog box with the Line and Page Breaks tab selected, click the Don't hyphenate option.
5. Click OK or press Enter.

Word will ignore the text in the paragraph or text in the selected paragraphs when hyphenating words in the document.

Automatically Hyphenating Words

1. Open Report 01.
2. Save the document with Save As and name it Ch 17, Ex 01.
3. Hyphenate words automatically in the report and limit consecutive hyphenations to 2 lines by completing the following steps:
   a. Click Tools, point to Language, and then click Hyphenation.
   b. At the Hyphenation dialog box, click the up-pointing triangle at the right of the Limit consecutive hyphens to text box until *2* displays in the text box.
   c. Click Automatically hyphenate document.
   d. Click OK.

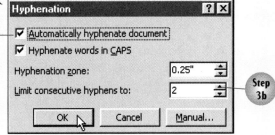

4. Save the document again with the same name (Ch 17, Ex 01).
5. Print and then close Ch 17, Ex 01.

The hyphen inserted during hyphenation is considered an *optional* hyphen. If the text is formatted and a hyphenated word no longer falls at the end of the text line, the optional hyphen is ignored. Later in this chapter, you will learn about the various types of hyphens.

Manually Hyphenating Words

If you want to control where a hyphen appears in a word during hyphenation, choose manual hyphenation. To do this, display the Hyphenation dialog box, and then click the Manual button. This displays the Manual Hyphenation dialog box as shown in figure 17.2. (The word in the Hyphenate at text box will vary.) At this dialog box, click Yes to hyphenate the word as indicated in the Hyphenate at text box; click No if you do not want the word hyphenated; or click Cancel to cancel hyphenation. Continue clicking Yes or No at the Manual Hyphenation dialog box. When the Office Assistant displays the message, *Hyphenation is complete.*, click in the document to remove the message. When hyphenating words, keep in mind the hyphenation guidelines shown in figure 17.3.

Manual Hyphenation Dialog Box

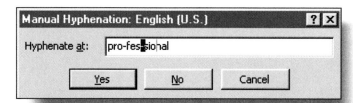

figure 17.2

Hyphenation Guidelines

Hyphenation Guidelines

Adapted from *The Paradigm Reference Manual* (Paradigm Publishing Inc., 1993)

One-Syllable Words: Do not divide one-syllable words such as *length, served,* or *thoughts.*

Multiple-Syllable Words: Divide multiple-syllable words between syllables, as in *publish.*

Note: Some divisions between syllables can confuse a reader, particularly if one or both parts may be read as words by themselves. Examples include *coin-sure, reed-ucate,* and *reap-portion.* In such cases, break the word at a different place *(co-insure, re-educate,* and *re-apportion).*

Prefixes, Suffixes: Generally, divide after a prefix and before a suffix. If the root word ends in a double consonant, divide after the double consonant (example: *bill-ing*). If adding a suffix results in a double consonant, divide between the doubled letters, as in *refer-ring.*

Consecutive Line Ends: Avoid dividing words at the ends of more than two consecutive lines.

Abbreviations, Numbers, Contractions: Do not divide except for abbreviations already containing hyphens, as in *CD-ROM.*

Names of People: Avoid dividing a person's name. But if it becomes necessary, hyphenate the name according to the guidelines for common words.

Dash: Do not divide before a dash or between the hyphens if the dash consists of two hyphens.

At the Manual Hyphenation dialog box, you can reposition the hyphen in the Hyphenate at text box. Word displays the word with syllable breaks indicated by a hyphen. The position where the word will be hyphenated displays as a blinking black bar. If you want to hyphenate at a different location in the word, position the mouse pointer at the desired location, and then click the left mouse button. If you are using the keyboard, press the left or right arrow key until the hyphen is positioned in the desired location. After positioning the hyphen, click Yes.

Manually Hyphenating Words

1. Open Report 03.
2. Save the document with Save As and name it Ch 17, Ex 02.
3. Manually hyphenate words in the document by completing the following steps:
   a. Click Tools, point to Language, and then click Hyphenation.
   b. At the Hyphenation dialog box, select the text *No limit* that displays in the Limit consecutive hyphens to text box, and then key 2.
   c. Click the Manual button.

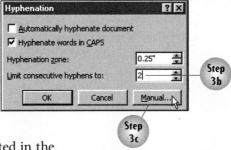

   d. At the Manual Hyphenation dialog box, make one of the following choices:
      • Click Yes to hyphenate the word as indicated in the Hyphenate at text box.
      • Move the hyphen in the word to a more desirable location, and then click Yes.
      • Click No if you do not want the word hyphenated.
   e. Continue clicking Yes or No at the Manual Hyphenation dialog box.
   f. When the Office Assistant displays the message, *Hyphenation is complete.*, click in the document to remove the message.
4. Save the document again with the same name (Ch 17, Ex 02).
5. Print and then close Ch 17, Ex 02.

If you want to remove all hyphens in a document, immediately click the Undo button on the Standard toolbar. To delete a few, but not all, of the optional hyphens inserted during hyphenation, use the Find and Replace dialog box. To do this, you would display the Find and Replace dialog box with the Replace tab selected, insert an optional hyphen symbol in the Find what text box, and make sure nothing displays in the Replace with text box. Complete the find and replace, clicking the Replace button to replace the hyphen with nothing or clicking the Find Next button to leave the hyphen in the document. The specific steps to do this are described in exercise 3.

exercise 3

Deleting Specific Optional Hyphens

1. Open Ch 17, Ex 02.
2. Save the document with Save As and name it Ch 17, Ex 03.
3. Delete the second, fourth, and sixth hyphens in the document by completing the following steps:
   a. Click Edit and then Replace.
   b. At the Find and Replace dialog box with the Replace tab selected, make sure there is no text in the Find what text box. If there is, press the Delete key. Make sure there is no formatting displayed below the Find what text box. If there is, click the More button and then click the No Formatting button.
   c. With the insertion point positioned in the Find what text box, make sure the dialog box is expanded (if not, click the More button), and then click the Special button.
   d. At the pop-up list of special characters that displays, click Optional Hyphen.
   e. Make sure there is no text in the Replace with text box and no formatting below the box.
   f. Click the Find Next button.
   g. When Word stops at the first occurrence of an optional hyphen (a hyphen inserted during hyphenation), click the Find Next button to leave the hyphen in the document and move to the next hyphen. (You may want to move down the Find and Replace dialog box so you can see some of the text in the document.)
   h. When Word stops at the second occurrence of an optional hyphen, click the Replace button.
   i. Continue clicking the Find Next button or Replace button until all hyphens have been found. (Replace the fourth and sixth optional hyphens. Leave the other hyphens in the document.)
   j. When the Office Assistant displays the message *Word has finished searching the document.*, click in the document to remove the message.
   k. Click the Close button to close the Find and Replace dialog box.
4. Save the document again with the same name (Ch 17, Ex 03).
5. Print and then close Ch 17, Ex 03.

Changing the Hyphenation Zone

Word uses a hyphenation zone of 0.25 inch from the right margin. If a word starts after the beginning of the hyphenation zone and continues beyond the end of the hyphenation zone, the word is wrapped to the next line. If a word starts at or before the beginning of the hyphenation zone and continues beyond the end of the hyphenation zone, it will be hyphenated during automatic hyphenation or presented for hyphenation during manual hyphenation.

If the hyphenation zone measurement is decreased, more words will be hyphenated. If the hyphenation zone measurement is increased, fewer words will be hyphenated. To change the hyphenation zone measurement, select the current measurement in the Hyphenation zone text box and then key the new measurement. You can also click the up- or down-pointing triangle after the Hyphenation zone text box to increase or decrease the hyphenation zone. After changing the hyphenation zone measurement, continue hyphenation by completing steps similar to those presented earlier.

Changing the Hyphenation Zone and Hyphenating Words in a Document

1. Open Para 02.
2. Save the document with Save As and name it Ch 17, Ex 04.
3. Change the left and right margins to 1.5 inches.
4. Change the hyphenation zone and then hyphenate the text in the document automatically by completing the following steps:
   a. Click Tools, point to Language, and then click Hyphenation.
   b. At the Hyphenation dialog box, click the up-pointing triangle at the right of the Hyphenation zone text box until *0.4"* displays in the text box.
   c. Click Automatically hyphenate document.
   d. Click OK.
5. Save the document again with the same name (Ch 17, Ex 04).
6. Print and then close Ch 17, Ex 04.

Step 4c

Step 4b

Hyphenation dialog box:
- ☑ Automatically hyphenate document
- ☑ Hyphenate words in CAPS
- Hyphenation zone: 0.4"
- Limit consecutive hyphens to: No limit
- OK | Cancel | Manual...

Inserting Hyphens

There are several ways that a hyphen is inserted in a document. The type of hyphen in a word like *co-worker* is called a *regular* hyphen. This hyphen is inserted by keying the minus sign on the keyboard. During hyphenation, Word will break hyphenated words, if necessary, at the hyphen.

A hyphen that you or Word inserts during hyphenation is considered an *optional* hyphen. An optional hyphen appears in the document screen and prints only if the word falls at the end of the text line. If text is adjusted and the word no longer falls at the end of the line, the optional hyphen is removed from the document screen and will not print. An optional hyphen can be inserted in a word by pressing Ctrl + -. If a word containing an optional hyphen falls at the end of the line, Word automatically breaks the word at the optional hyphen.

Inserting Optional Hyphens

1. Open Para 03.
2. Save the document with Save As and name it Ch 17, Ex 05.
3. Insert optional hyphens by completing the following steps:
   a. Position the insertion point between the letters *n* and *s* in the word *consider* that displays at the beginning of the second line in the second paragraph.
   b. Press Ctrl + -. (This inserts an optional hyphen and breaks *consider* between the first and second line of the paragraph.)
   c. Position the insertion point between the letters *n* and *n* in the word *beginning* that displays at the beginning of the fifth line in the second paragraph.
   d. Press Ctrl + -. (This inserts an optional hyphen and breaks *beginning* between the fourth and fifth line of the paragraph.)
4. Save the document again with the same name (Ch 17, Ex 05).
5. Print Ch 17, Ex 05.
6. With Ch 17, Ex 05 still open, change the left and right margins to 1.5 inches. (Notice how the optional hyphens are removed from *consider* and *beginning*.)
7. Save the document again with the same name (Ch 17, Ex 05).
8. Print and then close Ch 17, Ex 05.

Step 3a

Step 3c

In some text, such as telephone numbers and Social Security numbers, you may want to insert a *nonbreaking* hyphen rather than a regular hyphen. A nonbreaking hyphen tells Word that the text is to be considered a unit and not to break it between lines. A nonbreaking hyphen is inserted in text by pressing Ctrl + Shift + -.

Inserting Nonbreaking Hyphens

1. At a clear document screen, key the memo shown in figure 17.4. Insert a nonbreaking hyphen between the employee numbers and the telephone number. (Insert a nonbreaking hyphen by pressing Ctrl + Shift + -.)
2. Save the document and name it Ch 17, Ex 06.
3. Print and then close Ch 17, Ex 06.

figure

17.4 *Exercise 6*

DATE: February 21, 2001

TO: Lonnie Davidson

FROM: Dana Knowles

SUBJECT: NEW EMPLOYEE VERIFICATION

A New Employee Verification form has been received for Laurie Shipman, Alexander Yi, David White, and Naomi Roth. Please confirm the numbers—Laurie Shipman, 326-22-7842; Alexander Yi, 193-61-9849; David White, 355-90-6743; and Naomi Roth, 564-63-2417.

Many employees have asked for a toll-free number they can call from home to check on benefits. As a response to these requests, a toll-free number has been added which is 1-800-555-7800. Please provide the new employees with this number.

XX:Ch 17, Ex 06

Adding Bitmapped Graphics

Word recognizes a variety of picture formats dependent on the graphic filters installed with your program. Basically, there are two types of pictures—bitmaps and metafiles. Most clip art images are saved in a metafile format (named with a *.wmf* extension). Metafiles can be edited in Microsoft Word while bitmap files cannot. However, bitmaps can be edited in Microsoft Paint, Microsoft Photo Editor, or the program in which they were created. Metafiles can be ungrouped, converted to drawing objects, and then edited using tools on the Drawing toolbar. Pictures created in bitmap format are made from a series of small dots that form shapes and lines. Many scanned pictures are bitmapped. Bitmaps cannot be converted to drawing objects, but they can be scaled, cropped, and recolored using tools on the Picture toolbar.

Insert a bitmap image in a Word document by clicking Insert, pointing to Picture, and then clicking From File. At the Insert Picture dialog box, shown in figure 17.5, change to the folder containing the bitmap image, and then double-click the desired image in the list box.

figure

17.5

Insert Picture Dialog Box

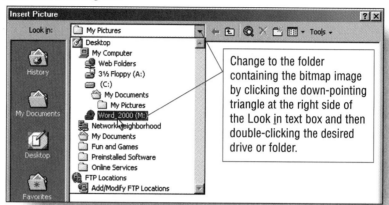

Change to the folder containing the bitmap image by clicking the down-pointing triangle at the right side of the Look in text box and then double-clicking the desired drive or folder.

Creating a Letterhead with a Bitmap Image

1. At a clear document screen, create a letterhead using a company bitmap logo by completing the following steps:
    a. Insert the CD that accompanies this textbook in the CD drive.
    b. Click Insert, point to Picture, and then click From File.
    c. At the Insert Picture dialog box, change to the drive containing the CD.
    d. Double-click *Waterfnt* in the list box. (This inserts the bitmap image in the document screen.)
2. Size and position the bitmap image by completing the following steps:
    a. Click the bitmap image to select it. (This displays black sizing handles around the image and also displays the Picture toolbar. If the Picture toolbar does not display, *right-click* the image, and then click Show Picture Toolbar at the shortcut menu.)
    b. Click the Format Picture button on the Picture toolbar.
    c. At the Format Picture dialog box, click the Size tab.
    d. At the Format Picture dialog box with the Size tab selected, select the current measurement in the Width text box, and then key **3.5**.

    Step 2c

Format Picture					
Colors and Lines	Size	Layout	Picture	Text Box
Size and rotate				
Height:	0.85"		Width:	3.5	

    Step 2d

    e. Click the Layout tab.
    f. At the Format Picture dialog box with the Layout tab selected, click Tight in the Wrapping style section.
    g. Click the Advanced button (located in the lower right corner of the dialog box).
    h. At the Advanced Layout dialog box with the Picture Position tab selected, click the Alignment option in the Horizontal section.
    i. Click the down-pointing triangle at the right side of the Alignment box (in the Horizontal section) and then click *Centered* at the drop-down list.
    j. Click the down-pointing triangle at the right side of the relative to box and then click *Page* at the drop-down list.

k. Make sure the measurement in the Absolute position text box (in the Vertical section) is *1"*. (If not, select the current measurement, and then key **1**.)

l. Click OK to close the Advanced Layout dialog box.

m. Click OK to close the Format Picture dialog box.

n. Click outside the bitmap image to deselect it.

3. Save the document and name it Ch 17, Ex 07.

4. Print and then close Ch 17, Ex 07.

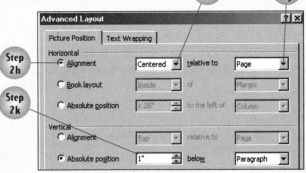

Using Bookmarks

In long documents, you may find marking a location in the document useful so you can quickly move the insertion point to the location. Create bookmarks for locations in a document at the Bookmark dialog box. When you create bookmarks, you can insert as many as needed in a document. To create a bookmark, position the insertion point at the location in the document where the bookmark is to appear, click Insert and then Bookmark. At the Bookmark dialog box shown in figure 17.6, key a name for the bookmark in the Bookmark name text box, and then click the Add button. Repeat these steps as many times as needed in a document to insert bookmarks.

figure 17.6

Bookmark Dialog Box

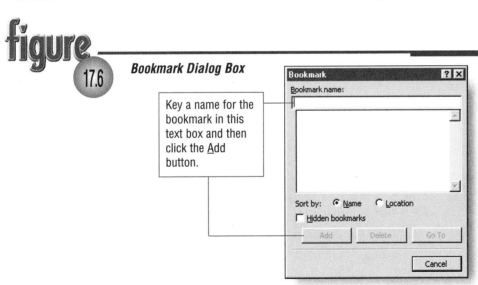

Key a name for the bookmark in this text box and then click the Add button.

Make sure you give each bookmark a unique name. A bookmark name can contain a maximum of 40 characters and can include letters, numbers, and the underscore character (_). You cannot use spaces in a bookmark name. When you insert a bookmark in a document, by default the bookmark is not visible. To make a bookmark visible, click Tools and then Options. At the Options dialog box, click the View tab. At the Options dialog box with the View tab selected, click Bookmarks in the Show section of the dialog box. (This inserts a check mark in the Bookmarks check box.) Complete similar steps to turn off the display of bookmarks. A bookmark displays as an I-beam marker.

You can also create a bookmark for selected text. To do this, select the text first and then complete the steps to create a bookmark. When you create a bookmark for selected text, a left bracket ([) indicates the beginning of the selected text and a right bracket (]) indicates the end of the selected text.

After bookmarks have been inserted in a document, you can move the insertion point to a specific bookmark. To do this, click Insert and then Bookmark. At the Bookmark dialog box, double-click the bookmark name in the list box. You can also click once on the bookmark name and then click the Go To button. When Word stops at the location of the bookmark, click the Close button to close the Bookmark dialog box. If you move the insertion point to a bookmark created with selected text, Word moves the insertion to the bookmark and selects the text.

Bookmarks in a document are deleted at the Bookmark dialog box (not the document). To delete a bookmark, display the Bookmark dialog box, select the bookmark to be deleted in the list box, and then click the Delete button.

exercise

Inserting Bookmarks in a Document

1. Open Report 01.
2. Turn on the display of bookmarks by completing the following steps:
   a. Click Tools and then Options.
   b. At the Options dialog box, click the View tab.
   c. Click Bookmarks in the Show section. (This inserts a check mark in the Bookmarks check box.)
   d. Click OK or press Enter.
3. Insert a bookmark at the beginning of the heading *Defining Desktop Publishing* by completing the following steps:
   a. Position the insertion point at the beginning of the line containing the heading *Defining Desktop Publishing*.
   b. Click Insert and then Bookmark.
   c. At the Bookmark dialog box, key **Define** in the Bookmark name text box.
   d. Click the Add button.
4. Insert a bookmark at the beginning of the following headings with the names listed by following steps similar to those in 3.

Initiating the Desktop Publishing Process	=	Initiate
Planning the Publication	=	Plan
Creating the Content	=	Create

5. Position the insertion point at the *Define* bookmark by completing the following steps:
   a. Click Insert and then Bookmark.
   b. At the Bookmark dialog box, double-click *Define* in the list box.
   c. When Word stops at the heading *Defining Desktop Publishing*, click the Close button to close the Bookmark dialog box.

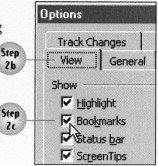

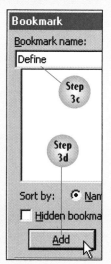

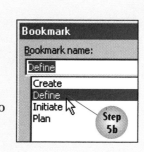

6. Complete steps similar to those in 5 to move the insertion point to the *Initiate, Plan*, and *Create* bookmarks.
7. Turn off the display of bookmarks by completing steps similar to those in 2.
8. Close the report without saving the changes.

Using AutoText

Word's AutoText feature is similar to the AutoCorrect feature you learned about in a previous chapter. With AutoCorrect, the text is automatically inserted in a document when the spacebar is pressed. For example, if you assigned the letters *HC* to *Hartland Corporation*, when you key **HC**, and then press the spacebar, *Hartland Corporation* is automatically inserted in the document. If you use text on a less frequent basis and do not want it automatically inserted in the document when you press the spacebar, use Word's AutoText feature. An AutoText entry is inserted in the document with an option from the AutoText side menu, the shortcut key, F3, or by pressing the Enter key.

Saving an AutoText Entry

The AutoText feature is useful for items such as addresses, company logos, lists, standard text, letter closing, or any other text that you use on a frequent basis. To save an AutoText entry, key the desired text and apply any necessary formatting. Select the text and then click Insert, point to AutoText, and then click New. At the Create AutoText dialog box shown in figure 17.7, key a short name for the text, and then click OK.

When you save selected text as an AutoText entry, the formatting applied to the text is also saved. If you are saving a paragraph or paragraphs of text that have paragraph formatting applied, make sure you include the paragraph mark with the selected text. To make sure the paragraph mark is included, turn on the display of nonprinting characters before selecting the text.

figure

17.7

Create AutoText Dialog Box

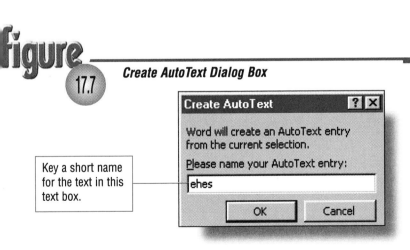

Key a short name for the text in this text box.

Create AutoText

Word will create an AutoText entry from the current selection.

Please name your AutoText entry:

ehes

OK   Cancel

An AutoText entry name can contain a maximum of 32 characters and can include spaces. Try to name the AutoText something that is short but also gives you an idea of the contents of the entry.

Inserting an AutoText Entry

An AutoText entry can be inserted in a document by keying the name of the AutoText and then pressing the Enter key or the shortcut key, F3; with an option from the AutoText side menu; or at the AutoCorrect dialog box with the AutoText tab selected. An AutoText entry name must be at least four characters in length to display the AutoText with the Enter key. The shortcut key, F3, can be used on an AutoText entry name of any length. To insert an AutoText entry with the Enter key, key the name given (at least four characters) to the AutoText entry (the full entry displays in a yellow box above the insertion point), and then press the Enter key. To insert an AutoText entry with the shortcut key, key the name given the AutoText entry, and then press F3.

To insert an AutoText entry with the AutoText side menu, click Insert, point to AutoText, point to Normal at the side menu, and then click the desired AutoText entry at the second side menu.

You can also insert an AutoText entry into a document at the AutoCorrect dialog box with the AutoText tab selected as shown in figure 17.8. To display this dialog box, click Insert, point to AutoText, and then click AutoText. At the AutoCorrect dialog box with the AutoText tab selected, key the name you gave the AutoText entry in the Enter AutoText entries here text box, and then click the Insert button.

figure
17.8

AutoCorrect Dialog Box with AutoText Tab Selected

One method for inserting an AutoText entry is to key the AutoText entry name in this text box and then to click the Insert button.

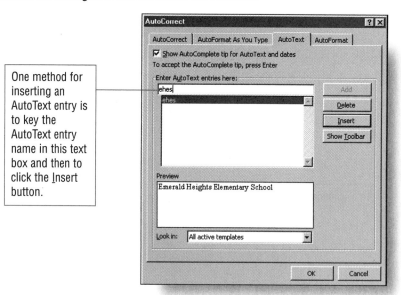

At the AutoCorrect dialog box with the AutoText tab selected, the Preview box displays the contents of the entry. This is useful if you cannot remember the name of the desired entry. Click each entry in the list box that displays below the Enter AutoText entries here text box and view the contents in the Preview box.

Creating AutoText Entries

1. At a clear document screen, create an AutoText entry for Emerald Heights Elementary School, by completing the following steps:
   a. Key **Emerald Heights Elementary School**.
   b. Select *Emerald Heights Elementary School*. (Be sure you do not include the paragraph symbol when selecting text. You may want to turn on the display of nonprinting characters.)
   c. Click <u>I</u>nsert, point to <u>A</u>utoText, and then click <u>N</u>ew.
   d. At the Create AutoText dialog box, key **ehes**.
   e. Click OK.
   f. Deselect the text.
   g. Close the document without saving it.

   > **Create AutoText** ? X
   >
   > Word will create an AutoText entry from the current selection.
   >
   > P̲lease name your AutoText entry:
   >
   > ehes
   >
   > OK   Cancel

   (Step 1d)

2. At a clear document screen, create an AutoText entry for the letter complimentary closing shown in figure 17.9 by completing the following steps:
   a. Key the text as shown in figure 17.9. (Insert your initials where you see the *XX*.)
   b. Select the text.
   c. Click <u>I</u>nsert, point to <u>A</u>utoText, and then click <u>N</u>ew.
   d. At the Create AutoText dialog box, key **cc**.
   e. Click OK.
   f. Deselect the text.
3. Close the document without saving it.
4. At a clear document screen, create the letter shown in figure 17.10 with the following specifications:
   a. While keying the letter, insert the *ehes* AutoText by keying **ehes** (this displays *Emerald Heights Elementary School* in a yellow box above the insertion point) and then pressing the Enter key.
   b. Insert the *cc* AutoText entry at the end of the letter by keying **cc** and then pressing F3.
5. When the letter is completed, save it and name it Ch 17, Ex 09.
6. Print and then close Ch 17, Ex 09.

Exercise 9

Very truly yours,

Blaine Dowler
Principal

XX:

figure

17.10   *Exercise 9*

September 5, 2001

Dear Parents:

The 2001 ehes Open House will be held Thursday, September 27. A short program explaining ehes opportunities and activities will be presented in the school gym. After the program, you can visit your student's classroom and speak with teachers. The program begins at 6:30 p.m. and the classroom visitations begin at 7:00 p.m.

During the school year, you can help make your student's school year a success by considering the following suggestions:

- Schedule a teacher conference within the first month of school and during each major grading period.
- Ask the teacher for expectations.
- Be sure you oversee your child's work and review any graded tests.
- Help your child set a time and place for homework. Be sure to provide support, materials, and encouragement.

During the classroom visitation, ask about each teacher's planning hour so you can schedule a private visitation when needed. Each of us at ehes look forward to a great year!

cc

Editing an AutoText Entry

An AutoText entry can be edited by inserting the entry in a document, making any necessary changes, and then saving it again with the same AutoText entry name. When the Office Assistant asks if you want to redefine the AutoText entry, click Yes.

Deleting an AutoText Entry

An AutoText entry can be removed from the AutoCorrect dialog box with the AutoText tab selected. To do this, display the AutoCorrect dialog box with the AutoText tab selected, select the entry to be deleted, and then click the Delete button.

Editing AutoText Entries

1. At a clear document screen, edit the *cc* AutoText entry by completing the following steps:
   a. Key **cc**.
   b. Press F3. (This inserts the complimentary close text.)
   c. Delete the name *Blaine Dowler* and then key **Linda Shing**.
   d. Delete the title *Principal* and then key **Superintendent**.
   e. Select the complimentary close text.
   f. Click Insert, point to AutoText, and then click New.
   g. At the Create AutoText dialog box, key **cc**.
   h. Click OK.
   i. At the message *Do you want to redefine the AutoText entry?*, click Yes.
   j. Deselect the text.

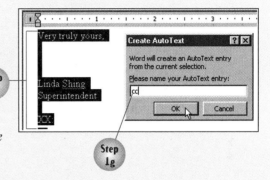

Step 1e

Step 1g

2. Close the document without saving it.
3. At a clear document screen, create an AutoText entry named *KSD* that includes the text shown in figure 17.11 by completing the following steps:
   a. Click the Center button on the Formatting toolbar.
   b. Key **KENTWOOD SCHOOL DISTRICT**.
   c. Press Enter.
   d. Key **200 Walton Boulevard**.
   e. Press Enter.
   f. Key **Kentwood, MI 48930**.
   g. Press Enter.
   h. Click the Align Left button on the Formatting toolbar.
   i. Press Enter.
   j. Select the text and the hard returns below the text.
   k. Change the font to 18-point Arial bold.
   l. With the text still selected, click Insert, point to AutoText, and then click New.
   m. At the Create AutoText dialog box, key **KSD**.
   n. Click OK.

Step 3m

4. Close the document without saving it.
5. At a clear document screen, create an AutoText entry named *ores* for Oak Ridge Elementary School.
6. Close the document without saving it.
7. At a clear document screen, create the letter shown in figure 17.12. Insert the AutoText entry where you see the AutoText entry name.
8. After creating the letter, save it and name it Ch 17, Ex 10.
9. Print and then close Ch 17, Ex 10.

10. At a clear document screen, delete the *ehes* AutoText entry by completing the following steps:

a. Click Insert, point to AutoText, and then click AutoText.

b. At the AutoCorrect dialog box with the AutoText tab selected, click *ehes* in the list box below the Enter AutoText entries here text box (you will need to scroll down the list to display *ehes*).

c. Click the Delete button.

d. Complete steps similar to those in 10b and 10c to delete the following AutoText entries: *cc, KSD,* and *ores*.

e. Click Close to close the AutoCorrect dialog box with the AutoText tab selected.

11. Close the document.

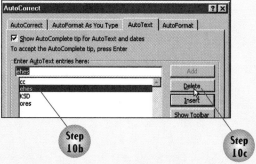

Step
10b

Step
10c

Exercise 10

KENTWOOD SCHOOL DISTRICT
200 Walton Boulevard
Kentwood, MI 48930

KSD

March 8, 2001

Dear Parents:

Child Psychologist Dr. Sandra White, from the University of Michigan, will be speaking at ehes and ores. Her topic is "Preparing all students for success in the 21st Century." Dr. White will speak at ehes Tuesday, April 10, from 7:00 to 8:30 p.m. in the multipurpose room. She will speak Thursday, April 12, from 7:30 to 8:30 p.m. in the gym at ores.

After speaking, Dr. White will accept questions from the audience. She will address the following issues:

- What knowledge, skills, attitudes, and maturity will be required of our students in the future world of work.
- The areas of education that need to be reconsidered to better prepare students for a future of fluctuating economy and global competition.
- The need for a comprehensive, integrated approach to education.

We are excited to have Dr. White as our guest speaker. The information she provides will help us and you make sound educational decisions.

cc

Inserting a Nonbreaking Space

As you key text in a document, Word makes line-end decisions and automatically wraps text to the next line. In some situations, word wrap may break up words or phrases on separate lines that should remain together. For example, a name such as *Daniel C. Lagasa* can be broken after, but should not be broken before, the initial *C*. The phrase *World War II* can be broken between *World* and *War*, but should not be broken between *War* and *II*.

To control what text is wrapped to the next line, a nonbreaking space can be inserted between words. When a nonbreaking space is inserted, Word considers the words as one unit and will not divide them. To insert a nonbreaking space between words, key the first word, press Ctrl + Shift + spacebar, and then key the second word.

If nonprinting characters are displayed, a normal space displays as a dot and a nonbreaking space displays as a degree symbol. To turn on the display of nonprinting characters, click the Show/Hide ¶ button on the Standard toolbar.

Inserting Nonbreaking Spaces

1. At a clear document screen, turn on the display of nonprinting characters (click Show/Hide ¶ button on the Standard toolbar), and then key the memo shown in figure 17.13. Insert nonbreaking spaces between the commands in the memo (for example, between *Ctrl + B* and *Ctrl + I*). Insert a nonbreaking space by pressing Ctrl + Shift + spacebar before and after the plus symbol in all the shortcut commands.
2. Save the memo and name it Ch 17, Ex 11.
3. Turn off the display of nonprinting characters.
4. Print and then close Ch 17, Ex 11.

Exercise 11

DATE: January 19, 2001

TO: All Administrative Assistants

FROM: Jolene Risse

SUBJECT: SHORTCUT COMMANDS

The transition to Word 2000 is almost complete. During the transition, I will continue offering helpful hints to all administrative assistants. Word offers a variety of shortcut keys and commands that you can use to quickly access certain features and functions. For example, to bold text press Ctrl + B, key text to be bolded, then press Ctrl + B again to turn off bold. To underline text, use the command Ctrl + U, and use Ctrl + I to italicize text.

In addition to the shortcut commands for applying character formatting, you can use shortcut commands to display certain dialog boxes. For example, use the command Ctrl + F to display the Find and Replace dialog box. Display the Open dialog box by pressing Ctrl + O. The command Ctrl + G will display the Find and Replace dialog box with the <u>G</u>o To tab selected.

If you have any questions regarding Word features, please call me at extension 710. I will be available between 9:00 a.m. and 12:00 noon and also between 1:00 p.m. and 4:30 p.m.

XX:Ch 17, Ex 11

Finding and Replacing Special Characters

In chapter 6, you learned about the find and replace feature and searched in a document for text and replaced it with other text. You also searched for formatting in a document and replaced it with other formatting. In addition to finding and replacing text and formatting, you can use the find and replace feature to search for special characters such as a nonbreaking space or an optional hyphen and to search for nonprinting elements such as a paragraph mark or tab character. To display a list of special characters and nonprinting elements, display the Find and Replace dialog box with the Replace tab selected, expand the dialog box, and then click the Special button. This displays a pop-up menu as shown in figure 17.14.

Special Button Pop-Up Menu

17.14

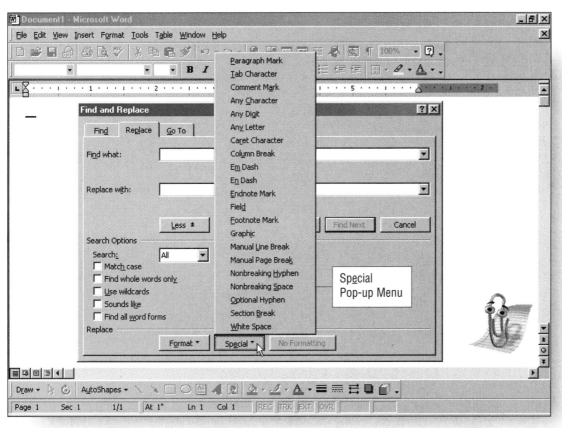

exercise 12

Finding and Replacing a Nonprinting Element

1. Open Ch 17, Ex 11.
2. Save the document with Save As and name it Ch 17, Ex 12.
3. Find all occurrences of the nonbreaking space and replace with a regular space by completing the following steps:
   a. Click Edit and then Replace.
   b. At the Find and Replace dialog box with the Replace tab selected, click the More button.
   c. With the insertion point positioned in the Find what text box (make sure there is no text in the text box and that the No Formatting button is dim), click the Special button that displays toward the bottom of the dialog box.
   d. At the pop-up menu that displays, click Nonbreaking Space. (This inserts ^s in the Find what text box.)
   e. Click in the Replace with text box (make sure there is no text in the text box and that the No Formatting button is dim) and then press the spacebar once. (This tells the Find and Replace feature to find a nonbreaking space and replace it with a regular space.)
   f. Click the Replace All button. (If a message displays telling you how many replacements were made, click the OK button.)
   g. When the replacements are made, click the Less button.
   h. Click the Close button to close the Find and Replace dialog box.
4. Save the document again with the same name (Ch 17, Ex 12).
5. Print and then close Ch 17, Ex 12.

[Dialog box labels:]

Field
Less ±
Footnote Mark
Graphic
Search Options
Search: All
Manual Line Break
☐ Match case
Manual Page Break
☐ Find whole words only
Nonbreaking Hyphen
☐ Use wildcards
Nonbreaking Space
☐ Sounds like
Optional Hyphen
☐ Find all word forms
Section Break
Replace
White Space
Format ▾   Special ▾   No Formatti

Step 3d

Step 3c

Creating a Dropped Capital Letter

In publications such as magazines, newsletters, and brochures, a graphic feature called *dropped caps* can be used to enhance the appearance of text. A drop cap is the first letter of the first word of a paragraph that is set into a paragraph. Drop caps identify the beginning of major sections or parts of a document.

Drop caps look best when set in a paragraph containing text set in a proportional font. The drop cap can be set in the same font as the paragraph text or it can be set in a complementary font. For example, a drop cap can be set in a sans serif font while the paragraph text is set in a serif font.

Figure 17.15 illustrates three paragraphs with different types of drop caps. The paragraph text and the drop cap in the first paragraph are set in Times New Roman. The drop caps in the second paragraph are set in Bookman Old Style and the paragraph text is set in Times New Roman. The drop cap in the third paragraph is set in Desdemona and the paragraph text is set in Times New Roman. The first paragraph shows the first letter of the paragraph as the drop cap. The first word of the paragraph is set as drop caps in the second paragraph. The first letter of the third paragraph is a drop cap that displays in the left margin of the paragraph.

figure 17.15 ***Paragraphs with Drop Caps***

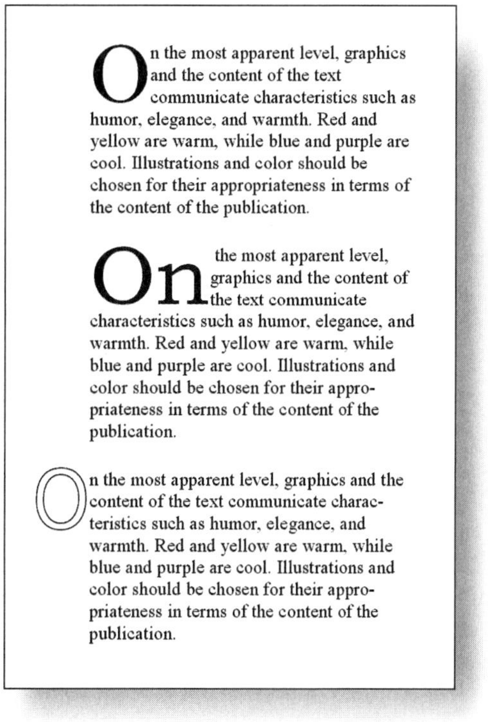
On the most apparent level, graphics and the content of the text communicate characteristics such as humor, elegance, and warmth. Red and yellow are warm, while blue and purple are cool. Illustrations and color should be chosen for their appropriateness in terms of the content of the publication.

On the most apparent level, graphics and the content of the text communicate characteristics such as humor, elegance, and warmth. Red and yellow are warm, while blue and purple are cool. Illustrations and color should be chosen for their appropriateness in terms of the content of the publication.

On the most apparent level, graphics and the content of the text communicate characteristics such as humor, elegance, and warmth. Red and yellow are warm, while blue and purple are cool. Illustrations and color should be chosen for their appropriateness in terms of the content of the publication.

Drop caps in Word are created through the Drop Cap dialog box shown in figure 17.16. To display this dialog box, click Format and then Drop Cap. At the Drop Cap dialog box, click the desired drop cap option, and then click OK or press Enter. When you create a drop cap, Word automatically changes the viewing mode from Normal to Page Layout.

figure
17.16   **Drop Cap Dialog Box**

exercise 13

Creating Drop Caps

1. Open Para 02.
2. Save the document with Save As and name it Ch 17, Ex 13.
3. Create a drop cap for the first paragraph by completing the following steps:
   a. Position the insertion point anywhere in the first paragraph.
   b. Click Format and then Drop Cap.
   c. At the Drop Cap dialog box, click Dropped in the Position section.
   d. Click OK or press Enter.
   e. Deselect the drop cap. (To do this with the mouse, click anywhere in the document screen outside the drop cap.)

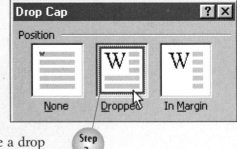

Step 3c

4. Complete steps similar to those in 3 to create a drop cap for the second paragraph.
5. Complete steps similar to those in 3 to create a drop cap for the third paragraph.
6. Save the document again with the same name (Ch 17, Ex 13).
7. Print and then close Ch 17, Ex 13.

If you want more than the first letter of a paragraph to be set in drop caps, you must select the word before displaying the Drop Cap dialog box.

exercise 14

Creating a Drop Cap on the First Word of a Paragraph

1. Open Para 05.
2. Save the document with Save As and name it Ch 17, Ex 14.
3. Create a drop cap for the first word of the first paragraph and change the font of the word by completing the following steps:
   a. Select the first word *(The)* of the first paragraph.
   b. Click Format and then Drop Cap.
   c. At the Drop Cap dialog box, click Dropped in the Position section.
   d. Click the down-pointing triangle at the right of the Font text box and then click *Desdemona* at the drop-down menu. (If Desdemona is not available, choose a similar decorative typeface.)
   e. Click OK or press Enter.
   f. Deselect the drop cap.
4. Save the document again with the same name (Ch 17, Ex 14).
5. Print and then close Ch 17, Ex 14.

To remove drop caps from a paragraph, position the insertion point in the paragraph, click Format and then Drop Cap. At the Drop Cap dialog box, click None in the Position section of the dialog box, and then click OK or press Enter.

exercise 15

Removing a Drop Cap

1. Open Ch 17, Ex 13.
2. Save the document with Save As and name it Ch 17, Ex 15.
3. Remove the drop cap from the second paragraph by completing the following steps:
   a. Position the insertion point anywhere in the second paragraph.
   b. Click Format and then Drop Cap.
   c. At the Drop cap dialog box, click None in the Position section of the dialog box.
   d. Click OK or press Enter.
4. Complete steps similar to those in 3 to remove the dropped cap from the third paragraph.
5. Save the document again with the same name (Ch 17, Ex 15).
6. Print and then close Ch 17, Ex 15.

Customizing Toolbars

Word 2000 contains customizable toolbars. For example, you can add to a toolbar buttons representing features you use on a consistent basis or remove buttons you do not need. You can also move buttons on a toolbar or reset the position of buttons.

Adding Buttons to and Removing Buttons from a Toolbar

To add a button to or remove a button from a toolbar, click the More Buttons button located at the right side of the toolbar and then click the Add or Remove Buttons option. This displays a drop-down list of button options. For example, clicking the More Buttons button located at the right side of the Standard toolbar and then clicking the Add or Remove Buttons option causes a drop-down list to display as shown in figure 17.17.

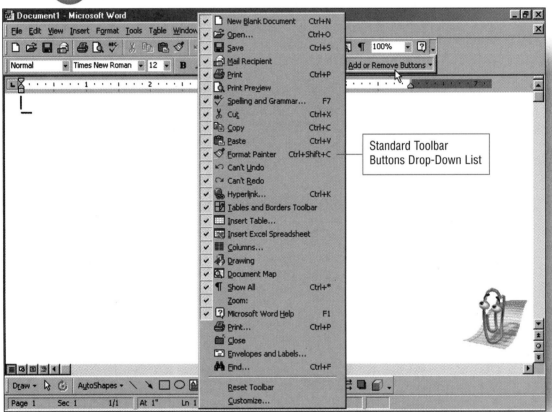

figure 17.17

Standard Toolbar Buttons Drop-Down List

To add a button to the toolbar, click the desired option at the drop-down list. This inserts the button at the right side of the toolbar. Another method for adding a button to a toolbar is to display the Customize dialog box with the Commands tab selected, click a category for the desired command, and then drag the command from the Commands box to the toolbar. To remove a button, click the desired option to remove the check mark. Another method for removing a button from a toolbar is to display the Customize dialog box and then drag the button off the toolbar.

Moving Buttons on a Toolbar

Buttons you add to a toolbar are inserted at the right side of the toolbar. You may want to move buttons to different locations on a toolbar. To do this, click Tools and then Customize. With the Customize dialog box displayed, drag a button to the desired position. You can also move a button from one toolbar to another.

Resetting Buttons on a Toolbar

You can reset buttons on a toolbar back to their original positions. To do this, display the Customize dialog box with the Toolbars tab selected, and then click the Reset button. At the Reset Toolbar dialog box, click OK.

Adding/Removing Buttons on the Standard Toolbar

1. Add a Close button to the Standard toolbar and remove the Document Map button by completing the following steps:
    a. At a clear document screen, click the More Buttons located at the right side of the Standard toolbar.
    b. Click the Add or Remove Buttons option.
    c. At the drop-down list that displays, click Document Map. (This removes the check mark from the option.)
    d. Click Close. (This inserts a check mark before the option.)
    e. Click outside the drop-down list to remove it from the screen. (Check the Standard toolbar and notice the Close button that displays at the right side of the toolbar.)
2. Drag the Close button on the Standard toolbar so it is positioned between the Open button and the Save button by completing the following steps:
    a. Click Tools and then Customize.
    b. With the Customize dialog box displayed, position the mouse pointer on the Close button, hold down the left mouse button, drag the icon representing the button so it is positioned between the Open button and Save button, and then release the mouse button.
    c. Click the Close button to close the Customize dialog box.
3. Add a Single Spacing button to the Formatting toolbar by completing the following steps:
    a. Click the More Buttons located at the right side of the Formatting toolbar.
    b. Click the Add or Remove Buttons option.
    c. At the drop-down list that displays, click Single Spacing. (This inserts a check mark before the option.)
    d. Click outside the drop-down list to remove it from the screen. (Check the Formatting toolbar and notice the Single Space button that displays at the right side of the toolbar.)

4. Move the Insert Clip Art button from the Drawing toolbar to the Standard toolbar by completing the following steps:
   a. Display the Drawing toolbar by clicking View, pointing to Toolbars, and then clicking Drawing.
   b. Display the Customize dialog box by clicking Tools and then Customize.
   c. Position the arrow pointer on the Insert Clip Art button on the Drawing toolbar, hold down the left mouse button, drag up so the button icon displays between the Spelling and Grammar button and the Cut button on the Standard toolbar, and then release the mouse button.
   d. Click the Close button to close the Customize dialog box.
5. Open Report 02.
6. Save the document with Save As and name it Ch 17, Ex 16.
7. Make the following changes to the document:
   a. Select the entire document, click the Single Space button on the Formatting toolbar (you added this button to the toolbar), and then deselect the text.
   b. Click the Insert Clip Art button on the Standard toolbar (you moved this button to the Standard toolbar).
   c. At the Insert ClipArt dialog box, search for a computer clip art image and then insert the image in the document. (Be sure to close the Insert ClipArt dialog box.)
   d. Size and/or move the image to a desirable location in the document (you choose the size and location). Make sure the text wraps around the image.
8. Save the document again with the same name (Ch 17, Ex 16).
9. Print Ch 17, Ex 16.
10. Close the document by clicking the Close button on the Standard toolbar. (You added this button to the Standard toolbar.)
11. Reset the Standard toolbar (removing the Close button and Insert Clip Art button, and adding the Document Map button) by completing the following steps:
    a. At a clear document screen, click Tools and then Customize.
    b. At the Customize dialog box, click the Toolbars tab.
    c. At the Customize dialog box with the Toolbars tab selected, make sure *Standard* is selected in the Toolbars list box.
    d. Click the Reset button.
    e. At the Reset Toolbar dialog box, click OK.
    f. Click Close to close the Customize dialog box.

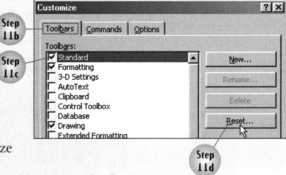

12. Complete steps similar to those in step 11 to reset the Formatting toolbar. (At the Customize dialog box, click *Formatting* in the Toolbars list box.)
13. Complete steps similar to those in step 11 to reset the Drawing toolbar. (At the Customize dialog box, click *Drawing* in the Toolbars list box.)

Using the Equation Editor

With Word's equation editor application called Microsoft Equation 3.0, you can create mathematical equations with proper formatting. The equation editor does the formatting for you, such as reducing the font size of exponents, applying italics to variables, and adjusting the spacing between equation elements.

Creating an Equation

To create an equation, you must access the equation editor application, Microsoft Equation 3.0. To do this, click Insert and then Object. At the Object dialog box with the Create New tab selected, double-click *Microsoft Equation 3.0* in the Object type list box. When you enter the equation editor, the screen displays as shown in figure 17.18.

Equation Editor Screen

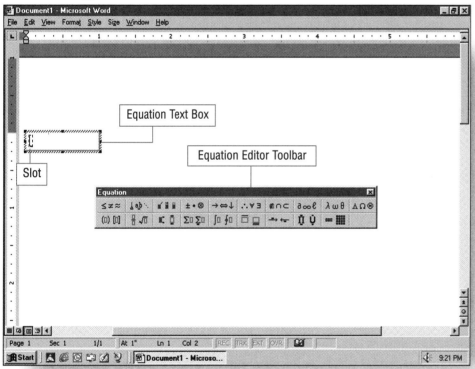

A text box displays in the upper left corner of the document screen. Key text for the equation in this box, or insert symbols and templates from the Equation Editor toolbar. The Equation Editor toolbar contains options for creating an equation. The top row on the toolbar contains symbols such as Greek characters that are used to write an equation. The bottom row of the toolbar contains templates. These templates contain such things as fractions and radicals, integrals, overbars and underbars, and arrows. Figure 17.19 identifies the name of each button on the Equation Editor toolbar.

Equation Editor Toolbar Buttons

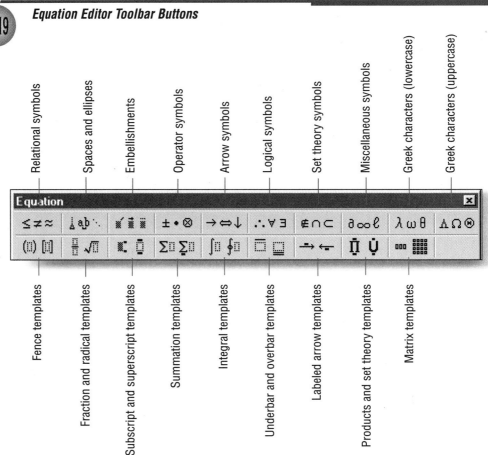

When you first open the equation editor, a text box is inserted in the upper left corner of the screen and the insertion point is positioned inside this box in a *slot* (a small box with a dashed border). The Equation Editor toolbar displays below this text box. With the insertion point inside the text box in the slot, key text or add symbols or templates with buttons on the Equation Editor toolbar.

As you enter text or insert symbols in the slot inside the text box, the slot expands. Some options from an Equation Editor toolbar button insert a slot such as the subscript and superscript options. To add an item from the Equation Editor toolbar, click the desired button on the toolbar. This causes a palette to display with a variety of options. Click one of the options on the palette and the symbol or character is inserted in the text box in the slot where the insertion point is located. When creating a symbol with the equation editor, you do not add spacing or formatting—the equation editor does that for you.

The steps to create equations in the exercises in this chapter are provided. For more information on writing extensive equations, please refer to the Microsoft Word Help feature.

exercise 17

Creating an Equation

1. At a clear document screen, create the equation shown in figure 17.20 by completing the following steps:
   a. At a clear document screen, click Insert and then Object.
   b. At the Object dialog box with the Create New tab selected, double-click *Microsoft Equation 3.0*.
   c. With the insertion point positioned in the slot inside the text box, key **A=P**. (Do not press the spacebar. The equation editor will determine the spacing.)
   d. Click the Fence templates button on the Equation Editor toolbar (the first button from the left in the bottom row).
   e. At the palette that displays, click the first option from the left in the top row.
   f. Key **1+**.
   g. Click the Fraction and radical templates button on the Equation Editor toolbar (the second button from the left in the bottom row).
   h. At the palette that displays, click the first option from the left in the top row.
   i. With the insertion point inside the top slot, key **1**.
   j. Position the tip of the arrow pointer inside the bottom slot and then click the left mouse button.
   k. Key **m**.
   l. Position the tip of the arrow pointer to the right of the right parenthesis and then click the left mouse button. (This moves the insertion point outside of the parentheses.)
   m. Click the Subscript and superscript templates button on the Equation Editor (the third button from the left in the bottom row).
   n. At the palette that displays, click the first option from the left in the first row.
   o. Key **nm**.
   p. Click in the document screen outside the text box and the Equation Editor toolbar. (This closes the equation editor and deselects the text box containing the equation.)
2. Save the document and name it Ch 17, Ex 17.
3. Print and then close Ch 17, Ex 17.

[Object dialog box showing Create New and Create from File tabs, Object type list: Microsoft Clip Gallery, Microsoft Drawing 1.01, Microsoft Equation 3.0, Microsoft Excel Chart, Microsoft Excel Worksheet, Microsoft Graph 2000 Chart, Microsoft Map, Microsoft Music Control — **Step 1b**]

[Equation box showing $A = P\left(1 + \frac{1}{m}\right)$ — **Step 1j**]

figure 17.20

Exercise 17

$$A = P\left(1 + \frac{1}{m}\right)^{nm}$$

Editing an Equation

An equation created with the equation editor can be edited. To do this, position the arrow pointer on the equation, and then double-click the left mouse button. This displays the equation in a text box and inserts the Equation Editor toolbar.

Click an equation once and black sizing handles display around the equation. Use these sizing handles to increase or decrease the size of the equation. To move an equation, select the equation, display the Picture toolbar, and then choose a text wrapping style. This changes the black sizing handles to white sizing handles. With white sizing handles displayed, position the arrow pointer in the equation, hold down the left mouse button, drag the equation to the desired location, and then release the mouse button.

Creating, Sizing, and Moving Equations

1. At a clear document screen, create the document shown in figure 17.21 by completing the following steps:
   a. Key the title and subtitle centered and bolded as shown in figure 17.21.
   b. After keying the subtitle, turn off bold, press Enter three times, and then return the alignment back to Left.
   c. Create the first equation shown in figure 17.21 by completing the following steps:
      1) Click Insert and then Object.
      2) At the Object dialog box with the Create New tab selected, double-click *Microsoft Equation 3.0*.
      3) With the insertion point positioned in the slot inside the text box, key **P=R**. (Do not press the spacebar. The equation editor will determine the spacing.)
      4) Click the Fence templates button on the Equation Editor toolbar (the first button from the left in the bottom row).
      5) At the palette that displays, click the second option from the left in the top row.
      6) Click the Fraction and radical templates button on the Equation Editor toolbar (the second button from the left in the bottom row).
      7) At the palette that displays, click the first option from the left in the top row.
      8) With the insertion point inside the top slot, key **1-**.
      9) Click the Fence templates button on the Equation Editor toolbar (the first button from the left in the bottom row).
      10) At the palette that displays, click the first button from the left in the top row.
      11) Key **1+i**.
      12) Position the tip of the arrow pointer immediately to the right of the right parenthesis but left of the right bracket and then click the left mouse button. (The blinking vertical bar should be only the length of the top row.)

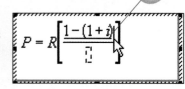

Step
1 c 12

      13) Click the Subscript and superscript templates button on the Equation Editor toolbar (the third button from the left in the bottom row).
      14) From the palette that displays, click the first button from the left in the top row.
      15) Key **-n**.

16) Position the tip of the arrow pointer in the bottom slot and then click the left mouse button.

17) Key **i**.

18) Click in the document screen outside the text box and the Equation Editor toolbar.

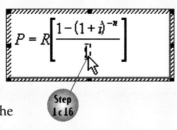

Step
1c 16

d. After creating the first equation, press the Enter key four or five times to separate the first equation from the second equation.

e. Save the document and name it Ch 17, Ex 18.

f. Complete the following steps to create the second formula in the figure:

1) Click Insert and then Object.

2) At the Object dialog box with the Create New tab selected, double-click *Microsoft Equation 3.0*.

3) With the insertion point positioned in the slot inside the text box, key **S=R**. (Do not press the spacebar. The equation editor will determine the spacing.)

4) Click the Fence templates button on the Equation Editor toolbar (the first button from the left in the bottom row).

5) At the palette that displays, click the second option from the left in the top row.

6) Click the Fraction and radical templates button on the Equation Editor toolbar (the second button from the left in the bottom row).

7) At the palette that displays, click the first option at the left in the first row.

8) Click the Fence templates button on the Equation Editor toolbar (the first button from the left in the bottom row).

9) At the palette that displays, click the first button from the left in the top row.

10) With the insertion point inside the top slot, key **1+i**.

11) Position the tip of the arrow pointer immediately to the right of the right parenthesis but left of the right bracket and then click the left mouse button. (The blinking vertical bar should be only the length of the top row.)

12) Click the Subscript and superscript templates button on the Equation Editor toolbar (the third button from the left in the bottom row).

13) From the palette that displays, click the first button from the left in the top row.

14) Key **n**.

15) Position the tip of the arrow point immediately to the right of the superscript number but left of the right bracket and then click the left mouse button.

16) Key **-1**.

17) Position the tip of the arrow pointer in the bottom slot and then click the left mouse button.

18) Key **i**.

19) Click in the document screen outside the text box and the Equation Editor toolbar.

Step
1f 11

Step
1f 15

Step
1f 17

g. Make the following changes to the first equation:

1) Click the first equation. (This displays black sizing handles around the equation.)

2) Using the middle sizing handle at the right side of the equation, increase the width of the equation approximately 0.5 inch.

3) Display the Picture toolbar. (To do this, right-click the equation, and then click Show Picture Toolbar at the shortcut menu.)

4) Click the Text Wrapping button on the Picture toolbar and then click Through.

5) With white sizing handles displayed around the equation, drag the equation to the middle of the left and right margins.
6) Click outside the equation to deselect it.

   h. Complete steps similar to those in 1g1 through 1g6 to size and move the second equation as shown in figure 17.21.

2. Save the document again with the same name (Ch 17, Ex 18).
3. Print and then close Ch 17, Ex 18.

figure

17.21

Exercise 18

MATH 145

Formulas for Mathematics of Finance

$$P = R \left[\frac{1 - (1 + i)^{-n}}{i} \right]$$

$$S = R \left[\frac{(1 + i)^{n} - 1}{i} \right]$$

chapter summary

➤ Word's hyphenation feature can help achieve a more balanced look when the right margin of a left-justified document is particularly ragged, or when the lines in justified paragraphs include large spaces.

➤ In addition to automatic or manual hyphenation, these options are also available at the Hyphenation dialog box: choose to hyphenate words that are in all capital letters, limit the number of consecutive lines that can end in hyphens, or tell Word to ignore text in selected text when hyphenating.

➤ To remove all manual or automatic hyphenations immediately after hyphenating, use the Undo feature. Delete specific hyphens at the Find and Replace dialog box with the Replace tab selected.

➤ The default hyphenation zone is 0.25 inch from the right margin. If the hyphenation zone is decreased at the Hyphenation dialog box, more words will be hyphenated. If the zone is increased, fewer words will be hyphenated.

➤ Keying a minus sign in a document inserts a *regular* hyphen. A hyphen inserted during the hyphenation process is called an *optional* hyphen. Insert a *nonbreaking* hyphen in words or groups of numbers that should be kept together on one line.

➤ Insert a bitmap image in a Word document by clicking Insert, pointing to Picture, and then clicking From File. At the Insert Picture dialog box, double-click the desired bitmap image.

➤ Insert a bookmark to mark a location in a document so you can later move the insertion point quickly to that location. Create or delete bookmarks at the Bookmark dialog box.

➤ Text that is used frequently can be saved as an AutoText entry and then inserted in a document. An AutoText entry is inserted in the document with the Enter key, the shortcut key F3, or at the AutoCorrect dialog box with the AutoText tab selected.

➤ When a nonbreaking space is inserted between words, Word considers these words as one unit and will not divide them. Insert a nonbreaking space with the shortcut command, Ctrl + Shift + spacebar.

➤ Use the find and replace feature to find special characters or nonprinting elements and replace with other special text.

➤ A dropped cap can be used to identify the beginning of major sections of a document. Create a dropped cap at the Drop Cap dialog box.

➤ Customize toolbars by adding, removing, and/or moving buttons. Return toolbars to the default buttons with the Reset button at the Customize dialog box.

➤ With Word's equation editor application called Microsoft Equation 3.0, you can create mathematical equations with proper formatting.

➤ To edit an equation created with the equation editor, position the arrow pointer on the equation, and then double-click the left mouse button.

commands review

	Mouse	Keyboard
Hyphenation dialog box	Tools, Language, Hyphenation	Tools, Language, Hyphenation
Remove all manual or automatic hyphens	Click Undo button on the Standard toolbar	Edit, Undo Hyphenation
Find and Replace dialog box with Replace tab selected	Edit, Replace	Edit, Replace
Insert an optional hyphen		Ctrl + -
Insert a nonbreaking hyphen		Ctrl + Shift + -
Display Insert Picture dialog box	Click Insert, point to Picture, then click From File	
Bookmark dialog box	Insert, Bookmark	Insert, Bookmark
AutoCorrect dialog box with AutoText tab selected	Insert, AutoText, AutoText	Insert, AutoText, AutoText
Insert a nonbreaking space		Ctrl + Shift + spacebar

Find and Replace dialog box	Edit, Replace	Edit, Replace
Drop Cap dialog box	Format, Drop Cap	Format, Drop Cap
Customize dialog box	Tools, Customize	Tools, Customize
Microsoft Equation 3.0	Insert, Object, then double-click *Microsoft Equation 3.0*	Insert, Object, choose *Microsoft Equation 3.0*, then choose OK

thinking offline

Completion: In the space provided at the right, indicate the correct term, command, or number.

1. This is the keyboard command to insert an optional hyphen when hyphenation is off.

2. This is the default measurement for the hyphenation zone.

3. Click this button on the Standard toolbar immediately after hyphenation if you want to delete all hyphens.

4. Do this to the hyphenation zone if you want to hyphenate more words in a document.

5. Click Tools, point to this option, and then click Hyphenation to display the Hyphenation dialog box.

6. Insert this in a document to mark a specific location.

7. If an AutoText entry name is less than four characters in length, key the AutoText entry name and then press this key on the keyboard to insert the full text.

8. This is the shortcut command from the keyboard to insert a nonbreaking space.

9. Click this button at the expanded Find and Replace dialog box to display a pop-up menu containing special characters and nonprinting elements.

10. Display the Drop Cap dialog box by clicking this option on the Menu bar and then clicking Drop Cap at the drop-down menu.

11. To add a button to or remove a button from a toolbar, click this button located at the right side of the toolbar.

12. Reset buttons on a toolbar back to their original positions by displaying this dialog box and then clicking the Reset button.

13. Display the equation editor screen by double-clicking this option at the Object dialog box with the Create New tab selected.

14. The bottom row of the Equation editor toolbar contains these.

15. When the equation editor is opened, a text box is inserted in the document and the insertion point is positioned inside a box called this. _____

16. In the space provided below, write the steps you would complete to create an AutoText entry for *Kellerman Manufacturing Corporation* with the name *kmc*.

_____

_____

working hands-on

Assessment 1

1. Open Para 04.
2. Save the document with Save As and name it Ch 17, SA 01.
3. Make the following changes to the document:
   a. Select the entire document and then change the font to 12-point Arial.
   b. Change the left and right margins for the document to 2 inches.
   c. Change the hyphenation zone to 0.5 inch and then hyphenate the text in the document automatically.
4. Save the document again with the same name (Ch 17, SA 01).
5. Print and then close Ch 17, SA 01.

Assessment 2

1. Open Report 01.
2. Save the document with Save As and name it Ch 17, SA 02.
3. Make the following changes to the report:
   a. Select the entire document and then change the font to 13-point Garamond.
   b. Set the title and the headings in 14-point Arial bold.
   c. Select the text in the body of the report (everything except the title) and then make the following changes:
      1) Change the line spacing to single.
      2) Change the spacing before and after paragraphs to 6 points.
      3) Change the paragraph alignment to justified.
   d. Hyphenate the document manually.
4. Save the document again with the same name (Ch 17, SA 02).
5. Print and then close Ch 17, SA 02.

Assessment 3

1. At a clear document screen, create a letterhead with a bitmap image with the following specifications:
   a. Insert the bitmap image named *Nature* located on the CD that accompanies this textbook. *(Hint: Do this by clicking Insert, pointing to Picture, and then clicking From File.)*
   b. Change the width of the image to 4 inches.
   c. Change the Wrapping style to Tight.

    d.   Change the horizontal alignment to centered relative to margins.

    e.   Change the vertical absolute position to 1 inch below the page.

2.   Save the document and name it Ch 17, SA 03.

3.   Print and then close Ch 17, SA 03.

Assessment 4

1.   Create an AutoText entry for *Stafford Annuity Mutual Funds* and use the initials *samf*.

2.   Key the document shown in figure 17.22 using the AutoText entry you created.

3.   Save the document and name it Ch 17, SA 04.

4.   Print and then close Ch 17, SA 04.

5.   At a clear document screen, delete the *samf* AutoText entry.

figure

17.22   *Assessment 4*

STAFFORD ANNUITY ASSOCIATION

The *samf* complement your traditional retirement savings by putting your after-tax dollars to work. The *samf* offer some very important advantages that can make your retirement dreams a reality including:

- No-loads
- Exceptionally low operating costs
- A low $250 initial investment
- Easy access to your money
- No marketing or distribution fees

The *samf* are backed by the investment expertise that has made Stafford Annuity Association one of the most respected companies in the financial industry.

Assessment 5

1.   At a clear document screen, create the memo shown in figure 17.23. Insert the current date at Date and Time dialog box or with a shortcut command. Insert nonbreaking spaces between the shortcut commands.

2.   Save the document and name it Ch 17, SA 05.

3.   Print and then close Ch 17, SA 05.

figure
17.23

Assessment 5

DATE: (current date)

TO: Administrative Assistants

FROM: Cynthia Stophel

SUBJECT: SHORTCUT COMMANDS

Shortcut commands can be used to format text, display dialog boxes, and insert special characters. For example, you can insert a nonbreaking space in text with Ctrl + Shift + space bar. You can insert a nonbreaking hyphen in a document with Ctrl + Shift + -. Shortcut commands can also be used to insert symbols. Press Alt + Ctrl + C to insert a copyright symbol. Insert a registered trademark with Alt + Ctrl + R.

A Word 2000 training session has been scheduled for next month. At this training, additional shortcut commands will be introduced.

XX:Ch 17, SA 05

Assessment 6

1. Open Para 03.
2. Save the document with Save As and name it Ch 17, SA 06.
3. Create a drop cap for the first letter of each paragraph.
4. Save the document again with the same name (Ch 17, SA 06).
5. Print and then close Ch 17, SA 06.

Assessment 7

1. At a clear document screen, create the document shown in figure 17.24 (center and bold the title and subtitle as shown). Create the equation by completing the following steps:
   a. Open Microsoft Equation 3.0.
   b. With the insertion point positioned in the slot inside the text box, key **r=1-**.
   c. Click the Fraction and radical templates button on the Equation Editor toolbar (the second button from the left in the bottom row).
   d. At the palette that displays, click the first option from the left in the first row.
   e. With the insertion point inside the top slot, key **6**.
   f. Click the Greek characters (uppercase) button (the last button in the top row).
   g. From the palette that displays, click the second option from the left in the fifth row.

h. Key **d**.
i. Click the Subscript and superscript templates button on the Equation Editor toolbar (the third button from the left in the bottom row).
j. From the palette that displays, click the first option from the left in the first row.
k. Key **2**.
l. Position the tip of the arrow pointer in the bottom slot and then click the left mouse button.
m. Key **n**.
n. Click the Fence templates button on the Equation Editor toolbar (the first button from the left in the bottom row).
o. At the palette that displays, click the first option from the left in the top row.
p. Key **n**.
q. Click the Subscript and superscript templates button on the Equation Editor toolbar (the third button from the left in the bottom row).
r. From the palette that displays, click the first option from the left in the first row.
s. Key **2**.
t. Position the tip of the arrow pointer outside the superscript slot but before the right parenthesis and then click the left mouse button.
u. Key **-1**.
v. Click in the document screen outside the text box and the Equation Editor toolbar.
w. Click the equation to select it and then increase the width and height approximately 1 inch.
x. With the equation still selected, display the Picture toolbar, choose a text wrapping style, and then move the equation to the middle of the screen.
2. Save the document and name it Ch 17, SA 07.
3. Print and then close Ch 17, SA 07.

Assessment 7

17.24

STATISTICS FORMULAS FOR CORRELATION ANALYSIS

Rank-Order Correlation

$$r = 1 - \frac{6\Sigma d^2}{n\left(n^2 - 1\right)}$$

Chapter 18

Creating Charts and Importing Data

P E R F O R M A N C E   O B J E C T I V E S

Upon successful completion of chapter 18, you will be able to:
- Create a chart with data in a Word table.
- Size and move a chart.
- Change the type of chart and choose a custom chart type.
- Change data in a chart.
- Add, delete, and customize chart elements.
- Import data from an Excel worksheet into a chart.
- Open, link, and embed an Excel worksheet in a Word document.
- Edit a linked worksheet.
- Modify an embedded Excel worksheet.

In chapter 13 you learned to create data in tables. While this does an adequate job of representing data, a chart can be created from data in a table to provide a more visual presentation of the data. A chart is sometimes referred to as a *graph* and is a picture of numeric data. A chart can be created with data in a table or data in a spreadsheet created in other programs such as Microsoft Excel. Charts are created with the Microsoft Graph Chart application. With Microsoft Graph, you can create a variety of charts including bar and column charts, pie charts, area charts, and much more.

Data can be imported and exported between applications within the Office suite. In this chapter, you will learn how to import data from an Excel worksheet into a chart and how to import data from an Excel worksheet into a Word table.

Creating a Chart

A chart can be created in Word by entering data in a datasheet provided by Microsoft Graph, or a chart can be created from data in a table or worksheet. In this chapter, you will learn how to create a chart using data from a table.

To create a chart in Word using data in a table, you would use the C_hart option from the _Picture side menu. For example, suppose you want to chart the data shown in the table in figure 18.1. To do this, you would complete the following steps:

1. Select the entire table.
2. Click Insert, point to Picture, and then click Chart.
3. The chart created by Microsoft Graph is inserted in the document below the table and a datasheet is inserted below the chart, as shown in figure 18.2. Click outside the chart to close Graph and remove the datasheet.

Table

Salesperson	April	May
A. Perez	20,405	19,340
J. White	28,966	29,485
L. Ching	41,309	25,340

Chart Based on Table

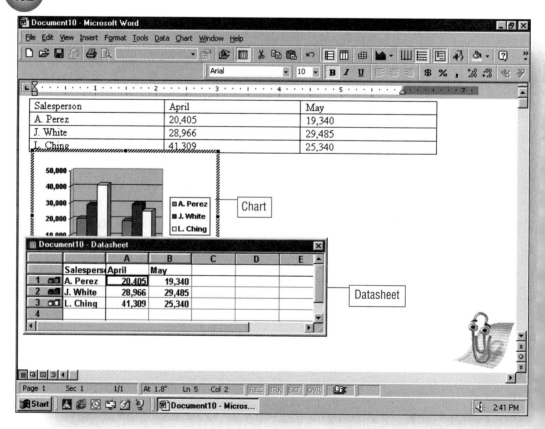

Chapter Eighteen

By default, Microsoft Graph charts the data in an orientation referred to as *data series in rows*. The text in the first row of the table is the category names. Text in the left column is the series names. Graph uses the series names as labels for the legend. For example, the names *A. Perez*, *J. White*, and *L. Ching* that display in the first column (except the first cell) are used for the legend. The legend is the box that labels the different colors used by each series of bars. The data in the first row, *April* and *May* (except the first cell), is used for the x-axis. The x-axis is the horizontal axis that runs along the bottom of the chart.

In a chart, such as the one shown in figure 18.2, the left side of the chart displays the values and is referred to as the z-axis. The z-axis is generally marked like a ruler and is broken into units by marks called *ticks*. Next to each tick mark is the amount of the value at that particular point on the axis. The values in the chart in figure 18.2 are broken into tick marks by ten thousands beginning with zero and continuing to 50,000. The values for the z-axis will vary depending on the data in the table.

exercise 1

Creating a Chart with Data in a Table

1. Open Table 02.
2. Save the document with Save As and name it Ch 18, Ex 01.
3. Create a chart by completing the following steps:
   a. Position the insertion point in any cell in the table.
   b. Select the table by clicking Table, pointing to Select, and then clicking Table.
   c. Click Insert, point to Picture, and then click Chart.
   d. When the datasheet and chart display, click outside the chart and the datasheet. (This closes Graph and removes the datasheet.)
4. Delete the table in the document by completing the following steps:
   a. Position the insertion point in any cell in the table.
   b. Click Table, point to Delete, and then click Table.
5. Save the document again with the same name (Ch 18, Ex 01).
6. Print and then close Ch 18, Ex 01.

Deleting a Chart

A chart created in Word can be deleted by clicking once in the chart to select it and then pressing the Delete key.

Sizing and Moving a Chart

Increase the size of a chart by selecting the chart and then dragging a sizing handle. When a chart is selected, white sizing handles display around the chart. If black sizing handles display around the chart, the chart can only be sized and not moved. To move a chart that displays with black sizing handles, display the Picture toolbar, click the Text Wrapping button on the Picture toolbar, and then click any wrapping option at the drop-down menu. This should change the black sizing handles to white sizing handles.

To move a chart, move the arrow pointer inside the chart (displays with a four-headed arrow attached), hold down the left mouse button, drag the chart to the desired location, and then release the mouse button.

Sizing and Moving a Chart

1. Open Ch 18, Ex 01.
2. Save the document with Save As and name it Ch 18, Ex 02.
3. Size and move the chart by completing the following steps:
    a. Change to the Print Layout view.
    b. Change the Zoom to Whole Page. To do this, click the down-pointing triangle at the right of the Zoom button on the Standard toolbar, and then click *Whole Page* at the drop-down menu.
    c. Click in the chart to select it. (If black sizing handles display around the chart, right-click the chart and then click Show Picture Toolbar. Click the Text Wrapping button on the Picture toolbar and then click T̲hrough at the drop-down list.)
    d. Drag the middle sizing handle at the right side of the chart to the right approximately 2 inches (using the measurements displayed toward the top of the screen on the horizontal ruler).
    e. Drag the middle sizing handle at the bottom of the chart down approximately 2 inches (using the measurements displayed at the left side of the screen on the vertical ruler).
    f. With the chart still selected, position the arrow pointer (displays with a four-headed arrow attached) inside the chart, hold down the left mouse button, drag the outline of the chart to the middle of the page, and then release the mouse button.
    g. Click outside the chart to deselect it.
    h. Change the Zoom back to 100%. To do this, click the down-pointing triangle at the right of the Zoom button, and then click *100%* at the drop-down menu.
4. Save the document again with the same name (Ch 18, Ex 02).
5. Print and then close Ch 18, Ex 02.

Changing the Chart Type

In Graph, 14 basic chart types are available along with built-in autoformats that can be applied to save time to get the desired look for the chart. Figure 18.3 shows an illustration and explanation of the 14 chart types.

figure

18.3 *Types of Charts*

Area	An Area chart emphasizes the magnitude of change, rather than time and the rate of change. It also shows the relationship of parts to a whole by displaying the sum of the plotted values.
Bar	A Bar chart shows individual figures at a specific time, or shows variations between components but not in relationship to the whole.
Bubble	A Bubble chart compares sets of three values in a manner similar to a Scatter chart, with the third value displayed as the size of the bubble marker.
Column	A Column chart compares separate (noncontinuous) items as they vary over time.
Cone	A Cone chart displays columns with a conical shape.
Cylinder	A Cylinder chart displays columns with a cylindrical shape.
Doughnut	A Doughnut chart shows the relationship of parts to the whole.
Line	A Line chart shows trends and change over time at even intervals. It emphasizes the rate of change over time rather than the magnitude of change.
Pie	A Pie chart shows proportions and relationships of parts to the whole.
Pyramid	A Pyramid chart displays columns with a pyramid shape.
Radar	A Radar chart emphasizes differences and amounts of change over time and variations and trends. Each category has its own value axis radiating from the center point. Lines connect all values in the same series.
Stock	A Stock chart shows four values for a stock—open, high, low, and close.
Surface	A Surface chart shows trends in values across two dimensions in a continuous curve.
XY (Scatter)	A Scatter chart either shows the relationships among numeric values in several data series or plots the interception points between x and y values. It shows uneven intervals of data and is commonly used in scientific data.

Chart Type

The default chart type created by Graph is a Column chart. This default chart type can be changed with the Chart Type button on the Graph Standard toolbar or at the Chart Type dialog box. (The chart must be displayed in Microsoft Graph for the Graph Standard toolbar to display. To display Microsoft Graph for an existing chart, double-click the chart.) To change the chart type with the Chart Type button, click the down-pointing triangle at the right side of the button, and then click the desired chart type at the drop-down list. The drop-down list contains a visual representation of chart types. Click the chart that represents the desired chart type. (If the Chart Type button is not visible on the Graph Standard toolbar, click the More Buttons button. This is the button that displays with two right-pointing arrows.)

A chart type can also be selected at the Chart Type dialog box with the Standard Types tab selected, as shown in figure 18.4. To display this dialog box, click Chart and then Chart Type.

figure
18.4

Chart Type Dialog Box with Standard Types Tab Selected

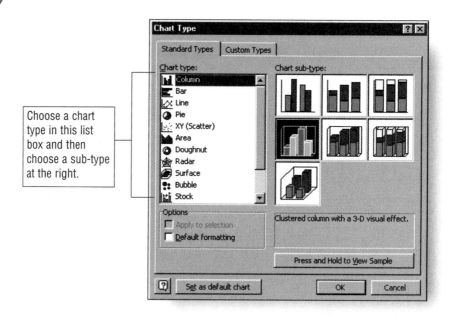

Choose a chart type in this list box and then choose a sub-type at the right.

The various chart types display in the Chart type list box. A description of the selected chart type displays in the lower right corner of the dialog box (above the Press and Hold to View Sample button). Click a different chart type in the Chart type list box and the description changes. When you click a different chart type, the sample charts that display in the Chart sub-type list box change. Graph provides chart sub-types that contain different combinations of enhancements for each chart type. With these sub-types, you can choose a chart with different enhancements or formatting without having to customize the chart yourself.

If you would like to see a sample of a particular chart, click the desired chart type in the Chart type list box and then click the desired sub-type chart in the Chart sub-type list box. Position the arrow pointer on the Press and Hold to View Sample button and hold down the left mouse button. This causes a sample chart to display in the selected chart type and sub-type chosen.

The default chart type is a Column chart. This default can be changed by clicking the desired chart type in the Chart type list box and then clicking the Set as default chart button that displays toward the bottom of the dialog box.

Changing the Chart Type

1. Open Ch 18, Ex 02.
2. Save the document with Save As and name it Ch 18, Ex 03.
3. Change the chart type to Line by completing the following steps:
   a. Make sure the view is Print Layout.
   b. Change the Zoom to Whole Page.
   c. Position the arrow pointer in the chart and then double-click the left mouse button.
   d. Close the datasheet. (To do this, click the View Datasheet button on the Graph Standard toolbar; or, click the Close button that displays in the upper right corner of the datasheet.)
   e. Click Chart and then Chart Type.
   f. At the Chart Type dialog box, click *Line* in the Chart type list box.
   g. Change the chart sub-type by clicking the first chart in the second row in the Chart sub-type list box. (Skip this step if the sub-type is already selected.)
   h. View a sample of how this sub-type chart will display by positioning the arrow pointer on the Press and Hold to View Sample button and then holding down the left mouse button. After viewing a sample of the selected Line chart, release the mouse button.
   i. Click OK to close the Chart Type dialog box.
   j. Click outside the chart to close Graph and deselect the chart.
4. Save the document again with the same name (Ch 18, Ex 03).
5. Print Ch 18, Ex 03.
6. With Ch 18, Ex 03 still open, complete the following steps:
   a. Double-click the chart.
   b. Click Chart and then Chart Type.
   c. At the Chart Type dialog box, click *Bar* in the Chart type list box.
   d. Click the first chart type in the second row in the Chart sub-type list box.

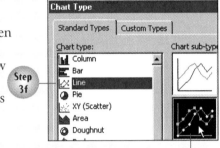

Step 3f

Step 3g

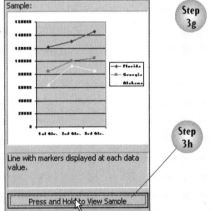

Step 3h

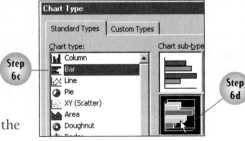

Step 6c

Step 6d

e. View a sample of how this sub-type chart will display by positioning the arrow pointer on the Press and Hold to View Sample button and then holding down the left mouse button. After viewing a sample of the selected Bar chart, release the mouse button.

f. Click OK to close the Chart Type dialog box.

g. Click outside the chart to close Graph and deselect the chart.

h. Change the Zoom to 100%.

7. Save the document again with the same name (Ch 18, Ex 03).

8. Print and then close Ch 18, Ex 03.

Choosing a Custom Chart Type

Graph offers a variety of preformatted custom charts. A custom chart can be chosen at the Chart Type dialog box with the Custom Types tab selected as shown in figure 18.5. To display this dialog box, double-click a chart to display the chart in Graph, click Chart and then Chart Type.

figure

18.5   *Chart Type Dialog Box with Custom Types Tab Selected*

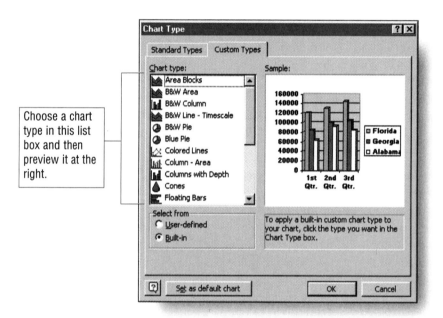

Choose a chart type in this list box and then preview it at the right.

You can also choose a custom chart for an existing chart with a shortcut menu. To do this, position the arrow pointer in a white portion of the chart (inside the chart but outside any chart element), and then click the *right* mouse button. At the shortcut menu that displays, click *Chart Type*. At the Chart Type dialog box, click the Custom Types tab. Click the desired custom chart type in the Chart type list box.

exercise 4

Choosing a Custom Chart Type

1. Open Ch 18, Ex 02.
2. Save the document with Save As and name it Ch 18, Ex 04.
3. Choose a custom chart type by completing the following steps:
   a. Double-click the chart. (This displays the chart in Graph.)
   b. Close the datasheet.
   c. Click Chart and then *Chart Type*.
   d. At the Chart Type dialog box, click the Custom Types tab.
   e. At the Chart Type dialog box with the Custom Types tab selected, click *B&W Column* in the Chart type list box.
   f. Click OK to close the Chart Type dialog box.
4. Click outside the chart. (This closes Graph and deselects the chart.)
5. Save the document again with the same name (Ch 18, Ex 04).
6. Print and then close Ch 18, Ex 04.

Changing Data in Cells

Graph uses data in cells to create a chart. In a Word table, this data can be changed and the chart will reflect the changes. If you use a table to create a chart, the information from the table is automatically inserted in the chart datasheet. When a chart is created, the datasheet displays over the chart. Data in the datasheet can be changed in a manner similar to a table. You can move the insertion point to cells within the datasheet, select the cell contents, and then make changes. In a datasheet, the mouse pointer displays as a white plus sign. If the datasheet has been closed, you can display it by clicking the View Datasheet button on the Graph Standard toolbar.

View Datasheet

To select a cell with the mouse, position the mouse pointer (white plus sign) in the desired cell, and then click the left mouse button. To select multiple cells, drag the mouse pointer across the cells. To select a row or column, click the row or column header. To select all cells in the datasheet, click the gray rectangle at the top left corner where row and column headings intersect. With a cell or cells selected, you can cut, copy, and/or paste data in cells using the Cut, Copy, or Paste buttons on the Graph Standard toolbar or options at the Edit drop-down menu.

exercise

Editing a Datasheet in a Chart

1. Open Ch 18, Ex 02.
2. Save the document with Save As and name it Ch 18, Ex 05.
3. Change the contents of certain cells in the datasheet by completing the following steps:
    a. Make sure the view is Print Layout and then change the Zoom to Whole Page.
    b. Double-click the chart.
    c. Position the mouse pointer (displays as a white plus sign) in the datasheet in the cell containing the amount *84560*, click the left mouse button (this selects the cell contents), and then key **98650**.
    d. Position the insertion point in the cell containing the amount *100540*, click the left mouse button, and then key **106540**.
    e. Position the insertion point in the cell containing the amount *104532*, click the left mouse button, and then key **110245**.
4. Click outside the chart. (This removes the datasheet, updates the chart, and deselects the chart.)
5. Change the Zoom to 100%.
6. Save the document again with the same name (Ch 18, Ex 05).
7. Print and then close Ch 18, Ex 05.

			A	
		State	1st Qtr.	2n(
1		Florida	121398	
2		Georgia	98650	
3		Alabama	64120	
4				

🟦 Ch 19, Ex 05.doc - Datasheet

Step 3c

Changing the Data Series

When a chart is created, Graph uses the data in the first row (except the first cell) to create the x-axis (the information along the bottom of the chart) and uses the data in the first column (except the first cell) to create the legend. For example, in the chart in figure 18.2, the names (*A. Perez, J. White,* and *L. Ching*) were used for the legend and the months (*April* and *May*) were used for the x-axis (along the bottom of the chart).

By Row

By Column

When a chart is created, the By Row button on the Graph Standard toolbar is active by default. This indicates that Graph uses the data in the first row (except the first cell) to create the x-axis for the chart. This can be changed by clicking the By Column button on the Graph Standard toolbar. Click the By Column button and the data in the first column (except the first cell) is used to create the x-axis. The active button on the Graph Standard toolbar displays with a light gray background. If the By Row or By Column button is not visible, click the More Buttons button on the Graph Standard toolbar (this button contains two right-pointing arrows).

exercise 6

Changing the Data Series in a Chart

1. Open Ch 18, Ex 02.
2. Save the document with Save As and name it Ch 18, Ex 06.
3. Change the data series from rows to column by completing the following steps:
   a. Make sure the view is Print Layout and then change the Zoom to Whole Page.
   b. Double-click the chart.
   c. Close the datasheet.
   d. Click the By Column button on the Graph Standard toolbar. (If the By Column button is not visible, click the More Buttons button.) (Notice that this changes the x-axis to the states [*Florida, Georgia, Alabama*]. If Georgia does not display in the x-axis, increase the width of the chart.)

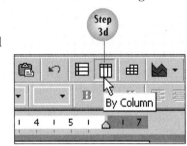

4. Click outside the chart.
5. Change the Zoom to 100%.
6. Save the document again with the same name (Ch 18, Ex 06).
7. Print and then close Ch 18, Ex 06.

Adding Chart Elements

When a chart is created by Graph, certain chart elements are automatically inserted, including a chart legend and labels for the axes. Other chart elements can be added, such as a chart title and data labels. These elements can be added to a chart with options at the Chart Options dialog box shown in figure 18.6. To display this dialog box, click Chart and then Chart Options. You can also display this dialog box by positioning the arrow pointer in a white portion of the chart (outside any chart elements), clicking the *right* mouse button, and then clicking *Chart Options* at the shortcut menu that displays.

18.6   *Chart Options Dialog Box with Titles Tab Selected*

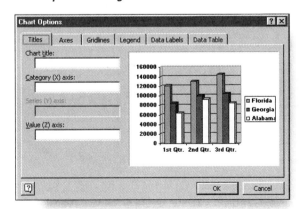

To add a chart element, click the desired tab at the Chart Options dialog box, and then choose the desired chart element. For example, to add a title to a chart, display the Chart Options dialog box, and then click the Titles tab. At the Chart Options dialog box with the Titles tab selected, click inside the Chart title text box, key the desired title, and then click the OK button to close the dialog box.

Creating a Pie Chart and Adding Chart Elements

1. Open Table 03.
2. Save the document with Save As and name it Ch 18, Ex 07.
3. Create a Pie chart with the data in the table by completing the following steps:
   a. Select the table.
   b. Click Insert, point to Picture, and then click Chart.
   c. When the datasheet and chart display, close the datasheet.
   d. Change to a Pie chart by completing the following steps:
      1) Click the down-pointing triangle at the right side of the Chart Type button. (If the Chart Type button is not visible, click the More Buttons button on the Graph Standard toolbar.)
      2) At the drop-down palette of chart type options, click the first pie chart option in the fifth row.
   e. Click the By Column button on the Graph Standard toolbar. (If the By Column button is not visible, click the More Buttons button on the Graph Standard toolbar.)

Step 3d1

Step 3d2

4. Add a title and data labels to the Pie chart and move the legend by completing the following steps:
   a. Click Chart and then Chart Options.
   b. At the Chart Options dialog box, click the Titles tab. (Skip this step if the Titles tab is already selected.)

   Step 4c

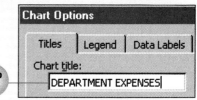

   c. At the Chart Options dialog box with the Titles tab selected, click inside the Chart title text box, and then key **DEPARTMENT EXPENSES**.
   d. Click the Data Labels tab.
   e. At the Chart Options dialog box with the Data Labels tab selected, click Show percent.

   Step 4d

   Step 4e

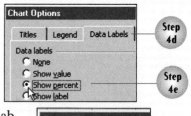

   f. Click the Legend tab.
   g. At the Chart Options dialog box with the Legends tab selected, click Left.
   h. Click OK to close the Chart Options dialog box.
   i. Click outside the chart to close Graph.
5. Delete the table in the document by completing the following steps:
   a. Position the insertion point in any cell in the table.
   b. Click Table, point to Delete, and then click Table.
6. Size and move the chart by completing the following steps:

   Step 4f

   Step 4g

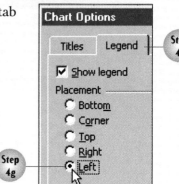

a. Make sure the view is Print Layout and then change the Zoom to Whole Page.
b. Click in the chart to select it. (If black sizing handles display around the chart, right-click the chart and then click Show Picture Toolbar. Click the Text Wrapping button on the Picture toolbar and then click Through at the drop-down list.)
c. Drag the middle sizing handle at the right side of the chart to the right approximately 2 inches (using the measurements displayed toward the top of the screen on the horizontal ruler).
d. Drag the middle sizing handle at the bottom of the chart down approximately 2 inches (using the measurements displayed at the left side of the screen on the vertical ruler).
e. With the chart selected, position the arrow pointer (displays with a four-headed arrow attached) inside the chart, hold down the left mouse button, drag the outline of the chart to the middle of the page, and then release the mouse button.
f. Click outside the chart to deselect it.
g. Change the Zoom back to 100%.
7. Save the document again with the same name (Ch 18, Ex 07).
8. Print and then close Ch 18, Ex 07.

Moving/Sizing Chart Elements

When additional elements are added to a chart, the chart can become quite full and elements may overlap. If elements in a chart overlap, an element can be selected and then moved. To select an element, position the arrow pointer on a portion of the element, and then click the left mouse button. This causes sizing handles to display around the element. Position the mouse pointer toward the edge of the selected element until it turns into an arrow pointer, hold down the left mouse button, drag the element to the desired location, and then release the mouse button. To change the size of an element, drag the sizing handles in the desired direction.

As you move the arrow pointer around a chart that is displayed in Graph, a yellow box will display when the arrow pointer is positioned on a chart or chart element. For example, if you position the arrow pointer on a chart legend, a yellow box displays next to the arrow pointer with the text *Legend*. This yellow box can help you position the arrow pointer correctly before selecting an element.

Deleting Chart Elements

Chart elements can be selected by clicking the desired element. Once an element is selected, it can be moved and it can also be deleted. To delete a selected element, press the Delete key. If you delete a chart element and then decide you want it redisplayed in the chart, immediately click the Undo button on the Graph Standard toolbar.

Moving and Sizing Chart Elements

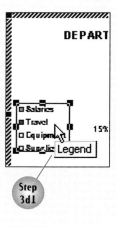

1. Open Ch 18, Ex 07.
2. Save the document with Save As and name it Ch 18, Ex 08.
3. Move and size chart elements by completing the following steps:
   a. Make sure the view is Print Layout and then change the Zoom to 50%.
   b. Double-click the chart.
   c. Close the datasheet.
   d. Move the legend to the right side of the chart by completing the following steps:
      1) Click the legend to select it. (Before clicking the legend, make sure a yellow box displays by the arrow pointer with the text *Legend*.)
      2) With the arrow pointer positioned in the legend, hold down the left mouse button, drag the outline of the legend to the right side of the chart, and then release the mouse button. (The legend will overlap the pie chart.)
   e. Move the pie to the left by completing the following steps:
      1) Select the pie. To do this, position the arrow pointer in a gray portion of the border that displays around the pie, and then click the left mouse button. (Before clicking the left mouse button, make sure a yellow box displays by the arrow pointer with the text *Plot Area*.) This should insert sizing handles around the square border around the pie. If not, try selecting the pie again.
      2) With the pie selected, position the arrow pointer inside the gray border surrounding the pie (not inside the pie), hold down the left mouse button, drag the outline of the pie to the left until it looks balanced with the legend, and then release the mouse button.
   f. With the pie still selected, increase the size of the pie by completing the following steps:
      1) Position the arrow pointer on the black sizing handle that displays in the bottom right corner of the selected pie until the pointer turns into a double-headed arrow pointing diagonally.
      2) Hold down the left mouse button, drag the pie border down and to the right to increase the size of the pie, and then release the mouse button. (You determine the size.)
      3) If the pie overlaps the legend, move the pie and/or move the legend.
   g. Click outside the chart to deselect it.
4. Save the document again with the same name (Ch 18, Ex 08).
5. Print and then close Ch 18, Ex 08.

Adding Gridlines

Gridlines can be added to a chart for the category, series, and value. Depending on the chart, some but not all of these options may be available. To add gridlines, display the Chart Options dialog box and then click the Gridlines tab. This displays the Chart Options dialog box with the Gridlines tab selected as shown in figure 18.7. At this dialog box, insert a check mark in those options for which you want gridlines.

figure

18.7 *Chart Options Dialog Box with Gridlines Tab Selected*

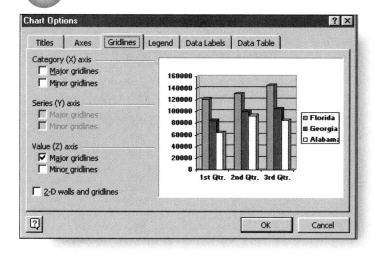

In addition to the options at the Gridlines dialog box, horizontal and/or vertical gridlines can be added to a chart with the Category Axis Gridlines button and the Value Axis Gridlines button on the Graph Standard toolbar. (If these buttons are not visible, click the More Buttons button on the Graph Standard toolbar.)

Category Axis
Gridlines

Value Axis
Gridlines

Adding Gridlines to a Chart

1. Open Ch 18, Ex 02.
2. Save the chart with Save As and name it Ch 18, Ex 09.
3. Add gridlines to the chart by completing the following steps:
   a. Make sure the view is Print Layout and then change the Zoom to Whole Page.
   b. Double-click the chart.
   c. Close the datasheet.
   d. Click Chart and then Chart Options.

e. At the Chart Options dialog box, click the Gridlines tab.

f. At the Chart Options dialog box with the Gridlines tab selected, insert a check mark in the two options in the *Category (X) axis* section and also the two options in the *Value (Z) axis* section.

g. Click OK to close the Chart Options dialog box.

h. Click outside the chart to close Graph and deselect the chart.

i. Change the Zoom to 100%.

4. Save the document again with the same name (Ch 18, Ex 09).

5. Print and then close Ch 18, Ex 09.

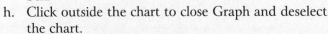

Formatting a Chart and Chart Elements

A variety of formatting options are available for a chart or elements in a chart. Formatting can include adding a pattern, changing background and foreground colors of the selected element or chart, changing the font, and changing the element alignment or placement. If you double-click a chart element, a formatting dialog box displays. For example, if you double-click in a chart (outside any specific chart element) the Format Chart Area dialog box displays. Click the Font tab and the dialog box displays as shown in figure 18.8. At this dialog box, choose a font face, style, and size for the text in the chart as well as a font color and a background. You can also display the Format Chart Area dialog box by clicking once to select the chart area, then clicking Format and then Selected Chart Area.

18.8 *Format Chart Area Dialog Box with Font Tab Selected*

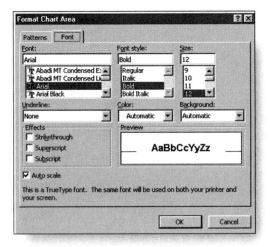

If you click the Patterns tab at the Format Chart Area dialog box, the dialog box displays as shown in figure 18.9. At this dialog box, you can add a border and/or pattern to the chart and change the border style.

figure

18.9   ***Format Chart Area with Patterns Tab Selected***

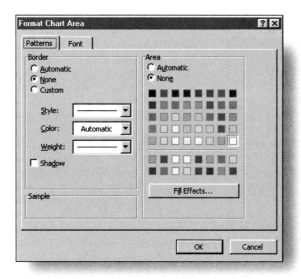

The font and pattern of chart elements can also be customized, along with additional formatting for specific elements. For example, if you double-click a chart title, the Format Chart Title dialog box displays. (You can also display this dialog box by clicking once on the title, then clicking Format and then Selected Chart Title.) This dialog box contains three tabs—Patterns, Font, and Alignment. Clicking the Patterns or the Font tab displays the same options as those available at the Format Chart Area dialog box. Click the Alignment tab and options for changing the text alignment (horizontal or vertical) display along with options for the title orientation.

Double-click a chart legend and the Format Legend dialog box displays with three tabs—Patterns, Font, and Placement. (You can also display this dialog box by clicking once on the legend, then clicking Format and then Selected Legend.) Clicking the Patterns or the Font tab displays the same options as those available at the Format Chart Area dialog box. Click the Placement tab to display options for specifying the location of the legend in relation to the chart.

Each chart element contains a formatting dialog box. To display this dialog box, double-click the desired chart element. For example, double-click text in either the x-axis or the z-axis and the Format Axis dialog box displays.

exercise 10

Customizing a Chart and Chart Elements

1. Open Ch 18, Ex 02.
2. Save the document with Save As and name it Ch 18, Ex 10.
3. Double-click the chart. (This displays the chart in Graph.)
4. Close the datasheet.
5. Customize the chart by completing the following steps:

   a. Double-click in the chart area outside any chart elements.
   b. At the Format Chart Area dialog box, make sure the Patterns tab is selected (if not, click the Patterns tab).
   c. At the Format Chart Area dialog box with the Patterns tab selected, click the Light Purple color (last color in the sixth row).
   d. Click the Font tab.
   e. At the Format Chart Area dialog box with the Font tab selected, click Garamond in the Font list box. (You will need to scroll down the Font list to display Garamond. If this typeface is not available, choose a similar serif typeface.)
   f. Click OK to close the Format Chart Area dialog box.

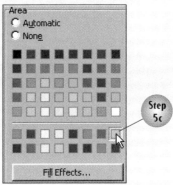

6. Customize the legend in the chart by completing the following steps:

   a. Double-click the legend. (This displays the Format Legend dialog box.)
   b. At the Format Legend dialog box click the Patterns tab. (Skip this step if the Patterns tab is already selected.)
   c. Click the Light Blue color (fifth color from the left in the fifth row).
   d. Click the Placement tab.
   e. At the Format Legend dialog box with the Placement tab selected, click Left.
   f. Click OK to close the Format Legend dialog box.

7. Click outside the chart to close Graph.
8. Save the document again with the same name (Ch 18, Ex 10).
9. Print and then close Ch 18, Ex 10.

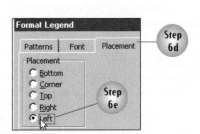

Customizing Elements in a Chart

1. At a clear document screen, key the headings and the first paragraph of the memo in figure 18.10.
2. With the insertion point positioned a double space below the first paragraph in the memo, create the table as shown in figure 18.10. After creating the table, move the insertion point below the table, and then press Enter twice.
3. Create a Pie chart for the table, change the position of the legend, and add a title by completing the following steps:
   a. Select the entire table.
   b. Click Insert, point to Picture, and then click Chart.
   c. When the datasheet and chart display, close the datasheet.
   d. Change to a Pie chart by completing the following steps:
      1) Click the down-pointing triangle at the right side of the Chart Type button. (If this button is not visible, click the More Buttons button on the Graph Standard toolbar.)
      2) At the drop-down palette of chart type options, click the first pie chart option in the fifth row.
   e. Click the By Column button on the Graph Standard toolbar. (If this button is not visible, click the More Buttons button on the Graph Standard toolbar.)
4. Add a title and data labels to the Pie chart by completing the following steps:
   a. Click Chart and then Chart Options.
   b. At the Chart Options dialog box, click the Titles tab. (Skip this step if the Titles tab is already selected.)
   c. At the Chart Options dialog box with the Titles tab selected, click inside the Chart title text box, and then key **Software Training**.
   d. Click the Data Labels tab.
   e. At the Chart Options dialog box with the Data Labels tab selected, click Show percent.
   f. Click OK to close the Chart Options dialog box.
   g. Click outside the chart to close Graph.

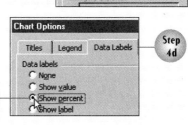

5. Delete the table in the document by completing the following steps:
   a. Position the insertion point in any cell in the table.
   b. Click Table, point to Delete, and then click Table.
6. Click in the chart to select it. (If black sizing handles display around the chart, right-click the chart and then click Show Picture Toolbar. Click the Text Wrapping button on the Picture toolbar and then click Square at the drop-down list.)
7. With the chart selected (white sizing handles display), move it so it is centered between the left and right margins.

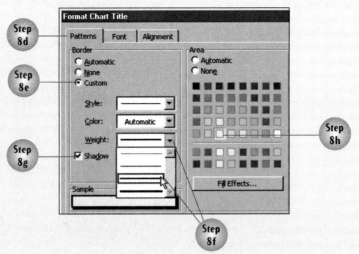

8. Change the font for the title and legend and add a border and shading by completing the following steps:
   a. Double-click the chart. (This displays the chart in Graph.) If necessary, close the datasheet.
   b. Double-click the title *Software Training*.
   c. At the Format Chart Title dialog box, click the Font tab, and then change the font to 10-point Times New Roman bold (or a similar serif typeface).
   d. Click the Patterns tab.
   e. Click the white circle before Custom in the Border section of the dialog box.
   f. Click the down-pointing triangle to the right of the Weight text box. From the drop-down menu that displays, click the third option.
   g. Click the check box before the Shadow option.
   h. Add a light yellow background color to the title by clicking the third color from the left in the fifth row.
   i. Click OK to close the Format Chart Title dialog box.
9. Format the legend in the chart with the same options as the title (except change the font to 6-point Times New Roman bold) by completing steps similar to those in step 8. (When changing the font, you will need to select the current number in the Size list box at the Format Legend dialog box with the Font tab selected and then key **6**.)
10. Select the gray border that displays behind the pie and then increase the size of the pie by dragging one of the corner sizing handles. Increase the size of the pie so it is easier to read but still fits inside the chart area.
11. Click outside the chart window to close Graph and deselect the chart.
12. Press Ctrl + End to move the insertion point to the end of the document and then press Enter enough times to move the insertion point approximately a double space below the chart.
13. Key the paragraph and the initials and document name displayed in figure 18.10 below the table.
14. Save the document and name it Ch 18, Ex 11.
15. Print and then close Ch 18, Ex 11.

figure

18.10 *Exercise 11*

DATE: (current date)

TO: Timothy Watson, Director

FROM: Dana Jordan, Administrative Assistant

SUBJECT: EMPLOYEE TRAINING SURVEY

All employee training surveys have been collected. I have analyzed the section of the survey dealing with training needs. The chart below shows the percentage of people requesting training on the specified software.

Software	Percentage
Word Processing	42
Spreadsheet	29
Product Assessment	18
Database	11

As you can see by the chart, word processing is the software most requested by employees for training. I will finish analyzing the rest of the survey by the end of next week.

XX:Ch 18, Ex 11

Changing Element Colors

A fill color can be added to a chart or a chart element with the Fill Color button on the Graph Standard toolbar. To add a fill color, select the chart or the chart element, and then click the down-pointing triangle at the right side of the Fill Color button on the Graph Standard toolbar. This displays a palette of color choices as shown in figure 18.11. Click the desired color on the palette. (If the Fill Color button is not visible, click the More Buttons button on the Graph Standard toolbar.)

Fill Color

figure

18.11 *Fill Color Palette*

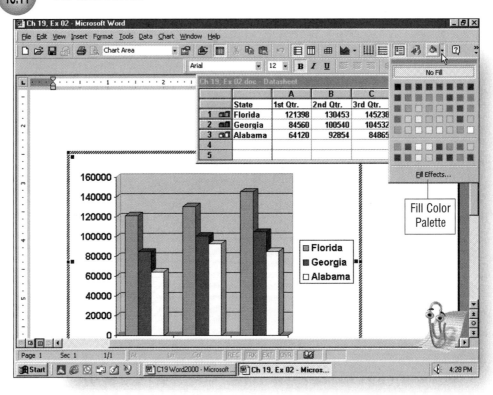

Fill Color
Palette

exercise 12

Changing Element Fill Colors in a Chart

1. Open Ch 18, Ex 02.
2. Save the document with Save As and name it Ch 18, Ex 12.
3. Change the colors of the bars in the chart by completing the following steps:
   a. Double-click the chart.
   b. Close the datasheet.
   c. Change the color of the blue bars (for Florida) to red
      by completing the following steps:
      1) Position the arrow pointer on any blue bar in the
         chart and then click the left mouse button. (This
         selects the three blue bars.)
      2) Click the down-pointing triangle at the right
         of the Fill Color button on the Graph
         Standard toolbar.
      3) At the color palette, click the Red
         color (first color from the left in the
         third row).

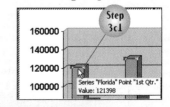

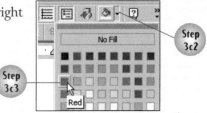

d. Change the color of the maroon bars (for Georgia) to blue by completing steps similar to those in step 3c. (Choose the Blue color in the second row, sixth from the left.)

e. Change the color of the light yellow bars (for Alabama) to green by completing steps similar to those in step 3c. (Choose the Green color in the second row, fourth from the left.)

f. Add a background color to the chart by completing the following steps:

   1) Select the entire chart. (To do this, position the arrow pointer inside the chart window but outside the chart, and then click the left mouse button.)

   2) Click the down-pointing triangle at the right of the Fill Color button.

   3) From the color palette that displays, click the Turquoise color in the fourth row, fifth from the left.

g. Click outside the chart window to close Graph and deselect the chart.

4. Save the document again with the same name (Ch 18, Ex 12).

5. Print and then close Ch 18, Ex 12.

Importing Data

In chapter 13 you learned to insert data in a Word table and in this chapter you learned to create a chart from data in a table. The Office suite contains an application called Excel, which is a complete spreadsheet program. While numbers can be calculated in a Word table, for extensive calculations, use Excel. In this section, you will import data from Excel into a chart and import, modify, and create worksheets in a table.

If Excel is not available, you will still be able to complete many of the exercises in this section. Two Excel worksheets have already been created and are available in the *Chapter 18* folder. To import and edit a worksheet, you will need access to Excel. Before completing exercises in this section, check with your instructor.

Importing Data into a Chart

Data in an Excel worksheet can be imported into a chart. To do this, you would complete these basic steps:

1. Click Insert and then Object.

2. At the Object dialog box with the Create New tab selected, double-click *Microsoft Graph 2000 Chart* in the Object type list box. (You will need to scroll down the list to display this program.)

3. With the default datasheet and chart displayed, click the Import File button on the Standard toolbar.

4. At the Import File dialog box, double-click the desired worksheet name.

5. At the Import Data Options dialog box, shown in figure 18.12, specify whether you want the entire worksheet or a specific range of cells, and then click OK.

6. Click in the document screen outside the chart and datasheet to return to the document and view the chart.

figure

Import Data Options Dialog Box

exercise 13

Importing an Excel Worksheet into a Chart

1. Open and save an Excel worksheet by completing the following steps:
   a. Open Excel by clicking the Start button on the Taskbar, pointing to Programs, and then clicking *Microsoft Excel*.
   b. In Excel, click the Open button on the Standard toolbar.
   c. At the Open dialog box, make sure the *Chapter 18* folder on your disk is the active folder, and then double-click *Excel Worksheet 01*.
   d. With Excel Worksheet 01 open, click File and then Save As.
   e. At the Save As dialog box, key **Excel Ch 18, Ex 13** and then press Enter.
   f. Click File and then Close to close Excel Ch 18, Ex 13.
   g. Click File and then Exit to exit Excel.
2. In Word, import Excel Ch 18, Ex 13 into a chart by completing the following steps:
   a. At a clear document screen, click Insert and then Object.
   b. At the Object dialog box with the Create New tab selected, double-click *Microsoft Graph 2000 Chart* in the Object type list box. (You will need to scroll down the list to display this program.)

   c. With the default datasheet and chart displayed, click the Import File button on the Standard toolbar.
   d. At the Import File dialog box, make sure the *Chapter 18* folder on your disk is the active folder, and then double-click *Excel Ch 18, Ex 13*.
   e. At the Import Data Options dialog box, make sure Entire sheet is selected in the Import section, and then click OK.
   f. Click in the document screen outside the chart and datasheet to return to the document and view the chart.

   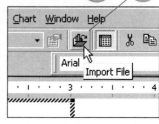

   Step 2b   Step 2c

3. Save the document with Save As and name it Ch 18, Ex 13.
4. Print and then close Ch 18, Ex 13.

Importing a Worksheet into a Table

Several methods are available for importing a Microsoft Excel worksheet into a Word document. The methods include opening the worksheet into a Word document, linking the worksheet to a Word document, or embedding the worksheet as an object. Consider the following when choosing a method:

- Open an Excel worksheet in a Word document in situations where the worksheet will not need to be edited.
- Link an Excel worksheet with a Word document in situations where the worksheet is continually updated in Excel and you want the updates to appear in the Word document.
- Embed an Excel worksheet in a Word document in situations where the worksheet will be edited in the Word document.

Opening a Worksheet into a Word Document

1. At a clear document screen, open an Excel worksheet by completing the following steps:
   a. Click the Open button on the Standard toolbar.
   b. At the Open dialog box, change the Files of type option to *All Files*.
   c. Make sure *Chapter 18* is the active folder.
   d. Double-click *Excel Worksheet 01*.
   e. At the Open Worksheet dialog box, make sure *Entire Workbook* displays in the Open document in Workbook list box, and then click OK.

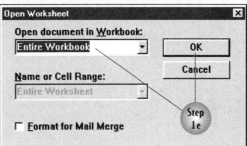

2. Make the following changes to the document:
   a. Press the Enter key three times. (This inserts blank lines above the worksheet and moves the worksheet down the screen.)
   b. Press the up arrow key twice.
   c. Click the Bold button on the Formatting toolbar and then key **2000 REGIONAL SALES**.
   d. If the gridlines do not display in the table, click T**a**ble and then Show **G**ridlines.
   e. Increase the size of the first column so the text does not wrap by completing the following steps:
      1) Position the mouse pointer on the column border between the first and second column (pointer turns into left- and right-pointing arrows with a double line between).
      2) Hold down the Shift key and the left mouse button.
      3) Drag the column border to the right approximately 0.25 inch.
      4) Release the mouse button and then the Shift key.
3. Save the document with Save As and name it Ch 18, Ex 14.
4. Print the document. (The worksheet border lines will not print.)
5. Close Ch 18, Ex 14.

Linking an Excel Worksheet with a Word Document

1. In Word, key the memo shown in figure 18.13. (Press the Enter key four times between the first and second paragraphs of text as shown in the figure. You will link an Excel worksheet in that location.)
2. Link an Excel worksheet with the Word document by completing the following steps:
   a. Open Excel by clicking the Start button on the Taskbar, pointing to Programs, and then clicking *Microsoft Excel*.
   b. In Excel, click the Open button on the Standard toolbar.
   c. At the Open dialog box, make sure the *Chapter 18* folder on your disk is the active folder, and then double-click *Excel Worksheet 02*.
   d. With Excel Worksheet 02 open, click File and then Save As.
   e. At the Save As dialog box, key **Excel Ch 18, Ex 15** and then press Enter.
   f. Select cells A1 through D7. (To do this, position the mouse pointer in cell A1, hold down the left mouse button, drag down to cell D7, and then release the mouse button.)
   g. Click the Copy button on the Standard toolbar.
   h. Make Word the active program (click the button on the Taskbar identifying Word).
   i. With Ch 18, Ex 15 open, position the insertion point between the first and second paragraphs of text in the body of the memo.
   j. Click Edit and then Paste Special.
   k. At the Paste Special dialog box, click *Microsoft Excel Worksheet Object* in the As list box.
   l. Click Paste link.
   m. Click OK to close the dialog box.

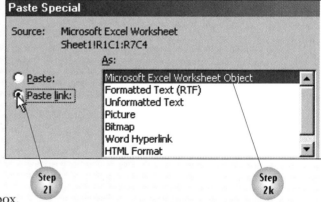

Step 2l

Step 2k

3. Save the Word document again with the same name (Ch 18, Ex 15).
4. Print and then close Ch 18, Ex 15. (The worksheet border lines will not print.)
5. Exit Word.
6. With Excel the active program, close Excel Ch 18, Ex 15.
7. Exit Excel by clicking File and then Exit.

figure

18.13   *Exercise 15*

DATE: January 11, 2001

TO: Raymond Farrel

FROM: Mindy O'Connell

SUBJECT: REGIONAL SALES

I am finalizing the 2000 yearly report this week. Lou gave me the following sales figures just this morning. Please look them over and let me know if they match the figures you calculated.

Paula asked for the final report two days before the budget meeting. If I can get your response by Monday, I can plug these figures into the report.

XX:Ch 18, Ex 15

exercise 16

Editing a Linked Worksheet

1. Open the Microsoft Excel program.
2. Open and edit *Excel Ch 18, Ex 15* by completing the following steps:
   a. In Excel, click the Open button on the Standard toolbar.
   b. At the Open dialog box, make sure *Chapter 18* on your disk is the active folder, and then double-click *Excel Ch 18, Ex 15*.
   c. Change some of the numbers in cells by completing the following steps:
      1) Position the mouse pointer (thick white plus sign) over the cell containing the number *$218,335* (cell C3) and then click the left mouse button.

      Step 2c2

      2) Key **230578** (over *$218,335*).
      3) Press the Enter key. (Notice that the number in cell D3 [the *Difference* column] automatically changed. This is because the cell contains a formula.)
      4) Change the number in cell B5 from *181,329* to *195,200*.
      5) Change the number in cell C7 from *197,905* to *188,370*. (Be sure to press the Enter key.)

	A	B	C	D
1		SALES FIGURES		
2	**State**	**Projected**	**Actual**	**Difference**
3	Florida	$238,450	230578	$ (20,115)
4	Georgia	$198,549	$210,698	$ 12,149
5	Alabama	$181,329	$175,320	$ (6,009)
6	Louisiana	$195,480	$156,700	$ (38,780)
7	Mississippi	$189,450	$197,905	$ 8,455

d. Save the revised worksheet by clicking the Save button on the Standard toolbar.
3. Close *Excel Ch 18, Ex 15* by clicking File and then Close.
4. Exit Microsoft Excel by clicking File and then Exit.
5. Open Word and then open Ch 18, Ex 15. (Notice how the numbers in the worksheet are updated to reflect the changes made to *Excel Ch 18, Ex 15*.)
6. Save the document with Save As and name it Ch 18, Ex 16.
7. Print and then close Ch 18, Ex 16.

Insert Microsoft Excel Worksheet

Embed an Excel worksheet in a Word document using the Insert Microsoft Excel Worksheet button located on the Standard toolbar. Click this button and a grid displays below the button. This grid is similar to the grid that displays when you click the Insert Table button. Select the desired number of rows and columns and then click the left mouse button. This opens the Microsoft Excel program and inserts the worksheet in the document. Figure 18.14 shows the embedded worksheet you will create in exercise 17. The Excel toolbars and Formula bar are identified in the figure.

figure
18.14
Embedded Excel Worksheet

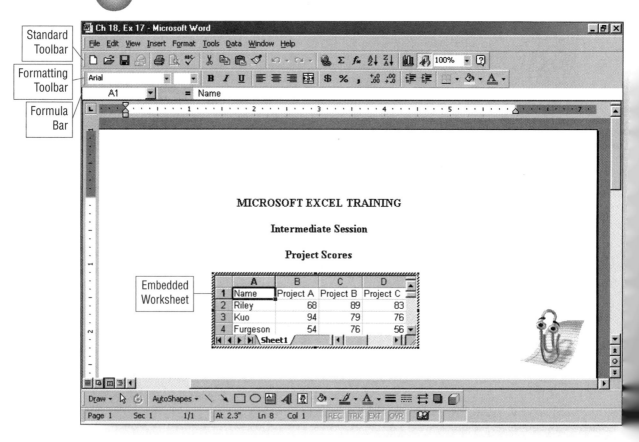

When an Excel worksheet is inserted in a Word document using the Insert Microsoft Excel Worksheet button, Excel opens and all the toolbars and Excel features are available for creating, modifying, or editing the worksheet. After creating or editing the worksheet, return to the Word by clicking in the document screen, outside the worksheet.

Embedding an Excel Worksheet in a Word Document

1. At a clear document screen, click the Center button on the Formatting toolbar, click the Bold button, and then key the three lines of text shown at the beginning of figure 18.15.
2. With the insertion point positioned a triple space below the text (centered), create the text shown in the table in the figure as an Excel worksheet by completing the following steps:
   a. Click the Insert Microsoft Excel Worksheet button on the Standard toolbar.
   b. Drag down and to the right until four rows and four columns are selected on the grid. (The numbers below the grid display as *4 x 4 Spreadsheet*.)
   c. Click the left mouse button.
   d. Key the text in the cells as shown in figure 18.15. (Key the text in the cells in the same manner as you would in a table.)
   e. When all the text is entered in the worksheet, click in the document screen outside the worksheet.
3. Save the document and name it Ch 18, Ex 17.
4. Print and then close Ch 18, Ex 17.

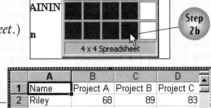

Exercise 17

Figure 18.15

MICROSOFT EXCEL TRAINING

Intermediate Session

Project Scores

Name	Project A	Project B	Project C
Riley	68	89	83
Kuo	94	79	76
Furgeson	54	76	56

One of the advantages to embedding an Excel worksheet in a Word document is the ability to modify the worksheet. To modify an embedded worksheet, open the Word document containing the worksheet, and then double-click the worksheet. This opens Microsoft Excel and provides all the toolbars and editing features of Excel.

Modifying an Embedded Excel Worksheet

1. Open Ch 18, Ex 17.
2. Save the document with Save As and name it Ch 18, Ex 18.
3. Add a column to the worksheet, insert a calculation to average the project scores, and apply formatting by completing the following steps:
   a. Double-click the worksheet. (This opens Microsoft Excel.)
   b. Increase the size of the worksheet so columns E and F display by completing the following steps:
      1) Position the mouse pointer on the small square black sizing handle that displays in the middle at the right side of the worksheet until the pointer turns into a double-headed arrow pointing left and right.
      2) Hold down the left mouse button, drag to the right so the right border jumps twice (approximately 2 inches), and then release the mouse button.
   c. Click once in cell E1 and then key **Average.**
   d. Insert a formula to calculate the average of the project scores by completing the following steps:
      1) Click once in cell E2.
      2) Click inside the white text box that displays immediately after an equals sign on the Formula bar. (The Formula bar displays above the Ruler. See figure 18.14.)
      3) Key **=AVERAGE(B2:D2)** and then press Enter.
   e. Copy the formula down to cells E3 and E4 by completing the following steps:
      1) Click once in cell E2 to make it active.
      2) Position the mouse pointer on the small black square that displays in the lower right corner of cell E2 until the pointer turns into a thin black cross. (The small black square is called the "fill handle.")
      3) With the mouse pointer displayed as a thin black cross, hold down the left mouse button, drag down to cell E4, and then release the mouse button.
   f. Decrease the size of the worksheet so column F is no longer visible by completing the following steps:
      1) Position the mouse pointer on the small square black sizing handle that displays in the middle at the right side of the worksheet until the pointer turns into a double-headed arrow pointing left and right.
      2) Hold down the left mouse button, drag to the left so the right border jumps once, and then release the mouse button.

g. Apply the following formatting to the cells:
   1) Select cells A1 through E1.
   2) Click the Bold button and then the Center button on the Formatting toolbar.
   3) Select cells B2 through E4.
   4) Click the Center button on the Formatting toolbar.
h. Click in the document screen outside the worksheet.
4. Save the document again with the same name (Ch 18, Ex 18).
5. Print and then close Ch 18, Ex 18.

chapter summary

➤ A chart can be created in Word with the Microsoft Graph Chart application.

➤ In a chart the x-axis is the horizontal axis that runs along the bottom of the chart. The left side of the chart generally displays values and is referred to as the z-axis.

➤ Delete a chart by selecting the chart and then pressing the Delete key.

➤ To change the size of a chart, click the chart to select it, and then use the sizing handles that display around the chart to increase or decrease the size.

➤ To move a chart, click the chart to select it, and then drag the chart to the desired location.

➤ Fourteen basic chart types are available in Microsoft Graph along with built-in autoformats. The 14 chart types are Area, Bar, Bubble, Column, Cone, Cylinder, Doughnut, Line, Pie, Pyramid, Radar, Stock, Surface, and XY (Scatter).

➤ The default chart type created by Graph is a Column chart.

➤ A chart type can be selected at the Chart Type dialog box with the Standard Types tab selected.

➤ A custom chart can be selected at the Chart Type dialog box with the Custom Types tab selected.

➤ Change data in the datasheet and the chart will reflect the change.

➤ Add chart elements at the Chart Options dialog box.

➤ A selected chart or chart element can be moved, sized, or deleted.

➤ Add gridlines to a chart at the Chart Options dialog box with the Gridlines tab selected.

➤ Format a chart or a chart element by double-clicking the chart or the element. This displays a formatting dialog box for the chart or specific element.

➤ Add fill color to a chart or a chart element with the Fill Color button on the Graph Standard toolbar.

➤ Data from an Excel worksheet can be imported into a chart.

➤ Several methods are available for importing a Microsoft Excel worksheet into a Word document such as opening the worksheet into a Word document, linking the worksheet to a Word document, or embedding the worksheet as an object.

➤ Open an Excel worksheet in a Word document in situations where the worksheet will not need to be edited. Link an Excel worksheet with a Word document in situations where the worksheet is continually updated. Embed an Excel worksheet in a Word document in situations where the worksheet will be edited in the Word document.

commands review

Mouse/Keyboard

Create a chart in Word	Select the table, click Insert, point to Picture, and then click Chart
Change chart type	Click Chart Type button on the Graph Standard toolbar, then click desired chart at the drop-down list
Display Chart Type dialog box	In Graph, click Chart and then Chart Type
Choose a custom chart type	In Graph, click Chart and then Chart Type. At Chart Type dialog box, click the Custom Types tab and then click the desired custom chart type in the Chart type list box
Turn on/off display of datasheet	Click View Datasheet button on Graph Standard toolbar
Display Chart Options dialog box	In Graph, click Chart and then Chart Options
Display formatting dialog box for a chart or a chart element	In Graph, double-click the chart or chart element
Display Object dialog box	Click Insert and then Object
Embed and Excel worksheet in in a Word document	Click the Insert Microsoft Excel Worksheet button on the Standard toolbar, drag down and to the right to create the desired number of rows and columns, and then click the left mouse button

thinking offline

Completion: In the space provided at the right, indicate the correct term, command, or number.

1. To create a chart, select a table, click Insert, point to this option, and then click Chart.

2. This is the horizontal axis that runs along the bottom of a chart.

3. Click this button on the Graph Standard toolbar to turn off the display of the datasheet.

4. Change the size of a selected chart by dragging these.

5. Make changes to a chart created in Word by editing the data in this.

6. If you double-click the title of a chart, this dialog box displays.

7. If you double-click the legend of a chart, this dialog box displays.

8. Use this type of chart to show proportions and relationships of parts to the whole.

9. Use this type of chart to show variations between components but not in relationship to the whole.

10. Do this to an Excel worksheet you want inserted in a Word document when the worksheet will be continually updated in Excel. _____

11. Do this to an Excel worksheet you want inserted in a Word document when the worksheet will be edited in Word. _____

12. In the space provided below, list the steps you would complete to create a default chart with data in a table.

_____

_____

_____

working hands-on

Assessment 1

1. Open Table 04.
2. Save the document with Save As and name it Ch 18, SA 01.
3. Select the table and then create a chart with the default settings.
4. After creating the chart, select the table, and then delete it.
5. Make the following changes to the chart:
   a. With the chart displayed in Graph, add the title *GROSS PRODUCT SALES*.
   b. Click outside the chart to close Graph.
   c. Make sure the view is Print Layout and then change the Zoom to Whole Page.
   d. Select the chart, increase the width and height of the chart approximately 2 inches, move the chart to the middle of the page, and then deselect the chart.
   e. Change the Zoom to 100%.
6. Save the document again with the same name (Ch 18, SA 01).
7. Print and then close Ch 18, SA 01.

Assessment 2

1. Open Ch 18, SA 01.
2. Save the document with Save As and name it Ch 18, SA 02.
3. Make sure the view is Print Layout and then change the Zoom to 50%.
4. Double-click the chart and then make the following changes to the chart:
   a. Change the color of each bar in the chart (you determine the colors).
   b. Add a light background color to the chart.
   c. Add a light background color (one that complements the chart background color) to the legend.
   d. Change the font for the title to a serif typeface of your choosing in a larger point size.
   e. Change the font for the legend to the same typeface (do not increase the size) as that used for the title.
5. Change the Zoom to 100%.
6. Save the document again with the same name (Ch 18, SA 02).
7. Print and then close Ch 18, SA 02.

Assessment 3

1. Open Table 05.
2. Save the document with Save As and name it Ch 18, SA 03.
3. Create a chart from the table with the following elements:
   a. Change the chart type to Line.
   b. Click the By Column button on the Graph Standard toolbar. (If this button is not visible, click the More Buttons button on the Graph Standard toolbar.)
   c. Add the chart title *Population Growth - 1960 to 1990*.
   d. Add major and minor gridlines to both axes.
   e. Click outside the chart window to close Graph.
   f. Make sure the view is Print Layout and then change the Zoom to Whole Page.
   g. Select and then delete the table (*not* the chart).
   h. Select the chart, increase the size of the chart (you determine the size), move the chart to the middle of the page, and then deselect the chart.
   i. Change the Zoom to 100%.
4. Save the document again with the same name (Ch 18, SA 03).
5. Print and then close Ch 18, SA 03.

Assessment 4

1. At a clear document screen, key the headings and the first paragraph of the memo in figure 18.16.
2. With the insertion point a double space below the first paragraph, create the table as shown in figure 18.16. After creating the table, move the insertion point below the table, and then press Enter twice.
3. Create a pie chart for the table with the following elements:
   a. Change the chart type to Pie.
   b. Click the By Column button on the Graph Standard toolbar.
   c. Add the title *Investment Assets* to the chart.
   d. Add percentage data labels to the pie.
4. Click outside the chart to close Graph.
5. Select the entire table (*not* the chart) and then delete it.
6. Select the chart, move it so it is positioned between the left and right margins of the document, and then deselect the chart.
7. Double-click the chart and then make the following changes:
   a. Decrease the size of the legend.
   b. Increase the size of the pie.
   c. Make sure chart elements do not overlap.
8. Click outside the chart to close Graph.
9. Press Ctrl + End to move the insertion point to the end of the document and then key the paragraph and the initials and document name below the chart as shown in figure 18.16.
10. Save the document and name it Ch 18, SA 04.
11. Print and then close Ch 18, SA 04.

figure
18.16   *Assessment 4*

DATE: (current date)

TO: Lee Hunter, Editor

FROM: Paula Diaz, Investment Coordinator

SUBJECT: INVESTMENT ASSETS

The charts presented in last month's newsletter to investors looked great. Presenting data in a chart has much more visual impact on readers than displaying it in a table. I would like the following pie chart included in the investment section of the newsletter.

Invested Assets	Percentage
Mortgage Loans	34
Bonds	26
Business Loans	20
Real Estate	13
Other	7

I am currently gathering data on stock market investments. If you want this information for the next newsletter, please let me know.

XX:Ch 18, SA 04

Assessment 5

1. Open Excel and then open Excel Worksheet 03.
2. Save the worksheet with Save As and name it Excel Ch 18, SA 05.
3. Close Excel Ch 18, SA 05 and then exit Excel.
4. In Word, at a clear document screen, key the memo shown in figure 18.17.
5. Link Excel Ch 18, SA 05 with the Word document so the worksheet displays between the first and second paragraphs.
6. Save the document and name it Ch 18, SA 05.
7. Print and then close Ch 18, SA 05.

figure

18.17   *Assessment 5*

DATE: February 2, 2001

TO: Geraldine Monahan

FROM: Jordan Washington

SUBJECT: MONTHLY QUOTAS

Below are the cumulative and net values for our funds for January, 2001. This information will be presented in the monthly corporate newsletter and will also be made available to potential customers.

These figures will be updated each month and will be available to all service representatives and customers.

XX:Ch 18, SA 05

Assessment 6

1. Open the Microsoft Excel program.
2. Open Excel Ch 18, SA 05 and make the following changes:
    a. Change the percentage in cell B3 from *8.3* to *8.4*.
    b. Change the percentage in cell C3 from *7.4* to *8.1*.
    c. Change the percentage in cell B5 from *17.4* to *17.3*.
    d. Change the percentage in cell C5 from *17.6* to *17.0*.
    e. Save the revised worksheet by clicking the Save button on the Excel Standard toolbar.
3. Close Excel Ch 18, SA 05.
4. Exit Microsoft Excel.
5. Open Word and then open Ch 18, SA 05. (Notice how the numbers in the worksheet are updated to reflect the changes made to Excel Ch 18, SA 05.)
6. Save the document with Save As and name it Ch 18, SA 06.
7. Print and then close Ch 18, SA 06.

Chapter 19

Formatting with Macros

PERFORMANCE OBJECTIVES

Upon successful completion of chapter 19, you will be able to:

- Record, run, pause, and delete macros.
- Assign a macro to a keyboard command.
- Assign a macro to a toolbar.
- Record and run a macro with fill-in fields.
- Edit a macro with Visual Basic.
- Copy and rename a macro project.

Word includes a time-saving feature called *macros* that automates the formatting of a document. The word *macro* was coined by computer programmers for a collection of commands used to make a large programming job easier and save time.

There are two basic steps involved in working with macros—recording a macro and running a macro. When you record a macro, all the keys pressed and the menus and dialog boxes displayed are recorded and become part of the macro. After a macro is recorded, you can run the macro to apply the macro formatting.

Recording a Macro

Recording a macro involves turning on the macro recorder, performing the steps to be recorded, and then turning off the recorder. To record a macro, click Tools, point to Macro, and then click Record New Macro. You can also double-click the REC button that displays on the Status bar. This displays the Record Macro dialog box shown in figure 19.1.

At the Record Macro dialog box, key a name for the macro in the Macro name text box. A macro name must begin with a letter and can contain only letters and numbers. Key a description for the macro in the Description text box located at the bottom of the dialog box. A macro description can contain a maximum of 255 characters and may include spaces.

By default, Word stores a macro in the Normal template document. Macros stored in this template are available for any document based on the Normal template. In a company or school setting where computers may be networked, consider storing macros in personalized documents or templates. Specify the location for macros with the Store macro in option at the Record Macro dialog box (refer to figure 19.1).

After keying the macro name, specifying where the macro is to be stored, and keying a description, click OK or press Enter to close the Record Macro dialog box. This displays the document screen with the Macro Record toolbar displayed as shown in figure 19.2. At this screen, perform the actions to be recorded. After all steps to be recorded have been performed, stop the recording of the macro by clicking the Stop Recording button on the Macro Record toolbar, or by double-clicking the REC button on the Status bar.

Stop Recording

When you record macros in exercises in this chapter, you will be instructed to name the macros beginning with your initials. An exercise step may instruct you, for example, to "record a macro named XXXInd01." Insert your initials in the macro name instead of the *XXX*. Recorded macros are stored in the Normal template document by default and display at the Macros dialog box. If the computer you are using is networked, macros recorded by other students will also display at the Macros dialog box. Naming a macro with your initials will enable you to distinguish your macros from the macros of other users.

Record Macro Dialog Box

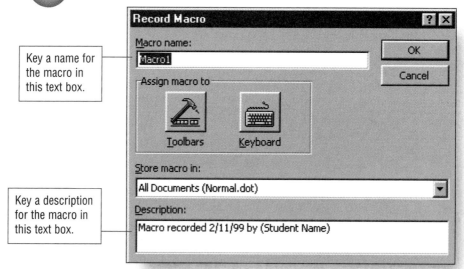

figure
19.2
Macro Record Toolbar

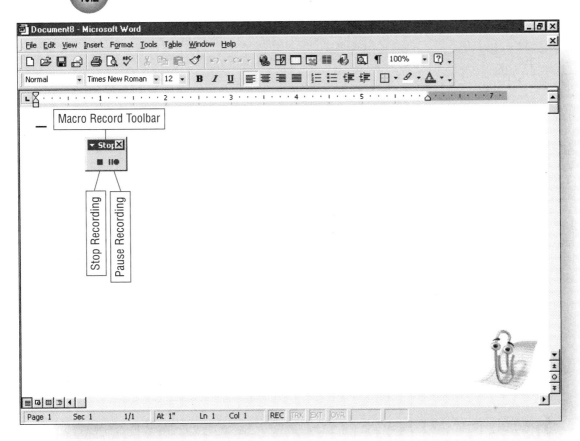

exercise 1

Recording Macros

1. Record a macro named XXXInd01 (where your initials are used instead of *XXX*) that indents text in a paragraph 0.5 inch and hang indents second and subsequent lines of the paragraph by completing the following steps:

   a. At a clear document screen, double-click the REC button on the Status bar.

   b. At the Record Macro dialog box, key **XXXInd01** in the Macro name text box.

   c. Click inside the Description text box and then key **Indent and hang text in paragraph**. (If there is any text located in the Description text box, select the text first, and then key **Indent and hang text in paragraph**.)

   d. Click OK.

e. At the document screen with the Macro Record toolbar displayed, complete the following steps:
   1) Click Format and then Paragraph.
   2) At the Paragraph dialog box, click the up-pointing triangle at the right side of the Left option until *0.5"* displays in the Left text box.
   3) Click the down-pointing triangle at the right side of the Special text box and then click *Hanging* at the drop-down list.
   4) Click OK or press Enter.
   f. Double-click the REC button on the Status bar.
2. Complete steps similar to those in 1 to create a macro named XXXInd02 that indents text in a paragraph 1 inch and hang indents second and subsequent lines of the paragraph.
3. Record a macro named XXXFormat01 (where your initials are used instead of *XXX*) that changes the top margin to 1.5 inches and the left and right margins to 1 inch by completing the following steps:
   a. Click Tools, point to Macro, and then click Record New Macro.
   b. At the Record Macro dialog box, key **XXXFormat01** in the Macro name text box.
   c. Click in the Description text box (or select existing text in the Description text box) and then key **Change top, left, and right margins**.
   d. Click OK.
   e. At the document screen with the Macro Record toolbar displayed, change the top margin to 1.5 inches and the left and right margins to 1 inch.
   f. Click the Stop Recording button on the Macro Record toolbar.
4. Close the document without saving it.

Running a Macro

After a macro has been recorded, it can be run in a document. To run a macro, click Tools, point to Macro, and then click Macros. At the Macros dialog box, click the desired macro name in the list box, and then click the Run button. You can also just double-click the desired macro name in the list box.

Running Macros

1. Open Survey 01.
2. Save the document with Save As and name it Ch 19, Ex 02.
3. Run the XXXFormat01 macro by completing the following steps:
   a. Click Tools, point to Macro, and then click Macros.
   b. At the Macros dialog box, click *XXXFormat01* in the Macro name list box, and then click the Run button.

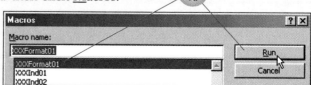

4. Run the XXXInd01 macro for the first numbered paragraph by completing the following steps:
   a. Position the insertion point anywhere in the paragraph that begins with *1*.
   b. Click <u>T</u>ools, point to <u>M</u>acro, and then click <u>M</u>acros.
   c. At the Macros dialog box, double-click *XXXInd01* in the list box.
5. Complete steps similar to those in 4 to run the macro for each of the numbered paragraphs (just the numbered paragraphs, not the lettered paragraphs).
6. Run the XXXInd02 macro for the lettered paragraph (a through d) after the first numbered paragraph by completing the following steps:
   a. Select paragraphs a through d below the first numbered paragraph.
   b. Click <u>T</u>ools, point to <u>M</u>acro, and then click <u>M</u>acros.
   c. At the Macros dialog box, double-click *XXXInd02* in the list box.

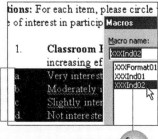

7. Complete steps similar to those in 6a through 6c to run the macro for the lettered paragraphs below each of the numbered paragraphs.
8. Save the document again with the same name (Ch 19, Ex 02).
9. Print and then close Ch 19, Ex 02.

Pausing and Then Resuming a Macro

When recording a macro, you can temporarily suspend the recording, perform actions that are not recorded, and then resume recording the macro. To pause the recording of a macro, click the Pause Recording button on the Macro Record toolbar. To resume recording the macro, click the Resume Recorder button (previously the Pause Recording button).

Pause
Recording

Deleting a Macro

If you no longer need a macro that has been recorded, it can be deleted. To delete a macro, display the Macros dialog box, click the macro name in the list box, and then click the <u>D</u>elete button. At the message asking if you want to delete the macro, click <u>Y</u>es. Click the Close button to close the Macros dialog box.

Deleting Macros

1. At a clear document screen, delete the XXXFormat01 macro by completing the following steps:
   a. Display the Macros dialog box.
   b. At the Macros dialog box, click *XXXFormat01* in the list box.
   c. Click the <u>D</u>elete button.
   d. At the message asking if you want to delete XXXFormat01, click <u>Y</u>es.
   e. Click the Close button to close the Macros dialog box.
2. Close the document.

Assigning a Macro

Consider assigning macros you use on a consistent basis either a shortcut command or to a toolbar. To run a macro that has been assigned to a keyboard command, just press the keys assigned to the macro. To run a macro assigned to a toolbar, just click the button.

Assigning a Macro a Keyboard Command

A macro can be assigned a keyboard command with a letter plus Alt + Ctrl, Ctrl + Shift, or Alt + Shift. Word has already used many combinations for Word functions. For example, pressing Ctrl + Shift + A changes selected text to all capital letters.

With the Alt + Ctrl combination, the following letters are available for assigning to a macro: A, B, G, H, J, Q, W, and X. With the Ctrl + Shift combination, the following letters are available for assigning to a macro: G, J, O, R, X, and Y. The following letters are available with the Alt + Shift combination: B, G, H, J, Q, S, V, W, Y, and Z.

Assign a keyboard command to a macro at the Record Macro dialog box. In exercise 4 you will record a macro and then assign the macro to a keyboard command. If you delete the macro, the keyboard command is also deleted. This allows you to use the key combination again.

exercise 4

Recording and Assigning a Keyboard Command to a Macro

1. Record a macro named XXXLtrhd01 that contains the letterhead text shown in figure 19.3 and assign it the keyboard command Alt + Shift + S by completing the following steps:
    a. At a clear document screen, double-click the REC button on the Status bar.
    b. At the Record Macro dialog box, key **XXXLtrhd01** in the Macro name text box.
    c. Click in the Description text box (or select existing text in the Description text box) and then key **St. Francis Letterhead**.
    d. Click the Keyboard button.
    e. At the Customize Keyboard dialog box with the insertion point positioned in the Press new shortcut key text box, press Alt + Shift + S.
    f. Click the Assign button.
    g. Click the Close button.

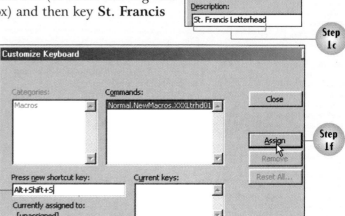

    h. At the document screen with the Macro Record toolbar displayed, create the letterhead shown in figure 19.3 by completing the following steps:

        1) Press Ctrl + E.
        2) Key **ST. FRANCIS MEDICAL CENTER.**
        3) Press Enter and then key **300 Blue Ridge Boulevard**.
        4) Press Enter and then key **Kansas City, MO 63009**.
        5) Press Enter and then key **(816) 555-2000**.
        6) Press Enter.
        7) Press Ctrl + L to return the paragraph alignment to left.
        8) Press Enter.
        9) Select (using the keyboard) the hospital name, address, and telephone number and then change the font to 18-point Goudy Old Style bold (or a similar serif typeface). (To select with the keyboard, press F8 and then use the arrow keys.)
       10) Deselect the text (using the keyboard). To do this, press the Esc key and then press an arrow key.
    i. Click the Stop Recording button on the Macro Record toolbar.

2. Close the document without saving changes.
3. At a clear document screen, run the XXXLtrhd01 macro by pressing Alt + Shift + S.
4. With the insertion point a double space below the letterhead, turn off the automatic numbering feature by completing the following steps:
    a. Click Tools and then AutoCorrect.
    b. At the AutoCorrect dialog box, click the AutoFormat As You Type tab.
    c. Remove the check mark from the Automatic numbered lists option.
    d. Click OK to close the dialog box.
5. Key the letter shown in figure 19.4. (Press the Tab key after keying the numbers *1.* and *2.* and the letters *a.* and *b.*)
6. After keying the letter, make the following changes:
    a. Change the top and bottom margins to 0.75 inch and the left and right margins to 1 inch.
    b. Run the XXXInd01 macro for the numbered paragraphs and the XXXInd02 macro for the lettered paragraphs.
7. If necessary, turn on the automatic numbering option. (For help, refer to step 4.)
8. Save the letter and name it Ch 19, Ex 04.
9. Print and then close Ch 19, Ex 04.

figure

19.3 *Exercise 4*

ST. FRANCIS MEDICAL CENTER
300 Blue Ridge Boulevard
Kansas City, MO 63009
(816) 555-2000

figure

19.4   *Exercise 4*

May 14, 2001

Mr. Victor Durham
Good Samaritan Hospital
1201 James Street
St. Louis, MO 62033

Dear Victor:

Congratulations on obtaining eight new nursing positions at your hospital. The attached registered nurse job description is generic. Depending on the specialty, additional responsibilities are added such as:

1.   Uses the nursing process to prescribe, coordinate, and delegate patient care from admission through discharge.
a.   Analyzes the patient's condition and reports changes to the appropriate health care provider.
b.   Observes patient for signs and symptoms, collects data on patient; reports and documents results.
2.   Teaches patient, family, staff, and students.
a.   Assumes responsibility for patient and family teaching and discharge planning.
b.   Participates in orientation of new staff and/or acts as preceptor.

I am interested in hearing about your recruitment plan. We are hiring additional medical personnel in the fall at St. Francis so I need to begin formulating a recruitment plan.

Sincerely,

Mariah Jackson

XX:Ch 19, Ex 04

Attachment

Assigning a Macro to the Toolbar

A macro that you use on a very regular basis can be added to a toolbar. To run a macro from a toolbar, just click the button. In exercise 5, you will assign a macro to the Standard toolbar. A macro can be assigned to any toolbar that is displayed.

An existing macro can also be assigned to a toolbar. To do this, display the Customize dialog box with the Commands tab selected. At this dialog box, click *Macros* in the Categories list box. Position the arrow pointer on the desired macro in the Macros list box, hold down the left mouse button, drag the outline of the button to the desired location on the desired toolbar, and then release the mouse button. Click the Close button to close the Customize dialog box.

A macro button can be removed from a toolbar with the Customize dialog box open. To do this, display the Customize dialog box. Position the arrow pointer on the button to be removed, hold down the left mouse button, drag the outline of the button off the toolbar, and then release the mouse button. Click Close to close the Customize dialog box. When a macro button is removed from a toolbar, the macro is not deleted. Delete the macro at the Macros dialog box.

Assigning a Macro to the Standard Toolbar

1. At a clear document screen, create a macro named XXXTab01 and assign it to the Standard toolbar by completing the following steps:
   a. Double-click the REC button on the Status bar.
   b. At the Record Macro dialog box, key **XXXTab01** in the Macro name text box.
   c. Click inside the Description text box (or select the text) and then key **Set left tabs at 0.5 and 1.0 and right tab with leaders at 5.5**.
   d. Click the Toolbars button.
   e. At the Customize dialog box with the Commands tab selected as shown in figure 19.5, position the arrow pointer on the XXXTab01 macro in the Commands list box. (This macro name may display as *Normal.NewMacros.XXXTab01*.) Hold down the left mouse button, drag the large mouse pointer representing the macro between the Spelling and Grammar button and the Cut button on the Standard toolbar, and then release the mouse button.

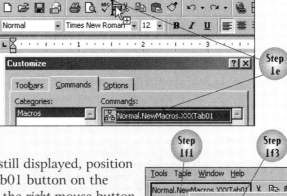

   f. Shorten the name of the macro by completing the following steps:
      1) With the Customize dialog box still displayed, position the arrow pointer on the XXXTab01 button on the Standard toolbar, and then click the *right* mouse button.
      2) At the drop-down list that displays, click Name. (This moves the insertion point inside the text box containing the full macro name.)
      3) Delete the existing name, key **T01** in the Name text box, and then press Enter.

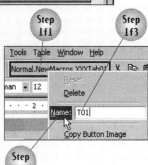

g. Click the Close button to close the Customize dialog box.

h. At the document screen with the Macro Record toolbar displayed, complete the necessary steps to set left tabs at the 0.5-inch mark and the 1-inch mark and a right tab with preceding leaders at 5.5-inch mark. (You must do this at the Tabs dialog box, not on the Ruler.)

i. After setting the tabs, click the Stop Recording button on the Macro Record toolbar.

2. Close the document without saving it.

3. At a clear document screen create the document shown in figure 19.6 by completing the following steps:

a. Click the T01 button on the Standard toolbar.

b. Key the text as shown in figure 19.6. (Key the first column of text at the first tab stop, not the left margin.)

4. Save the document and name it Ch 19, Ex 05.

5. Print and then close Ch 19, Ex 05.

6. Remove the T01 button from the Standard toolbar by completing the following steps:

a. At a clear document screen, click Tools and then Customize.

b. At the Customize dialog box, position the arrow pointer on the T01 button on the Standard toolbar, hold down the left mouse button, drag the outline of the button off the toolbar, and then release the mouse button.

c. Click the Close button to close the Customize dialog box.

Step 6b

figure

19.5 *Customize Dialog Box*

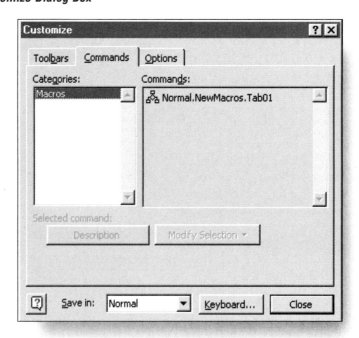

figure

19.6 *Exercise 5*

COLEMAN DEVELOPMENT CORPORATION

Mandy Armstead. . . . . Chief Executive Officer

Stephanie Branson. . . . . President

Brandon Kent . . . . Vice President

Conrad Wheeler. . . . . Vice President

Selene Resnick . . . . Vice President

Aurora Madsen . . . . Vice President

Paul O'Shea . . . . Development Manager

Recording a Macro with Fill-In Fields

In chapter 12, you inserted a Fill-in field in a document that prompted the
operator to insert information at the keyboard during a merge. A Fill-in field can
also be inserted in a macro that requires input from the keyboard. To insert a Fill-
in field in a macro, begin the recording of the macro. At the point where the Fill-
in field is to be inserted, click Insert and then Field. At the Field dialog box with
(All) selected in the Categories list box as shown in figure 19.7, scroll down the
Field names list box until *Fill-in* is visible and then click it. Add information
telling the operator what text to enter at the keyboard by clicking in the
Description text box and then keying the prompt message surrounded by
parentheses. When the macro is run, key the desired text specified by the prompt
message.

figure

Field Dialog Box

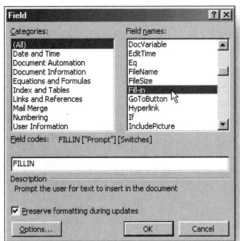

exercise 6

Recording a Macro with Fill-In Fields

1. At a clear document screen, record a macro for inserting notary signature information by completing the following steps:
    a. Double-click the REC button on the Status bar.
    b. At the Record Macro dialog box, key **XXXNotary** (where your initials are used instead of the *XXX*) in the <u>M</u>acro name text box.
    c. Click in the <u>D</u>escription text box (or select existing text in the <u>D</u>escription text box) and then key **Notary signature information**.
    d. Click the <u>K</u>eyboard button.
    e. At the Customize Keyboard dialog box with the insertion point positioned in the Press <u>n</u>ew shortcut key text box, press Alt + Ctrl + A.
    f. Click the <u>A</u>ssign button.
    g. Click the Close button.
    h. At the document screen with the Macro Record toolbar displayed, key the text shown in figure 19.8 up to the text *(name of person)*. (Do not key the text *(name of person)*.)
    i. Insert a Fill-in field by completing the following steps:

    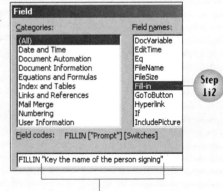

        1) Click <u>I</u>nsert and then <u>F</u>ield.
        2) At the Field dialog box with (All) selected in the <u>C</u>ategories list box, scroll down the Field <u>n</u>ames list box until *Fill-in* is visible and then click it.
        3) Click in the Description text box (contains the word *FILLIN*) one space to the right of *FILLIN* and then key **"Key the name of the person signing"**.

4) Click the OK button.
5) At the Microsoft Word dialog box, key **(name of person)** in the text box, and then click OK.

j. Continue keying the notary signature information shown in figure 19.8 up to the text *(day)* and then insert a Fill-in field by completing steps similar to those in 1i that tells the operator to key the current day.

Microsoft Word
Key the name of the person signing

|(name of person)|

Step
1i5

k. Continue keying the notary signature information shown in figure 19.8 up to the text *(month)* and then insert a Fill-in field by completing steps similar to those in 1i that tells the operator to key the current month.

l. Continue keying the notary signature information shown in figure 19.8 up to the text *(expiration date)* and then insert a Fill-in field by completing steps similar to those in 1i that tells the operator to key the expiration date.

m. When all the notary signature information is keyed, end the recording of the macro by double-clicking the REC button on the Status bar.

2. Close the document without saving it.

figure

19.8   *Exercise 6*

STATE OF CALIFORNIA   )
) ss.
COUNTY OF LOS ANGELES   )

On this day personally appeared before me (name of person), known to me to be the individual described in and who executed the aforesaid instrument, and acknowledged that he/she signed as his/her free and voluntary act and deed for the uses and purposes therein mentioned.

Given under my hand and official seal this (day) of (month), 2001.

_____
NOTARY PUBLIC in and for the State of California
My appointment expires (expiration date)

Running a Macro with Fill-In Fields

1. Open Legal 03.
2. Save the document with Save As and name it Ch 19, Ex 07.
3. Complete the following find and replaces:
    a. Find all occurrences of *NAME* and replace with *LOREN HOUSTON*. (Be sure to replace only the occurrences of *NAME* in all uppercase letters. *Hint: Expand the Find and Replace dialog box and insert a check mark in the Match case option.*)
    b. Find the one occurrence of *ADDRESS* and replace with *102 Marine Drive, Los Angeles, CA.* (Be sure to replace only the occurrence of *ADDRESS* in all uppercase letters and not the occurrence of *address* in all lowercase letters.)
4. Run the following macros:
    a. Run the XXXInd01 macro for the numbered paragraphs and the XXXInd02 macro for the lettered paragraphs.
    b. Move the insertion point to the end of the document a double space below the text and then run the XXXNotary macro by completing the following steps:
        1) Press Alt + Ctrl + A.
        2) When the macro stops and prompts you for the name of person, key **SYLVIA WHITT**, and then click OK.
        3) When the macro stops and prompts you for the day, key **12th**, and then click OK.
        4) When the macro stops and prompts you for the month, key **March**, and then click OK.
        5) When the macro stops and prompts you for the expiration date, key **12/31/03**, and then click OK.
5. Save the document again with the same name (Ch 19, Ex 07).
6. Print and then close Ch 19, Ex 07.

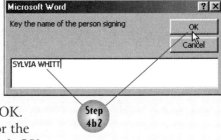

Step 4b2

Editing a Macro

In Word, a macro is created with Visual Basic and can be edited using the Visual Basic Editor. To edit a macro, display the Macros dialog box, select the macro to be edited, and then click the Edit button. This displays the macro in the Visual Basic Editor as shown in figure 19.9. (The macro displayed in figure 19.9 is the one you will be creating and then editing in exercise 8.)

figure

19.9 *Visual Basic Editor*

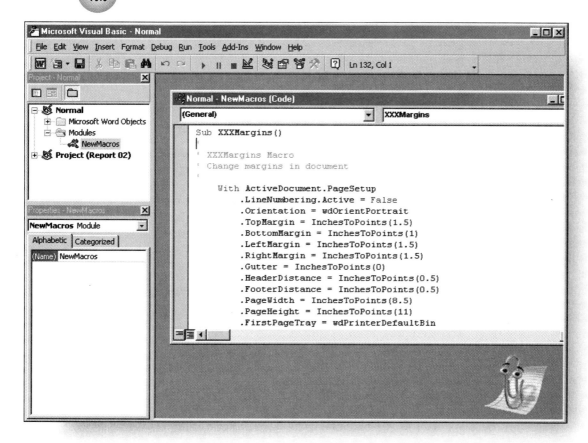

To edit the macro, remove unwanted steps from the list box, add steps, or change existing steps. When all changes are made, click the Save Normal button on the Visual Basic Editor Standard toolbar (third button from the left) or click File and then Save Normal. Close the Visual Basic Editor by clicking File and then Close and Return to Microsoft Word.

Recording, Running, and Editing a Macro

1. At a clear document screen, record a macro that changes the top, left, and right margins by completing the following steps:
   a. Double-click the REC button on the Status bar.
   b. At the Record Macro dialog box, key **XXXMargins** (where your initials are used instead of the *XXX*) in the Macro name text box.

c. Click inside the Description text box and then key **Change margins in
    document**. (If there is any text located in the Description text box, select the text
    first, and then key **Change margins in document**.)
d. Click OK.
e. At the document screen with the Macro Record toolbar displayed, complete the
    following steps:
    1) Click File and then Page Setup.
    2) At the Page Setup dialog box with the Margins tab selected, change the top,
       left, and right margins to 1.5 inches.
    3) Click OK to close the dialog box.
f. Turn off recording by double-clicking the REC button on the Status bar.
2. Close the document without saving it.
3. Open Report 02.
4. Save the document with Save As and name it Ch 19, Ex 08.
5. Run the XXXMargins macro by completing the following steps:
    a. Display the Macros dialog box.
    b. At the Macros dialog box, double-click *XXXMargins* in the list box.
6. Save the document again with the same name (Ch 19, Ex 08).
7. Print Ch 19, Ex 08.
8. With Ch 19, Ex 08 still open, edit the XXXMargins macro so it changes the left and
    right margins to 1 inch by completing the following steps:
    a. Display the Macros dialog box.
    b. At the Macros dialog box, click
        XXXMargins in the list box,
        and then click the Edit button.
    c. At the Visual Basic Editor,
        make the following changes:
        1) Edit the step *.LeftMargin =
           InchesToPoints(1.5)* so it
           displays as *.LeftMargin =
           InchesToPoints(1)*.
        2) Edit the step *.RightMargin =
           InchesToPoints(1.5)* so it
           displays as *.RightMargin =
           InchesToPoints(1)*.
    d. Click the Save Normal button
        on the Visual Basic Editor
        Standard toolbar (third button
        from the left).
    e. Close the Visual Basic Editor by
        clicking File and then Close and
        Return to Microsoft Word.

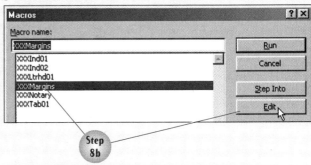

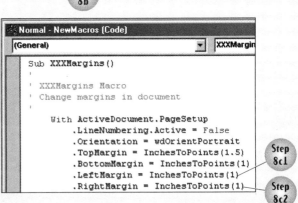

9. Run the XXXMargins macro.
10. Save the document again with the same name (Ch 19, Ex 08).
11. Print and then close Ch 19, Ex 08.

Organizing Macros

The macros you recorded in this chapter were inserted in the Normal template document by default. The macros recorded in the Normal template document are stored in a macro project named NewMacros. A macro project is a collection of macros stored in a document or template.

The macro project can be copied from the Normal template document to another template or document and renamed with options at the Organizer dialog box shown in figure 19.10. To display this dialog box, display the Macros dialog box, and then click the Organizer button.

figure

19.10   *Organizer Dialog Box*

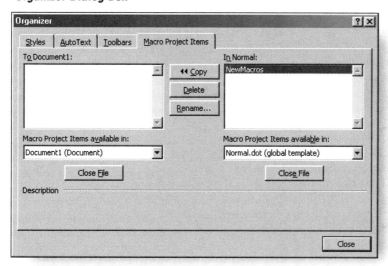

Copying and Renaming a Macro Project

To copy a macro project, open the template or document into which you want the macro project copied and then display the Organizer dialog box. At the Organizer dialog box, click the Copy button. When a macro project is copied to another document or template, it can be renamed. To do this, click the *NewMacros* project name and then click the Rename button. At the Rename dialog box, key the desired name for the macro project in the New name text box, and then click OK.

exercise

9

Copying and Renaming a Macro Project

1. Save a document as a template document by completing the following steps:
    a. At a clear document screen, click File and then Save As.
    b. At the Save As dialog box, click the down-pointing triangle at the right side of the Save as type list box, and then click *Document Template*. (This automatically changes the folder to the *Microsoft Templates* folder.)

c. Select the name in the File name box and then key **Legal Template**.
d. Press Enter or click the Save button.
2. With the Legal Template document open, copy macros in the NewMacros project from the Normal template document to the Legal Template document and rename the macro project by completing the following steps:
    a. Display the Macros dialog box.
    b. At the Macros dialog box, click the Organizer button.
    c. At the Organizer dialog box, make sure *Normal.dot (global template)* displays in the Macro Project Items available in box located at the right and *Legal Template (Template)* displays in the Macro Project Items available in box located at the left.

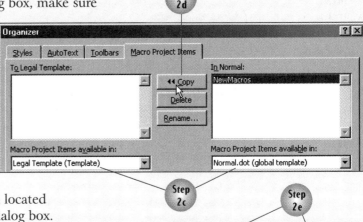

Step 2d

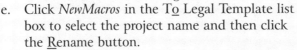

Step 2c

    d. Click the Copy button located in the middle of the dialog box.
    e. Click *NewMacros* in the To Legal Template list box to select the project name and then click the Rename button.

Step 2e

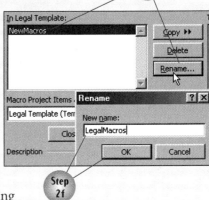

    f. At the Rename dialog box, key **LegalMacros** in the New name text box, and then click OK.
    g. Click the Close button (that displays in the lower right corner of the dialog box) to close the Organizer dialog box.

Step 2f

3. Delete macros from the LegalMacros project by completing the following steps:
    a. Display the Macros dialog box.
    b. At the Macros dialog box, click the down-pointing triangle at the right side of the Macros in option box, and then click *Legal Template (template)* at the drop-down list.
    c. Click *XXXLtrhd01* in the Macro name list box, click the Delete button, and then click Yes at the question asking if you want to delete the macro.
    d. Delete the XXXTab01 macro.
    e. Close the Macros dialog box.
4. Save and then close the Legal Template document.
5. Open the Legal Template document, insert a document, and run a macro by completing the following steps:
    a. Click File and then New.
    b. At the New dialog box with the General tab selected, double-click *Legal Template*.
    c. At the document screen, insert the document named Legal 01. (*Hint: Click Insert and then File.*)
    d. Run the XXXMargins macro by completing the following steps:
        1) Display the Macros dialog box.

2) Click the down-pointing triangle at the right side of the Macros in option box, and then click *Legal Template (template)* at the drop-down list.

3) Click *XXXMargins* in the M̲acro name list box and then click the R̲un button.

4) Close the Macros dialog box.

6. Save the document with Save As and name it Ch 19, Ex 09.

7. Print and then close Ch 19, Ex 09.

8. Display the New dialog box with the General tab selected, delete Legal Template, and then close the dialog box.

chapter summary

➤ Word's Macro feature is primarily used for executing a series of commands or applying formatting.

➤ Recording a macro involves turning on the macro recorder, performing the steps to be recorded, and then turning off the recorder.

➤ Run a macro by displaying the Macros dialog box and double-clicking the desired macro name.

➤ You can temporarily suspend the recording of a macro by clicking the Pause Recording button on the Macro Record toolbar.

➤ Delete a macro by displaying the Macros dialog box, clicking the macro name to be deleted, and then clicking the D̲elete button.

➤ Assign a keyboard command to a macro at the Record Macro dialog box.

➤ To run a macro that has been assigned a keyboard command, press the keys assigned to the macro.

➤ A macro can be added to a toolbar. To run a macro assigned to a toolbar, just click the button.

➤ Insert a Fill-in field in a macro that requires keyboard entry during the running of the macro.

➤ A macro is created with Visual Basic and can be edited using the Visual Basic Editor. To display a macro in the Visual Basic Editor, display the Macros dialog box, click the macro to be edited, and then click the E̲dit button.

➤ By default, macros are saved in the Normal template. Copy a macro project from the Normal template to other templates and rename a macro project with options at the Organizer dialog box.

commands review

Mouse/Keyboard

Macros dialog box	Click Tools, point to Macro, click Macros
Display Record Macro dialog box	Double-click REC button on Status bar; or click Tools, point to Macro, and then click Record New Macro
Display Customize dialog box	Click Tools and then Customize
Display the Field dialog box	Click Insert and then Field
Display Visual Basic Editor	Display the Macros dialog box, click the desired macro, and then click the Edit button
Display Organizer dialog box	Display the Macros dialog box and then click the Organizer button

thinking offline

Completion: In the space provided at the right, indicate the correct term, command, or number.

1. Double-click this button on the Status bar to display the Record Macro dialog box.

2. To temporarily suspend the recording of a macro, click this button on the Macro Record toolbar.

3. Assign a keyboard command to a macro at this dialog box.

4. Assign a macro to a toolbar with options from this dialog box.

5. Insert this field in a macro that requires keyboard entry during the running of the macro.

6. Edit a macro using this editor.

7. Copy a macro project from the Normal template into another template with options at this dialog box.

8. In the space provided below, list the steps needed to record a macro that changes the font to 18-point Arial bold. Name the macro Font18.

9. In the space provided below, list the steps needed to run the Font18 macro.

_____

_____

_____

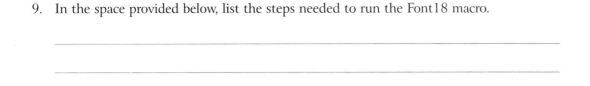

Assessment 1

1. At a clear document screen, record a macro named XXXLtrhd02 (where your initials are used instead of the *XXX*) that contains the letterhead text shown in figure 19.11 and assign it the keyboard command, Alt + Ctrl + G. (The text in figure 19.11 is set in 18-point Goudy Old Style bold.)
2. Close the document without saving it.
3. At a clear window, run the XXXLtrhd02 macro.
4. With the insertion point a double space below the letterhead, key the letter shown in figure 19.12. Use the Bullets button on the Formatting toolbar to insert the bullets as shown in the document. (Make sure the letter fits on one page. If not, change the top and bottom margins to 0.75 inch and the left and right margins to 1 inch.)
5. Save the letter and name it Ch 19, SA 01.
6. Print and then close Ch 19, SA 01.

figure

19.11 **Assessment 1**

GOOD SAMARITAN HOSPITAL
1201 James Street
St. Louis, MO 62033
(816) 555-1201

figure
19.12   *Assessment 1*

May 17, 2001

Ms. Mariah Jackson
St. Francis Medical Center
300 Blue Ridge Boulevard
Kansas City, MO 63009

Dear Mariah:

The registered nurse job description was very timely. I was able to use the basic outline to create a job description for the hospital. For one of the positions, the following information was included:

- Functions with the awareness of safety needs and implements appropriate safety measure.
- Demonstrates adherence to all unit hospital safety standards.
- Follows established standards in emergency situations.
- Recognizes, communicates, delegates, and coordinates management of emergent situations.
- Demonstrates awareness of legal issues on all aspects of patient care and unit function and takes action to limit or reduce risks.
- Completes unusual occurrence form for all patient incidents.
- Adheres to organizational standards in the area of patient confidentiality.

The information was provided by our legal department. Safety and legal issues are an integral part of medical services.

Very truly yours,

Victor Durham

XX:Ch 19, SA 01

Assessment 2

1. At a clear document screen, run the XXXTab01 macro and then create the document shown in figure 19.13. (Key the text in the first column at the first tab stop, not the left margin.)
2. After creating the document, save it and name it Ch 19, SA 02.
3. Print and then close Ch 19, SA 02.

figure
19.13   *Assessment 2*

McCORMACK FUNDS CORPORATION

Public Relations Department, Extension Numbers

Roger Maldon 129

Kimberly Holland 143

Richard Perez 317

Sharon Rawlins 211

Earl Warnberg 339

Susan Fanning 122

Assessment 3

1. At a clear document screen, record a macro named XXXNotSig that includes the information shown in figure 19.14. Include Fill-in fields in the macro where you see the text in parentheses.
2. After recording the macro, close the document without saving it.
3. Open Contract 02.
4. Save the document with Save As and name it Ch 19, SA 03.
5. Make the following changes to the document:
   a. Move the insertion point to the end of the document, press the Enter key twice, and then insert the following information at the left margin:

   _____
   LLOYD KOVICH, President
   Reinberg Manufacturing

   _____
   JOANNE MILNER, President
   Labor Worker's Union

   b. Move the insertion point to the end of the document, press the Enter key three times, and then run the XXXNotSig macro and insert the following information when prompted:

```
(name 1)   =   LLOYD KOVICH
(name 2)   =   JOANNE MILNER
(county)   =   Ramsey County
```

6. Save the document again with the same name (Ch 19, SA 03).
7. Print and then close Ch 19, SA 03.

Assessment 3

STATE OF MINNESOTA   )
) ss.
COUNTY OF RAMSEY   )

   I certify that I know or have satisfactory evidence that (name 1) and (name 2) are the persons who appeared before me, and said persons acknowledge that they signed the foregoing Contract and acknowledged it to be their free and voluntary act for the uses and purposes therein mentioned.

_____

NOTARY PUBLIC in and for the State of
Minnesota residing in (county)

Assessment 4

1. At a clear document screen, record a macro named XXXQuizFormat that does the following:
    a. Changes the font to 12-point Bookman Old Style (or a similar serif typeface).
    b. Changes the left paragraph indent to 0.3 inch.
    c. Adds 12 points of spacing before paragraphs.
2. Close the document without saving it.
3. Open Quiz.
4. Save the document with Save As and name it Ch 19, SA 04.
5. Select the entire document and then run the XXXQuizFormat macro.
6. Save the document again with the same name (Ch 19, SA 04).
7. Print Ch 19, SA 04.
8. With Ch 19, SA 04 still open, edit the XXXQuizFormat macro as follows:
    a. At the Visual Basic Editor, edit the step *.LeftIndent = InchesToPoints (0.3)* so it displays as *.LeftIndent = InchesToPoints (0.5)*. (You may need to scroll down the macro to display this macro line.)
    b. Edit the step *.RightIndent = InchesToPoints (0)* so it displays as *.RightIndent = InchesToPoints (0.5)*.
    c. Edit the step *.SpaceBefore = 12* so it displays as *.SpaceBefore = 24*.
9. After closing the Visual Basic Editor, select the entire document, and then run the XXXQuizFormat macro.
10. Center and bold the title *CHAPTER QUIZ*.
11. Save the document again with the same name (Ch 19, SA 04).
12. Print and then close Ch 19, SA 04.
13. At a clear document screen, display the Macros dialog box, delete all macros that begin with your initials, and then close the dialog box.

Chapter 20

Formatting with Styles

PERFORMANCE OBJECTIVES

Upon successful completion of chapter 20, you will be able to:

- Format a document with the AutoFormat feature.
- Format text with the Style Gallery.
- Create and apply styles.
- Assign a shortcut key combination to a style.
- Modify a style.
- Remove, rename, and delete a style.
- Create a cross-reference.

Some documents, such as company newsletters, reports, or brochures, may be created on a regular basis. These documents should maintain a consistency in formatting each time they are created. For example, a newsletter should maintain a consistency from issue to issue, and a company report should contain consistent formatting each time one is created. Formatting that is applied to a variety of documents on a regular basis or that maintains a consistency within a publication can be applied to text using a *style*. In Word, a style is a set of formatting instructions saved with a specific name in order to use the formatting instructions over and over.

In chapter 9, you learned to apply predesigned styles using the Style Button on the Standard toolbar and also at the Style dialog box. In this chapter, you will learn to format text with the AutoFormat feature, format text with styles from the Style Gallery, create and apply styles, assigned a shortcut key combination to styles, and modify and delete styles.

Formatting Text with Styles

As you learned in an earlier chapter, a Word document, by default, is based on the Normal template document. Within a normal template document, a Normal style is applied to text by default. This Normal style sets text in the default font (this may vary depending on what you have selected or what printer you are using), uses left alignment and single spacing, and turns on the Widow/Orphan control. In addition to this Normal style, other predesigned styles are available in a document based on the Normal template document. These styles can be displayed by clicking the down-pointing triangle to the right of the Style button on the Formatting toolbar.

Other template documents also contain predesigned styles. If you choose a different template document from the New dialog box, click the down-pointing triangle to the right of the Style button on the Formatting toolbar to display the names of styles available for that particular template document.

Styles can be changed and/or applied to text in three ways. The quickest way to apply styles to text in a document is with Word's AutoFormat feature. The advantage to using AutoFormat is that Word automatically applies the styles without you having to select them. The disadvantage is that you have less control over the styles that are applied.

Another method you can use to apply styles is to select a new template at the Style Gallery dialog box. The advantage to this is that you can preview your document as it will appear if formatted with various templates, and then apply the desired template. The disadvantage is that you have less control over the selection of styles.

A third method for applying styles to text is to make changes to those styles available in the template upon which your document is based. The advantage to this method is that you can format a document any way you want by creating and selecting styles. The disadvantage is that you have to create and/or select a style for each element in the document that you want formatted.

Formatting with AutoFormat

Word provides a variety of predesigned styles in the Normal template document that can be applied to text in a document. With this feature, called AutoFormat, Word goes through a document paragraph by paragraph and applies appropriate styles. For example, Word changes the font and size for heading text and adds bullets to listed items. The formatting is done automatically; all you do is sit back and watch Word do the work.

A document can be formatted by displaying the AutoFormat dialog box shown in figure 20.1. To display this dialog box, click Format and then AutoFormat. At the AutoFormat dialog box with the AutoFormat now option selected, click OK. This applies formatting to the open document. Figure 20.2 shows Report 01 with formatting applied to text with the AutoFormat feature.

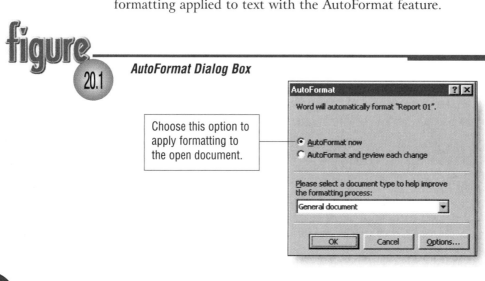

figure

20.1

AutoFormat Dialog Box

Choose this option to apply formatting to the open document.

figure 20.2

Document Formatted with AutoFormat

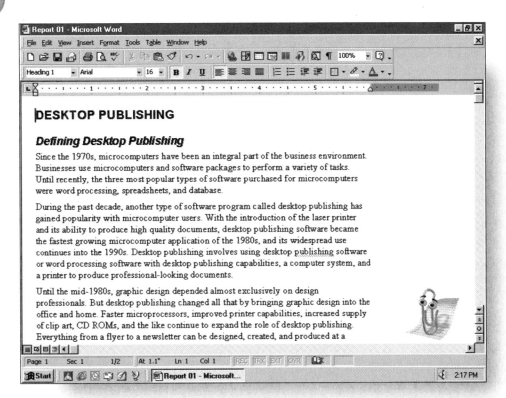

Formatting a Document with AutoFormat

1. Open Report 01.
2. Save the document with Save As and name it Ch 20, Ex 01.
3. Automatically format the document by completing the following steps:
   a. Click Format and then AutoFormat.
   b. At the AutoFormat dialog box, make sure the AutoFormat now option is selected (if not, click this option), and then click OK.
4. Save the document again with the same name (Ch 20, Ex 01).
5. Print and then close Ch 20, Ex 01.

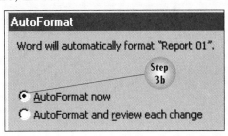

When AutoFormat applies styles to a document, it also makes corrections as follows:

- Uses formatting rules to find and format headings, body text, lists, superscript, subscript, addresses, and letter closings.
- Replaces straight quotes and apostrophes with typesetting quotation marks.
- Deletes extra paragraph marks.
- Replaces horizontal spaces inserted with the spacebar or the Tab key with indents.
- Replaces hyphens, asterisks, or other characters used to list items with a bullet (•).

If, after automatically formatting a document, you want to undo the changes, immediately click the Undo button on the Standard toolbar.

Reviewing/Rejecting Formatting Changes

At the AutoFormat dialog box, you can choose to review and then accept or reject changes made by AutoFormat. To do this, you would complete the following steps:

1. Open the document you want to automatically format, click Format and then AutoFormat.
2. At the AutoFormat dialog box, click the AutoFormat and review each change option, and then click OK.
3. After Word automatically applies the styles, the AutoFormat dialog box displays with the message:
   Formatting completed. You can now:
   - *Accept or reject all changes.*
   - *Review and reject individual changes.*
   - *Choose a custom look with Style Gallery.*
   At this message, click the Review Changes button.
4. At the Review AutoFormat Changes dialog box, shown in figure 20.3, accept or reject the changes, and then click the Cancel button.
5. At the next dialog box, click the Accept All button.

Review AutoFormat Changes Dialog Box

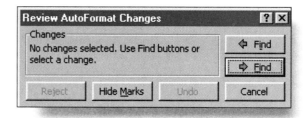

When Word displays the document for review, temporary revision marks are displayed. Revision marks are described in figure 20.4.

AutoFormat Revision Marks

This revision mark	Means
Blue paragraph mark	a style was applied to the paragraph.
Red paragraph mark	the paragraph mark was deleted.
Strikethrough character (-)	text or spaces were deleted.
Underline (_)	the underline character (displays in blue) was added.
Vertical bar in left margin	text or formatting was changed in that line.

As you review changes in a document, Word selects text with formatting applied. If you want to reject the formatting, click the Reject button, and then click the ➡ Find button to find the next formatting. If you want to leave the formatting as displayed, click the ➡ Find button to find the next formatting. If you want to find the previous formatting, click the ⬅ Find. To hide the revision marks in a document, click the Hide Marks button.

If the Review AutoFormat Changes dialog box is in the way of text you want to see in the document, position the mouse pointer in the title bar of the dialog box, hold down the left mouse button, drag the outline of the dialog box to a new location, and then release the mouse button.

Formatting Specific Portions of a Document with AutoFormat

1. Open Contract 02.
2. Save the document with Save As and name it Ch 20, Ex 02.
3. Format the document with the AutoFormat feature and reject some formatting by completing the following steps:

   a. Click Format and then AutoFormat.

   b. At the AutoFormat dialog box, click the AutoFormat and review each change option, and then click OK.

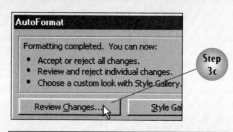

   c. After Word automatically applies the styles, the AutoFormat dialog box displays with the message:

   Formatting completed. You can now:
   - *Accept or reject all changes.*
   - *Review and reject individual changes.*
   - *Choose a custom look with Style Gallery.*

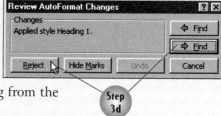

   At this message, click the Review Changes button.

   d. At the Review AutoFormat Changes dialog box, click the → Find button once, and then click the Reject button. (This removes the formatting from the first line of the title.)

   e. Click the → Find button once and then click the Reject button. (This removes the formatting from the second line of the title.)

   f. Click the Cancel button to close the dialog box.

   g. At the AutoFormat dialog box, click the Accept All button.
4. Select the two lines of the title and then change the font size to 14 points.
5. Save the document again with the same name (Ch 20, Ex 02).
6. Print and then close Ch 20, Ex 02.

Changing AutoFormat Options

Word follows certain rules when formatting text with AutoFormat. You can make changes to these rules. To do this, click the Options button at the AutoFormat dialog box or click Tools and then AutoCorrect. At the AutoCorrect dialog box, click the AutoFormat tab. Either method displays the dialog box shown in figure 20.5.

figure

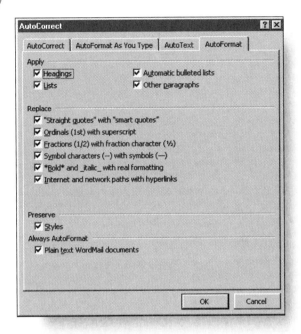

At the AutoCorrect dialog box with the AutoFormat tab selected, remove the check mark from a check box if you do not want the option active, or insert a check mark if you do want the option active.

Formatting Text with the Style Gallery

As you learned in an earlier chapter, each document is based on a template, with the Normal template document the default. The styles applied to text with AutoFormat are the styles available with the Normal template document. Word also provides predesigned styles with other template documents. You can use the Style Gallery dialog box to apply styles from other templates to the current document. This provides you with a large number of predesigned styles for formatting text. To display the Style Gallery dialog box shown in figure 20.6, click Format and then Theme. At the Theme dialog box, click the Style Gallery button (located at the bottom of the dialog box).

figure

20.6

Style Gallery Dialog Box

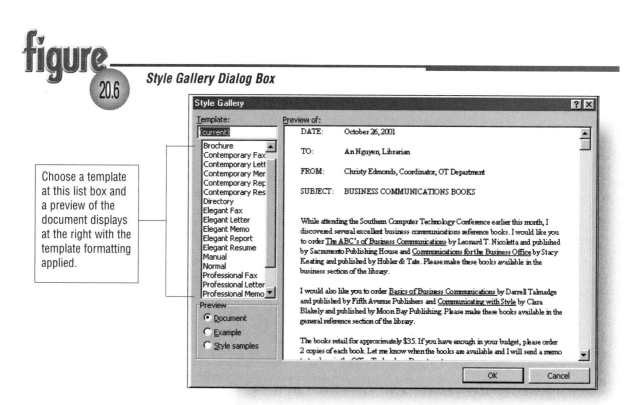

Choose a template at this list box and a preview of the document displays at the right with the template formatting applied.

At the Style Gallery dialog box, the template documents are displayed in the Template list box. The open document is displayed in the Preview of section of the dialog box. With this section, you can choose templates from the Template list box and see how the formatting is applied to the open document.

At the bottom of the Style Gallery dialog box, the Document option is selected in the Preview section. If you click Example, Word will insert a sample document in the Preview of section that displays the formatting applied to the document. Click Style samples and styles will display in the Preview of section of the dialog box rather than the document or sample document.

exercise

Formatting a Memo with Styles from a Memo Template

1. Open Memo 01.
2. Save the document with Save As and name it Ch 20, Ex 03.
3. Format the memo at the Style Gallery by completing the following steps:
   a. Click Format and then Theme.
   b. At the Theme dialog box, click the Style Gallery button (located at the bottom of the dialog box).
   c. At the Style Gallery dialog box, click *Elegant Memo* in the Template list box.
   d. Click OK or press Enter.
   e. At the memo, properly align the text after the *FROM:* heading.
4. Save the document again with the same name (Ch 20, Ex 03).
5. Print and then close Ch 20, Ex 03.

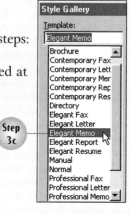

exercise 4

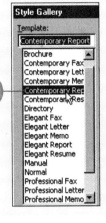

Formatting a Document with Styles from a Report Template

1. Open Contract 02.
2. Save the document with Save As and name it Ch 20, Ex 04.
3. Format the contract at the Style Gallery by completing the following steps:
   a. Click Format and then Theme.
   b. At the Theme dialog box, click the Style Gallery button (located at the bottom of the dialog box).
   c. At the Style Gallery dialog box, click *Contemporary Report* in the Template list box.
   d. Click OK or press Enter.
4. Save the document again with the same name (Ch 20, Ex 04).
5. Print and then close Ch 20, Ex 04.

Creating Styles

If all the styles predesigned by Word do not contain the formatting you desire, you can create your own style. A style can be created in two ways. You can either apply the desired formatting instructions to a paragraph and then save those instructions in a style, or you can specify the formatting instructions for a particular style without applying them to text. The first method is useful if you want to see how text appears when certain formatting instructions are applied to it. The second method is often used when you know the particular format that you want to use for certain paragraphs.

When you create your own style, you must give the style a name. When naming a style, avoid using the names already used by Word. The list of style names will display in the Styles list box at the Style dialog box if *All styles* is selected in the List text box. When naming a style, try to name it something that gives you an idea what the style will accomplish. Consider the following when naming a style:

- A style name can contain a maximum of 213 characters.
- A style name can contain spaces and commas.
- A style name is case-sensitive. Uppercase and lowercase letters can be used.
- Do not use the backslash (\), braces ({}) or a semicolon (;) when naming a style.

Creating a Style by Example

A style can be created by formatting text first and then using the Style button on the Formatting toolbar or the Style dialog box to create the style. To do this, position the insertion point in a paragraph of text containing the formatting you wish to include in the style, and then click the down-pointing triangle to the right of the Style button on the Formatting toolbar. Make sure the *Normal* style is selected in the drop-down list, key a unique name for the style, and then press Enter. This creates the style and also displays the style in the Style button. The new style will be visible in the Style drop-down list from the Formatting toolbar as well as the Style dialog box.

A style can also be created by example using the Style dialog box. To do this, position the insertion point in a paragraph of text containing the formatting you wish to include in the style, then click Format and then Style. At the Style dialog box, click the New button. At the New Style dialog box, key a name for the style in the Name text box, and then click OK or press Enter. At the Style dialog box, click the Close button.

Creating Styles by Example

1. Open Style.
2. Save the document with Save As and name it Sty 01.
3. Create a style by example named Title 1 by completing the following steps:
   a. Position the insertion point anywhere in the title *TITLE OF DOCUMENT*.
   b. Click the down-pointing triangle to the right of the Style button on the Formatting toolbar.
   c. Make sure the word *Normal* is selected. If not, select the word *Normal*.
   d. Key **Title 1** and then press Enter.
4. Create a style by example named Subtitle 1 using the Subtitle of Document text by completing steps similar to those in 3.
5. Select all the text in the document and then delete it. (This removes the text but keeps the styles you created.)
6. Save the document again with the same name (Sty 01).
7. Close Sty 01.

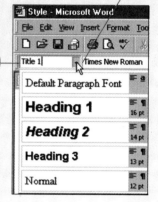

Creating a Style Using the Style Dialog Box

A style can be created before you use it rather than creating it by example. To do this, use options from the Style dialog box shown in figure 20.7. The Style dialog box can be used to create a style by applying the desired formatting instructions to text or by entering the specific formats without applying them to text.

To create a style at the Style dialog box, you would display the Style dialog box, and then click the New button. At the New Style dialog box, key a name for the style in the Name text box, and specify whether you are creating a paragraph or character style at the Style type option. Click the Format button and then click the desired formatting options. These options are displayed in figure 20.8. When all formatting has been selected, click the Close button.

Style Dialog Box

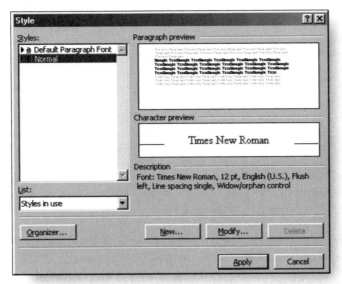

Style Formatting Options

Choose this	To select this type of formatting
Font	Font, style, size, color, superscript, subscript, and character spacing.
Paragraph	Paragraph alignment, indentations, spacing, and line spacing. (Not available for character styles.)
Tabs	Tab stop measurements, alignment, leaders, or clear tabs.
Border	Border location, color, style, and shading. (Not available for character styles.)
Language	Language that the spell checker, thesaurus, and grammar checker use for the current paragraph.
Frame	Horizontal and vertical positioning of object, size of object, and text wrapping style.
Numbering	Bulleted and numbered paragraphs in various styles. (Not available for character styles.)

exercise 6

Creating Styles at the Styles Dialog Box

1. Open Sty 01.
2. Create a style using the Style dialog box named Indent 1 that indents text 0.5 inch and adds 12 points of space after the paragraph by completing the following steps:

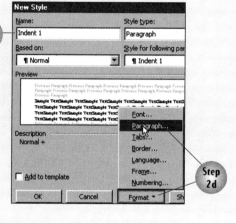

Step 2c

Step 2d

   a. Click Format and then Style.
   b. At the Style dialog box, click the New button.
   c. At the New Style dialog box, key **Indent 1** in the Name text box.
   d. Click the Format button that displays toward the bottom of the dialog box and then click Paragraph at the pop-up list.
   e. At the Paragraph dialog box, click the up-pointing triangle to the right of the Left text box until *0.5"* displays in the text box.
   f. Click the up-pointing triangle to the right of the After text box until *12 pt* displays in the text box.
   g. Click OK to close the Paragraph dialog box.
   h. Click OK to close the New Style dialog box.
   i. Click Close to close the Style dialog box.
3. Create a style named Font 1, using the Style dialog box, that changes the font to Century Schoolbook by completing the following steps:
   a. Click Format and then Style.
   b. At the Style dialog box, click the New button.

Step 3c

Step 3d

Step 3e

   c. At the New Style dialog box, key **Font 1** in the Name text box.
   d. Click the down-pointing triangle at the right side of the Style type text box and then click *Character* at the drop-down list.
   e. Click the Format button that displays toward the bottom of the dialog box and then click Font at the pop-up list.
   f. At the Font dialog box, click *Century Schoolbook* in the Font list box, *Regular* in the Font style list box, and *12* in the Size list box.
   g. Click OK or press Enter to close the Font dialog box.
   h. Click OK or press Enter to close the New Style dialog box.
   i. Click Close to close the Style dialog box.
4. Save the document again with the same name (Sty 01).
5. Close Sty 01.

Applying a Style

A style can be applied to the paragraph where the insertion point is positioned. You can also select several paragraphs and then apply a paragraph style. If you are applying a style that contains character formatting, you must select the text first, and then apply the style. A style can be applied using the Style button on the Formatting toolbar or the Style dialog box.

To apply a style using the Style button, position the insertion point in the paragraph to which you want the style applied, or select the text, then click the down-pointing triangle to the right of the Style button. At the drop-down list of styles, click the desired style.

To apply a style using the Style dialog box, position the insertion point in the paragraph to which you want the style applied, or select the text, and then click Format and then Style. At the Style dialog box, click the desired style in the Styles list box. (To view the entire list of styles offered by Word, click the down-pointing triangle at the right side of the List text box, and then click *All styles*.) With the desired style selected, click the Apply button.

exercise 7

Applying Styles in a Document Using the Style Button and the Style Dialog Box

1. Open Sty 01.
2. Save the document with Save As and name it Ch 20, Ex 07.
3. Insert the document named Quiz into the Ch 20, Ex 07 document. *(Hint: Use the File option from the Insert drop-down menu to do this.)*
4. Position the insertion point on any character in the title *CHAPTER QUIZ* and then apply the Title 1 style.
5. Select the text in the document (except the title) and then complete the following steps:
   a. Apply the Font 1 style.
   b. Apply the Indent 1 style by completing the following steps:
      1) Click Format and then Style.
      2) At the Style dialog box, scroll down the Styles list box until *Indent 1* is visible, and then click it.
      3) Click the Apply button.
   c. Deselect the text.
6. Save the document again with the same name (Ch 20, Ex 07).
7. Print and then close Ch 20, Ex 07.

Assigning a Shortcut Key Combination to a Style

A style can be applied quickly in a document if a shortcut key has been assigned to the style. You can use the letters A through Z, numbers 0 through 9, the Delete and Insert keys, combined with the Ctrl, Alt, and Shift keys to create a shortcut key combination. Word has already assigned shortcut key combinations to many features. If you assign a shortcut key combination to a style that is already used by Word, the message *Currently assigned to (name of feature)* displays. When this happens, choose another shortcut key combination. To create a shortcut key combination for a style, you would complete the following steps:

1. Open the document containing the style to which you want to assign a shortcut key combination.
2. Click Format and then Style.
3. At the Style dialog box, click the style for which you want to assign a shortcut key combination in the Styles list box.
4. Click the Modify button.
5. At the Modify Style dialog box, click the Shortcut Key button.
6. At the Customize Keyboard dialog box shown in figure 20.9, key the shortcut key combination in the Press new shortcut key text box.
7. Click the Assign button.
8. Click the Close button to close the Customize Keyboard dialog box.
9. At the Modify Style dialog box, click OK.
10. At the Style dialog box, click the Close button.

figure

20.9

Customize Keyboard Dialog Box

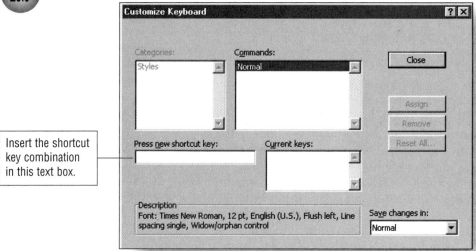

Insert the shortcut key combination in this text box.

exercise

8

Assigning Shortcut Key Combinations to Styles

1. Open Sty 01.
2. Save the document with Save As and name it Sty 02.
3. Create the shortcut key combination, Alt + F, for the Font 1 style by completing the following steps:
   a. Click Format and then Style.
   b. At the Style dialog box, click *Font 1* in the Styles list box. (You will need to scroll up the list box to display this style.)
   c. Click the Modify button.
   d. At the Modify Style dialog box, click the Shortcut Key button.

e. At the Customize Keyboard dialog box, hold down the Alt key and press the letter F (*Alt + F* will display in the Press new shortcut key text box).
   f. Click the Assign button.
   g. Click the Close button to close the Customize Keyboard dialog box.
   h. Click OK to close the Modify Style dialog box.
   i. Click Close to close the Style dialog box.

4. Create the shortcut key combination, Alt + I, for the Indent 1 style by completing steps similar to those in 3.
5. Create the shortcut key combination, Alt + S, for the Subtitle 1 style by completing steps similar to those in 3.
6. Create the shortcut key combination, Alt + T, for the Title 1 style by completing steps similar to those in 3.
7. Save the document again with the same name (Sty 02).
8. Close Sty 02.

exercise 9

Applying Styles in a Document with Shortcut Key Combinations

1. Open Sty 02.
2. Save the document with Save As and name it Ch 20, Ex 09.
3. Insert the document Report 01 into the Ch 20, Ex 09 document.
4. Select the entire document and then change line spacing to single.
5. Position the insertion point on any character in the title *DESKTOP PUBLISHING* and then apply the Title 1 style by pressing Alt + T.
6. Position the insertion point on any character in the subtitle *Defining Desktop Publishing* and then apply the Subtitle 1 style by pressing Alt + S.
7. Apply the Subtitle 1 style to the following headings:

   Initiating the Desktop Publishing Process
   Planning the Publication
   Creating the Content

8. Save the document again with the same name (Ch 20, Ex 09).
9. Print and then close Ch 20, Ex 09.

To remove a shortcut key combination from a style, display the Customize Keyboard dialog box for the specific style and then click the Remove button.

Removing a Shortcut Key Combination

1. Open Sty 02.
2. Save the document with Save As and name it Sty 03.
3. Remove the shortcut key combination, Alt + I, by completing the following steps:

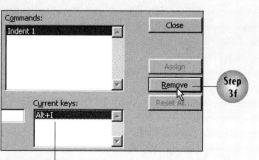

   a. Click Format and then Style.
   b. At the Style dialog box, click *Indent 1* in the Styles list box. (You will need to scroll up the list to display this style.)
   c. Click the Modify button.
   d. At the Modify Style dialog box, click the Shortcut Key button.
   e. At the Customize Keyboard dialog box, click *Alt + I* in the Current keys list box.
   f. Click the Remove button.
   g. Click the Close button to close the Customize Keyboard dialog box.
   h. At the Modify Style dialog box, click OK.
   i. At the Style dialog box, click the Close button.
4. Save the document again with the same name (Sty 03).
5. Close Sty 03.

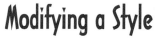

Step 3f

Step 3e

Modifying a Style

Once a style has been created, you can modify the style by changing the formatting instructions that it contains either with the Style button on the Formatting toolbar or the Style dialog box. When you modify a style by changing the formatting instructions, all text to which that style has been applied is changed accordingly. To modify a style using the Style button on the Formatting toolbar, you would complete the following steps:

1. Open the document containing a style you want to modify.
2. Reformat text with the formatting instructions you want changed in the style.
3. Select the text.
4. Click the down-pointing triangle to the right of the Style button on the Formatting toolbar.
5. At the drop-down list of styles, click the style name you want to modify.
6. When Word displays the Modify Style dialog box shown in figure 20.10, click the Update the style to reflect recent changes? option.
7. Click OK to close the dialog box.

figure

20.10

Modify Style Dialog Box

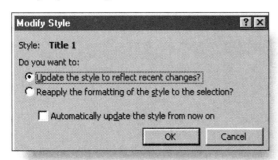

You can also modify a style at the Style dialog box. To modify a style at the Style dialog box, you would complete the following steps:

1. Open the document containing the style you want to modify.
2. Click F̲ormat and then S̲tyle.
3. At the Style dialog box, click the style name you want to modify in the S̲tyles list box.
4. Click the M̲odify button.
5. At the Modify Style dialog box shown in figure 20.11, add or delete formatting options by clicking the F̲ormat button, and then changing the appropriate options.
6. When all changes have been made, click OK to close the Modify Style dialog box.
7. At the Style dialog box, click the Close button.

figure

20.11

Modify Style Dialog Box

Modifying Styles

1. Open Ch 20, Ex 09.
2. Save the document with Save As and name it Ch 20, Ex 11.
3. Modify the Title 1 style by completing the following steps:
   a. Select the title *DESKTOP PUBLISHING*.
   b. Change the font to 18-point Arial bold.
   c. Display the Paragraph dialog box and then change the spacing after the paragraph to 6 points.
   d. With the text still selected, click the down-pointing triangle to the right of the Style button.
   e. At the drop-down list of styles, click *Title 1*.
   f. At the Modify Style dialog box, click the Update the style to reflect recent changes? option.
   g. Click OK to close the Modify Style dialog box.
   h. Deselect the text.

   Step 3f →

   ```
   Modify Style
   Style:  Title 1
   Do you want to:
   ⦿ Update the style to reflect recent changes?
   ⚬ Reapply the formatting of the style to the selection?
   ```

4. Modify the Subtitle 1 style by completing the following steps:
   a. Click Format and then Style.
   b. At the Style dialog box, click *Subtitle 1* in the Styles list box.
   c. Click the Modify button.
   d. At the Modify Style dialog box, change the font to 14-point Arial bold by completing the following steps:
      1) Click the Format button located toward the bottom of the dialog box.
      2) At the pop-up list that displays, click *Font*.
      3) At the Font dialog box, click *Arial* in the Font list box, *Bold* in the Font style list box, and *14* in the Size list box.
      4) Click OK or press Enter to close the Font dialog box.
   e. At the Modify Style dialog box, change the spacing before and after the paragraph to 6 points by completing the following steps:
      1) Click the Format button located toward the bottom of the dialog box.
      2) Click *Paragraph* at the pop-up list.
      3) At the Paragraph dialog box, click once on the up-pointing triangle to the right of the After text box. (This inserts *6 pt* in the text box.)
      4) Click once on the up-pointing triangle at the right of the Before text box. (This inserts *6 pt* in the text box.)
      5) Click OK or press Enter.
   f. At the Modify Style dialog box, click OK.
   g. Click the Close button to close the Style dialog box.
5. Check the page breaks in the document and, if necessary, adjust the page breaks.
6. Save the document again with the same name (Ch 20, Ex 11).
7. Print and then close Ch 20, Ex 11. (The title should print in 18-point Arial bold and the four headings should print in 14-point Arial bold.)

Removing a Style from Text

You may apply a style to text in a document and then change your mind and wish to remove the style. If you decide to remove the style immediately after applying it (before performing some other action), click the Undo button on the Standard toolbar. You can also click Edit and then Undo Style. When a style is removed, the style that was previously applied to the text is applied once again (usually this is the Normal style).

You can also remove a style from text by applying a new style. Only one style can be applied at a time to the same text. For example, if you applied the Heading 1 style to text and then later decide you want to remove it, position the insertion point in the text containing the Heading 1 style, and then apply the Normal style.

Renaming a Style

As you create more and more styles in a particular document, you may find that you need to rename existing styles to avoid duplicating style names. When a style is renamed, the formatting instructions contained within the style remain the same. Any text to which the style has been applied reflects the new name. You can rename styles that you create as often as needed, but you cannot rename Word's standard styles. To rename a style, click the Modify button at the Style dialog box. At the Modify Style dialog box, key the new name for the style, and then click OK to return to the Style dialog box. At the Style dialog box, click the Close button.

Modifying Styles

1. Open Sty 01.
2. Save the document with Save As and name it Sty 04.
3. Modify the Title 1 style by completing the following steps:
   a. Click Format and then Style.
   b. At the Style dialog box, click *Title 1* in the Styles list box.
   c. Click the Modify button.
   d. At the Modify Style dialog box, change the font to 18-point Arial bold by completing the following steps:
      1) Click the Format button that displays toward the bottom of the dialog box.
      2) Click *Font* at the pop-up list.
      3) At the Font dialog box, click *Arial* in the Font list box, *Bold* in the Font style list box, and *18* in the Size list box.
      4) Click OK to close the Font dialog box.
   e. Click the Format button located toward the bottom of the dialog box and then click *Paragraph* at the pop-up list.
   f. At the Paragraph dialog box, change the spacing after the paragraph to 12 points.
   g. Click OK to close the Paragraph dialog box

h. At the Modify Style dialog box, click OK.
i. Click the Close button to close the Style dialog box.
4. Modify the Subtitle 1 style so the font is 14-point Arial bold and the space after the paragraph is 12 points by completing steps similar to those in 3.
5. Modify the Font 1 style by completing the following steps:
   a. Key **This is sample text**.
   b. Select *This is sample text.*
   c. Apply the Font 1 style to the text. (To do this, click the down-pointing triangle to the right of the Style button on the Formatting toolbar, and then click *Font 1*.)
   d. With the text still selected, change the font to 12-point Bookman Old Style. (If this typeface is not available, choose a similar serif typeface [other than Century Schoolbook and Times New Roman].)
   e. Click the down-pointing triangle to the right of the Style button on the Formatting toolbar.
   f. At the drop-down list of styles, click *Font 1*.
   g. At the Modify Style dialog box, click the Update the style to reflect recent changes? option, and then click OK or press Enter.
6. With the text still selected, press the Delete key.
7. Save the document again with the same name (Sty 04).
8. Close Sty 04.

Deleting a Style

A style can be deleted in a document and any style to which that style is applied is returned to the Normal style. To delete a style, display the Style dialog box, select the style name you want to delete in the Styles list box, and then click the Delete button. At the message asking if you want to delete the style, click Yes. Click the Close button to close the Style dialog box. You can delete styles that you create, but you cannot delete Word's standard styles.

You can delete several styles at once at the Organizer dialog box. To do this, you would complete the following steps:

1. Open the document containing the styles you want to delete.
2. Click Format and then Style.
3. At the Style dialog box, click the Organizer button.
4. At the Organizer dialog box, select the style names you want deleted in the In list box at the left side of the dialog box.
5. Click the Delete button.
6. At the question asking if you want to delete the first style, click Yes to All. (This tells Word to delete all selected styles.)
7. Click the Close button to close the Organizer dialog box.

Deleting Styles

1. Open Sty 04.
2. Insert the document named Report 02 into the Sty 04 document.
3. Save the document with Save As and name it Ch 20, Ex 13.
4. Delete the Indent 1 style by completing the following steps:
   a. Click Format and then Style.
   b. At the Style dialog box, click *Indent 1* in the Styles list box.
   c. Click the Delete button.
   d. At the message asking if you want to delete the style, click Yes.
   e. Click the Close button to close the Style dialog box.
5. Select the entire document and then apply the Font 1 style.
6. Apply the Title 1 style to the title *DESKTOP PUBLISHING DESIGN*.
7. Apply the Subtitle 1 style to the headings *Designing a Document* and *Creating Focus*.
8. Save the document again with the same name (Ch 20, Ex 13).
9. Print and then close Ch 20, Ex 13.

Creating a Cross-Reference

A cross-reference in a Word document refers the reader to another location within the document. This feature is useful in a long document or a document containing related information. Insert a cross-reference to move to a specific location within the document. To insert a cross-reference, you would follow these basic steps:

1. Move the insertion point to the location where the cross-reference is to display.
2. Key introductory text such as *For more information, please refer to*.
3. Click Insert and then Cross-reference.
4. At the Cross-reference dialog box, shown in figure 20.12, identify the reference type, where to refer, and the specific text.
5. Click the Insert button and then click the Close button.

figure
20.12

Cross-reference Dialog Box

The reference identified in the Cross-reference dialog box displays immediately after the introductory text. To move to the specified reference, position the mouse pointer over the introductory text (pointer turns into a hand), and then click the left mouse button.

exercise
14

Inserting a Cross-Reference in a Document

1. Open Report 06.
2. Save the document with Save As and name it Ch 20, Ex 14.
3. Apply the specified styles to the following headings:

THE TECHNOLOGY OF DESKTOP PUBLISHING	=	Heading 1
WHAT IS DESKTOP PUBLISHING?	=	Heading 2
BASIC HARDWARE	=	Heading 2

4. Insert a cross-reference by completing the following steps:
   a. Position the insertion point immediately following the period at the end of the last sentence in the document.
   b. Press the spacebar once and then key **(For more information, refer to**.
   c. Press the spacebar once.
   d. Click Insert and then Cross-reference.
   e. At the Cross-reference dialog box, make sure *Heading* displays in the Reference type box. (If it does not, click the down-pointing triangle at the right side of the Reference type list box, and then click *Heading* at the drop-down list.)
   f. Click *BASIC HARDWARE* in the For which heading box.
   g. Click the Insert button.

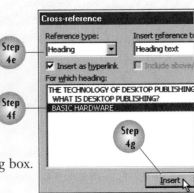

Step 4e

Step 4f

Step 4g

    h.   Click the Close button to close the dialog box.

    i.   At the document, key a period followed by the closing parenthesis.

5. Move to the reference text by positioning the mouse pointer over *BASIC HARDWARE* until the mouse pointer turns into a hand and then click the left mouse button.

6. Save the document again with the same name (Ch 20, Ex 14).

7. Print and then close Ch 20, Ex 14.

chapter summary

➤ Formatting that is applied to a variety of documents on a regular basis or that maintains a consistency within a publication can be applied to text using a *style*. A style is a set of formatting instructions saved with a specific name in order to use the formatting over and over.

➤ When the formatting instructions contained within a style are changed, all the text to which the style has been applied is automatically updated.

➤ Styles are created for a particular document and are saved with the document.

➤ In addition to the Normal style that is applied to text by default, other predesigned styles are available in a document based on the Normal template document. Other template documents also contain predesigned styles.

➤ Styles can be changed and/or applied to text in three ways: 1) use Word's AutoFormat feature; 2) select a new template at the Style Gallery dialog box; or 3) make changes to styles available in the template upon which your document is based.

➤ When formatting with the AutoFormat feature, you can review and then accept or reject changes.

➤ At the Style Gallery dialog box, you can see the effects of styles on the open document in the Preview section.

➤ A new style can be created in two ways: apply the desired formatting instructions to a paragraph and then save those instructions in a style; or, specify the formatting instructions for a style without applying the formatting to text.

➤ A style can be applied to the paragraph where the insertion point is positioned, or select several paragraphs and then apply a paragraph style.

➤ Apply a style using the Style button on the Formatting toolbar or the Style dialog box.

➤ A style can be applied quickly in a document if a shortcut key combination has been assigned to the style.

➤ Modify a style by changing the formatting instructions that it contains either with the Style button on the Formatting toolbar or the Style dialog box.

➤ Delete a style from a document or rename a style at the Style dialog box.

➤ Remove a style from text by applying a new style, since only one style can be applied at a time to the same text.

➤ Create a cross-reference in a document to refer the reader to another location within the document.

commands review

	Mouse/Keyboard
Format a document with AutoFormat	Click Format, AutoFormat, then click OK
Undo AutoFormat changes	Immediately click the Undo button on the Standard toolbar
Display Style Gallery dialog box	Click Format, then Theme; at the Theme dialog box, click the Style Gallery button
Display Style dialog box	Click Format, Style
Display Cross-reference dialog box	Click Insert, Cross-reference

thinking offline

Completion: In the space provided at the right, indicate the correct term, symbol, or command.

1. By default, a Word document is based on this template document.

2. The predesigned styles based on the default template document are displayed by clicking this button on the Formatting toolbar.

3. The quickest way to apply styles in a document is with this feature.

4. To display the AutoFormat dialog box, click this option on the Menu bar, and then click AutoFormat.

5. If, after automatically formatting a document, you want to remove the formatting, immediately click this button on the Standard toolbar.

6. This is the maximum number of characters a style name can contain.

7. Create a new style at this dialog box.

8. Delete several styles at once at this dialog box.

9. Insert this in a document to refer the reader to another location within the document.

10. In the space provided below, list the steps you would complete to create a style named Document Font that changes the font to 12-point Bookman Old Style (or a similar serif typeface).

working hands-on

Assessment 1

1. Open Report 03.
2. Save the document with Save As and name it Ch 20, SA 01.
3. Automatically format the document at the AutoFormat dialog box.
4. Save the document again with the same name (Ch 20, SA 01).
5. Print and then close Ch 20, SA 01.

Assessment 2

1. Open Notice 01.
2. Save the document with Save As and name it Ch 20, SA 02.
3. Format the document at the Style Gallery with the Professional Report template.
4. Save the document again with the same name (Ch 20, SA 02).
5. Print and then close Ch 20, SA 02.

Assessment 3

1. Open Sty 03.
2. Save the document with Save As and name it Ch 20, SA 03.
3. Make the following changes to the document:
   a. Change the alignment to center and then key **KENTWOOD SCHOOL DISTRICT**.
   b. Press the Enter key and then key **September Newsletter**.
   c. Press the Enter key and then key **David Olmsted, Editor**.
   d. Press the Enter key three times.
   e. Change the alignment to left.
4. Insert the document named News 01 into the Ch 20, SA 03 document.
5. Make the following changes to the document:
   a. Change the left and right margins to 1 inch.
   b. Delete the blank line below each of the following headings: *Welcome Back*, *Double Shifting*, and *Emergency Kits*.
   c. Apply the Title 1 style to the following text:

      KENTWOOD SCHOOL DISTRICT
      September Newsletter
      David Olmsted, Editor

   d. Apply the Subtitle 1 style to the following text:

      Welcome Back
      Double Shifting
      Emergency Kits

6. Save the document again with the same name (Ch 20, SA 03). (Make sure the document fits on one page. If not, consider decreasing slightly the left and right margins or the top and bottom margins.)
7. Print and then close Ch 20, SA 03.

Assessment 4

1. Open Ch 20, SA 03.
2. Save the document with Save As and name it Ch 20, SA 04.
3. Make the following changes to the document:
   a. Modify the Title 1 style so the font is 16-point Arial bold.
   b. Modify the Subtitle 1 style so the font is 14-point Arial bold and the space after the paragraph is 6 points.
4. Make sure the document fits on one page. If it does not, consider decreasing the top and bottom margins to approximately 0.75 inch.
5. Save the document again with the same name (Ch 20, SA 04).
6. Print and then close Ch 20, SA 04.

Assessment 5

1. Open Report 03.
2. Save the document with Save As and name it Ch 20, SA 05.
3. Select the entire document and then change to single line spacing.
4. Apply the specified styles to the following headings:

MODULE 1: DEFINING NEWSLETTER ELEMENTS	=	Heading 1
Designing a Newsletter	=	Heading 2
Defining Basic Newsletter Elements	=	Heading 2
MODULE 2: PLANNING A NEWSLETTER	=	Heading 1
Defining the Purpose of a Newsletter	=	Heading 2

5. Insert a cross-reference following the period at the end of the first paragraph that contains the text *For more information, refer to* and refers readers to the *Defining the Purpose of a Newsletter* heading.
6. Move to the reference text using the cross-reference.
7. Save the document again with the same name (Ch 20, SA 05).
8. Print and then close Ch 20, SA 05.

Performance Assessments
Unit Four

ENHANCING THE PRESENTATION OF TEXT

DEMONSTRATING YOUR SKILLS

In this unit, you have learned to enhance documents with special features such as hyphenation, line numbering, AutoText, and drop caps. You also learned to enhance the presentation of data by inserting data into a chart and to automate the formatting of text using macros and styles.

Assessment one 1

1. Create the following AutoText entries:
   a. Create an AutoText entry for *Government Obligations Fund* and use the initials *gof*.
   b. Create an AutoText entry for *Prime Obligations Fund* and use the initials *pof*.
   c. Create an AutoText entry for *Tax Free Obligations Fund* and use the initials *tfof*.
2. Key the document shown in figure U4.1 using the AutoText entries you created.
3. Save the document and name it Unit 4, PA 01.
4. Print and then close Unit 4, PA 01.
5. At a clear document screen, delete the *gof*, *pof*, and *tfof* autotext entries.

LIFETIME ANNUITY FUNDS

The Board of Directors and Shareholders
gof
pof
tfof

We have audited the statements of net assets of the *gof*, *pof*, and *tfof* as of September 30, 2000, and the related statements of operations, the statements of changes in net assets and the financial highlights for each of the periods presented.

In our opinion, the financial statements and the financial highlights present fairly, in all material respects, the financial position of the *gof*, *pof*, and *tfof* as of September 30, 2000, and the results of their operations, changes in their net assets, and the financial highlights for each of the periods are in conformity with generally accepted accounting principles.

Figure U4.1 • Assessment 1

Assessment 2

1. At a clear document screen, create a macro named Formhead that is assigned the shortcut command, Alt + Ctrl + H, which selects text and changes the font to 14-point Arial bold. *(Hint: At a clear document screen, key **This is a heading**. This gives you text to select when recording the macro.)*
2. Close the document without saving it.
3. At a clear document screen, open Report 01.
4. Save the document with Save As and name it Unit 4, PA 02.
5. Make the following changes to the report:
   a. Select the entire document then change the font to 12-point Century Schoolbook (or a similar serif typeface).
   b. Select the text in the document except the title, change the line spacing to single, and then change the paragraph spacing before and after to 6 points.
   c. Run the Alt + Ctrl + H macro for the title and the four headings.
   d. Hyphenate words in the document manually.
6. Save the document again with the same name (Unit 4, PA 02).
7. Print and then close Unit 4, PA 02.

Assessment three

1. At a clear document screen, record a macro named CWInfo that includes the copyright information shown in figure U4.2. Include Fill-in fields in the macro where you see the text in parentheses.
2. After recording the macro, close the document without saving it.
3. Open Contract 02.
4. Save the document with Save As and name it Unit 4, PA 03.
5. Change the top, bottom, left, and right margins to 0.8 inch.
6. Move the insertion point to the end of the document, press the Enter key once, and then run the CWInfo macro and insert the following information when prompted:

    (name) = *Richard Viera*
    (date) = *March 22, 2001*

7. Save the document again with the same name (Unit 4, PA 03).
8. Print and then close Unit 4, PA 03.

This document is the sole property of Reinberg Manufacturing and may not be reproduced, copied, or sold without express written consent of a legal representative of Reinberg Manufacturing.

Prepared by: (name)
Date: (date)

Figure U4.2 • Assessment 3

Assessment four

1. Open Table 06.
2. Save the document with Save As and name it Unit 4, PA 04.
3. Create a Column chart with the table with the following elements:
   a. Add the title, *REVENUE SOURCES*, to the chart.
   b. Select and then delete the table.
   c. Change the Zoom to Whole Page.
   d. Increase the size of the chart. (You determine the size. Make sure it fits within the margins.)
   e. Move the chart to the middle of the page.
   f. Change the Zoom back to 100%.
4. Save the document again with the same name (Unit 4, PA 04).
5. Print and then close Unit 4, PA 04.

Assessment 5

1. Open Table 07.
2. Save the document with Save As and name it Unit 4, PA 05.
3. Create a Pie chart for the table with the following elements:
   a. Change the chart type to a two-dimensional pie.
   b. Make sure the data is displayed properly in the Pie chart. *(Hint: You may need to click the By Column button on the Graph Standard toolbar.)*
   c. Add the title *EXPENDITURES*.
   d. Add percent data labels to the pieces of the pie in the chart.
   e. Select and then delete the table.
   f. Increase the size of the chart (you determine the size; make sure it fits within the margins).
   g. Change the Zoom to Whole Page.
   h. Move the chart to the middle of the page.
   i. Change the Zoom back to 100%.
4. Save the document again with the same name (Unit 4, PA 05).
5. Print and then close Unit 4, PA 05.

Assessment 6

1. At a clear document screen, create the following styles:
   a. Create a style named Title Formatting that changes text to a sans serif typeface (you determine the typeface) in 16-point size and bold type style.
   b. Create a style named Heading Formatting that changes text to a sans serif typeface (use the same typeface as the previous style) in 12-point size and bold type style.
2. Save the document and name it Unit 4, PA 06.
3. With Unit 4, PA 06 still open, insert the file named Report 05 into Unit 4, PA 06.
4. Make the following changes to the document:
   a. Select the entire document and then set a tab at 0.25 inch on the Ruler.
   b. Complete a spelling check on the document.
   c. Apply the Title Formatting style to the title *STRUCTURED PUBLICATIONS*.

    d.   Apply the Heading Formatting style to the following headings:

> *Cover*
> *Title Page*
> *Copyright Page*
> *Preface*
> *Table of Contents*
> *Body Text*
> *Appendix*
> *Bibliography*
> *Glossary*
> *Index*

5.   Check the page break and, if necessary, adjust the page break.
6.   Save the document again with the same name (Unit 4, PA 06).
7.   Print Unit 4, PA 06.
8.   With Unit 4, PA 06 still open, save the document with Save As and name it Unit 4, PA 06 Second.
9.   Make the following changes to the document:
    a.   Edit the Title Formatting style so it changes text to a serif font (you choose the font) set in 16-point size and bold type style.
    b.   Edit the Heading Formatting style so it changes text to a serif font (you choose the font) set in 14-point size and bold type style.
10.   Save the document again with the same name (Unit 4, PA 06 Second).
11.   Print and then close Unit 4, PA 06 Second.

CREATING ORIGINAL DOCUMENTS

Assessment 7 seven

Situation: You work for Lifetime Annuity Association and you have been asked by your supervisor to create a document that shows customers' average household expenditures. Include the following information:

<u>Average Household Expenditures</u>

This pie chart shows how a typical two-paycheck household with an average after-tax income of $42,000 spends its annual income. How does your family's spending compare?

Include this information in the pie chart:

Expenditure	Percent of Income
Housing	33%
Transportation	18%
Food	16%
Insurance	13%
Health Care	4%
Other	16%

When determining your family's life insurance needs, you will want to consider if your coverage will be adequate 5, 10, or even 15 years from now. Your family's financial needs may change over the years and inflation will gradually erode the value of your policy.

When creating the document, consider what typeface you will use, where you will place elements on the page, and how you will create the pie chart. Include a title for this document. Save the document and name it Unit 4, PA 07. Print and then close Unit 4, PA 07.

Assessment 8eight

Make sure you are connected to the Internet and then use a search engine (you choose the search engine) to search for companies on the Web that provide information, services, and/or products for designing documents. Key words you might consider using to search the Web include:

> *desktop publishing*
> *document design*
> *typeface*
> *electronic design*

Find at least three Web sites that interest you and then create a report in Word about the sites that includes the following:

- Type of site (company, personal, magazine, etc.)
- Site name, address, and URL
- A brief description of the site
- Products, services, and/or information available at the site

Include any other additional information pertinent to the sites. Apply formatting to enhance the document. When the document is completed, save it and name it Unit 4, PA 08. Print and then close Unit 4, PA 08.

Unit five

ORGANIZING TEXT IN DOCUMENTS

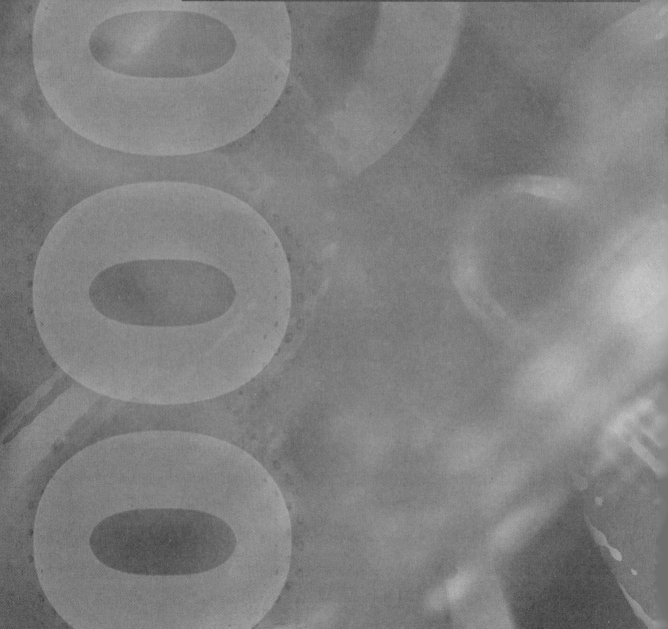

MICROSOFT® WORD 2000

MOUS SKILLS—UNIT FIVE

Coding No.	SKILL	Pages
W2000E.1	**Working with paragraphs**	
W2000E.1.3	Sort lists, paragraphs, tables	704-715
W2000E.2	**Working with documents**	
W2000E.2.9	Work with master documents and subdocuments	740-748
W2000E.2.10	Create and modify a table of contents	803-811
W2000E.2.12	Create and modify an index	812-822
W2000E.5	**Using mail merge**	
W2000E.5.3	Sort records to be merged	716-718
W2000E.6	**Using advanced features**	
W2000E.6.1	Insert a field	754-755
W2000E.6.4	Create and modify form	753-771
W2000E.6.5	Create and modify a form control	
	(e.g., add an item to a drop-down list)	761-767
W2000E.7	**Collaborating with workgroups**	
W2000E.7.1	Insert comments	782-785
W2000E.7.3	Create multiple versions of a document	794-798
W2000E.7.4	Track changes to a document	777-782
W2000E.7.5	Set default file location for workgroup templates	791-794
W2000E.7.6	Round Trip documents from HTML	791

Chapter 21

Sorting and Selecting

PERFORMANCE OBJECTIVES

Upon successful completion of chapter 21, you will be able to:

- Sort text in paragraphs, columns, tables, and data source documents.
- Sort on more than one field.
- Select specific information from a document.

Word is primarily a word processing program, but it also includes some basic database functions. With a database program, you can alphabetize information or arrange numbers numerically and select specific records from a document.

In Word, you can sort text in paragraphs, text in rows in tables, or records in a data source. Sorting can be done alphabetically, numerically, or by date. You can also select specific records from a data source to be merged with a main document. Word can perform the three types of sorts shown in figure 21.1.

figure

21.1   *Types of Sorts*

Alphanumeric: In an alphanumeric sort, Word arranges the text in the following order: special symbols such as @ and # first, numbers second, and letters third. You can tell Word to sort text in all uppercase letters first, followed by words beginning with uppercase letters, and then words beginning with lowercase letters.

Numeric: In a numeric sort, Word arranges the text in numeric order and ignores any alphabetic text. Only the numbers 0 through 9 and symbols pertaining to numbers are recognized. These symbols include $, %, ( ), a decimal point, a comma, and the symbols for the four basic operations: + (addition), - (subtraction), * (multiplication), and / (division).

Date: In a date sort, Word sorts dates that are expressed in common date format, such as 05-15-01; 05/15/01; May 15, 2001; or 15 May 2001. Word does not sort dates that include abbreviated month names without periods. Dates expressed as a month, day, or year by themselves are also not sorted.

Sorting Text in Paragraphs

Text arranged in paragraphs can be sorted by the first character of the paragraph. This character can be a number, a symbol (such as $ or #), or a letter. The paragraphs to be sorted can be keyed at the left margin or indented with the Tab key. Unless you select paragraphs to be sorted, Word sorts the entire document.

Paragraphs can be sorted either alphanumerically, numerically, or by date. In an alphanumeric sort, punctuation marks or special symbols are sorted first, followed by numbers, and then text. If you sort paragraphs either alphanumerically or numerically, dates are treated as regular numbers.

To sort text in paragraphs, open the document containing the paragraphs to be sorted. (If the document contains text you do not want sorted with the paragraphs, select the paragraphs.) Click Table and then Sort. This displays the Sort Text dialog box shown in figure 21.2. At this dialog box, make sure *Paragraphs* displays in the Sort by text box, Ascending is selected, and then click OK or press Enter.

Sort Text Dialog Box

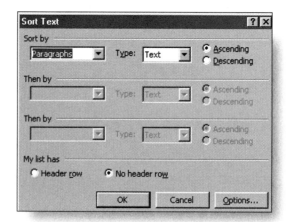

The Sort by option at the Sort Text dialog box has a default setting of *Paragraphs*. This default setting changes depending on the text in the document. For example, if you are sorting a table, the Sort by option has a default setting of *Column 1*. If you are sorting only the first word of each paragraph in the document, leave the Sort by option at the default of *Paragraphs*.

The Type option at the Sort Text dialog box has a default setting of *Text*. This can be changed to *Number* or *Date*. Figure 21.1 specifies how Word will sort numbers and dates. When Word sorts paragraphs that are separated by two hard returns (two strokes of the Enter key), the hard returns are removed and inserted at the beginning of the document.

Sorting Paragraphs Alphabetically

1. Open Bibliography.
2. Save the document with Save As and name it Ch 21, Ex 01.
3. Sort the paragraphs alphabetically by the last name by completing the following steps:
   a. Click Table and then Sort.
   b. At the Sort Text dialog box, make sure *Paragraphs* displays in the Sort by text box and the Ascending option is selected.
   c. Click OK or press Enter.
   d. Deselect the text.
   e. Delete the hard returns at the beginning of the document.
   f. Add space below each paragraph by completing the following steps:
      1) Press Ctrl + A to select the entire document.
      2) Click Format and then Paragraph.
      3) At the Paragraph dialog box with the Indents and Spacing tab selected, click the up-pointing triangle at the right side of the After text box (in the Spacing section) until *12 pt* displays in the text box.
      4) Click OK to close the dialog box.
4. Save the document again with the same name (Ch 21, Ex 01).
5. Print and then close Ch 21, Ex 01.

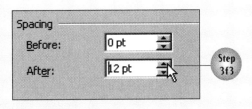

Changing Sort Options

The Sort by options will also vary depending on options at the Sort Options dialog box shown in figure 21.3. To display the Sort Options dialog box, open a document containing text to be sorted, click Table and then Sort. At the Sort Text dialog box, click the Options button.

Sort Options Dialog Box

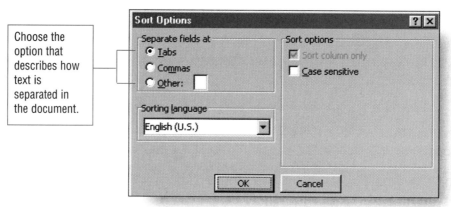

Choose the option that describes how text is separated in the document.

The Separate fields at section of the dialog box contains three options. The first option, Tabs, is selected by default. At this setting, Word assumes that text to be sorted is divided by tabs. This can be changed to Commas or Other. With the Other setting, you can specify the character that divides text to be sorted. For example, suppose a document contains first and last names in paragraphs separated by a space and you want to sort by the last name. To do this, you would click Other at the Sort Options dialog box, and then press the spacebar. (This inserts a space, which is not visible, in the Other text box.) If names are separated by a comma, click Commas as the separator.

The Sort Options dialog box contains two choices in the Sort Options section. The first choice, Sort column only, sorts only the selected column. This choice is dimmed unless a column of text is selected. If a check mark appears in the Case sensitive check box, Word will sort text so that a word whose first letter is a capital letter is sorted before any word with the same first letter in lowercase. This option is available only if *Text* is selected in the Type text box at the Sort dialog box.

When you make changes at the Sort Options dialog box, the choices available with Sort by at the Sort Text dialog box will vary. For example, if you click Other at the Sort Options dialog box, and then press the spacebar, the choices for Sort by at the Sort Text dialog box will include *Word 1, Word 2, Word 3*, etc.

exercise 2

Sorting Text Alphabetically by First and Last Name

1. At a clear document screen, key the text shown in figure 21.4. Begin each line of text at the left margin.
2. After keying the text, save the document and name it Ch 21, Ex 02.
3. With Ch 21, Ex 02 still open in the document screen, sort the text alphabetically by first name by completing the following steps:
   a. Click T<u>a</u>ble and then <u>S</u>ort.
   b. At the Sort Text dialog box, make sure *Paragraphs* displays in the Sort by text box and the <u>A</u>scending option is selected.
   c. Click OK or press Enter.
   d. Deselect the text.
4. Save the document again with the same name (Ch 21, Ex 02).
5. Print Ch 21, Ex 02.
6. With Ch 21, Ex 02 still displayed in the document screen, sort the text by the last name (second word) by completing the following steps:

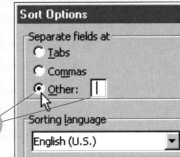

   a. Click T<u>a</u>ble and then <u>S</u>ort.
   b. At the Sort Text dialog box, click the <u>O</u>ptions button.
   c. At the Sort Options dialog box, click <u>O</u>ther, and then press the spacebar. **Step 6c**
   d. Click OK or press Enter.
   e. At the Sort Text dialog box, click the down-pointing triangle at the right side of the Sort by option, and then click *Word 2* at the drop-down list.
   f. Make sure the <u>A</u>scending option is selected.

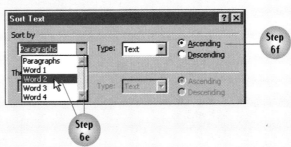

   g. Click OK or press Enter.
   h. Deselect the text.
7. Save the document again with the same name (Ch 21, Ex 02).
8. Print and then close Ch 21, Ex 02.

Step 6e

Step 6f

Exercise 2

Paul O'Shea, Development Manager
Nicole Clark, Director
Jack Takagawa, Assistant Director
Darryl Ellis, Trainer
Lynette Lagasi, Trainer
Timothy Watson, Director
Erica Torres, Director
Andrea Okamato, Director

Sorting Text in Columns

Text arranged in columns with tabs between the columns can be sorted alphabetically or numerically. Text in columns must be separated with tabs. When sorting text in columns, Word sorts by *fields*. Text keyed at the left margin is considered *Field 1*, text keyed at the first tab is considered *Field 2,* and so on. To sort text arranged in columns, display the Sort Text dialog box, and then click the Options button. At the Sort Options dialog box, make sure Tabs is selected in the Separate fields at section of the dialog box, and then click OK or press Enter. At the Sort Text dialog box, display the appropriate field number in the Sort by text box, and then click OK or press Enter.

When sorting text in columns, only one tab can be inserted between columns when keying the text. If you press the Tab key more than once between columns, Word recognizes each tab as a separate column. In this case, the field number you specify may correspond to an empty column rather than the desired column.

Sorting Text in Columns

1. At a clear document screen, create the document shown in figure 21.5 by completing the following steps:
   a. Set left tabs on the Ruler at the 0.5-inch mark, the 2.5-inch mark, and the 5-inch mark.
   b. Key the text in columns as shown in figure 21.5. Press the Tab key before keying each entry in the first column. (Be sure to press the Tab key before keying the first column.) Do not press the Enter key after the last entry *(2988)* in the third column.
2. Save the document and name it Ch 21, Ex 03.

3. With Ch 21, Ex 03 still displayed in the document screen, sort the first column alphabetically by last name by completing the following steps:
   a. Select the text in all three columns *except* the headings.
   b. Click T<u>a</u>ble and then <u>S</u>ort.
   c. At the Sort Text dialog box, click the <u>O</u>ptions button.
   d. At the Sort Options dialog box, click <u>T</u>abs in the Separate fields at section of the dialog box.

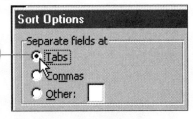

   e. Click OK or press Enter to close the Sort Options dialog box.
   f. At the Sort Text dialog box, click the down-pointing triangle at the right side of the Sort by text box, and then click *Field 2* at the drop-down list. (*Field 2* is the first tab.)
   g. Make sure <u>A</u>scending is selected.
   h. Click OK or press Enter.
   i. Deselect the text.

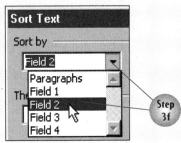

4. Save the document again with the same name (Ch 21, Ex 03).
5. Print Ch 21, Ex 03.
6. With Ch 21, Ex 03 still open in the document screen, sort the third column of text numerically by completing the following steps:
   a. Select the text in all three columns except the headings.
   b. Click T<u>a</u>ble and then <u>S</u>ort.
   c. At the Sort Text dialog box, click the <u>O</u>ptions button.
   d. At the Sort Options dialog box, click <u>T</u>abs in the Separate fields at section of the dialog box.
   e. Click OK or press Enter to close the Sort Options dialog box.
   f. At the Sort Text dialog box, click the down-pointing triangle at the right side of the Sort by text box, and then click *Field 4* at the drop-down list. (*Field 4* is the third tab.)
   g. Make sure *Number* displays in the Type text box. (If not, click the down-pointing triangle at the right side of the Type text box, and then click *Number* from the drop-down list.)
   h. Make sure <u>A</u>scending is selected.
   i. Click OK or press Enter.
   j. Deselect the text.
7. Save the document again with the same name (Ch 21, Ex 03).
8. Print and then close Ch 21, Ex 03.

figure

21.5   *Exercise 3*

Employee	Department	Ext.
Clark, Nicole	Human Resources	3221
Takagawa, Jack	Human Resources	4120
Watson, Timothy	Administrative Services	1094
Torres, Erica	Research	5530
Baxter, Lisa	Administrative Services	2287
Marcus, Leigh	Support Services	5338
Gibson, Todd	Research	2988

exercise 4

Sorting Text by Date

1. At a clear document screen, create the document shown in figure 21.6. (Set left tabs for the columns, including the first column. You determine the tab settings. Be sure to press the Tab key before keying each entry in the first column.)
2. Save the document and name it Ch 21, Ex 04.
3. With Ch 21, Ex 04 still displayed in the document screen, sort the second column by date by completing the following steps:
   a. Select the text in all three columns *except* the title.
   b. Click T̲able and then S̲ort.
   c. At the Sort Text dialog box, click the O̲ptions button.
   d. At the Sort Options dialog box, click T̲abs in the Separate fields at section of the dialog box.
   e. Click OK or press Enter to close the Sort Options dialog box.
   f. At the Sort Text dialog box, click the down-pointing triangle at the right side of the Sort by text box, and then click *Field 3* at the drop-down list. (*Field 3* is the second tab.)
   g. Make sure *Date* appears in the T̲ype text box and A̲scending is selected.
   h. Click OK or press Enter.
   i. Deselect the text.
4. Save the document again with the same name (Ch 21, Ex 04).
5. Print and then close Ch 21, Ex 04.

Step 3g

Step 3f

Sort Text dialog box:

Sort Text

Sort by

Field 3 — Type: Date — Ascending / Descending

Paragraphs / Field 1 / Field 2 / Field 3 / Field 4 — Type: Text — Ascending / Descending

figure
21.6

Exercise 4

TRAINING SCHEDULE

Desktop Publishing	09/05/01	1:00 - 3:00 p.m.
Word Processing	10/04/01	9:00 - 11:00 a.m.
Database Management	08/23/01	1:30 - 3:30 p.m.
Spreadsheet	09/12/01	2:00 - 3:30 p.m.

Sorting on More than One Field

When sorting text, you can sort on more than one field. For example, in the text shown in the columns in figure 21.7, you can sort the text alphabetically by school name and then tell Word to sort the last names alphabetically within the school names. To do this, you would tell Word to sort on *Field 3* (the second tab), and then sort on *Field 2* (the first tab). Word sorts the second column of text (*Field 3*) alphabetically by school name and then sorts the names in the first column of text (*Field 2*) by last name. This results in the columns displaying as shown in figure 21.8.

figure
21.7

Columns

Employee	School	Ext.
Sandifer, Tara	Oakridge E. S.	6644
Dean, Jennifer	Emerald Heights E. S.	4435
Long, Christine	Oakridge E. S.	1203
Dowler, Blaine	Emerald Heights E. S.	3203
Anderson, Louise	Oakridge E. S.	6554

figure
21.8 *Sorted Columns*

Employee	School	Ext.
Dean, Jennifer	Emerald Heights E. S.	4435
Dowler, Blaine	Emerald Heights E. S.	3203
Anderson, Louise	Oakridge E. S.	6554
Long, Christine	Oakridge E. S.	1203
Sandifer, Tara	Oakridge E. S.	6644

Notice that the school names in the second column in figure 21.8 are alphabetized and that the last names *within* the school names are alphabetized. For example, *Anderson* is sorted before *Long* within *Oakridge E. S.*

exercise

Sorting on Two Fields

1. Open Ch 21, Ex 03.
2. Save the document with Save As and name it Ch 21, Ex 05.
3. Make sure there is no blank line at the end of the document. If there is, delete it.
4. Sort the text in columns alphabetically by department and then alphabetically by last name by completing the following steps:
   a. Select the text in all three columns *except* the headings.
   b. Display the Sort Text dialog box.
   c. At the Sort Text dialog box, click the Options button.
   d. At the Sort Options dialog box, click Tabs in the Separate fields at section of the dialog box.
   e. Click OK or press Enter to close the Sort Options dialog box.
   f. At the Sort Text dialog box, click the down-pointing triangle at the right side of the Sort by text box, and then click *Field 3* at the drop-down list. (*Field 3* is the second tab.)
   g. Click the down-pointing triangle at the right side of the Then by text box and then click *Field 2* at the drop-down list.
   h. Make sure Ascending is selected.
   i. Click OK or press Enter.
   j. Deselect the text.
5. Save the document again with the same name (Ch 21, Ex 05).
6. Print and then close Ch 21, Ex 05.

Specifying a Header Row

The Sort Text dialog box contains the option Header row in the My list has section. If a document contains only columns of text with headings, you can use this option to tell Word to sort all text except for the headings of the columns.

Sorting Text in Columns with a Header Row

1. Open Ch 21, Ex 05.
2. Save the document with Save As and name it Ch 21, Ex 06.
3. Sort the third column of text numerically by the extension number by completing the following steps:
    a. With the columns displayed in the document screen, position the insertion point anywhere within the document.
    b. Display the Sort Text dialog box.
    c. At the Sort Text dialog box, click Header row in the My list has section of the dialog box.
    d. Click the Options button.
    e. At the Sort Options dialog box, make sure Tabs is selected in the Separate fields at section of the dialog box. (If not, click Tabs.)
    f. Click OK or press Enter to close the Sort Options dialog box.
    g. At the Sort Text dialog box, click the down-pointing triangle at the right side of the Sort by text box, and then click *Ext.* at the drop-down list.
    h. Make sure *Number* displays in the Type list box and Ascending is selected.
    i. If there is any text displayed in the Then by text box, click the down-pointing triangle to the right of the box, and then click *(none)* at the drop-down list.
    j. Click OK or press Enter.
    k. Deselect the text.
4. Save the document again with the same name (Ch 21, Ex 06).
5. Print and then close Ch 21, Ex 06.

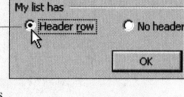

Sorting Text in Tables

Sorting text in columns within tables is very similar to sorting columns of text separated by tabs. The same principles that apply to sorting columns of text also apply to sorting text within table columns. If a table contains a header row, you can tell Word not to include the header row when sorting by clicking Header row at the Sort dialog box. (The Sort Text dialog box becomes the Sort dialog box when sorting a table.) You can also select the cells in the table, except the header row, and then complete the sort.

If Header row is selected at the Sort dialog box, the information in the header row becomes the Sort by options. For example, in the table shown in figure 21.9, if Header row is selected, the Sort by options are *Salesperson, January Sales,* and *February Sales*.

Table

Salesperson	January Sales	February Sales
Tirado, Jessica	120,440.35	130,302.45
Stanton, Kenneth	149,895.05	155,784.25
Madison, Ramon	180,320.40	193,100.55
Fiscus, Marlana	200,345.10	210,450.25

Sorting Text Alphabetically in a Table

1. Open Table 03.
2. Save the document with Save As and name it Ch 21, Ex 07.
3. Sort the text alphabetically in the first column by completing the following steps:

a. Position the insertion point anywhere within the table.
b. Click T<u>a</u>ble and then <u>S</u>ort.
c. At the Sort dialog box, click Header <u>r</u>ow in the My list has section of the dialog box.

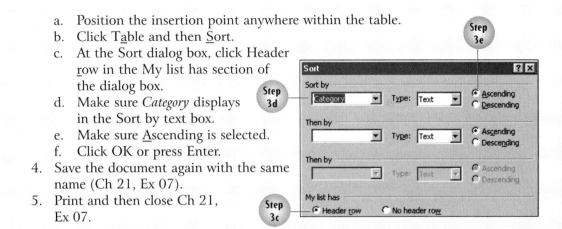

d. Make sure *Category* displays in the Sort by text box.
e. Make sure <u>A</u>scending is selected.
f. Click OK or press Enter.
4. Save the document again with the same name (Ch 21, Ex 07).
5. Print and then close Ch 21, Ex 07.

In exercise 7, you selected Header <u>r</u>ow at the Sort dialog box. You can also sort text in a table by first selecting the cells you want sorted and then displaying the Sort dialog box.

Sorting Selected Text in a Table

1. Open Table 04.
2. Save the document with Save As and name it Ch 21, Ex 08.
3. Sort the numbers in the second column in descending order by completing the following steps:
    a. Select all the cells in the table except the cells in the first row.
    b. Click T<u>a</u>ble and then <u>S</u>ort.
    c. At the Sort dialog box, click the down-pointing triangle at the right side of the Sort by text box, and then click *Column 2* at the drop-down list.

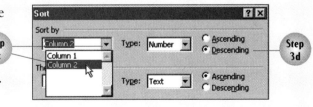

    d. Click <u>D</u>escending.
    e. Click OK or press Enter.
4. With the insertion point positioned anywhere in the table, display the Table AutoFormat dialog box, and then apply the *Classic 2* format.
5. Save the document again with the same name (Ch 21, Ex 08).
6. Print and then close Ch 21, Ex 08.

Sorting Records in a Data Source

In an earlier chapter, you learned how to create a data source document. When a data source document is opened from a main document, the Database toolbar displays below the Formatting toolbar. You can also display the Database toolbar without opening the main document by clicking View, pointing to Toolbars, and then clicking Database. Another method is to right-click the Standard or Formatting toolbar and then click Database.

Records in a data source can be sorted with the Sort Ascending and Sort Descending buttons on the Database toolbar. In addition to sorting with the buttons on the Database toolbar, you can sort a data source as you learned in the previous section of this chapter, "Sorting Text in Tables." This is because a data source is established in a table.

Sort
Ascending

Sort
Descending

Sorting Text in a Data Source Using the Database Toolbar

1. Sort the records in the Client list ds document alphabetically by last name by completing the following steps:
   a. Open Client list ds.
   b. Save the document with Save As and name it Ch 21, Ex 09.
   c. Display the Database toolbar by right-clicking the Standard toolbar and then clicking Database at the drop-down list.
   d. Position the insertion point in any cell in the *LastName* column.
   e. Click the Sort Ascending button on the Database toolbar.
   f. Turn off the display of the Database toolbar by right-clicking the Standard toolbar and then clicking Database at the drop-down list.

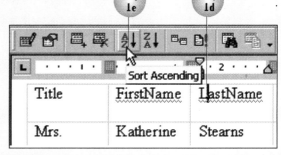

2. Save the document again with the same name (Ch 21, Ex 09).
3. Print and then close Ch 21, Ex 09.

Text in a data source document can also be sorted like text in a normal table. In exercise 10, you will sort the records numerically by Zip Code.

exercise 10

Sorting Text Numerically in a Data Source Document

1. Sort the records in the Client list ds document numerically by Zip Code by completing the following steps:
   a. Open Client list ds.
   b. Save the document with Save As and name it Ch 21, Ex 10.
   c. Position the insertion point in any cell in the table.
   d. Display the Sort dialog box.
   e. At the Sort dialog box, click Header row in the My list has section of the dialog box.
   f. Click the down-pointing triangle at the right side of the Sort by text box and then click *PostalCode* at the drop-down list. (You will need to scroll down the list to display *PostalCode*.)
   g. Make sure *Number* displays in the Type text box.
   h. Make sure Ascending is selected. (If not, click Ascending.)
   i. Click OK or press Enter.
   j. Deselect the text.
2. Save the document again with the same name (Ch 21, Ex 10).
3. Print and then close Ch 21, Ex 10.

Sorting at the Query Options Dialog Box

In addition to the two methods just described for sorting records in a data source, you can also sort records at the Query Options dialog box with the Sort Records tab selected. To display the Query Options dialog box shown in figure 21.10, open a main document, and then click the Mail Merge Helper button on the Mail Merge toolbar. At the Mail Merge dialog box, click the Query Options button. At the Query Options dialog box, click the Sort Records tab.

figure
21.10

Query Options Dialog Box with Sort Records Tab Selected

exercise 11

Sorting Text in a Data Source Document at the Query Options Dialog Box

1. Sort the records alphabetically by City in the Client list ds data source document attached to the Open house md main document by completing the following steps:
   a. Open Open house md.
   b. Click the Mail Merge Helper button on the Mail Merge toolbar.
   c. At the Merge dialog box, click the Query Options button.
   d. At the Query Options dialog box, click the Sort Records tab.
   e. At the Query Options dialog box with the Sort Records tab selected, click the down-pointing triangle at the right side of the Sort by text box, and then click *City* at the drop-down list.
   f. Make sure Ascending is selected.
   g. Click OK or press Enter.
   h. At the Merge dialog box, click the Close button.
   i. Click the Edit Data Source button on the Mail Merge toolbar.
   j. At the Data Form dialog box, click the View Source button.
2. With the data source document displayed, click the Print button on the Standard toolbar.
3. Close Client list ds without saving the changes.
4. Close Open house md without saving the changes.

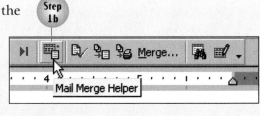

Step 1b

Mail Merge Helper

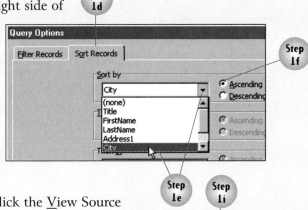

Step 1d

Step 1f

Step 1e

Step 1i

Edit Data Source

Selecting Records

If you have created a main document and a data source document to produce personalized form letters, there may be situations that arise where you want to merge the main document with specific records in the data source. For example, you may want to send a letter to customers with a specific Zip Code or who live in a certain city.

With options from the Query Options dialog box with the Filter Records tab selected, shown in figure 21.11, you can select records for merging with the main document that meet certain criteria. For example, in exercise 12, you will select records of clients with a Zip Code higher than 10300.

figure
21.11

Query Options Dialog Box with Filter Records Tab Selected

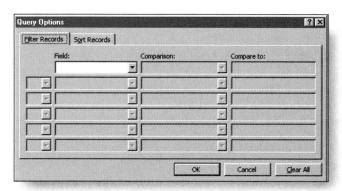

When you select a field from the Field drop-down list, Word automatically inserts *Equal to* in the Comparison text box. There are other comparisons you can make. Clicking the down-pointing triangle to the right of the Comparison text box causes a drop-down list to display with these additional options: *Not equal to, Less than, Greater than, Less than or equal, Greater than or equal, is blank*, and *is not blank*. Use one of these options to create a select equation. For example, select all customers with a Zip Code higher than 90543 by clicking *PostalCode* at the Field drop-down list. Click the down-pointing triangle at the right of the Comparison text box and then click *Greater than*. Key **90543** in the Compare to text box.

exercise 12

Selecting Records with Specific Zip Codes

1. Select the records with a Zip Code higher than 10300 in the Client list ds data source document attached to the Open house md main document and then merge the records to a new document by completing the following steps:
   a. Open Open house md.
   b. Click the Mail Merge Helper button on the Mail Merge toolbar.
   c. At the Mail Merge Helper dialog box, click the Query Options button.
   d. At the Query Options dialog box, make sure the Filter Records tab is selected.

   e. Click the down-pointing triangle at the right of the Field text box, click the down-pointing triangle at the bottom of the vertical scroll bar until *PostalCode* is displayed, and then click *PostalCode*. (When *PostalCode* is inserted in the Field text box, Word inserts *Equal to* in the Comparison text box and positions the insertion point in the Compare to text box.)
   f. With the insertion point positioned in the Compare to text box, key **10300**.
   g. Click the down-pointing triangle at the right of the Comparison text box, and then click *Greater than* at the drop-down list.

h. Click OK or press Enter.
   i. At the Mail Merge Helper dialog box, click the <u>M</u>erge button.
   j. At the Merge dialog box, make sure *New document* displays in the Me<u>r</u>ge to text box, and then click the <u>M</u>erge button.
2. Save the merged document and name it Ch 21, Ex 12.
3. Print and then close Ch 21, Ex 12.
4. Close Open house md without saving the changes.

When a field is selected from the field drop-down list, Word automatically inserts *And* in the first box at the left side of the dialog box. This can be changed, if needed, to *Or*. With the *And* and *Or* options, you can specify more than one condition for selecting records. For example, in exercise 13, you will select all records of clients living in the cities of *Hopkinton* or *Bow*. If the Client list ds document contained another field such as a specific financial plan for each customer, you could select all customers in a specific city that subscribe to a specific financial plan. For this situation, you would use the *And* option.

If you want to clear the current options at the Query Options dialog box with the <u>F</u>ilter Records tab selected, click the <u>C</u>lear All button. This clears any text from text boxes and leaves the dialog box on the screen. Click Cancel if you want to close the Query Options dialog box without specifying any records.

exercise 13

Selecting Records Containing Specific Cities

1. Select the records in the Client list ds data source document attached to the Open house md main document that contain the city Hopkinton or Bow by completing the following steps:
   a. Open Open house md.
   b. Click the Mail Merge Helper button on the Mail Merge toolbar.
   c. At the Mail Merge Helper dialog box, click the <u>Q</u>uery Options button.
   d. At the Query Options dialog box, make sure the <u>F</u>ilter Records tab is selected.
   e. Click the down-pointing triangle to the right of the Field text box, click the down-pointing triangle at the bottom of the vertical scroll bar until *City* is displayed, and then click *City*.

   f. With the insertion point positioned in the Compare to text box, key **Hopkinton**.
   g. Click the down-pointing triangle to the right of the text box containing the word *And* (at the left side of the dialog box) and then click *Or* at the drop-down list.
   h. Click the down-pointing triangle to the right of the second Field text box, click the down-pointing triangle at the bottom of the vertical scroll bar until *City* is displayed, and then click *City*.
   i. With the insertion point positioned in the second Compare to text box (the one below the box containing *Hopkinton*), key **Bow**.

j. Click OK or press Enter.
k. At the Mail Merge Helper dialog box, click the Merge button.
l. At the Merge dialog box, make sure *New document* displays in the Merge to text box, and then click the Merge button.
2. Save the merged document and name it Ch 21, Ex 13.
3. Print and then close Ch 21, Ex 13.
4. Close Open house md without saving the changes.

chapter summary

➤ Word is a word processing program that includes some basic database functions. With the database functions, you can alphabetize information, arrange numbers numerically, or select specific records from a data source.

➤ Word lets you sort text in paragraphs, text in table rows, or records in a data source. You can also select specific records from a data source to be merged with a main document.

➤ Word can perform these three types of sorts: alphanumeric, numeric, and date.

➤ Text arranged in paragraphs can be sorted by the first character of the paragraph at the Sort Text dialog box.

➤ The Sort by option at the Sort Text dialog box has a default setting of *Paragraph*. This default setting changes depending on the text in the document and the options specified at the Sort Options dialog box.

➤ Text arranged in columns with tabs between the columns can be sorted alphabetically or numerically. Text keyed at the left margin is considered *Field 1*, text keyed at the first tab is considered *Field 2*, and so on.

➤ When sorting text, you can sort on more than one field.

➤ Use the option Header row in the My list has section of the Sort Text dialog box to tell Word to sort all text in columns except for the headings of the columns.

➤ Sorting text in columns within tables is very similar to sorting columns of text separated by tabs.

➤ Records in a data source can be sorted in the same way as text in a table, or use the Sort Ascending and Sort Descending buttons on the Database toolbar.

➤ Records can also be sorted at the Query Options dialog box with the Sort Records tab selected.

➤ With options from the Query Options dialog box with the Filter Records tab selected, specific records can be selected for merging with the main document.

commands review

	Mouse/Keyboard
Display Sort Text dialog box	Table, Sort
Display Sort Options dialog box	Table, Sort, Options

thinking offline

Completion: In the space provided at the right, indicate the correct term, command, or number.

1. With the sorting feature, you can sort text in paragraphs, records in a data source, or this type of text.

2. These three types of sorts can be performed by Word's sort feature: alphanumeric, numeric, and this.

3. Sort text in paragraphs at this dialog box.

4. This is the default selection at the Separate fields at section of the Sort Options dialog box.

5. When sorting columns, text keyed at the first tab is considered to be this field number.

6. Click this option at the Sort Text dialog box to tell Word not to include the column headings in the sort.

7. With the insertion point positioned in a table, clicking Table, and then Sort causes this dialog box to display.

8. Select specific records from a data source to be merged with the main document from this dialog box.

9. To complete the last step to select all customers from a data source that have a balance higher than $500, key **500** at this text box.

working hands-on

Assessment 1

1. At a clear document screen, create the document shown in figure 21.12.
2. Save the document and name it Ch 21, SA 01.
3. Sort the names (not the title) alphabetically by last name.
4. Save the sorted document again with the same name (Ch 21, SA 01).
5. Print and then close Ch 21, SA 01.

figure

21.12   *Assessment 1*

KENTWOOD SCHOOL DISTRICT

Shing, Linda, Superintendent
Valenzuela, Rodney, Assistant Superintendent
Brennan, Sarah, Curriculum Specialist
Goodrow, Gabriel, Support Specialist
Griffin-Leon, Janet, Information Specialist
Olmsted, David, Newsletter Editor
Long, Christine, Assistant Newsletter Editor

Assessment 2

1. At a clear document screen, create the document shown in figure 21.13. (Set tabs for each column of text in the document.)
2. Save the document and name it Ch 21, SA 02.
3. Sort the columns of text alphabetically by last name in the first column. *(Hint: Select the columns of text but not the title, subtitle, and headings.)*
4. Print Ch 21, SA 02.
5. Sort the columns of text by the date of hire in the third column.
6. Print Ch 21, SA 02.
7. Sort the columns of text alphabetically by the department name and then alphabetically by last name.
8. Save the document again with the same name (Ch 21, SA 02).
9. Print and then close Ch 21, SA 02.

figure

21.13   *Assessment 2*

COLEMAN DEVELOPMENT CORPORATION

New Employees

Employee	Department	Hire Date
Wilson, Grace	Financial Services	02/03/99
Prada, Craig	Human Resources	04/14/99
McClure, Anthony	Administrative Services	03/10/99
Sok, Neay	Financial Services	02/10/99
Woodhouse, Leanne	Support Services	04/07/99
Tucker, Sandra	Human Resources	03/24/99
Mattila, Diana	Administrative Services	02/17/99

Assessment 3

1. Open Table 02.
2. Save the document with Save As and name it Ch 21, SA 03.
3. Sort the text alphabetically by *State* in the first column of the table. (Make sure no text displays in the Then by text box.)
4. Print Ch 21, SA 03.
5. Sort the text numerically by *1st Qtr.* in ascending order in the second column of the table.
6. Display the Table AutoFormat dialog box and apply a table formatting of your choosing to the table.
7. Save the document again with the same name (Ch 21, SA 03).
8. Print and then close Ch 21, SA 03.

Assessment 4

1. Create a main document for envelopes that has the Client list ds data source document attached and then merge the envelope with those records in Client list ds with the city *Concord*. Merge to a new document.
2. Save the merged document and name it Ch 21, SA 04.
3. Print and then close Ch 21, SA 04.
4. Close the envelope main document without saving the changes.

Chapter 22

Creating Outlines, Master Documents, and Subdocuments

PERFORMANCE OBJECTIVES

Upon successful completion of chapter 22, you will be able to:

- Display a document in Outline view.
- Create an outline.
- Assign headings in an outline.
- Collapse and expand outline headings.
- Organize an outline.
- Number an outline.
- Navigate in a document using the Document Map feature.
- Create a master document and subdocuments.
- Expand, collapse, open, close, rearrange, split, combine, remove, and rename subdocuments.

Word's outlining feature will format headings within a document as well as let you view formatted headings and body text in a document. With the outlining feature you can quickly see an overview of a document by collapsing parts of a document so that only the headings show. With headings collapsed, you can perform such editing functions as moving or deleting sections of a document.

Word also includes the Document Map feature. This feature is similar to the outlining feature. The Document Map is a separate pane that displays an outline of the document's headings. In Document Map, you can change heading levels and jump to specific headings in a document.

For some documents such as a book or procedures manual, consider creating a master document. A master document contains a number of separate documents called subdocuments. In this chapter, you will learn how to create a master document using subdocuments.

Creating an Outline

To create an outline, you identify particular headings and subheadings within a document as certain heading levels. The Outline view is used to assign particular heading levels to text. You can also enter text and edit text while working in Outline view. To change to Outline view, click the Outline View button at the left side of the horizontal scroll bar, or click <u>V</u>iew, and then <u>O</u>utline. Figure 22.1 shows the Report 01 document as it will appear in exercise 1 with heading formatting applied in Outline view.

Outline View

Document in Outline View

Outlining Toolbar

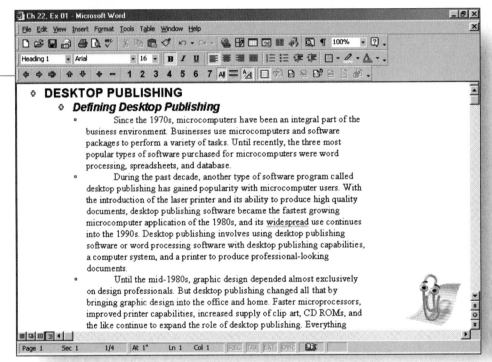

In figure 22.1, the title *DESKTOP PUBLISHING* is identified as a first-level heading, the heading *Defining Desktop Publishing* is identified as a second-level heading, and the paragraphs following are normal text.

When a document contains headings and text that have been formatted in the Outline view, each paragraph is identified as a particular heading level or as normal text. Paragraphs are identified by *outline selection symbols* that appear in the selection bar at the left side of the screen. Figure 22.2 describes the three outline selection symbols and what they indicate.

22.2 *Outline Selection Symbols*

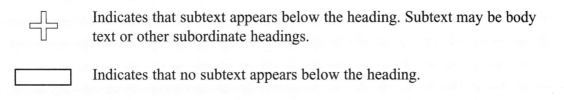

Indicates that subtext appears below the heading. Subtext may be body text or other subordinate headings.

Indicates that no subtext appears below the heading.

Indicates the paragraph is normal text.

The outline selection symbols can be used to select text in the document. To do this, position the arrow pointer on the outline selection symbol next to text you want to select until it turns into a four-headed arrow, and then click the left mouse button.

Assigning Headings

When a document is displayed in Outline view, the Outlining toolbar displays below the Formatting toolbar as shown in figure 22.1. Use buttons on this toolbar to assign various level headings and outline numbers to paragraphs.

When you initially display a document in Outline view, each paragraph is identified as a normal text paragraph. To identify certain paragraphs as heading levels, use the arrow buttons at the left side of the Outlining toolbar. These buttons are described in figure 22.3 along with the other buttons on the Outlining toolbar. (The master and subdocument buttons on the Outlining toolbar are described later in this chapter.)

figure

22.3 *Outlining Toolbar Buttons*

Button	Name	Action
⇦	Promote	Promotes heading (and its body text) by one level; promotes body text to the heading level of the preceding heading.
⇨	Demote	Demotes heading by one level; demotes body text to the heading level below the preceding heading.

	Demote to Body Text	Demotes heading to body text.
	Move Up	Moves selected paragraph(s) to appear before first visible paragraph that precedes selected paragraph(s).
	Move Down	Moves selected paragraph(s) to appear after first visible paragraph that follows selected paragraph(s).
	Expand	Expands first heading level below currently selected heading.
	Collapse	Collapses body text into heading and then collapses lowest heading levels into higher heading levels.
	Show Headings 1 through 7	Displays all headings and text through lowest level button chosen.
	Show All Headings	Displays all text if some collapsed; displays only headings if all text already expanded.
	Show First Line Only	Switches between displaying all body text or only first line of each paragraph.
	Show Formatting	Displays outline with or without character formatting.

Promote

To change a paragraph that is identified as normal text to a first-level heading, position the insertion point on any character in the text (or select the text), and then click the Promote button on the Outlining toolbar. This applies the Heading 1 style to the paragraph. The Heading 1 style is a style that has been predefined by Word. This style displays in the Style button on the Formatting toolbar (first button at left side). The Heading 1 style sets the text in 16-point Arial bold.

Demote

To change a paragraph to a second-level heading, position the insertion point anywhere within the text, and then click the Demote button. This applies the Heading 2 style to the text. The Heading 2 style sets text in 14-point Arial bold italic and indents the text 0.5 inch. Figure 22.4 shows the formatting that is applied for each heading level.

figure
22.4   *Heading Formatting*

Heading 1	16-point Arial bold; 12 pt spacing before paragraph and 3 pt after
Heading 2	14-point Arial bold italic; 12 pt spacing before paragraph and 3 pt after
Heading 3	13-point Arial; 12 pt spacing before paragraph and 3 pt after
Heading 4	14-point Times New Roman bold; 12 pt spacing before paragraph and 3 pt after
Heading 5	13-point Times New Roman bold italic; 12 pt spacing before paragraph and 3 pt after
Heading 6	11-point Times New Roman bold; 12 pt spacing before paragraph and 3 pt after
Heading 7	12-point Times New Roman; 12 pt spacing before paragraph and 3 pt after
Heading 8	12-point Times New Roman italic; 12 pt spacing before paragraph and 3 pt after
Heading 9	11-point Arial; 12 pt spacing before paragraph and 3 pt after

exercise

Formatting a Document with Buttons on the Outlining Toolbar

1. Open Report 01.
2. Save the document with Save As and name it Ch 22, Ex 01.
3. Change to the Outline view by clicking the Outline View button at the left side of the horizontal scroll bar.
4. Promote and demote heading levels by completing the following steps:
   a. Position the insertion point anywhere in the title *DESKTOP PUBLISHING* and then click the Promote button on the Outlining toolbar. (*Heading 1* will display in the Style button on the Formatting toolbar.)

   b. Position the insertion point anywhere in the heading *Defining Desktop Publishing* and then click the Demote button on the Outlining toolbar. (*Heading 2* will display in the Style button on the Formatting toolbar.)

   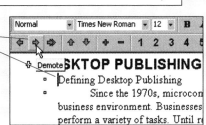

    c.   Position the insertion point anywhere in the heading *Initiating the Desktop Publishing Process* and then click the Promote button on the Outlining toolbar. (*Heading 2* will display in the Style button on the Formatting toolbar.)

    d.   Position the insertion point anywhere in the heading *Planning the Publication* and then click the Promote button on the Outlining toolbar. (*Heading 2* will display in the Style button on the Formatting toolbar.)

    e.   Position the insertion point anywhere in the heading *Creating the Content* and then click the Promote button on the Outlining toolbar. (*Heading 2* will display in the Style button on the Formatting toolbar.)

5. Save the document again with the same name (Ch 22, Ex 01).

6. Print and then close Ch 22, Ex 01.

You can also promote or demote a heading in the Outline view by dragging the selection symbol to the left or right 0.5 inch. For example, to demote text identified as a Heading 1 to Heading 2, position the arrow pointer on the plus symbol before the Heading 1 text until it turns into a four-headed arrow, hold down the left mouse button, drag the mouse to the right until a gray vertical line displays down the screen, and then release the mouse button.

Complete similar steps to promote a heading. For example, to promote a Heading 2 to a Heading 1, position the arrow pointer on the plus symbol before the Heading 2 text until it turns into a four-headed arrow, hold down the left mouse button, drag the mouse to the left until a gray vertical bar displays with a small square attached, and then release the mouse button.

Demote to
Body Text

Another way to demote a heading is to position the insertion point in the heading text, and then click the Demote to Body Text button on the Outlining toolbar.

Demoting Headings in a Document

1. Open Ch 22, Ex 01.

2. Save the document with Save As and name it Ch 22, Ex 02.

3. Make sure the document displays in Outline view and then demote the heading *Creating the Content* to Heading 3 level by completing the following steps:

    a.   Press Ctrl + End to move the insertion point to the end of the document and then scroll up in the document until *Creating the Content* is visible (located toward the end of the document).

    b.   Position the mouse pointer on the plus symbol that displays before *Creating the Content* until the mouse pointer turns into a four-headed arrow.

    c.   Hold down the left mouse button, drag the mouse to the right until a gray vertical line displays down the screen, and then release the mouse button.

4. Demote the heading *Planning the Publication* to a Heading 3 level by completing steps similar to those in step 3.
5. Save the document again with the same name (Ch 22, Ex 02).
6. Print and then close Ch 22, Ex 02.

Collapsing and Expanding Outline Headings

One of the major benefits of working in the Outline view is the ability to see a condensed outline of your document without all of the text in between headings or subheadings. Word lets you collapse a heading level in an outline. This causes any text or subsequent lower heading levels to disappear temporarily. When heading levels are collapsed, viewing the outline of a document is much easier. For example, when an outline is collapsed, you can see an overview of the entire document and move easily to different locations in the document. You can also move headings and their subordinate headings to new locations in the outline.

The ability to collapse and expand headings in an outline provides flexibility in using Word's outline feature. One popular use of this capability is to move quickly from one portion of a document to another. For example, if you are working at the beginning of a lengthy document and want to move to a particular section, but you cannot remember the name of the heading in that section or the page number on which it is located, switch to the Outline view, collapse the entire outline, position the insertion point in the desired heading, and then expand the outline.

Another popular use of the collapse and expand feature is in maintaining consistency between various headings. While creating a particular heading, you may need to refer to the previous heading. To do this, switch to the Outline view, collapse the outline, and the previous heading is visible.

To collapse the entire outline, click the Show Heading button containing the number of headings desired. For example, if a document contains three heading levels, clicking the Show Heading 2 button on the Outlining toolbar will collapse the outline so only Heading 1 and Heading 2 text is displayed.

Show Heading

Click the Show All Headings button to deactivate the button and the document collapses displaying only heading text, not body text. Click the Show All Headings button again to activate it and the document expands to show all heading levels and body text. If you click the Show All Headings button to deactivate it, the document would display as shown in figure 22.5. (The document in figure 22.5 is the document from figure 22.1.) When a heading is collapsed, a gray horizontal line displays beneath it.

Show All Headings

figure

22.5 *Collapsed Outline*

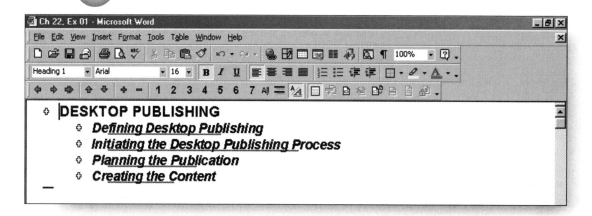

exercise 3

Collapsing an Outline

1. Open Ch 22, Ex 01.
2. Save the document with Save As and name it Ch 22, Ex 03.
3. Make the following changes to the document:
   a. Make sure the document displays in Outline view.
   b. Click the Show All Headings button on the Outlining toolbar to deactivate it.
   c. With the outline collapsed, click the white plus symbol preceding *Defining Desktop Publishing*.
   d. With the heading selected, press the Delete key. (This deletes the heading and all text below the heading.)
4. Save the document again with the same name (Ch 22, Ex 03).
5. Print and then close Ch 22, Ex 03. (This will print the collapsed outline, not the entire document.)

Collapse

Expand

To collapse all of the text beneath a particular heading (including the text following any subsequent headings), position the insertion point within the heading, and then click the Collapse button on the Outlining toolbar. To make the text appear again, click the Expand button on the Outlining toolbar. For example, if you collapsed the first second-level heading shown in the document in figure 22.1, the document would display as shown in figure 22.6.

figure
22.6 *Collapsed Second-Level Heading*

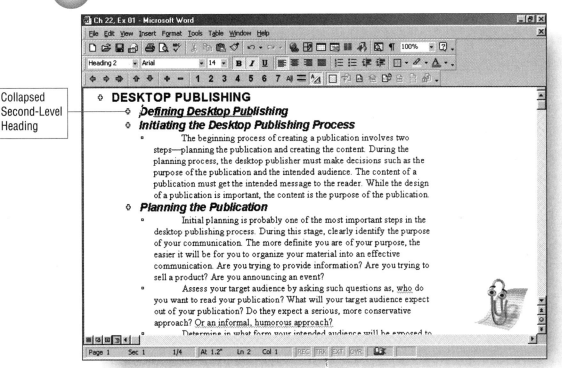

Collapsed
Second-Level
Heading

Collapsing and Expanding an Outline

1. Open Report 04.
2. Save the document with Save As and name it Ch 22, Ex 04.
3. Make the following changes to the document:
   a. Change to the Outline view.
   b. Promote the title *MODULE 3: DESIGNING A NEWSLETTER* to Heading 1.
   c. Demote the heading *Applying Desktop Publishing Guidelines* to Heading 2.
   d. Promote the title *MODULE 4: CREATING NEWSLETTER LAYOUT* to Heading 1.
   e. Demote the heading *Choosing Paper Size and Type* to Heading 2.
   f. Promote the heading *Choosing Paper Weight* to Heading 2.
   g. Promote the heading *Creating Margins for Newsletters* to Heading 2.

4. Collapse and expand the document by completing the following steps:

   a. Position the insertion point anywhere in the title *MODULE 3: DESIGNING A NEWSLETTER* and then click the Collapse button on the Outlining toolbar. (This collapses the text in the first module so only the title and heading display.)

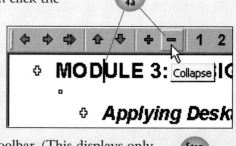

   b. Click the Expand button to expand the display of the text in the first module.

   c. With the insertion point still positioned anywhere in the title *MODULE 3: DESIGNING A NEWSLETTER,* click the Show Heading 1 button on the Outlining toolbar. (This displays only the two titles.)

   d. Click the Show Heading 2 button on the Outlining toolbar. (This displays the titles and headings.)

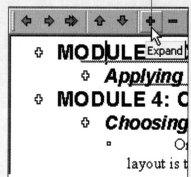

   e. Click the Expand button on the Outlining toolbar.

   f. Click the Show First Line Only button on the Outlining toolbar. (This displays only the first line of each paragraph in the first module.)

   g. Click the Show First Line Only button to deactivate it.

   h. Click the Show Heading 2 button on the Outlining toolbar. (This displays the titles and headings.)

   i. Click the white plus symbol preceding *Choosing Paper Weight.*

   j. With the heading selected, press the Delete key. (This deletes the heading and all text below the heading.)

   k. Click the Show All Headings button on the Outlining toolbar to activate it and display the entire document.

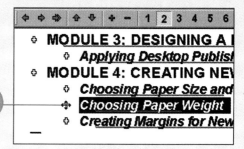

5. Save the document again with the same name (Ch 22, Ex 04).

6. Print and then close Ch 22, Ex 04.

Organizing an Outline

Collapsing and expanding headings within an outline is only part of the versatility offered by Word's outline feature. It also offers you the ability to rearrange an entire document by reorganizing an outline. Whole sections of a document can quickly be rearranged by moving the headings at the beginning of those sections. The text that is collapsed beneath the headings is moved at the same time.

For example, to move a second-level heading below other second-level headings, you would collapse the outline, select the second-level heading to be moved, and then click the Move Down button on the Outlining toolbar until the second-level heading is in the desired position.

Move Down

If headings are collapsed, you only need to select the heading and move it to the desired location. Any subsequent text that is hidden is moved automatically. You can also move headings in a document by positioning the arrow pointer on the plus symbol before the desired heading until it turns into a four-headed arrow, holding down the mouse button, dragging the heading to the desired location, and then releasing the mouse button. As you drag the mouse, a gray horizontal line displays in the document with an arrow attached. Use this horizontal line to help you move the heading to the desired location.

Moving Headings in a Document

1. Open Ch 22, Ex 01.
2. Save the document with Save As and name it Ch 22, Ex 05.
3. Make the following changes to the document:
   a. With the document displayed in Outline view, click the Show Heading 2 button on the Outlining toolbar.
   b. Move *Creating the Content* above *Planning the Publication* by completing the following steps:
      1) Position the insertion point anywhere in the heading *Creating the Content*.
      2) Click once on the Move Up button on the Outlining toolbar.

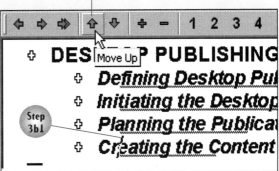

   c. Move the heading *Initiating the Desktop Publishing Process* below *Planning the Publication* by completing the following steps:
      1) Position the arrow pointer on the white plus symbol immediately left of the heading *Initiating the Desktop Publishing Process* until it turns into a four-headed arrow.

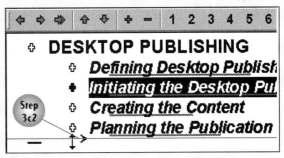

      2) Hold down the left mouse button, drag the mouse down until the gray horizontal line with the arrow attached is positioned below *Planning the Publication*, and then release the mouse button.
      3) Deselect the text.
4. Save the document again with the same name (Ch 22, Ex 05).
5. Print Ch 22, Ex 05. (Only the title and headings will print.)
6. Click the Show All Headings button on the Outlining toolbar to display the document text and then close the document.

Numbering an Outline

Headings in an outline can be automatically numbered with options from the Bullets and Numbering dialog box with the Outline Numbered tab selected. If headings in an outline are moved, inserted, or deleted, the headings are automatically renumbered by Word. Heading numbers become part of the document and display in the Normal and Print Layout views as well as the Outline view.

To number headings in an outline, display the document in the Outline view and then select the document text. With the document selected, click Format, and then Bullets and Numbering. At the Bullets and Numbering dialog box, click the Outline Numbered tab. At the Bullets and Numbering dialog box with the Outline Numbered tab selected, as shown in figure 22.7, click the desired numbering method, and then click OK.

figure

22.7

Bullets and Numbering Dialog Box with Outline Numbered Tab Selected

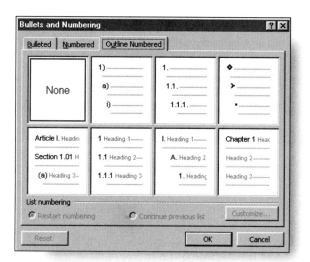

exercise

6

Numbering Headings in an Outline

1. Open Ch 22, Ex 04.
2. Save the document with Save As and name it Ch 22, Ex 06.

3. Make the following changes to the document:
   a. Click the Show Heading 2 button on the Outlining toolbar.
   b. Add numbering by completing the following steps:
      1) Press Ctrl + A to select all text in the document.
      2) Click Format, and then Bullets and Numbering.
      3) At the Bullets and Numbering dialog box, click the Outline Numbered tab.
      4) At the Bullets and Numbering dialog box with the Outline Numbered tab selected, click the third numbering option from the left in the bottom row.
      5) Click OK to close the dialog box.
   c. Move the title *MODULE 3: DESIGNING A NEWSLETTER* (and all the headings below it) below the title *MODULE 4: CREATING NEWSLETTER LAYOUT* (and all the headings below it).
   d. Change the module 3 title to module 4 and change the module 4 title to module 3 (since these titles were reversed).
4. Save the document again with the same name (Ch 22, Ex 06).
5. With the document still collapsed, print the document.
6. Close Ch 22, Ex 06.

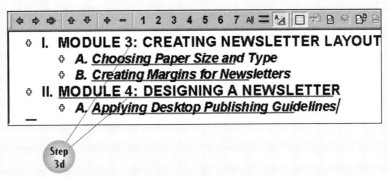

Document Mapping

Word 2000 includes a Document Map feature you can use to navigate easily in a document and keep track of your location within the document. The Document Map displays any headings that are formatted with Word's heading styles (Heading 1 through 9) or outline-level paragraph format. If there are no headings formatted with headings styles or outline levels, Document Map searches for paragraphs that look like headings, such as short lines set in a larger type size. If no headings are found, the Document Map pane is blank.

The Document Map is a separate pane that displays the outline of a document. To display the Document Map pane, click the Document Map button on the Standard toolbar. This displays the Document Map pane at the left side of the document as shown in figure 22.8. Figure 22.8 displays the document named Ch 22, Ex 04. The document Ch 22, Ex 04 contains headings with heading styles applied with buttons on the Outlining toolbar.

Document Map

figure
22.8

Document Map Pane

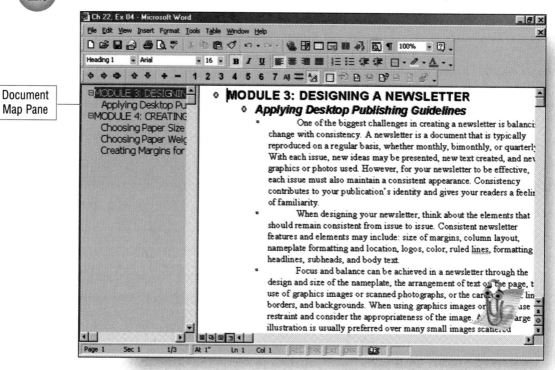

Document Map Pane

In the Document Map pane in figure 22.8, not all of the heading text is visible. To display the entire heading, position the arrow pointer on the heading and the heading text displays in a yellow box.

In exercise 7, you will display the Document Map for Report 01 and also Report 03. Neither of these documents contains headings that are formatted with Word's heading styles. However, Document Map will search the document and then display the short lines in the Document Map pane.

exercise
7

Displaying the Document Map Pane in a Document

1. Open Report 01.
2. Display the Document Map pane and move to different locations in the document by completing the following steps:
   a. Click the Document Map button on the Standard toolbar.

Step 2a

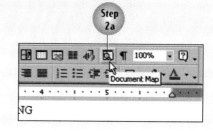

b. Click the heading *Creating the Content* that displays in the Document Map pane.
c. Click the heading *Defining Desktop Publishing* that displays in the Document Map pane.
d. Remove the Document Map pane by clicking the Document Map button on the Standard toolbar.

3. Close Report 01.
4. Open Report 03.
5. Display the Document Map pane and move to different locations in the document by completing the following steps:
   a. Click the Document Map button on the Standard toolbar.
   b. Click the heading *MODULE 2: PLANNING A NEWSLETTER*.
   c. Click the heading *MODULE 1: DEFINING NEWSLETTER ELEMENTS*.
   d. Remove the Document Map pane by clicking the Document Map button on the Standard toolbar.
6. Close Report 03.

If Word's heading styles have been applied to a document's heading, many of the same options on the Outlining toolbar are available in the Document Map pane. To display the options available, position the arrow pointer on a heading in the Document Map pane and then click the right mouse button. This displays the shortcut menu shown in figure 22.9.

figure

22.9 **Document Map Shortcut Menu**

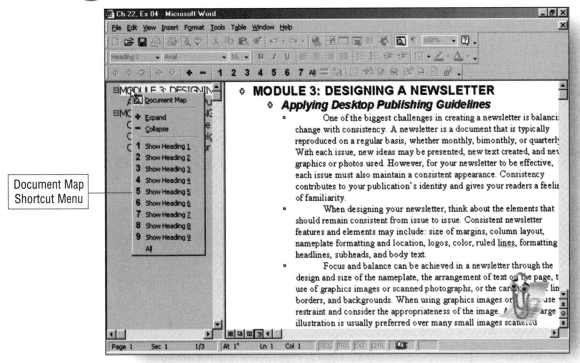

Document Map Shortcut Menu

At the shortcut menu, click the desired option. For example, to collapse text within a heading, position the arrow pointer on the heading, click the *right* mouse button, and then click the <u>C</u>ollapse option at the shortcut menu. This collapses the text so only the heading displays where the insertion point is positioned.

Collapsing and Expanding a Document Using the Document Map Pane

1. Open Ch 22, Ex 04.
2. Display the Document Map pane and collapse and expand the document by completing the following steps:
   a. Click the Document Map button on the Standard toolbar.
   b. Collapse the document so only first-level headings are displayed by completing the following steps:
      1) Position the arrow pointer on the heading *MODULE 3: DESIGNING A NEWSLETTER* that displays in the Document Map pane and then click the *right* mouse button.

         Step 2b2

      2) At the shortcut menu that displays, click the left mouse button on *Show Heading <u>1</u>*.
   c. Show first- and second-level headings. To do this, position the arrow pointer on either of the two headings in the Document Map pane, click the *right* mouse button, and then click *Show Heading <u>2</u>* at the shortcut menu.
   d. Position the arrow pointer on the heading *Creating Margins for Newsletters* and then click the left mouse button. (This moves the insertion point to that heading in the document window.)
   e. Expand the document by positioning the arrow pointer on any heading in the Document Map pane, clicking the *right* mouse button, and then clicking the left mouse button on *A<u>l</u>l* at the shortcut menu.
3. Remove the Document Map pane by clicking the Document Map button on the Standard toolbar.
4. Close Ch 22, Ex 04.

Creating a Master Document and Subdocuments

For projects containing a variety of parts or sections such as a reference guide or book, consider using a *master document*. A master document contains a number of separate documents referred to as *subdocuments*. A master document might be useful in a situation where several people are working on one project. Each person prepares a document for their part of the project and then the documents are included in a master document. A master document allows for easier editing of subdocuments. Rather than opening a large document for editing, you can open a subdocument, make changes, and those changes are reflected in the master document.

Create a new master document or format an existing document as a master document at the Outline view and the Master Document view. When you change to the Outline view, the Outlining toolbar displays with buttons for working with master documents and subdocuments. These buttons are shown in figure 22.10. The names and functions of some of the Outlining toolbar buttons for working with master documents and subdocuments may vary depending on what is selected in the document. Some buttons may display activated and others deactivated. An activated button displays on the toolbar with a light gray background.

figure

22.10   *Outlining Toolbar Buttons*

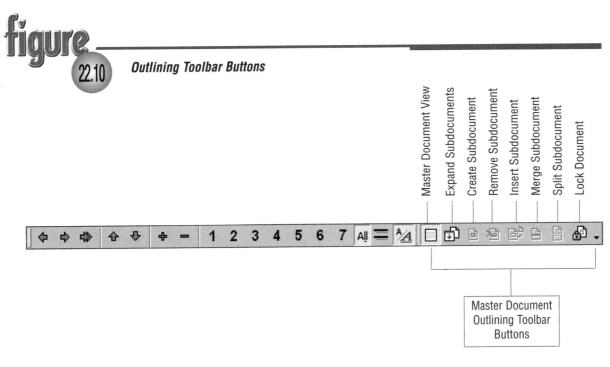

Master Document View
Expand Subdocuments
Create Subdocument
Remove Subdocument
Insert Subdocument
Merge Subdocument
Split Subdocument
Lock Document

Master Document Outlining Toolbar Buttons

When Outline View is selected, the Master Document View button on the Outlining toolbar is automatically activated (displays with a light gray background). With this button activated, collapsed subdocuments display surrounded by a light gray border line, and subdocument icons display.

Master Document View

Creating a Master Document

To create a master document, start at a clear document screen, and then key the text for the document; or, open an existing document. Identify the subdocuments by completing the following steps:

1. Change to the Outline view.
2. Make sure the Master Document View button is activated (light gray background).
3. Make sure heading level styles are applied to headings in the document.
4. Select the heading and text to be divided into a subdocument.
5. Click the Create Subdocument button on the Outlining toolbar. (Text specified as a subdocument displays surrounded by a thin gray line border and a subdocument icon displays in the upper left corner of the border.)

Create Subdocument

Word creates a subdocument for each heading at the top level within the selected text. For example, if selected text begins with Heading 1 text, Word creates a new subdocument at each Heading 1 in the selected text.

Save the master document in the same manner as a normal document. Word automatically assigns a document name to each subdocument using the first characters in the subdocument heading.

Opening and Closing a Master Document and Subdocument

Open a master document at the Open dialog box in the same manner as a normal document. Subdocuments in a master document display collapsed in the master document as shown in figure 22.11. This figure displays the master document named Master Doc Ch 22, Ex 09 that you will create in exercise 9. Notice that Word automatically converts subdocument names into hyperlinks. To open a subdocument, click the subdocument hyperlink. This displays the subdocument and also displays the Web toolbar.

figure

22.11

Master Doc Ch 22, Ex 09

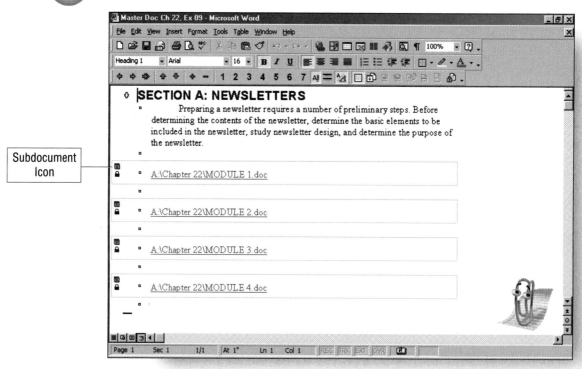

Subdocument Icon

To close a subdocument, click File and then Close or click the Close button that displays at the right side of the Menu bar. If you made any changes to the document, you will be asked if you want to save the changes. Closing a subdocument redisplays the master document and the subdocument hyperlink displays in a different color (identifying that the hyperlink has been used). Close a master document in the normal manner. You may also want to turn off the display of the Web toolbar.

Expanding/Collapsing Subdocuments

Open a master document and subdocuments are automatically collapsed. To expand subdocuments, click the Expand Subdocuments button on the Outlining toolbar. To collapse expanded subdocuments, click the Collapse Subdocuments button on the Outlining toolbar.

Expand
Subdocuments

Collapse
Subdocuments

Locking/Unlocking a Subdocument

By default, a subdocument is unlocked so that the subdocument can be viewed or edited. If you want a subdocument available for viewing but not editing, lock the subdocument by clicking the Lock Document button on the Outlining toolbar. Word will automatically lock a subdocument if the subdocument name is set as a read-only document or if another user is currently working on the subdocument.

When subdocuments are collapsed, all subdocuments appear to be locked. A lock icon displays below the subdocument icon at the left side of the subdocument name. A document is only locked if the lock icon displays below the subdocument icon when subdocuments are expanded.

Lock
Document

exercise 9

Creating a Master Document and Expanding/Collapsing Subdocuments

1. At a clear document screen, change the line spacing to double, and then key the text shown in figure 22.12. (Press the Enter key after keying the text.)
2. Move the insertion point to the end of the document and then insert the document named Report 03. (To do this, click Insert and then File. At the Insert File dialog box, make sure the *Chapter 22* folder is active, and then double-click *Report 03*.)
3. With the insertion point positioned at the end of the document, insert the document named Report 04. (Use Insert and then File.)
4. Make the following changes to the document:
   a. Move the insertion point to the beginning of the document.
   b. Change to Outline view.
   c. Make sure the Master Document View button on the Outlining toolbar is active (displays with a light gray background). If it is not active, click the Master Document View button.

d. Format the title with a style by completing the following steps:

1) Position the insertion point on any character in the title *SECTION A: NEWSLETTERS*.

2) Click the down-pointing triangle at the right side of the Style button (located at the left side of the Formatting toolbar).

3) At the drop-down menu that displays, click *Heading 1*.

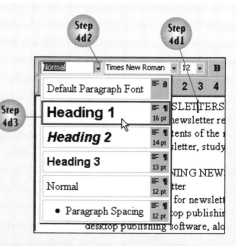

e. Complete steps similar to those in 4d to apply the specified styles to the following headings:

MODULE 1: DEFINING NEWSLETTER ELEMENTS	=	Heading 2
Designing a Newsletter	=	Heading 3
Defining Basic Newsletter Elements	=	Heading 3
MODULE 2: PLANNING A NEWSLETTER	=	Heading 2
Defining the Purpose of a Newsletter	=	Heading 3
MODULE 3: DESIGNING A NEWSLETTER	=	Heading 2
Applying Desktop Publishing Guidelines	=	Heading 3
MODULE 4: CREATING NEWSLETTER LAYOUT	=	Heading 2
Choosing Paper Size and Type	=	Heading 3
Choosing Paper Weight	=	Heading 3
Creating Margins for Newsletters	=	Heading 3

5. Save the document and name it Master Doc Ch 22, Ex 09.

6. Create subdocuments with the module text by completing the following steps:

a. Position the mouse pointer on the selection symbol (white plus sign) that displays immediately left of the heading *MODULE 1: DEFINING NEWSLETTER ELEMENTS* until the pointer turns into a four-headed arrow, and then click the left mouse button.

b. Scroll through the document until the *MODULE 4: CREATING NEWSLETTER LAYOUT* heading displays.

c. Hold down the Shift key, position the mouse pointer on the selection symbol (white plus sign) immediately left of the title until the

pointer turns into a four-headed arrow, and then click the left mouse button. (This selects all the text in modules 1, 2, 3, and 4.)

d. With the text selected, click the Create Subdocument button on the Outlining toolbar.

7. Save the document again with the same name (Master Doc Ch 22, Ex 09).

8. Close Master Doc Ch 22, Ex 09.

9. Open Master Doc Ch 22, Ex 09 and then complete the following steps:

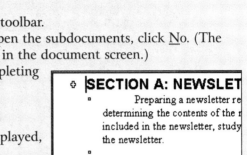

Step 6d

a. Print Master Doc Ch 22, Ex 09 by completing the following steps:
   1) Click the Print button on the Standard toolbar.
   2) At the question asking if you want to open the subdocuments, click <u>N</u>o. (The document will print collapsed as shown in the document screen.)

b. Edit the MODULE 1 subdocument by completing the following steps:

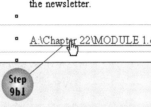

SECTION A: NEWSLET

   1) Click the *A:\Chapter 22\MODULE 1.doc* hyperlink.
   2) With the *MODULE 1.doc* document displayed, edit the title so it reads *MODULE 1: DEFINING ELEMENTS*.
   3) Change the heading *Designing a Newsletter* so it displays as *Designing*.
   4) Change the heading *Defining Basic Newsletter Elements* so it displays as *Defining Basic Elements*.

Step 9b1

c. Save the subdocument by clicking the Save button on the Standard toolbar.

d. Close the subdocument.

e. Clicking the module hyperlink automatically turned on the display of the Web toolbar. Turn off this toolbar by clicking <u>V</u>iew, pointing to <u>T</u>oolbars, and then clicking *Web*. Drag the Outlining toolbar to the left so it is positioned under the Formatting toolbar.

f. Expand the subdocuments by clicking the Expand Subdocuments button on the Outlining toolbar.

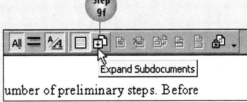

Step 9f

g. Print page 1 of the master document.

h. Collapse the subdocuments by clicking the Collapse Subdocuments button on the Outlining toolbar.

10. Save the document again with the same name (Master Doc Ch 22, Ex 09).

11. Close Master Doc Ch 22, Ex 09.

figure

22.12 *Exercise 9*

SECTION A: NEWSLETTERS

Preparing a newsletter requires a number of preliminary steps. Before determining the contents of the newsletter, determine the basic elements to be included in the newsletter, study newsletter design, and determine the purpose of the newsletter.

Rearranging Subdocuments

Many of the features of a master document are similar to an outline. For example, expanding and collapsing an outline is very similar to expanding and collapsing subdocuments. Also, like headings in an outline, expanded subdocuments in a master document can be moved or rearranged.

To rearrange the order of a subdocument, position the mouse pointer on the subdocument icon, hold down the left mouse button (mouse pointer turns into a four-headed arrow), drag to the location where you want the subdocument moved, and then release the mouse button. As you drag with the mouse, a dark gray horizontal line displays identifying where the subdocument will be inserted. Use this dark gray line to insert the subdocument in the desired location.

Removing a Subdocument

Remove a subdocument from a master document by clicking the subdocument icon and then pressing the Delete key. This removes the subdocument from the master document but not from the original location. For example, in exercise 10, you will remove the MODULE 3 subdocument from the Master Doc Ch 22, Ex 09 master document, but the document named MODULE 3 still displays on your disk.

Splitting/Combining Subdocuments

Spit
Subdocument

Merge
Subdocument

A subdocument can be split into smaller subdocuments or subdocuments can be combined into one. To split a subdocument, expand subdocuments, select the specific text within the subdocument, and then click the Split Subdocument button on the Outlining toolbar. Word assigns a document name based on the first characters in the subdocument heading.

To combine subdocuments, expand subdocuments, and then click the subdocument icon of the first subdocument to be combined. Hold down the Shift key and then click the subdocument icon of the last subdocument (subdocuments must be adjacent). With the subdocuments selected, click the Merge Subdocument button on the Outlining toolbar. Word saves the combined subdocuments with the name of the first subdocument.

Renaming a Subdocument

If you need to rename a subdocument, do it through the master document. To rename a subdocument, display the master document containing the subdocument, and then click the subdocument hyperlink. With the subdocument displayed, click File and then Save As. At the Save As dialog box, key a new name for the subdocument, and then press Enter or click the Save button. This renames the document in its original location as well as within the master document.

Rearranging, Splitting, Removing, and Renaming Subdocuments

1. Open Master Doc Ch 22, Ex 09.
2. Save the document with Save As and name it Master Doc Ch 22, Ex 10.
3. Make the following changes to the master document:
    a. Move the MODULE 4 subdocument above the MODULE 3 subdocument by completing the following steps:
        1) Position the arrow pointer on the subdocument icon that displays to the left of the A:\Chapter 22\MODULE 4.doc subdocument. (The pointer turns into an arrow pointing up and to the right.)
        2) Hold down the left mouse button, drag up so the dark gray horizontal line displays between the MODULE 2 and MODULE 3 subdocuments, and then release the mouse button.

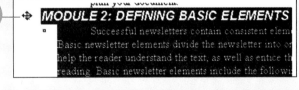

    b. Print Master Doc Ch 22, Ex 10. (At the prompt asking if you want to open the subdocuments, click No.)
    c. Remove the A:\Chapter 22\MODULE 3.doc subdocument by completing the following steps:
        1) Click the subdocument icon that displays to the left of the A:\Chapter 22\MODULE 3.doc subdocument.
        2) Press the Delete key.
    d. Split the MODULE 1 subdocument by completing the following steps:
        1) Click the Expand Subdocuments button on the Outlining toolbar.
        2) Move the insertion point to the MODULE 1 subdocument.
        3) In the MODULE 1 subdocument, edit the heading *Defining Basic Elements* so it displays as *MODULE 2: DEFINING BASIC ELEMENTS*.
        4) Change the heading style of the heading *MODULE 2: DEFINING BASIC ELEMENTS* from Heading 3 to Heading 2. *(Hint: Use the Style button on the Formatting toolbar.)*
        5) Position the mouse pointer on the selection symbol (white plus sign) that displays immediately left of the heading *MODULE 2: DEFINING BASIC ELEMENTS* until the pointer turns into a four-headed arrow, and then click the left mouse button.

        > **Step 3d5** ⟶ **MODULE 2: DEFINING BASIC ELEMENTS**
        > Successful newsletters contain consistent elem...
        > Basic newsletter elements divide the newsletter into or...
        > help the reader understand the text, as well as entice th...
        > reading. Basic newsletter elements include the followi...

        6) With the text selected, click the Split Subdocument button on the Outlining toolbar.
        7) Click the Collapse Subdocuments button on the Outlining toolbar. At the question asking if you want to save the changes to the master document, click OK.

e. Rename the MODULE 1 subdocument by completing the following steps:
   1) Click the *A:\Chapter 22\MODULE 1.doc* hyperlink.
   2) With the subdocument open, click File and then Save As.
   3) At the Save As dialog box, key **NEW MOD 1** and then press Enter.
   4) Close the subdocument.
f. Rename and edit the MODULE 5 subdocument by completing the following steps:
   1) Click the *A:\Chapter 22\MODULE 5.doc* hyperlink.
   2) With the subdocument open, click File and then Save As.
   3) At the Save As dialog box, key **NEW MOD 2** and then press Enter.
   4) Close the subdocument.
g. Rename and edit the MODULE 2 subdocument by completing the following steps:
   1) Click the *A:\Chapter 22\MODULE 2.doc* hyperlink.
   2) With the subdocument open, edit the *MODULE 2: PLANNING A NEWSLETTER* heading so it reads *MODULE 3: PLANNING A NEWSLETTER.*
   3) Click File and then Save As.
   4) At the Save As dialog box, key **NEW MOD 3** and then press Enter.
   5) Close the subdocument.
h. Rename the MODULE 4 subdocument by completing the following steps:
   1) Click the *A:\Chapter 22\MODULE 4.doc* hyperlink.
   2) With the subdocument open, click File and then Save As.
   3) At the Save As dialog box, key **NEW MOD 4** and then press Enter.
   4) Close the subdocument.
4. Save the master document again with the same name (Master Doc Ch 22, Ex 10).
5. Print the master document with the subdocuments collapsed.
6. Close Master Doc Ch 22, Ex 10.

chapter summary

➤ Word's outlining feature will format headings within a document as well as let you view formatted headings and body text in a document.

➤ To create an outline, first identify particular headings and subheadings within a document as certain heading levels. The Outline view is used to assign particular heading levels to text.

➤ When a document contains headings and text that have been formatted in the Outline view, the paragraphs are identified by one of the *outline selection symbols* that appear in the selection bar at the left side of the screen.

➤ The outline selection symbols can be used to select text in the document.

➤ When a document is displayed in Outline view, the Outlining toolbar displays below the Formatting toolbar. Use buttons on the Outlining toolbar to assign various level headings to paragraphs.

➤ When a paragraph is identified as a first-level heading, the Heading 1 style is applied to that paragraph.

➤ Heading 2 style is applied to a paragraph identified as a second-level heading.

➤ The advantage of working in the Outline view is the ability to see a condensed outline of your document without all of the text in between headings or subheadings. Another benefit of working in the Outline view is in maintaining consistency between various headings.

➤ Word's outline feature offers you the ability to rearrange an entire document by rearranging an outline.

➤ Headings in an outline can be automatically numbered with options from the Bullets and Numbering dialog box with the Outline Numbered tab selected. If headings in an outline are moved, inserted, or deleted, the headings are automatically renumbered.

➤ Use the Document Map feature to navigate easily in a document and keep track of your location within a document. The Document Map is a separate pane that displays the outline of a document. Display the Document Map pane by clicking the Document Map button on the Standard toolbar.

➤ A master document contains a number of separate documents called subdocuments.

➤ Create a master document or format an existing document as a master document at the Outline view and the Master Document view.

➤ The Outlining toolbar contains buttons for working with master documents and subdocuments.

➤ Clicking the Create Subdocument button on the Outlining toolbar causes Word to create a subdocument for each heading at the top level within the selected text.

➤ Save a master document in the normal manner. Word automatically assigns a document name to each subdocument using the first characters in the subdocument heading.

➤ Using buttons on the Outlining toolbar, you can expand and collapse subdocuments, lock and unlock subdocuments, and rearrange, remove, split, combine, and rename subdocuments.

commands review

	Mouse/Keyboard
Change to Outline view	Click Outline View button at left side of horizontal scroll bar; or click View, Outline
Document Map pane	Click Document Map button on Standard toolbar
Change to Master Document view	Click the Master Document View button on the Outlining toolbar

thinking offline

Matching: In the space provided at the left, write the letter of the term that matches the description. (Terms may be used more than once.)

Ⓐ Document Map Ⓕ Outline Numbered Ⓚ Print Layout view
Ⓑ Expand Ⓖ Outline selection symbols Ⓛ Show Heading 1
Ⓒ Heading 1 Ⓗ Outline view Ⓜ Show Heading 2
Ⓓ Heading 2 Ⓘ Outlining toolbar Ⓝ Subdocument toolbar
Ⓔ Master Document view Ⓙ Plus symbol

_____ 1. This toolbar displays in Outline view below the Formatting toolbar.

_____ 2. This heading style applies 14-point Arial bold italic formatting to text.

_____ 3. This symbol appears in the selection bar at the left side of the screen and indicates that subtext appears below the heading.

_____ 4. This feature will display the outline of a document in a separate pane.

_____ 5. This heading style applies 16-point Arial bold formatting to text.

_____ 6. Click this button on the Outlining toolbar to display only first-level headings.

_____ 7. Automatically number headings in an outline with options from the Bullets and Numbering dialog box with this tab selected.

_____ 8. These appear in the selection bar at the left side of the screen.

_____ 9. Click this Outlining toolbar button to make text in the first heading level below the currently selected heading appear.

_____ 10. In Outline view and this view, collapsed subdocuments display surrounded by a light gray border line and subdocument icons display.

_____ 11. Expand subdocuments with the Expand Subdocuments button on this toolbar.

working hands-on

Assessment 1

1. Open Report 03.
2. Save the document with Save As and name it Ch 22, SA 01.
3. Make the following changes to the document:
   a. Change to the Outline view.

b. Promote or demote the following titles, headings, or subheadings as identified below:

MODULE 1: DEFINING NEWSLETTER ELEMENTS	=	Heading 1
Designing a Newsletter	=	Heading 2
Defining Basic Newsletter Elements	=	Heading 2
MODULE 2: PLANNING A NEWSLETTER	=	Heading 1
Defining the Purpose of a Newsletter	=	Heading 2

   c. Collapse the outline so only the two heading levels are displayed.
4. Save the document again with the same name (Ch 22, SA 01).
5. Print and then close Ch 22, SA 01. (This will print the collapsed outline, not the entire document.)

Assessment 2

1. Open Ch 22, SA 01.
2. Save the document with Save As and name it Ch 22, SA 02.
3. Make the following changes to the document:
   a. Collapse the outline and then move the module 1 title and the headings below it after the module 2 title and the heading below it.
   b. Renumber the modules (module 2 becomes 1 and module 1 becomes 2).
   c. Move the section *Designing a Newsletter* below the section *Defining Basic Newsletter Elements*.
4. With the outline still collapsed, save the document again with the same name (Ch 22, SA 02).
5. Print and then close Ch 22, SA 02.

Assessment 3

1. Open Ch 22, SA 01.
2. Save the document with Save As and name it Ch 22, SA 03.
3. Make the following changes to the document:
   a. Display only level-one and level-two headings in the document.
   b. Select all the text in the document.
   c. Add numbering to the outline.
   d. Delete the section *Designing a Newsletter*.
   e. Expand the document.
4. Save the document again with the same name (Ch 22, SA 03).
5. Print and then close Ch 22, SA 03.

Assessment 4

1. Open Report 01.
2. Save the document with Save As and name it Master Doc Ch 22, SA 04.
3. Make the following changes to the document:
    a. Delete the title *DESKTOP PUBLISHING* and the blank line below the title.
    b. Change to the Outline view.
    c. Apply the Heading 1 style to the following headings:

    > *Defining Desktop Publishing*
    > *Initiating the Desktop Publishing Process*
    > *Planning the Publication*
    > *Creating the Content*

    d. Make sure the Master Document View button on the Outlining toolbar is activated.
    e. Create subdocuments by selecting the entire document and then clicking the Create Subdocument button on the Outlining toolbar.
4. Save the document again with the same name (Master Doc Ch 22, SA 04).
5. Close Master Doc Ch 22, SA 04.
6. Open Master Doc Ch 22, SA 04 and then print the document. (Subdocuments will be collapsed.)
7. Close Master Doc Ch 22, SA 04.

Assessment 5

1. Open Master Doc Ch 22, SA 04.
2. Save the document with Save As and name it Master Doc Ch 22, SA 05.
3. Make the following changes to the document:
    a. Move the *Planning the Publication* subdocument above the *Initiating the Desktop Publishing Process* subdocument.
    b. Remove the *Defining Desktop Publishing* subdocument.
4. Save the document again with the same name (Master Doc Ch 22, SA 05).
5. Print Master Doc Ch 22, SA 05. (At the prompt asking if you want to open the subdocuments, click No.)
6. Close Master Doc Ch 22, SA 05.

Chapter 23

Creating Fill-In Forms

PERFORMANCE OBJECTIVES

Upon successful completion of chapter 23, you will be able to:
- Create a form template.
- Fill in a form document.
- Print, edit, and customize a form.
- Draw a table in a form template.

Many businesses use preprinted forms that are generally filled in by hand, with a typewriter, or using a computer. These forms require additional storage space and also cost the company money. With Word's form feature, you can create your own forms, eliminating the need for preprinted forms.

In this chapter, you will learn how to create a template document for a form that includes text boxes, check boxes, and pull-down lists. You will learn how to save the form as a protected document and then open the form and key information in the fill-in boxes. You will create basic form documents in this chapter. For ideas on creating advanced forms, please refer to Word's Help feature.

In chapter 12, you learned how to create fill-in fields in a main document. The main document containing fill-in fields also required a data source for other variable information. Creating a form does not require a main document or a data source. The form is created as a template document that contains fill-in fields. Information is keyed in the fields when a document based on the form template is opened.

Creating a Form

In Word, a *form* is a protected document that includes fields where information is entered. A form document contains *form fields* that are locations in the document where one of three things is performed: text is entered, a check box is turned on or off, or information is selected from a drop-down list. There are three basic steps that are completed when creating a form:

1. Create a form document based on a template and build the structure of the form.
2. Insert form fields where information is to be entered at the keyboard.
3. Save the form as a protected document.

Creating the Form Template

A form is created as a template so that anyone who fills in the form is working on a copy of the form, not the original. The original is the template document that is saved as a protected document. In this way, a form can be used over and over again without changing the original form. When a form is created from the template form document that has been protected, information can only be keyed in the fields designated when the form was created.

Word provides a Forms toolbar with buttons you can use to easily insert a text box, check box, or other form fields into a form template document. To display the Forms toolbar shown in figure 23.1, position the arrow pointer on either the Standard or Formatting toolbar, click the *right* mouse button, and then click *Forms* at the drop-down list. You can also display the Forms toolbar by clicking View, pointing to Toolbars, and then clicking Forms.

Forms Toolbar

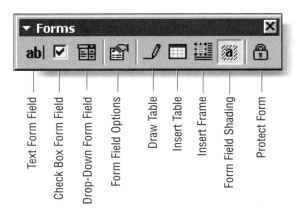

Figure 23.2 shows an example of a form document created with the form feature. (You will create this form in exercise 1.) You can create forms that contain fields for text, such as the fields *Name:*, *Address:*, *Date of Birth:*, etc., shown in figure 23.2. Forms can also contain check boxes, such as the boxes after *Yes* and *No*, shown in figure 23.2. Forms can also contain drop-down lists (not used in the form shown in figure 23.2). You will learn about drop-down lists later in this chapter.

Generally, a form is created based on the default template document (called the Normal template). The form is created and then saved as a protected template document. To learn how to create a form document, complete exercise 1.

Changing File Locations

By default, Word saves template documents in a *Templates* subfolder within the Microsoft Office program. In this chapter, you will create form template documents and save them to this subfolder. In some situations, you may want to change the location of template documents. Do this at the Options dialog box with the File Locations tab selected. At the Options dialog box, click the *User templates* in the File types list box, and then click the Modify button. At the Modify Location dialog box, specify the desired folder, and then click OK. Click OK to close the Options dialog box.

Creating a Form Document

1. Create the form shown in figure 23.2 as a template document by completing the following steps:
   a. Click File and then New.
   b. At the New dialog box with the General tab selected, make sure *Blank Document* is selected in the list box.
   c. Click Template in the Create New section at the bottom right corner of the dialog box.
   d. Click OK or press Enter.
   e. At the document screen, make sure the default font is 12-point Times New Roman. (If it is not, display the Font dialog box, change the size to 12, and then click the Default button. At the question asking if you want to change the default font, click Yes.)
   f. Key the beginning portion of the form shown in figure 23.2 up to the colon after *Name:*. After keying the colon, press the spacebar once, and then insert a form field where the name will be keyed by completing the following steps:
      1) Turn on the display of the Forms toolbar by clicking View, pointing to Toolbars, and then clicking Forms.
      2) At the Forms toolbar, click the Text Form Field button. (The form field displays as a shaded area in the document screen.)

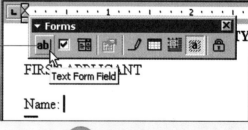

   g. After inserting the form field, press the Enter key, and then create the remaining text and text form fields as shown in figure 23.2. To create the check boxes after *Yes* and *No*, position the insertion point where you want the check box to display, and then click the Check Box Form Field button on the Forms toolbar.

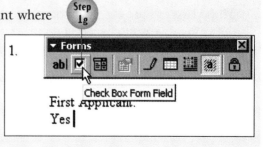

   h. After the form is completed, protect the document by clicking the Protect Form button on the Forms toolbar.
   i. Turn off the display of the Forms toolbar by clicking the Close button located at the right side of the Forms toolbar Title bar.
2. Save the document with Save As and name it XXX Template Document. (Use your initials in place of the *XXX*.)
3. Print XXX Template Document. (The form field gray shading will not print.)
4. Close XXX Template Document.

Exercise 1

LIFETIME ANNUITY INSURANCE APPLICATION

FIRST APPLICANT

Name:
Address:
Date of Birth:
Occupation:

SECOND APPLICANT

Name:
Address:
Date of Birth:
Occupation:

1. During the past 3 years, have you for any reason consulted a doctor or been hospitalized?

    First Applicant: Second Applicant:
    Yes ☐   No ☐   Yes ☐   No ☐

2. Have you ever been treated for or advised that you had any of the following: heart, lung, nervous, kidney, or liver disorder; high blood pressure; drug abuse, including alcohol; cancer or tumor; AIDS, or any disorder of your immune system; diabetes?

    First Applicant: Second Applicant:
    Yes ☐   No ☐   Yes ☐   No ☐

These answers are true and complete to the best of my knowledge and belief. To determine my insurability, I authorize any health care provider or insurance company to give any information about me or my physical or mental health.

FIRST APPLICANT'S SIGNATURE   SECOND APPLICANT'S SIGNATURE

_____   _____

Filling in a Form Document

After a template form document is created, protected, and saved, the template can be used to create a personalized form document. When you open a form template document that has been protected, the insertion point is automatically inserted in the first form field. Key the information for the data field and then press the Tab key to move the insertion point to the next form field. You can move the insertion point to a preceding form field by pressing Shift + Tab. To fill in a check box form field, move the insertion point to the check box, and then press the spacebar. Complete the same steps to remove an *X* from a check box form field. As an example of how to fill in a form template, complete exercise 2.

Filling in a Template Form Document

1. Create a form with the XXX Template Document form template by completing the following steps:
    a. Click File and then New.
    b. At the New dialog box with the General tab selected, double-click the *XXX Template Document* icon (where your initials display instead of the *XXX*).
    c. Word displays the form document with the insertion point positioned in the first form field after *Name*. Key the name **Dennis Utley** (as shown in figure 23.3).
    d. Press the Tab key or the Enter key to move to the next form field.
    e. Fill in the remaining text and check box form fields as shown in figure 23.3. Press the Tab key to move the insertion point to the next form field. Press Shift + Tab to move the insertion point to the preceding form field. (To insert the *X* in a check box, move the insertion point to the check box, and then press the spacebar.)
2. When the form is completed, save the document and name it Ch 23, Ex 02.
3. Print and then close Ch 23, Ex 02.

figure

23.3   *Exercise 2*

LIFETIME ANNUITY INSURANCE APPLICATION

FIRST APPLICANT

Name: Dennis Utley
Address: 11315 Lomas Drive, Seattle, WA 98123
Date of Birth: 02/23/59
Occupation: Accountant

SECOND APPLICANT

Name: Geneva Utley
Address: 11315 Lomas Drive, Seattle, WA 98123
Date of Birth: 09/04/62
Occupation: Social Worker

1. During the past 3 years, have you for any reason consulted a doctor or been hospitalized?

    First Applicant: Second Applicant:
    Yes ☐   No ☒   Yes ☐   No ☒

2. Have you ever been treated for or advised that you had any of the following: heart, lung, nervous, kidney, or liver disorder; high blood pressure; drug abuse, including alcohol; cancer or tumor; AIDS, or any disorder of your immune system; diabetes?

    First Applicant: Second Applicant:
    Yes ☐   No ☒   Yes ☐   No ☒

These answers are true and complete to the best of my knowledge and belief. To determine my insurability, I authorize any health care provider or insurance company to give any information about me or my physical or mental health.

FIRST APPLICANT'S SIGNATURE   SECOND APPLICANT'S SIGNATURE

_____   _____

Printing a Form

After the form fields in a form document have been filled in, the form can be printed in the normal manner. In some situations, you may want to print just the data (not the entire form) or print the form and not the fill-in data.

If you are using a preprinted form that is inserted in the printer, you will want to print just the data. Word will print the data in the same location on the page as it appears in the form document. To print just the data in a form, click Tools and then Options. At the Options dialog box, click the Print tab. At the Options dialog box with the Print tab selected, click Print data only for forms in the Options for current document only section (this inserts a check mark in the check box), and then click OK or press Enter. Click the Print button on the Standard toolbar. After printing only the data, complete similar steps to remove the check mark from the Print data only for forms check box.

To print only the form without the data, you would click File and then New. At the New dialog box, select the desired template document in the Template list box, and then click OK or press Enter. With the form document displayed in the document screen, click the Print button on the Standard toolbar, and then close the document.

Printing Only Data in a Form Document

1. Open Ch 23, Ex 02.
2. Print only the data in the form fields by completing the following steps:
   a. Click Tools and then Options.
   b. At the Options dialog box, click the Print tab.
   c. At the Options dialog box with the Print tab selected, click Print data only for forms in the Options for current document only section. (This inserts a check mark in the check box.)
   d. Click OK or press Enter.
   e. Click the Print button on the Standard toolbar.
3. After printing, remove the check mark from the Print data only for forms option by completing the following steps:
   a. Click Tools and then Options.
   b. At the Options dialog box with the Print tab selected, click Print data only for forms in the Options for current document only section. (This removes the check mark from the check box.)
   c. Click OK or press Enter.
4. Close Ch 23, Ex 02 without saving the changes.

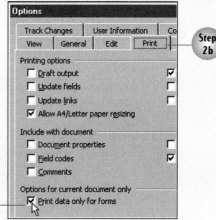

Editing a Form Template

When a form template is created and then protected, the text in the template cannot be changed. If you need to make changes to a form template, you must open the template document, unprotect the document, and then make the changes. After making the changes, protect the document again.

Protect Form

To unprotect a template document, click the Protect Form button on the Forms toolbar to deactivate it. You can also unprotect a document by clicking Tools and then Unprotect Document. Make any necessary changes to the document and then protect it again by clicking the Protect Form button on the Forms toolbar or by clicking Tools and then Protect Document.

Editing a Template Form

1. Add the text shown in figure 23.4 to the XXX Template Document form template by completing the following steps:
   a. Click the Open button on the Standard toolbar.
   b. At the Open dialog box, click the down-pointing triangle to the right of the Look in text box. From the drop-down list that displays, click the drive where the *Templates* folder is located. (If you have Microsoft Office installed on a hard-drive system, click *(C:)*, double-click *Program Files*, double-click *Microsoft Office*, and then double-click *Templates*. If this is not the correct path, try clicking *(C:)*, double-clicking *Windows*, double-clicking *Application Data*, double-clicking *Microsoft*, and then double-clicking *Templates*. This path will vary if you have only Word installed and not Microsoft Office. If you are using Word on a network system, check with your instructor to determine the location of the *Templates* folder.)
   c. With the *Templates* folder selected, click the down-pointing triangle to the right of the Files of type text box (located at the bottom left corner of the dialog box), and then click *All Files*.
   d. Double-click *XXX Template Document* in the list box (where *XXX* indicates your initials).
   e. Display the Forms toolbar.
   f. Unprotect the template document by clicking the Protect Form button on the Forms toolbar to deactivate it.

   g. Add the paragraph and the check boxes shown in figure 23.4 to the form.
   h. Protect the document again by clicking the Protect Form button on the Forms toolbar.
   i. Turn off the display of the Forms toolbar.
   j. Save the document with the same name (XXX Template Document).
2. Print and then close XXX Template Document.

figure
23.4 *Exercise 4*

3. During the past 3 years, have you for any reason been denied life insurance by any other insurance company?

First Applicant: Second Applicant:
Yes ☐   No ☐   Yes ☐   No ☐

Customizing Form Field Options

A drop-down list, text box, or check box form field is inserted in a document with default options. You can change these default options for each form field. Options at the Drop-Down Form Field Options dialog box can be used to create form fields with drop-down lists.

Creating Form Fields with Drop-Down Lists

When creating form fields for a form document, there may be some fields where you want the person entering the information to choose from specific options, rather than keying the data. To do this, create a form field with a drop-down list. To do this, open the template document, unprotect the template document, key the field name, and then click the Drop-Down Form Field button on the Forms toolbar. After inserting the drop-down form field, click the Form Field Options button on the Forms toolbar. This displays the Drop-Down Form Field Options dialog box shown in figure 23.5.

Drop-Down
Form Field

Form Field Options

figure
23.5 *Drop-Down Form Field Options Dialog Box*

Key an item in this text box that you want included in the drop-down list and then click the Add button.

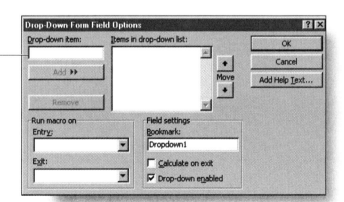

At the Drop-Down Form Field Options dialog box, key the first option you want to display in the drop-down list, and then click the Add button. Continue in this manner until all drop-down list items have been added and then click OK or press Enter to close the Drop-Down Form Field Options dialog box. Protect and then save the template document. A drop-down form field in a form document displays as a gray box with a down-pointing arrow at the right side of the box. You can remove drop-down items at the Drop-Down Form Field Options dialog box by selecting the item in the Items in drop-down list box and then clicking the Remove button.

When filling in a form field in a form template document that contains a drop-down list, position the insertion point in the drop-down form field, and then complete one of the following steps:

- Click the down-pointing triangle at the right side of the form field.
- Press F4.
- Press Alt + down arrow key.

When you choose one of the methods above, a drop-down list displays with the choices for the form field. Click the desired choice, or press the up or down arrow key to select the desired choice, and then press the Enter key.

Changing Text Form Field Options

To change options for a text form field, position the insertion point on the text form field you want to change and then click the Form Field Options button on the Forms toolbar. This displays the Text Form Field Options dialog box shown in figure 23.6.

figure
23.6 **Text Form Field Options Dialog Box**

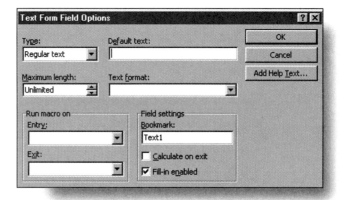

At the Text Form Field Options dialog box, you can change the type of text that is to be inserted in the form field. The default setting at the Type text box is *Regular text*. This can be changed to *Number, Date, Current date, Current time*, or *Calculation*.

If you change the Type option, Word will display an error message if the correct type of information is not entered in the form field. For example, if you change the form field type to *Number* in the Type text box, only a number can be entered in the form field. If something other than a number is entered, Word displays an error message, the entry is selected, and the insertion point stays in the form field until a number is entered.

If a particular text form field will generally need the same information, key that information in the Default text text box. This default text will display in the form field. If you want to leave the default text in the form document, just press the Tab key or the Enter key when filling in the form. If you want to change the default text, key the new text over the default text when filling in the form.

With the Maximum length option at the Text Form Field Options dialog box, you can specify an exact measurement for a form field. This option has a setting of *Unlimited* by default.

Formatting options for text in a form field can be applied with options at the Text format text box. For example, if you want text to display in all uppercase letters, click the down-pointing triangle at the right side of the Text format text box, and then click *Uppercase* at the drop-down list. When you key text in the form field while filling in the form, the text is converted to uppercase letters as soon as you press the Tab key or Enter key. The Text format options will vary depending on what is selected in the Type text box.

Changing Check Box Form Field Options

Check Box form field options can be changed at the Check Box Form Field Options dialog box shown in figure 23.7. To display this dialog box, position the insertion point on a check box form field and then click the Form Field Options button on the Forms toolbar.

23.7   *Check Box Form Field Options Dialog Box*

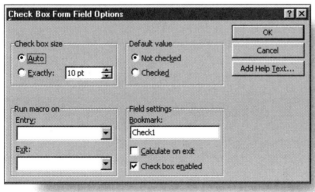

By default, Word inserts a check box in a form template document in the same size as the adjacent text. This is because <u>A</u>uto is selected at the Check box size section of the Check Box Form Field Options dialog box. If you want to specify an exact size for the check box, click <u>E</u>xactly, and then key the desired point measurement in the <u>E</u>xactly text box.

A check box form field is empty by default. If you want the check box to be checked by default, click the <u>C</u>hecked option in the Default value section of the dialog box.

exercise 5

Creating a Form with Text Fields, Check Boxes, and Drop-Down Lists

1. Create the form shown in figure 23.8 as a template document by completing the following steps:
   a. Click <u>F</u>ile and then <u>N</u>ew.
   b. At the New dialog box with the General tab selected, make sure *Blank Document* is selected in the list box.
   c. Click <u>T</u>emplate in the Create New section at the bottom right corner of the dialog box.
   d. Click OK or press Enter.
   e. At the document screen, make sure the default font is 12-point Times New Roman. (If it is not, display the Font dialog box, change the size to 12, and then click the <u>D</u>efault button. At the question asking if you want to change the default font, click <u>Y</u>es.)
   f. Turn on the display of the Forms toolbar.
   g. Key the title of the form, **APPLICATION FOR PREFERRED INSURANCE,** centered and bolded. Press the Enter key twice, turn off bold, and then return the paragraph alignment to left. Key **Date:**, press the spacebar once, and then insert a text form field that inserts the current date by completing the following steps:

   Step 1g2

   Form Field Options

   1) Click the Text Form Field button on the Forms toolbar.
   2) Click the Form Field Options button on the Forms toolbar.
   3) At the Text Form Field Options dialog box, click the down-pointing triangle at the right side of the Ty<u>p</u>e text box, and then click *Current date* at the drop-down list.
   4) Click OK or press Enter to close the Text Form Field Options dialog box.
   5) Press the right arrow key to deselect the field and move the insertion point to the right side of the field. (You can also position the mouse pointer immediately right of the field and then click the left mouse button.)

   Text Form Field Options

   Ty<u>p</u>e:

   Regular text

   Regular text
   Number
   Date
   Current date
   Current time
   Calculation

   Step 1g3

   h. Press the Enter key twice, key **Name:**, press the spacebar once, and then create the text form field. Do the same for **Address:** and **Date of Birth:**.

764

Chapter Twenty-Three

i. Key **Social Security Number:** and then create a text form field that allows a maximum of 11 characters (the number required for the Social Security number including the hyphens) by completing the following steps:

    1) Press the spacebar once after keying **Social Security Number:**.

    2) Click the Text Form Field button on the Forms toolbar.

    3) Click the Form Field Options button on the Forms toolbar.

    4) At the Text Form Field Options dialog box, select *Unlimited* that displays in the <u>M</u>aximum length text box, and then key **11**.

    5) Click OK or press Enter to close the Text Form Field Options dialog box.

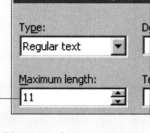

    6) Press the right arrow key to deselect the field and move the insertion point to the right side of the field. (You can also position the mouse pointer immediately right of the field and then click the left mouse button.)

j. Press the Enter key twice, key **Gender:**, and then press the Tab key. Create the text and check boxes after *Gender:* as shown in figure 23.8.

k. After creating the check box after *Male*, press the Enter key twice, key **Nonprofit Employer:**, press the spacebar once, and then create a drop-down form field with three choices by completing the following steps:

    1) Click the Drop-Down Form Field button on the Forms toolbar.

    2) Click the Form Field Options button on the Forms toolbar.

    3) At the Drop-Down Form Field Options dialog box, key **College** in the <u>D</u>rop-down item text box.

    4) Click the <u>A</u>dd button.

    5) Key **Public School** in the <u>D</u>rop-down item text box.

    6) Click the <u>A</u>dd button.

    7) Key **Private School** in the <u>D</u>rop-down item text box.

    8) Click the <u>A</u>dd button.

    9) Click OK or press Enter to close the Drop-Down Form Field Options dialog box.

    10) Press the right arrow key to deselect the field and move the insertion point to the right side of the field. (You can also position the mouse pointer immediately right of the field and then click the left mouse button.)

l. Press the Enter key twice, key **How are premiums to be paid?**, press the spacebar once, and then create a drop-down form field with the choices *Annually, Semiannually,* and *Quarterly* by completing steps similar to those in 1k.

m. Continue creating the remainder of the form as shown in figure 23.8.

n. After the form is completed, protect the document by clicking the Protect Form button on the Forms toolbar.

o. Close the Forms toolbar.

2. Save the document and name it XXX Ch 23, Ex 05. (Use your initials in place of the *XXX.*)

3. Print and then close XXX Ch 23, Ex 05.

figure 23.8

Exercise 5

APPLICATION FOR PREFERRED INSURANCE

Date:

Name:

Address:

Date of Birth:

Social Security Number:

Gender: Female ☐   Male ☐

Nonprofit Employer:

How are premiums to be paid?

1.   Will this insurance replace any existing insurance or annuity?
         Yes ☐   No ☐

2.   Within the past 3 years has your driver's license been suspended, revoked, or have you been convicted for driving under the influence of alcohol or drugs?
         Yes ☐   No ☐

3.   Do you have any intention of traveling or residing outside the United States or Canada within the next 12 months?
         Yes ☐   No ☐

Signature of proposed insured:

_____   Date _____

exercise 6

Filling in a Template Form Document

1. Create a form with the XXX Ch 23, Ex 05 form template by completing the following steps:
   a. Click <u>F</u>ile and then <u>N</u>ew.
   b. At the New dialog box, double-click *XXX Ch 23, Ex 05* (where your initials are displayed instead of the *XXX*).
   c. Word displays the form document with the insertion point positioned in the *Name:* form field. Fill in the text and check boxes as shown in figure 23.9. (Press the Tab key to move the insertion point to the next form field. Press Shift + Tab to move the insertion point to the preceding form field.) To fill in the form fields with drop-down lists, complete the following steps:
      1) With the insertion point in the drop-down list form field, click the down-pointing arrow at the right side of the text box.
      2) Click the desired option at the drop-down list.
2. When the form is completed, save the document and name it Ch 23, Ex 06.
3. Print and then close Ch 23, Ex 06.

figure

23.9   *Exercise 6*

APPLICATION FOR PREFERRED INSURANCE

Date: (current date)

Name: Jennifer Reynolds

Address: 2309 North Cascade, Renton, WA 98051

Date of Birth: 12/18/63

Social Security Number: 411-23-6800

Gender: Female ☒   Male ☐

Nonprofit Employer: Public School

How are premiums to be paid? Quarterly

1. Will this insurance replace any existing insurance or annuity?
                  Yes ☒   No ☐

2. Within the past 3 years has your driver's license been suspended, revoked, or have you been convicted for driving under the influence of alcohol or drugs?

    Yes ☐   No ☒

3. Do you have any intention of traveling or residing outside the United States or Canada within the next 12 months?

    Yes ☐   No ☒

Signature of proposed insured:

_____   Date _____

Creating Tables in a Form Template

A table can be very useful when creating a form with form fields. A table can be customized to create a business form such as an invoice or a purchase order. Figure 23.10 shows an example of a form you will create in exercise 7 using the table feature.

Creating a Form Using the Table Feature

1. Create the form shown in figure 23.10 as a template document and name it XXX Ch 23, Ex 07 (where *XXX* are your initials), by completing the following steps:
    a. Click File and then New.
    b. At the New dialog box with the General tab selected, make sure *Blank Document* is selected in the list box.
    c. Click Template in the Create New section at the bottom right corner of the dialog box.
    d. Click OK or press Enter.
    e. At the document screen, make sure the default font is 12-point Times New Roman. (If it is not, display the Font dialog box, change the size to 12, and then click the Default button. At the question asking if you want to change the default font, click Yes.)
    f. Display the Forms toolbar.
    g. Click the Draw Table button on the Forms toolbar.

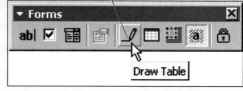

h. Use the buttons on the Tables and Borders toolbar to draw the table lines as shown in figure 23.10.

i. Change the text alignment to Align Center for specific cells by completing the following steps:

   1) Select the cells that will contain the text *Date*, *Description*, *Amount*, and *Ref #*.

   2) Click the down-pointing triangle at the right side of the Align Top Left button on the Tables and Borders toolbar.

   3) At the drop-down palette of choices, click Align Center (second option from the left in the second row).

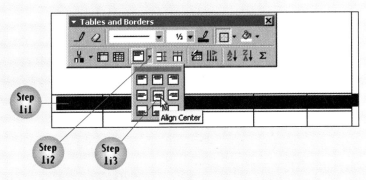

j. Turn off the display of the Tables and Borders toolbar.

k. Key the text in the cells as shown in figure 23.10. Insert text form fields as shown in the figure. (To insert the three text form fields in the Date column, insert the first text form field and then press the Enter key. This moves the insertion point down to the next line within the cell. Continue in this manner until all three text form fields are inserted. Complete similar steps for the three text form fields in the Description, Amount, and Ref # columns.)

l. After the table is completed, protect the document by clicking the Protect Form button on the Forms toolbar.

m. Close the Forms toolbar.

2. Save the document and name it XXX Ch 23, Ex 07. (Use your initials in place of the *XXX*.)

3. Print and then close XXX Ch 23, Ex 07.

figure

23.10   *Exercise 7*

GOOD SAMARITAN HOSPITAL
1201 James Street
St. Louis, MO 62033
(818) 555-1201

Account Number:

Invoice Number: **Date:**

Date	Description	Amount	Ref #

exercise 8

Filling in a Template Table Form

1. Create a form with the XXX Ch 23, Ex 07 form template by completing the following steps:
   a. Click File and then New.
   b. At the New dialog box, double-click *XXX Ch 23, Ex 07* (where your initials are displayed instead of the *XXX*).
   c. Word displays the form document with the insertion point positioned in the first form field. Fill in the text and check boxes as shown in figure 23.11. (Press the Tab key to move the insertion point to the next form field. Press Shift + Tab to move the insertion point to the preceding form field.)
2. When the form is completed, save the document and name it Ch 23, Ex 08.
3. Print and then close Ch 23, Ex 08.

figure 23.11   *Exercise 8*

GOOD SAMARITAN HOSPITAL
1201 James Street
St. Louis, MO 62033
(818) 555-1201

Account Number: 3423-001

Invoice Number: 342   **Date:** 04/30/99

Date	Description	Amount	Ref #
04/13/99	Bed linens	$984.50	5403
04/21/99	Hospital slippers	$204.00	9422
04/23/99	Hospital gowns	$750.25	6645

chapter summary

- You can create your own forms with Word's form feature, thus eliminating the need for preprinted forms.
- A form is created as a template document that contains fill-in fields. Information based on the form template is keyed in the fields when a document is opened.
- A form document contains *form fields* where one of three actions is performed: text is entered, a check box is turned on or off, or information is selected from a drop-down list.
- Three basic steps are involved in creating a form: 1) create a form document based on a template and build the structure of the form; 2) insert form fields where information is to be entered at the keyboard; and 3) save the form as a protected document.
- Create a template document by clicking Template at the New dialog box.
- Word provides a Forms toolbar with buttons you can use to easily insert a text box, check box, or other form field into a form template document.
- After a template form document is created, protected, and saved, the template can be used to create a personalized form document.
- After the form fields have been filled in, the form can be printed in the normal manner, or you can print just the data from the Options dialog box with the Print tab selected.
- When a form template is created and then protected, the text in the template cannot be changed. To edit a template document, you must open the document, unprotect it, make the necessary changes, and then protect the document again.
- Use options at the Drop-Down Form Field Options dialog box to create form fields with drop-down lists.
- Change options for a text form field at the Text Form Field Options dialog box.
- Change check box form field options at the Check Box Form Field Options dialog box.
- Click the Draw Table button on the Forms toolbar and then draw table lines to create a form.

commands review

	Mouse/Keyboard
New dialog box	File, New
Text Form Field Options dialog box	Position insertion point on text form field, then click Form Field Options button on Forms toolbar.
Check Box Form Field Options dialog box	Position insertion point on check box form field, then click Form Field Options button on Forms toolbar.
Drop-Down Form Field Options dialog box	Position insertion point on drop-down form field, then click Form Field Options button on Forms toolbar.

Completion: In the space provided at the right, indicate the correct term, command, or number.

1. Generally, a form is created based on this default template document.

2. A fill-in form can include text boxes, check boxes, and/or these.

3. This is the third basic step performed when creating a form document.

4. To display the Text Form Field Options dialog box, position the insertion point on a text form field, and then click this button on the Forms toolbar.

5. To protect a document, click this button on the Forms toolbar.

6. If you want the user to fill in a form by choosing from specific options, create this type of form field.

7. To fill in a check box form field, move the insertion point to the check box, and then press this key on the keyboard.

8. The default setting for a text form field can be changed to *Number, Date, Current time, Calculation*, or this.

9. This is the default setting for the <u>M</u>aximum length option at the Text Form Field Options dialog box.

10. When filling in a form template document, press this key to move the insertion point to the next form field.

11. This Word feature can be used to create a business form such as an invoice or purchase order.

working hands-on

Assessment 1

1. Create the form shown in figure 23.12 as a template document named XXX Ch 23, SA 01. Insert text form fields and check box form fields in the document as shown in figure 23.12.

2. Print and then close XXX Ch 23, SA 01.

figure

23.12   *Assessment 1*

GOOD SAMARITAN HOSPITAL

APPLICATION FOR FUNDING

Project Title:

Department Applying:

Facility: SFH ☐   LC ☐   SCC ☐

Contact Person(s):

Check the statement(s) that best describe(s) how this proposal will meet the eligibility criteria:

☐   Improved patient care outcomes

☐   Cost reduction

☐   Improved customer satisfaction

☐   Reduced outcome variation

☐   Compliance with quality standards

_____   _____
Signature   Date

_____   _____
Department   Extension

Assessment 2

1. Create a form with the XXX Ch 23, SA 01 form template. Insert the following information in the form:

> Project Title: *Quality Improvement Project*
> Department Applying: *Pediatrics*
> Facility: (check SFH)
> Contact Person(s): *Alyce Arevalo*
> Check all the statements describing the proposal except *Cost reduction*.

2. When the form is completed, save the document and name it Ch 23, SA 02.
3. Print and then close Ch 23, SA 02.

Assessment 3

1. Create the form shown in figure 23.13 as a template document named XXX Ch 23, SA 03. Customize the table as shown in figure 23.13. Insert text form fields and check box form fields in the table shown in the figure.
2. Print and then close XXX Ch 23, SA 03.

Assessment 3

LIFETIME ANNUITY

PROFESSIONAL LIABILITY INSURANCE APPLICATION

Name:

Address:

County:	**SSN:**	**DOB:**

Type of Deduction:
☐ Flat
☐ Participating

Deduction Amount:
☐ None   ☐ $2,500
☐ $1,000   ☐ $5,000

Check if this insurance is to be part of a program.
☐ AANA   ☐ AAOMS   ☐ APTA-PPS   ☐ None

Check your specific professional occupation.

☐ Chiropractor   ☐ Medical Technician
☐ Dental Anesthesia   ☐ Nurse
☐ Dental Hygienist   ☐ Nurse Practitioner
☐ Dietitian/Nutritionist   ☐ Occupational Therapist
☐ Laboratory Director   ☐ Optometrist
☐ Medical Office Assistant   ☐ Paramedic/EMT

Signature:	**Date:**

Assessment 4

1. Create a form with the XXX Ch 23, SA 03 form template. Insert the following information in the form:

> Name: *Steven Katori*
> Address: *11502 South 32nd Street, Bellevue, WA 98049*
> County: *King*
> SSN: *230-52-9812*
> DOB: *11/20/60*
>
> Type of Deduction: (check *Flat*)
> Deduction Amount: (check $1,000)
> Part of insurance program? (check *None*)
> Occupation: (check *Nurse Practitioner*)

2. When the form is completed, save the document and name it Ch 23, SA 04.
3. Print and then close Ch 23, SA 04.

Assessment 5

1. Delete the XXX Template Document form document created in exercise 1 by completing the following steps:
   a. Click File and then New.
   b. At the New dialog box, position the arrow pointer on the XXX Template Document template form, and then click the *right* mouse button.
   c. From the pop-up menu that displays, click Delete.
   d. At the question asking if you want to delete the document, click Yes.
2. Complete similar steps to delete the other template documents containing your initials created in this chapter.

Chapter 24

Working with Shared Documents

PERFORMANCE OBJECTIVES

Upon successful completion of chapter 24, you will be able to:

- Track changes to a document.
- Accept/reject changes to a document.
- Create, view, delete, and print comments.
- Send and route documents.
- Set the file location for Workgroup templates.
- Create multiple versions of a document.

Computers within a company can be connected by a private network referred to as an *intranet*. With an intranet, employees within a company can send e-mail, send a document out for review by more than one person, track changes to a document, route a document to a series of people, create multiple versions of a document, and create a master document using subdocuments. An intranet is a powerful communication tool providing employees with the ability to exchange information. In this chapter, you will learn how to create comments, send and route documents, and create multiple versions of a document.

Tracking Changes to a Document

In a business, a person may create a document that needs to be reviewed by other employees. When more than one person is reviewing a document and making editing changes, consider using the tracking feature. With the tracking feature on, deleted text is not removed from the document but instead displays with a line through it and in a different color. Inserted text displays with an underline below and in a different color. Word uses a different color (up to eight) for each author making changes to the document. In this way, the person looking at the document can identify which author made what change.

Track Changes

Turn on tracking by clicking the Track Changes button on the Reviewing toolbar. To display this toolbar, shown in figure 24.1, *right-click* on the Standard toolbar and then click *Reviewing* at the drop-down list.

figure

24.1

Reviewing Toolbar

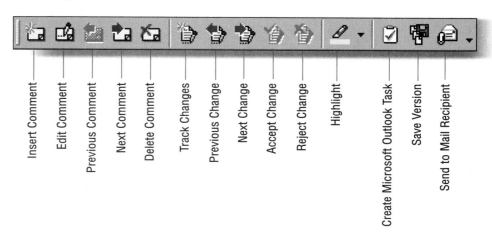

You can also turn on tracking by clicking <u>T</u>ools, pointing to <u>T</u>rack Changes, and then clicking <u>H</u>ighlight Changes. This displays the Highlight Changes dialog box shown in figure 24.2. At this dialog box, insert a check mark in the <u>T</u>rack changes while editing check box, and then click OK. When tracking is on, the letters *TRK* display in black on the Status bar (located toward the bottom of the screen).

figure

24.2

Highlight Changes Dialog Box

Insert a check mark in this check box to turn on tracking.

To turn off tracking, click the Track Changes button on the Reviewing toolbar to deactivate it. You can also turn off tracking by displaying the Highlight Changes dialog box and removing the check mark from the <u>T</u>rack changes while editing check box.

With tracking on, changes made to a document display in the document and in a different color. Additionally, Word inserts a vertical line outside the left margin beside the line containing a change.

Tracking Changes to a Document

1. Open Contract 02.
2. Save the document with Save As and name it Ch 24, Ex 01.
3. Make changes to the contract and track the changes by completing the following steps:

Step 3b

   a. Turn on the display of the Reviewing toolbar by *right-clicking* on the Standard toolbar and then clicking *Reviewing* at the drop-down list. (Skip this step if the Reviewing toolbar is already displayed.)
   b. Click the Track Changes button on the Reviewing toolbar.
   c. Delete *4,000* in paragraph number 3 in the *TRANSFERS AND MOVING EXPENSES* section (the text will not be removed from the screen—instead, a line will display through the text).
   d. Key **6,000** immediately after *4,000*.
   e. Delete *two (2)* in paragraph number 3 in the *SICK LEAVE* section and key **three (3)** immediately after *two (2)*.
   f. Turn off tracking by clicking the Track Changes button on the Reviewing toolbar.
4. Save the document again with the same name (Ch 24, Ex 01).
5. Print and then close Ch 24, Ex 01.

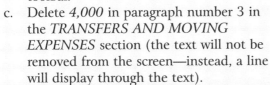

3. Employees transferring to anot force shall be provided with o up to 4,0006,000 pounds at no

Step 3c   Step 3d

3. An employee shall report to his least two (2)three (3) hours prio

Step 3e

You can display information on tracking changes by positioning the mouse pointer on a change. After approximately one second, a yellow box displays above the change. This yellow box contains the author's name, date, time, and the type of change (for example, whether it was a deletion or insertion).

If changes are made to the document by another person with different User Information, the changes display in a different color. In the next exercise, you will pretend to be another author, change User Information, and then make changes to the contract. To change User Information, click Tools and then Options. At the Options dialog box, click the User Information tab. This displays the dialog box as shown in figure 24.3. At the Options dialog box with the User Information tab selected, key different information in the Name, Initials, and Mailing address text boxes.

figure

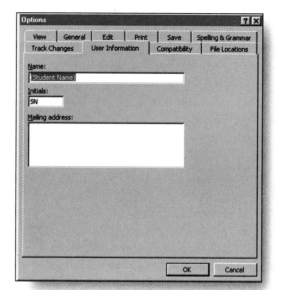

24.3   *Options Dialog Box with User Information Tab Selected*

exercise 2

Tracking Changes to a Document Made by Another Author

(Note: Check with your instructor before completing this exercise to determine if you can change User Information.)

1.   Open Ch 24, Ex 01.
2.   Save the document with Save As and name it Ch 24, Ex 02.
3.   Make additional changes to the contract and track the changes by completing the following steps:
   a.   Click Tools and then Options.
   b.   At the Options dialog box, click the User Information tab.
   c.   At the Options dialog box with the User Information tab selected, make a note of the current name, initials, and mailing address. (You will reenter this information later in this exercise.)
   d.   Key **David Wells** in the Name text box.
   e.   Press the Tab key. (This moves the insertion point to the Initials text box.)
   f.   Key **DW**.
   g.   Click OK to close the Options dialog box.
   h.   Make sure the Reviewing toolbar is displayed and then turn on tracking by clicking the Track Changes button.

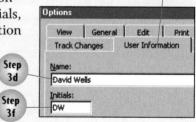

i. Make the following changes to the contract:

1) Add the text **up to $5,000** to the end of the sentence in paragraph number 4 in the *TRANSFERS AND MOVING EXPENSES* section.

2) Delete paragraph number 5 in the *SICK LEAVE* section.

j. Turn off tracking by clicking the Track Changes button on the Reviewing toolbar.

4. Change the User Information back to the information that displayed before you keyed *David Wells* and the initials *DW* by completing the following steps:

a. Click <u>T</u>ools and then <u>O</u>ptions.

b. At the Options dialog box, make sure the User Information tab is selected.

c. At the Options dialog box with the User Information tab selected, key the original name in the <u>N</u>ame text box.

d. Press the Tab key and then key the original initials in the <u>I</u>nitials text box.

e. Click OK to close the dialog box.

5. Save the document again with the same name (Ch 24, Ex 02).

6. Print and then close Ch 24, Ex 02.

4. Each employee requested by **RM** to expenses <u>up to $5,000</u>.

Step 3i1

5. ~~If~~ **RM,** ~~at any time, grants additional LWU will deem this a precedence rec other case.~~

Step 3i2

Moving to the Next/Previous Change

In a longer document containing several changes, use buttons on the Reviewing toolbar to move the insertion point to a change in the document. Click the Previous Change button on the Reviewing toolbar to move to the previous change in the document or click the Next Change button to move to the next change in the document.

Previous Change

Next Change

Accepting/Rejecting Changes

Changes made to a document can be accepted or rejected. Click the Accept Change button on the Reviewing toolbar to accept the change or click the Reject Change button to reject the change. You can also position the mouse pointer over the change and then click the *right* mouse button. This causes a pop-up menu to display with several options. To accept the change, click Acc<u>e</u>pt Change and to reject the change, click <u>R</u>eject Change.

Accept Change

Reject Change

exercise 3

Accepting/Rejecting Changes in a Document

1. Open Ch 24, Ex 02.
2. Save the document with Save As and name it Ch 24, Ex 03.
3. Accept some changes and reject others by completing the following steps:
    a. Accept the change from *4,000* to *6,000* by completing the following steps:
        1) Make sure the Reviewing toolbar is displayed. (If not, *right-click* on the Standard toolbar and then click *Reviewing*.)
        2) Click the Next Change button on the Reviewing toolbar.
        3) With the *4,000* selected, click the Accept Change button on the Reviewing toolbar.
    b. Accept the *6,000* by completing steps similar to those in 3a.

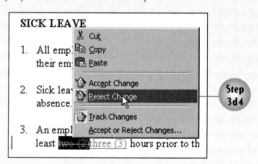

Step 3a3

    c. Click the Next Change button on the Reviewing toolbar and then accept the change adding *up to $5,000* to the end of the sentence in paragraph number 4 in the *TRANSFERS AND MOVING EXPENSES* section.
    d. Reject the change from *two (2)* to *three (3)* by completing the following steps:
        1) Click the Next Change button on the Reviewing toolbar.
        2) Position the mouse pointer over *two (2)*. (This text is selected.)
        3) Click the *right* mouse button.
        4) At the pop-up menu that displays, click Reject Change.
        5) Position the mouse pointer over *three (3)*, click the *right* mouse button, and then click Reject Change.
    e. Reject the change deleting paragraph number 5 in the *SICK LEAVE* section.
    f. Deselect the text.

Step 3d4

4. Save the document again with the same name (Ch 24, Ex 03).
5. Print and then close Ch 24, Ex 03.

Inserting Comments

If you want to make comments in a document you are creating, or if a reviewer wants to make comments in a document written by someone else, insert a comment. A comment includes the initials of the person whose name was entered as the user information and a number. (In a school setting, this may not be your name.) For example, if *Linda Chambers* is the user's name, the first comment in a document would be named *LC1*. You can determine the user name by displaying the Options dialog box with the Information tab selected (as learned in the previous section of this chapter).

Creating a Comment

A comment is similar to a footnote or endnote in that a reference mark is inserted in a document and comment text is keyed at a comment pane. A comment mark will not display in the document screen by default. To show comment marks, turn on the display of nonprinting characters. You can also display comment marks by displaying the Options dialog box, clicking the View tab, clicking H̲idden text, and then clicking OK.

To create a comment, select the text or item on which you want to comment or position the insertion point at the end of the text, click I̲nsert and then Co̲mment. This changes the selected text to highlighted text (yellow background) and opens the comment pane shown in figure 24.4. At the comment pane, key comment text, and then click the C̲lose button.

You can also insert a comment in a document by clicking the Insert Comment button on the Reviewing toolbar. To display this toolbar, *right-click* on the Standard toolbar or the Formatting toolbar and then click *Reviewing* at the drop-down list that displays. If you do not select text before creating a comment, Word will select the closest word to the insertion point.

Insert Comment

figure
24.4

Comment Pane

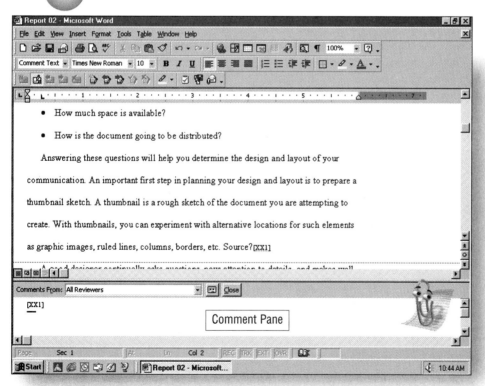

Viewing Comment Text

If you turn on the display of nonprinting characters or hidden text, the comment mark is visible but not the comment text entered in the comment pane. To view the comment text, click <u>V</u>iew and then <u>C</u>omments. This displays the comment pane with the comment text. After viewing the comment text, click <u>C</u>lose to close the comment pane. You can also display the comment pane by *right-clicking* the comment mark and then clicking <u>E</u>dit Comment at the pop-up menu. Another method for displaying the comment pane is to click the Edit Comment button on the Reviewing toolbar. Word will locate the next comment in the document and then display that text in the comment pane.

Edit Comment

Deleting a Comment

Delete a comment in the same manner as a footnote or endnote is deleted. To delete a comment, select the comment mark and then press the Delete key. When the mark is deleted, the corresponding comment text is also deleted. You can also delete a comment mark and its corresponding text by positioning the mouse pointer on the comment mark and then clicking the Delete Comment button on the Reviewing toolbar. Another method is to position the mouse pointer on a comment mark, click the *right* mouse button, and then click Delete Co<u>m</u>ment at the drop-down list.

Delete Comment

Printing a Comment

A document containing comments can be printed with the comments, or you can choose to print just the comments and not the document. To print a document and comments, display the Print dialog box, and then click the <u>O</u>ptions button. This displays the Print dialog box with the Print tab selected. At this dialog box, click <u>C</u>omments (this inserts a check mark in the check box), and then click OK or press Enter. Click OK or press Enter again to close the Print dialog box and send the document to the printer.

To print only comments in a document, display the Print dialog box. At the Print dialog box, click the down-pointing triangle at the right side of the Print <u>w</u>hat option and then click *Comments* at the drop-down list. Click OK or press Enter to close the Print dialog box and send the comments to the printer. Comments are printed on a separate page from the document. The page number where the comment occurs in the document is printed along with the comment mark and the comment text.

Creating Comments in a Document

1. Open Report 02.
2. Save the document with Save As and name it Ch 24, Ex 04.
3. Make sure the Reviewing toolbar displays. (If not, right-click on the Standard toolbar, and then click *Reviewing* at the drop-down list.)
4. Turn on the display of comment marks by completing the following steps:
   a. Click <u>T</u>ools and then <u>O</u>ptions.

b. At the Options dialog box, click the View tab.
c. At the Options dialog box with the View tab selected, click Hidden text in the Formatting marks section.
d. Click OK or press Enter.

5. Create a comment at the end of the first paragraph below the bulleted items on the first page in the report by completing the following steps:
   a. Position the insertion point at the end of the first paragraph below the bulleted items on the first page in the report.
   b. Key **Source?**.
   c. Select *Source?*.
   d. Click the Insert Comment button on the Reviewing toolbar.
   e. At the Comment pane, key **Please add the source for the information in this paragraph.**
   f. Click the Close button.

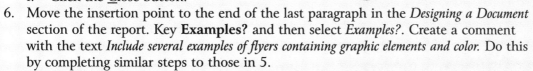

6. Move the insertion point to the end of the last paragraph in the *Designing a Document* section of the report. Key **Examples?** and then select *Examples?*. Create a comment with the text *Include several examples of flyers containing graphic elements and color.* Do this by completing similar steps to those in 5.
7. Move the insertion point to the end of the last paragraph in the report. Key **Illustrations** and then select *Illustrations*. Create a comment with the text, *Add several illustrations of focal points in a document.*, by completing steps similar to those in 5.
8. Save the document again with the same name (Ch 24, Ex 04).
9. Print the document and the comments by completing the following steps:
   a. Display the Print dialog box.
   b. At the Print dialog box, click the Options button.
   c. At the Print dialog box with the Print tab selected, click Comments. (This inserts a check mark in the Comments check box and the Hidden text check box.)
   d. Click OK or press Enter.
   e. At the Print dialog box, click OK or press Enter.

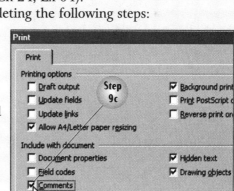

10. Turn off the display of comment marks by completing steps similar to those in 4.
11. Turn off the printing of comments by completing the following steps:
    a. Display the Print dialog box.
    b. At the Print dialog box, click the Options button.
    c. At the Print dialog box with the Print tab selected, click Comments, and then click Hidden text.
    d. Click OK or press Enter.
    e. Click the Close button to close the Print dialog box.
12. Turn off the display of the Reviewing toolbar.
13. Close Ch 24, Ex 04.

Sending and Routing Documents

In a corporate or business setting, you may work on a project with others in a group. In a situation where a number of people are working on individual documents that will be combined into a larger document, sending and routing documents can be very helpful. In Word, you can send a document to a project member in an Outlook e-mail message or route a document to several project members, one after the other.

To complete exercises in this section, you will need to have Outlook available on your system. System configurations can be quite varied. You may find that your screen does not exactly match what you see in figures in this section. Steps in exercises may need to be modified to accommodate your system. Before completing exercises in this section, please check with your instructor for any modifications or changes to information and exercises.

Sending a Document

E-mail

To send a document as an Outlook e-mail message, open the document in Word, and then click the E-mail button on the Standard toolbar. (You can also click File, point to Send To, and then click Mail Recipient.) This displays the e-mail header below the Formatting toolbar as shown in figure 24.5. When the e-mail header displays, Outlook is automatically opened.

figure

24.5

E-mail Header

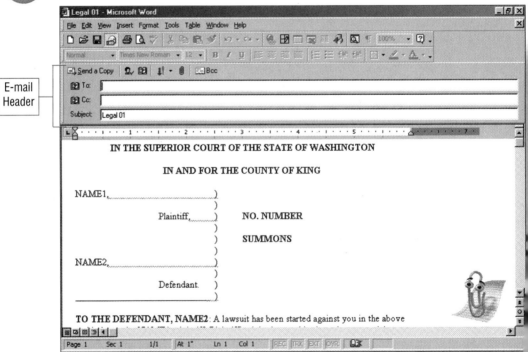

At the e-mail header, fill in the recipient information and then click the Send button. Word sends a copy of the document to the recipient and closes the e-mail header. The original document remains open for editing. When the document is saved, the e-mail information is saved with the document.

In the To text box in the e-mail header, key the e-mail address of the person to receive the document. If the e-mail name and address have been established in an address folder, click the book icon that displays immediately before To and the Select Recipients dialog box displays. At this dialog box, shown in figure 24.6, select the name to receive the document in the list box that displays at the left side of the dialog box, and then click the To button. This inserts the name in the Message recipients list box. Click OK to close the dialog box.

Address Book

figure

24.6 **Select Recipients Dialog Box**

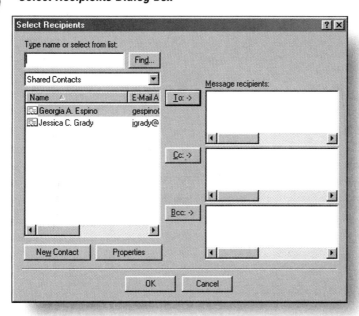

The e-mail header contains buttons you can use to customize the e-mail message. The button names and descriptions are shown in figure 24.7.

24.7 *E-mail Header Buttons*

Button	Name	Function
Send a Copy	Send	Sends a copy of the document to the recipient
	Check Names	Checks name to ensure that Outlook recognizes the e-mail address
	Address Book	Displays the Address Book dialog box
	Set Priority	Sets the message priority level
	Attach File	Displays the Insert Attachment dialog box where you can choose a document you want attached to the e-mail
Bcc	Toggle Bcc	Displays a Bcc text box (*Bcc* refers to *blind carbon copy*) where the name you key in the Bcc text box receives a copy of the document but the original recipient does not know

In the exercises in this chapter, you will send the e-mail to your instructor. If your system is networked and your computer is not part of an intranet system, skip the step instructing you to click the Send button.

exercise 5

Creating and Printing an Outlook E-Mail Message

(Note: Before completing this exercise, check to see if you can send e-mail messages. If you cannot, consider completing all the steps in the exercise except step 3d.)

1. Open Legal 01.
2. Save the document with Save As and name it Ch 24, Ex 05.
3. Create the Ch 24, Ex 05 document as an Outlook e-mail by completing the following steps:

a. Click the E-mail button on the Standard toolbar.
b. At the e-mail header, key your instructor's name in the To text box. (Depending on how the system is configured, you may need to key your instructor's e-mail address.)
c. Click the down-pointing triangle at the right side of the Set Priority button and then click High Priority at the drop-down list.
d. Click the Send button.
e. If necessary, click the E-mail button on the Standard toolbar to turn off the display of the e-mail header.

Step 3a

Step 3c

Step 3d

Step 3b

4. Save the document again with the same name (Ch 24, Ex 05).
5. Close the Ch 24, Ex 05 document.

Routing a Document

Routing a document differs from sending a document in that the first recipient receives the document, makes comments or changes, and then sends it to the next person on the list. In this way, one document is edited by several people rather than several people editing versions of the same document.

To route a document, open the document, click File, point to Send To, and then click Routing Recipient. This displays the Routing Slip dialog box shown in figure 24.8. At the Routing Slip dialog box, click the Address button and the Address Book dialog box shown in figure 24.9 displays.

24.8   *Routing Slip Dialog Box*

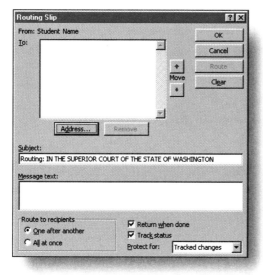

figure 24.9

Address Book Dialog Box

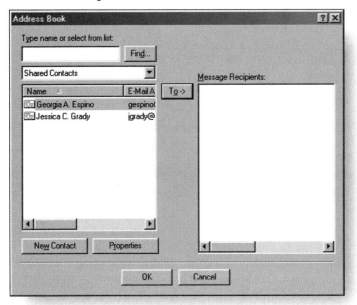

At the Address Book dialog box, double-click the name of each recipient in the order they are to receive the document. Double-clicking a name inserts the name in the list box that displays at the right side of the dialog box. When all names are displayed in the list box, click OK. At the Routing Slip dialog box, make sure the names are displayed in the proper order. (If not, click one of the Move buttons to move the names into the proper order.) Key a message in the Message text box. Make sure One after another is selected in the Route to recipients section, and then click the Route button that displays at the right side of the dialog box.

exercise 6

Routing a Document

1. Open Ch 24, Ex 05.
2. Route the document by completing the following steps:
   a. Click File, point to Send To, and then click Routing Recipient.
   b. At the Routing Slip dialog box, click the Address button.
   c. At the Address Book dialog box, double-click any names that display in the list box at the left side of the dialog box. (If there are no names, skip this step.)
   d. Click OK to close the Address Book dialog box.
   e. At the Routing Slip dialog box, click the Route button to route the document to the first recipient. (Depending on your system configuration, you may not be able to send this e-mail. If that is the case, click the Cancel button instead of the Route button.)
3. Close Ch 24, Ex 05.

Sending a Document on a "Round Trip"

If you send a document on a company intranet, the person receiving the document will probably open and edit the document in the application in which it was created. For example, if you are sending a Word document to a colleague, he or she will open and edit the document in Word.

Situations may arise where you need to send a document to a person who does not have the application in which the document was created. In this situation, save the document in HTML file format. To do this, click File and then Save as Web Page. At the Save As dialog box, key a name for the document in the File name text box, and then click the Save button.

The person receiving the document does not need the originating application to view and/or edit the document. The receiver can open the document in his or her Web browser and then view and even edit the document in the browser (rather than the originating application). When the document is returned to you and opened in the originating application, all of the formatting and functionality of the document is retained. Office refers to this process as a "round trip." The document is saved in a specific application, saved in HTML file format, viewed and edited in a Web browser, and then returned to the originating application without losing any formatting or functionality.

Creating a Template

A document that will be used in the future as a framework for other documents can be saved as a template. To save a document as a template, display the Save As dialog box, change the Save as type option to *Document Template*, key a name for the template, and then press Enter.

Changing the Default File Location for Workgroup Templates

By default a template is saved in the *Templates* folder and will display at the New dialog box with the General tab selected. You can save a template in a folder other than the default by specifying the folder. If you are working in a company setting with an intranet, consider saving templates that will be shared on the network in the *Workgroup templates* file location. You can specify the file location for Workgroup templates at the Options dialog box. To do this, you would complete the following steps:

1. At a clear document screen, click Tools and then Options.
2. At the Options dialog box, click the File Locations tab.
3. At the Options dialog box with the File Locations tab selected as shown in figure 24.10, click *Workgroup templates* in the File types list box.
4. Click the Modify button.
5. At the Modify Location dialog box, specify the desired drive and/or folder in the Look in list box, and then click OK.
6. Click OK to close the Options dialog box.

figure

24.10

Options Dialog Box with File Locations Tab Selected

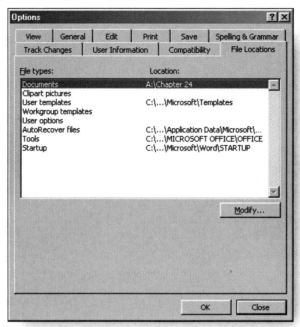

In exercise 7, you will be change the location of Workgroup templates to a *Templates* folder you will create on your disk. In a company setting, the Workgroup templates location would probably be a folder on the network. Before completing exercise 7, check with your instructor to determine if you can change file locations.

Changing File Location and Creating a Template Document

1. Create a *Templates* folder on your disk by completing the following steps:
   a. Display the Open dialog box.
   b. Make active the drive where your disk is located (do not make *Chapter 24* the active folder).
   c. Click the Create New Folder button on the Open dialog box toolbar.
   d. At the New Folder dialog box, key **Templates** in the Name text box.
   e. Click OK or press Enter to close the dialog box.
   f. Click the Cancel button to close the Open dialog box.
2. At a clear document screen, specify the *Templates* folder on your disk as the location for Workgroup templates by completing the following steps:
   a. Insert your disk (containing the *Templates* folder) in the appropriate drive.
   b. Click Tools and then Options.

c. At the Options dialog box, click the File Locations tab.
d. At the Options dialog box with the File Locations tab selected, make a note of the current location for *Workgroup templates* that displays in the File types list box (the location may be blank). (You will be returning the location back to this default at the end of the exercise.)
e. Click *Workgroup templates* in the File types list box.
f. Click the Modify button.
g. At the Modify Location dialog box, click the down-pointing triangle at the right side of the Look in list box and then click *3½ Floppy (A:)* (or the drive letter where your disk is located).
h. Double-click the *Templates* folder.
i. Click OK to close the Modify Location dialog box.
j. Click OK to close the Options dialog box.

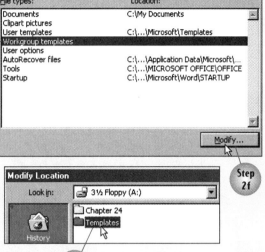

3. Open Legal 01.
4. Save the document as a template named Summons in the *Templates* folder on your disk by completing the following steps:
   a. Click File and then Save As.
   b. At the Save As dialog box, click the down-pointing triangle at the right side of the Save as type list box, and then click *Document Template*. (This automatically changes the folder to the *Microsoft Templates* folder.)
   c. Change to the *Templates* folder on your disk by completing the following steps:
      1) Click the down-pointing triangle at the right side of the Save in list box.
      2) At the drop-down list that displays, click the drive where your disk is located.
      3) Double-click the *Templates* folder.
   d. Select the name in the File name box and then key **Summons**.
   e. Press Enter or click the Save button.
5. Close the Summons template.
6. Open the Summons template by completing the following steps:
   a. Click File and then New.
   b. At the New dialog box with the General tab selected, double-click *Summons*.
7. With the Summons template document open, make the following find and replaces:
   a. Find *NAME1* and replace with *AMY GARCIA*.
   b. Find *NAME2* and replace with *NEIL CARLIN*.
   c. Fine *NUMBER* and replace with *C-98002*.
8. Save the document in the *Chapter 24* folder on your disk and name it Ch 24, Ex 07.
9. Print and then close Ch 24, Ex 07.
10. Remove the Summons template from the New dialog box by completing the following steps:
    a. Click File and then New.

b. At the New dialog box with the General tab selected, *right-click* on the *Summons* icon.
c. At the shortcut menu that displays, click the Delete option.
d. At the Confirm File Delete message, click Yes.
e. Click Cancel to close the New dialog box.
11. Return the Workgroup templates back to the default location by completing the following steps:
a. At a document screen, click Tools and then Options.
b. At the Options dialog box, click the File Locations tab.
c. At the Options dialog box with the File Locations tab selected, click *Workgroup templates* in the File types list box.
d. Click the Modify button.
e. At the Modify Location dialog box, change to the default *Workgroup templates* folder. (If the default location was blank, select any text currently displayed in the Folder name text box and then press the Delete key.)
f. Click OK to close the Modify Location dialog box.
g. Click OK to close the Options dialog box.

Sumn | **New**
Scan for Viruses
Open
Add to Zip
Add to Summons.zip
Cut
Copy
Create Shortcut
Delete
Properties

Step 10c

Creating Multiple Versions of a Document

Use Word's versioning feature to save multiple versions of a document in the same document. This saves disk space because only the differences between the versions are saved, not the entire document. You can create, review, open, and delete versions of a document. Creating versions is useful in a situation where you want to maintain the original document and use it as a "baseline" to compare with future versions of the document.

Saving a Version of a Document

To save a version of a document, click File and then Versions. This displays the Versions in (Document Name) dialog box shown in figure 24.11.

figure

24.11   *Versions in (Document Name) Dialog Box*

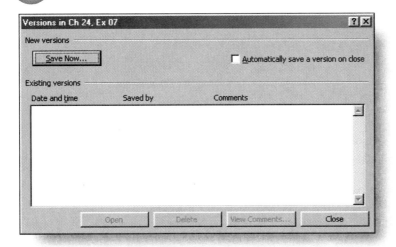

At the Versions in (Document Name) dialog box, click the Save Now button. This displays the Save Version dialog box shown in figure 24.12. At this dialog box, key a comment about the version in the Comments on version text box, and then click OK. This removes the dialog box and returns you to the document. When a version is saved, a *File Versions* icon displays at the right side of the Status bar. To review the version information, display the Versions in (Document Name) dialog box.

figure

24.12   *Save Version Dialog Box*

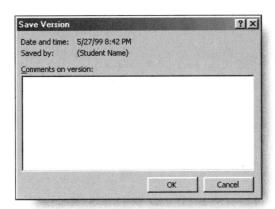

Saving Versions of a Document

1. Open Contract 02.
2. Save the document with Save As and name it Ch 24, Ex 08.
3. Create a version of the original document by completing the following steps:
   a. Click File and then Versions.
   b. At the Versions in Ch 24, Ex 08 dialog box, click the Save Now button.
   c. At the Save Version dialog box, key **First draft of contract** in the Comments on version text box.
   d. Click OK.

Save Version	
Date and time:	2/8/99 9:32 AM
Saved by:	(Student Name)
Comments on version:	
First draft of contract	

Step
3c

4. Make the following editing changes to the contract:
   a. Delete paragraph number 5 in the *TRANSFERS AND MOVING EXPENSES* section.
   b. Add the text *and ten (10) hours of sick leave after 10 years of employment with RM* at the end of the sentence in paragraph number 1 in the *SICK LEAVE* section.
5. Create another version of the document that contains the edits by completing the following steps:
   a. Click File and then Versions.
   b. At the Versions in Ch 24, Ex 08 dialog box, click the Save Now button.
   c. At the Save Version dialog box, key **Second draft of contract** in the Comments on version text box.
   d. Click OK.
6. Make the following editing changes to the contract:
   a. Change *4,000* to *8,000* in paragraph number 3 in the *TRANSFERS AND MOVING EXPENSES* section.
   b. Delete paragraph number 2 in the *SICK LEAVE* section. (When you delete paragraph number 2, the remaining paragraphs are automatically renumbered.)
7. Create another version of the document with the comment *Third draft of contract*.
8. Close Ch 24, Ex 08.

Opening an Earlier Version

You can open an earlier version of a document and view it next to the current version. To do this, open the document containing the versions, and then display the Versions in (Document Name) dialog box. Click the desired earlier version in the Existing versions list box and then click the Open button. This opens the earlier version in a new window and tiles the two documents.

Saving a Version as a Separate Document

If you try to save an earlier version, the Save As dialog box will display. This dialog box displays so you will key a new name for the version document rather than overwriting the original. Key a new name for the version at the Save As dialog box and then press Enter or click the Save button.

Deleting a Version

Delete a version of a document at the Versions in (Document Name) dialog box. To delete a version, display the dialog box, click the version name in the Existing versions list box, and then click the <u>D</u>elete button. At the Confirm Version Delete message, click <u>Y</u>es.

Opening, Saving, Deleting, and Comparing Versions

1. Open Ch 24, Ex 08.
2. Open an earlier version by completing the following steps:
   a. Click <u>F</u>ile and then V<u>e</u>rsions.
   b. At the Versions in Ch 24, Ex 08 dialog box, click the first draft of contract version in the Existing versions list box.
   c. Click the <u>O</u>pen button. (This opens the earlier version in a new window and tiles the two documents.)

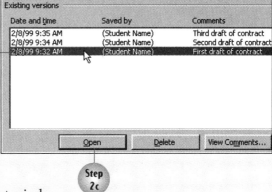

Step 2b

Step 2c

3. After viewing the documents, save the earlier version as a separate document by completing the following steps:
   a. Make sure the earlier version document window is active (and no text is selected). (The earlier version will probably display in the bottom window and will contain the word *version* somewhere in the Title bar.)
   b. Click <u>F</u>ile and then Save <u>A</u>s.
   c. At the Save As dialog box, key **Contract First Draft**.
   d. Press Enter or click the <u>S</u>ave button.
4. Close the Contract First Draft document.
5. Maximize the Ch 24, Ex 08 window.
6. Delete the second draft version of the document by completing the following steps:
   a. Click <u>F</u>ile and then V<u>e</u>rsions.
   b. At the Versions in Ch 24, Ex 08 dialog box, click the second draft of contract version in the Existing versions list box.
   c. Click the <u>D</u>elete button.
   d. At the Confirm Version Delete message, click <u>Y</u>es.
   e. At the Versions in Ch 24, Ex 08 dialog box, click the Close button.

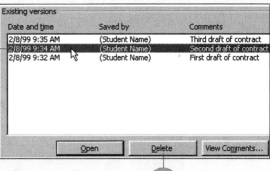

Step 6b

Step 6c

7. Save the document again with the same name (Ch 24, Ex 08).
8. Close Ch 24, Ex 08.

9. Compare the first draft document with the latest version by completing the following steps:
   a. Open the document named Contract First Draft.
   b. Click Tools, point to Track Changes, and then click Compare Documents.
   c. At the Select File to Compare With Current Document dialog box, double-click the document named Ch 24, Ex 08.
10. Save the document with Save As and name it Ch 24, Ex 09.
11. Print and then close Ch 24, Ex 09.

chapter summary

➤ Use the tracking feature when more than one person is reviewing a document and making editing changes.

➤ When tracking is on, deleted text is not removed but instead displays with a line through it and in a different color. Inserted text displays with an underline below and in a different color.

➤ Display information on tracking changes such as author's name, date, time, and type of change by positioning the mouse pointer on a change. After approximately one second, a yellow box displays with the information.

➤ Change user information at the Options dialog box with the User Information tab selected.

➤ Move to the next change in a document by clicking the Next Change button on the Reviewing toolbar. Click the Previous Change button to move to a previous change in the document.

➤ Changes made to a document can be accepted or rejected.

➤ If you want to make comments in a document you are creating, or if a reviewer wants to make comments in a document written by someone else, insert a comment. A comment includes the initials of the person whose name was entered as the user information and a number.

➤ Create a comment at a comment pane.

➤ A document containing comments can be printed with the comments, or you can choose to print just the comments and not the document.

➤ Send a document in an Outlook e-mail message in a situation where a number of people are working on individual documents that will be combined into a larger document.

➤ When a document is routed, one document is edited by several people rather than several people editing versions of the same document.

➤ Use the versioning feature to save multiple versions of a document in the same document.

➤ Save a version of a document and delete a version of a document at the Version in (Document Name) dialog box.

➤ An earlier version of a document can be opened and then viewed next to the current version.

commands review

	Mouse/Keyboard
Turn on tracking	Click the Track Changes button on Reviewing toolbar; or click Tools, point to Track Changes, then click Highlight Changes.
Display a comment pane	Click the Insert Comment button on Reviewing toolbar; or click Insert and then click Comment
View comments	Click View and then Comments
Delete a comment	Select comment mark, press Delete key; or, position mouse pointer on comment mark, then click the Delete Comment button on Reviewing toolbar; or, position the mouse pointer on comment mark, click the *right* mouse button, then click Delete Comment
Display E-mail header	Click the E-mail button on the Standard toolbar
Display Routing Slip dialog box	Click File, point to Send To, then click Routing Recipient
Display Address Book dialog box	At the Routing Slip dialog box, click Address button
Display Options dialog box	Click Tools and then Options.
Display Version in (Document Name) dialog box	Click File and then Versions
Display Save Version dialog box	At the Version in (Document Name) dialog box, click Save Now button

thinking offline

Completion: In the space provided at the right, indicate the correct term, command, or number.

1. Turn on tracking by clicking this button on the Reviewing toolbar.

2. With tracking turned on in a document, deleted text is not removed but instead displays in this manner.

3. With tracking turned on in a document, inserted text displays in this manner.

4. When tracking is turned on in a document, these letters display in black on the Status bar.

5. To create a comment, click this button on the Reviewing toolbar.

6. Key comment text at this location.

7. To view comment text in a document, click View and then this.

8. To display the e-mail header, click this button on the Standard toolbar.

9. Click File, point to Send To, and then click Routing Recipient and this dialog box displays.

10. At this dialog box with the File Locations tab selected, you can specify a location for Workgroup templates. _____

11. Use this feature to save multiple versions of a document in the same document. _____

12. Display the Save Version dialog box by clicking this button at the Version in (Document Name) dialog box. _____

13. In the space provided below, list the steps you would complete to insert the comment *Please include additional resources.* into a document.

_____

_____

_____

working hands-on

Assessment 1

1. Open Mortgage.
2. Save the document with Save As and name it Ch 24, SA 01.
3. Make changes to the document and track the changes by completing the following steps:
   a. Turn on tracking.
   b. Change *ten (10)* in the *Delinquency* paragraph to *fifteen (15)*.
   c. Delete the words *charge computed as if Buyers had prepaid in full* that display at the end of the *Demand for Full Payment* paragraph.
   d. Insert the words *and safe* between *good* and *condition* in the second sentence in the *Use of the Collateral* paragraph.
   e. Turn off tracking.
4. Save the document again with the same name (Ch 24, SA 01).
5. Print and then close Ch 24, SA 01.

Assessment 2

1. Open Ch 24, SA 01.
2. Save the document with Save As and name it Ch 24, SA 02.
3. Make additional changes to the document and track the changes by completing the following steps:
   a. Display the Options dialog box with the User Information tab selected and then complete the following steps:.
      1) Make a note of the current name, initials, and mailing address. (You will reenter this information later in this assessment.)
      2) Key **Mildred Brown** in the Name text box.
      3) Key **MB** in the Initials text box.
   b. Close the Options dialog box.
   c. Turn on tracking.
   d. Make the following changes to the document:
      1) Insert the word *all* between *pay* and *reasonable* in the last sentence in the *Delinquency* paragraph.
      2) Delete the words *at the time of the default or any time after default* in the first sentence in the *Demand for Full Payment* paragraph.

       3) Insert the words *unless agreed upon by Sellers* between *Contract* and the period that ends the last sentence in the *Use of the Collateral* paragraph.
  e. Turn off tracking.
  f. Display the Options dialog box with the User Information tab selected, change back to the information that displayed before you keyed *Mildred Brown* and the initials *MB*, and then close the dialog box.
4. Save the document again with the same name (Ch 24, SA 02).
5. Print and then close Ch 24, SA 02.

Assessment 3

1. Open Ch 24, SA 02.
2. Save the document with Save As and name it Ch 24, SA 03.
3. Accept the following changes in the document:
  a. Accept the change from *ten (10)* to *fifteen (15)* in the *Delinquency* paragraph.
  b. Accept the change deleting the words *charge computed as if Buyers had prepaid in full* that display at the end of the *Demand for Full Payment* paragraph.
  c. Accept the change inserting the word *all* between *pay* and *reasonable* in the last sentence in the *Delinquency* paragraph.
  d. Accept the change inserting the words *unless agreed upon by Sellers* between *Contract* and the period that ends the last sentence in the *Use of the Collateral* paragraph.
4. Reject the following changes in the document:
  a. Reject the change inserting the words *and safe* between *good* and *condition* in the second sentence in the *Use of the Collateral* paragraph.
  b. Reject the change deleting the words *at the time of the default or any time after default,* in the first sentence in the *Demand for Full Payment* paragraph.
5. Save the document again with the same name (Ch 24, SA 03).
6. Print and then close Ch 24, SA 03.

Assessment 4

1. Open Report 01.
2. Save the document with Save As and name it Ch 24, SA 04.
3. Make the following changes to the report:
  a. Select the entire document and then change the font to 13-point Garamond (or a similar serif typeface).
  b. Set the title and the headings in 14-point Arial bold.
  c. Select the text in the body of the report (everything except the title) and then make the following changes:
    1) Change the line spacing to single.
    2) Change the spacing before and after paragraphs to 6 points.
    3) Change the paragraph alignment to justified.
  d. Create a comment at the end of the second paragraph in the *Defining Desktop Publishing* section of the report. Key the words **Color printers?**, select the words, and then create the comment with the following text: *Include information on color printers.*
  e. Create a comment at the end of the last paragraph in the *Planning the Publication* section of the report. Key the word **Examples**, select the word, and then create the comment with the following text: *Include examples of effective designs.*
4. Save the document again with the same name (Ch 24, SA 04).
5. Print the document and the comments. (After printing the document and the comments, be sure to remove the check marks in the Comments and Hidden text check boxes at the Print dialog box with the Print tab selected.)
6. Close Ch 24, SA 04.

Assessment 5

1. Open Mortgage.
2. Save the document with Save As and name it Ch 24, SA 05.
3. Create the Ch 24, SA 05 document as an Outlook e-mail message by completing the following steps:
   a. Display the e-mail header.
   b. Key your instructor's name (or e-mail address) in the To text box.
   c. Identify the document as low priority.
   d. If possible, send the e-mail message to your instructor.
   e. Close the e-mail header.
4. Save the document again with the same name (Ch 24, SA 05).
5. Close Ch 24, SA 05.

Assessment 6

1. Open Legal 01.
2. Save the document with Save As and name it Ch 24, SA 06.
3. Create a version of the original document by completing the following steps:
   a. Display the Versions in Ch 24, SA 06 dialog box.
   b. Click the Save Now button to display the Save Version dialog box.
   c. At the Save Version dialog box, key **First draft of Summons** in the Comments on version text box.
   d. Click OK to close the dialog box.
4. Make the following editing changes to the document:
   a. Delete the words *a copy of which is* at the end of the first paragraph and replace them with *two copies of which are.*
   b. Insert the word *written* between the words *without* and *notice* located at the end of the first sentence in the second paragraph.
5. Create another version of the document with the comment *Second draft of Summons.*
6. Make the following editing changes to the document:
   a. Delete the sentence *A default judgment is one where the plaintiff, NAME1, is entitled to what plaintiff asks for because you have not responded.* that displays at the end of the second paragraph.
   b. Insert the words *null and* between the words *be* and *void* located at the end of the third paragraph.
7. Create another version of the document with the comment *Third draft of Summons.*
8. Open the First draft of Summons version of the document. *(Hint: Be sure to do this at the Versions in Ch 24, SA 06 dialog box.)*
9. After viewing the first draft version, save the version as a separate document named *Summons First Draft.*
10. Close the Summons First Draft document.
11. Maximize the Ch 24, SA 06 window.
12. Delete the second draft version of the document. *(Hint: Be sure to do this at the Versions in Ch 24, SA 06 dialog box.)*
13. Save the document again with the same name (Ch 24, SA 06).
14. Compare the first draft document with the latest version.
15. Save the document with Save As and name it Ch 24, SA 06 Com Doc.
16. Print and then close Ch 24, SA 06 Com Doc.

Chapter 25

Creating Specialized Tables and Indexes

PERFORMANCE OBJECTIVES

Upon successful completion of chapter 25, you will be able to:

- Create, compile, and update a table of contents.
- Create, compile, and update an index.
- Create, compile, and update a table of figures.
- Create, compile, and update a table of authorities.

A book, textbook, report, or manuscript often includes sections such as a table of contents, index, and table of figures in the document. Creating these sections can be tedious when done manually. With Word, these functions can be automated to create the sections quickly and easily. In this chapter, you will learn the steps to mark text for a table of contents, index, table of figures, and table of authorities, and then compile the table or list.

Creating a Table of Contents

A table of contents appears at the beginning of a book, manuscript, or report and contains headings and subheadings with page numbers. Figure 25.1 shows an example of a table of contents.

figure
25.1   *Table of Contents*

TABLE OF CONTENTS

Text to be included in a table of contents can be identified by applying a heading style or text can be marked as a field entry. The advantage to using styles to mark text for a table of contents is that it is quick. The disadvantage is that the headings in the document will display with the formatting applied by the style.

The advantage to marking headings for a table of contents as a field entry is that no formatting is applied to the heading in the document. The disadvantage is that it takes more time to mark headings.

Marking Table of Contents Entries as Styles

A table of contents can be created by applying heading styles to text to be included in the table of contents. When creating a table of contents, there are two steps involved in creating the table of contents:
1. Apply the appropriate styles to the text that will be included in the table of contents.
2. Compile the table of contents in the document.

Word automatically includes text that is formatted with a heading style in a table of contents. In chapter 22 you learned that Word contains nine heading styles that can be applied to text. If you have already applied these styles to create an outline, the same headings are included in the table of contents. If the styles have not previously been applied, you can apply them with the Style button on the Formatting toolbar, or with buttons on the Outlining toolbar in the Outline view. To apply styles for a table of contents, position the insertion point on any character in the text you want included in the table of contents, click the down-pointing triangle to the right of the Style button on the Formatting toolbar, and then click the desired style. Continue in this manner until all styles have been applied to titles, headings, and subheadings in the document.

Compiling a Table of Contents

After the necessary heading styles have been applied to text that you want included in the table of contents, the next step is to compile the table of contents. To do this, position the insertion point where you want the table to appear, then click Insert and then Index and Tables. At the Index and Tables dialog box, click the Table of Contents tab. This displays the Index and Tables dialog box as shown in figure 25.2. At this dialog box, make any desired changes, and then click OK.

figure
25.2

Index and Tables Dialog Box with Table of Contents Tab Selected

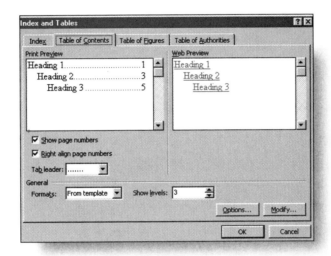

At the Index and Tables dialog box with the Table of Contents tab selected, a sample table of contents displays in the Print Preview section. You can change the table of contents format by clicking the down-pointing triangle at the right side of the Formats list box (located in the General section). At the drop-down list that displays, click the desired format. When a different format is selected, that format displays in the Print Preview section. Page numbers in a table of contents will display after the text or aligned at the right margin depending on what options are selected. The number of levels displayed depends on the number of heading levels specified in the document.

Tab leaders help guide the reader's eyes from the table of contents heading to the page number. The default tab leader is a period. To choose a different leader, click the down-pointing triangle at the right side of the Tab leader text box, and then click the desired leader character from the drop-down list.

If you want the table of contents to print on a page separate from the document text, insert a section break that begins a new page between the table of contents and the title of the document. If the beginning of the text in the document, rather than the table of contents, should be numbered as page 1, change the starting page number for the section. A table of contents is generally numbered with lowercase Roman numerals.

Word automatically displays headings in a table of contents as hyperlinks. Position the mouse pointer on a heading in a table of contents and the mouse pointer turns into a hand. Click the left mouse button and the specific heading in the document displays.

Applying Styles and Compiling a Table of Contents

1. Open Report 01.
2. Save the document with Save As and name it Ch 25, Ex 01.
3. Apply heading styles to the title, headings, and subheadings by completing the following steps:
   a. With the insertion point positioned at the beginning of the document, press the Enter key once. (This adds room for the table of contents you will be inserting later.)
   b. Select the entire document and then change the line spacing to single.
   c. Position the insertion point on any character in the title *DESKTOP PUBLISHING*, click the down-pointing triangle to the right of the Style button on the Formatting toolbar, and then click *Heading 1*.
   d. Position the insertion point on any character in the heading *Defining Desktop Publishing*, click the down-pointing triangle to the right of the Style button on the Formatting toolbar, and then click *Heading 2*.
   e. Apply the Heading 2 style to the following headings:
      Initiating the Desktop Publishing Process
      Planning the Publication
      Creating the Content
4. Position the insertion point immediately left of the *D* in *DESKTOP PUBLISHING* and then insert a section break by completing the following steps:
   a. Click Insert and then Break.
   b. At the Break dialog box, click Next page.
   c. Click OK or press Enter.
5. With the insertion point positioned below the section break, insert page numbering and change the beginning number to 1 by completing the following steps:
   a. Click Insert and then Page Numbers.
   b. At the Page Numbers dialog box, click the down-pointing triangle at the right side of the Alignment option, and then click *Center* at the drop-down list.
   c. Click the Format button (in the dialog box, not on the Menu bar).
   d. At the Page Number Format dialog box, click Start at. (This inserts 1 in the Start at text box.)

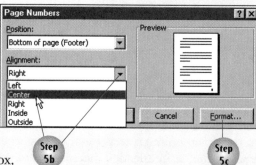

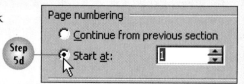

e. Click OK or press Enter to close the Page Number Format dialog box.

f. At the Page Numbers dialog box, click OK or press Enter.

6. Compile and insert a table of contents at the beginning of the document by completing the following steps:

a. Position the insertion point at the beginning of the document (on the new page).

b. Turn on bold, key **TABLE OF CONTENTS** centered, and then turn off bold.

c. Press the Enter key once and then change the paragraph alignment back to left.

d. Click Insert and then Index and Tables.

e. At the Index and Tables dialog box, click the Table of Contents tab.

f. At the Index and Tables dialog box with the Table of Contents tab selected, click the down-pointing triangle at the right side of the Formats list box, and then click *Formal* at the drop-down list.

g. Click OK or press Enter.

7. Position the insertion point on any character in the title *TABLE OF CONTENTS*, and then apply the Heading 1 style. (This will change the font to 16-point Arial bold and also change the alignment to left.)

8. Insert page numbering in the Table of Contents page by completing the following steps:

a. Click Insert and then Page Numbers.

b. At the Page Numbers dialog box, click the Format button.

c. At the Page Number Format dialog box, click the down-pointing triangle at the right side of the Number format text box, and then click *i, ii, iii, ...* at the drop-down list.

d. Click Start at. (This inserts *i* in the Start at text box.)

e. Click OK or press Enter to close the Page Number Format dialog box.

f. At the Page Numbers dialog box, click OK or press Enter.

9. Save the document again with the same name (Ch 25, Ex 01).

10. Print the table of contents page. (Check with your instructor to see if you should print the other pages of the document.)

11. Close Ch 25, Ex 01. (If a message displays asking if you want to save the changes to the document, click Yes.)

Marking Table of Contents Entries as Fields

you do not want style formatting to be applied to the title, headings, or
bheadings in a document but you do want to create a table of contents for the
cument, mark text for the table as fields. When text is marked for a table of
ntents, a field code is inserted in the document. (This code should be visible in
e document screen. If it is not, click the Show/Hide ¶ button on the Standard
olbar.)

To mark a title in a document for a table of contents, position the insertion point at the beginning of the title, then click Insert and then Field. At the Field dialog box, shown in figure 25.3, click *Index and Tables* in the Categories list box, and click *TC* in the Field names list box. Position the mouse pointer inside the Field codes text box to the right of the *TC* and then click the left mouse button. Key the title surrounded by quotation marks followed by \l1. The first character after the backslash is a lowercase L and the second character is the number 1. Click OK or press Enter to close the dialog box.

Field Dialog Box

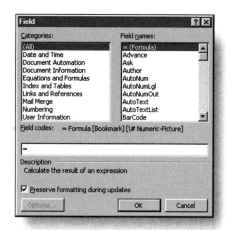

The field code { **TC** *"TITLE OF DOCUMENT"* **\l1** } (where the document title is inserted between the quotation marks) is inserted at the beginning of the document title. The backslash and the lowercase L are referred to as a *switch*. This switch tells Word that the character after the switch is the heading level for the table of contents. If you were marking a heading for level 2 in the table of contents, you would enter a **2** after the \l switch. After marking text for a table of contents, compile the table of contents as described earlier in this chapter.

Marking Headings as Fields and Then Compiling a Table of Contents

1. Open Report 03.
2. Save the document with Save As and name it Ch 25, Ex 02.
3. Mark the titles and headings as fields for a table of contents by completing the following steps:
   a. With the insertion point positioned at the beginning of the document, press the Enter key once. (This adds room for the table of contents you will be inserting later.)
   b. Position the insertion point at the beginning of the title *MODULE 1: DEFINING NEWSLETTER ELEMENTS* and then mark it as a field for the table of contents by completing the following steps:
      1) Click Insert and then Field.

2) At the Field dialog box, click *Index and Tables* in the Categories list box.
3) Click *TC* in the Field names list box.
4) Position the mouse pointer **Step 3b2** inside the Field codes text box to the right of the *TC* and then click the left mouse button.
5) Key "**MODULE 1: DEFINING NEWSLETTER ELEMENTS**"\l1. **Step 3b5** (The first character after the backslash is a lowercase L and the second character is the number 1.)

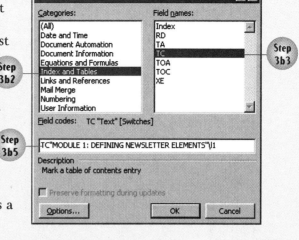

6) Click OK or press Enter. (If the field code is not visible, click the Show/Hide ¶ button on the Standard toolbar.)

c. Position the insertion point at the beginning of the heading *Designing a Newsletter* and then mark it as a field for the table of contents by completing the following steps:
1) Click Insert and then Field.
2) At the Field dialog box, click *Index and Tables* in the Categories list box.
3) Click *TC* in the Field names list box.
4) Position the mouse pointer inside the Field codes text box to the right of the *TC* and then click the left mouse button.
5) Key "**Designing a Newsletter**"\l2. (The first character after the backslash is a lowercase L and the second character is the number 2.)
6) Click OK or press Enter.

d. Complete steps similar to those in 3b or 3c to mark the following text as a field with the specified level:

Defining Basic Newsletter Elements	=	Level 2
MODULE 2: PLANNING A NEWSLETTER	=	Level 1
Defining the Purpose of a Newsletter	=	Level 2

4. Position the insertion point immediately left of the { that begins the field code before the title *MODULE 1: DEFINING NEWSLETTER ELEMENTS* and then insert a section break that begins a new page. *(Hint: Refer to exercise 1, step 4.)*
5. With the insertion point positioned below the section break, insert page numbering at the bottom center of each page of the section and change the starting number to 1. *(Hint: Refer to exercise 1, step 5.)*
6. Compile and insert a table of contents at the beginning of the document by completing the following steps:
   a. Position the insertion point at the beginning of the document (on the new page).
   b. Key **TABLE OF CONTENTS** centered and bolded.
   c. Press the Enter key once, turn off bold, and then change the paragraph alignment back to left.
   d. Click Insert and then Index and Tables.
   e. At the Index and Tables dialog box, click the Table of Contents tab.
   f. At the Index and Tables dialog box with the Table of Contents tab selected, click the down-pointing triangle at the right side of the Formats list box, and then click *Fancy* at the drop-down list.

g. Click the Options button.

h. At the Table of Contents Options dialog box, click Table entry fields. (This option is located in the bottom left corner of the dialog box.)

i. Click OK or press Enter to close the Table of Contents Options dialog box.

j. Click OK or press Enter to close the Index and Tables dialog box.

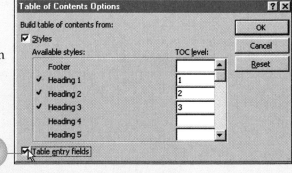

7. Insert page numbering on the Table of Contents page at the bottom center. *(Hint: Refer to exercise 1, step 8.)*

8. Check the page breaks in the document and, if necessary, adjust the page breaks.

9. Save the document again with the same name (Ch 25, Ex 02).

10. Print the table of contents page. (Before printing, make sure that hidden text will not print. To do this, click the Options button at the Print dialog box. At the Print dialog box with the Print tab selected, make sure there is no check mark in the Hidden text option. Check with your instructor to see if you should print the entire document.)

11. Close Ch 25, Ex 02. (If a message displays asking if you want to save the changes to the document, click Yes.)

Updating or Replacing a Table of Contents

If you make changes to a document after compiling a table of contents, you can either update the existing table of contents or replace the table of contents with a new one. To update the current table of contents, position the insertion point anywhere within the current table of contents (this causes the table of contents to display with a gray background), and then press F9. (This is the Update Field key.) At the Update Table of Contents dialog box shown in figure 25.4, click Update page numbers only if the changes occur only to the page numbers, or click Update entire table if changes were made to headings or subheadings within the table. Click OK or press Enter to close the dialog box.

Update Table of Contents Dialog Box

If you make extensive changes to the document, you may want to replace the entire table of contents. To do this, position the insertion point anywhere within the current table of contents (this causes the table of contents to display with a gray background), then click Insert and then Index and Tables. At the Index and Tables dialog box, make sure the Table of Contents tab is selected, and then click OK or press Enter. At the prompt asking if you want to replace the existing table of contents, click Yes.

exercise 3

Updating a Table of Contents

1. Open Ch 25, Ex 01.
2. Save the document with Save As and name it Ch 25, Ex 03.
3. Select the entire document and then change the line spacing to double.
4. Update the table of contents by completing the following steps:
   a. Using keys on the keyboard (rather than the mouse), position the insertion point anywhere within the current table of contents. (This causes the table of contents to display with a gray background. Use keys on the keyboard rather than the mouse to move the insertion point because headings in a table of contents are hyperlinks and clicking with the mouse moves the insertion point to the heading in the document.)
   b. Press F9. (This is the Update Field key.)
   c. At the Update Table of Contents dialog box, make sure Update page numbers only is selected, and then click OK or press Enter.
5. Save the document again with the same name (Ch 25, Ex 03).
6. Print the table of contents page. (Check with your instructor to see if you should print the entire document.)
7. Close Ch 25, Ex 03. (If a message displays asking if you want to save the changes to the document, click Yes.)

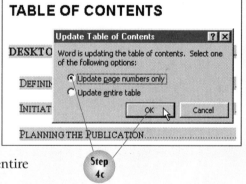

Deleting a Table of Contents

A table of contents that has been compiled in a document can be deleted. To do this, select the entire table of contents in the normal manner, and then press the Delete key. When the insertion point is positioned on any character in the table of contents, the entire table of contents displays with a gray background. This does not select the table. To delete the table, you must select it in the normal manner using either the mouse or the keyboard.

Creating an Index

An index is a list of topics contained in a publication, and the pages where those topics are discussed. Word lets you automate the process of creating an index in a manner similar to that used for creating a table of contents. When creating an index, you mark a word or words that you want included in the index. Creating an index takes some thought and consideration. The author of the book, manuscript, or report must determine the main entries desired and what subentries will be listed under main entries. An index may include such items as the main idea of a document, the main subject of a chapter or section, variations of a heading or subheading, and abbreviations. Figure 25.5 shows an example of an index.

figure

25.5 *Index*

INDEX

Marking Text for an Index

A selected word or words can be marked for inclusion in an index. Before marking words for an index, determine what main entries and subentries are to be included in the index. Selected text is marked as an index entry at the Mark Index Entry text box.

To mark text for an index, select the word or words, click Insert, and then click Index and Tables. At the Index and Tables dialog box, click the Index tab. At the Index and Tables dialog box with the Index tab selected, as shown in figure 25.6, click the Mark Entry button. At the Mark Index Entry dialog box, shown in figure 25.7, the selected word(s) appears in the Main entry text box. Make any necessary changes to the dialog box, and then click the Mark button. (When you click the Mark button, Word automatically turns on the display of nonprinting characters and displays the index field code.) Click Close to close the Mark Index Entry dialog box.

figure

25.6 *Index and Tables Dialog Box with Index Tab Selected*

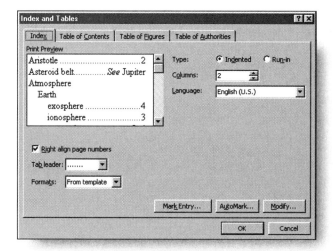

figure

25.7 *Mark Index Entry Dialog Box*

At the Mark Index Entry dialog box, the selected word or words display in the Main entry text box. If the text is a main entry, leave it as displayed. If, however, the selected text is a subentry, key the main entry in the Main entry text box, click in the Subentry text box, and then key the selected text. For example, suppose a publication includes the terms *Page layout* and *Portrait*. The words *Page layout* are to be marked as a main entry for the index and *Portrait* is to be marked as a subentry below *Page layout*. To mark these words for an index, you would complete the following steps:

1. Select *Page layout*.
2. Click Insert and then Index and Tables.
3. At the Index and Tables dialog box, make sure the Index tab is selected, and then click the Mark Entry button.
4. At the Mark Index Entry dialog box, click the Mark button.
5. With the Mark Index Entry dialog box still displayed on the screen, click in the document to make the document active, and then select *Portrait*.
6. Click the Mark Index Entry dialog box Title bar to make it active.
7. Select *Portrait* in the Main entry text box and then key **Page layout**.
8. Click in the Subentry text box and then key **Portrait**.
9. Click the Mark button.
10. Click Close.

The main entry and subentry do not have to be the same as the selected text. You can select text for an index, type the text you want to display in the Main entry or Subentry text box, and then click Mark.

At the Mark Index Entry dialog box, you can apply bold and/or italic formatting to the page numbers that will appear in the index. To apply formatting, click Bold and/or Italic to insert a check mark in the check box.

The Options section of the Mark Index Entry dialog box contains several options, with Current page the default. At this setting, the current page number will be listed in the index for the main and/or subentry. If you click Cross-reference, you would key the text you want to use as a cross-reference for the index entry in the Cross-reference text box. For example, you could mark the word *Monospaced* and cross-reference it to *Typefaces*.

Click the Mark All button at the Mark Index Entry dialog box to mark all occurrences of the text in the document as index entries. Word marks only those entries whose uppercase and lowercase letters exactly match the index entry.

Marking Words for an Index

1. Open Report 01.
2. Save the document with Save As and name it Ch 25, Ex 04.
3. Make the following changes to the document:
   a. Number pages at the bottom center of each page.
   b. Set the title *DESKTOP PUBLISHING* and the headings *Defining Desktop Publishing*, *Initiating the Desktop Publishing Process*, *Planning the Publication*, and *Creating the Content* in 14-point Times New Roman bold.
4. Mark the word *software* in the first paragraph for the index as a main entry and mark *word processing* in the first paragraph as a subentry with *software* as the main entry by completing the following steps:

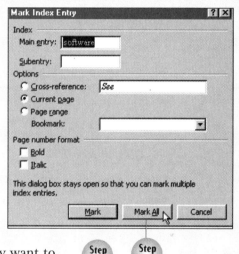

   a. Select *software* (located in the last sentence of the first paragraph).
   b. Click Insert and then Index and Tables.
   c. At the Index and Tables dialog box, click the Index tab.
   d. Click the Mark Entry button.
   e. At the Mark Index Entry dialog box, click the Mark All button.
   f. With the Mark Index Entry dialog box still displayed, click in the document to make the document active, and then select *word processing* (located in the last sentence of the first paragraph). (You may want to drag the dialog box down the screen so more of the document text is visible.)

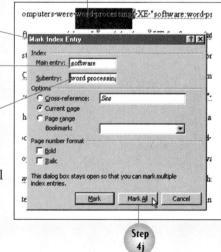

   g. Click the Mark Index Entry dialog box Title bar to make it active.
   h. Select *word processing* in the Main entry text box and then key **software**.
   i. Click in the Subentry text box and then key **word processing**.
   j. Click the Mark All button.
   k. With the Mark Index Entry dialog box still displayed, complete steps similar to those in 4f through 4j to mark the *first* occurrence of the following words as main entries or subentries for the index:

In the first paragraph in the *Defining Desktop Publishing* section:

spreadsheets	=	subentry (main entry = *software*)
database	=	subentry (main entry = *software*)

In the second paragraph in the *Defining Desktop Publishing* section:

publishing	=	main entry
desktop	=	subentry (main entry = *publishing*)

In the second paragraph in the *Defining Desktop Publishing* section:

printer	=	main entry
laser	=	subentry (main entry = *printer*)

In the third paragraph in the *Defining Desktop Publishing* section:

design	=	main entry

In the fourth paragraph in the *Defining Desktop Publishing* section:

traditional	=	subentry (main entry = *publishing*)

In the first paragraph in the *Initiating the Desktop Publishing Process* section:

publication	=	main entry
planning	=	subentry (main entry = *publication*)
creating	=	subentry (main entry = *publication*)
intended audience	=	subentry (main entry = *publication*)
content	=	subentry (main entry = *publication*)

In the third paragraph in the *Planning the Publication* section:

message	=	main entry

   l.   Click Close to close the Mark Index Entry dialog box.
   m.   Click the Show/Hide ¶ button on the Standard toolbar to turn off the display of nonprinting characters.
5.   Save the document again with the same name (Ch 25, Ex 04).
6.   Close Ch 25, Ex 04.

Compiling an Index

After all necessary text has been marked as a main entry or subentry for the index, the next step is to compile the index. An index should appear at the end of a document, generally beginning on a separate page. To compile the index, position the insertion point at the end of the document, and then insert a page break. With the insertion point positioned below the page break, key **INDEX** centered and bolded, and then press the Enter key. With the insertion point positioned at the left margin, click Insert and then Index and Tables. At the Index and Tables dialog box, click the Index tab. At the Index and Tables dialog box with the Index tab selected, select the desired formatting, and then click OK or press Enter.

Word compiles the index and then inserts it at the location of the insertion point with the formatting selected at the Index and Tables dialog box. Word also inserts a section break above and below the index text.

At the Index and Tables dialog box with the Index tab selected, you can specify how the index entries will appear. The Print Preview section shows how the index will display in the document. The Columns option has a default setting of 2. At this setting, the index will display in two newspaper columns. This number can be increased or decreased.

By default, numbers are right aligned in the index. If you do not want numbers right aligned, click the Right align page numbers check box to remove the check mark. The Tab leader option is dimmed for all formats except *Formal*. If you click *Formal* in the Formats list box, the Tab leader option displays in black. The default tab leader character is a period. To change to a different character, click the down-pointing triangle at the right of the text box, and then click the desired character.

In the Type section, the Indented option is selected by default. At this setting, subentries will appear indented below main entries. If you click Run-in, subentries will display on the same line as main entries.

Click the down-pointing triangle at the right side of the Formats list box and a list of formatting choices displays. At this list, click the desired formatting and the Print Preview box will display how the index will appear in the document.

exercise 5

Compiling an Index

1. Open Ch 25, Ex 04.
2. Save the document with Save As and name it Ch 25, Ex 05.
3. Compile the index and insert it in the document by completing the following steps:
   a. Position the insertion point at the end of the document.
   b. Insert a page break.
   c. With the insertion point positioned below the page break, key **INDEX** centered and bolded.
   d. Press the Enter key, turn off bold, and then change the paragraph alignment back to left.
   e. Click Insert and then Index and Tables.
   f. At the Index and Tables dialog box, click the Index tab.
   g. At the Index and Tables dialog box with the Index tab selected, click *Classic* in the Formats list box, and then click OK or press Enter.
   h. Select the title *INDEX* and then set it in 14-point Times New Roman bold.
4. Save the document again with the same name (Ch 25, Ex 05).
5. Print the index (last page). (Check with your instructor to see if you should print the entire document.)
6. Close Ch 25, Ex 05.

Creating a Concordance File

Words that appear frequently in a document can be saved as a concordance file. This saves you from having to mark each reference in a document. A concordance file is a regular Word document containing a single, two-column table with no text outside the table. In the first column of the table, you enter words you want to index. In the second column, you enter the main entry and subentry that should appear in the index. To create a subentry, separate each main entry from a subentry by a colon. Figure 25.8 shows an example of a completed concordance file.

25.8 *Concordance File*

World War I	World War I
Technology	Technology
technology	Technology
teletypewriters	Technology: teletypewriters
motion pictures	Technology: motion pictures
television	Technology: television
Radio Corporation of America	Radio Corporation of America
coaxial cable	Coaxial cable
telephone	Technology: telephone
Communications Act of 1934	Communications Act of 1934
World War II	World War II
radar system	Technology: radar system
computer	Computer
Atanasoff Berry Computer	Computer: Atanasoff Berry Computer
Korean War	Korean War
Columbia Broadcasting System	Columbia Broadcasting System
Cold War	Cold War
Vietnam	Vietnam
artificial satellite	Technology: artificial satellite
Communications Satellite Act of 1962	Communications Satellite Act of 1962

In the concordance file shown in figure 25.8, the text as it appears in the
ument is inserted in the first column (such as *World War I*, *Technology*, and
nology). The second column contains the text as it should appear in the index
ifying whether it is a main entry or subentry. For example, the text *motion
res* in the concordance file will appear in the index as a subentry under the
n entry *Technology*.

After a concordance file has been created, it can be used to quickly mark text
an index in a document. To do this, open the document containing text you
t marked for the index, then click Insert and then Index and Tables. At the
ex and Tables dialog box with the Index tab selected, click the AutoMark
on. At the Open Index AutoMark File dialog box, double-click the
cordance file name in the list box.

Word turns on the display of nonprinting characters, searches through the
ument for text that matches the text in the concordance file, and then marks
cordingly. After marking text for the index, insert the index in the document
escribed earlier.

When creating the concordance file in exercise 6, Word's AutoCorrect feature
automatically capitalize the first letter of the first word entered in each cell.
igure 25.9, you can see that many of the first words in the first column do not
n with a capital letter. Before completing the exercise consider turning off this
oCorrect capitalization feature. To do this, click Tools and then AutoCorrect.
he AutoCorrect dialog box click the *Capitalize first letter of sentences* check box
emove the check mark. Click OK to close the dialog box.

Creating a Concordance File

1. At a clear document screen, create the text shown in figure 25.9 as a concordance file
   by completing the following steps:
   a.   Click Table, point to Insert, and then click Table.
   b.   At the Insert Table dialog box, key **2** in the Number of columns text box, and
        then click OK. (This inserts a table in the document containing two rows and two
        columns.)
   c.   Key the text in the cells as shown in figure 25.9. Press the Tab key to move to the
        next cell. (If you did not remove the check mark before the *Capitalize first letter of
        sentences* option at the AutoCorrect dialog box, the *n* in the first word in the first
        cell *newsletters* is automatically capitalized. Delete the capital *N*, key an **n**, press
        the down arrow key [this will capitalize it again], and then click the Undo button.
        You will need to repeat this for each cell entry in the first column that should
        begin with a lowercase letter.)
2. Save the document and name it Ch 25, Concord File.
3. Print and then close Ch 25, Concord File.

figure

25.9   *Exercise 6*

newsletters	Newsletters
software	Software
desktop publishing	Software: desktop publishing
word processing	Software: word processing
printers	Printers
laser	Printers: laser
design	Design
communication	Communication
consistency	Design: consistency
elements	Elements
Nameplate	Elements: nameplate
Logo	Elements: logo
Subtitle	Elements: subtitle
Folio	Elements: folio
Headlines	Elements: headlines
Subheads	Elements: subheads
Byline	Elements: byline
Body Copy	Elements: body copy
Graphics Images	Elements: graphics images
audience	Newsletters: audience
purpose	Newsletters: purpose
focal point	Newsletters: focal point

If you removed the check mark before the *Capitalize first letter of sentences* option at the AutoCorrect dialog box, you may need to turn this feature back on. To do this, click Tools and then AutoCorrect. At the AutoCorrect dialog box, click the *Capitalize first letter of sentences* check box to insert the check mark, and then click OK to close the dialog box.

Compiling an Index Using a Concordance File

1. Open Report 03.
2. Save the document with Save As and name it Ch 25, Ex 07.
3. Make the following changes to the document:
   a. Select the entire document and then change the font to 12-point Century Schoolbook (or a similar serif typeface).
   b. Set the titles and headings in the document in 14-point Century Schoolbook bold.
4. Mark text for the index using the concordance file by completing the following steps:
   a. Click Insert and then Index and Tables.
   b. At the Index and Tables dialog box, click the AutoMark button.
   c. At the Open Index AutoMark File dialog box, double-click *Ch 25, Concord File* in the list box.
5. Compile and insert the index in the document by completing the following steps:
   a. Position the insertion point at the end of the document.
   b. Insert a page break.
   c. Key **INDEX** bolded and centered.
   d. Press the Enter key, turn off bold, and then return the paragraph alignment to left.
   e. Click Insert and then Index and Tables.
   f. At the Index and Tables dialog box, click the Index tab.
   g. At the Index and Tables dialog box with the Index tab selected, click the down-pointing triangle at the right side of the Formats list box, and then click *Formal* at the drop-down list.
   h. Click OK to close the dialog box.
   i. Click the Show/Hide ¶ button on the Standard toolbar to turn off the display of nonprinting characters.
   j. Set the title *INDEX* in 14-point Century Schoolbook bold.
6. Check the page breaks in the document and, if necessary, adjust the page breaks.
7. Save the document again with the same name (Ch 25, Ex 07).
8. Print the index (last page). (Check with your instructor to see if you should print the entire document.)
9. Close Ch 25, Ex 07.

⌐dating or Replacing an Index

‹you make changes to a document after inserting an index, you can either
›date the existing index or replace the index with a new one. To update an
‹ex, position the insertion point anywhere within the index (displays with a
‹y background), and then press F9.

Replace an index in the same manner as replacing a table of contents. To do
›s, position the insertion point anywhere within the current index (this causes
‹ index to display with a gray background), then click Insert and then Index
‹ Tables. At the Index and Tables dialog box, make sure the Index tab is
‹cted, and then click OK or press Enter. At the prompt asking if you want to
‹ace the existing index, click Yes.

Updating an Index

1. Open Ch 25, Ex 07.
2. Save the document with Save As and name it Ch 25, Ex 08.
3. Insert a page break at the beginning of the title *MODULE 2: PLANNING A NEWSLETTER*.
4. Update the index by completing the following steps:
   a. Position the insertion point on any character in the index.
   b. Press F9.
5. Save the document again with the same name (Ch 25, Ex 08).
6. Print only the index. (Check with your instructor to see if you should print the entire document.)
7. Close Ch 25, Ex 08.

Deleting an Index

An index that has been compiled in a document can be deleted. An index is deleted in the same manner as a table of contents. To delete an index, select the entire index using either the mouse or the keyboard, and then press the Delete key.

Creating a Table of Figures

A document that contains figures should include a list (table) of figures so the reader can quickly locate a specific figure. Figure 25.10 shows an example of a table of figures. A table of figures can be created using a variety of methods. The easiest method is to mark figure names as captions and then use the caption names to create the table of figures.

25.10 *Table of Figures*

TABLE OF FIGURES

Creating Captions

There are a variety of methods you can use to create a caption for text. One method you can use to create a caption is to select the text, click Insert and then Caption. At the Caption dialog box shown in figure 25.11, make sure *Figure 1* displays in the Caption text box and the insertion point is positioned after *Figure 1*. Key the name for the caption, and then click OK or press Enter. Word inserts *Figure 1 (caption name)* below the selected text.

25.11   **Caption Dialog Box**

Key a caption in this text box after *Figure 1*.

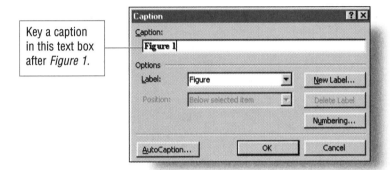

Compiling a Table of Figures

Once figures have been marked as captions in a document, a table of figures can be compiled and inserted in the document. A table of figures is compiled in a document in a manner similar to a table of contents. A table of figures generally displays at the beginning of the document, after the table of contents.

To compile a table of figures in a document containing figures marked as captions, position the insertion point at the beginning of the document and then insert a section break that begins a new page. (If the document contains a table of contents, position the insertion point between the table of contents and the title of the document.) Move the insertion point above the section break and then key **TABLE OF FIGURES** bolded and centered. Press the Enter key and then turn off bold and change the paragraph alignment back to left. Click Insert and then Index and Tables. At the Index and Tables dialog box, click the Table of Figures tab. At the Index and Tables dialog box with the Table of Figures tab selected, as shown in figure 25.12, make any necessary changes, and then click OK or press Enter.

figure

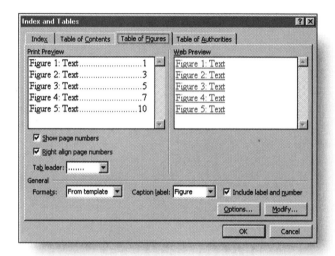

The options at the Index and Tables dialog box with the Table of Figures tab selected are similar to those options available at the dialog box with the Table of Contents tab selected. For example, you can choose a format for the table of figures from the Formats list box, change the alignment of the page number, or add leaders before page numbers.

exercise

Creating a List of Figures

1. Open Report 06.
2. Save the document with Save As and name it Ch 25, Ex 09.
3. Add the caption *Figure 1 Basic Hardware* to the bulleted text, and the lines above and below the bulleted text, that displays in the middle of page 2 by completing the following steps:

   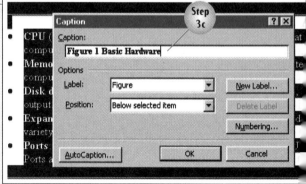

   a. Move the insertion point to the middle of page 2 and then select the horizontal lines and the bulleted text between the two lines.
   b. Click Insert and then Caption.
   c. At the Caption dialog box, press the spacebar once, and then key **Basic Hardware**. (The insertion point is automatically positioned in the Caption text box, immediately after *Figure 1*.)

      d.   Click OK or press Enter.

4.   Complete steps similar to those in 3 to create the caption *Figure 2 Input Devices* for the bulleted text toward the bottom of the second page. (Be sure to include the lines above and below the bulleted text.)

5.   Complete steps similar to those in 3 to create the caption *Figure 3 Output Devices* for the bulleted text that displays at the bottom of the second page and the top of the third page (the location may vary slightly). (Be sure to include the lines above and below the bulleted text.)

6.   Compile and insert a table of figures at the beginning of the document by completing the following steps:

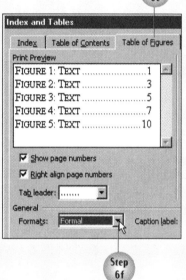

Step 6e

      a.   Position the insertion point at the beginning of the document, press the Enter key, and then insert a page break.

      b.   Move the insertion point above the page break and then key **TABLE OF FIGURES** bolded and centered.

      c.   Press the Enter key, turn off bold, and then change the paragraph alignment back to left.

      d.   Click Insert and then Index and Tables.

      e.   At the Index and Tables dialog box, click the Table of Figures tab.

      f.   At the Index and Tables dialog box with the Table of Figures tab selected, click the down-pointing triangle at the right side of the Formats list box, and then click *Formal* at the drop-down list

Step 6f

      g.   Click OK or press Enter.

7.   Check the page breaks in the document and, if necessary, adjust the page breaks.

8.   Save the document with the same name (Ch 25, Ex 09).

9.   Print the Table of Figures page. (Check with your instructor to see if you should print the entire document.)

10.   Close Ch 25, Ex 09.

Updating or Replacing a Table of Figures

A table of figures can be updated in the same manner as updating a table of contents. To update a table of figures, position the insertion point anywhere within the current table of figures (this causes the table of figures to display with a gray background), and then press F9. At the Update Table of Figures dialog box, click Update page numbers only if the changes occur only to the page numbers, or click Update entire table if changes were made to headings or subheadings within the table. Click OK or press Enter to close the dialog box.

If you make extensive changes to the document, you may want to replace the entire table of figures. To do this, position the insertion point anywhere within the current table of figures, then click Insert and then Index and Tables. At the Index and Tables dialog box, make sure the Table of Figures tab is selected, and then click OK or press Enter. At the prompt asking if you want to replace the existing table of figures, click Yes.

Deleting a Table of Figures

A table of figures that has been compiled in a document can be deleted. A table of figures is deleted in the same manner as a table of contents. To delete a table of figures, select the entire table of figures using either the mouse or the keyboard, and then press the Delete key.

Creating a Table of Authorities

A table of authorities is a list of citations identifying the pages where the citations appear in a legal brief or other legal document. Word provides many common categories under which citations can be organized. Word includes Cases, Statutes, Other Authorities, Rules, Treatises, Regulations, and Constitutional Provisions. Within each category, Word alphabetizes the citations. Figure 25.13 shows an example of a table of authorities.

figure

25.13   *Table of Authorities*

TABLE OF AUTHORITIES

CASES

Mansfield v. Rydell, 72 Wn.2d 200, 433 P.2d 723 (1983) 3
State v. Fletcher, 73 Wn.2d 332, 124 P.2d 503 (1981) 5
Yang v. Buchwald, 21 Wn.2d 385, 233 P.2d 609 (1991) 7

STATUTES

RCW 8.12.230(2) 4
RCW 6.23.590 7
RCW 5.23.103(3) 10

Some thought goes into planning a table of authorities. Before marking any text in a legal document, you need to determine what section headings you want and what should be contained in the sections.

When marking text for a table of authorities, you need to find the first occurrence of the citation, mark it as a full citation with the complete name, and then specify a short citation. To mark a citation for a table of authorities, you would complete the following steps:

1. Select the first occurrence of the citation.
2. Click Insert and then Index and Tables.
3. At the Index and Tables dialog box, click the Table of Authorities tab.
4. At the Index and Tables dialog box with the Table of Authorities tab selected, click the Mark Citation button.
5. At the Mark Citation dialog box shown in figure 25.14, edit and format the text in the Selected text box as you want it to appear in the table of authorities. Edit and format the text in the Short citation text box so it matches the short citation you want Word to search for in the document.
6. Click the down-pointing triangle at the right of the Category text box and then click the category from the drop-down list that applies to the citation.
7. Click the Mark button to mark the selected citation or click the Mark All button if you want Word to mark all long and short citations in the document that match those displayed in the Mark Citation dialog box.
8. The Mark Citation dialog box remains in the document screen so you can mark other citations. To find the next citation in a document, click the Next Citation button. (This causes Word to search through the document for the next occurrence of text commonly found in a citation such as *in re* or *v.*)
9. Select the text for the next citation and then complete steps 5 through 7.
10. After marking all citations, click the Close button.

25.14   **Mark Citation Dialog Box**

Edit and format text in this text box as you want it to appear in the table of authorities.

Edit and format text in this text box so it matches the short citation you want Word to search for in the document.

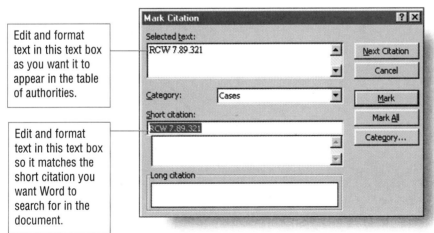

Compiling a Table of Authorities

Once citations have been marked in a document, the table of authorities can be compiled and inserted in the document. A table of authorities is compiled in a document in a manner similar to a table of contents or figures. A table of authorities generally displays at the beginning of the document. To compile a table of authorities in a document containing text marked as citations, you would complete the following steps:

1. Position the insertion point at the beginning of the document and then press the Enter key twice.
2. Position the insertion point at the beginning of the title of the document and then insert a section break that begins a new page.
3. Position the insertion point at the beginning of the document and then key **TABLE OF AUTHORITIES** centered and bolded.
4. Press the Enter key and then turn off bold and change the paragraph alignment back to left.
5. Click Insert and then Index and Tables.
6. At the Index and Tables dialog box, click the Table of Authorities tab.
7. At the Index and Tables dialog box with the Table of Authorities tab selected, choose the desired formatting.
8. Click OK or press Enter.

If you want the table of authorities to print on a page separate from the document text, insert a section break that begins a new page between the table of authorities and the title of the document. If the beginning of the text in the document, rather than the table of authorities, should be numbered as page 1, change the starting page number for the section.

The Index and Tables dialog box with the Table of Authorities tab selected contains options for formatting a table of authorities. The Use passim option is active by default (the check box contains a check mark). When it is active, Word replaces five or more page references to the same authority with *passim*. With the Keep original formatting check box active, Word will retain the formatting of the citation as it appears in the document. Click the Tab leader option if you want to change the leader character.

By default, Word compiles all categories for the table of authorities. If you want to compile citations for a specific category, select that category from the Category drop-down list.

exercise 10

Compiling a Table of Authorities

1. Open Legal Brief.
2. Save the document with Save As and name it Ch 25, Ex 10.
3. Mark *RCW 7.89.321* as a statute citation by completing the following steps:
   a. Select *RCW 7.89.321*. (This citation is located toward the middle of the second page. *Hint: Use the Find feature to help you locate this citation.*)
   b. Click Insert and then Index and Tables.
   c. At the Index and Tables dialog box, click the Table of Authorities tab.
   d. At the Index and Table dialog box with the Table of Authorities tab selected, click the Mark Citation button.
   e. At the Mark Citation dialog box, click the down-pointing triangle at the right side of the Category text box, and then click *Statutes* at the drop-down list.
   f. Click the Mark All button.
   g. Click Close.

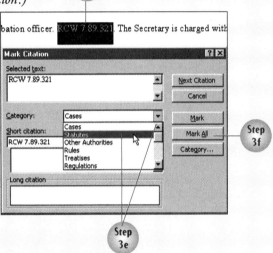

4. Complete steps similar to those in 3 to mark *RCW 7.53.443* as a statute citation. (This citation is located toward the middle of the second page.)
5. Complete steps similar to those in 3 to mark *RCW 7.72A.432(2)* as a statute citation. (This citation is located toward the top of the third page.)
6. Complete steps similar to those in 3 to mark *RCW 7.42A.429(1)* as a statute citation. (This citation is located toward the top of the third page.)
7. Mark *State v. Connors, 73 W.2d 743, 430 P.2d 199 (1974)* as a case citation by completing the following steps:
   a. Select *State v. Connors, 73 W.2d 743, 430 P.2d 199 (1974)*. (This citation is located toward the bottom of the second page. *Hint: Use the Find feature to help you locate this citation.*)
   b. Click Insert and then Index and Tables.
   c. At the Index and Tables dialog box with the Table of Authorities tab selected, click the Mark Citation button.
   d. At the Mark Citation dialog box, click the down-pointing triangle at the right side of the Category text box, and then click *Cases* at the drop-down list.
   e. Click in the Short citation text box and then key **State v. Connors**.
   f. Click the Mark All button.
   g. Click Close.

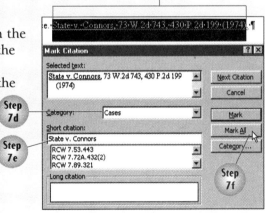

8. Complete steps similar to those in 7 to mark *State v. Bertelli*, *63 W.2d 77, 542 P.2d 751 (1971)*. Enter *State v. Bertelli* as the short citation. (This citation is located toward the bottom of the second page.)

9. Complete steps similar to those in 7 to mark *State v. Landers*, *103 W.2d 432, 893 P.2d 2 (1984)*. Enter *State v. Landers* as the short citation. (This citation is located toward the top of the third page.)

10. Turn on page numbering and compile the table of authorities by completing the following steps:
    a. Position the insertion point at the beginning of the document and then press the Enter key once.
    b. Position the insertion point immediately left of the *S* in *STATEMENT OF CASE* and then insert a section break that begins a new page.
    c. With the insertion point positioned below the section break, turn on page numbering at the bottom center of each page and change the starting number to 1.
    d. Position the insertion point above the section break and then key **TABLE OF AUTHORITIES** centered and bolded.
    e. Press the Enter key, turn off bold, and then change the paragraph alignment back to left.
    f. Click Insert and then Index and Tables.
    g. At the Index and Tables dialog box, click the Table of Authorities tab.
    h. At the Index and Tables dialog box with the Table of Authorities tab selected, click the down-pointing triangle at the right side of the Formats list box, and then click *Formal* at the drop-down list.
    i. Click OK or press Enter.

11. With the insertion point positioned anywhere in the table of authorities, turn on page numbering at the bottom center of each page and change the numbering format to lowercase Roman numerals.

12. Turn off the display of nonprinting characters.

13. Save the document again with the same name (Ch 25, Ex 10).

14. Print the table of authorities. (Check with your instructor to see if you should print the entire document.)

15. Close Ch 25, Ex 10.

Updating or Replacing a Table of Authorities

A table of authorities can be updated in the same manner as updating a table of contents or figures. To update a table of authorities, position the insertion point anywhere within the current table of authorities (this causes the table of authorities to display with a gray background), and then press F9. At the Update Table of Authorities dialog box, click Update page numbers only if the changes occur only to the page numbers, or click Update entire table if changes were made to citations in the document. Click OK or press Enter to close the dialog box.

If you make extensive changes to the document, you may want to replace the entire table of authorities. To do this, position the insertion point anywhere within the current table of authorities, then click Insert and then Index and Tables. At the Index and Tables dialog box, make sure the Table of Authorities tab is selected, and then click OK or press Enter. At the prompt asking if you want to replace the existing table of authorities, click Yes.

Deleting a Table of Authorities

A table of authorities that has been compiled in a document can be deleted. A table of authorities is deleted in the same manner as a table of contents. To delete a table of authorities, select the entire table of authorities using either the mouse or the keyboard, and then press the Delete key.

chapter summary

➤ Word contains options for automating the creation of a table of contents, index, list, or table of authorities.

➤ Text to be included in a table of contents can be identified by applying a heading style, or text can be marked as a field entry.

➤ Two steps are involved in creating a table of contents: apply the appropriate styles to the text that will be included, and compile the table of contents in the document.

➤ To compile the table of contents, position the insertion point where you want it to appear, display the Index and Tables dialog box with the Table of Contents tab selected, make any desired changes, and then click OK.

➤ If you want the table of contents to print on a page separate from the document text, insert a section break that begins a new page between the table of contents and the title of the document. You may need to adjust the page numbering also.

➤ If you make changes to a document after compiling a table of contents, you can either update the existing table of contents or replace it. An index, a table of figures, or a table of authorities can be updated in the same manner.

➤ To delete a table of contents, select the entire table of contents, and then press the Delete key. Delete an index, a table of figures, or a table of authorities in the same manner.

➤ An index is a list of topics contained in a publication and the pages where those topics are discussed. Word lets you automate the process of creating an index in a manner similar to that for creating a table of contents.

➤ Mark text for an index at the Index and Tables dialog box with the Index tab selected.

➤ After all necessary text has been marked as a main entry or subentry for the index, the next step is to compile the index so that it appears at the end of the document beginning on a separate page.

➤ Word provides a variety of formatting choices for an index at the Formats list box at the Index and Tables dialog box.

➤ Words that appear frequently in a document can be saved as a concordance file so that you need not mark each reference in a document.

- A concordance file is a regular document containing a single, two-column table created at the Insert Table dialog box.
- A table of figures can be created using a variety of methods. The easiest method is to mark figure names as captions and then use the caption names to create the table of figures.
- A table of figures is compiled in a document in a manner similar to a table of contents and generally displays at the beginning of the document, after the table of contents.
- A table of authorities is a list of citations identifying the pages where the citations appear in a legal brief or other legal document.
- When marking text for a table of authorities, find the first occurrence of the citation, mark it as a full citation with the complete name, and then specify a short citation at the Index and Tables dialog box.
- A table of authorities is compiled in a document in a manner similar to a table of contents or figures. A table of authorities generally displays at the beginning of the document.

commands review

	Mouse/Keyboard
Display Index and Tables dialog box	Insert, Index and Tables
Display Insert Table dialog box	Table, Insert, Table

thinking offline

Matching: In the space provided at the left, write the letter of the term or terms that match the description. (Terms may be used more than once.)

- Ⓐ Table of contents
- Ⓑ Index
- Ⓒ Table of figures
- Ⓓ Table of authorities
- Ⓔ Concordance file
- Ⓕ Index and Tables dialog box
- Ⓖ Fields
- Ⓗ Compiling
- Ⓘ Captions
- Ⓙ Main entries
- Ⓚ Subentries
- Ⓛ Marking

_____ 1. Helps save time when marking text for an index.

_____ 2. Identifies citations in a legal brief.

_____ 3. Generally placed at the end of a document.

_____ 4. This is the next step in creating a table of contents after applying the necessary heading styles.

_____ 5. If included in a document, it usually follows the table of contents.

_____ 6. Generally placed at the beginning of a document.

_____ 7. The easiest way to create a table of figures is to use these.

_____ 8. If you do not want style formatting applied in a document, mark text for the table of contents as these.

_____ 9. Choose a preformatted table of contents at this dialog box.

_____ 10. This is a list of topics contained in a publication.

working hands-on

Assessment 1

1. Open Report 04.
2. Save the document with Save As and name it Ch 25, SA 01.
3. Make the following changes to the document:
   a. Apply the following styles:

MODULE 3: DESIGNING A NEWSLETTER	=	Heading 1
Applying Desktop Publishing Guidelines	=	Heading 2
MODULE 4: CREATING NEWSLETTER LAYOUT	=	Heading 1
Choosing Paper Size and Type	=	Heading 2
Choosing Paper Weight	=	Heading 2
Creating Margins for Newsletters	=	Heading 2

   b. Number the pages at the bottom center of each page.
   c. Compile the table of contents. (Include a title for the table of contents.)
   d. Number the table of contents page at the bottom center of the page. (Change the number to a lowercase Roman numeral.)
4. Save the document again with the same name (Ch 25, SA 01).
5. Print the table of contents page. (Check with your instructor to see if you should print the entire document.)
6. Close Ch 25, SA 01.

Assessment 2

1. At a clear document screen, create the text shown in figure 25.15 as a concordance file.
2. Save the document and name it Ch 25, SA Concord File.
3. Print and then close Ch 25, SA Concord File.
4. Open Ch 25, SA 01.
5. Save the document with Save As and name it Ch 25, SA 02.
6. Make the following changes to the document:
   a. Mark text for an index using the concordance file Ch 25, SA Concord File.
   b. Compile the index at the end of the document.
7. Save the document again with the same name (Ch 25, SA 02).
8. Print the index. (Check with your instructor to see if you should print the entire document.)
9. Close Ch 25, SA 02.

figure

25.15 *Assessment 2*

NEWSLETTER	Newsletter
newsletter	Newsletter
consistency	Newsletter: consistency
element	Elements
margins	Elements: margins
column layout	Elements: column layout
nameplate	Elements: nameplate
location	Elements: location
logos	Elements: logos
color	Elements: color
ruled lines	Elements: ruled lines
Focus	Elements: focus
balance	Elements: balance
graphics images	Graphics images
photos	Photos
Headlines	Newsletter: headlines
subheads	Newsletter: subheads
White space	White space
directional flow	Newsletter: directional flow
paper	Paper
size	Paper: size
type	Paper: type
weight	Paper: weight
stock	Paper: stock
margin size	Newsletter: margin size

Assessment 3

1. Open Ch 25, SA 02.
2. Save the document with Save As and name it Ch 25, SA 03.
3. Insert a page break at the beginning of the title *MODULE 4: CREATING NEWSLETTER LAYOUT.*
4. Update the table of contents and the index.
5. Save the document again with the same name (Ch 25, SA 03).
6. Print the table of contents and then the index. (Check with your instructor to see if you should print the entire document.)
7. Close Ch 25, SA 03.

Performance Assessments
Unit Five

DEMONSTRATING YOUR SKILLS

In this unit, you have learned to organize text in documents using sorting and selecting features; manage documents with tracking, routing, and versioning features; format text into outlines, master documents, and subdocuments; create fill-in business forms; and create a table of contents, index, table of figures, and table of authorities.

Assessment one 1

1. Open Mortgage.
2. Save the document with Save As and name it Unit 5, PA 01.
3. Sort the paragraphs alphabetically by the first word of each paragraph. (After the sorting is completed, delete the hard returns that are moved to the beginning of the document.)
4. Save the sorted document again with the same name (Unit 5, PA 01).
5. Print and then close Unit 5, PA 01.

Assessment two 2

1. Open Table 07.
2. Save the document with Save As and name it Unit 5, PA 02.
3. Sort the text alphabetically in the first column.
4. Apply the Colorful 3 table formatting to the table.
5. Save the document again with the same name (Unit 5, PA 02).
6. Print and then close Unit 5, PA 02.

Assessment three **3**

1. Open Report 04.
2. Save the document with Save As and name it Unit 5, PA 03.
3. Make the following changes to the document:
   a. Change to the Outline view.
   b. Apply the Heading 1 style to the titles in the document and apply the Heading 2 style to the headings in the document.
   c. Collapse the outline so only two heading levels display.
   d. Move the module 3 section below the module 4 section and then renumber the modules (3 becomes 4 and 4 becomes 3).
   e. Move the heading *Creating Margins for Newsletters* above the heading *Choosing Paper Size and Type*.
4. With the outline still collapsed, save the document again with the same name (Unit 5, PA 03).
5. Print and then close Unit 5, PA 03.

Assessment four **4**

1. Open Report 05.
2. Save the document with Save As and name it Master Doc Unit 5, PA 04.
3. Make the following changes to the document:
   a. Complete a spell check on the document.
   b. Apply the following styles:

STRUCTURED PUBLICATIONS	=	Heading 1
Cover	=	Heading 2
Title Page	=	Heading 2
Copyright Page	=	Heading 2
Preface	=	Heading 2
Table of Contents	=	Heading 2
Body Text	=	Heading 2
Appendix	=	Heading 2
Bibliography	=	Heading 2
Glossary	=	Heading 2
Index	=	Heading 2

   c. Change to the Outline view. (Make sure the Master Document View button is active.)
   d. Select the document from the title *Cover* to the end of the document and then create subdocuments with the selected text.
4. Save the document again with the same name (Master Doc Unit 5, PA 04).
5. Close Master Doc Unit 5, PA 04.
6. Open Master Doc Unit 5, PA 04.

7. Print Master Doc Unit 5, PA 04. (At the prompt asking if you want to open the subdocuments, click <u>N</u>o.)
8. Make the following changes to the document:
   a. Move the *Glossary* subdocument above the *Bibliography* subdocument.
   b. Remove the *Title Page* subdocument.
9. Save the document again with the same name (Master Doc Unit 5, PA 04).
10. Print Master Doc Unit 5, PA 04. (At the prompt asking if you want to open the subdocuments, click <u>N</u>o.)
11. Close Master Doc Unit 5, PA 04.

Assessment 5

1. Open Job Desc.
2. Save the document with Save As and name it Unit 5, PA 05.
3. Make the following changes to the document:
   a. Select the paragraphs of text (excluding the title and subtitle) and then apply bullets and change the spacing before paragraphs to 6 points.
   b. Set the entire document in 12-point Bookman Old Style (or a similar serif typeface).
   c. Bold and center align the title *JOB DESCRIPTION* and the subtitle *REGISTERED NURSE*.
   d. Turn on tracking and then make the following changes:
      1) Insert the word *supervise,* between the words *plan,* and *implement* in the first bulleted paragraph.
      2) Change the words *to plan of care* in the fourth bulleted paragraph to *care plan*.
   e. Display the Options dialog box with the User Information tab selected, change the name to *Sylvia Yuan,* the initials to *SY,* and then close the dialog box.
   f. Make the following tracking changes:
      1) Insert the words *any and all* between the words *reports* and *changes* in the second bulleted paragraph.
      2) Delete the bulleted paragraph that reads *Performs documentation that is timely, accurate, and complete*.
   g. Turn off tracking.
   h. Display the Options dialog box with the User Information tab selected, change back to the information that displayed before you keyed *Sylvia Yuan* and the initials *SY,* and then close the dialog box.
4. Save the document again with the same name (Unit 5, PA 05).
5. Print Unit 5, PA 05.

6. With Unit 5, PA 05 still open, accept the following changes in the document:
   a. Accept the change to *care plan* from *to plan of care* in the fourth bulleted paragraph.
   b. Accept the change inserting the words *any and all* between the words *reports* and *changes* in the second bulleted paragraph.
7. Reject the following changes in the document:
   a. Reject the change inserting the word *supervise* between the words *plan,* and *implement* in the first bulleted paragraph.
   b. Reject the change deleting the bulleted paragraph that reads *Performs documentation that is timely, accurate, and complete.*
8. Save the document with Save As and name it Unit 5, PA 05 Rev.
9. Print and then close Unit 5, PA 05 Rev.

Assessment six

1. Open Report 04.
2. Make the following changes to the report:
   a. Select the text from beginning of the document to just before the title *MODULE 4: CREATING NEWSLETTER LAYOUT.* (This includes all of Module 3).
   b. Copy and paste the selected text it into a new document.
   c. Save the new document and name it Unit 5, PA 06.
   d. Make Report 04 the active document and then close it.
   e. With Unit 5, PA 06 the active document, make the following changes:
      1) Set the entire document in a 12-point serif typeface (other than Times New Roman).
      2) Set the title and the one heading in 14-point Arial bold.
   f. Move the insertion point to the end of the second paragraph in the document, key the words **Newsletter examples**, select the words, and then create the comment with the following text: *Include examples of corporate newsletters.*
   g. Move the insertion point to the end of the last paragraph in the document, key the words **Price of color**, select the words, and then create the comment with the following text: *Please find out the price of adding one color, two colors, or more colors, to a newsletter.*
3. Save the document again with the same name (Unit 5, PA 06).
4. Print the document and the comments.
5. Close Unit 5, PA 06.

Assessment 7

1. Create the table form shown in figure U5.1 as a template document named XXX Unit 5, PA 07 (where your initials are inserted in place of the *XXX*). Customize the table as shown in figure U5.1. Insert text form fields in the table as shown in the figure.
2. Print and then close XXX Unit 5, PA 07.

REDWOOD COMMUNITY COLLEGE
312 South 122nd Street
Mendocino, CA 94220
(707) 555-7880

Name: **Date:**

Department:

Description	Qty.	Cost

ure U5.1 • Assessment 7

Assessment eight

1. Create a form with the XXX Unit 5, PA 07 form template. Insert the following information in the form:

> Name: *Ronald Jarvis*
> Date: (key the current date)
> Department: *Public Relations*
>
> Description: *Transfer Brochure*
> Qty.: *400*
> Cost: *$225.00*
>
> Description: *Technology Degree Brochure*
> Qty.: *250*
> Cost: *$179.50*
>
> Description: *College Newsletter*
> Qty.: *2,000*
> Cost: *$150.50*

2. When the form is completed, save the document and name it Unit 5, PA 08.
3. Print and then close Unit 5, PA 08.

Assessment nine

1. At a clear document screen, create the text shown in figure U5.2 as a concordance file.
2. Save the document and name it Unit 5, Concord File.
3. Print and then close Unit 5, Concord File.
4. Open Report 02.
5. Save the document with Save As and name it Unit 5, PA 09.
6. Make the following changes to the document:
   a. Mark text for an index using the concordance file, Unit 5, Concord File.
   b. Compile the index at the end of the document.
   c. Mark the title and headings for a table of contents.
   d. Compile the table of contents at the beginning of the document.
7. Save the document again with the same name (Unit 5, PA 09).
8. Print the table of contents and the index. (Check with your instructor to see if you should print the entire document.)
9. Close Unit 5, PA 09.

message	Message
publication	Publication
design	Design
Flier	Flier
letterhead	Letterhead
newsletter	Newsletter
intent	Design: intent
audience	Design: audience
layout	Design: layout
thumbnail	Thumbnail
principles	Design: principles
focus	Design: focus
balance	Design: balance
proportion	Design: proportion
contrast	Design: contrast
directional flow	Design: directional flow
consistency	Design: consistency
color	Design: color
White space	White space
white space	White space
Legibility	Legibility

Figure U5.2 • Assessment 9

CREATING ORIGINAL DOCUMENTS

ssessment 10

ten

Situation: You are an administrative assistant at Rockford Medical Center and you have been asked by your supervisor to create a directory with the information displayed below. After creating the directory, sort the text alphabetically by last name. Save the document and name it Unit 5, PA 10. Print Unit 5, PA 10. With Unit 5, PA 10 still open, sort the text numerically by extension, and then save the document with the same name. Print and then close Unit 5, PA 10.

Grogan, Avery	President	2005
Cartagena, Eduardo	Vice President	2012
Gaines, Jessica	Vice President	2056
Elmore, Marcus	Vice President	2089
Bevan-Church, Chloe	Director	2971
Sackett, Joel	Director	2702
Lyons, Melissa	Director	2311
Lee, Sang	Director	2482
Soileau, Victoria	Director	2766
Oslakovic, Craig	Director	2515

Assessment 11 eleven

Situation: You are an administrative assistant in the vocational department at Redwood Community College. You have been asked by your supervisor to create a fill-in form template for advisory committees that contains the following information (you determine the layout of the form and the types of form fields used):

ADVISORY COMMITTEE MEMBER APPLICATION

Committee Requested: Science, Social Studies, Arts, or Health and Fitness

Name:
Company Address:
Telephone:
Job Title:
Years of Experience:
Gender: Male or Female

After creating the form template, save the template document as XXX Unit 5, PA 11. Use the XXX Unit 5, PA 11 form template to create a filled-in form. You make up information to fill in the form fields. After the form is filled in, save it and name it Unit 5, PA 11. Print and then close Unit 5, PA 11.

Assessment 12 twelve

1. Display the New dialog box.
2. At the New dialog box, delete the following template form documents:

    XXX Unit 5, PA 07 (where your initials display rather than *XXX*)
    XXX Unit 5, PA 11 (where your initials display rather than *XXX*)

3. Close the New dialog box.

Appendix A

Proofreaders' Marks

Proofreaders' Mark		Example		Revised
#	Insert space	letter to the		letter to the
ℐ	Delete	the commands is		the command is
lc /	Lowercase	lc he is Branch Manager		he is branch manager
or UC ☰	Uppercase	cap Margaret simpson		Margaret Simpson
¶	New paragraph	¶ The new product		The new product
no ¶	No paragraph	the meeting.		the meeting. Bring the
		no ¶ Bring the		
∧	Insert	pens, and clips		pens, and clips
⊙	Insert period	a global search.		a global search.
⊐	Move right	⊐ With the papers		With the papers
⊏	Move left	⊏ access the code		access the code
⊐⊏	Center	⊐ Chapter Six ⊏		Chapter Six
∽	Transpose	It is raesonable		It is reasonable
sp	Spell out	sp 475 Mill Ave		475 Mill Avenue
...	Stet (do not delete)	I am very pleased		I am very pleased
⌒	Close up	regret fully		regretfully
ss	Single-space	The margin top		The margin top
		ss		is 1 inch.
		is 1 inch.		
ds	Double-space	ds Paper length is		Paper length is
		set for 11 inches.		
				set for 11 inches.
ts	Triple-space	ts The F8 function		The F8 function
		key turns on Extend		
				key turns on Extend
bf	Boldface	bf Boldface type		**Boldface** type
		provides emphasis.		provides emphasis.
ital	Italics	ital Use italics for terms		Use *italics* for terms
		to be defined.		to be defined.

Appendix B

Formatting a Memo

The formatting for an interoffice correspondence, referred to as a *memo*, can vary. Microsoft Word 2000 offers three memo templates, each with different formatting for the memo headings. Many companies design their own formatting for a memo. In some exercises in this textbook, you will be required to key and format a memo. When asked to format a memo, use the formatting shown below.

Include reference initials at the end of the memo as shown below, along with the document name. The reference initials are indicated by the *XX*. In this textbook, insert your initials instead of the *XX*.

1-inch top margin

DATE: September 27, 2001
ds
TO: Adam Mukai, Vice President
ds
FROM: Carol Jenovich, Director
ds
SUBJECT: NEW EMPLOYEES
ts

Two new employees have been hired to work in the Human Resources Department. Lola Henderson will begin work on October 1 and Daniel Schriver will begin October 15.
ds
Ms. Henderson has worked for three years as an administrative assistant for another company. Due to her previous experience, she was hired as a program assistant.
ds
Mr. Schriver has just completed a one-year training program at Gulf Community College. He was hired as an Administrative Assistant I.
ds
I would like to introduce you to the new employees. Please schedule a time for a short visit.
ds
XX:Memo

Appendix C

Formatting a Business Letter

A variety of formatting styles can be applied to a business letter. Some common business letter styles include block style, modified block style, and simplified. In some exercises in this textbook, you will be required to key and format a business letter. When asked to format a business letter, use the block style shown below. Include your initials at the end of the letter, followed by the document name. The business letter shown below is formatted with standard punctuation. Standard punctuation includes a colon after the salutation and a comma after the complimentary close.

2-inch top margin

December 5, 2001

5 Enters (Returns)

Mr. Paul Reinke
Iverson Medical Center
1290 South 43rd Street
Houston, TX 77348
    ds
Dear Mr. Reinke:
    ds
During the entire month of January, our laser printer, Model No. 34-454, will be on sale. We are cutting the original price by 33 percent!
    ds
When you purchased your computer system from our store last month, you indicated an interest in a laser printer. Now is your chance, Mr. Reinke, to purchase a high-quality laser printer at a rock-bottom price. Once you have seen the quality of print produced by a laser printer, you will not be satisfied with any other type of printer.
    ds
Visit our store at your convenience and see a demonstration of this incredible printer. We are so confident you will purchase the printer that we are enclosing a coupon for a free printer cartridge worth over $25.
    ds
Very truly yours,

4 Enters (Returns)

Gina Cerazzo, Manager
    ds
XX: Block Letter
    ds
Enclosure

Index